For guidance on selecting the right study plan for you, see Ch. 2.

GET MORE PRACTICE AND SCORE YOUR EXAMS BY REGISTERING AT KAPTEST.COM/MOREONLINE

For guidance on selecting the right study plan for you, see Ch. 2.

GET MORE PRACTICE AND SCORE YOUR EXAMS BY REGISTERING AT KAPTEST.COM/MOREONLINE

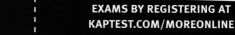

2-MONTH STUDY PLAN

- 4 practice exams
- 20 online quizzes
- 4–6 hours each week

For each Rapid Review chapter, begin by completing the Test What You Already Know section.

Based on your results, you will be given instructions about next steps.

At the end of each chapter, complete the Test What You Learned section before moving on to the next topic.

WEEK 1 (4–5 hours)

Practice Exam 1

Review Practice Exam 1

WEEK 2 (4–6 hours)

Chapters 1–2

Chapter 3 (Rapid)

Chapter 7 (Comprehensive)

1200–1450 Online Quizzes 1–5

(cont.)

1-MONTH STUDY PLAN

- 2 practice exams
- 8 online quizzes
- 5–9 hours each week

For each Rapid Review chapter, begin by completing the Test What You Already Know section.

Based on your results, you will be given instructions about next steps.

At the end of each chapter, complete the Test What You Learned section before moving on to the next topic.

WEEK 1 (5–7 hours)

Practice Exam 1

Review Practice Exam 1

Chapters 1–2

WEEK 2 (6–8 hours)

Chapters 3–4 (Rapid)

Chapters 7–8 (Comprehensive)

1200–1450 Online Quizzes 1–2

1450–1750 Online Quizzes 1–2

(cont.)

2-WEEK STUDY PLAN

- 2 practice exams
- 10–15 hours each week

For each Rapid Review chapter, begin by completing the Test What You Already Know section.

Based on your results, you will be given instructions about next steps.

At the end of each chapter, complete the Test What You Learned section before moving on to the next topic.

WEEK 1 (10–15 hours)

Day 1 (3–4 hours)

Practice Exam 1

Day 2–3 (1–3 hours)

Review Practice Exam 1

Chapters 1–2

Day 4–5 (3–4 hours)

Chapter 3 (Rapid)

Chapter 7 (Comprehensive)

Day 6–7 (3–4 hours)

Chapter 4 (Rapid)

Chapter 8 (Comprehensive)

(cont.)

2-WEEK STUDY PLAN

WEEK 2 (10–15 hours)

Day 8–9 (3–4 hours)
   Chapter 5 (Rapid)
   Chapter 9 (Comprehensive)

Day 10–11 (3–4 hours)
   Chapter 6 (Rapid)
   Chapter 10 (Comprehensive)

Day 12–13 (3–5 hours)
   Chapter 11 (Free-Response)
   Practice Exam 2

Day 14 (1–2 hours)
   Review Practice Exam 2

1-MONTH STUDY PLAN

WEEK 3 (7–9 hours)
   Chapters 5–6 (Rapid)
   Chapters 9–10 (Comprehensive)
   1750–1900 Online Quizzes 1–2
   1900–Present Online Quizzes 1–2

WEEK 4 (5–6 hours)
   Chapter 11 (Free-Response)
   Practice Exam 2
   Review Practice Exam 2

2-MONTH STUDY PLAN

WEEK 3 (4–6 hours)
   Chapter 4 (Rapid)
   Chapter 8 (Comprehensive)
   1450–1750 Online Quizzes 1–5

WEEK 4 (4–6 hours)
   Chapter 5 (Rapid)
   Chapter 9 (Comprehensive)
   1750–1900 Online Quizzes 1–5

WEEK 5 (5–6 hours)
   Chapter 11 (Free-Response)
   Practice Exam 2
   Review Practice Exam 2

WEEK 6 (4–6 hours)
   Chapter 6 (Rapid)
   Chapter 10 (Comprehensive)
   1900–Present Online Quizzes 1–5

WEEK 7 (4–5 hours)
   Practice Exam 3
   Review Practice Exam 3

WEEK 8 (4–5 hours)
   Practice Exam 4 or 5
   Review Practice Exam 4 or 5

AP®
World History: Modern
Prep Plus
2020 & 2021

Lead Editor:
Katy Haynicz-Smith, MA

Contributing Editor:
M. Dominic Eggert

Special thanks to our writers and reviewers on this edition: Laura Aitcheson, Naomi Beesen, Steve Bartley, Leslie Buchanan, Sterling Davenport, Mark Feery, Paula Fleming, Christina Giangrandi, Craig Harman, Peter Haynicz-Smith, Melissa McLaughlin, Kathryn Sollenberger, Glen Stohr, Alexandra Strelka, Amanda Swearingen, and Caroline Sykes.

Additional special thanks to the following for their contributions to this text: Joanna Graham, Adam Grey, Maria Hauser, Jesika Islam, Rebecca Knauer, Mandy Luk, Jenn Moore, Camellia Mukherjee, Kristin Murner, Monica Ostolaza, Rebecca Truong, Oscar Velazquez, Robert Verini, Shayna Webb-Dray, and Amy Zarkos.

AP® is a registered trademark of the College Board, which was not involved in the production of, and does not endorse, this product.

TABLE OF CONTENTS

Table of Contents

PART 1

Getting Started

CHAPTER 1

What You Need to Know About the AP World History: Modern Exam

Congratulations—you have chosen Kaplan to help you get a top score on your AP World History: Modern exam. Kaplan understands your goals and what you're up against: conquering a tough exam while participating in everything else that high school has to offer.

You expect realistic practice, authoritative advice, and accurate, up-to-date information on the exam. And that's exactly what you'll find in this book. To help you reach your goals, we have conducted extensive research and have incorporated insights from an AP Expert who has over 15 years of experience with AP World History.

ABOUT THE AP EXPERT

Christina Gentile Giangrandi earned a Bachelor of Arts *cum laude* in History and Secondary Education from Hofstra University and Master of Arts from Stony Brook University. She has taught AP World History in the Smithtown Central School District since 2004, in addition to teaching the New York State Global History course and a Holocaust, Genocide, and Human Rights elective course. She has served as an AP Reader for the College Board and has attended numerous professional development courses and study tours to further her knowledge of world history. She is also the author of *Barron's AP Q&A World History*, published in 2018.

ABOUT THIS BOOK

In preparing for the AP exam, you build a solid foundation of knowledge about world history in the years 1200 to the present. While this knowledge is critical to your learning, keep in mind that just being able to recall isolated facts, dates, and events does not ensure success on the exam. World history is about big ideas, such as how various civilizations developed and how different regions of the world are interconnected. The College Board (the maker of the AP exam) asks you to apply the knowledge you've learned at a higher level in order to show evidence of college-level abilities.

That's where this book comes in. This guide offers much more than a review of basic content. We'll show you how to put your knowledge to brilliant use on the AP exam through structured practice and efficient review of the areas you need to work on most. We'll explain the ins and outs of the exam structure and question formats so you won't experience any surprises. We'll even give you test-taking strategies that successful students use to earn high scores.

Are you ready for your adventure in the study and mastery of everything AP World History: Modern? Good luck!

EXAM STRUCTURE

The main goal of the College Board (the makers of the AP exam) is to help students think like historians. To that end, some skills and methods you'll be expected to demonstrate are:

- Analyzing primary and secondary sources

- Explaining and analyzing historical processes, developments, and events

- Making connections using historical reasoning (specifically, comparison, causation, continuity, and change)

- Developing historical arguments

AP World History: Modern is broken down into four historical periods:

Period	Units	Exam Weighting
c. 1200 to c. 1450	The Global Tapestry	8–10%
	Networks of Exchange	8–10%
c. 1450 to c. 1750	Land-Based Empires	12–15%
	Transoceanic Interconnections	12–15%
c. 1750 to c. 1900	Revolutions	12–15%
	Consequences of Industrialization	12–15%
c. 1900 to the Present	Global Conflict	8–10%
	Cold War and Decolonization	8–10%
	Globalization	8–10%

The AP World History: Modern exam is 3 hours and 15 minutes long and is divided into two sections:

Section	Part	Exam Weighting	Timing
I	Part A: Multiple-Choice (55 Questions)	40%	55 minutes
	Part B: Short-Answer (3 Questions)	20%	40 minutes
II	Part A: Document-Based (1 Question)	25%	60 minutes (includes a recommended 15-minute reading period)
	Part B: Long Essay (1 Question)	15%	40 minutes

EXAM SCORING

Once you complete your AP exam, it will be sent to the College Board for grading. Student answer sheets for the multiple-choice section (Section I, Part A) are scored by machine. Scores are based on the number of questions answered correctly. No points are deducted for wrong answers, and no points are awarded for unanswered questions.

The free-response sections (Section I, Part B and Section II) are evaluated and scored by hand by trained AP readers. Rubrics based on each specific free-response prompt are released on the AP central website after the exams are administered.

After your total scores from Sections I and II are calculated, your results are converted to a scaled score from 1 to 5. The range of points for each scaled score varies depending on the difficulty of the exam in a particular year, but the significance of each value is constant from year to year. According to the College Board, AP scores should be interpreted as follows:

5 = Extremely well qualified

4 = Very well qualified

3 = Qualified

2 = Possibly qualified

1 = No recommendation

Colleges will generally not award course credit for any score below a 3, with more selective schools requiring a 4 or 5. Note that some schools will not award college credit regardless of your score. Be sure to research schools that you plan to apply to so you can determine the score you need to aim for on the AP exam.

Registration and Fees

To register for the exam, contact your school guidance counselor or AP Coordinator. If your school does not administer the AP exam, contact the College Board for a listing of schools that do.

There is a fee for taking AP exams. The current cost can be found at the official exam website listed below. For students with acute financial need, the College Board offers a fee reduction. In addition, most states offer exam subsidies to cover all or part of the remaining cost for eligible students. To learn about other sources of financial aid, contact your AP Coordinator.

For more information on all things AP, contact the Advanced Placement Program:

Phone: (888) 225-5427 or (212) 632-1780

Email: apstudents@info.collegeboard.org

Website: https://apstudent.collegeboard.org/home

CHAPTER 2

How to Get the Score You Need

HOW TO GET THE MOST OUT OF THIS BOOK

Kaplan's *AP World History: Modern Prep Plus* contains precisely what you'll need to get the score you want in the time you have to study. The unique format of this book allows you to customize your prep experience to make the most of your time.

Start by going to **kaptest.com/moreonline** to register your book and get a glimpse of the additional online resources available to you.

Book Features

Specific Strategies

This chapter features both general test-taking strategies and strategies tailored specifically to the AP World History: Modern exam. You'll learn about the types of questions you'll see on the official exam and how to best approach them to achieve a top score.

Customizable Study Plans

We recognize that every student is a unique individual, and there is no single recipe for success that works for everyone. To give you the best chance to succeed, we have developed three customizable study plans. Each offers guidance on how to make the most of your available study time. In addition, we have split this book into "Rapid Review" and "Comprehensive Review" sections for each historical period. There is guidance in both the study plans and the Rapid Review sections to help you determine how to best move through this book and optimize your study time.

Rapid Review

Chapters 3–6 aim to cover the most high-yield content in the shortest amount of time. Each Rapid Review chapter begins with a "Test What You Already Know" section containing a multiple-choice quiz and a checklist of key terms; this combination allows you to see where you stand with this historical period before you even begin studying the content. The "Next Steps" chart (example shown below) will guide you in customizing your further study. In the middle of the Rapid Review chapter, the section entitled "Essential Content" contains a summary of key takeaways and a complete list of definitions for all of the key terms. Finally, the "Test What You Learned" section contains another multiple-choice quiz and the same key terms checklist so you can see how you're doing after some studying.

If You Got...	Do This
80% or more of the Test What You Already Know assessment correct	• Read definitions in this chapter for all the key terms you didn't check off. • Complete the Test What You Learned assessment in this chapter.
50% or less of the Test What You Already Know assessment correct	• Read the comprehensive review for this period. • If you are short on time, read only the High-Yield sections. • Complete the Practice Set assessment. • Read through all of the key term definitions in this chapter. • Complete the Test What You Learned assessment in this chapter.
Any other result	• Read the High-Yield sections in the comprehensive review of this period. • Read definitions in this chapter for all the key terms you didn't check off. • Complete the Test What You Learned assessment in this chapter.

Comprehensive Review

Chapters 7–10 feature the same time periods as the Rapid Review chapters, but they offer a more detailed look at all of the important topics tested on the AP exam. You'll be directed to these Comprehensive Review chapters, for studying the High-Yield topics or for reading the complete chapter, based on your results in the corresponding Rapid Review chapter.

The Comprehensive Review chapters are like an abbreviated version of a textbook you would use in class. The key terms in bold are the same ones that appear in the Rapid Review chapters, and those checklists are in the same order the terms appear in the Comprehensive Review chapters. Chapter 11 is an in-depth review of the free-response section of the exam, including sample essays and grading rubrics. High-Yield icons appear throughout the Comprehensive Review chapters to help you recognize when information is absolutely essential to know. You will also see AP Expert Notes that highlight important connections between topics and provide tips about how to better apply your knowledge on the official exam.

Full-Length Practice Exams

In addition to all of the exam-like practice questions featured in the chapter quizzes, we have provided five full-length practice exams. These full-length exams mimic the multiple-choice and free-response questions on the real AP exam. Taking a full-length practice exam gives you an idea of what it's like to answer exam-like questions for about three hours. Granted, that's not exactly a fun experience, but it is a helpful one. And the best part is that it doesn't count; mistakes you make on our practice exams are mistakes you won't make on your real exam.

After taking each practice exam, you'll score your multiple-choice and free-response sections using the answers and explanations. Then, you'll navigate to the scoring section in your online resources and input your raw scores to see what your overall score would be with a similar performance on the official exam.

Online Quizzes

While this book contains hundreds of exam-like multiple-choice questions, you may still find yourself wanting additional practice on particular topics. That's what the online quizzes are for! Your online resources contain additional quizzes for each historical period. Go to **kaptest.com/moreonline** to find them all.

CHOOSING THE BEST STUDY PLAN FOR YOU

There's a lot of material to review before the AP exam, so it's essential to have a solid game plan that optimizes your available study time. The sheet in the front of the book consists of three separable bookmarks, each of which covers a specific, customizable study plan. You can use one of these bookmarks both to hold your place in the book and to keep track of your progress in completing one of these study plans. But how do you choose the study plan that's right for you?

Fortunately, all you need to know to make this decision is how much time you have to prep. If you have two months or more with plenty of time to study, then we recommend using the Two-Month Study Plan. If you only have about a month, or if you have more than a month but your time will be split among competing priorities, you should probably choose the One-Month Study Plan. Finally, if you have less than a month to prep, your best bet is the Two-Week Study Plan.

Regardless of your chosen plan, you have flexibility in how you follow the instructions. You can stick to the order and timing that the plan recommends or tailor those recommendations to fit your particular study schedule. For example, if you have six weeks before your exam, you could use the One-Month Study Plan but spread out the recommended activities for Week 1 across the first two weeks of your studying.

After you've made your selection, tear out the perforated study plan page, separate the bookmark that contains your choice of plan, and use it to keep track of both your place in the book and your progress in the plan. You can further customize any of the study plans by skipping over chapters or sections that you've already mastered or by adjusting the recommended time to better suit your schedule. Don't forget to also use the guidelines in the Rapid Review chapters to further customize how you study.

STRATEGIES FOR EACH QUESTION TYPE

The AP World History: Modern exam can be challenging, but with the right strategic mindset, you can get yourself on track for earning the score you need to qualify for college credit or advanced placement. Let's review some strategies that, along with the content review and practice questions in the rest of this book, will help you succeed on the AP exam.

Section I

Multiple-Choice Questions

The multiple-choice section (Part A of Section I) consists of question sets that typically contain three or four questions and can focus on any historical period from circa 1200 to the present. A primary or secondary source is provided for each question set, which could be a passage, image, graph, or map. The questions assess your ability to understand and analyze historical texts and interpretations, as well as your ability to make larger historical connections. Keep in mind that even if a question set is based on a specific historical period, the individual questions may require you to make connections to other periods and events.

The questions range from easy and medium to difficult with no distinct pattern to their appearance within the exam. In other words, the easiest question may be the last one, so make sure to go through all of the exam questions! A solid strategy for the multiple-choice section is to do multiple passes:

1. On your first pass, answer all of the questions that you know and are sure about.

2. Next, go back through the remaining questions. If you can eliminate at least two answer choices and the topic is familiar, take your best educated guess. If you look at the question and do not remember the topic, mark the question with an X in your exam booklet and move on. (If you skip a question, make sure that you skip that line on the answer grid!)

3. Go back through the exam for a third time to answer the questions you marked with an X. Again, try to eliminate at least two choices, and take an educated guess. If you're still not sure, at this point, just bubble in an answer for the question; remember that there is no penalty for guessing on these multiple-choice questions.

4. With the time remaining, remove any extraneous marks in your answer grid (such as any X's you may have left), and make sure that the answers you have bubbled in correspond to the correct numbers in the test booklet.

✔ **AP Expert Note**

Know when and how to guess

The AP exam does not deduct points for wrong answers, so never leave a multiple-choice question unanswered! A blind guess gives you a 1 in 4 (25 percent) chance of getting the correct answer. Even better, every incorrect answer you can confidently eliminate increases those odds: eliminate one answer choice and your chances improve to 33 percent, two and you're at 50 percent.

When eliminating incorrect choices, look for ones that are out of the given time period or region or are not related to specific categories (e.g., the question asked for economic factors, and the answer choice mentions law codes). If you end up guessing on that question, at least you have now improved your odds.

Lastly, do *not* change an answer you have made unless you are absolutely sure that your initial answer is incorrect. Research shows that your first attempt is usually the correct one.

Short-Answer Questions

In Part B of Section I, you will have three short-answer questions to answer, each of which will have multiple parts. The short-answer section allows you to demonstrate what you know best since you get to choose which historical examples to discuss in relation to the prompts. While two of the short-answer prompts are required, for the third and final question, you get to choose between two prompts.

According to the College Board, a high-scoring response to a short-answer question will accomplish all tasks outlined in the question. You must answer each part of the question with complete sentences and provide specific historical examples in order to receive full credit. Make sure you go beyond simply quoting or paraphrasing historical evidence and really explain its meaning or significance. In composing your answer, you do not need to develop and support a thesis statement, but you do need to synthesize your ideas into cohesive paragraphs.

In Chapter 11, you'll learn a straightforward Kaplan Method you can apply to every free-response question. In general, take time to analyze all of the parts of each short-answer question. Then, before you begin writing your response, create a plan of which historical examples you will use for each part. You will have plenty of opportunities to practice writing responses to short-answer questions on the practice exams, so be sure to complete those sections to the best of your ability for the most exam-like experience.

Section II

The Document-Based Question

The first part of Section II is the document-based question (DBQ). This essay asks you to think like a historian and develop an argument based on evidence. You will be provided a specific prompt and seven related documents; these will vary in length and format, and may include text, graphs, and images. Essentially, you must take these sources and draw conclusions based on your analytical skills. The task at hand is less about remembering facts and more about analyzing and organizing information logically. You are expected to make sophisticated connections; therefore, it is essential to demonstrate your knowledge of larger historical themes (rather than just isolated events, dates, and people) in order to earn the highest scores.

If the DBQ prompt and accompanying documents cover something well outside the mainstream, don't panic! The exam writers do this on purpose. The other essay on the exam—the long essay question—will evaluate your knowledge of history, but the DBQ evaluates your ability to work with historical material, even material with which you're less familiar. Writing the DBQ is a skill that can be learned much like any other skill, and this book will help you hone that skill.

The Long Essay Question

The second part of Section II is the long essay question (LEQ). You will answer one of three prompts, each of which focuses on different time periods. Make sure to choose the prompt that best show-cases the extent of your knowledge.

The LEQ assesses your ability to apply knowledge of history in a complex, analytical manner. You will be asked to develop an argument about a historical process or development—thus, you will need to supply relevant historical examples as evidence to support a claim you make about the long essay question prompt. High-scoring long essay responses do not merely list information that is related to the prompt; the critical component of the long essay is your ability to develop a supported argument. See Chapter 11 for scoring rubrics and special strategies for both the DBQ and LEQ.

Pacing

The multiple-choice section, Part A of Section I, consists of 55 questions to be completed in 55 minutes. Since you will need to analyze primary and secondary sources for each question set, you'll want to move quickly but thoroughly through the multiple-choice section; don't linger on any one question for more than 30 seconds or so.

In Part B of Section I, you have 40 minutes to answer three short-answer questions. Aim to spend about 13 minutes on each question, including both planning and writing. Apply any extra time you have at the end of the section to reread your responses, looking for quick errors to fix (such as a missing word or punctuation mark).

The 100 minutes for Section II of the exam is divided into two parts. The first 15 minutes is the suggested reading and organizing time for the document-based question, and the last 85 minutes is the suggested essay writing time, to be split between the two essays. It is recommended that you spend 45 minutes writing the document-based question and 40 minutes writing the long essay question. The proctor may make timing announcements, but you will not be forced to move from reading and planning to writing, or from the DBQ to the LEQ, if you're not yet ready.

Practice, Practice, Practice

Now you've learned about the structure of the exam sections and the types of questions you'll encounter, but to maximize your scoring potential, you'll need to practice these question types. The quizzes in the Rapid Review section (Chapters 3–6), the practice sets in the Comprehensive Review section (Chapters 7–10), the free-response chapter (Chapter 11), the full-length exams, and the additional quizzes in your online resources provide the perfect opportunity to practice your skills with hundreds of exam-like questions!

> ✔ **AP Expert Note**
>
> **Practice your Test Day mindset**
>
> Having the right mindset plays a large part in how well people do on a test. Students who practice consciously reframing feelings of nervousness as excitement when taking tests can approach their AP exams with a more confident attitude; this helps sharpen their focus and often leads to higher scores. Practice developing a confident mindset—no matter what, you've prepared for this exam and you *can* do well. As you work your way through the exam, devote your attention to just one question at a time, and don't be afraid to pause and take a few refocusing deep breaths as needed. You've got this!

COUNTDOWN TO THE EXAM

This book contains detailed review, guidance, and practice for you to utilize in the weeks leading up to your AP exam. In the final few days before your exam, we recommend the following steps.

Three Days Before the Exam

Take a full-length practice exam under timed conditions. Use the techniques and strategies you've learned in this book. Approach the exam strategically, actively, and confidently. (Note that you should *not* take a full-length practice exam with fewer than 48 hours left before your real exam. Doing so will probably exhaust you and hurt your score.)

Two Days Before the Exam

Go over the results of your latest practice exam. Don't worry too much about your score or whether you got a specific question right or wrong. Instead, examine your overall performance on the different topics, choose a few of the topics where you struggled the most, and brush up on them one final time.

Know exactly where you're going to take the official exam, how you're getting there, and how long it takes to get there. It's probably a good idea to visit your testing center sometime before the day of your exam so that you know what to expect: what the rooms are like, how the desks are set up, and so on.

The Night Before the Exam

Do not study! You cannot cram for a test as extensive as the AP Exam. Worse, pulling an all-nighter will simply deplete your stamina ahead of the exam. If you feel you must review some AP material, only do so for a little while and stick to broad review (such as the Essential Content sections of this book). The best, most effective way to prepare for the AP Exam at this point is to rest the night before.

Get together an "AP Exam Kit" containing the following items:

- A few No. 2 pencils (Pencils with slightly dull points fill the ovals better; mechanical pencils are NOT permitted.)
- A few pens with black or dark blue ink (for the free-response questions)
- Erasers
- A watch (as long as it doesn't have Internet access, have an alarm, or make noise)
- Your 6-digit school code (Home-schooled students will be provided with their state's or country's home-school code at the time of the exam.)
- Photo ID card
- Your AP Student Pack
- If applicable, your Student Accommodation Letter verifying that you have been approved for a testing accommodation such as braille or large-type exams

Make sure that you don't bring anything that is *not* allowed in the exam room. You can find a complete list at the College Board's website (https://apstudent.collegeboard.org/home). Your school may have additional restrictions, so make sure you get this information from your school's AP Coordinator prior to the exam.

Again, try to relax. Read a good book, take a hot shower, watch something you enjoy. Go to bed early and get a good night's sleep.

The Morning of the Exam

Wake up early, leaving yourself plenty of time to get ready without rushing. Dress in layers so that you can adjust to the temperature of the testing room. Eat a solid breakfast: something substantial, but nothing too heavy or greasy. Don't drink a lot of caffeine. Read something as you eat breakfast, such as a newspaper or a magazine; you shouldn't let the exam be the first thing you read that day.

Leave extra early so that you can ensure you are on time to the testing location. Allow yourself extra time for any traffic, mass transit delays, and/or detours.

During the Exam

Breathe. Don't get shaken up. If you find your confidence slipping, remind yourself how well you've prepared. You know the structure of the exam; you know the material covered on it; you've had practice with every question type.

If something goes really wrong, do not panic! If you accidentally misgrid your answer page or put the answers in the wrong section, raise your hand and tell the proctor. He or she may be able to arrange for you to regrid your exam after it's over, when it won't cost you any time.

After the Exam

You might walk out of the AP exam thinking that you blew it. This is a normal reaction. Lots of people—even the highest scorers—feel that way. You tend to remember the questions that stumped you, not the ones that you knew. Keep in mind that almost nobody gets everything correct. You can still score a 4 or 5 even if you get some multiple-choice questions incorrect or miss several points on a free-response question.

We're positive that you will have performed well and scored your best on the exam because you followed the Kaplan strategies outlined in this chapter and reviewed all the content provided in the rest of this book. Be confident and celebrate the fact that, after many hours of hard work and preparation, you have just completed the AP World History: Modern exam!

PART 2

Rapid Review

CHAPTER 3

1200 to 1450

LEARNING OBJECTIVES

- Explain how states interact with peoples who do not identify with a state.

- Analyze the influence of politics on how states come into being, grow, and falter.

- Describe interactions between states and stateless societies.

- Describe the role of the arts in both changing and reflecting society.

- Describe the effects, both positive and negative, of legal systems and independence movements on race, class, and gender.

TIMELINE

Date	Region	Event
1127–1279	East Asia	Southern Song Dynasty in China
1192–1333	East Asia	Kamakura shogunate in Japan
1204	Mid East	Sack of Constantinople by Crusaders
1205	East Asia	Mongol conquests begin
1206	South Asia	Delhi Sultanate in India begins
1227	East Asia	Death of Genghis Khan
1230	West Africa	Empire of Mali begins
1250	North Africa	Mamluk Sultanate in Egypt begins
1258	Mid East	Siege of Baghdad by Mongols
1271–1295	East Asia	Marco Polo's expeditions to China
1279–1368	East Asia	Yuan Dynasty in China
1299	Mid East	Ottoman Empire begins
1300	Central Africa	Kingdom of Kongo begins
1315–1317	Europe	The Great Famine takes place
1325–1354	Africa & Asia	Travels of Ibn Battuta
1330s	East Asia	Outbreak of bubonic plague in China
1337–1453	Europe	The Hundred Years' War
1347	Europe	Bubonic plague reaches Europe via Sicily
1368–1644	East Asia	Ming Dynasty in China
1428	Central America	Mexica (Aztec) Empire founded
1438	South America	Inca Empire founded
1453	Mid East	Fall of Constantinople to Ottomans

TEST WHAT YOU ALREADY KNOW

Part A: Quiz

Questions 1–2 refer to the passage below.

"Genghis Khan divided his Tartars by captains of ten, captains of a hundred, and captains of a thousand, and over [the] captains of a thousand, he placed one colonel, and over one whole army he authorized two or three dukes, but so that all should have special regard unto one of the said dukes.

And when they join battle against any other nation, unless they do all consent to retreat, every man who flees is put to death. And if one or two, or more, of ten proceed manfully to the battle, but the remainder of those ten draw back and follow not the company, the remainder are to be slain. Also, if one among ten or more has been taken prisoner, their fellows, if they rescue them not, are punished with death."

John of Plano Carpini, excerpt of letter to Pope Innocent IV, circa 1245

1. Which of the following sources would be most useful in evaluating the accuracy of John of Plano Carpini's account in the passage?

   (A) An account by Pope Innocent IV of his reaction to the letter

   (B) An account by a Chinese adviser to the Great Khan

   (C) An account by a modern Mongol scholar analyzing the letter

   (D) An account by another member of John of Plano Carpini's party

2. Based on the passage and your knowledge of world history, which of the following statements best describes a similarity between the impact of the British and Mongol empires?

   (A) They both brought all of the Asian mainland under their singular political and military control.

   (B) They both fostered interregional cultural and technological transfers through the creation of a global economic system.

   (C) They both eventually collapsed due to successful rebellions by the conquered peoples of their empire.

   (D) They both instilled a common language across the conquered populations within their imperial domain.

Questions 3–4 refer to the map below.

MAIN TRANS-SAHARAN CARAVAN ROUTES CIRCA 1400

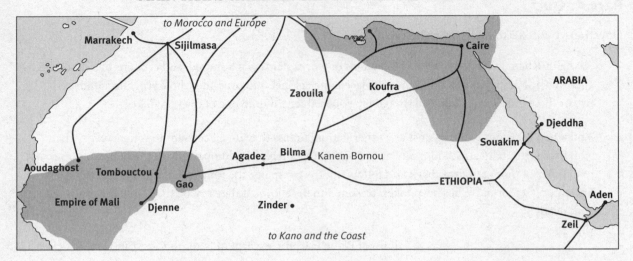

3. Which of the following facilitated the development of the trade networks depicted in the map?

   (A) The conversion of African kings, elites, and traders to Islam created a common cultural identity that facilitated trade.

   (B) The Mongol conquests reinvigorated Silk Road trade, which in turn supported other trade networks throughout the world.

   (C) The Portuguese expansion along the West African coast in search of a sea route to India pushed trade networks eastward.

   (D) The gold mines of the Mali Empire attracted Middle Eastern merchants who were eager to introduce Islam to West Africa.

4. The map reflects which of the following characteristics of trans-Saharan trade?

   (A) The importance of state-sponsored commercial infrastructure to facilitate interregional trade

   (B) The importance of money economies and new forms of credit to fostering the growth of trade

   (C) The interconnectedness of the Eastern and Western Hemisphere in terms of the global circulation of goods

   (D) The dependence of merchants on technology and environmental knowledge to sustain trade routes

Questions 5–6 refer to the passage below.

"13. Besides, we excommunicate and anathematize those false and impious Christians who, against Christ and the Christian people, furnish the Saracens* with arms, irons, and timbers for their galleys. We decree that any who sell galleys or ships to the Saracens, or accept positions on their piratical craft, or give them aid, counsel, or support with regard to their [war] machines to the disadvantages of the holy land shall be punished with the loss of all their goods and shall be the slaves of those who capture them. We command that this decree be published anew every Sunday and Christian feast day in all the maritime cities. . . .

14. We forbid all Christians for the next four years to send their ships, or permit them to be sent, to lands inhabited by Saracens, in order that a larger supply of vessels may be on hand for those who wish to go to the aid of the holy land, and also that the Saracens may be deprived of that not inconsiderable aid which they have been accustomed to receiving from this."

*Saracen was a common term used among Christian authors in the Middle Ages to refer to Arab Muslims.

Pope Innocent III, *Decrees of the Fourth Lateran Council*, 1215

5. Christians trading with "the Saracens," as alluded to in the passage, was part of which of the following processes?

   (A) The development of European maritime technology in order to facilitate transport to and from East Asia

   (B) The growth of European awareness of and interest in Asia through exposure to Islamic societies

   (C) The strengthening of the feudal system thanks to the knightly class participating in the Crusades

   (D) The continuing failure of economic sanctions to weaken Islamic kingdoms

6. Which of the following was the most direct result of the general attitude toward "false" Christians reflected in the passage?

   (A) The Crusades failed to retake the Holy Land, leading to the rise of the self-flagellant movement as a critique of the Church.

   (B) The authority of the papacy was undermined, leading to a succession of popes residing at Avignon, rather than Rome.

   (C) The Byzantine Empire was alienated from Western Europe, which isolated them in the face of later Turkish advances.

   (D) The works of the ancient Greek philosophers were synthesized with Christian ideas to make discussion of them acceptable.

Questions 7–9 refer to the map below.

ZHENG HE'S VOYAGES

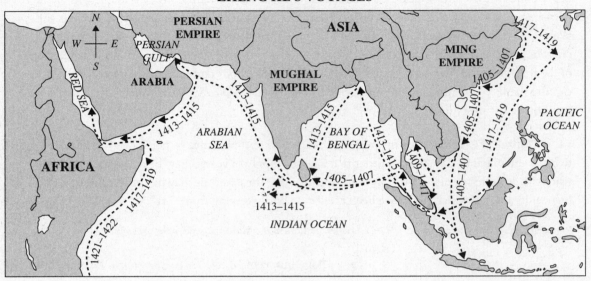

7. The particular routes and years of the voyages depicted on the map best support which of the following statements?

   (A) The Chinese sought to incorporate trading ports around the Indian Ocean into their tributary system.

   (B) The Silk Route included a maritime path in addition to its overland route across Afro-Eurasia.

   (C) Christopher Columbus and Ferdinand Magellan could not have accomplished what they did without East Asian navigators.

   (D) The Song Dynasty possessed the naval technology and organization structure to conduct transoceanic voyages.

8. A historian might argue that the voyages depicted on this map reflect a turning point in world history primarily because Zheng He's treasure fleet

   (A) drew resources away from the Chinese army at a time when the Mongols under Temujin's leadership were a rising threat

   (B) was the last great achievement of the Yuan Dynasty prior to its overthrow by the Red Turban Rebellion

   (C) demonstrated that the Yuan Dynasty's minimal taxation policy left it unable to fund foreign expeditions over the long-term

   (D) marked the last chance that China had to expand its influence into the Indian Ocean before the arrival of Europeans

9. The fears that motivated the end of the voyages depicted on the map are best understood in the context of which of the following?

   (A) Kublai Khan's conquest of China

   (B) The outbreak of the Hundred Years' War

   (C) The sack of Constantinople

   (D) The downfall of the Mali Empire

Questions 10–11 refer to the passage below.

"Bruges, in Flanders, the western terminus of the before-mentioned highway of commerce, was during the last centuries of the Middle Ages approximately what London is to the world of today. It was, beside Venice, the actual world-mart of the Continent, a centre where Italians, Spaniards, Portuguese, Frenchmen, and High- and Low-Germans—a motley throng—congregated to exchange their goods. Thither the Hanseatic* merchant transported wood and other forest products; building stones and iron, the latter being still forged in primitive forest smithies; and copper from the rich mines of Falun, the ore from which was usually sold or mortgaged to the Lubeck merchants. From the Baltic countries, he imported grain, and from Scandinavia, herring and cod—all natural products, in exchange for which he sent his own manufactured goods to the respective countries. In Bruges, he represented the entire northern region, both in the giving and the receiving of merchandise, for only through his instrumentality could the gifts of the East, such as oil, wine, spices, silk, and other articles of luxury, which were usually transported through the Alpine passes and thence down the Rhine to Bruges, be distributed among the northern nations. This applies also to the highly prized textiles of Flanders, which in those days were sometimes sold at fabulous prices."

*Stretching from the North Sea to the Baltic, the Hanseatic League was an organization of towns and guilds that coordinated trade and defense agreements.

H. Denicke, a German historian, *Rise of the Hanseatic League*, 1905

10. The activities described in the passage illustrate which of the following interregional interactions in the period circa 1200–1450?

    (A) The rise of trading organizations to fill the void created by weak, decentralized states

    (B) The importance of state-sponsored infrastructure in promoting international commerce

    (C) The development of financial innovations to facilitate commerce, such as banks and bills of exchange

    (D) The growth in cities as Europe transitioned from a feudal agricultural economy to a modern industrialized economy

11. Which of the following additional pieces of information would be most directly useful in determining whether the passage is accurate in comparing Bruges to early twentieth-century London?

    (A) Information on the origin and comparative value of the goods passing through Bruges and London in their respective periods

    (B) Information on the population total of Bruges and London in comparison to other cities of their respective periods

    (C) Information on the volume of Hanseatic League trade passing through Bruges and London in their respective periods

    (D) Information on the amount of taxes collected in Bruges and in London during their respective periods

Questions 12–15 refer to the image below.

MEXICO VALLEY UNDER MEXICA RULE, CIRCA 1519

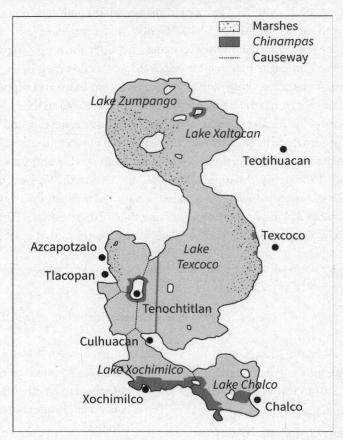

Pictured are the major towns within the Mexico Valley on the eve of Spanish conquest, including the island capital of the Aztecs (Mexica), Tenochtitlan.

12. The location of cities depicted on the map best reflects which of the following characteristics of the Mexica?

(A) Their location enabled them to conveniently defend urban areas from outside invaders.

(B) Their use of draft animals enabled them to construct large cities with monumental architecture.

(C) They used technologies to adapt to their environment and improve agricultural production.

(D) They needed to import food crops from North America due to a lack of areas for cultivation.

13. Which of the following factors contributed to urban revival in Mexica civilization?

(A) The need for protection from invasions plaguing the countryside

(B) The rise of commerce and increase in agricultural productivity

(C) The concentration of industrial labor in cities

(D) The decline in trade and lower levels of production

14. Which of the following best describes the Mexica civilization?

(A) The empire had a tributary relationship with conquered groups.

(B) The decentralized government was divided into individual city-states.

(C) The empire was highly centralized with bureaucratic institutions.

(D) The government had little control beyond Tenochtitlan.

15. The map best illustrates which of the following patterns of world history?

(A) Cities are often self-sufficient and have little contact with surrounding areas.

(B) Cities are often economic centers rather than residential areas.

(C) Cities are often built in locations that provide access to lakes, swamps, and islands.

(D) Cities often serve as centers of commerce, religious rituals, and political institutions.

Part B: Key Terms

The following is a list of the major people, places, and events for 1200 to 1450. You will very likely see many of these on the AP World History: Modern exam.

For each key term, ask yourself the following questions:

- Can I describe this key term?
- Can I discuss this key term in the context of other events?
- Could I correctly answer a multiple-choice question about this key term?
- Could I correctly answer a free-response question about this key term?

Check off the key terms if you can answer "yes" to at least three of these questions.

Cultural Developments and Belief Systems

☐ Neo-Confucianism   ☐ Eastern Orthodox Church   ☐ Sunni

☐ Catholic Church   ☐ Shi'a

Civilizations in the Americas

☐ *Chinampa*   ☐ *Mit'a*

Civilizations in East Asia

☐ Mandate of Heaven   ☐ Grand Canal   ☐ Champa rice

Islamic Golden Age

☐ Al-Andalus   ☐ Astrolabe   ☐ Trans-Saharan trade

Europe during the Late Middle Ages

☐ Feudalism   ☐ Bills of exchange   ☐ Crusades

Nomadic and Traveling Empires

☐ Ottoman   ☐ Mongols   ☐ Genghis Khan

Civilizations in Africa

☐ Mansa Musa   ☐ Swahili city-states

Interregional Economic and Cultural Exchange

☐ Melaka   ☐ Ibn Battuta   ☐ Marco Polo

☐ Bubonic plague

Recovery and Renaissance in Asia and Europe

☐ Renaissance

3

Next Steps

Step 1: Tally your correct answers from Part A, and review the quiz explanations at the end of this chapter.

1.	B	6.	C	11.	A
2.	B	7.	A	12.	C
3.	A	8.	D	13.	B
4.	D	9.	D	14.	A
5.	B	10.	A	15.	D

_____ out of 15 questions

Step 2: Count the number of key terms you checked off in Part B.

_____ out of 26 key terms

Step 3: Read the Key Takeaways in this chapter.

Step 4: Consult the table below and follow the instructions based on your performance.

If You Got...	Do This
80% or more of the Test What You Already Know assessment correct (12 or more questions from Part A and 21 or more key terms from Part B)	• Read definitions in this chapter for all the key terms you didn't check off. • Complete the Test What You Learned assessment in this chapter.
50% or less of the Test What You Already Know assessment correct (7 or fewer questions from Part A and 13 or fewer key terms from Part B)	• Read the comprehensive review for this period in Chapter 7. • If you are short on time, read only the High-Yield sections. • Complete the Practice Set assessment at the end of Chapter 7. • Read through all of the key term definitions in this chapter. • Complete the Test What You Learned assessment in this chapter.
Any other result	• Read the High-Yield sections in the comprehensive review of this period in Chapter 7. • Read definitions in this chapter for all the key terms you didn't check off. • Complete the Test What You Learned assessment in this chapter.

ESSENTIAL CONTENT

Key Takeaways: 1200 to 1450

1. The spread of religion, aided by the increase in trade, often acted as a unifying social force. Throughout East Asia, the development of Neo-Confucianism solidified a cultural identity. Islam created a new cultural world known as Dar al-Islam, which transcended political and linguistic boundaries in Asia and Africa. Christianity and the Catholic Church served as unifying forces in Europe.

2. Centralized empires like the Arab Caliphates and the Song Dynasty built on the successful models of the past, while decentralized areas (Western Europe and Japan) developed political organization to more effectively deal with their unique issues. The peoples of the Americas saw new, large-scale political structures develop, such as the Inca Empire in the Andes and the Mississippian culture in North America.

3. The movement of people greatly altered the world politically and demographically. Traveling groups, such as the Turks and Mongols, disrupted much of Asia's existing political structure. Turkic peoples founded the Mumluk and Delhi Sultanates. The recovery from the Mongol period introduced political structures that defined many areas for centuries to follow.

4. There was tremendous growth in long-distance trade. Technological developments such as the compass improved shipbuilding technology, and gunpowder shaped the development of the world. Trade through the Silk Road, the Indian Ocean, the trans-Saharan routes, and the Mediterranean Sea led to the spread of ideas, religions, and technology. Interregional cultural exchanges, represented by early world travelers like Ibn Battuta and Marco Polo, increased due to the Mongol Conquests.

5. War, disease, and famine caused massive social and political upheaval throughout Eurasia. The Black Death killed over a third of the European population, and the resulting labor shortfall increased the bargaining power of peasants, diminishing the system of feudalism. The Mongol Conquests led to a massive death toll from Korea to Russia to the Middle East, weakening many regions for centuries to come as European powers expanded outward.

6. Western Europe and China saw significant economic and political recoveries. The Italian city-states grew prosperous enough to support the burgeoning Renaissance, which was partly inspired by ancient Greek works recovered from Islamic scholars. The Ming Dynasty experienced a cultural flowering that resulted in great works of art. The Ming also supported major naval expeditions by Zheng He.

Key Terms: 1200 to 1450

Remember that the AP World History exam tests you on the depth of your knowledge, not just your ability to recall facts. While we have provided brief definitions here, you will need to know these terms in even more depth for the AP exam, including how terms connect to broader historical themes and understandings.

Cultural Developments and Belief Systems

Neo-Confucianism: Popular during the Tang Dynasty; fused elements of Buddhism and Confucianism.

Catholic Church: The largest of the three main branches of Christianity; centered in Rome and led by the pope; found most often in Europe, the Americas, sub-Saharan Africa, and parts of East Asia.

Eastern Orthodox Church: The third largest of the three main branches of Christianity; originally based in the Byzantine Empire; found most often in Russia, Eastern Europe, the Balkans, and parts of Central Asia.

Shi'a: One of the two main branches of Islam; rejects the first three Sunni caliphs and regards Ali, the fourth caliph, as Muhammad's first true successor; most commonly found in Iran, but otherwise constitutes 10 to 15 percent of Muslims worldwide.

Sunni: One of the two main branches of Islam; commonly described as orthodox and differs from Shi'a in its understanding of the Sunnah and in its acceptance of the first three caliphs; is by far the most common branch of Islam worldwide.

Civilizations in the Americas

Chinampa: A form of Mesoamerican agriculture in which farmers cultivated crops in rectangular plots of land on lake beds; hosted corns, beans, chilis, squash, tomatoes, and more; provided up to seven harvests per year.

Mit'a: A mandatory public service system in the Inca Empire requiring all people below the age of 50 to serve for two months out of the year; not to be confused with the *mita*, a forced labor system practiced by conquistadors in the former Inca Empire.

Civilizations in East Asia

Mandate of Heaven: Ancient Chinese concept stating that the right to rule was granted by the heavens; used to explain the rise of every Chinese dynasty, including the Qing in 1644.

Grand Canal: World's longest canal, connecting the fertile Huang He River to the highly populated cities in the north; allowed grain to be shipped easily.

Champa rice: Introduced to China from Vietnam; allowed the Chinese to have two harvests per year, dramatically improving output; combined with an improved infrastructure, led to a significant growth of the Chinese population.

Islamic Golden Age

Al-Andalus: Islamic state located in modern-day Spain; led by the Berbers; renowned for its achievements in science, mathematics, and trade.

Astrolabe: Introduced to the Islamic world in the 700s, where it was perfected by mathematicians; used by astronomers and navigators to determine latitude through inclination.

Trans-Saharan trade: Trade network starting in the 400s and 500s; thrived due to an organized network of camel caravans carrying gold, salt, cloth, slaves, and other valuables; allowed the kingdoms of Ghana and Mali to thrive, and as Islam spread to Africa, allowed its teachings to impact the lives of kings and traders.

Europe during the Late Middle Ages

Feudalism: Political and economic system that developed as a result of the decentralization and collapse of the Western Roman Empire; lords, usually noblemen, protected vassals in exchange for mandatory labor or military service; vassals received a fief, or grant of land.

Bills of exchange: Written guarantees of payment that were essentially the forerunners of modern-day bank checks; helped facilitate trade; known as *sakk* in the Islamic world; also used in China during this period.

Crusades: Holy wars launched by Pope Urban II in 1095 that called for Christians to reclaim the Holy Land of Israel from Muslims; its four campaigns, lasting over 100 years, were unsuccessful; stimulated European-Muslim trade and reintroduced Europeans to wisdom that had been last taught during the Classical period.

Nomadic and Traveling Empires

Ottomans: Group of Anatolian Turks who, in their dedication to Islam, attacked the weakening Byzantine Empire and captured Constantinople in 1453; expanded to create an empire in the Middle East and Southeast Europe; collapsed after World War I.

Mongols: Group of Central Asian nomads from Mongolia who, under the leadership of Genghis Khan, conquered large portions of the Asian continent; four empires, centered on Russia, China, Persia, and the Central Asian steppes, were led by Khan's successors until the Mongol Empire collapsed into disunity and civil war.

Genghis Khan: Mongol clan leader who united the clans and made the Mongols the most feared force in Asia; under his leadership, the Mongol Empire expanded greatly into China, Persia, Central Asia, and Tibet; sons ruled the Four Khanates that followed; grandson, Kublai Khan, became leader of the Yuan Dynasty in 1271.

Civilizations in Africa

Mansa Musa: Ruling from 1312 to 1337, he was the most famous of the Mali emperors; capital city, Timbuktu, was a center of trade, culture, and education; most famous for going on pilgrimage to Mecca (a practice that few Muslims in his time actually did) carrying a large caravan with satchels of gold, which he used to fund schools and mosques across North Africa.

Swahili city-states: Cities in East Africa (present-day Somalia, Kenya, and Tanzania) that became bustling ports due to interchanges between Bantu and Arab mariners; in an effort to facilitate trade, the Bantus created a hybrid language, Swahili, that allowed them to communicate with the Arabs (a language that is still spoken by over 80 million East Africans).

Interregional Economic and Cultural Exchange

Melaka: Located in modern-day Malaysia; port city that became a waystation for sea traders from China and India in the fourteenth century.

Bubonic plague: Disease that spread from China to Europe through rats and decimated Europe's population; ended the feudal system and led many people to question religion; also known as the Black Plague or the Black Death.

Ibn Battuta: Islamic traveler who, in the fourteenth century, visited the kingdom of Mansa Musa in the Mali Empire; his writings stimulated an interest in African trade.

Marco Polo: Venetian merchant who spent over 20 years traveling the Silk Road through the Mongol Empire, where he actually served on the court of its ruler, Kublai Khan; his efforts stimulated interest in trade with China.

Recovery and Renaissance in Asia and Europe

Renaissance: A period of artistic and scientific self-discovery and relearning of Classical wisdom, particularly from the fourteenth through the sixteenth centuries; stimulated by the Crusades and soldiers' exposure to Muslim advances in math, science, and the arts; also led to questioning of the nature of religion and natural phenomena.

TEST WHAT YOU LEARNED

Part A: Quiz

Questions 1–2 refer to the passage below.

"Nokhor, or Ongcor [Angkor], was the capital of the ancient kingdom of Cambodia, or Khmer, formerly so famous among the great states of Indo-China, that almost the only tradition preserved in the country mentions that empire as having had twenty kings who paid tribute to it, as having kept up an army of five or six million soldiers, and that the buildings of the royal treasury occupied a space of more than 300 miles.

In the province still bearing the name of Ongcor, which is situated eastward of the great lake Touli-Sap . . . there are, on the banks of the Mekon, and in the ancient kingdom of Tsiampois (Cochin-China), ruins of such grandeur*, remains of structures which must have been raised at such an immense cost of labour, that, at the first view, one is filled with profound admiration, and cannot but ask what has become of this powerful race, so civilised, so enlightened, the authors of these gigantic works?"

*A succession of Khmer rulers changed the state religion between Buddhism and Hinduism, after years of wars with Buddhist and Hindu neighbors. The ruins at Angkor, particularly the temples, display a fusion of Buddhist and Hindu imagery, as rulers often expanded or defaced the temples to emphasize the change in governance.

H. Mouhot, *Travels in the Central Parts of Indo-China (Siam), Cambodia, and Laos*, 1864

1. Historians posit that Hindu/Buddhist empires, such as the one discussed in the passage, represent the ways in which religion and state formation are connected. The example of the Khmer Empire is most similar to which of the following?

   (A) The expulsion of Jews in the Iberian Peninsula

   (B) The sacking of Constantinople in the Fourth Crusade

   (C) The adoption of Islam by elites in Western Africa

   (D) The spread of Islam along the Silk Road and Spice Route

2. A modern historian researching the Khmer Empire would benefit most from which of the following in evaluating the passage?

   (A) Access to all of the rest of the cited author's works

   (B) Further travel accounts by Europeans in the nineteenth century

   (C) Satellite analysis of the temples of Angkor

   (D) Primary source material from the Khmer Imperial period

Questions 3–4 refer to the map below.

BAGHDAD, 150–300 C.E.

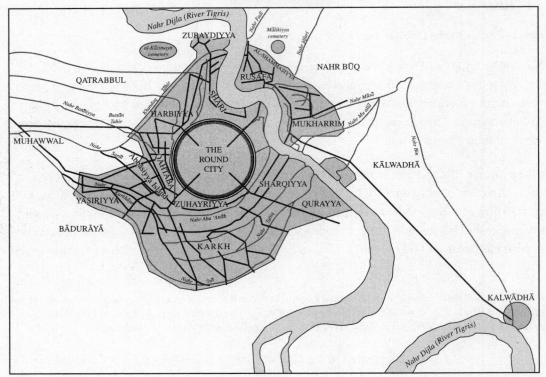

The map depicts canals (light lines) and highways (dark lines) built into the early city of Baghdad.

3. A historian would most likely use the map of early Baghdad to support which of the following statements about commercial exchange in the period 1200–1450?

   (A) The Eastern Hemisphere was connected through long-existing land and water routes.

   (B) Novel disease pathogens spread along trade routes, decreasing populations.

   (C) Religious beliefs transformed as they diffused along trade routes.

   (D) Technologies such as printing and gunpowder were exchanged alongside goods.

4. Cities along the Silk Road, such as Baghdad, experienced growth due to which of the following?

   (A) Advances in domestic manufacturing and production

   (B) Increased demand for Asian manufactured goods

   (C) A mass movement of people from rural areas to cities

   (D) Strong centralized government infrastructure projects

Questions 5–6 refer to the passage below.

"History is filled with the sound of silken slippers going downstairs and wooden shoes coming up."

Quote attributed to Voltaire, French Enlightenment writer, historian, and philosopher, circa 1740

5. A proponent of the idea presented in the excerpt—that history is full of cycles in which the elite are overthrown by an underclass that subsequently become the new elite—would most likely use which of the following as an example?

(A) The sack of Constantinople in 1204

(B) The rise of the Ghanaian Empire

(C) The Chinese Red Turban Rebellion

(D) The split of the Romans and Byzantines

6. A historian evaluating the concept in the excerpt for the time period 1200–1450 would benefit most from which of the following?

(A) Records of political change across the period in one region

(B) Records of population growth in the Americas and Europe

(C) Primary source accounts of governments in the period

(D) Primary source accounts of religious and social change

Questions 7–9 refer to the map below.

WEST AFRICAN TRADE ROUTES

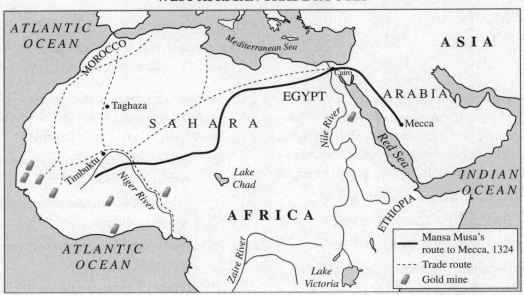

7. Musa I (also known as Mansa Musa) made a notable pilgrimage to Mecca and worked to spread Islam throughout his reign. This is an example of which of the following?

   (A) Forced conversion of conquered populations

   (B) The spread of Islam facilitating trade relationships

   (C) Religious conflict between native African religions

   (D) A sectarian split between Sunni and Shi'a in Africa

8. A modern historian evaluating the economic strength of the Malian Empire would benefit most from which of the following?

   (A) The production of gold in troy ounces at the height of the empire

   (B) The number of trading caravans that departed Timbuktu annually

   (C) Economic records from Mali and its closest neighboring states

   (D) Records of the gold expenditure during Musa I's pilgrimage to Mecca

9. Based on your knowledge of world history, the information in the map could best be used to support which of the following arguments?

   (A) Social and cultural changes often spread along trade routes.

   (B) Religious conflict in northern Africa dampened trade relationships.

   (C) The movement of populations was facilitated by shared religion.

   (D) Strong imperial states conquered weaker states along trading routes.

Questions 10–11 refer to the map below.

MAP OF THE GRAND CANAL, CHINA

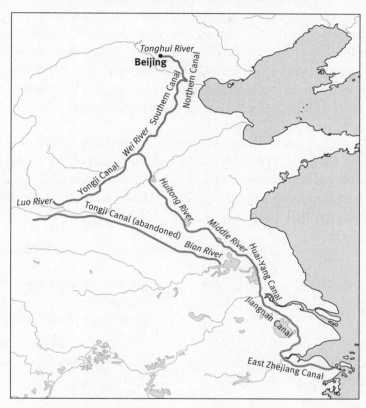

10. Over the course of millennia, the Grand Canal went through periods of use and disuse. In the 1200s and 1400s, it was expanded and modernized by the Song and Ming Dynasties, leading to which of the following effects?

    (A) Domestic economic growth encouraged by ease of transport

    (B) Increased diffusion of industrial technologies from Europe

    (C) Increased international trade with neighboring countries in Asia

    (D) The growth of state-owned enterprise in the Chinese economy

11. The economic impact of the Grand Canal in China is most similar to the economic impact of which of the following?

    (A) The spread of bubonic plague in Western Europe in the 1300s

    (B) The establishment of the Inca road system in South America

    (C) The establishment of the Silk Road across Asia and the Middle East

    (D) The establishment of the Hanseatic League in Northern Europe

Questions 12–15 refer to the passage below.

"That [Europe's] nations could so quickly overcome such a fearful concussion in their external circumstances, and, in general, without retrograding more than they actually did, could so develop their energies in the following century, is a most convincing proof of the indestructibility of human society as a whole. To assume, however, that it did not suffer any essential change internally, because in appearance everything remained as before, is inconsistent with a just view of cause and effect. . . . We, for our parts, are convinced that in the history of the world the Black Death is one of the most important events which have prepared the way for the present state of Europe.

He who studies . . . may perhaps find some proofs of this assertion in the following observations:—at that time, the advancement of the hierarchy was, in most countries, extraordinary; for the Church acquired treasures and large properties in land, even to a greater extent than after the Crusades; but experience has demonstrated that such a state of things is ruinous to the people, and causes them to retrograde, as was evinced on this occasion."

J. F. C. Hecker, a medical writer, *The Black Death, and The Dancing Mania*, 1888

12. Which of the following best illustrates Hecker's description of Europe as "retrograding" during this period?

   (A) The Black Death's seemingly inexplicable cause led to a new crusade with Muslims in the Holy Land serving as scapegoats.

   (B) The Black Death created a scarcity in the labor supply that led to a decline in serfdom in both Western and Eastern Europe.

   (C) The Black Death sparked the self-flagellation movement as the religious authority of the Catholic Church came into question.

   (D) The Black Death led to widespread deforestation and the clearing of primeval land as refugees fled to the countryside.

13. Despite outward appearances as described by Hecker, Europe's internal change was best illustrated by which of the following?

   (A) The death of two-thirds of Europe's population in the first five years of the plague alone

   (B) The overthrow of the English monarchy by dissatisfied nobles in Parliament

   (C) The initiation of the Hundred Years' War between France and England

   (D) The resulting labor shortage that led to workers demanding higher wages

14. Which of the following best explains Hecker's characterization of the Catholic Church gaining assets during this time period?

(A) The Church's additional lands and money allowed it to finance further crusades, which proved to be military disasters.

(B) The Church's newfound resources allowed it to administer medicine to more plague victims and lessen the plague's lethality.

(C) The Church's increased wealth fostered institutional corruption that eventually sparked the Protestant Reformation.

(D) The Church's vast sums of capital allowed it to finance the arts and architecture that made the Renaissance possible.

15. The reference in the first paragraph to the fact that Europeans "could so develop their energies in the following century" is best understood in the context of which of the following?

(A) The artistic masterpieces and scientific discoveries of the Renaissance

(B) The initial crusades into the Middle East renewing European interest in Classical culture

(C) The exploration of new ideas in politics and philosophy in the Enlightenment

(D) The development of English and French national identities during the Hundred Years' War

3

Part B: Key Terms

This key terms list is the same as the list in the Test What You Already Know section earlier in this chapter. Based on what you have now learned, again ask yourself the following questions:

- Can I describe this key term?
- Can I discuss this key term in the context of other events?
- Could I correctly answer a multiple-choice question about this key term?
- Could I correctly answer a free-response question about this key term?

Check off the key terms if you can answer "yes" to at least three of these questions.

Cultural Developments and Belief Systems

- ☐ Neo-Confucianism
- ☐ Eastern Orthodox Church
- ☐ Sunni
- ☐ Catholic Church
- ☐ Shi'a

Civilizations in the Americas

- ☐ *Chinampa*
- ☐ *Mit'a*

Civilizations in East Asia

- ☐ Mandate of Heaven
- ☐ Grand Canal
- ☐ Champa rice

Islamic Golden Age

- ☐ Al-Andalus
- ☐ Astrolabe
- ☐ Trans-Saharan trade

Europe During the Late Middle Ages

- ☐ Feudalism
- ☐ Bills of exchange
- ☐ Crusades

Nomadic and Traveling Empires

- ☐ Ottoman
- ☐ Mongols
- ☐ Genghis Khan

Civilizations in Africa

- ☐ Mansa Musa
- ☐ Swahili city-states

Interregional Economic and Cultural Exchange

☐ Melaka   ☐ Ibn Battuta   ☐ Marco Polo

☐ Bubonic plague

Recovery and Renaissance in Asia and Europe

☐ Renaissance

Next Steps

Step 1: Tally your correct answers from Part A, and review the quiz explanations at the end of this chapter.

1. C	6. A	11. B
2. D	7. B	12. C
3. A	8. C	13. D
4. B	9. A	14. C
5. C	10. A	15. A

_____ out of 15 questions

Step 2: Count the number of key terms you checked off in Part B.

_____ out of 26 key terms

Step 3: Compare your Test What You Already Know results to these Test What You Learned results to see how exam-ready you are for this period.

For More Practice:

- Read (or reread) the comprehensive review for this period in Chapter 7.

- Complete the Practice Set assessment at the end of Chapter 7.

- Go to kaptest.com to complete the online quiz questions for 1200 to 1450.

  ○ Haven't registered your book yet? Go to kaptest.com/moreonline to begin.

ANSWERS AND EXPLANATIONS

Test What You Already Know

1. B

In evaluating the accuracy of a primary source, the most useful tool for evaluating it is another primary source, preferably one not connected to the first document. Thus, **(B)** is correct. While a secondary source can be useful in terms of consulting experts on the accuracy of a given source or author, primary sources are still best evaluated by comparing them to concrete evidence, such as other eyewitness accounts, so (A) and (C) are incorrect. While (D) is tempting, an unconnected primary source would be more useful since he or she would not possess the same background and biases as John of Plano Carpini's party.

2. B

Both the British Empire and the Mongol Empire established periods of economic and political stability by conquering large swaths of the world. Known as the *Pax Britannica* and *Pax Mongolica* respectively, these periods enabled trade to flourish within a large zone of common administration. This trade also allowed for the flow of culture and technology between world regions. Thus, **(B)** is correct. At their maximum extent, the British ruled nearly a quarter of the Earth's land area, but they never ruled all of Asia; in fact, nineteenth century Russia was a British geopolitical rival. Similarly, the Mongols never extended their control of Asia across all of India. (A) is incorrect. Rebellions only overthrew some of the Mongol successor states after the unified empire had already collapsed due to disputes over succession, while Britain generally decolonized peacefully. (C) is incorrect. While the British Empire spread English as a common language, the Mongols did not forcibly spread their own or any other language. (D) is incorrect.

3. A

Circa 1200, Islam had expanded throughout North and West Africa. It provided a common cultural identity for elites from various nations, easing diplomacy and facilitating the expansion of trade networks. Thus, **(A)** is correct. While tempting, (B) is incorrect; the map is labeled as depicting trade networks circa 1400, but the Mongol Empire had fractured into various khanates by 1294, and Silk Road trade largely broke down over the fourteenth century. Likewise, (C) is incorrect because the Portuguese did not begin their expansion along the West African coastline until 1415. (D) is incorrect because Islam was already practiced in West Africa circa 1230, when Sundiata Keita established the Mali Empire.

4. D

Trans-Saharan trade circa 1400 depended on merchants having both the technology and environmental knowledge to travel across the Sahara Desert. The technology included the camel, as the more globally common horse was unsuited to the extreme conditions of the Sahara. The environmental knowledge included travel time and distance of particular routes, as well as management of water resources. Thus, **(D)** is correct. (A) is incorrect because there was little state-sponsored commercial infrastructure around the Sahara (especially compared to other regions; e.g., the Inca road network in the Andes). While Mali was known for its gold exports during this period as a form of hard money, (B) is incorrect because the map focuses on trade routes, not the economies that revolved around them. (C) is incorrect because the Columbian Exchange occurred nearly a century after the trans-Sahara routes of 1400.

5. B

During the Crusades, Western Europe's elites personally experienced the diverse luxury goods and literature of the Eastern Roman Empire and the Muslim caliphate. This, plus increased shipping capacity for troop movements, boosted the already-growing trade volumes with the eastern Mediterranean and led to increased interaction with all the civilizations to the south and east of Europe. Therefore, **(B)** is correct. While navigational technology improved in Europe due to the Crusades, the Holy Land is in the Middle East, not East Asia, so (A) is incorrect. (C) is incorrect because the Crusades actually weakened feudalism: the knightly class loosened its hold on its landed estates due to prolonged absences, war deaths, and sales to raise travel funds. (D) is incorrect because it reverses cause and effect. The sanctions against trade with Islamic kingdoms cannot be a continuing failure because the decree is establishing them.

6. C

The Eastern Roman (Byzantine) Empire had been fighting the Islamic armies for centuries and had hoped the

Western crusaders would join with them in a Christian coalition. However, in 1204, in a climax to increasingly hostile sectarian tensions, crusaders sacked the imperial capital of Constantinople. The punitive attitude toward Christians diverging from Catholic doctrine is reflected in the passage; **(C)** is correct. (A) is incorrect because the self-flagellant movement arose in response to the Black Death. Also, the Crusades did retake the Holy Land, but they could not hold onto it indefinitely. (B) is incorrect because the Avignon Papacy was rooted in a conflict between the Church and France over the extent of the papacy's secular authority. (D) is incorrect because, while philosophers like Thomas Aquinas synthesized ancient Greek philosophy and Christian revelation, discussion of those ancient works was not previously unacceptable. They had merely been lost until reintroduced to Europe by the Islamic world.

7. A

The treasure fleets were an attempt by the Ming Dynasty to project Chinese wealth and power around the Indian Ocean, thus enticing various trading ports and states to become Chinese tributaries. Therefore, **(A)** is correct. The map does not depict the Silk Road maritime routes, so (B) is incorrect. (C) is a speculative statement that cannot be supported using the information presented in the map. (D) is incorrect because it attributes the voyages depicted on the map to the incorrect Chinese dynasty: Zheng He commanded these fleets during the Ming Dynasty, not the Song Dynasty.

8. D

From 1405 to 1433, the Ming Dynasty sponsored seven massive naval expeditions in order to reinforce Chinese presence in the Indian Ocean, impose imperial control over trade, and impress foreign peoples with the authority of the Ming Dynasty. However, Confucian officials convinced the Chinese emperor that the voyages were too expensive and unprofitable, especially because of renewed concern over the northern Mongol border. Thus, in 1433, the voyages ended. This contraction of Chinese influence left the Indian Ocean uncontested when Portugal sent its first ship to India in 1498. Thus, **(D)** is correct. While the Mongols were a factor in the decline of the treasure fleets, (A) is incorrect because Temujin is another name for Genghis Khan, who died in the thirteenth century. (B) and (C) are incorrect because the Ming, not the Yuan, sponsored Zheng He.

9. D

Confucian officials in the court of the Ming emperor believed that Zheng He's voyages were too expensive and not worth the cost of investment, as the money could be better spent elsewhere. This fear of lavish spending is justified in light of the Mali Empire's downfall, as overspending by a series of kings spurred internal unrest and the collapse of their empire. Thus, **(D)** is correct. The Mongol conquest of Song China took many decades and was a hard-fought conflict, which does not reflect either party weakened by excessive spending; (A) is incorrect. The outbreak of the Hundred Years' War was caused by tensions between English and French kings over territory in Scotland and Flanders, as well as the issue of dynastic succession. (B) is incorrect. (C) is incorrect because the 1204 sack of Constantinople primarily resulted from a sectarian religious conflict between Eastern Orthodox Christians and Roman Catholics.

10. A

The Hanseatic League was a trading organization that filled a void created by the weak, decentralized states common to Western and Northern Europe in the period circa 1200 to 1450. The passage illustrates the varieties of goods that flowed through Europe during a time when states were weak; this flow was made possible by the Hanseatic League, so **(A)** is correct. Nothing in the passage is suggestive of commercial infrastructure playing a vital role in commerce, making (B) incorrect. While the activities of a Hanseatic merchant are discussed in the passage, nothing related to banks or bills of exchange is mentioned; (C) is incorrect. While the passage describes Europe shifting away from feudal agriculture to a commercial economy, industrialization did not begin until the eighteenth century, so (D) is also incorrect.

11. A

The passage compares Bruges to early twentieth-century London as the "world-mart" of its day, a market where goods from all across the world are bought and sold. To determine whether this is an accurate comparison, more information on the origin and comparative value of the goods (such as spices) being sold in each city during their respective periods would be useful. Thus, **(A)** is correct. (B) is incorrect because the question is comparing the trade of both cities, not anything to do with their populations. (C) is incorrect because the question is asking about the diversity and richness of the goods traded in both cities, not about the Hanseatic League, which declined over the centuries and, in particular, after the formation of the German Empire in 1871. (D) is incorrect because tax revenue is not necessarily indicative of the diversity of goods being traded in a city, and there are other potential sources of tax revenue besides trade.

12. C

The Mexica, or Aztec, people built causeways to connect their capital, Tenochtitlan, to the mainland and used *chinampas*, or floating gardens, to create more land for farming. **(C)** is correct. (A) is incorrect because they did not have natural barriers, such as mountains, to provide protection from invaders. (B) is incorrect because the Americas lacked draft animals for heavy labor in the pre-Columbian era. The Mexica were able to sustain their population with their food production, making (D) incorrect.

13. B

Cities flourished as centers of trade in part because of agricultural innovations, such as the *chinampas* depicted on the map. While the Mexica did not invent *chinampas*, they were the first to use them at a large scale, leading to increased yields that could support a growing population. **(B)** is correct. In times of invasions, cities are more vulnerable because wealth is concentrated in one location, so the factors described in (A) would not lead to urban revival. (C) is incorrect because industrialization did not occur until the late eighteenth century. (D) is incorrect because, if trade was declining, cities would decline as well due to fewer commercial transactions.

14. A

The Mexica were militaristic and conquered surrounding groups, forcing them to pay tribute in the form of goods or people; **(A)** is correct. The government was centralized under the rule of an emperor, making (B) incorrect. (C) is incorrect because, although the empire was centralized, they lacked an organized bureaucracy. The government controlled much of modern-day Mexico, so (D) is incorrect.

15. D

In many civilizations through world history, cities have tended to have multiple roles, including seats of government, trading hubs, and religious centers; this is due to the fact that there is a large concentration of people in these urban areas. **(D)** is correct. (A) is incorrect because rural areas usually provide food and supplies for urban markets. (B) is incorrect because people live in cities in addition to conducting business there. (C) is incorrect because cities do not necessarily have access to lakes, swamps, and islands.

Test What You Learned

1. C

Rulers across the world in this period fused religion and state identity to create a durable governing foundation so that the legitimacy of state power would not be questioned. The Khmer Empire exemplifies the ways in which religion and government changed and shifted together. Similarly, rulers such as Mansa Musa used changes in religion to strengthen their rule. Mansa Musa adopted Islam in Western African states along the trans-Saharan trade route and created new relationships with neighboring states based on shared religion. **(C)** is correct. (A) is incorrect because the Jewish people did not rule in the Iberian peninsula; they were a minority given a choice between forced conversion and exile. The Crusaders sacked Constantinople in 1204, but both sides of that conflict were of the same religion, Christianity, so no major religious change occurred based on a shift in governance; (B) is incorrect. Islam did spread along the Silk Road and Spice Route, but that diffusion did not directly stem from changes in state religion, so (D) is incorrect.

2. D

Primary sources are invaluable in researching the lived reality of cultures over time because they come directly from the time and place being studied. In contrast, secondary sources always come from a later time (and sometimes a different place), so they encode the biases, preconceived notions, suppositions, and mistakes of their authors and their authors' distinct cultures. Thus, to evaluate this secondary source, primary sources would be most helpful; **(D)** is correct. While a literary historian might want to read the rest of the author's works, the best way to evaluate a passage of this kind is by corroborating it with primary sources, so (A) is incorrect. (B) is incorrect for similar reasons as (A); looking at European travel accounts would give historical insight into that period, but not the Khmer Empire itself. Satellite analysis of Angkor is itself primary source analysis, but would not cover the entire scope of the Khmer Empire, only the remains of its capital city, so (C) is incorrect.

3. A

All of the choices are true, but the only one directly supported by the map is **(A)**. The map contains roads, canals, and the Tigris River, which feeds into the Persian Gulf. This offers proof that land routes and water routes ran through Baghdad even in the early common era, and this could be extrapolated forward to the era in the question, though more evidence would be needed for the conclusion to be proven and not merely proposed. This is an example of supporting evidence, not conclusive proof. While pathogens, religions, and technologies did flow along trade routes as noted, those conclusions are not directly supported by the map alone and would require additional source material for evidence. (B), (C), and (D) are incorrect.

4. B

As the Afro-Eurasian market for Asian goods expanded, the trading cities grew to meet the expanded demand and increased volume of trading caravans; **(B)** is correct. Manufacturing was expanded in Asia, notably China with iron and steel, but it was not a major part of the economy of the trading cities, so (A) is incorrect. There was a movement from rural to urban areas much later during the Industrial Revolution, but not in the period in the question; (C) is incorrect. The trading cities belonged to many different states or were independent; the trade route was not directly created by governments. (D) is thus incorrect.

5. C

The Red Turban Rebellion, an uprising of Chinese peasants upset over Mongol domination and high taxation, best reflects Voltaire's idea of a historical cycle where the elite are overthrown by an underclass that subsequently become the new elite. The Mongols had once been steppe nomads poor enough that they were forced to make clothes from the pelts of field mice. Later, even with the fragmentation of their empire, they ruled China under the banner of the Yuan Dynasty. Zhu Yuanzhang, a peasant turned Red Turban, would overthrow them and become the first Ming emperor. Therefore, **(C)** is correct. The sack of Constantinople weakened the Byzantine Empire, but the Crusaders only looted the city; they did not take power, so (A) is incorrect. The Ghanaian Empire arose organically from villages along a trade network; thus, (C) is incorrect. The Byzantine Empire was created as the Roman Empire shrank, and the Byzantines thought of themselves as Roman; this is an example of reorganization, not rebellion. Thus, (D) is incorrect.

6. A

Analyzing change over time in a single area would allow the historian to find a concrete example of the phenomenon; if it is true, then the analysis could be applied to other regions for further testing. This is a common technique that allows scholars to see effects that were likely happening across broader areas, without making their inquiry too broad and getting bogged down in too much data. The important thing is the scope of the source, either through time, or across multiple regions, or both. **(A)** is correct. Records of population growth could be used to support conclusions about governments and change, but not by themselves; (B) is incorrect. Primary source accounts of governments could be used indirectly to see changes over time, but like the population records, these are best used as supporting sources. (C) is incorrect. Religious and social changes often cross political boundaries and are not a reliable indication of governmental change; (D) is incorrect.

7. B

Situated at the western end of the Trans-Saharan trade route, the Malian conversion to and spread of Islam contributed to trade and diplomatic relationships with neighboring states and exposure to the broader Islamic world (Dar al-Islam); **(B)** is correct. The Ottomans practiced forced conversion, but the Malians did not; (A) is incorrect. Islam spread in Africa from the Arabian peninsula and supplanted native African religions, especially in states in Northern Africa, but we cannot know if it caused conflict among the native religions. The wide acceptance of a foreign religion like Islam indicates an atmosphere of religious tolerance, though more evidence would be needed to prove that. (C) is incorrect. Both Shi'a and Sunni make a pilgrimage to Mecca (hajj), so we cannot make a judgment about sectarian splits in Africa from this example alone; (D) is incorrect.

8. C

Analyzing Malian production, building, and trade relationships compared to its closest neighbors would give us the most accurate picture of the empire relative to its contemporaries; **(C)** is correct. Knowing gold production weights would not tell us the relative value of that gold during the Malian Imperial period, so (A) is incorrect here. However, that information could be useful in another context, for example in an analysis of relative gold production among states in the period. Trading caravans leaving one city would give us a lopsided picture of the total imperial economy; (B) is incorrect. The expenditure of gold along the pilgrimage route to Mecca is one of the legendary aspects of Musa I and his reign, but it does not significantly indicate the economic strength of the Malian Empire; (D) is incorrect.

9. A

Islam spread into Africa from the Arabian peninsula after its founding in the seventh century, eventually making it to the western end of the continent. The map shows one result, as an Islamic leader makes a pilgrimage back to the Arabian peninsula. Trade routes are typically created by non-state actors and follow the boundaries of geography, particularly in arid regions like northern Africa. **(A)** is correct. Most of the northern African states were Islamic; (B) is incorrect. The map does not indicate a movement of populations, and we cannot support that inference from the evidence here; (C) is incorrect. Similarly, while we could find examples of stronger states conquering weaker neighbors, or forcing them into tributary relationships, this map would not work as evidence for that claim; (D) is incorrect.

10. A

Starting before the common era and continuing in stages to the present, successive dynasties sponsored the construction and expansion of the Grand Canal, with the goal of improving trade between the northern and southern regions of China. Most of the major Chinese rivers are not navigable by trade vessels. By the 1200s (the Song Dynasty), advances in agricultural production coupled with transportation innovations like the Grand Canal led to economic growth. **(A)** is correct. (B) is incorrect because the canal was built before European industrialization, which began around 1750. In this era, China was exporting innovations to Europe, like gunpowder and paper. The main aim and effect of the Grand Canal was more efficiently moving products internally within Chinese markets, not internationally; (C) is incorrect. State-owned enterprise was a feature of twentieth-century China, not thirteenth- to fifteenth-century China; (D) is incorrect.

11. B

The main effect of the Grand Canal and the Inca road system was the facilitation of intra-regional trade by state

sponsored infrastructure; **(B)** is correct. The spread of plague in Europe affected the economy negatively and was not caused by infrastructure development, so (A) is incorrect. The Silk Road crossed national boundaries and created prosperity across countries and regions, not in only one; (C) is incorrect. The Hanseatic League fostered inter-regional trade between different states and independent cities, not intra-regional trade within one governmental entity; (D) is incorrect.

12. C

The Black Death (bubonic plague) spread through infected fleas carried by rodents, but Europeans at the time did not understand this disease vector. Instead interpreting the plague as divine punishment and viewing the Church as powerless to stop it, many Europeans turned to whipping themselves as penance for their sins. Thus, **(C)** is correct. While the crusades continued in piecemeal fashion into the early fifteenth century, Muslims in the Holy Land were not specifically targeted as scapegoats for the plague. Rather, Jews and other minorities within Europe were. So (A) is incorrect. Although the labor scarcity created by the plague helped end serfdom in Western Europe, it did not do so in Eastern Europe, which suffered comparatively less population loss. That makes (B) incorrect. Europe was largely deforested prior to the plague; the widespread population loss from the plague actually led to reforestation. (D) is incorrect because it suggests the opposite.

13. D

While the societies and institutions of Western Europe had outwardly endured the plague unaltered, internally they had changed due to, for example, a labor shortage. Workers were able to demand higher wages and greater political rights, such as freedom of movement, which contributed to undermining feudalism. Thus, **(D)** is correct. Only one-third of the population died in the first five years of the plague, not two-thirds; (A) is incorrect. The English Civil War did not take place until the seventeenth century. In fact, the plague strengthened the power of monarchies throughout Europe; (B) is incorrect. While tempting due to the plague's impact on the course of the conflict, especially in terms of French manpower loss, (C) is incorrect because the start of the Hundred Years' War predates the outbreak of the plague in Europe by a decade.

14. C

Hecker offers a negative characterization of the Catholic Church gaining new lands and money during the plague, suggesting it led to retrogression. In fact, the introduction of added wealth spurred a culture of corruption and wealth-seeking within the Church that helped spark the Protestant Reformation a century and a half later. Thus, **(C)** is correct. (A) is incorrect because there were only nine official crusades conducted by the Catholic Church, the last of which ended in 1291. Later crusades were regional or national affairs, not overseen by the Church. (B) is incorrect because medical science in this time period was unable to treat the plague. (D) is incorrect because, while the financial gains made by the Church did help fund various Renaissance projects later on, Hecker is referencing a negative outcome for the Church, not a positive one.

15. A

In the context of the passage, Hecker is referring to near-term positive developments for European civilization after it suffered greatly from the Black Death. The Renaissance was a period of artistic and scientific self-discovery in Europe, particularly from the fourteenth through the sixteenth centuries. Thus, **(A)** is correct. The First Crusade was called for in 1095, long before the plague; (B) is incorrect. The Enlightenment took place in the seventeenth and eighteenth centuries—too late for Hecker; (C) is incorrect. Although (D) is tempting in the context of the war strengthening English and French identity and government, it is too limited to be correct. The Renaissance had a widespread impact throughout the European continent.

CHAPTER 4

1450 to 1750

LEARNING OBJECTIVES

- Describe the interrelationships between various economic exchange networks.

- Explain changes in the way governments work and are structured.

- Analyze the effects of labor reform movements, including changes in labor systems.

- Describe the impact of technological and scientific progress on populations.

- Describe the effect of exchange networks on culture across regions.

- Explain how industrialization and globalization were shaped by technology.

TIMELINE

Date	Region	Event
1403–1433	East Asia	Voyages of Zheng He
1453	Mid East	Ottoman conquest of Constantinople
1456	Europe	Johannes Gutenberg introduces printing press
1464	West Africa	Songhai Empire established
1492	Caribbean	European explorers reach the New World
1501–1736	Mid East	Safavid Dynasty in Iran
1517	Europe	Protestant Reformation begins
1526	South Asia	Mughal Empire established
1543	Europe	Copernicus publishes theory of heliocentrism
1588	Europe	England defeats the Spanish Armada
1618–1648	Europe	Thirty Years War; ended with Peace of Westphalia
1603	East Asia	Tokugawa shogunate established
1636	East Asia	Qing Dynasty established
1652	South Africa	Cape Town Colony is established
1650–1800	Europe	Enlightenment

TEST WHAT YOU ALREADY KNOW

Part A: Quiz

Questions 1–2 refer to the image below.

WORLD SILVER TRADE: PRODUCTION, EXPORTS, AND IMPORTS

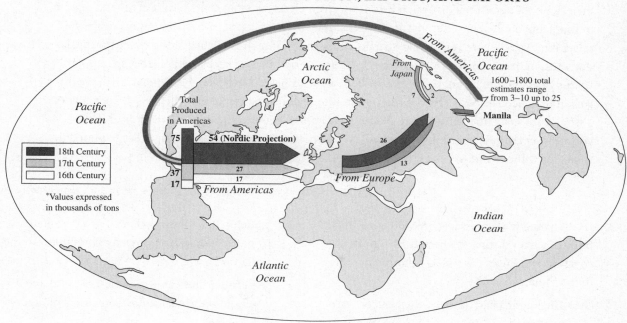

1. The development of the trade networks depicted on the map most directly pertains to which of the following about the silver trade from the sixteenth through eighteenth centuries?

   (A) The demand for silver in China drove the trade networks.

   (B) Spain was unable to attain a supply of silver.

   (C) The Ottoman Empire served as the middle-man in the silver trade.

   (D) The Ming Dynasty was strengthened due to the inflation caused by silver.

2. Which of the following was the most direct consequence of the silver trade depicted on the map above?

   (A) The Spanish empire used its great wealth to modernize its feudal economy.

   (B) A global trade system developed, the first between all major centers of civilization.

   (C) Britain waged the Opium War to force China off the silver standard.

   (D) Gold declined in value, increasing the volume of the Atlantic slave trade.

Questions 3–4 refer to the passage below.

"My Honourable Friends,

. . . For a Fort, at my first arrival I received it as very Necessary; but experience teaches me we are refused it to our advantage. If [the King] would offer me ten, I would not accept one. . . . the Charge is greater than the trade can bear; for to maintain a garrison will eat the Profit. It is not an hundred men can keep it; for the Portugal, if he once see you undertake that course, will set his rest upon it to supplant you. A war and traffic are incompatible. By my consent, you shall no way engage your selves but at sea, where you are like to gain as often as to lose. It is the beggaring of the Portugal, notwithstanding his many rich residences and territories, that he keeps soldiers that spends it; yet his garrisons are mean. He never Profited by the Indies, since he defended them. Observe this well. It hath been also the error of the Dutch, who seek Plantation here by the Sword. They turned a wonderful stock, they prowl in all Places, they Possess some of the best; yet their dead [fields] consume all the gain. Let this be received as a rule that if you will Profit, seek it at Sea, and in quiet trade; for without controversy it is an error to affect Garrisons and Land wars in India."

Sir Thomas Roe, excerpt from letter to the East India Company, 1616

3. As discussed in the passage, how did emerging trade practices during the period 1450 to 1750 contribute to England's rise as a dominant power in the Indian Ocean?

   (A) The English had defeated their major competitors, the Chinese, in the Opium War.

   (B) England used joint-stock companies of private investors, who traded flexibly for profit rather than for royal prestige.

   (C) The Ottoman Empire had great difficulty retaining its position as the dominant power in the Indian Ocean.

   (D) The Portuguese voluntarily withdrew their economic interests from the region.

4. Which of the following later events resulted from the East India Company's monopoly of the India trade?

   (A) The American Revolution of 1776, as a result of the East India Company's monopoly on tea

   (B) Russian penetration of Central Asia in 1847, as a result of England's expansion in India

   (C) The Indian Rebellion of 1857, as a result of England's control over India's sovereignty

   (D) The settlement of Australia in 1788, as a result of an overflow of English criminals sent to India

Questions 5–6 refer to the passage below.

"Why, I asked, should we not admire the angels themselves and the beatific choirs more? At long last, however, I feel that I have come to some understanding of why man is the most fortunate of living things and, consequently, deserving of all admiration; of what may be the condition in the hierarchy of beings assigned to him, which draws upon him the envy, not of the brutes alone, but of the astral beings and of the very intelligences which dwell beyond the confines of the world. . . .

But when this work was done, the Divine Artificer still longed for some creature which might comprehend the meaning of so vast an achievement, which might be moved with love at its beauty and smitten with awe at its grandeur. When, consequently, all else had been completed (as both Moses and Timaeus testify), in the very last place, He bethought Himself of bringing forth man. Truth was, however, that there remained no archetype according to which He might fashion a new offspring, nor in His treasure-houses the wherewithal to endow a new son with a fitting inheritance, nor any place, among the seats of the universe, where this new creature might dispose himself to contemplate the world. All space was already filled; all things had been distributed in the highest, the middle and the lowest orders. Still, it was not in the nature of the power of the Father to fail in this last creative élan; nor was it in the nature of that supreme Wisdom to hesitate through lack of counsel in so crucial a matter; nor, finally, in the nature of His beneficent love to compel the creature destined to praise the divine generosity in all other things to find it wanting in himself."

Giovanni Pico della Mirandola, *Oration on the Dignity of Man*, 1486

5. The ideas expressed in the passage best reflect which of the following characteristics of the Renaissance?

    (A) A celebration of Chinese and Islamic art

    (B) A development of the new art form chiaroscuro

    (C) A growing acceptance of atheism

    (D) A view of humankind as creative and rational

6. Which of the following best explains the origin of the Renaissance in Italy?

    (A) Italian city-states were geographically isolated from most of Europe.

    (B) The Protestant Reformation weakened the Church's control over society.

    (C) Northern Italy helped supply and transport goods during the Crusades.

    (D) Political power in Italy was highly centralized.

Questions 7–8 refer to the passage below.

"Cortes advanced some four leagues beyond the great wall of Tlascala, despite the entreaties of the cacique of Yxtacamaxtitlan, who again warned him against the Tlascalans and offered to conduct him to Mexico by way of Cholula.

Accompanied by six horsemen, he rode about half a league ahead of his army, while a body of light infantry acted as scouts, supported by a vanguard of musketeers and crossbowmen. The artillery was placed in the centre, and the rear was brought up by some two thousand Indians in charge of the baggage and provisions. The first hostile encounter was with a small body of Indians, armed with the maquahuitl and rodela, who attacked the Spaniards with great courage, showing no fear either of firearms or horses. They succeeded in unhorsing one man, who afterwards died of his wounds, and two horses were killed outright. . . . The Indians finally withdrew in good order. Four Spaniards were wounded in this engagement while the Indians had seventeen killed and an immense number of wounded."

Francis Augustus MacNutt, *Fernando Cortes and the Conquest of Mexico, 1485–1547*, 1909

7. The description of the battle in the passage most directly reflects which of the following historical developments in the period 1450 to 1750?

   (A) The Columbian Exchange caused the spread of disease pathogens from the Old World to the New World.

   (B) The Columbian Exchange involved crops brought over from Europe to the Americas.

   (C) The Columbian Exchange did not include significant exchanges of culture between the New and Old World.

   (D) The Columbian Exchange included a transfer of livestock to the Americas.

8. Based on your knowledge of world history, how did Mexica social structure <u>differ</u> most strongly from other social structures during the period 1450 to 1750?

   (A) Mexica rulers claimed that their authority derived from divine sources.

   (B) Mexica women could become property owners.

   (C) Slavery was institutionalized in Mexica society.

   (D) Most Mexica commoners were farmers.

Questions 9–10 refer to the passage below.

"An attempt by Father Collado and some Japanese Christians to rescue Father Flores from his imprisonment in the Dutch Factory still further inflamed the Shōgun's ire. Accordingly, Gonroku, who was severely censured, was ordered to return to Nagasaki, and there to see to it that the two priests and Hirayama, the Japanese captain, were burned alive—or rather slowly roasted to death, while the same sentence was also passed upon all the *religieux* in prison as well as upon those who harboured them. . . .

'Three days after the Great Martyrdom,' we are told, 'by order of the Governor, all the bodies, with images, rosaries, and all the objects of religion seized among the Christians, were cast together into a great pit, as pestiferous objects. . . .'

Although annual galleons came from Macao in that and the following year, yet on October 6th, 1637, an Edict forbade 'any foreigner to travel in the empire, lest Portuguese with passports bearing Dutch names might enter it.'"

James Murdoch, *A History of Japan, Vol. 2*, 1903

9. The passage is best understood in the context of which of the following developments in seventeenth-century Japan?

(A) The Tokugawa shogunate became more interested in expansionist policies, resulting in the colonization of Korea.

(B) The Tokugawa shogunate implemented strict isolationist policies that halted all overseas trade routes entirely.

(C) The Tokugawa shogunate banned Christianity to prevent Spanish and Portuguese colonization attempts.

(D) The Tokugawa shogunate's contact with the West allowed for an influx of ideas and ushered in Japan's Industrial Revolution.

10. The Tokugawa shogunate's effort to sustainably manage natural resources was most similar to which of the following during the period 1450 to 1750?

(A) King Louis XIV's forestry program intended to maintain France's timber

(B) The British government's emissions restrictions to fight the Great London Smog

(C) The Ottoman Empire's efforts to reduce overfishing in the Mediterranean region

(D) The United States' designation of protected lands such as Yellowstone National Park

Questions 11–13 refer to the map below.

THE MING AND QING DYNASTIES OF CHINA, 1644–1760

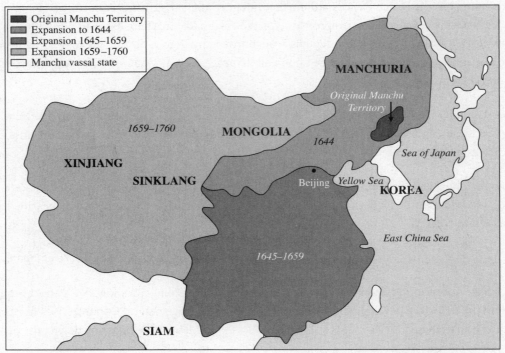

11. Which of the following best explains the changes on the map between 1644 and 1760?

   (A) The decline of surrounding land empires led to a power vacuum in East Asia.

   (B) The Manchu used gunpowder technology and effective military strategies.

   (C) The Taiping Rebellion had weakened the central government as provincial governors then commanded their own armies.

   (D) The Ming Dynasty's high taxes incited a rebellion of provincial governors that left the empire vulnerable to conquest.

12. Which of the following challenges occurred as a result of the changes shown on the map?

   (A) The Manchu had to legitimize their rule and accommodate diverse ethnic groups.

   (B) Increased population led to a strain on resources and a civil war.

   (C) The Manchu had to secure their borders from attacks by neighboring land empires.

   (D) Ethnic and religious diversity led to the fall of the dynasty in the late eighteenth century.

13. How did the Qing Empire shown on the map differ from European empires in the period 1450–1750?

(A) The Qing Empire was less centralized than European empires due to the Qing's large land area.

(B) European maritime empires were in a period of decline as they lost overseas territories.

(C) The Qing Empire was less tolerant of the religious beliefs and customs of conquered groups.

(D) European empires controlled overseas colonies and trading posts.

Questions 14–15 refer to the table below.

POPULATION OF ICELAND, 1095–1790

Year	Population
1095	77,500
1311	72,000
1703	50,000
1790	38,000

14. Which of the following best explains the overall population trend shown in the table?

   (A) The spread of epidemic diseases, such as bubonic plague, showed lack of immunity.

   (B) The Little Ice Age contributed to the contraction of settlements in the Northern Hemisphere.

   (C) The colonization of the Americas led to widespread migration out of Iceland.

   (D) The raids by Vikings led to the relocation of many in the Northern Hemisphere.

15. Which of the following was an effect of the trend suggested by the table?

   (A) Agricultural practices changed.

   (B) New trade routes were established.

   (C) The family size in Iceland increased.

   (D) A lack of resources led to civil war.

Part B: Key Terms

The following is a list of the major people, places, and events for 1450 to 1750. You will very likely see many of these on the AP World History: Modern exam.

For each key term, ask yourself the following questions:

- Can I describe this key term?
- Can I discuss this key term in the context of other events?
- Could I correctly answer a multiple-choice question about this key term?
- Could I correctly answer a free-response question about this key term?

Check off the key terms if you can answer "yes" to at least three of these questions.

The Age of Exploration

☐ Christopher Columbus

The Development of the Global Economy

☐ Conquest of Constantinople

☐ Caravel

☐ Lateen sail

☐ Carrack

☐ Fluyt

☐ Joint-stock companies

Columbian Exchange

☐ Columbian Exchange

☐ Mercantilism

☐ Sugar cultivation

State-Building

☐ Gunpowder

☐ Mughal Empire

☐ Songhai

☐ Creoles

☐ *Mestizos*

☐ *Mulattos*

☐ Manchu

☐ Peter the Great

☐ Tokugawa shogunate

☐ *Daimyo*

Systems of Forced Labor

☐ Triangular trade

☐ *Encomienda*

☐ *Haciendas*

Intellectual Changes

☐ Printing press

☐ Protestant Reformation

☐ Peace of Westphalia

Scientific Revolution

☐ Scientific Revolution

Next Steps

Step 1: Tally your correct answers from Part A, and review the quiz explanations at the end of this chapter.

1.	A	6.	C	11.	B
2.	B	7.	D	12.	A
3.	B	8.	B	13.	D
4.	C	9.	C	14.	B
5.	D	10.	A	15.	A

_____ out of 15 questions

Step 2: Count the number of key terms you checked off in Part B.

_____ out of 27 key terms

Step 3: Read the Key Takeaways in this chapter.

Step 4: Consult the table below and follow the instructions based on your performance.

If You Got...	Do This
80% or more of the Test What You Already Know assessment correct (12 or more questions from Part A and 22 or more key terms from Part B)	• Read definitions in this chapter for all the key terms you didn't check off. • Complete the Test What You Learned assessment in this chapter.
50% or less of the Test What You Already Know assessment correct (7 or fewer questions from Part A and 13 or fewer key terms from Part B)	• Read the comprehensive review for this period in Chapter 8. • If you are short on time, read only the High-Yield sections. • Complete the Practice Set assessment at the end of Chapter 8. • Read through all of the key term definitions in this chapter. • Complete the Test What You Learned assessment in this chapter.
Any other result	• Read the High-Yield sections in the comprehensive review of this period in Chapter 8. • Read definitions in this chapter for all the key terms you didn't check off. • Complete the Test What You Learned assessment in this chapter.

ESSENTIAL CONTENT

Key Takeaways: 1450 to 1750

1. The Americas became part of the global trade network, spurred by the Columbian Exchange. New diseases, crops, people, and cultures were distributed throughout the world.

2. Technological improvements in shipbuilding and gunpowder weapons allowed European empires to form and exercise a more prominent role in world affairs, eventually leading to colonialism.

3. Indigenous populations in the Americas died by the millions due to their exposure to previously unknown European diseases. This led to the forced migration of African people to work the sugar plantations in the New World, changing social structures and creating the Triangular Trade route.

4. New social structures emerged in the Americas based on racial hierarchies, such as those of the *peninsulares*, Creoles, *mestizos*, and *mulattos* of the Spanish colonies.

5. Land-based empires in Asia grew to their greatest extent in the Qing Empire of China, the Mughal Empire, and the Ottoman Empire. Meanwhile, maritime powers like the Portuguese and the Dutch spread throughout the world following the voyages of Magellan, de Gama, and Columbus.

6. Social changes occurred in Europe as the Renaissance, the Protestant Reformation, and the Scientific Revolution challenged the power of the Catholic Church and weakened traditional bases of authority, while also creating the conditions for rapid growth in European economies and populations in later centuries.

Key Terms: 1450 to 1750

Remember that the AP World History exam tests you on the depth of your knowledge, not just your ability to recall facts. While we have provided brief definitions here, you will need to know these terms in even more depth for the AP exam, including how terms connect to broader historical themes and understandings.

The Age of Exploration

Christopher Columbus: Italian navigator who attempted to find a westward route to Asia under the sponsorship of Ferdinand and Isabella of Spain; first European to discover the New World.

The Development of the Global Economy

Conquest of Constantinople: In 1453, the Ottomans conquered the Byzantine capital and ended the Eastern Roman Empire, giving rise to the Ottoman Empire, which lasted until WWI.

Caravel: Inspired by the Arab dhow, a compact ship of Portuguese origin that featured triangular sails and a sternpost rudder making it capable of crossing oceans; used during the Age of Exploration.

4

Lateen sail: Triangular sail that allowed ships to sail against the wind, increasing maneuverability and making early oceanic sailing possible.

Carrack: Large sailing vessel with multiple masts with a large cargo capacity; stable in rough seas, which enabled voyages of several months through difficult waters; originally developed in Europe by the Portuguese in the fourteenth and fifteenth centuries.

Fluyt: Dutch-built cargo ship with comparatively light construction, usually unarmed; allowed for quick construction and smaller crew requirements, which facilitated the growth of Dutch maritime trade.

Joint-stock companies: Large, investor-backed companies that sponsored European exploration and colonization in the seventeenth and eighteenth centuries; precursors to modern corporations; a famous example is the British East India Company.

Columbian Exchange

Columbian Exchange: Beginning with the explorations of Christopher Columbus, the interchange of plants, animals, pathogens, and people between the Old World and the New World.

Mercantilism: Economic system focused on maintaining a positive balance of exports to imports that encouraged domestic employment;

measured the economic strength of a state relative to its neighboring states.

Sugar cultivation: Specialized resource extraction process that relied on African slave labor after indigenous populations were decimated by disease; foreshadowed the intensive manufacturing of the Industrial Revolution.

State-Building

Gunpowder: Chemical explosive developed by the Chinese; spread along trade routes like the Silk Road; Europeans introduced a slow-burning propellant to maximize the potential of explosive weapons.

Mughal Empire: Empire that reunified India in 1526, advocated religious tolerance, and sponsored great art and architecture projects; later collapsed because of Hindu/Muslim conflict and the competition of European traders.

Songhai: Successor of the Mali Empire in West Africa in the 1500s; instituted administrative and economic reforms throughout their realm; conquered by the Moroccans in 1591.

Creoles: Persons of Spanish blood who were born in the Americas; descended from the *peninsulares* who came from the continent.

Mestizos: Persons of mixed European and indigenous descent in the Spanish colonies.

Mulattos: Persons of mixed African and Spanish descent in the Spanish colonies.

Manchu: Nomadic group from Northeast China who were the principal rulers of the Qing Dynasty; created a multiethnic Chinese state; later came into conflict with Europeans, particularly the Russian Empire.

Peter the Great: Tsar of Russia from 1682 to 1725, he rapidly modernized Russia under autocratic rule; moved the capital to St. Petersburg to provide better access to Europe.

Tokugawa shogunate: Ruled Japan from 1600 to 1867; isolated Japan from the rest of the world, banned Christianity, and ejected foreign merchants other than a small number of Dutch and Chinese ships annually.

Daimyo: The class of lords in a feudal system centered on the relationship between lord and warrior or peasant, which was reformed during the Tokugawa shogunate.

Systems of Forced Labor

Triangular trade: Trade route between Europe and Africa (manufactured goods), Africa and the New World (enslaved peoples), and the New World and Europe (raw materials like precious metals, sugar, and other agricultural products).

Encomienda: Spanish system of land grants that allowed colonists in the Americas to force labor from indigenous populations.

Haciendas: Spanish system of landed estates in the colonies; owners practiced the *encomienda* system and later the *repartimiento* system of labor, where workers were paid.

Intellectual Changes

Printing press: Invented in Europe by Johannes Gutenberg in 1456; made mass literacy possible and contributed to several important social movements, such as the Protestant Reformation and the Enlightenment.

Protestant Reformation: Movement questioning the practices of the Catholic Church during a period of social upheaval, particularly the selling of indulgences; commonly held to start with Martin Luther in Germany and his 95 Theses at Wittenburg; led to other reformers like John Calvin in Switzerland and John Wesley in England.

Peace of Westphalia: Series of treaties in 1648 that ended the Thirty Years' War; laid the basis for the modern state system.

Scientific Revolution

Scientific Revolution: Period in which scientists challenged traditional accounts of reality by investigating the nature of natural phenomena like astronomical events; led to the scientific method and progress in all of the natural sciences; early figures such as Galileo Galilei were persecuted by the Catholic Church.

TEST WHAT YOU LEARNED

Part A: Quiz

Questions 1–2 refer to the passage below.

> "Whereas Hindustan has now become the center of security and peace, and the land of justice and beneficence, a large number of people, especially learned men and lawyers, have immigrated and chosen this country for their home. Now we, the principal Ulamas, who are not only well versed in the several departments of the law and in the principles of jurisprudence, and well-acquainted with the edicts which rest on reason or testimony, but are also known for our piety and honest intentions, have duly considered the deep meaning, *first*, of the verse of the Qoran (Sur. IV, 62) '*Obey God, and obey the prophet, and those who have authority among you*,' and *secondly*, of the genuine tradition . . . and *thirdly*, of several other proofs based on reasoning or testimony; and we have agreed that . . . *Abul Fath Jalaluddin Muhammad Akbar Padishah i ghazi*, whose kingdom God perpetuate, is a most just, a most wise, and a most God-fearing king.* Should therefore, in future, a religious question come up, . . . and His Majesty, in his penetrating understanding and clear wisdom, be inclined to adopt, for the benefit of the nation and as a political expedient, any of the conflicting opinions which exist on that point, and issue a decree to that effect, we do hereby agree that such a decree shall be binding on us and on the whole nation."

*The "king" referred to is Emperor Akbar I, who ruled the Mughal Empire from 1556–1605.

> Abu al-Fazl ibn Mubarak, "Infallibility Decree of 1579," issued by Islamic scholars in the Mughal Empire, *The Ain i Akbari*, c. 1590, translated by Henry Blochmann, 1873

1. The document is best understood in the context of which of the following trends?

   (A) The separation of religious authority from government authority

   (B) The use of religion as a justification for imperial expansion

   (C) The decline in religious observance following the Enlightenment

   (D) The convergence of diverse populations within vast empires

2. A historian might use this document to corroborate which of the following statements about Emperor Akbar I's position regarding religion?

   (A) He required everyone in the empire to convert to Islam and punished those who refused to comply.

   (B) He created his own sect of Islam that incorporated elements of Hinduism and promoted religious tolerance.

   (C) He permitted Christian missionaries to enter India and eventually converted to Christianity himself.

   (D) He left the Islamic faith and established the first secular government in India.

Questions 3–4 refer to the map below.

PORTUGUESE TRADING POSTS, CIRCA 1480–1550

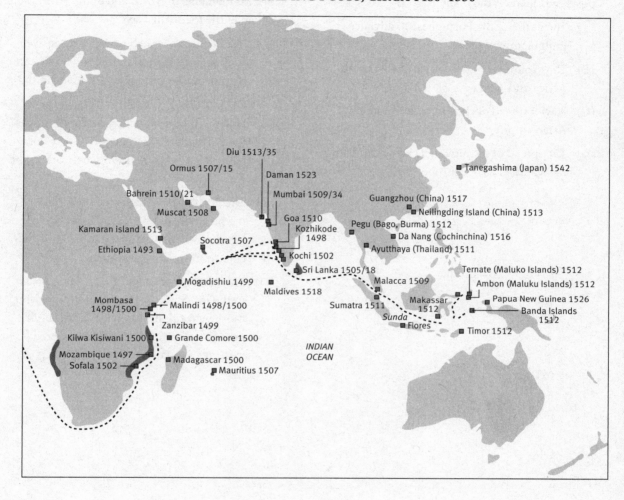

Diu 1513/35
Ormus 1507/15
Daman 1523
Tanegashima (Japan) 1542
Bahrein 1510/21
Mumbai 1509/34
Guangzhou (China) 1517
Muscat 1508
Neilingding Island (China) 1513
Goa 1510
Kamaran island 1513
Kozhikode 1498
Pegu (Bago, Burma) 1512
Da Nang (Cochinchina) 1516
Socotra 1507
Ethiopia 1493
Kochi 1502
Ayutthaya (Thailand) 1511
Sri Lanka 1505/18
Ternate (Maluko Islands) 1512
Mogadishiu 1499
Ambon (Maluku Islands) 1512
Maldives 1518
Malacca 1509
Mombasa
Papua New Guinea 1526
1498/1500
Malindi 1498/1500
Sumatra 1511
Makassar
Banda Islands
Zanzibar 1499
1512
1512
Kilwa Kisiwani 1500
Grande Comore 1500
Sunda
Timor 1512
Mozambique 1497
INDIAN
Flores
Sofala 1502
OCEAN
Madagascar 1500
Mauritius 1507

4

3. Which of the following most directly contributed to the distribution of the Portuguese trading posts indicated on the map?

   (A) The desire of the Portuguese to advance Enlightenment ideals

   (B) The expansion of the Jewish diaspora into Africa and Asia

   (C) A widespread decline in the economies of Asian empires

   (D) The spread of technological advances from the Middle East to Europe

4. The Portuguese trading network along the Indian Ocean most strongly differed from European settlements in North and South America in which of the following ways?

   (A) The Portuguese established an extensive trading post network in the Indian Ocean region, but they did not participate in the colonization of the Americas.

   (B) Unlike those who colonized the Americas, the Portuguese relied on joint-stock companies to fund their trading network in the Indian Ocean region.

   (C) The Portuguese established their trading post network primarily for economic reasons, whereas religious missions drove colonization in the Americas.

   (D) The Portuguese established trading posts in the Indian Ocean to control trade, while those who colonized the Americas built permanent settlements and conquered existing populations.

Questions 5–6 refer to the passage below.

"During the reign of Shun Chih, of the people of T'eng-i, seven in ten were opposed to the Manchu Dynasty. The officials dared not touch them; and subsequently, when the country became more settled, the magistrates used to distinguish them from the others by always deciding any cases in their favor: for they feared lest these men should revert to their old opposition. And thus it came about that one litigant would begin by declaring himself to have been a 'rebel,' while his adversary would follow up by showing such statement to be false; so that before any case could be heard on its actual merits, it was necessary to determine the status both of plaintiff and defendant, whereby indefinite labor was entailed upon the Registrars.

Now it chanced that the yamen of one of the officials was haunted by a fox, and the official's daughter was bewitched by it. Her father, therefore, engaged the services of a magician, who succeeded in capturing the animal and putting it into a bottle; but just as he was going to commit it to the flames, the fox cried out from inside the bottle, 'I'm a rebel!' at which the bystanders were unable to suppress their laughter."

Pu Songling, excerpt from *Strange Stories from a Chinese Studio*,
1740, translated by Herbert A. Giles, 1880

5. The story is best understood in the context of which of the following developments in Chinese history?

    (A) The conquest of China by the Mongol Empire

    (B) The suppression of traditional Chinese culture by the Manchus

    (C) The transition from the Ming Dynasty to the Qing Dynasty

    (D) The modernization of the Chinese legal system

6. The use of the term "rebels" in the story most likely refers to which of the following groups?

    (A) Members of prominent Chinese families who wanted to upend the existing social hierarchy

    (B) Han Chinese who considered neighboring populations such as the Manchus to be uncivilized and brutish

    (C) Proponents of the Qing Dynasty seeking to justify their support of the Manchu conquest

    (D) Bureaucrats appointed to implement the legal and political reforms enacted by the Qing Dynasty

Questions 7–8 refer to the image below.

SUGAR-MAKING IN HISPANIOLA, 1590

7. The image best represents which one of the following sixteenth-century trends in North and South America?

   (A) The creation of economic opportunities for indigenous populations

   (B) A voluntary reduction in the Atlantic slave trade

   (C) The use of forced labor in the production of cash crops

   (D) The influence of indigenous imagery in artwork of the period

8. Which of the following best explains the role that sugar would come to play in the global economy?

   (A) It contributed to the triangular trade networks that developed between North America, Europe, and Africa.

   (B) It was introduced to Europe and Asia via the Columbian Exchange, which caused a sharp spike in global demand.

   (C) It was expensive to produce, making it a luxury product that only the richest consumers could afford to purchase.

   (D) It had only a minor impact on the global economy because few people outside of Europe and North America consumed it.

Questions 9–10 refer to the image below.

LEONARDO DA VINCI, *VITRUVIAN MAN*, 1490

9. The image above is best understood in the context of which of the following developments?

   (A) The Protestant Reformation

   (B) The invention of the printing press

   (C) The founding of the Sikh religion

   (D) The Italian Renaissance

10. The image best represents which of the following characteristics of European thought during the fifteenth and sixteenth centuries?

   (A) A shift toward realism, scientific study, and humanist thought

   (B) Increased religious devotion and faith in the Catholic Church

   (C) Equality between men and women in the social hierarchy

   (D) A rejection of influences from other cultures or time periods

4

Questions 11–13 refer to the passage below.

"Those that arrived at these Islands from the remotest parts of Spain, and who call themselves Christians, steered two courses mainly to destroy and exterminate this People from the face of the Earth. The first whereof was raising an unjust, bloody, cruel war. The other was by putting them to death . . .

Now the ultimate end and scope that incited the Spaniards to endeavor the desolation of this People, was Gold only . . . their insatiable greed and ambition, the greatest ever seen in the world, is the cause of their villainies. And also, the wealth of the lands, and the humility and patience of the Inhabitants, made the approach easier. They treated them (I speak of things which I was an Eye Witness of, without the least fallacy) not as Beasts . . . but as the most abject dung and filth of the Earth; and an infinite number of People died without understanding the true Faith or Sacraments. And this also is as really true as the preceeding narration (which the very Tyrants and cruel Murderers cannot deny) that the Spaniards never received any injury from the Indians . . . until they were compelled to take up arms, provoked by the repeated injuries, violent torments, and unjust butcheries."

Bartolomé de Las Casas, Spanish missionary,
Brief Account of the Destruction of the Indies, 1542

11. Spanish treatment of indigenous Americans as described in the passage contributed most directly to which of the following?

(A) The independence of Latin American colonies

(B) Widespread slave rebellions throughout the Americas

(C) The rise of the trans-Atlantic slave trade

(D) The development and spread of Enlightenment ideas

12. Which of the following factors contributed most directly to the situation described in the passage?

(A) The Spanish view of indigenous populations as an inferior group

(B) The desire of the Spanish to spread Christianity

(C) Competition among European conquerors for control of the indigenous populations

(D) Retaliation for large-scale rebellions by indigenous peoples

13. Which of the following would most directly lead to the end of the labor system described in the passage?

(A) The spread of Enlightenment ideas

(B) The overthrow of colonial governments by slaves

(C) The colonization of Africa

(D) The Atlantic Revolutions

Questions 14–15 refer to the passage below.

"The Tsar had sent out orders to the governments of the different provinces of the empire requiring each of them to send his quota of artificers and laborers to assist in building the city. This they could easily do, for in those days all the laboring classes of the people were little better than slaves, and were almost entirely at the disposal of the nobles, their masters. In the same manner, he sent out agents to all the chief cities in western Europe, with orders to advertise there for carpenters, masons, engineers, ship-builders, and persons of all other trades likely to be useful in the work of building the city. These men were to be promised good wages and kind treatment, and were to be at liberty at any time to return to their prospective homes."

Jacob Abbot, *Peter the Great*, 1859

14. Which of the following best describes Peter the Great's motivation for constructing St. Petersburg, the city mentioned in the passage?

   (A) He wanted to revitalize a sluggish economy through government spending on a public works project.

   (B) He wanted to replace Moscow as the capital city after it was destroyed during a Mongol invasion.

   (C) He wanted to build a new center for religious devotion following his conversion to Catholicism.

   (D) He wanted to move the capital westward in order to increase contact between Russia and Europe.

15. The attitude toward foreign workers described in the passage differs most strongly from that of which of the following states during the period 1450–1750?

   (A) The Songhai Empire in West Africa

   (B) The Tokugawa shogunate in Japan

   (C) The Qing Dynasty in China

   (D) The Safavid Dynasty in Persia

Part B: Key Terms

This key terms list is the same as the list in the Test What You Already Know section earlier in this chapter. Based on what you have now learned, again ask yourself the following questions:

- Can I describe this key term?
- Can I discuss this key term in the context of other events?
- Could I correctly answer a multiple-choice question about this key term?
- Could I correctly answer a free-response question about this key term?

Check off the key terms if you can answer "yes" to at least three of these questions.

The Age of Exploration

☐ Christopher Columbus

The Development of the Global Economy

☐ Conquest of Constantinople

☐ Caravel

☐ Lateen sail

☐ Carrack

☐ Fluyt

☐ Joint-stock companies

Columbian Exchange

☐ Columbian Exchange

☐ Mercantilism

☐ Sugar cultivation

State-Building

☐ Gunpowder

☐ Mughal empire

☐ Songhai

☐ Creoles

☐ *Mestizos*

☐ *Mulattos*

☐ Manchu

☐ Peter the Great

☐ Tokugawa shogunate

☐ *Daimyo*

Systems of Forced Labor

☐ Triangular trade

☐ *Encomienda*

☐ *Haciendas*

Intellectual Changes

☐ Printing press

☐ Protestant Reformation

☐ Peace of Westphalia

Scientific Revolution

☐ Scientific Revolution

Next Steps

Step 1: Tally your correct answers from Part A and review the quiz explanations at the end of this chapter.

1.	D	6.	B	11.	C
2.	B	7.	C	12.	A
3.	D	8.	A	13.	A
4.	D	9.	D	14.	D
5.	C	10.	A	15.	B

_____ out of 15 questions

Step 2: Count the number of key terms you checked off in Part B.

_____ out of 27 key terms

Step 3: Compare your Test What You Already Know results to these Test What You Learned results to see how exam-ready you are for this period.

For More Practice:

- Read (or reread) the comprehensive review for this period in Chapter 8.

- Complete the Practice Set assessment at the end of Chapter 8.

- Go to kaptest.com to complete the online quiz questions for 1450 to 1750.

  ○ Haven't registered your book yet? Go to kaptest.com/moreonline to begin.

ANSWERS AND EXPLANATIONS

Test What You Already Know

1. A

The Chinese economy was the world's largest in this period, but the country lacked domestic silver or gold resources. This had led to the earliest invention of paper money, but misuse of that currency resulted in an inflationary spiral in the Ming Dynasty in the late 1400s—just as Japan and then Spanish America discovered and exploited their large silver reserves. China stabilized its money by switching from paper to silver. This led to a great demand for silver over the next few centuries. Therefore, **(A)** is correct. As the map shows, although most New World silver seems to be exported to Europe, a large fraction of it was then traded further east, to China, for the luxury goods that could not be paid for with any other exchange. (B) is contradicted by the map: the world's largest sources of silver were the mines in Spanish Peru and Mexico. Although some silver passed through Ottoman lands and seas in the course of world trade, as in (C), the Silk Road routes were increasingly bypassed by European ships trading silver for Chinese goods directly by sea. Ironically, given its inflationary history with paper money, the Ming Dynasty actually experienced serious inflation due to an excessive importation of silver. Because high inflation does not strengthen any economy, (D) is incorrect.

2. B

The silver trade was a primary component in the first truly global trade system, so called because of the growing unification of the Eastern and Western hemispheres' economies after European expansion. **(B)** is correct. This is best illustrated by the small but significant trade route across the Pacific Ocean between Mexico, Peru, the Philippines, and China—the first to connect the New World with the eastern and western halves of the Old World. Spain did not modernize internally despite its huge reserves of precious metals from America. Rather, it continued subsidizing its elite landholding classes and paying cash for talented foreigners to conduct its trade, imperial administration, and imperial wars. Thus, (A) is incorrect. (C) mixes up its history: the Opium Wars were in the 1800s and sought to balance the silver trade between England and China, not end it. It is true that, as silver became available in large quantities, gold declined somewhat in relative value, as in (D); however,

that had little to do with the expansion of the slave trade in this period, which was based on demand for plantation commodities paid for with manufactured goods.

3. B

Unlike Portugal, whose royal government financed all of its expeditions in the Indian Ocean, the relatively impoverished British rulers used joint-stock companies, in which prosperous investors—not the crown—funded the expeditions. Thus, **(B)** is correct. As Roe's letter says, this allowed the English captains to separate the idea of controlling monopoly territories (e.g., by setting up expensive fortified trading stations) from the concept of seeking the best markets and trading agreements with local powers. Other factors in England's rise were its generally stronger trading economy in the Atlantic and its successful competitions with France and the Netherlands. Another factor was Portugal's struggle with Spain and its increasing focus on its profitable empire in Brazil and Africa. (A) is out of period and region: the Opium Wars were in the 1800s, and China was not primarily engaged in Indian Ocean trade. Although the Ottoman Empire had trading links to the Indian Ocean via its provinces on the Red Sea and Persian Gulf, it had never been the dominant naval or political power across the entire ocean basin as stated. Thus, (C) is incorrect. As noted, the Portuguese over time focused more on their Atlantic and African imperial holdings, but Portugal only abandoned its colonial ports at Goa in India and Macau in China in the late twentieth century. Thus, (D) is incorrect.

4. C

Ironically, given the close of Roe's letter, the British East India Company eventually did invest in "garrisons and land wars in India" in the eighteenth century. By the 1800s, this had led to a monopolistic business empire that ruled India as a private venture, supported indirectly by British military and legal institutions. General abuses of Indian sovereignty, culture, and privileges led to a rebellion of the East India Company's native troops in 1857. Although this Rebellion was unsuccessful in expelling the British, it did lead to the fall of the East India Company. **(C)** is correct. The Boston Tea Party, a 1773 riot against the company's tea monopoly, contributed to the American Revolution but certainly didn't cause it; (A) is incorrect. (B) is incorrect; it took place in conjunction with British expansion in India, and the two European empires in Asia engaged in border conflicts called "The Great Game," but Russia's interest in its southern neighbors was not dependent on the vulnerability of India. (D) is incorrect because Australia was initially set up as a penal colony after the American Revolution eliminated North America as a place for transporting English criminals.

5. D

Even though the Church was still quite powerful during the Renaissance, the growing power of merchant families and increasing interest in rediscovering the Greco-Roman past led to increasingly secular attitudes. Emerging humanist philosophies depicted humankind as creative and rational, and the printing revolution supported a corresponding rise in literacy and interest in gaining knowledge. **(D)** is correct. Because the Renaissance marks a period of increasing interest and resurgence of Greco-Roman styles, not Chinese and Islamic art, (A) is incorrect. (B) is incorrect because chiaroscuro is an art form that developed just after the Renaissance during the sixteenth century in Mannerism and Baroque art. While attitudes were increasingly secular in outlook, stating that atheism became accepted by more and more Europeans goes too far; (C) is incorrect.

6. C

By supplying trade routes during the Crusades, not only did Italy prosper immensely, but exposure to Muslim advances in math, science, and the arts stimulated an interest in relearning Classical wisdom, making **(C)** correct. Indeed, contact with Eastern regions allowed for new ideas and a period of artistic and scientific self-discovery. (A) is incorrect because Italy was a center of commerce where goods and ideas were exchanged. (B) is incorrect because the Protestant Reformation began after the Renaissance had already emerged in Italy. Further, the Church was one of the leading patrons of Renaissance artists, including Michelangelo. Lastly, political power in Italy was characterized by many competitive city-states; thus, (D) is incorrect.

7. D

The Columbian Exchange was the exchange of plants, animals, pathogens, and people between the Old World and the New World. In the passage, the Aztecs in the battle indicated "no fear either of firearms or horses," perhaps indicating their lack of familiarity with such forms of

warfare. Horses were a central component of the Columbian Exchange, making **(D)** correct. It is true that Europeans brought diseases such as measles and tuberculosis as they explored other regions, yet that is not depicted in the passage. Therefore, (A) is incorrect. The Columbian Exchange did include a transfer of crops, but this primarily involved the introduction of crops indigenous to the Americas to other regions through trade. Such crops included the potato, tomato, maize, and tobacco. Further, the exchange of crops is not depicted in the passage. Therefore, (B) is incorrect. (C) is incorrect because cultural exchange was one of the most significant immediate impacts of the Columbian Exchange. One such example is the concept of private property, brought to the New World by European colonizers.

8. B

In Mexica society, unlike in many other societies during this period, it was common for women to own property or occupy formal religious roles. Therefore, **(B)** is correct. Although Mexica rulers indeed claimed that their rule was divinely inspired and that they themselves had divine origins, this assertion was relatively common in other cultures, making (A) incorrect. (C) is incorrect because although the Mexica had slaves, especially enslaved prisoners of war, the institution of slavery was fairly common among other societies; for example, the slave trade between Africa and the Western Hemisphere expanded throughout this period. Similarly, while most Mexica commoners did work in agriculture, this was very common worldwide during this period, making (D) incorrect as well.

9. C

Following an earlier period during which Christianity was seen as a useful tool in combating the influence of Buddhism, the Tokugawa shogunate began to perceive Christianity as a threat to its authority and began persecuting missionaries. Thus, **(C)** is correct. Japan colonized Korea during the twentieth century, after the reign of the Tokugawa shogunate; (A) is incorrect. The Tokugawa shoguns did severely limit European trade with Japan; however, not all overseas trade was stopped. Carefully controlled trade with China, Korea, Taiwan, and some Dutch merchants was allowed. Therefore, (B) is incorrect. The Tokugawa shogunate ensured very limited contact between Japan and the outside world. Thus, (D) is incorrect.

4

10. A

Both the Tokugawa shogunate and the French government under Louis XIV created laws to manage timber resources; **(A)** is correct. Both (B) and (D) are true; however, they did not occur during the period from 1450 to 1750. The emissions restrictions to fight the Great London Smog was enacted in 1956. Yellowstone didn't become the first national park until 1872. The Ottoman Empire did not try to reduce overfishing. Therefore, (C) is incorrect.

11. B

When you are unsure of the right answer, use your world history knowledge to eliminate potential options. (A) is incorrect because no land empire previously controlled these areas (Tibet, Mongolia, and Xinjiang) just prior to Manchu expansion. In fact, the Mongols were the only land empire to control these regions, and their empire fell before 1450. (C) is incorrect because the Taiping Rebellion took place during the Qing Dynasty, not the Ming Dynasty. (D) is incorrect because the Ming Dynasty had low taxes, partly due to backlash against the Yuan Dynasty taxing the Han Chinese to fund further Mongol conquests. Thus, **(B)** is correct because it is the only option not yet eliminated. The Manchu were able to expand by using gunpowder weapons and strategies adapted from their experiences fighting other nomadic tribes.

12. A

Expansion caused the Manchu to incorporate groups that were not ethnically Chinese, such as Turkish-speaking groups in Central Asia. Additionally, any new government had to demonstrate its right to rule. Thus, **(A)** is correct. The conquered areas were not heavily populated because these areas were of the steppe and the Tibetan Plateau. In addition, there was no civil war. Thus, (B) is incorrect. The Manchu had few threats from their neighbors, Russia and the Mughals, making (C) incorrect. (D) is incorrect because the Qing Dynasty fell in the early twentieth century, and this was mainly due to foreign influence and peasant rebellions, rather than ethnic and religious diversity.

13. D

The Qing Empire was land-based. In contrast, most European empires were maritime and spread across the globe, including colonies and trading posts; **(D)** is correct. (A) is incorrect because the Qing Empire was centralized due to its bureaucracy, and it was more centralized than European empires that were sea-based. In fact, European empires were difficult to centralize due to the locations of their territories across the globe. European maritime empires were thriving during this time period; they were expanding rather than losing territory, making (B) incorrect. (C) is incorrect because the Qing Empire embraced religious diversity and was usually tolerant of conquered groups, as shown by its continuation of Chinese policies and promotion of Confucian ideology.

14. B

During the Little Ice Age, global cooling occurred. This led to the abandonment of farms in Northern Europe due to the shorter growing season, ports freezing over, and the inability to grow certain crops in cooler climates. **(B)** is correct. The bubonic plague impacted Europe in the mid-fourteenth century, so the plague would not explain population decline through 1790; (A) is incorrect. (C) is incorrect because the colonization of the Americas had little impact on Iceland. (D) is incorrect because the Vikings settled in Iceland and Greenland when the climate was warmer, before the Little Ice Age.

15. A

Global cooling during the Little Ice Age led to changes in farming. These changes included the cultivation of potatoes because they thrive in cool climates and the abandonment of farms in Northern Europe. **(A)** is correct. There was no correlation between the rise of entirely new trade routes and the declining population of Iceland, although fishing may have been relied on more due to less available farmland; (B) is incorrect. The population was declining, so the average family size likely remained consistent or possibly decreased due to famine; (C) is incorrect. This population decline did not necessarily mean fewer resources, making (D) incorrect.

Test What You Learned

1. D

The document was issued during the Mughal Empire, which came into being as the result of a Muslim conquest of India, or "Hindustan" as it is referred to in the passage. This conquest, like those within other large empires, led to a convergence of the traditional beliefs and practices of the indigenous culture with those of the conquering culture. Passages like this one demonstrated a need to clarify how those different cultural and religious practices would be reconciled in the legal and political spheres—in this case, by having the "king" Akbar resolve any conflicts. Thus, **(D)** is correct. (A) is incorrect because the passage reflects the opposite trend: the blending, not the separation, of religious and government authority. (B) is incorrect because the passage does not reflect a desire for imperial expansion, just for finding a method to resolve religious disputes. While the authors of the document refer to their use of "reason," the Enlightenment was a European phenomenon rather than a South Asian one, and it began around 100 years after this document was written; (C) is incorrect.

2. B

The Mughal emperor Akbar I was known for promoting religious tolerance through his abolition of the non-Muslim tax, his promotion of Hindu government officials, and his encouragement of religious intermarriage. Historians often credit these efforts with the relative peace and stability of the Mughal Empire during Akbar I's reign. Akbar I eventually founded his own religious sect known as the Divine Faith, which combined elements of Islam and Hinduism. Thus, **(B)** is correct. (A), (C), and (D) are incorrect because they are contrary to fact: Akbar I remained a Muslim and saw himself as head of state *and* religion, but he was not militant about his religious beliefs and promoted tolerance of other religions rather than forced conversion.

3. D

The Portuguese trading posts along the coastline of the Indian Ocean resulted from a combination of factors, including the development of new seafaring technology that made it possible for Portuguese explorers to sail around the horn of Africa and discover a sea route to Asia. The Portuguese made these advancements due to the spread of similar technology from Asia and the Middle East to Europe; thus, **(D)** is correct. (A) is incorrect because Portuguese colonizers were not motivated by a desire to spread Enlightenment ideals; instead, they were primarily motivated by economic interests, while some were also motivated by a desire to spread Christianity. (B) is incorrect because, while Jews were being expelled from Spain and Portugal around this time and many moved eastward into the Ottoman Empire, the subsequent expansion of the Jewish diaspora did not impact Portuguese imperialism. (C) is incorrect because the Asian empires were not experiencing a widespread economic

decline; in fact, Portugal wanted to establish a trading network in the Indian Ocean to take advantage of the lucrative trade that already existed there.

4. D

The Portuguese trading posts established along the Indian Ocean were geographically compact because the Portuguese wanted to control trade in the region, rather than to conquer and colonize as was the aim of European settlements in the Americas. Thus, **(D)** is correct. The Portuguese also participated in the exploration and colonization of the Americas, primarily in South America, so (A) is incorrect. (B) is incorrect because it was other European nations, primarily England and the Netherlands, that relied on joint stock companies to fund colonization. (C) is incorrect because both the trading network in the Indian Ocean and European colonization in the Americas were motivated primarily by economic interests, although in both cases some colonizers were motivated by a desire to spread Christianity.

5. C

The setting of the story is the early "Manchu" Dynasty, which is synonymous with the Qing Dynasty—that is, the government established by the Manchu invaders after they had conquered the Ming Dynasty in the mid-sixteenth century. The Manchu were far outnumbered by the Han Chinese, and so they feared a large-scale uprising by Ming loyalists. In the story, this fear led to a court system that was highly deferential to such loyalists. Thus, the story reflects the transition from the Ming Dynasty to the Qing Dynasty, and **(C)** is correct. (A) is incorrect because the Mongol conquest of China occurred in the thirteenth century, long before the Manchu Dynasty referenced in the story. (B) is incorrect because the story reflects a way in which the Manchu were deferential to traditional Chinese culture, which was common during the transition period. (D) is incorrect because the story does not reflect the modernization of the Chinese legal system; if anything, it indicates that the legal system of the time was subject to a peculiarity (giving deference to former "rebels") at odds with a modern sense of justice. Also, the Qing Dynasty eventually undertook a comprehensive reform of the legal system, but not until the early twentieth century.

6. B

The story mentions opposition to the Manchu (or Qing) Dynasty and implies that the "rebels" were people who

4

opposed the Manchu conquest of China. Typically, these people would have been Han Chinese, many of whom considered the Manchu a barbaric foreign invader. Thus, **(B)** is correct. (A) is incorrect because it was not characteristic of the time period for members of the elite class to advocate for extreme changes to the existing social structure, as they typically benefited from it. (C) and (D) are incorrect for a similar reason: because the "rebels" opposed the Manchu (or Qing) Dynasty, the term would not have referred to Qing supporters or bureaucrats.

7. C

The image depicts more than a dozen men engaged in various stages of the sugar-making process. Based on their physiques, they appear to perform strenuous labor frequently, and their minimal attire suggests that they are working in a warm climate. These details are consistent with the importation of African slaves to work on sugar plantations in the Caribbean where the island of Hispaniola is located. **(C)** is correct. (A) is incorrect because, even though the image shows people working, this work was conducted for the economic gain of the colonizers who operated the plantation, not that of the workers. The Atlantic slave trade was generally expanding during this time period, and any temporary reductions were not likely to have been the result of voluntary limitations on the slave trade, so (B) is incorrect. (D) is incorrect because there is nothing about this engraving that reflects the art or culture of Native Americans; the workers it depicts were most likely from Africa, since by 1590 most of the indigenous population had died from smallpox or other European diseases.

8. A

Sugar was a key component of the triangular trade between North America, Europe, and Africa. Slaves were imported from Africa to the Caribbean to work on sugar plantations. The sugar they produced was exported to North America or Europe and used to make rum and other consumable goods, which were then traded in Africa for more slaves. Thus, **(A)** is correct. (B) is incorrect because sugar was introduced to the Americas by Europeans, not the other way around. (C) is incorrect because the cultivation of sugar in the Americas caused the price of sugar to drop due to the use of slave labor as well as improved agricultural conditions and practices. By the seventeenth century, sugar was becoming a staple of an ordinary diet rather than a luxury good that only the rich could afford. (D) is incorrect because it is contrary to fact: sugar had

a significant impact on the global economy, in direct and indirect ways, regardless of who was consuming it (which was not, in any case, limited to Europeans and North Americans).

9. D

Leonardo da Vinci was one of the most prolific artists of the Italian Renaissance, a period of increased social, political, cultural, and scientific learning that lasted approximately from 1300 to 1600. Thus, **(D)** is correct. Although the Protestant Reformation was influenced by social and cultural changes already underway during the Renaissance, neither da Vinci nor his artwork is associated with the Protestant Reformation, which began in Germany, not Italy, just a few years before da Vinci's death; (A) is incorrect. (B) is incorrect because the invention of the printing press is generally associated with the spread of writing and literacy, not art. (C) is incorrect because Sikhism was founded in India and incorporates elements of Hinduism and Islam, neither of which are associated with Leonardo da Vinci or his art.

10. A

Art created during the Renaissance tended to reflect an interest in realism and nature, an appreciation for the human body and its beauty, and an emphasis on reason and logical thought. In the *Vitruvian Man*, Leonardo da Vinci sought to relate the proportions of the human body to the geometric figures of a circle and of a square. Because this comparison represents the heightened interest in science and nature characteristic of Renaissance art, **(A)** is correct. (B) is incorrect because none of the imagery in the *Vitruvian Man* is representative of religious devotion; moreover, the Renaissance was generally characterized by a decrease in allegiance to the Catholic Church, as reflected by the Protestant Reformation and other similar movements. (C) is incorrect because men were still largely dominant over women in social and political spheres throughout the Renaissance. (D) is incorrect because Renaissance artists and thinkers drew inspiration from ancient Greece and Rome, as well as the contemporary Islamic world.

11. C

Spanish cruelty and disease led to population decline in the Americas, which then led to a labor shortage and the importation of African slaves; **(C)** is correct. (A) is incorrect because Latin-American independence did not occur until the early nineteenth century. It was the result of the actions of the Creoles (those of Spanish descent) rather than the indigenous populations. (B) is incorrect because most slave rebellions in the Americas happened much later, at a point when African slaves had replaced native populations as the majority of forced laborers. (D) is incorrect because the Enlightenment developed in the late seventeenth and early eighteenth centuries; additionally, it began in Europe, not the Americas.

12. A

The Spanish viewed the indigenous populations as barbarians due to their polytheistic religion, lack of advanced weapons, and cultural traditions that the Spanish did not understand. Because of this view, the Spanish felt their conquest was justified. **(A)** is correct. (B) is incorrect because, although some among the Spanish wanted to spread Christianity, the primary motivation of the Spanish conquistadors was the acquisition of wealth. (C) is incorrect because the Spanish were not in direct competition with other Europeans for control of the Indies at this time; the French and English settled in North America, and the Portuguese were granted Brazil by the Treaty of Tordesillas. (D) is incorrect because rebellions by indigenous populations were not widespread and were often put down easily.

13. A

The Enlightenment ideas of liberty and equality led to the questioning of slavery and the eventual emancipation of slaves in the mid-nineteenth century; **(A)** is correct. (B) is incorrect because the only successful slave revolt was in Haiti; most slave rebellions were not successful in freeing slaves. (C) is incorrect because the colonization of Africa occurred after the end of the Atlantic slave trade and led to new forms of coerced labor. (D) is incorrect because the Atlantic Revolutions achieved independence for the colonies. However, the governments that were established did not abolish slavery immediately (except in Haiti, which was an exception).

14. D

During his reign, Peter the Great implemented programs and policies designed to modernize Russia. Peter was strongly influenced by Western culture and, as part of his modernization efforts, he wanted to reposition the capital to a location that would provide his country with better access to Europe. Thus, he undertook the construction of St. Petersburg, the city described in the passage, making **(D)** correct. (A) is incorrect because Peter was not trying to bolster a failing economy; in addition, the strategy of using government spending to revive a sluggish economy is primarily a twentieth-century idea. Although Russia had previously been conquered by the Mongols and was under their control until the late fifteenth century, (B) is incorrect because Moscow had been a thriving city for several hundred years when Peter the Great ordered the capital moved to St. Petersburg. Finally, (C) is incorrect because Peter was a member of the Russian Orthodox Church; he never converted to Catholicism, and his primary motivation for building St. Petersburg was not religious devotion.

15. B

The passage describes Peter the Great offering to provide "good wages and kind treatment" to foreign workers, especially highly skilled workers, who assisted in the construction of St. Petersburg. Peter's attitude toward foreign workers is generally positive and consistent with his eagerness to accept foreign influence, especially European influence, in order to modernize Russia. This attitude differs strongly from that of the Tokugawa shogunate, which adopted an isolationist stance; it expelled most foreigners from Japan, closed Japan to most foreign trade, and forbade Japanese citizens from traveling abroad. Thus, **(B)** is correct. The remaining choices are incorrect because they do not indicate states with a negative view toward foreign workers or their influence. The Songhai Empire, (A), and the Safavid Dynasty, (D), relied heavily on foreign trade to support their economies, indicating a willingness to cooperate with foreigners. Similarly, the Qing Dynasty, (C), also engaged in foreign trade.

CHAPTER 5

1750 to 1900

LEARNING OBJECTIVES

- Describe the effects, both positive and negative, of legal systems and independence movements on race, class, and gender.

- Describe the interaction of specialized labor systems and social hierarchies.

- Demonstrate ways in which economic systems, and values and ideologies, have influenced each other.

- Explain how production and commerce develop and change.

- Explain how societies can be changed or challenged over time.

- Describe the impact of ideology and belief on populations.

- Assess the impact of technology and exchange networks on the environment.

TIMELINE

Date	Region	Event
1756–1763	Europe, Americas, West Africa, & South Asia	Seven Years' War (French & Indian War)
1760–1820	Americas & Europe	First Industrial Revolution
1775–1781	North America	American Revolution
1776	Europe	*The Wealth of Nations* published
1776	North America	Declaration of Independence published
1789	Europe	*Declaration of the Rights of Man and of the Citizen* published
1789–1799	Europe	French Revolution
1792	Europe	*A Vindication of the Rights of Woman* published
1803–1814	Europe	Napoleonic Era (France)
1804	Caribbean	Haitian independence
1810–1829	Americas & Caribbean	Wave of independence movements throughout Latin America
1815	Americas	Simón Bolívar's Jamaica Letter published
1839–1879	Middle East	Tanzimât Movement reforms Ottoman Empire
1839–1842	East Asia	First Opium War in China
1848	Europe	*The Communist Manifesto* published
1848	Europe	Revolutions of 1848/Springtime of the Peoples (Italy and Germany)
1850–1864	East Asia	Taiping Rebellion in China
1853	East Asia	Commodore Perry visits Japan
1856–1860	East Asia	Second Opium War in China
1857	South Asia	Indian Rebellion of 1857
1861	Asia	Emancipation of Russian serfs
1865	North America	Slavery abolished in the United States
1868	East Asia	Meiji Restoration in Japan
1870–1914	Americas, Europe, Asia	Second Industrial Revolution
1871	Europe	Unification of Italy
1871	Europe	Unification of Germany
1882	North America	Chinese Exclusion Act passed (United States)
1885	Central Africa	Congo Free State established
1885	South Asia	Indian National Congress founded
1894–1895	East Asia	First Sino-Japanese War
1897	Europe	Zionist movement begins
1898	Caribbean, Asia-Pacific	Spanish-American War
1899–1901	East Asia	Boxer Rebellion in China
1899–1902	South Africa	Boer War

TEST WHAT YOU ALREADY KNOW

Part A: Quiz

Questions 1–3 refer to the map below.

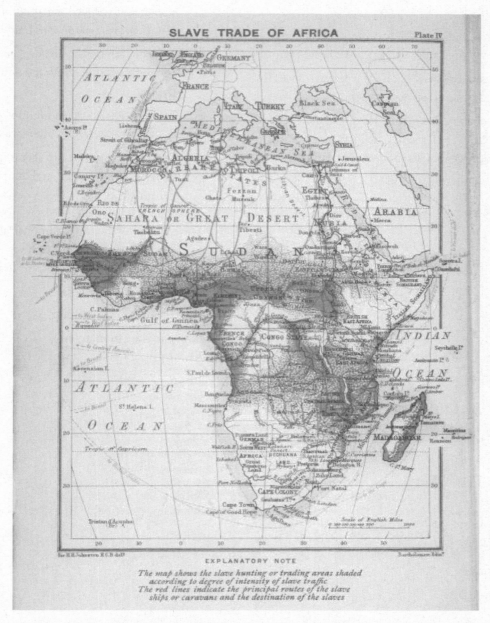

Explanatory note at bottom of map reads: The map shows the slave hunting or trading areas shaded according to degree of intensity of slave traffic. The lines indicate the principal routes of the slave ships or caravans and the destination of the slaves.

1. The routes depicted on the map best reflect which of the following characteristics of the transatlantic slave trade?

   (A) It served as a catalyst for Christianity becoming the dominant religion in North Africa.

   (B) It caused geographic centers of trade in West Africa to shift toward coastal regions.

   (C) It focused heavily on transporting slaves to India and other Asian regions.

   (D) It enabled the formation of permanent European settlements, such as Cape Colony in South Africa, to support slave traders.

2. Which of the following additional pieces of information would be most directly useful in assessing the extent to which the routes depicted on the map affected people living in Africa?

   (A) Information on technological developments that reduced the amount of manual labor required on plantations

   (B) Information on the distance covered by the routes compared to the total area of the continent

   (C) Information on the amount of African countries acquired by European colonizers

   (D) Information on the number of people born in Africa in the eighteenth and nineteenth centuries

3. The increase of the trade demonstrated on the map during the eighteenth century was most strongly influenced by which of the following?

   (A) Industrialization

   (B) Plantation agriculture

   (C) Absolute monarchies

   (D) Laissez-faire capitalism

Questions 4–6 refer to the passage below.

"Where the money is to come from which will defray this enormous annual expense of three millions sterling, and all those other debts, I know not; unless the author of *Common Sense*, or some other ingenious projector, can discover the Philosopher's Stone, by which iron and other base metals may be transmuted into gold. Certain I am that our commerce and agriculture, the two principal sources of our wealth, will not support such an expense. The whole of our exports from the Thirteen United Colonies, in the year 1769, amounted only to £2,887,898 sterling; which is not so much, by near half a million, as our annual expense would be were we independent of Great Britain."

Charles Inglis, Loyalist and Anglican clergyman of Trinity Church in New York City, New York, 1776

4. Based on this passage and your knowledge of world history, which of the following best describes the primary motivations of proponents of the American Revolution?

   (A) They were concerned that Great Britain would not allow the colonies to share the economic developments of the Industrial Revolution.

   (B) They had aspirations to expand money-making industries such as metalwork in the colonies.

   (C) They believed in abstract ideals, as described by philosophers such as Montesquieu and Locke.

   (D) They desired to attain freedom from the Anglican church and practice their faith with simplicity instead of ornamentation.

5. Compared to the economic considerations of the American Revolution discussed in the passage, the primary economic considerations of the French Revolution <u>differed</u> in that the French Revolution

   (A) was caused by tensions in a colonial relationship with a distant imperial power

   (B) was led by the wealthiest members of society, who were the main proponents of political change

   (C) was fueled by widespread discontent over feudal obligations to nobles and to the crown

   (D) based much of its revolutionary rhetoric on Enlightenment ideas and philosophies

6. The financial situation described in the passage is best understood in the context of which of the following systems?

   (A) Mercantilism

   (B) Feudalism

   (C) Monarchism

   (D) Liberalism

Questions 7–9 refer to the following two images.

<u>Image 1</u>

PORTRAIT OF THE EMPEROR MEIJI, 1888

<u>Image 2</u>

NEGOTIATIONS AMONG THE JAPANESE, CHINESE, AND KOREANS, YOSAI (WATANABE) NOBUKAZU, 1894

Japanese print showing negotiations between the Japanese (on the left), Chinese (on the right), and Koreans (behind the table) to end the Sino-Japanese War, 1894

7. <u>Image 1</u> is best understood as an example of which of the following?

   (A) The use of the Japanese emperor as a figurehead by European imperial powers

   (B) The blending of traditional Japanese and Western clothing styles and furnishings

   (C) The implementation of centralized rule for the first time in Japanese history

   (D) The adoption of Western cultural elements as a result of increased interactions

8. <u>Image 2</u> best illustrates the fact that Japan in the period 1750–1900 experienced

   (A) rapid industrialization and imperialism

   (B) interference of European powers in East Asian affairs

   (C) the creation of an alliance with China

   (D) a modernized military that sought to conquer China

9. Taken together, the two images best illustrate which of the following continuities in the first half of the twentieth century?

   (A) The rejection of foreign cultural traditions as a result of isolation

   (B) The increased cooperation of industrializing powers in an effort to reduce trade barriers

   (C) The expansion of an empire due to the demand for natural resources

   (D) The rise of a nationalist movement sparked by the desire for independence

5

Questions 10–12 refer to the passage below.

"As we consider the various classes of which the State is composed, we are convinced that the laws of our empire which have wisely provided for the upper and middle classes, and have fixed with precision their rights and obligations, have not reached the same degree of success in relation to the peasants bound to the soil, who, either through ancient laws or custom, have been hereditarily subjected to the authority of the landlords. Indeed, the rights of landowners over their serfs have hitherto been very extensive and very imperfectly defined by the laws, which have been supplemented by tradition, custom, and the good will of the landlords.

This system has at best established patriarchal relations based upon the fairness and benevolence of the landowners and an affectionate docility on the part of the peasants, but as manners have lost their simplicity, the paternal ties between the landlords and the peasants have been weakened. Furthermore, as the seigniorial authority falls into the hands of those exclusively intent on their own selfish advantage, those relations of mutual good will have tended to give way and open the door to arbitrariness, burdensome to the peasants and hostile to their prosperity. This has served to develop in them an indifference to all progress.

These facts did not fail to impress our predecessors of glorious memory, and they took measures to improve the lot of the peasants; but these measures have had little effect, since they were either dependent for their execution on the individual initiative of such landlords as might be animated by a liberal spirit or were merely local in their scope, or adopted as an experiment."

Excerpt from a proclamation of Tsar Alexander II, 1861

10. Based on the information in the passage, the abolition of serfdom in Russia was most similar to the abolition of slavery in the United States in that

(A) both permitted landowners to determine how abolition would ultimately be carried out on their land

(B) both required government intervention due to the natural self-interest of lords and slaveowners, respectively

(C) neither process happened gradually, which made peaceful implementation more difficult to achieve

(D) neither process could be completed without the cooperation of affected property owners

11. Which of the following best describes the circumstances of former serfs <u>immediately following</u> the abolition of serfdom described in the passage?

(A) Most serfs won political rights, exempting them from taxation.

(B) Most serfs embarked on successful careers as industrial capitalists.

(C) Most serfs moved to cities to work in the factories.

(D) Most serfs did not prosper and remained impoverished.

5

12. A historian studying the period could use the passage to support which of the following claims about Alexander II?

    (A) He felt that the laws had addressed the needs of many citizens.

    (B) He felt that the laws had failed all citizens to some degree.

    (C) He felt that the laws provided clarity to all citizens.

    (D) He felt the legal system required a massive overhaul.

Questions 13–15 refer to the image below.

POLITICAL CARTOON PUBLISHED IN *PUCK* MAGAZINE IN THE AFTERMATH OF THE BOXER REBELLION IN CHINA, UNITED STATES, 1900

The cartoon, which is captioned "The real trouble will come with the 'wake,'" shows international powers (Britain, Russia, Austria, Italy, Germany, and France) as animals that are subjugating the Chinese dragon, as the United States, represented by the eagle, looks on.

13. A historian would most likely use this image to study which of the following in the period 1750–1900?

    (A) European states' responses to uprisings

    (B) Chinese views of economic imperialism

    (C) Tactics used by imperial powers to conquer territories

    (D) Advances in military technology as a result of industrialization

14. Which of the following was the most immediate direct effect of the events illustrated in the image?

    (A) China adopted communism with a capitalist economy.

    (B) Reform movements led to rapid Chinese industrialization.

    (C) European powers took control of China's government.

    (D) China's monarchy was overthrown in a revolution.

15. China's political climate led to which of the following in the early twentieth century?

    (A) Cooperation among European states and China in response to the Great Depression

    (B) Competition by European powers over access to China during World War I

    (C) New forms of economic imperialism practiced by European powers in China

    (D) Expansion of China's borders at the expense of European powers

Part B: Key Terms

The following is a list of the major people, places, and events for 1750 to 1900. You will very likely see many of these on the AP World History: Modern exam.

For each key term, ask yourself the following questions:

- Can I describe this key term?
- Can I discuss this key term in the context of other events?
- Could I correctly answer a multiple-choice question about this key term?
- Could I correctly answer a free-response question about this key term?

Check off the key terms if you can answer "yes" to at least three of these questions.

Revolutions and Independence Movements

- ☐ Enlightenment
- ☐ American Revolution
- ☐ French Revolution
- ☐ Maroon
- ☐ Haitian Revolution
- ☐ Latin American independence movements

Nationalism and the Nation State

- ☐ Nationalism

Industrialization

- ☐ Adam Smith
- ☐ Factory system
- ☐ Global division of labor
- ☐ First Industrial Revolution
- ☐ Second Industrial Revolution
- ☐ Railroads

Reactions to Industrialization

- ☐ Liberalism
- ☐ Socialism
- ☐ Communism

Reform in Asian States

- ☐ Tanzimât Movement
- ☐ First Opium War
- ☐ Second Opium War
- ☐ Self-Strengthening Movement
- ☐ Taiping Rebellion
- ☐ Boxer Rebellion
- ☐ Meiji Restoration

Imperialism and Its Impact

- ☐ Imperialism
- ☐ Indian Rebellion of 1857
- ☐ Congo Free State
- ☐ Social Darwinism

Legacies of Imperialism

- ☐ Indentured servants
- ☐ Chinese Exclusion Act

Emancipation

- ☐ Emancipation of slaves
- ☐ Feminism

Next Steps

Step 1: Tally your correct answers from Part A, and review the quiz explanations at the end of this chapter.

1. B	6. A	11. D
2. C	7. D	12. A
3. B	8. A	13. A
4. C	9. C	14. D
5. C	10. B	15. B

_____ out of 15 questions

Step 2: Count the number of key terms you checked off in Part B.

_____ out of 31 key terms

Step 3: Read the Key Takeaways in this chapter.

Step 4: Consult the table below and follow the instructions based on your performance.

If You Got...	Do This
80% or more of the Test What You Already Know assessment correct (12 or more questions from Part A and 25 or more key terms from Part B)	• Read definitions in this chapter for all the key terms you didn't check off. • Complete the Test What You Learned assessment in this chapter.
50% or less of the Test What You Already Know assessment correct (7 or fewer questions from Part A and 15 or fewer key terms from Part B)	• Read the comprehensive review for this period in Chapter 9. • If you are short on time, read only the High-Yield sections. • Complete the Practice Set assessment at the end of Chapter 9. • Read through all of the key term definitions in this chapter. • Complete the Test What You Learned assessment in this chapter.
Any other result	• Read the High-Yield sections in the comprehensive review of this period in Chapter 9. • Read definitions in this chapter for all the key terms you didn't check off. • Complete the Test What You Learned assessment in this chapter.

ESSENTIAL CONTENT

Key Takeaways: 1750 to 1900

1. The ideals of the Enlightenment inspired a wave of independence movements and revolutions throughout the Americas and Europe that promoted liberty and other democratic values. These new governments, however, extended full legal and political rights to only a limited class of people.

2. The concept of the nation-state become a new aspect of cultural identity. In Europe, nationalist movements led to the unification of Italy and Germany. In other parts of the world, such as Russia, China, Japan, and the Ottoman Empire, nationalism prompted rebellions and reform movements.

3. Industrialization increased economic interdependence between different regions of the world. Industrialized nations in Europe and the Americas sought to colonize portions of Africa and Asia to obtain raw materials and to open up new markets for trade.

4. Populations grew, and many people migrated to cities in search of work in factories. Wage laborers were more desirable than forced labor in this new market-driven economy, so slaves and serfs were emancipated. The working class emerged, and workers organized into unions to advocate for improving dangerous and oppressive working conditions.

5. New political and economic ideologies emerged in response to industrialization. Liberalism promoted limited government interference with the free market, whereas socialism and communism advocated for government regulation and increased political power for the working class.

6. Women gained some economic opportunities as a result of industrialization, but were paid considerably less than their male counterparts. These new economic opportunities and Enlightenment ideals prompted women to fight for political rights as well, though these rights would not become realized until the twentieth century in most parts of the world.

Key Terms: 1750 to 1900

Remember that the AP World History exam tests you on the depth of your knowledge, not just your ability to recall facts. While we have provided brief definitions here, you will need to know these terms in even more depth for the AP exam, including how terms connect to broader historical themes and understandings.

Revolutions and Independence Movements

Enlightenment: Post-Renaissance period in European history devoted to the study and exploration of new ideas in science, politics, the arts, and philosophy.

American Revolution: Conflict between American colonists and the British government, caused by growing resentments based on taxation and governing policies; Revolutionary War lasted from 1775 to 1781; ultimately ended in American independence and the first large-scale democracy since ancient Greece.

French Revolution: Conflict between the Third Estate (peasants, townsfolk, and merchants) and the First and Second Estates (clergy and nobility, respectively) for political and social control; inspired by the American Revolution; various political factions competed for control of the government, with Napoleon Bonaparte ultimately seizing power in a coup.

Maroon: Term for a nineteenth-century escaped slave in the Americas who established his or her own settlement away from plantations, causing tensions with colonial authorities; term is also used to describe the slaves' present-day descendants.

Nationalism and the Nation State

Nationalism: The tendency of people to see themselves as part of a broader community with unifying forces such as common heritages, cultures, languages, religions, and customs; this sense of national identity and pride both fueled the expansion of empires and often occurred as a reaction against foreign rule.

Industrialization

Adam Smith: Scottish economist whose 1776 work *The Wealth of Nations* advocated a laissez-faire policy toward economics (minimal government interference), making him one of the fathers of modern capitalism.

Factory system: System of labor that uses rigorous mechanization and large numbers of unskilled workers to mass-produce goods that were once made skillfully by hand; developed during the Industrial Revolution; the use of interchangeable parts simplified assembly but made work repetitive.

Global division of labor: The system in which industrialized societies utilized the raw materials of less industrialized societies (e.g., cotton from India, rubber from Brazil, metals from Central Africa) to facilitate large-scale manufacturing and transportation; the growth of these industrialized societies provided an impetus for imperialist conquests later in the nineteenth century.

Haitian Revolution: Slave revolt that lasted from 1791–1804 led by Toussaint L'Ouverture; the former French colony of Saint-Domingue became the independent nation of Haiti, the second independent nation in the Western Hemisphere and the world's first black republic.

Latin American independence movements: Movements against Spanish colonial rule in Central and South America in the 1810s and 1820s, which led to the independence of every nation in the region; inspired by the success of the Haitian Revolution; key leaders were Simón Bolívar, José de San Martín, and Bernardo O'Higgins.

First Industrial Revolution: Rapid development and industrial production that occurred in European countries and the United States between 1760 and 1820; the development of the steam engine allowed steamships and early locomotives to rapidly increase the speed at which goods, people, and ideas spread.

Second Industrial Revolution: Continuing industrialization that occurred between 1870 and 1920, which included revolutionary new methods of producing steel, chemicals, and electrical power; changed society in Western Europe, Japan, and the United States by introducing new ways of working and living.

Railroads: Steam-powered locomotives invented in England in the 1820s; started a "transportation revolution" in which mass-produced goods could be transported overland more quickly and inexpensively than ever before; by 1900, virtually every industrialized nation had a well-developed railroad system.

Reactions to Industrialization

Liberalism: Political and economic ideology based on Enlightenment philosophies that advocated for constitutional government, separation of powers, and natural rights, as well as limited government involvement in the regulation of the new industrialized economy.

Socialism: Utopian ideal developed in response to the poor working conditions faced by factory workers; in this radical form of society, the workers would run the economy in a self-sufficient manner and share everything fairly, thereby eliminating the wealthy classes.

Communism: Extreme form of socialism in which governments centrally plan the economy; inspired by *The Communist Manifesto* (1848), which advocated the overthrow of the bourgeoisie (capitalists) by the proletariat (workers).

Reform

Tanzimât Movement: Period of reform in the Ottoman Empire, lasting from 1839 to 1879, that resulted in a modernized infrastructure, a new legal code modeled after the French system, and religious equality under the law.

First Opium War: Conflict waged between China and Great Britain in 1839 after Chinese customs officials refused British imports of Indian opium due to the addictive effects it had on Chinese workers; this war weakened the Qing Dynasty and made China more vulnerable to unequal trade with the West.

Second Opium War: Conflict between China, Great Britain, and France that lasted from 1856 to 1860; spurred by the desire of the European powers to further weaken China's position in trade negotiations, to legalize the opium trade, and to expand the export of indentured workers from China.

Self-Strengthening Movement: Attempt by China, in the 1860s and 1870s, to modernize its military and economy under its own terms; changes were minimal due to imperial resistance.

Taiping Rebellion: Christian-based uprising led by Chinese scholar Hong Xiuquan that lasted from 1850 to 1864; the violent reaction by the imperial court left China financially strained and caused the bloodiest civil war in world history.

Boxer Rebellion: Movement undertaken by a secret society of Chinese and backed by Empress Cixi that sought to rid China of foreigners and foreign influence; the Boxers were defeated by a multinational force that included the United States, Russia, and Japan.

Meiji Restoration: Successful rebellion in which young reform-minded Japanese sought to overthrow the isolationist Tokugawa shogunate and restore the power of Emperor Meiji; sparked by contact between Japan and the United States; following the restoration, Japan experienced rapid industrialization and modernization.

Imperialism and Its Impact

Imperialism: Policy of a country extending its rule over other countries, often by force; the world saw a wave of imperialism from 1750 to 1900 in particular, which was spurred by industrial countries' need for raw materials and for markets for their goods, as well as justified by various cultural, racial ideologies about the superiority of imperial powers.

Social Darwinism: Popular nineteenth-century theory used to justify capitalism and imperialism; drew on evolutionary theorist Charles Darwin's view of "survival of the fittest."

Indian Rebellion of 1857: Conflict fought in India between the British and the Indian soldiers in British service; the British victory strengthened the legitimacy of their rule.

Legacies of Imperialism

Indentured servants: System of labor in which workers are contracted to work for a fixed period of time, usually for a low wage, in exchange for land or other assistance.

Emancipation

Emancipation of slaves: Process by which slavery was abolished and slaves were granted their freedom; partly the result of a new political movement that found slavery to be incompatible with Enlightenment ideals; between the 1830s and the 1880s, every industrialized nation and its colonies gradually abolished slavery, turning to other labor systems such as wage labor and indentured servitude.

Congo Free State: Colony in Central Africa established in 1885 by Belgium's King Leopold II; despite the name "Free State," it consisted of a series of large rubber plantations worked by forced labor in brutal weather and working conditions; in the 1960s, it declared independence, became the nation of Zaire, and is currently known as the Democratic Republic of the Congo.

Chinese Exclusion Act: Law enacted in the United States in 1882 that severely limited immigration from China, which had been prevalent earlier in the nineteenth century during the time of the California Gold Rush and the construction of the Transcontinental Railroad.

Feminism: Movement undertaken by women that emerged as a result of the economic changes that occurred following industrialization; challenged established gender roles and advocated for increased political and legal rights.

5

TEST WHAT YOU LEARNED

Part A: Quiz

Questions 1–3 refer to the passage below.

"Ever since the restoration of the Meiji Dynasty in 1876, the Japanese have followed to the letter the fifth and concluding command of the famous Imperial Rescript, issued by the reigning Mikado when he took his seat upon the throne vacated by the banished Tokugawa Shogunate. This clause, in all the naïveté and ingenuousness of the guilelessly honest, asserts simply that 'We shall endeavor to raise the prestige and honor of our country by seeking knowledge throughout the world.' Upon the command of their new and greatly beloved Mikado the Japanese began to 'seek knowledge throughout the world.' And the one man who was ever in the van, leading and and pointing the way—the long, dim, unknown, mysterious road of Western civilization—was Yukichi Fukuzawa."

Joseph Sale, American journalist, "The Moral Code of Yukichi Fukuzawa," 1907

1. Based on the passage and your knowledge of world history, which of the following changes in Japan occurred during the Meiji Dynasty?

   (A) The division of Japan into spheres of influence

   (B) The advancement of military and manufacturing technology

   (C) The expansion of the feudal system of labor and land ownership

   (D) The reduction of army and naval forces

2. Which of the following characteristics of the Meiji Dynasty best explains why Japan was opened to trade with the West?

   (A) Commodore Matthew Perry's diplomacy was both effective and well-received.

   (B) Emperor Meiji sought to avoid being forced into colonization.

   (C) Japan recognized a demand for Western goods and technology.

   (D) The stagnant political climate of the Meiji period left Japan vulnerable to foreign influence.

3. The political philosophy reflected in the passage most directly contributed to which of the following?

   (A) A general acknowledgment of Japan's inability to modernize quickly

   (B) The continuation of global power concentrated among Western nations

   (C) A shift in power that provided the emperor with extensive authority

   (D) Increased displeasure among some samurai, which led to an unsuccessful rebellion

Questions 4–6 refer to the following passage.

"You, O King, live beyond the confines of many seas, nevertheless, impelled by your humble desire to partake of the benefits of our civilisation, you have dispatched a mission respectfully bearing your memorial [message of goodwill]. Your envoy has crossed the seas and paid his respects at my court on the anniversary of my birthday. To show your devotion, you have also sent offerings of your country's produce.

I have perused your memorial. The earnest terms in which it is couched reveal a respectful humility on your part, which is highly praiseworthy. In consideration of the fact that your ambassador and his deputy have come a long way with your memorial and tribute, I have shown them high favour and have allowed them to be introduced into my presence. To manifest my indulgence, I have entertained them at a banquet and made them numerous gifts. I have also caused presents to be forwarded to the naval commander and 600 of his officers and men, although they did not come to Peking, so that they too may share in my all-embracing kindness.

As to your entreaty to send one of your nationals to be accredited to my Celestial Court, and to be in control of your country's trade with China, this request is contrary to all usage of my dynasty. It cannot possibly be entertained. It is true that Europeans, in the service of the dynasty, have been permitted to live at Peking—but they are compelled to adopt Chinese dress, they are strictly confined to their own precincts and are never permitted to return home. You are presumably familiar with our dynastic regulations.

It behoves you, O King, to respect my sentiments and to display even greater devotion and loyalty in future, so that, by perpetual submission to our Throne, you may secure peace and prosperity for your country hereafter."

Qing Emperor, letter to King George III of England, 1793

4. Which of the following provided justification for the Qing Dynasty policies described in the <u>third paragraph</u>?

   (A) Laissez-faire

   (B) Isolationism

   (C) Communism

   (D) Democracy

5. Which of the following best describes the effect of the Opium Wars in the nineteenth century?

   (A) They served as the catalyst for the Taiping Rebellion.

   (B) They led to the restoration of the emperor, the downfall of the shogunate, and an industrialization program.

   (C) They led to China adopting the French legal code and, eventually, installing a "puppet" emperor.

   (D) They led to China's sovereignty being weakened in order to facilitate free trade.

6. The Revolution of 1911 that overthrew the Qing Dynasty is most similar to which of the following?

   (A) The French Revolution

   (B) The Paris Commune

   (C) The American Revolution

   (D) The Young Turk Revolution

Questions 7–9 refer to the graph below.

POPULATION OF EUROPE AND THE AMERICAS, 1750–1900

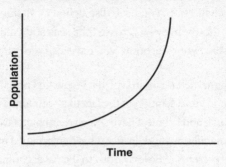

5

7. Which of the following statements could be supported by the information shown in the graph?

   (A) The end of famines prevented death due to starvation.

   (B) Antibiotics prevented deaths from infections.

   (C) Increased food production led to better diets.

   (D) A reduction in environmental pollution improved air quality.

8. Which of the following additional pieces of information would be most directly useful in assessing the extent to which the population growth shown on the graph contributed to a shift in global perspective?

   (A) Information on the population in locations beyond Europe and the Americas

   (B) Information on the amount of foreign investment in the Americas by 1900

   (C) Information on interactions among countries as populations increased

   (D) Information on conflicting political ideologies that emerged prior to 1750

9. By 1900, which of the following emerged in large part as a reaction to the exponential population growth illustrated in the graph?

   (A) The creation of new languages

   (B) New forms of governance

   (C) Changes in religious traditions

   (D) Shifts in migration patterns

Questions 10–12 refer to the passage below.

"The essential point in dealing with Africans is to establish a respect for the European. Upon this—the prestige of the white man—depends his influence, often his very existence, in Africa. If he shows by his surroundings, by his assumption of superiority, that he is far above the native, he will be respected, and his influence will be proportionate to the superiority he assumes and bears out by his higher accomplishments and mode of life. In my opinion—at any rate with reference to Africa—it is the greatest possible mistake to suppose that a European can acquire a greater influence by adopting the mode of life of the natives. In effect, it is to lower himself to their plane, instead of elevating them to his."

F. D. Lugard, British colonial administrator, *The Rise of Our East African Empire*, 1893

10. The passage is best understood in the context of which of the following historical events?

    (A) The mass conversion of Africans to Christianity

    (B) The expansion of the transatlantic slave trade

    (C) The establishment of transoceanic empires by industrializing powers

    (D) The transformation of Africa's economy due to industrial technology

11. F. D. Lugard's view of natives most directly reflects the influence of which of the following?

    (A) The political and social theories of Karl Marx and Friedrich Engels

    (B) Predominant ideologies regarding race and international relations

    (C) Enlightenment ideas generated by highly educated Europeans

    (D) Capitalist economic theories that support privately owned enterprises

12. Which of the following was a direct effect of interactions among Africans and Europeans as described in the passage?

    (A) The outbreak of violent resistance movements among Africans

    (B) The abandonment of African cultural and religious traditions

    (C) The stimulation of Africa's economy due to industrialization

    (D) The elevation of impoverished Africans to higher status

5

Questions 13–15 refer to the image below.

"THE WORLD'S CONSTABLE," 1905

This U.S. political cartoon shows President Theodore Roosevelt as a constable standing between Europe and Latin America, with a club labeled "The New Diplomacy."

13. The image can best be used as evidence for which of the following developments that took place circa 1900?

   (A) The increase of U.S. influence and decline of Spanish and Portuguese influence

   (B) The diplomacy used to expand Western transoceanic empires as violent conflicts declined

   (C) The use of warfare and diplomacy to expand American colonies in Africa

   (D) The establishment of settler colonies in Africa by industrializing powers

14. According to the image, President Theodore Roosevelt was advocating an approach to governance that most clearly reflected the principles of

   (A) liberalism

   (B) communism

   (C) neocolonialism

   (D) nationalism

15. The foreign policies reflected in the image had which of the following effects on U.S. interactions with Latin American countries in the late nineteenth century?

(A) They reflected Latin American countries' desire to have the United States' protection from European influence.

(B) They contributed to failed infrastructure projects, such as the initial Panama Canal project.

(C) They provided the United States with additional justification for intervention in Latin America.

(D) They made it difficult to secure future economic interests in Central and South America.

Part B: Key Terms

This key terms list is the same as the list in the Test What You Already Know section earlier in this chapter. Based on what you have now learned, again ask yourself the following questions:

- Can I describe this key term?
- Can I discuss this key term in the context of other events?
- Could I correctly answer a multiple-choice question about this key term?
- Could I correctly answer a free-response question about this key term?

Check off the key terms if you can answer "yes" to at least three of these questions.

Revolutions and Independence Movements

- ☐ Enlightenment
- ☐ American Revolution
- ☐ French Revolution
- ☐ Maroon
- ☐ Haitian Revolution
- ☐ Latin American independence movements

Nationalism and the Nation State

- ☐ Nationalism

Industrialization

- ☐ Adam Smith
- ☐ Factory system
- ☐ Global division of labor
- ☐ First Industrial Revolution
- ☐ Second Industrial Revolution
- ☐ Railroads

Reactions to Industrialization

- ☐ Liberalism
- ☐ Socialism
- ☐ Communism

Reform in Asian States

- ☐ Tanzimât Movement
- ☐ First Opium War
- ☐ Second Opium War
- ☐ Self-Strengthening Movement
- ☐ Taiping Rebellion
- ☐ Boxer Rebellion
- ☐ Meiji Restoration

Imperialism and Its Impact

- ☐ Imperialism
- ☐ Social Darwinism
- ☐ Indian Rebellion of 1857
- ☐ Congo Free State

Legacies of Imperialism

☐ Indentured servants ☐ Chinese Exclusion Act

Emancipation

☐ Emancipation of slaves ☐ Feminism

Next Steps

Step 1: Tally your correct answers from Part A, and review the quiz explanations at the end of this chapter.

1. B	6. A	11. B
2. B	7. C	12. A
3. D	8. C	13. A
4. B	9. D	14. C
5. D	10. C	15. C

_____ out of 15 questions

Step 2: Count the number of key terms you checked off in Part B.

_____ out of 31 key terms

Step 3: Compare your Test What You Already Know results to these Test What You Learned results to see how exam-ready you are for this period.

For More Practice:

- Read (or reread) the comprehensive review for this period in Chapter 9.

- Complete the Practice Set assessment at the end of Chapter 9.

- Go to kaptest.com to complete the online quiz questions for 1750 to 1900.

  ○ Haven't registered your book yet? Go to kaptest.com/moreonline to begin.

ANSWERS AND EXPLANATIONS

Test What You Already Know

1. B

Slave trading with Europeans began in coastal regions of Africa, causing previously established African trade routes to shift; **(B)** is correct. North Africa remained predominantly Islamic despite European imperialism, while sub-Saharan Africa largely Christianized in the twentieth century, well after the end of the transatlantic slave trade. Thus, (A) is incorrect. Also, the map suggests that relatively little slave trading occurred in regions of Northern Africa such as Egypt and Algeria. It also suggests that relatively few slaves were sent to India and other Asian regions and that relatively little slave trading occurred near Cape Colony in South Africa. Therefore, (C) and (D) are incorrect.

2. C

During the "Scramble for Africa" (1875–1914), European empires utilized well-traveled routes as they overtook the entire continent, with the exception of Ethiopia and Liberia. The fact that the majority of African territory was colonized, along with the information depicted in the map, demonstrates the great extent to which people throughout Africa were affected by slave trade routes. Therefore, **(C)** is correct. Technological developments such as the cotton gin greatly impacted plantations, but this information is not directly relevant to the routes' impact on African people, so (A) is incorrect. (B) is incorrect because while the distance covered by the routes would indicate the amount of terrain affected by trade, it would not provide the most direct information about the extent to which people's lives were changed. The number of people born in Africa in the 1700s and the 1800s would be an interesting data point, but it would not indicate *how* those people were affected by the slave trade; (D) is incorrect.

3. B

Sugar, tobacco, and cotton were especially labor-intensive cash crops, meaning plantation owners required cheap labor to make large profits. Their primary source of labor was African slaves, who were transported to the Americas through the transatlantic slave trade. Therefore, **(B)** is correct. Industrialization began with the nineteenth-century Industrial Revolution, postdating this map; (A) is incorrect. Although absolute monarchy was the primary political system in Europe during this period, it did not directly affect the economics of the slave trade, making (C) incorrect. European countries of this time period adhered to mercantilist principles rather than laissez-faire capitalism; (D) is also incorrect.

4. C

Charles Inglis, the Loyalist author of this passage, describes how the colonies' economic dependence on Great Britain should have otherwise deterred these leaders from embarking on such a risky revolution. Thomas Paine (the author of the popular pamphlet *Common Sense*) and other leaders of the American Revolution were inspired by Enlightenment philosophers—including Montesquieu, Locke, and Rousseau—and were not primarily motivated by economic considerations. Therefore, **(C)** is correct. (A) is incorrect; the Industrial Revolution began in the 1780s, after the American Revolution had ended. Although the passage mentions metal, the American revolutionaries were not primarily motivated by a desire to improve the colonies' industries; (B) is incorrect. (D) is also incorrect; it describes the Puritans' religious motivations to create their settlements in Massachusetts in the seventeenth century.

5. C

Although serfdom was no longer present in late eighteenth-century France, many of the obligations and taxes of the feudal period continued to burden peasants up to the revolution. Thus, **(C)** is correct. Unlike the American Revolution, France's revolution was primarily an internal struggle resulting from dramatic social divisions and economic inequality. Thus, (A) is incorrect. While the wealthiest members of society were at the forefront of the American Revolution, the wealthy typically resisted the French Revolution, which was led primarily by the Third Estate. While a catchall category for people who were not nobles or clergy, politically the Third Estate was primarily led by the *bourgeoisie*. Thus, (B) is incorrect. Enlightenment philosophers and ideals such as natural rights, the separation of powers, and the social contract inspired both revolutions. Therefore, (D) is incorrect.

5

6. A

The 13 British colonies primarily provided England with their natural resources instead of growing their own industries; this reflects the system of mercantilism, making **(A)** correct. Feudalism was a medieval social system, which generally required peasants to serve vassals, who in turn served nobles; this system is not reflected in the passage, so (B) is incorrect. (C) is incorrect because monarchism is a political system, in which a monarch such as King George III of Great Britain rules over his people. (D) is incorrect because economic liberalism is a system that advocates for free trade and minimal government regulation of the economy, which contrasts with the mercantilist trade described in the passage.

7. D

The style of the uniform and the chair shown in the image are Western, which is the result of increased contact with Westerners following Matthew Perry's visit and the Treaty of Kanagawa; **(D)** is correct. (A) is incorrect because the Japanese emperor in the Meiji period ruled independently. Additionally, Japan's government was never controlled by foreigners. (B) and (C) are incorrect because the clothing and furnishings shown in the image do not reflect any traditional Japanese elements and there was centralized rule under the Tokugawa shogunate.

8. A

Image 2 depicts Japanese leaders positioned in aggressive stances while negotiating with Chinese and Korean representatives. The Japanese leaders are dressed in Western-style clothes, which were made possible by the booming Japanese industrialization movement and their contact with the Western world. The image reflects how Japan rapidly industrialized and attempted to gain more territory to acquire natural resources in the late nineteenth century; **(A)** is correct. European powers are not pictured and were not involved in negotiations, so (B) is incorrect. (C) is incorrect because Japan and China had just fought a war and were attempting to conclude it, so it would be unlikely that they would suddenly become allies. (D) is incorrect because Japan never completely conquered China, although it did take over some parts of eastern China in the 1930s and early 1940s.

9. C

Image 1 shows Western-style dress and furnishings, which reflect more frequent interactions with Westerners. Image 2 also includes Western-style clothing, and the Japanese leaders are leaning forward, displaying confidence in their ability to expand the Japanese empire. In the decades leading up to World War II, upon increased contact with industrialized Western countries, Japan sought to expand its empire and gain resources, such as oil and iron ore, in order to fuel industrialization; **(C)** is correct. The images show that Japan adopted Western technology and cultural elements, so (A) is incorrect. (B) is incorrect because the early twentieth century was characterized by global conflict rather than cooperation. (D) is incorrect because Japan was never controlled by Western powers, so there was no need for an independence movement.

10. B

In the passage, Alexander II mentions that previous tsars had attempted to improve the situation of the serfs but that these efforts had failed because they were too dependent on the cooperation of landlords, who had a financial interest in maintaining the serfdom. Similarly, in the United States, it was unusual for slave owners to voluntarily relinquish their slaves due to their own financial self-interest. Thus, the abolition of both serfdom and slavery required government intervention, making **(B)** correct. (A) contradicts the passage and is not a characteristic of American slavery either, so it is incorrect. Based on the previous reforms mentioned in the passage, the abolition of serfdom was a gradual process, making (C) incorrect. (D) is incorrect because the abolition was government-mandated and, therefore, did not depend on the cooperation of affected property owners, which was the problem with the previous reforms in Russia.

11. D

In 1861, Tsar Alexander II abolished serfdom, and the government compensated landowners for the loss of land and serfs. The serfs gained their freedom, and their labor obligations were gradually cancelled. However, few serfs prospered, and most were desperately poor, matching **(D)**. Former serfs won very few political rights and had to pay a redemption tax for most of the land they received—and receiving that land was often a painfully slow process. Thus, (A) is incorrect. Very few serfs were able to move beyond an agrarian existence, so (B) and (C) are incorrect.

5

12. A

In the first paragraph of the excerpt, Alexander II offered his opinion that the "laws of our empire have wisely provided for the upper and middle classes," leaving only lower-class peasants in need of assistance. Because he believed many citizens' needs were addressed by the laws, **(A)** is correct. Since he felt that the upper and middle classes were served well by their laws, (B) is incorrect. By the same logic, he said that the laws gave upper- and middle-class citizens (but not peasants) a clear sense of their "rights and obligations," making (C) incorrect. Since he believed that only the peasants could be substantially better served by Russian laws, (D) is incorrect.

13. A

In response to the growth of Western economic privilege in China, a secret society of Chinese attacked Western soldiers and workers in 1900. The cartoon shows that European states were at odds with one another but joined together to defeat the Boxers, making **(A)** correct. (B) is incorrect because the cartoon was published in the U.S. magazine *Puck*. The titles of graphics such as this one can contain important details, such as publication location. (C) is incorrect because China was not conquered and, since this is a cartoon, it would not be useful in determining specific tactics. The image is not focused on military technologies, so (D) is incorrect.

14. D

The Qing Dynasty survived the Boxer Rebellion. However, the monarchy was overthrown about 10 years later due to economic imperialism by Western powers, a lack of industrialization, and the desire to implement a more stable government; **(D)** is correct. (A) is incorrect because while China did eventually have a communist revolution in 1949, this was after the overthrow of the Qing in 1911, so it is not the most immediate effect. (B) is incorrect because China's reform movements failed; industrialization did not occur on a large scale until economic reforms were made in the 1970s. China's government was never controlled by European powers, which were mainly interested in economic control, so (C) is incorrect.

15. B

In the early twentieth century, World War I broke out. There was a struggle for control of spheres of influence in China, resulting in Germany losing its sphere to Japan. Thus, **(B)** is correct. European states focused on domestic policies during the Great Depression, so (A) is incorrect. (C) is incorrect because economic imperialism in the twentieth century did not differ from previous forms, so it would not be "new." (D) is incorrect because China did not expand beyond the borders established by the Qing Dynasty. If it had, that expansion would have been at the expense of China's neighboring countries, not European countries.

Test What You Learned

1. B

After opening to Western influence, Japan sent its leaders abroad to "seek knowledge throughout the world," as stated in the passage. One of the areas Japanese leaders gained much knowledge in was modern advances in military and manufacturing technology. **(B)** is correct. (A) is incorrect because European powers divided China, not Japan, into spheres of influence. The feudal system was abolished prior to the Meiji Dynasty, making (C) incorrect. Throughout the Meiji Dynasty, Japan expanded rather than reduced military forces; (D) is incorrect.

2. B

The nineteenth century saw contact and conflict between Western powers and East Asian empires that often turned violent, with the result of land ceded to Western powers, such as Britain. Emperor Meiji agreed to open trade, not due to Commodore Perry's diplomatic tactics, but rather to avoid being forced into a trade relationship with the United States—or worse, becoming a colony. Therefore, **(B)** is correct and (A) is incorrect. Prior to Commodore Perry's arrival, Japan was not interested in learning more about Western goods or technology, making (C) incorrect. (D) is incorrect because the Meiji period was characterized by rapid modernization and dramatic political, social, and economic change.

3. D

After the Tokugawa shogunate was overthrown, some samurai were displeased not just with the loss of their privileges, but also with the mass adoption of Western ways by Japan. The resulting Satsuma Rebellion (1877) saw traditionalist samurai launch a brief civil war, during which the government's army of peasant conscripts defeated the rebels. Thus, **(D)** is correct. (A) and (B) are incorrect because the rapidity of the industrialization and modernization of Japan impressed the rest of the world, and the rise of Japan as an imperial power altered the global balance of power as the twentieth century began. (C) is incorrect because while the emperor was nominally restored to authority, real power was held in the hands of nobles.

4. B

The Qing Dynasty wanted very little commercial or cultural exchange with the outside world in the eighteenth century, continuing the isolationist policy of the previous Ming Dynasty. Accordingly, in the third paragraph, the Qing emperor declares that having a British diplomat come to his court to control trade with China would be unacceptable, or "contrary to all usage of my dynasty." The emperor also makes clear that when Europeans are allowed in his court, it is "in the service of the dynasty" and they are "compelled" to assimilate to Chinese customs. Thus, **(B)** is correct. Laissez-faire refers to unregulated trade, which is not relevant to the policies observed in this passage; (A) is incorrect. China would not become a communist country until the post-imperial period in 1949, making (C) incorrect. China was still a feudal empire at the time of the letter, so (D) is also incorrect.

5. D

The Opium Wars most directly resulted in the weakening of Chinese sovereignty as it related to trade, as tariffs were removed and foreigners were granted special rights and privileges. Thus, **(D)** is correct. While the outbreak of the Taiping Rebellion resulted, in part, from the First Opium War, the rebellion was still ongoing when the Second Opium War broke out. Therefore, (A) is incorrect. (B) is incorrect because the downfall of the shogunate and the restoration of the emperor describes the Meiji Restoration, which happened in Japan. (C) is incorrect because it was the Ottoman Empire that adopted the French legal code and saw a soft takeover by the Young Turks.

6. A

The French Revolution saw the internal revolt against a monarchy, the establishment of a republic, and eventually a failure of the initial revolution and rollback of its ideas. The Revolution of 1911, also called the Xinhai Revolution, likewise saw its gains diminished as violence soon broke out and China descended into civil war and rule by warlords. Therefore, **(A)** is correct. The Paris Commune was a revolutionary socialist government. While one of Sun Yat-sen's Three Principles of the People was socialism, it was not as prominent, and his revolution's Republic

of China was not crushed by a large native army. Thus, (B) is incorrect. Sun Yat-sen took over his home country rather than fighting for independence from it, making (C) incorrect. (D) is incorrect because the Young Turks installed a puppet sultan for them to rule through, while Sun Yat-sen and his fellow revolutionaries overthrew their monarchy and established a republic.

7. C

The graph shows population growth in the eighteenth and nineteenth centuries, with an even sharper uptick at the end of the nineteenth century. Innovations in food production led to more robust, diverse diets, which fueled these larger populations; **(C)** is correct. (A) is incorrect because, despite increased food production, famines continued due to poverty. (B) is incorrect because antibiotics were not available until the early twentieth century. Environmental pollution was unregulated until the late twentieth century, so (D) is incorrect.

8. C

The exponential increase in the global population from 1750 to 1900 greatly influenced the ways in which countries interacted with one another as well as how they developed internally. Having a timeline of interactions as well as information about the types of interactions would better frame a shift in global perspective, making **(C)** correct. While information about the population in Africa, Asia, and Australia would be helpful for comparison, it would not provide information about economic or political changes, so (A) is incorrect. Foreign economic interest in the Americas was just one of many factors in shifting global perspectives; (B) is incorrect. (D) is incorrect because it is the implementation of the ideologies rather than the ideas themselves that influence global interactions.

9. D

The latter half of the eighteenth century through the nineteenth century saw booming populations across Europe. The pressures of growing populations and the need for increased resources led to migration movements from Europe to the Americas, as well as from China to the United States. **(D)** is correct. (A) is incorrect because population growth would not have any bearing on language. Government forms remained relatively stable or became more inclusive without changing the structure of power, so (B) is incorrect. (C) is incorrect because no new religious traditions formed in this era as a result of population growth.

10. C

Interactions among Africans and Europeans at this time were the result of widespread colonization, and the British author of this excerpt is outlining power relations that came out of this "Scramble for Africa"; **(C)** is correct. (A) is incorrect because, even though some Africans adopted Christianity, it is not referred to in the passage and did not occur on a massive scale. (B) is incorrect because the slave trade was abolished by the time this document was written and before Europeans traveled to inland regions of Africa. The passage does not examine economic changes, making (D) incorrect.

11. B

Racial ideologies of this time period, such as Social Darwinism and the White Man's burden, contributed to the philosophy that Europeans were superior to Africans; **(B)** is correct. Marx, and his collaborator Engels, developed Marxism, which called for social equality, the abolition of private property, and an overthrow of the existing system; (A) is incorrect. (C) is incorrect because Enlightenment ideas promoted equality, emancipation, and liberty rather than superiority and subjugation. Capitalist theories dictated decisions in business rather than interactions with natives, so (D) is incorrect.

12. A

Colonization and European claims of superiority caused multiple rebellions, making **(A)** correct. (B) is incorrect because African peoples retained many cultural traditions even as new ideas were brought by Europeans. (C) and (D) are incorrect because, while Europeans did bring industry to Africa, it was to benefit European economies, and African people were exploited for work in mines and on plantations.

13. A

The Spanish and Portuguese lost their colonies in the Americas through revolutions, which led to greater American economic and political influence, particularly in Latin America. Additionally, President Theodore Roosevelt was known for his "big stick diplomacy," which was a combination of peaceful negotiation and forceful action as needed. **(A)** is correct. (B) is incorrect because there was continued use of violence between colonists and colonizers, including military interventions by the United States. The cartoon focuses on the United States, which did not expand in Africa, making (C) incorrect. (D) is incorrect because the United States did not expand its influence to Africa. Following the Spanish-American War, the United States acquired Cuba, Puerto Rico, and the Philippines. This spread U.S. influence in both Latin America and Asia, but not Africa.

14. C

Neocolonialism is when a foreign country exerts influence on economic, political, or cultural affairs, which characterized the relationship between the United States and Latin America in the nineteenth and twentieth centuries; **(C)** is correct. (A) is incorrect because liberalism is an ideology that promotes reforms and human progress. (B) is incorrect because communism is an ideology that promotes control of the means of production by the masses and tries to promote social equality. (D) is incorrect because nationalism is when individuals have patriotic feelings toward their country and may feel they are superior to others.

15. C

In 1904, President Roosevelt issued an extension, or corollary, to the Monroe Doctrine. The Monroe Doctrine stated that "the American continents . . . are henceforth not to be considered as subjects for future colonization by any European powers." The Roosevelt Corollary gave the United States the right to intervene in the Western Hemisphere, which matches **(C)**. (A) is incorrect because many Latin Americans protested U.S. intervention. While a French company did fail to complete a canal across Panama in the 1880s, that initial project was not influenced by U.S. foreign policies, making (B) incorrect. (D) is incorrect because the Roosevelt Corollary made it possible for the United States to protect its significant economic investments throughout Latin America.

CHAPTER 6

1900 to the Present

LEARNING OBJECTIVES

- Analyze the influence of politics on states.

- Describe how societies rise and change because of race, class, and gender.

- Describe the impact of ideologies and beliefs on social hierarchies.

- Explain changes in social structures over time.

- Describe the role of the arts in both changing and reflecting society.

TIMELINE

Date	Region	Event
1904–1905	East Asia	Russo-Japanese War
1910–1920	Americas	Mexican Revolution
1911–1912	East Asia	Chinese Revolution
1914–1918	Europe, North America, Africa, & Asia	World War I
1917	Asia	Bolshevik Revolution
1918–1920	Asia	Russian Civil War
1919	Europe	Treaty of Versailles
1921–1928	Asia	Lenin's New Economic Policy
1922	Europe	King of Italy deposed; fascist government established by Mussolini
1923	Mid East	Republic of Turkey is established; end of the Ottoman Empire
1928–1932	Asia	First of Stalin's Five-Year Plans
1929	Global	Great Depression begins
1931	East Asia	Japanese invade Manchuria
1933	Europe	Hitler's rise to power
1935	South Asia	Government of India Act
1937	East Asia	Beginning of Second Sino-Japanese War
1939	Europe	German invasion of Poland
1945	Europe & East Asia	End of World War II
1947	South Asia	Partition of India
1948	Europe	Marshall Plan
1948	Mid East	Creation of Israel
1948	South Africa	Apartheid established in South Africa
1949	Europe & North America	NATO founded
1949	Europe	Division of Germany
1949	East Asia	People's Republic of China established
1950–1953	East Asia	Korean War
1955	Europe	Warsaw Pact signed
1956	Americas, Africa, & Asia	Non-Aligned Movement founded
1958–1961	East Asia	China's Great Leap Forward
1959	Caribbean	Cuban Revolution
1962	North America & Caribbean	Cuban Missile Crisis
1966–1976	East Asia	China's Cultural Revolution

Date	Region	Event
1973	Mid East	Arab-Israeli War
1975	East Asia	End of Vietnam War
1979	Mid East	Iranian Revolution
1980–1988	Mid East	Iran-Iraq War
1989	Europe	Fall of Berlin Wall
1990–1991	Mid East	Gulf War
1991	Europe & Asia	Fall of Soviet Union; end of the Cold War
2001	North America	9/11 Attacks by al-Qaeda
2003–2011	Mid East	Iraq War
2008–2010	Global	Economic crisis
2010–2012	Mid East and North Africa	Arab Spring

TEST WHAT YOU ALREADY KNOW

Part A: Quiz

Questions 1–2 refer to the passage below.

"In a telegram addressed to the Emperor by the members of the Council of the Empire on the night of the 28th February [1905], the state of affairs was described as follows:—

'Owing to the complete disorganisation of transport and to the lack of necessary materials, factories have stopped working. Forced unemployment, and the acute food crisis due to the disorganisation of transport, have driven the popular masses to desperation. This feeling is further intensified by hatred towards the Government and grave suspicions against the authorities, which have penetrated deeply into the soul of the nation. All this has found expression in a popular rising of elemental dimensions, and the troops are now joining the movement. The Government, which has never been trusted in Russia, is now utterly discredited and incapable of coping with the dangerous situation.'"

General A.I. Denikin, *The Russian Turmoil: Memoirs: Military, Social, and Political*, 1922

1. The events described in the passage are best understood in the context of which of the following historical developments?

    (A) The success of the working class had prompted resentment from the elites.

    (B) Russia's rapid industrialization had resulted in poor living conditions for the working class.

    (C) The Bolshevik Revolution had stirred widespread anti-capitalist feelings.

    (D) The onset of the Cold War had led Russian groups to publicly demonstrate.

2. Which of the following was a direct consequence of the events depicted in the passage?

    (A) Tsarist rule was immediately dismantled.

    (B) Tsarist rule persisted until the end of World War II.

    (C) Socialism was largely replaced by nationalism among the working class.

    (D) Russian revolutionary efforts expanded further.

6

Questions 3–4 refer to the image below.

"THE NEW RELIGION," 1966

Political cartoon depicting the Cultural Revolution launched in 1966 by Mao Zedong. Mao Zedong, drawn as a Budda-like figure, is being carried by devoted followers.

3. Based on the intended purpose of this political cartoon, it is most likely that the artist saw the Cultural Revolution as

   (A) a way to legitimize the Chinese Communist Party's authority

   (B) a rejection by Mao Zedong of the anti-religious aspects of communism

   (C) an effort to rally domestic support for Chinese forces in the Korean War

   (D) the consolidation by Mao Zedong of his base of political power

4. Which of the following best describes one consequence of the Cultural Revolution?

   (A) Literature, historical monuments, cultural sites, and religious sites were destroyed.

   (B) China experienced a return to traditional values, culture, and customs.

   (C) China was transformed from an agrarian to an industrial economy.

   (D) A cultural climate emerged that was more tolerant of diverse political ideologies.

Questions 5–7 refer to the passage below.

"The Purposes of the United Nations are:

1 To maintain international peace and security, and to that end: to take effective collective measures for the prevention and removal of threats to the peace, and for the suppression of acts of aggression or other breaches of the peace, and to bring about by peaceful means, and in conformity with the principles of justice and international law, adjustment or settlement of international disputes or situations which might lead to a breach of the peace;

2 To develop friendly relations among nations based on respect for the principle of equal rights and self-determination of peoples, and to take other appropriate measures to strengthen universal peace;

3 To achieve international co-operation in solving international problems of an economic, social, cultural, or humanitarian character, and in promoting and encouraging respect for human rights and for fundamental freedoms for all without distinction as to race, sex, language, or religion; and

4 To be a centre for harmonizing the actions of nations in the attainment of these common ends."

Charter of the United Nations, 1945

5. Which of the following conflicts most directly motivated the international community to form the United Nations?

    (A) The Korean War

    (B) The Cold War

    (C) World War I

    (D) World War II

6. A historian would cite which of the following as a primary reason for the failure of the League of Nations?

    (A) The refusal of the United States and Soviet Union to join as members

    (B) Global economic fallout from the Great Depression

    (C) Multiple conflicts which overtaxed the league's joint military forces

    (D) The rising global threat of communism

7. The United Nations is committed to all of the following goals except

    (A) the promotion of personal freedoms

    (B) the use of diplomacy to resolve conflict

    (C) cooperation among nations through international trade

    (D) the pursuit of self-governance

Questions 8–10 refer to the passage below.

"Since the FSLN was formed in the early 1960s, the Sandinistas have looked to Cuba for ideological inspiration, strategic guidance, tactical training, material support, and sanctuary.

Guatemala's Guerrilla Army of the Poor (EGP) and El Salvador's Popular Liberation Forces (FPL) have already undertaken the kinds of actions recommended by Cuba and are planning more. Ecuador's Socialist Revolutionary Party (PSRE) has reportedly planned an attack on the Nicaraguan Embassy in Quito, to be carried out with support from the Chilean Movement of the Revolutionary Left (MIR). The MIR also reportedly has a support apparatus in Costa Rica that helps train Nicaraguan guerrillas. Radical groups in Peru and Colombia are reportedly considering sending volunteers to Nicaragua to fight with the FSLN guerrillas. All the Central American guerrilla groups probably provide the Sandinistas with safesites, documents, and assistance in travel and border crossing."

Memorandum Prepared in the Central Intelligence Agency, 1978

8. The reference in the first paragraph to "ideological inspiration" is best understood in context of which of the following twentieth-century developments?

   (A) U.S. military strategy in the Vietnam War

   (B) U.S. support for right-wing governments in Latin America

   (C) The demolition of the Berlin Wall in Germany

   (D) Soviet influence emerging in the Western Hemisphere

9. The radical groups in Peru and Columbia referenced in the second paragraph would most likely support which of the following?

   (A) Central American guerrilla groups standing against Soviet influence

   (B) Central American governments and embassies

   (C) El Salvador's Popular Liberation Forces (FPL)

   (D) Opposition groups to the Chilean Movement of the Revolutionary Left (MIR)

10. The events described in the passage represent a reaction most directly <u>against</u> which of the following?

   (A) Capitalism

   (B) Marxism

   (C) Nationalism

   (D) Anti-colonialism

6

Questions 11–13 refer to the passage below.

"1. Ghana's vain and egocentric Kwame Nkrumah is driven by his dreams of primacy in a united Africa and of a world role as a leading figure among the nonaligned states. . . . He now seems convinced that the West is essentially hostile to his aspirations while the countries of the [Communist] Bloc are his firm allies in the fight against "neocolonialism."

2. To achieve his goals, Nkrumah has tried to make himself the principal spokesman of anti-colonialism, and this has made for a strong ideological bond between him and the Bloc. . . . However, while he has a strong affinity for Socialist doctrines, as adapted to the African milieu, he is primarily concerned with advancing his own designs. He certainly believes he can use Bloc aid and support without becoming so tied to the Communists that he must take orders from them."

CIA internal memo, "Orientation of Nkrumah Regime," 1963

11. The passage about Nkrumah is best understood in the context of which of the following?

(A) The spread of communist ideologies

(B) Emerging ideologies of anti-imperialism

(C) The diffusion of industrial technologies

(D) New economic policies imposed by Europeans

12. The views in the passage best illustrate which of the following processes?

(A) The development of transnational movements to unite people across national boundaries

(B) The rise of religious movements to redefine the relationship between individuals and the state

(C) The shift in the global balance of power from Europe to Africa and Asia

(D) The end of European influence on the African economy

13. Kwame Nkrumah's proposed solution to Africa's problems as described in the passage was hindered mostly by which of the following?

(A) Arguments over the use of free-market policies and participation in the United Nations

(B) European legal systems that continued after African nations achieved autonomy

(C) Ethnic and tribal disputes resulting from artificial boundaries created by Europeans

(D) Rebellions against imperial rule that weakened nationalist ideologies

Questions 14–15 refer to the graph below.

MALARIA MORTALITY RATES, 1900–1997

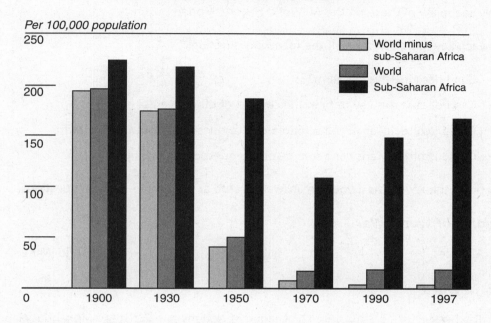

14. The difference in mortality rates of sub-Saharan Africa and the world minus sub-Saharan Africa shown on the graph best illustrates which of the following?

    (A) The lack of effective treatments for diseases like malaria

    (B) The increase in epidemic diseases due to improved transportation

    (C) The eradication of malaria outside of sub-Saharan Africa

    (D) The persistence of diseases associated with poverty

15. The overall trend shown on the graph is a result of which of the following twentieth-century developments?

    (A) Epidemic diseases

    (B) The Green Revolution

    (C) Medical innovations

    (D) Increased food supply

6

Part B: Key Terms

The following is a list of the major people, places, and events for 1900 to the Present. You will very likely see many of these on the AP World History: Modern exam.

For each key term, ask yourself the following questions:

- Can I describe this key term?
- Can I discuss this key term in the context of other events?
- Could I correctly answer a multiple-choice question about this key term?
- Could I correctly answer a free-response question about this key term?

Check off the key terms if you can answer "yes" to at least three of these questions.

Origins of World War I

- ☐ Alliances
- ☐ Militarism
- ☐ World War I

World War I

- ☐ Total war
- ☐ League of Nations
- ☐ Mohandas Gandhi

Global Depression

- ☐ World War II
- ☐ Great Depression

Rise of Fascist and Totalitarian States

- ☐ Fascism
- ☐ Adolf Hitler
- ☐ Joseph Stalin
- ☐ Benito Mussolini

World War II

- ☐ Firebombing
- ☐ United Nations
- ☐ Cold War
- ☐ Atomic bomb

Revolutions

- ☐ Vladimir Lenin
- ☐ Great Leap Forward
- ☐ Fidel Castro
- ☐ Mao Zedong

The Cold War

- ☐ Proxy wars
- ☐ NATO
- ☐ Non-Aligned Movement
- ☐ Vietnam
- ☐ Warsaw Pact
- ☐ European Union

Independence and Nationalist Movements

☐ Indian National Congress ☐ Indian/Pakistan partition ☐ Ho Chi Minh

☐ Muhammad Ali Jinnah ☐ Algeria

Political Reform and Economic Changes

☐ Deng Xiaoping ☐ Tiananmen Square

Technology, Populations, and the Environment

☐ Green Revolution ☐ Cholera

Social and Cultural Changes

☐ Liberation theology in Latin America

Next Steps

Step 1: Tally your correct answers from Part A, and review the quiz explanations at the end of this chapter.

1. B	6. A	11. B
2. D	7. C	12. A
3. D	8. D	13. C
4. A	9. C	14. D
5. D	10. A	15. C

_____ out of 15 questions

Step 2: Count the number of key terms you checked off in Part B.

_____ out of 36 key terms

Step 3: Read the Key Takeaways in this chapter.

Step 4: Consult the table below and follow the instructions based on your performance.

If You Got...	Do This
80% or more of the Test What You Already Know assessment correct (12 or more questions from Part A and 29 or more key terms from Part B)	• Read definitions in this chapter for all the key terms you didn't check off. • Complete the Test What You Learned assessment in this chapter.
50% or less of the Test What You Already Know assessment correct (7 or fewer questions from Part A and 18 or fewer key terms from Part B)	• Read the comprehensive review for this period in Chapter 10. • If you are short on time, read only the High-Yield sections. • Complete the Practice Set assessment at the end of Chapter 10. • Read through all of the key term definitions in this chapter. • Complete the Test What You Learned assessment in this chapter.
Any other result	• Read the High-Yield sections in the comprehensive review of this period in Chapter 10. • Read definitions in this chapter for all the key terms you didn't check off. • Complete the Test What You Learned assessment in this chapter.

6

ESSENTIAL CONTENT

Key Takeaways: 1900 to the Present

1. Military conflicts are central to understanding the course of the twentieth century and the current system of states and international organizations. The world wars led to rapid advances in technology, including medical technology, which has helped the global population increase to over seven billion. Some current regional conflicts like those in the Middle East are the legacy of the world wars.

2. Revolutions and nationalist movements played an important role, especially in the period of decolonization after WWII. Some existing countries experienced revolutions, like China and Russia, while other countries were created through nationalist movements, like Vietnam. Some current regional conflicts are the legacy of these movements, such as the dispute between India and Pakistan over Kashmir.

3. In the second half of the twentieth century into the present, political and economic reforms reshaped interstate relations, and the world economy became more integrated. The fall of the Soviet Union, the opening of Chinese trade with the United States in the 1970s, the formation of the European Union, and the population and industrial growth of states have led to significant structural changes.

4. Advances in computer technology, especially the growth of the Internet from the 1990s to the present, have changed economic and social structures. While this technology brought about new ways of communication and has fundamentally changed economies in the developed world, it has also led to new types of crime, such as hacking and identity theft.

5. Over the course of the twentieth century, social structures changed to include more rights for minority groups and women. The decline of traditional social structures has been caused by many factors, such as changes in the workforce, new concepts of human rights in the post-WWII period, and the rapid growth and industrialization of the global south.

6. Globalization in the economic and cultural spheres also increased, including the advent of mass culture based on new communications technologies like radio, television, and the Internet. This has accelerated changes caused by the other significant events in the period, such as the world wars, the expansion of human rights, and the interconnection of global trade.

Key Terms: 1900 to the Present

Remember that the AP World History exam tests you on the depth of your knowledge, not just your ability to recall facts. While we have provided brief definitions here, you will need to know these terms in even more depth for the AP exam, including how terms connect to broader historical themes and understandings.

Origins of World War I

Alliances: A formal system of treaties binding participant states to mutual military aid in the case of attack by a third party.

Militarism: System of national organization that prioritizes military spending and glorifies conflict and military service; examples include the British Empire and the Soviet Union.

World War I: Global conflict that began in Europe in 1914 and continued until November 1918, concluding with the Treaty of Versailles in 1919.

World War I

Total war: Style of warfare which reorders national economies toward war and includes civilians as targets; movement away from rules of limited engagement in the seventeenth and eighteenth centuries; common examples are World War I and World War II.

League of Nations: International organization created after World War I as part of the peace effort; weakened by the absence of the United States, which never joined, and the Soviet Union, which was expelled; precursor to the United Nations; dissolved prior to World War II.

Mohandas Gandhi: Leader of the Indian Independence Movement known for a strategy of nonviolent resistance and civil disobedience; inspired later leaders like Martin Luther King, Jr., and the Dalai Lama.

Global Depression

World War II: Global conflict from 1939 to 1945 between the Axis powers (Germany, Italy, and Japan) and the Allied powers (Britain, France, the Soviet Union, and the United States); led to the collapse of the European and Japanese empires and changed the world's political and economic structure.

Great Depression: Global economic depression sparked by the collapse of the American stock market in 1929; led to the rise of fascism and WWII; affected the global economy but was especially severe in Europe, which was still recovering from WWI.

Rise of Fascist and Totalitarian States

Fascism: Governmental system organized around extreme nationalism, militarism, and consolidation of state power in a single charismatic leader.

Benito Mussolini: Leader of Italy's Blackshirts and key proponent of fascism as an anti-communist movement; deposed King Vittorio Emmanuel II and established a fascist government in 1922.

Adolf Hitler: Austrian-born German leader who planned to restore Germany to its prewar status through militarism, ultranationalism, extreme violence, and anti-Semitism; appointed chancellor in 1933; leader of the National Socialist German Workers Party (NSDAP), commonly called the Nazi Party.

Joseph Stalin: Took control of Russia after the death of Vladimir Lenin; created a system of one-man dictatorial rule known as Stalinism; oversaw mass purges and pogroms in Soviet Russia until his death in 1953.

World War II

Firebombing: Use of incendiary bombs during warfare, often directed at cities and other civilian targets; used extensively during World War II.

Atomic bomb: Developed in the United States during World War II and used against the Japanese cities of Hiroshima and Nagasaki, sparking an arms race that continued into the Cold War.

United Nations: International organization founded in 1945 with the intent of settling postwar concerns and the creation of a new global order based on mutual peacekeeping; mostly focused on human rights in the modern era.

Cold War: Ideological struggle between the capitalist United States and the communist Soviet Union from 1949 to 1993 that included many other states in proxy wars and alliance networks, like NATO and the Warsaw Pact.

Revolutions

Vladimir Lenin: Leader of the Bolsheviks in Russia during World War I; seized power in 1917 and created the Union of Soviet Socialist Republics (USSR).

Mao Zedong: Leader of the Chinese Communist Party in the 1920s and 1930s; reemerged in the 1940s to fight the Nationalists (Kuomintang) under Chiang Kai-shek; leader of China from 1949–1976; promoted mass purges and modernization programs, following the Stalinist example.

Great Leap Forward: Mao Zedong's plan starting in 1958 to collectivize all aspects of the economy, most notably by having communal houses with backyard furnaces for steel production; led to millions of deaths from starvation.

Fidel Castro: Guerrilla leader of Cuba who deposed Cuban dictator Fulgencio Batista in 1959; allied Cuba with the Soviet Union; led the country until his resignation in favor of his brother Raul Castro in 2008.

The Cold War

Proxy wars: Regional conflicts that typically involve tacit or hidden support from major powers who are antagonistic to one another but not openly at war; were particularly common during the Cold War era; sometimes directly involved the armed forces of major powers (e.g., the Vietnam War and the United States, and the Soviet occupation of Afghanistan in the 1980s).

Vietnam: Southeast Asian nation that formed after the French defeat at Dien Bien Phu in 1954; divided into North and South Vietnam, site of an important proxy war during the Cold War; unified into one country after U.S. withdrawal in 1973 and communist victory in 1975.

NATO: North Atlantic Treaty Organization, founded in 1949 by the nations of North America and Europe to counter the spread of communism in Eastern Europe.

Warsaw Pact: Alliance formed in 1955 by the Soviet Union and seven Eastern Bloc countries to counteract the growing influence of NATO.

Non-Aligned Movement: International organization formed during decolonization to promote a middle path for newly independent nations between the United States and the Soviet Union in the Cold War.

6

European Union: Supranational organization in Europe promoting common economic regulation and growth; grew out of the European Economic Community, which was founded in 1957; commonly referred to as the EU.

Independence and Nationalist Movements

Indian National Congress: Political party founded in 1885 by British-educated Hindu leaders that pushed for Indian independence along the model of a federal state.

Muhammad Ali Jinnah: Muslim political leader who supported the creation of an independent Muslim nation as a counter to the federal idea of the Indian National Congress; became the first leader of Pakistan after partition.

Indian/Pakistan partition: Creation of Muslim-majority Pakistan and Hindu-majority India after Great Britain granted India independence in 1947; led to mass migration, a refugee crisis, and hundreds of thousands of civilian deaths.

Algeria: Former French colony and the largest nation in Northwest Africa; gained independence in 1962; still closely connected with France economically and culturally.

Ho Chi Minh: Vietnamese nationalist leader who fought against the Japanese during the Axis occupation of French Indochina in World War II, then fought the French after the war, then fought the American-supported regime in South Vietnam to create a unified communist Vietnam in 1975.

Political Reform and Economic Changes

Deng Xiaoping: Leader of communist China from Mao Zedong's death in 1976 to his own death in 1997; instituted the Four Modernizations to introduce capitalist reform in China.

Tiananmen Square: Large public square in Beijing, China. Site of a 1989 conflict between students protesting for democratic reform and the Chinese military defending the leadership of Deng Xiaoping.

Technology, Populations, and the Environment

Green Revolution: Technological movement in the 1960s and 70s that introduced new agricultural techniques and high-yield seed strains in an attempt to boost food production in developing countries.

Cholera: Acute bacterial infection of the small intestine associated with inadequate sanitation and unsanitary drinking water; associated with poverty and developing nations.

Social and Cultural Changes

Liberation theology in Latin America: Movement in the Roman Catholic Church that argued for Church attention to focus on world issues of poverty, human rights, and economic justice.

TEST WHAT YOU LEARNED

Part A: Quiz

Questions 1–3 refer to the map below.

THE VOYAGES OF BRITISH H.M.S. *ORVIETO*, 1915–1918

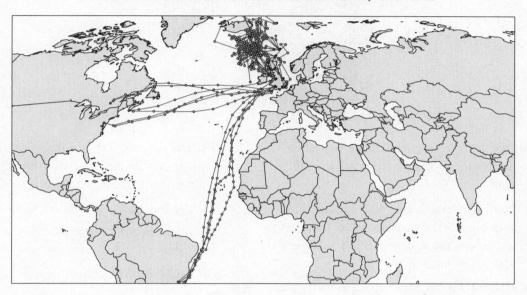

1. The travels of the H.M.S. *Orvieto* depicted on the map best reflect which of the following developments during the World War I era?

    (A) The severing of relations between Britain and India

    (B) The interconnection between international trade and war efforts

    (C) The vast reach of British imperial territory

    (D) The declining role of sea transportation in the world economy

2. The German response to the actions of British ships like the H.M.S. *Orvieto* best illustrates which of the following principles?

    (A) Containment

    (B) Totalitarianism

    (C) Proxy war

    (D) Total war

3. Which of the following best characterizes Great Britain's international relations in the time period immediately <u>after</u> the one depicted in the map and before World War II?

    (A) Great Britain faced opposition to its imperial rule in numerous overseas colonies.

    (B) Great Britain isolated itself and refused to join international organizations.

    (C) Great Britain granted full independence to its overseas colonies.

    (D) Great Britain's main foreign policy goal was to contain the spread of communism.

Questions 4–6 refer to the image below.

WORLD TRADE, 1929-1933

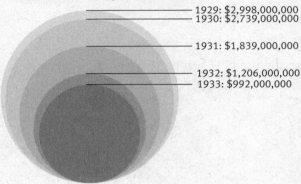

1929: $2,998,000,000
1930: $2,739,000,000

1931: $1,839,000,000

1932: $1,206,000,000
1933: $992,000,000

4. Which of the following was a major impact on colonial territories of the trend depicted in the diagram?

   (A) Many territories were granted independence because the governments of industrialized capitalist countries could no longer support them.

   (B) Demand for raw materials expanded while demand for finished goods dropped.

   (C) Local economies were devastated because exports of certain raw materials were vulnerable to fluctuations in the world market.

   (D) Economic and social tensions caused many colonies to revolt and establish independent communist governments.

5. Which of the following best describes the response of many national governments to the conditions reflected in the diagram?

   (A) Reaffirming Enlightenment ideals

   (B) Adopting a more active role in the economy

   (C) Establishing strict isolationist policies

   (D) Abandoning international trade organizations

6. The conditions reflected in the diagram would most directly result in which of the following?

   (A) The outbreak of World War II

   (B) The escalation of the Cold War

   (C) The breakdown of land-based empires

   (D) The redrawing of old colonial boundaries

Questions 7–9 refer to the passage below.

"Are these the beginnings of profound changes in the Soviet state? Or are they token gestures, intended to raise false hopes in the West, or to strengthen the Soviet system without changing it? We welcome change and openness; for we believe that freedom and security go together, that the advance of human liberty can only strengthen the cause of world peace. There is one sign the Soviets can make that would be unmistakable, that would advance dramatically the cause of freedom and peace.

General Secretary Gorbachev, if you seek peace, if you seek prosperity for the Soviet Union and Eastern Europe. . . . Come here to this gate! Mr. Gorbachev, open this gate! Mr. Gorbachev, tear down this wall!"

Ronald Reagan, address at the Brandenburg Gate, June 12, 1987

7. The reference in the <u>first paragraph</u> to "change and openness" is best understood in the context of which of the following late twentieth-century developments?

   (A) The rise of the Green Revolution

   (B) An increase in liberalization policies

   (C) A renewed focus on environmentalism

   (D) The goals of the Non-Aligned Movement

8. Which of the following factors contributed the most to the political climate described by Reagan?

   (A) The state of the Soviet communist economy

   (B) The Soviet invasion of Korea

   (C) The reunification of Germany

   (D) The proliferation of nuclear weapons

9. The economic conditions in the Soviet Union <u>before</u> the changes mentioned by Reagan were most similar to which of the following?

   (A) Post–World War II Japan

   (B) The New Deal in the United States

   (C) The impact of NAFTA on its member nations

   (D) The Great Leap Forward in China

6

Questions 10–12 refer to the passage below.

". . . The Allende Government can be expected to move sooner or later to seek to weaken U.S. influence in the Organization of American States and to reduce the effectiveness of the Organization as one generally cooperative with U.S. objectives. Allende's present decision to keep Chile in the OAS is in line with this purpose. Chile's actions will develop as a matter of timely opportunity. . . .

Problem: Chilean continuation in or exclusion from the OAS

Considerations:

1. While Allende was highly critical of the OAS in his campaign platform, he has since stated his intention of keeping Chile in the OAS.
2. The only precedent for excluding a member from participation in the OAS is the Cuban case. . . .
3. Allende has not explicitly identified his Government as Marxist/Leninist, describing it rather as a leftist/socialist coalition.
4. Allende is intent on closer relations, including economic, with the 'socialist' countries, but has not spoken of military alignment. (He has already resumed full relations with Cuba and established commercial relations with North Korea.) . . .
6. Moreover, Allende, unlike Castro, is the product of constitutional election and at present is governing within the framework of constitutional institutions."

> John Hugh Crimmins, Acting Chairman Ad Hoc Interagency Working Group on
> Chile, Memorandum for Mr. Henry A. Kissinger, National Security Adviser, December 4, 1970

10. Crimmins's memorandum is best understood in the context of which of the following?

    (A) The turmoil following former colonies' creation of governments after independence

    (B) The trend toward institutions granting equal rights and representation for diverse groups

    (C) The lack of democratic and representative governments in Latin America

    (D) The impact of the ongoing worldwide conflict between political ideologies

11. The references in the passage to the "Organization of American States" (or "OAS") best reflect which of the following twentieth-century trends?

    (A) The establishment of international coalitions that sought to distance themselves from the world superpowers

    (B) The development of international organizations to help maintain peace and cooperation

    (C) The emergence of competition for economic dominance among different intercontinental organizations

    (D) The emergence of complicated alliance systems that created unstable political conditions

12. Chile's objection to U.S. dominance of the OAS, as alluded to in the passage, is similar to the ideologies behind the Mexican Revolution in which of the following ways?

(A) Both advocated socialist principles.

(B) Both were protesting neocolonialist practices.

(C) Both resented the United States' involvement in major wars.

(D) Both preferred conflicts to be settled by the League of Nations.

Questions 13–15 refer to the passage below.

[Line 1] "Whereas recognition of the inherent dignity and of the equal and inalienable rights of all members of the human family is the foundation of freedom, justice and peace in the world,

[Line 2] Whereas disregard and contempt for human rights have resulted in barbarous acts which have outraged the conscience of mankind, and the advent of a world in which human beings shall enjoy freedom of speech and belief and freedom from fear and want has been proclaimed as the highest aspiration of the common people,

[Line 3] Whereas it is essential, if man is not to be compelled to have recourse, as a last resort, to rebellion against tyranny and oppression, that human rights should be protected by the rule of law. . . .

[Line 4] Now, Therefore THE GENERAL ASSEMBLY proclaims THIS UNIVERSAL DECLARATION OF HUMAN RIGHTS as a common standard of achievement for all peoples and all nations, to the end that every individual and every organ of society, keeping this Declaration constantly in mind, shall strive by teaching and education to promote respect for these rights and freedoms and by progressive measures, national and international, to secure their universal and effective recognition and observance, both among the peoples of Member States themselves and among the peoples of territories under their jurisdiction."

United Nations, "Universal Declaration of Human Rights," 1948

13. The ideas referred to in <u>Line 1</u> are most directly the result of which of the following?

(A) Atlantic Revolutions

(B) The Enlightenment

(C) The Cold War

(D) The Renaissance

14. The "barbarous acts" referred to in Line 2 are best understood in the context of which of the following?

(A) Imperial expansion by European powers

(B) The spread of communism during the Cold War

(C) The annihilation of specific populations during the world wars

(D) Coerced labor systems and resistance to imperial rule

15. Which of the following resulted from ideas similar to those expressed in the passage?

(A) Increased participation in political and professional roles by groups that were previously marginalized

(B) The justification for violent rebellions against neocolonialist policies in Africa and Latin America

(C) Increased intervention by governments in national economies and international trade policies

(D) The abolition of women's suffrage and emancipation of coerced laborers on Caribbean plantations

Part B: Key Terms

This key terms list is the same as the list in the Test What You Already Know section earlier in this chapter. Based on what you have now learned, again ask yourself the following questions:

- Can I describe this key term?
- Can I discuss this key term in the context of other events?
- Could I correctly answer a multiple-choice question about this key term?
- Could I correctly answer a free-response question about this key term?

Check off the key terms if you can answer "yes" to at least three of these questions.

Origins of World War I

☐ Alliances   ☐ Militarism   ☐ World War I

World War I

☐ Total war   ☐ League of Nations   ☐ Mohandas Gandhi

Global Depression

☐ World War II   ☐ Great Depression

Rise of Fascist and Totalitarian States

☐ Fascism   ☐ Adolf Hitler   ☐ Joseph Stalin
☐ Benito Mussolini

World War II

☐ Firebombing   ☐ United Nations   ☐ Cold War
☐ Atomic bomb

Revolutions

☐ Vladimir Lenin   ☐ Great Leap Forward   ☐ Fidel Castro
☐ Mao Zedong

The Cold War

☐ Proxy wars   ☐ NATO   ☐ Non-Aligned Movement
☐ Vietnam   ☐ Warsaw Pact   ☐ European Union

Independence and Nationalist Movements

☐ Indian National Congress ☐ Indian/Pakistan partition ☐ Ho Chi Minh

☐ Muhammad Ali Jinnah ☐ Algeria

Political Reform and Economic Changes

☐ Deng Xiaoping ☐ Tiananmen Square

Technology, Populations, and the Environment

☐ Green Revolution ☐ Cholera

Social and Cultural Changes

☐ Liberation theology in Latin America

Next Steps

Step 1: Tally your correct answers from Part A, and review the quiz explanations at the end of this chapter.

1. **B**	6. **A**	11. **B**
2. **D**	7. **B**	12. **B**
3. **A**	8. **A**	13. **B**
4. **C**	9. **D**	14. **C**
5. **B**	10. **D**	15. **A**

_____ out of 15 questions

Step 2: Count the number of key terms you checked off in Part B.

_____ out of 36 key terms

Step 3: Compare your Test What You Already Know results to these Test What You Learned results to see how exam-ready you are for this period.

For More Practice:

- Read (or reread) the comprehensive review for this period in Chapter 10.

- Complete the Practice Set assessment at the end of Chapter 10.

- Go to kaptest.com to complete the online quiz questions for 1900 to the Present.

  ○ Haven't registered your book yet? Go to kaptest.com/moreonline to begin.

ANSWERS AND EXPLANATIONS

Test What You Already Know

1. B

The poor living conditions caused by Russia's rapid industrialization in the last decade of the nineteenth century led to the organization of new socialist parties, such as the Marxist Social Democratic Party and the Social Revolutionaries. Spurred by the bad economic conditions described in the passage, in January 1905, on so-called Bloody Sunday, socialist protesters marched to the Winter Palace in St. Petersburg. This event sparked more protests throughout Russia; **(B)** is correct. While there was resentment between the working class and the elite, (A) is incorrect because it does not accurately characterize the events in the passage. While the Bolshevik Revolution did stir anti-capitalist sentiment among many Russians, this revolution would not occur until 1917, so (C) is incorrect. (D) is incorrect because the Cold War would not get underway until much later, following World War II.

2. D

The Russian Revolution of 1905 directly ignited strikes and uprisings throughout the country, but it also more generally spurred Russian revolutionary efforts to continue. Thus, **(D)** is correct. (A) and (B) are incorrect because tsarist rule continued in Russia, but only until the Revolution of 1917, culminating in the execution of the tsar and his family in 1918. (C) is incorrect because socialism continued to be the primary philosophy of the revolutionary movement in Russia after 1905.

3. D

The political cartoon depicts Mao Zedong as a Buddha-like figure, leading a procession of people reading from a book titled *Mao's Thought*, a reference to Mao's famous *Little Red Book*. Thus, it is most likely that the artist saw the Cultural Revolution as an effort by Mao Zedong to consolidate his political power base, installing himself as the head of a personality cult—thus the cartoon's title: "The New Religion." **(D)** is correct. The cartoon is centered on Mao Zedong as a figure of religious importance, not the Chinese Communist Party at large, the symbols of which merely adorn Mao; (A) is incorrect. The use of a hammer and sickle emblem as prayer beads is evidence of the author's satirical intent, not of Mao Zedong's rejection of the anti-religious aspects of communism. Mao himself is depicted at the center of "The New Religion." So, (B) is incorrect. The cartoon is dated to 1966, while the Korean War ended in 1953. (C) is incorrect.

4. A

The Cultural Revolution sought to destroy anything perceived as undermining communist ideals, by eliminating what were known as the "Four Olds"—old customs, old culture, old habits, and old ideas. Included were art and literature from previous periods in Chinese history. Thus, **(A)** is correct and (B) is incorrect. The aims of the Great Leap Forward are described by (C), which makes that choice incorrect. The Cultural Revolution enforced ideological purity and repressed divergent thinking; (D) is incorrect.

5. D

The United Nations was formed in 1945 as a result of World War II, making **(D)** correct. Fifty-one countries started the international organization, which was committed to maintaining international peace and security, developing friendly relations among nations, and promoting social progress. The Korean War began in 1950, after the United Nations had been well established, making (A) incorrect. The Cold War refers to the tension between the Eastern Bloc (the Soviet Union and satellite nations) and the Western Bloc (the United States and its Western European allies). It lasted approximately from the end of World War II until the collapse of the Soviet Union in 1991; (B) is incorrect. The international organization founded after World War I to promote peace was called the League of Nations, not the United Nations, making (C) incorrect.

6. A

The League of Nations, the organization preceding the United Nations, was doomed to fail when the United States and Soviet Union, two of the most powerful countries at the time, refused to join; **(A)** is correct. (B) is incorrect because, while the Great Depression did negatively affect the global economy, the League of Nations was not involved in international commerce enough to be affected. The League of Nations had no force, making it powerless in military conflicts; (C) is incorrect. The global spread of communism did not become a significant issue until after World War II, when the League of Nations was replaced by the United Nations; therefore, (D) is also incorrect.

7. C

While the charter does generally reference economic relations between countries, international trade is not an explicit purpose of the UN itself; therefore, **(C)** is correct. The UN charter outlines its mission of promoting personal freedoms in the form of human rights, (A), preventing military aggression through diplomacy, (B), and increasing "friendly relations among nations based on respect for the principle of equal rights and the self determination of peoples," (D).

8. D

The passage states that in the early 1960s, the Sandinistas looked to Cuba for ideological inspiration. Cuba, under the leadership of Fidel Castro, had recently established close ties with the Soviet Union, after which the United States viewed Castro's Cuba as a threat, especially since this was the first time the Soviet Union had wielded significant influence in the Western Hemisphere. **(D)** is correct. (A) is incorrect because the Sandinistas shared a similar ideology to the communists in Vietnam, with both groups opposing the United States. U.S. support for right-wing governments in Latin America was an effort to oppose the left-wing groups mentioned in the passage, making (B) incorrect. (C) is incorrect because the demolition of the Berlin Wall would not occur until 1989.

9. C

The radical groups in Peru and Columbia, as referenced in the second paragraph, supported the leftist guerrillas in Nicaragua. Another leftist group that these groups shared a common ideology with was the Popular Liberation Forces (FPL) in Ecuador. Thus, **(C)** is correct. The Central American guerrilla groups in this passage generally supported communism; as such, they would not have opposed Soviet influence, making (A) incorrect. According to the passage, it was a leftist group, Ecuador's Socialist Revolutionary Party (PSRE), that planned an attack on the Nicaraguan embassy. More broadly, the passage indicates that the radical groups opposed Central American governments, making (B) incorrect. Similarly, such groups shared a common goal with Chile's Movement of

the Revolutionary Left (MIR)—not with their opposition groups, so (D) is incorrect.

10. A

The passage describes the events of Cuban-supported leftist groups in Central and South America and their efforts to support communism in the region. As such, these events can be best seen as a reaction against capitalism; **(A)** is correct. Marxism advocated for the overthrow of the moneyed classes, which would be followed by a "workers' state." The groups in this passage did not oppose Marxism, but rather supported it, making (B) incorrect. (C) and (D) are incorrect because these groups generally supported both nationalism and anti-colonialism, preferring for their countries to be able to govern without outside influence.

11. B

Nkrumah, as an African nationalist, would be against imperialism. Although the CIA memo takes a hostile tone when describing Nkrumah, it does note that Nkrumah is "primarily concerned with advancing his own designs" of pan-Africanism rather than spreading communism, even if the memo treats the concept of neocolonialism derisively. Thus, **(B)** is correct. (A) is incorrect because Nkrumah does not advocate for the adoption of communist ideology but instead is described as allying with the Communist Bloc against the West. (C) is incorrect because industrial technologies did not spread to Africa until relatively recently. In the 1960s, many African colonies became independent so they would no longer be subject to undue European economic influence, making (D) incorrect.

12. A

Nkrumah espoused a philosophy of pan-Africanism and thus advocated for the unity of all Africans, across national boundaries. **(A)** is correct. As a nationalist, Nkrumah was looking for a political solution rather than a religious one, making (B) incorrect. (C) is incorrect because, while European influence declined in the post–World War II era, the United States and the Soviet Union became global superpowers and involved Africa and Asia in their ideological conflict. (D) is incorrect because, even after independence, many mines and plantations continued to be owned by Europeans; this persistent economic dominance is known as neocolonialism.

13. C

When European imperialists carved up Africa during the Berlin Conference in the late nineteenth century, they disregarded tribal and ethnic affiliations. This led to some groups being divided by new political boundaries and some rival tribes finding themselves within the same colony. Civil war and border disputes broke out after independence because the new nations had generally kept the European-imposed borders, and minority groups often suffered oppression. Therefore, **(C)** is correct. Although free-market policies were disputed during the Cold War, when socialism enjoyed popularity in many places around the globe, (A) is incorrect because countries typically joined the United Nations willingly. European legal systems did not prevent African unity, making (B) incorrect. Nkrumah proposed African unity in the aftermath of imperial rule to strengthen newly independent countries; (D) is incorrect.

14. D

Malaria is treatable, which is why it has declined globally, but in many places in sub-Saharan Africa it is deadly because of lack of access to antibiotics due to poverty. **(D)** is correct. (A) is incorrect because there are effective treatments; otherwise, the rates in other parts of the world would not have decreased. (B) is incorrect because transportation has improved across the twentieth century; if that contributed to the spread of diseases, the trend would be upward in all regions. (C) is incorrect because eradication would indicate that malaria was completely wiped out, and while it has diminished greatly, there are still cases in the world outside of sub-Saharan Africa.

15. C

Medical innovations and antibiotics led to a significant decline in global malaria cases; **(C)** is correct. (A) is incorrect because epidemic diseases are highly communicable and malaria is transmitted mainly by mosquitoes. The Green Revolution is associated with increased agricultural yields rather than the reduction of disease, making (B) incorrect. (D) is incorrect because increased food supply does not closely correlate with the decline of malaria.

Test What You Learned

1. B

The map shows the movements of a British ship during World War I to locations where fighting was not occurring; these voyages must have been related to obtaining supplies during the war effort. Indeed, ships such as the H.M.S. *Orvieto* accompanied Allied civilian ships in order to protect them against German U-boat attacks. Even during peacetime, European countries such as Great Britain did not have sufficient raw materials to supply their factories and thus developed international trade relations, usually involving less developed nations and territorial possessions supplying raw materials for industry in more developed nations. **(B)** correctly reflects the importance of these trade relations. (A) is incorrect because Britain still ruled India during World War I; India did not become autonomous until after World War II. Though the British Empire was large and spanned multiple continents, the map does not depict the extent of these colonies, making (C) incorrect. (D) is incorrect because sea transportation was vital to the world economy in the early twentieth century; although railroads and automobiles could be used overland, sea travel was the only way to transport goods or people across oceans before the development of jets.

2. D

Germany attempted to interrupt Allied supply lines using their U-boats to attack both military and civilian ships. The principle of waging an extreme form of war that does not distinguish between combatants and noncombatants is total war, so **(D)** is correct. Total war also entails utilizing all of a country's resources and industry toward the war effort, resulting in a large impact on the lives of all citizens. (A) is incorrect because containment refers to the attempt to stop the spread of communism during the Cold War. (B), totalitarianism, is incorrect because this term refers to a state in which one leader or political party holds total control over citizens, often engaging in policing or terror to silence opposition. (C) is incorrect because a proxy war refers to conflicts that broke out as a result of countries' affiliations with or interference from superpowers during the Cold War.

3. A

Politically, the interwar period was a time of attempts at international cooperation (as in the League of Nations), the rise of authoritarian states in the wake of economic depression, and the continuation of imperial conflicts. Japan invaded Manchuria and Italy invaded Ethiopia, while Great Britain encountered resistance to its rule in colonial possessions such as India, Ireland, South Africa, and Egypt. **(A)** correctly describes Great Britain's empire in the interwar period. (B) is incorrect because Great Britain joined the League of Nations and was very much involved in affairs of its empire during this period. (C) is incorrect because Great Britain controlled parts of its empire, notably India, until after the end of World War II. (D) is incorrect because "containing the spread of communism" better reflects the geopolitical conflicts of the post–World War II era; although democratic nations felt threatened by communism between the world wars, as during the Red Scare in the United States, concerns about communism were mainly tied to domestic issues rather than its international spread.

4. C

The diagram depicts the reduction in world trade as a result of the Great Depression. Many colonial territories relied on exporting one or two main products, leaving them vulnerable to fluctuations in the global market. Global demand for rubber, for example, dramatically decreased during the Depression, due in part to a dip in car tire manufacturing. This was disastrous for colonial economies, making **(C)** correct. Both (A) and (D) are incorrect because the Great Depression did not directly lead to independence or communist revolutions; this occurred more after World War II, when imperial governments were weakened. (B) is incorrect because all global trade and manufacturing contracted, lessening the need for finished goods and raw materials alike.

5. B

In response to the global economic crisis spurred by the Great Depression, many countries adopted policies in which the government had an increased role in the economy. Socialist principles and extreme government control flourished in the midst of economic turmoil, contributing to the rise of fascist states. Democratic countries also attempted to improve their economies through government interventions, such as the New Deal in the United States. **(B)** is correct. (A) is incorrect because Enlightenment ideals were more influential during the political revolutions of the late eighteenth and nineteenth centuries. Although many countries did adopt protectionist policies to salvage their economies by restricting imports, strict isolationism was no longer possible in the global economy, so (C) is incorrect. (D) is incorrect because most international trade organizations developed after World War II.

6. A

The diagram depicts the diminishing world economy in the midst of the Great Depression. Factors contributing to World War II included expansionism, nationalism, and the rise of fascist and totalitarian states; the latter were able to ferment in the political and economic instability that emerged after World War I and were exacerbated by the Great Depression. **(A)** is correct. (B) and (D) are incorrect because they reflect developments that occurred after World War II, during the postwar ideological conflict of democratic and communist superpowers and the breakdown of colonial empires. (C) is incorrect because traditional land-based empires, such as Russia, China, and the Ottoman Empire, collapsed in the years of political turmoil before, during, and after World War I, not as a result of the Great Depression.

7. B

Reagan's speech is directly addressing the policies of Soviet leader Mikhail Gorbachev. One such policy was *glasnost*, or "openness," which entailed cultural and intellectual freedom, leading to increased freedom for the press. *Perestroika*, or "restructuring," introduced some aspects of capitalism into the existing economic system. More liberal economic and political policies were also being adopted by formerly restrictive governments in Latin America and East Asia. Thus, **(B)** is correct. (A) is incorrect because the Green Revolution refers to improved agricultural production due to new farming principles, which is not related to Reagan's speech about the decline of communism. Likewise, (C) is not related to the content of Reagan's speech. (D) is incorrect because it refers to the association of countries that remained neutral during the Cold War, but the Non-Aligned Movement does not reflect the growing liberalization to which Reagan alludes.

8. A

Reagan is admonishing Gorbachev to signal the decline of Cold War tensions by tearing down the Berlin Wall, which for decades had separated Berlin into a democratic west and communist east. Reagan's speech is in the midst of the thawing of Cold War tensions; the Communist Party was seeking increasingly liberal policies while trying to hold together the collapsing Soviet Union in light of its struggling economy and internal pressures. **(A)** is correct because it reflects one of the factors that would lead to the collapse of the Soviet Union. (B) is incorrect because

6

the Soviet Union's involvement with Korea dated back to its support in the 1950s for the communist North during the Korean War; the Soviet Union did not invade Korea during the decline of the Cold War. (C) is incorrect because the reunification of Germany was a result of the collapse due to the loss of Soviet control of East Germany. While nuclear buildup certainly characterized the Cold War era, (D) is incorrect because the collapse of the Soviet Union was during a period of nuclear deescalation.

9. D

Before liberalization at the end of the Cold War era, the Communist Party tightly controlled the government and politics of the Soviet Union, repressing dissent and establishing a command economy that resulted in economic stagnation and deprivation. Similar government and economic policies existed in communist China; as the Soviet Union employed Five-Year Plans to attempt to increase industrial and agricultural production, China's Great Leap Forward in the 1950s and 1960s attempted similar government-led economic restructuring. **(D)** is correct. (A) is incorrect because Japan adopted rapid industrialization during and after its occupation at the end of World War II using free market principles rather than adopting communism. (B) is incorrect because, although the United States government was increasingly involved in the economy during the New Deal, these programs were aimed at stabilization and recovery in the wake of the Great Depression. The government did not engage in policies such as collectivization and a planned economy as in the Soviet Union and China. (C) is incorrect because NAFTA represents a trade agreement among free-market countries.

10. D

The memorandum concerns the U.S. strategy towards Chile. The memo discusses Chile's government under Allende in terms of being "Marxist/Leninist" or "leftist/socialist," and it speculates about Chile's relationship with the "'socialist' countries." This concern for Chile's political status is best understood in the midst of the ideological tensions of the Cold War, when both the United States and Soviet superpowers sought to limit the influence of the other's ideology, so **(D)** is correct. (A) is incorrect because Chile was an independent nation in 1970, having gained independence from Spain during the Latin American independence movements in the nineteenth century. (B) is incorrect because the memo does not discuss rights

for diverse groups. (C) is incorrect because many Latin American countries had some form of representative government; the memo itself acknowledges that Allende was "constitutional[ly] elect[ed]."

11. B

The Organization of American States (OAS) includes most countries in North and South America as members and works to facilitate cooperation among the nations; this reflects the growth of such international organizations especially in the post–World War II era. **(B)** is correct. (A) is incorrect because it better reflects the Non-Aligned Movement of states that sought to remain neutral during the Cold War. (C) is incorrect because intercontinental organizations, such as OAS and ASEAN, did not typically engage in competition with each other, but sought cooperation. (D) is incorrect because these international organizations did not consist of complicated alliances or lead to political instability; this choice best reflects the political climate leading up to World War I, rather than the passage at hand.

12. B

In the first paragraph, Crimmins claims that Chile is expected to "seek to weaken U.S. influence in the OAS." The powerful United States had dominated the other countries in the Americas, through both political and economic means, since the nineteenth century. The Mexican Revolution protested conditions in Mexico that favored the elites and that led to exploitative influence of foreign investments. Thus, the objections of both Chile and Mexico revolve around the perception of exploitative economic and political dominance by foreign countries, which are central characteristics of "neocolonialism." **(B)** is correct. (A) is incorrect because although both Chile and Mexico were influenced by socialism, Chile's objections to the OAS were not specifically socialist. (C) and (D), wars and the League of Nations, do not reflect concerns of Chile or Mexico during the relevant time periods.

13. B

Inalienable rights, freedom, and justice were ideas of the Enlightenment that were gradually incorporated into governments. Thus, **(B)** is correct. (A) is incorrect because the Atlantic Revolutions sought to incorporate Enlightenment ideas into governments. (C) is incorrect because the Cold War was an ideological struggle between capitalist and communist systems. (D) is incorrect because the

Renaissance focused on individual potential, but did not significantly examine the relationship between people and government.

14. C

This document was written in the aftermath of World War II and the Holocaust, during which Jews and other minority groups were systematically murdered. **(C)** is correct. (A) is incorrect because some nations who drafted the document had participated in imperial expansion in the first half of the twentieth century; they would thus be unlikely to consider their nations' actions as disregarding of human rights. While the tensions of the Cold War were growing at this time, concerns about the international spread of communism did not become prominent until later in the Cold War; (B) is incorrect. Legal coerced labor

systems, such as slavery and serfdom, had largely ended by this point, making (D) incorrect.

15. A

The protection of the rights of ethnic, religious, social, or political groups, as promoted in the passage, led to greater participation in government; **(A)** is correct. (B) is incorrect because resistance to economic imperialism usually took the form of economic nationalism, which includes policies to protect domestic goods, not violent rebellion. The trend in the last half of the twentieth century was toward free-market economic systems, making (C) incorrect. (D) is incorrect because women's suffrage was extended, not abolished, in the period after World War II, and slavery had ended in the mid-nineteenth century.

PART 3

Comprehensive Review

CHAPTER 7

1200 to 1450

CULTURAL DEVELOPMENTS AND BELIEF SYSTEMS

AP World History: Modern explores the story of humanity beginning in the year 1200. AP students are expected to investigate important people, developments, and events from 1200 to the present, as well as to demonstrate historical thinking skills: analyzing primary and secondary sources, developing historical arguments, and making connections across time periods and geographical regions. Before we begin a detailed review of what was occurring in the world circa 1200 onward, we need to first review the various belief systems and philosophies that span continents and millennia and that have impacted history in ways both big and small.

> ✔ **AP Expert Note**
>
> ### Focus on larger historical themes and connections
>
> This book will discuss many people, places, and events throughout world history. Keep in mind that these are what the test maker, the College Board, refers to as illustrative examples. They demonstrate certain historical patterns, processes, and themes, but you aren't expected to memorize them all, and you shouldn't panic if you come across examples on the exam that you haven't studied. World history is about big ideas, like how various civilizations developed and how differing regions of the world are interconnected, and the AP exam primarily tests your critical thinking skills and ability to reason like a historian.

Shinto

Shinto is the indigenous religion of Japan. The early Japanese people believed that *kami*—spirits—were present in their natural surroundings. These beliefs coalesced into the Shinto religion. People built shrines to honor *kami*, and Japanese emperors claimed to descend from the supreme Shinto deity, the sun goddess Amaterasu.

Hinduism

Hinduism originated in India, but its creation cannot be linked to a specific time or person; it is a belief system that evolved over time. Hinduism actually refers to a wide variety of beliefs and practices that developed in South Asia. Hinduism is often described as not only a religion, but a way of life.

At the most basic level, Hindus believe they have a *dharma* (roughly translated as duty) to perform in life. If all follow their *dharma*, the world works smoothly. If it is violated, the natural order falls out of sync. This *dharma* is determined by birth and one's stage in life. If one follows his or her *dharma*, then karma (the sum of all good and bad deeds performed) will be the result. It is the accumulation of good karma that allows someone to move up in the level of *saṃsāra* in their next life.

Hinduism is a polytheistic religion that believes in Brahma, the creator god, and his various incarnations including Vishnu, Shiva, and Devi. Bhakti is a popular practice in which followers have a personal devotion to a particular deity. Hindus believe they will be reincarnated (reborn) after death. The new position they assume in the next life will depend on how well they performed their *dharma* in the past life. The ultimate goal for Hindus is to end the cycle of reincarnation by finally reaching *moksha*, or oneness with the universe.

Buddhism

The founder of Buddhism is Siddhartha Gautama, who lived from approximately 563 B.C.E. to 483 B.C.E. He was raised as a prince in a small state near present-day Nepal. After living a sheltered life, he decided to leave the palace in search of answers to questions such as: "Why is there so much suffering in the world?" and "Is there a way out of suffering?" According to Buddhist teachings, after meditating under a bodhi tree, the prince reached enlightenment and became known as the Buddha (translated variously as "Awakened One" or "Enlightened One").

The Buddha made a crucial decision that helped transform his ideas from the thoughts of one man into a world religion: he decided to teach what he had learned to others. The Buddha taught that there were four noble truths:

1. All life is suffering.
2. Suffering is caused by desire.
3. There is a way out of suffering.
4. The way out of suffering is to follow the Eightfold Path.

The ultimate goal for Buddhists is to reach *nirvana*, which is the release from the cycles of reincarnation and the achievement of union with the universe. Buddhism took the central ideas of Hinduism, such as *dharma*, karma, and *saṃsāra*, but altered them significantly. According to Buddhism, people do not need rituals, and gods and goddesses are not necessary; everyone can seek enlightenment on his or her own, and no one is an outcast by birth. This belief challenges the historically established caste system in India.

Daoism

Some claim that the Chinese sage Laozi founded the Daoist school of thought during the sixth century B.C.E., around the same time as Confucius. The literal translation of *the Dao* is "the way." According to Daoism, all life is interdependent, and human beings should exist in harmony with nature. Its advice is to relax and be in harmony with the Dao. In order to solve the problems of the day, Daoists taught the concept of *wu wei*, which means act by not acting. Do nothing and problems will solve themselves, like in nature. Be like water—soft and yielding—but at the same time, very naturally powerful.

Daoists believe it is useless to try to build institutions to govern men, because institutions (or anything that rewards knowledge) are dangerous. Institutions lead to competition and, eventually, to fighting. The less government interference, the better; the ideal state is a small, self-sufficient town. The ultimate goal, according to Daoists, should be to cultivate the virtues of patience, selflessness, and concern for all.

In Chinese society, Daoism provided a counterpoint to the proper behavior of Confucianism; it encouraged people to relax and just let things happen. It allowed the Chinese, essentially, to be Confucian at work and Daoist while not at work. The Daoist attitude toward war was that it should be used only for defensive purposes. The Han Chinese followed this idea by stationing troops along the Great Wall to maintain the safety of trade routes.

Confucianism

Confucius (551–479 B.C.E.) was a philosopher who believed that the key to ending the chaos of his time and to bringing back peace was to find the right kind of leadership to rule China. His two most important concepts were *ren* (appropriate feelings) and *li* (correct actions), which must be used together in order to have any effect. Additionally, filial piety (respect for one's parents) was a key concept. Confucianism became the most influential philosophy in China, and its ideas spread to Korea and Japan, where they also had significant influence.

Confucius taught that order would be achieved when people knew their proper roles and relationships to others. Rulers would govern by moral example. People would learn to behave properly through the example of those superior to them. According to Confucius, there are five key relationships: ruler and ruled, father and son, husband and wife, older brother and younger brother, and friends.

Neo-Confucianism, a remodeled form of Confucianism, developed in the ninth century as a response to Buddhism and Daoism. It rejected mysticism in favor of a rationalist approach, emphasizing individual self-improvement and the goodness of humanity. Nevertheless, it also reworked some concepts and principles from Buddhism. Neo-Confucianism dominated Chinese philosophy from the late Tang Dynasty until the twentieth century, and it spread to Japan, Vietnam, and Korea.

Judaism

Between 1200 and 1150 B.C.E., the civilizations bordering the eastern Mediterranean Sea suffered a violent societal collapse known as the Late Bronze Age collapse. Nearly every city in the region was destroyed in quick succession. Due to this cataclysm, the Canaanite city-state system in the Levant (the eastern coast of the Mediterranean Sea) broke down. Neighboring groups incorporated the remnants of this system into their own cultures. One such group lived in the south Levant, in highland settlements neighboring those city-states: the Hebrews, speakers of the ancient Hebrew language. The Hebrews trace their origin to the patriarch Abraham, whom they believe God called to found a new nation in Canaan. Although the Hebrews were sporadically conquered by neighboring empires such as the Assyrians, Babylonians, and Romans, they maintained their cultural identity through their religion, Judaism.

Uprisings against the Romans in the years 66 and 135 were violently suppressed with large military campaigns. Many Jews were killed and their holiest temple was leveled. In 135, the Romans drove the Jews out of their homeland. This scattering of the Jews is referred to as the Diaspora. Jews survived in scattered communities around the Mediterranean region, Persia, and Central Asia. (The terms *Hebrews*, *Israelites*, and *Jews* are sometimes used interchangeably in historical texts. In the present day, members of this ethnic and religious group are most commonly referred to as Jews.)

The Hebrews believe that they are protected by YHWH (God), a name considered too holy a word to say out loud. According to the Torah, the Hebrews are God's chosen people. They entered into a covenant with God; they were forbidden from worshiping any other god and were obligated to follow certain religious laws, like the Ten Commandments. Some of these commandments include a prohibition against murder, adultery, or theft. Most important, the Hebrews followed a mono-theistic tradition, which claims there is only one creator (God) who made the world and all life. As a monotheistic religion, Judaism greatly influenced the development of Christianity and Islam.

Christianity

Christianity centers on the figure of Jesus, who was born to Jewish parents between 6 and 4 B.C.E. Teachings describe Jesus as being concerned with the growing cosmopolitan nature of Jewish society and as preaching a simple message of love and compassion. Christian tradition also attributes to Jesus the power to perform miracles, such as healing the sick and raising the dead. Jesus taught that all people were equal and that the faithful would experience eternal life in heaven with God. These ideas especially appealed to the lower classes, slaves, and women. Given that there was ongoing tension between Rome and its Jewish subjects, Jesus's teachings alarmed Roman authorities; in order to quell a potential rebellion, they had Jesus executed by crucifixion around the year 30. Followers believed that Jesus rose from the dead and that he was the son of God. As such, they compiled a body of writings about his life and his messages, which became the New Testament. Over the following centuries, Christianity gradually spread across the Roman Empire, and the world.

Several schisms have affected Christianity since its formation. Two of the three major Christian denominations—the **Catholic Church** and the **Eastern Orthodox Church**—disagreed over religious practices, such as the worship of idols (images of saints). Their respective leaders, the pope and the patriarch, excommunicated each other in 1054 in what became known as the East-West Schism. Originally a core aspect of the Eastern Roman (Byzantine) Empire, the Eastern Orthodox form of Christianity later spread to the Slavic people and Russia. Protestantism, the third major Christian denomination, saw its inception in 1517 with the publication of Martin Luther's *Ninety-five Theses*. Its development and characteristics will be discussed in Chapter 8.

Islam

Prior to the introduction of Islam, inhabitants of the Arabian Peninsula, or Bedouins, lived in nomadic tribes led by sheikhs. Settlements arose along trade routes, as Arabs transported products between the Mediterranean Sea and the Indian Ocean. Although patriarchy dominated Arabian social structures, women were allowed to inherit property, initiate divorce agreements, and participate in business dealings. Most Arabs practiced a polytheistic form of religion, which included a principal god, Allah, although idol worship of lesser deities was commonplace as Allah was viewed as a remote figure. This changed with the coming of Muhammad.

Born in 570 in Mecca, Muhammad later married a merchant widow named Khadija. Together, they traveled on caravans and met Jews, Zoroastrians, and Christians. Muslims believe that the angel Gabriel revealed to Muhammad that he had been selected to be Allah's messenger. Muhammad believed and preached that all people were to submit to one all-powerful, all-knowing God: Allah. All would face a final day of judgment; those who had submitted to Allah would go to a heavenly paradise, and those who had not would go to a fiery hell. He also taught that he was the last of a long line of prophets from the Jewish and Christian scriptures that included Abraham, Moses, David, and Jesus.

Muhammad's message was not met with enthusiasm in Mecca; he and his followers migrated to Medina in 622, on a journey known as the *Hegira* (or *Hijrah*). Muhammad's message proved popular in Medina, where he was viewed as a prophet and a political leader. In 630, after further organizing his new religion, he and his followers returned to Mecca, capturing the city. After his death, Muhammad's revelations were written down by his followers in the Quran, which is believed to be the actual words of God as revealed to Muhammad. The word *Islam* means "submission to Allah."

By the time of Muhammad's death in 632, much of Arabia was under Islamic control. However, Muhammad did not designate a successor, and Muslim followers disagreed over who Muhammad's successor should be. One group, the **Shi'a**, believed that the Muslim leader should be a descendant of Muhammad. The other group, the **Sunni**, believed that the wisest member of the strongest tribe should succeed Muhammad. Although Muhammad's father-in-law Abu Bakr was chosen to be the first caliph, and he served as the political and religious leader of the Arab Empire, the split between Shi'a and Sunni Muslims led to religious and political divisions in the Muslim world that endure today.

Islam is based on five duties—called pillars—that define the faith:

1. Statement of faith: "There is no god but Allah, and Muhammad is the messenger of Allah."
2. Pray five times a day facing Mecca.
3. Give alms (charity) to the poor.
4. Fast during the holy month of Ramadan.
5. Make a pilgrimage, or *hajj*, to Mecca during one's lifetime, if able.

Islam is a universal religion that promises salvation to all who believe and follow its principles. Islam appealed to women because the Quran afforded women equal status to men before God, outlawed female infanticide, and permitted wives to keep their dowries. However, the Quran allowed inheritance to be restricted to male offspring. It also restricted women's social experiences in order to protect the legitimacy of offspring. In general, though, Islam appealed to the poor and powerless, and it fostered a strong sense of brotherhood.

The Importance of Context

This section has touched upon major religions in world history in order to provide important context for how cultural beliefs have shaped historical developments. The following sections will go into more detail about post-1200 history, starting with an overview of early civilizations. Please note that, even though the focus of *AP World History: Modern* is on years 1200 to the present, there are times when discussing pre-1200 context will be necessary to properly situate events, people, and developments within world history.

CIVILIZATIONS IN THE AMERICAS

Mexica Empire

The Mexica (also known as Aztec) people occupied territory in Mesoamerica, and the capital city Tenochtitlán was located in what today is Mexico City. A militant warrior tradition characterized their culture. They developed a system of feudalism, which had similarities to that of Japan and Europe. The Mexica were ruled by a single monarch, who exerted power over local rulers.

The Mexica had an agricultural economy, with cacao beans sometimes used as currency. They practiced **chinampa** agriculture, where farmers cultivated crops in rectangular plots of land on lake beds. A priestly class oversaw polytheistic religious rituals, which sometimes included human sacrifice. Although Mexica society was patriarchal, women were able to own property and agree to business contracts.

✔ **AP Expert Note**

Be aware of proper terminology

You may have noticed that a civilization traditionally described as *Aztec* is now primarily called *Mexica*. The term *Aztec* was popularized by earlier historians, but in recent years there has been a shift to a more accurate term, given that both the people of central Mexico and their later Spanish conquerors referred to this civilization as the Mexica people. Changes in terminology are the result of historical evidence being analyzed and debated. On the AP exam, especially in the free-response sections, be prepared to use the most accurate, current terminology.

Inca Empire

Indigenous clans in the Andean highlands of South America developed a rich and complex culture, leading to the rise of an empire in the fifteenth century. These people, the Incas, conquered a large territory and absorbed many groups in central and western South America. In 90 years, the Inca Empire grew into a stretch of land that covered over 3,000 miles. The Chimor Empire, stretching along 620 miles of coastline, was the only regional rival of the Inca. Eventually conquered by the Inca after a war in the late fifteenth century, their territory and ruling elite were incorporated into the Inca Empire.

Despite its large size, the Inca Empire was centralized, led by a king and a privileged class of nobles. The capital city was Cuzco, in present-day Peru, but the Incas also occupied other large urban centers. The Inca Empire had a mandatory public service system, called the **mit'a**, where people had to serve for two months out of the year. This system allowed the Inca to develop an extensive road system, as well as provide armies that overwhelmed targets of imperial conquest.

The Inca lacked steel or iron; their weapons were typically made of wood, bone, stone, and copper. Surviving descriptions of the rope bridges that connected mountains and hilltops suggest the bridges were sturdy enough for conquistadors to gallop their horses across them at full speed.

The Inca economy was rooted in agriculture, as the people had adapted to the steep, rugged terrain of the Andes with the use of extensive irrigation techniques. The coca plant was viewed as sacred, and message runners would chew on leaves to maintain their energy across long distances. Inca religion was polytheistic, based on worship of the sun, and incorporated ancestor worship. They developed a system of record-keeping called *quipu*; it used knotted strings to record numeric data, such as tax obligations and census records. Descent was traced along parallel lines, father to son and mother to daughter.

Maya City-States

From approximately 250 B.C.E. to 900, the Maya Empire occupied territory in modern-day Belize, Guatemala, Honduras, and southern Mexico. The Maya cosmos was divided into three parts: the heavens above, humans at the center, and the underworld below. Similar to the Egyptians, the Maya people built impressive pyramids, meant to be portals to the heavens. Warfare was imbued with sacred significance, as religious rituals would precede battle. The Maya also made huge contributions to mathematics and astronomy, particularly the concept of zero, as well as a modern calendar with 365 days.

In their postclassical period, from 950 to 1539, the Maya civilization persisted in a much-reduced form. Many of their cities and lands were abandoned, due to a combination of factors ranging from warfare to disease. The Maya settlements gradually shifted toward the Gulf coast. The Spanish conquest of the Maya took most of the seventeenth century. In contrast to the Inca or Mexica, the Maya were not unified into a single state or empire.

Cahokia

Primarily located in the present-day American Midwest, the Cahokia Mounds are remnants of a pre-Columbian settlement of the Mississippian culture. The Mississippians existed from approximately the eleventh century to the mid-sixteenth century. Cahokia, their largest city, located near present day St. Louis, is believed to have been an important religious center. The Mississippians lacked a writing system, and due to a general lack of contact with Europeans until Old World diseases had thoroughly disrupted their society, little is known about them in comparison to other American Indian civilizations of the era. The Mississippians worked stone and copper. Their agriculture was centered around corn. They participated in trade networks that stretched from the Gulf of Mexico to the Atlantic, from the Great Lakes to the Rocky Mountains.

CIVILIZATIONS IN EAST ASIA

Chinese Empire

Commonalities across Dynasties

High-Yield

A succession of different dynasties ruled China all through its history until the 1912 proclamation of the Republic of China. Three dynasties are of note in this period: the Song, Yuan, and Ming. The latter two will be discussed later in this chapter along with the Mongols, due to the involvement of the Mongols in the development of these dynasties. Certain elements are common to all three Chinese dynasties.

First, there is the **Mandate of Heaven**, an ancient Chinese concept stating that the right to rule was granted by the heavens. Because this power was divinely given, there was a direct connection between ruler and god. However, if justice and order were not maintained, then the mandate could be revoked. Events such as floods, earthquakes, and peasant rebellions were indications from the gods that the end neared for a dynasty.

Second, there is the imperial bureaucracy and the civil service examination system. By the time of the Song, the exam allowed for the entry of gentry and commoners to the bureaucracy.

Third, there is the **Grand Canal**, an economically vital series of waterways that linked the Yellow and Yangtze Rivers. This canal, the world's longest, connected the fertile Huang He River to the highly populated cities in the north, allowing grain to be shipped easily. Farmers also took advantage of the Grand Canal's complex irrigation networks and improved road networks; accordingly, the increased food supply facilitated population growth. Maintaining and occasionally expanding the Grand Canal was a vital duty of the Chinese imperial state.

Fourth, Neo-Confucianism was at the forefront of Chinese philosophy and was also influential in Japan and Korea. Delegations from the "outside," such as Japan or Siam (present-day Thailand), had to show great deference to the Chinese emperor in his presence with the *kowtow*, a prostrate bow during which one touches one's head to the ground multiple times. This symbolized the Chinese perception that they were superior to all foreigners.

Song Dynasty

Political Development

The founding of the Song Dynasty is traditionally dated to 960, but it was not until 979 that it had reestablished centralized control over China, ending the "Five Dynasties and Ten Kingdoms" period. The Song Dynasty deemphasized a military approach to security; instead, it reestablished the tribute system with its nomad neighbors, in which the Chinese provided nomads with gifts in exchange for peace. Despite this system, peace did not endure. The Song's scholar-controlled army was often ineffective, and an excess of paper money in circulation caused inflation. Thus, the Song can be divided into two periods: the Northern Song (960–1127) and the Southern Song (1127–1279).

By 1126, China had lost the northern half of the empire to the semi-nomadic Jurchen, also known as the Jin Dynasty. The Song imperial court relocated the capital to Lin'an (present-day Hangzhou), south of the Yangtze River. Despite this defeat, the Southern Song held out against both the Jurchen and later the Mongols for decades. However, military threats from the north continued, and finally the most powerful of all northern groups invaded, absorbing the Song Dynasty into the new Mongol Empire in the thirteenth century.

Economic and Technological Development

The economic revolution, which began under the Tang Dynasty, continued under Song rule. Following Vietnamese agricultural practices, Chinese farmers began to cultivate **champa rice**, which improved crop yields. The population continued to increase, until it reached 115 million people in 1200 (as compared to 45 million people in 600). The earliest joint-stock companies developed in Song China, as investors sought fortunes in domestic and international shipping.

Several technological developments occurred. The first gunpowder weapons were developed by the Song. Iron and copper production grew massively. The capital of Kaifeng became a manufacturing center for cannons, movable type printing, water-powered mills, looms, and high-quality porcelain. After the Song lost control of Northern China, the Southern Song established their capital at Hangzhou, and commerce soared there as well. Ocean trade with East Africa, Southeast Asia, India, and Persia grew, especially due to naval innovations such as cotton sails and the magnetic compass. Because trade was so successful, copper supplies dwindled; paper currency and letters of credit, known as flying cash, emerged as forms of monetary compensation.

Cultural Development

The civil service exam system retained great prominence during Song rule. It checked the power of the landed aristocracy and fostered the development of a powerful elite known as the scholar-gentry. Ceramics, painting, and sculpture grew in prominence during the Song Dynasty, as did poetry. The spread of gunpowder resulted in the development of fireworks. Buddhism declined as Neo-Confucianism rose in popularity.

Korea

Korean history can be divided into two dynasties for much of world history: the Goryeo Dynasty (918–1392) and the Joseon Dynasty (1392–1897). The Goryeo unified the Korean Peninsula into one political body; the modern name of Korea is derived from Goryeo. Ruled by families from the military class, Goryeo notably resisted conquest by the Mongols for nearly three decades, until it eventually pledged allegiance to the Mongols as a client. The royal family began to inter-marry with Mongol princesses from the Yuan Dynasty. Weakened by decades of warfare and Mongol influence in their government, the Goryeo were overthrown and the Joseon Dynasty was established.

Japan

Political Development

Japan's geography as a group of islands led to the development of small, independent communities. In the Heian Period (794–1185), the Japanese emperor installed the new capital of Heian (modern-day Kyoto). During this era, the weakness of Japan's centralized government led local aristocrats to recruit samurai. These warriors followed their lord's orders and defended his interests, and they developed a strict warrior code called *bushido* ("the way of the warrior").

After several centuries of civil conflicts, a Japanese noble, Minamoto no Yoritomo, created a form of feudal military government. Under this Kamakura shogunate (1192–1333), the emperor became a symbolic figurehead, and the shogun, the supreme military general, controlled a centralized military government. The shogun divided Japanese land into regional feudal fiefdoms based on military power. Regional military leaders called *daimyo* led groups of samurai warriors. When the Mongols attempted to invade Japan in the thirteenth century, they encountered this military and political system.

Economic Development

Japan was a predominantly agrarian society with an artisan class of weavers, carpenters, and iron-workers. Trade, which focused on markets in larger towns and foreign exchange with Korea and China, developed during the Kamakura Period.

Most Japanese people were peasants, who worked on land owned by a lord or by a Buddhist monastery. Though their freedom was limited, peasants could keep what remained of their harvest after they paid their tax quota. Those unable to pay became landless laborers known as *genin*, who could be bought and sold with the land. As slaves, they performed jobs such as burying the dead or curing leather; eventually, these jobs would be associated with the *burakumin* outcast group.

Cultural Development

Although Shintoism remained a significant force in Japan, its society also welcomed Chinese and Korean influences. The Japanese people adopted Confucianism and Buddhism, as well as Chinese technology and script. Japan also developed its own version of Buddhism known as Zen Buddhism, which added a strong aesthetic dimension.

In early Japanese society, women could inherit or own land. Over time, however, women lost much of their legal and social power. Many women, however, such as Murasaki Shikibu, created literary works, including her famous novel *The Tale of Genji*.

ISLAMIC GOLDEN AGE

The Islamic Golden Age spanned from the eighth to the fourteenth centuries. It was a period of notable cultural, intellectual, and military achievement. The Islamic world stretched from Spain to India, present-day Turkey to East Africa, Central Asia to Southeast Asia. However, internal political fragmentation as well as the Mongol Conquests would bring an end to this golden age.

Political Development

After the first four caliphs, the Umayyad Dynasty took control in 661 and transformed the caliphate into a hereditary monarchy, with its government centered in Damascus. With its military expertise and the weakness of the Byzantine and Persian Empires, the Umayyad Dynasty continued to conquer additional territories—including Syria, Egypt, Persia, North Africa, Spain (which became known as **Al-Andalus**), and Byzantine territory in West Asia. The Umayyad caliphates set up a bureaucratic structure in which local administrators governed the conquered areas. All cultures were tolerated as long as they obeyed the rules of Islam, paid their taxes, and did not revolt. Arabic became the language of administration, business, law, and trade, and many conquered peoples converted to Islam.

7

The Abbasid Dynasty (750–1517) overthrew the Umayyads in 750 and moved the imperial capital to Baghdad. At the time, Baghdad was the second largest city in the world next to Chang'an. The size of the Abbasid Empire made it difficult to control. Eventually, the remaining Umayyad prince settled in Spain and established a separate caliphate there. Berber tribesmen controlled much of the northern African coast, and the Mamluks revolted and gained control over Egypt from 1250 to 1517. Thus, by the mid-ninth century, the Abbasid political authority had become mostly symbolic, and the caliphate was broken into smaller states.

Despite this, the culture of the Muslim world created a common bond from Spain to many parts of Africa, the Middle East, Central and South Asia, and Southeast Asian islands. The term *Dar al-Islam* ("the home of Islam") refers to these areas in which a Muslim traveler or trader found himself welcome regardless of his homeland.

Economic Development

Trade flourished throughout the caliphate and beyond, as Muslim merchants relied on a common set of principles. Improved irrigation led to increased agricultural production and tax revenue. Many types of agriculture, including sugarcane, citrus fruits, and coffee, spread throughout the Islamic empire. Artisans flourished in the cities, as urban areas became centers for manufacturing pottery, fabrics, and rugs. Paper, which was introduced from China, emerged as a form of currency.

Cultural Development

Mosques, hospitals, and schools were built throughout the empire. Scholars developed intellectual fields such as algebra and medicine, and developed innovations such as the **astrolabe** and the concepts of latitude and longitude. Muslim scholars also reexamined the works of Greek philosophers such as Plato and Aristotle. Scholars at the House of Wisdom, built in Baghdad during the rule of the fifth Abbasid caliph Harun al-Rashid, sought out Greek and Persian texts and translated them into Arabic. One fourteenth-century Moroccan geographer, Ibn Khaldun, wrote an economics, ethnography, world history, and sociology text called *Muqaddimah* or *Prolegomena* ("Introduction"). Universities were established in Cordoba, Toledo, and Granada. In art and architecture, calligraphy and geometric shapes known as arabesques replaced depictions of idols.

Influence

Even though the Islamic Golden Age declined and ended with the Mongol invasions, the influence of Islam continued to spread throughout the period. Islam spread to West Africa through **trans-Saharan trade**, to East Africa and Southeast Asia through Indian Ocean trade, to Central Asia and China through the Silk Road trade, and to India through the migrations of the Turks. By the conclusion of this period, *Dar al-Islam* had developed into one of the most dominant influences throughout the world.

EUROPE DURING THE LATE MIDDLE AGES

Political Development

Compared to Byzantium, China, and the Islamic world, Western Europe remained politically decentralized following the decline and fall of the Western Roman Empire. Instead, Europe developed a system of **feudalism**, in which lords gave lands to vassals in exchange for military service and loyalty. This system allowed various lords and vassals to compete for power, in the absence of central authority. The one centralizing power in this period was the Roman Catholic Church and its ruler, the pope. By the thirteenth century, the Church owned approximately one-third of European land.

The absence of a strong central authority led many peasants to seek protection on large estates. These peasants became serfs; they had the right to work a portion of the land and could pass that right on to their children, but they could not leave their land. Serfs could keep a portion of their harvests, but they sent the majority of their earnings to their lord. In addition, serfs paid taxes for using their lord's mill, provided labor during agricultural off-seasons, and sent gifts on holidays to their lords. Lords' estates became large, walled manors that were economically self-sufficient. They maintained mills, bakeries, and breweries. They had private armies served by knights.

Birth largely determined one's social status. Marriage was the key to political power, and marital alliances were crucial to a family's continued social success. Women also entered convents, where some women could exercise leadership skills. Noblewomen had more power and authority than peasant women and could inherit land if they were widowed or without sons.

However, feudalism was not a uniform system. There were regional variations that are important to distinguish. French feudalism perhaps best fits the classic decentralized model described above. English feudalism developed along different, more organizationally cohesive lines. The Magna Carta, written in 1215, outlined specific rights and duties that the monarchy, English nobility, and Church all had to observe. The Italian city-states boasted a feudalism that was more socially fluid, with birth not necessarily cementing social status.

In Eastern Europe, feudalism developed along more stringent lines than in France. The development of serfdom there firmly anchored the peasantry to the land they worked. In many towns and villages throughout Russia, serfdom functionally continued until the Communist Revolution in 1918.

Cultural Development

Christianity was the principal source of religious, moral, and cultural authority throughout the Middle Ages, and strong papal leadership contributed to this authority. The Roman Catholic Church developed a strong hierarchy, which consisted of a pope, cardinals, archbishops, bishops, and priests. Monasteries, building complexes where monks dwelled, also developed throughout Europe. These

7

sites often maintained large landholdings and served as refuges for individuals in need. Monks preserved classical knowledge by hand-copying great works of literature and philosophy.

The end of the Medieval Warm Period, which lasted from roughly 950 to 1250, meant that the European climate cooled. Crop yields shrank and food prices rose as nations like France experienced their first famines in centuries. The Great Famine of 1315–1317 killed millions across Europe. Food shortages were so severe that widespread incidents of cannibalism and of children being abandoned may have provided the basis for fairy tales like Hansel and Gretel.

From 1337 to 1453, the English and French fought the Hundred Years' War. This conflict resulted in England losing its possessions in continental Europe save for Calais in northern France, and it led to a rejection of French culture in England. Both kingdoms developed their national identities due to their long-running clash with one another, with France gaining a national heroine in Joan of Arc. The French monarchy gained greater power as the formerly loosely bound kingdom centralized in order to prosecute the war. The growth of power in both monarchies, especially in terms of collecting taxes and organizing professional armies, contributed to the decline of feudalism in Western Europe.

Economic Development

As Europeans interacted with other regions, they adopted new agricultural techniques, such as the three-field system of crop rotation, and foreign agricultural technologies, such as iron plows, watermills, and horse harnesses. These innovations increased crop production and population sizes in Europe.

While the traditional feudal economy was solely based on agriculture in the countryside, a new premodern economy was evolving by 1100. During the early medieval period, the old Roman towns decreased in size. Now, after centuries of decline, increased trade began to stimulate the growth of commercial cities in the heart of Europe. Most often located on riversides, these towns grew into marketplaces and adopted foreign financial innovations, such as banks and **bills of exchange**. Some representative examples of these new urban centers included:

- Bruges: Located on a river system that connected the North Sea with Central Europe along the Rhine River, its cross-channel trade brought raw wool from England, which was converted into clothing to sell.

- Hamburg: A major port on the North Sea. Hamburg was part of the Hanseatic League, an alliance of trading cities and their merchant guilds, which controlled trade along the Northern European coast. The League regulated taxes and created rules for fair trade among the member cities.

- Florence: Central Italian city that controlled the flow of goods through the peninsula. Called the Republic of Florence, this city-state became a center for banking and commerce by 1300.

Service providers and craftspeople set up businesses in these towns, further stimulating growth. Among those providing services were barbers, blacksmiths, coopers (barrel makers), jewelers, leatherworkers (tanners), innkeepers, and merchants of beer and wine. These cities began to plan their growth, regulate business, and collect taxes. Wealthy towns in Italy invested in new buildings and statuary for beautification.

The Crusades

The **Crusades** were a series of Christian holy wars conducted against infidels—nonbelievers. The most significant crusade was a massive expedition led by the Roman Catholic Church to recapture Palestine, the land of Christian origins, from the Muslims. Pope Urban II launched the Crusades in 1095, when he urged Christian knights to take up arms and seize the Holy Land. After the First Crusade, the Christians captured Edessa, Antioch, and Jerusalem and divided that territory into feudal states. However, the Muslim forces reorganized under the leadership of Saladin and retook Jerusalem in 1187. The Fourth Crusade never made it to the Holy Land. The crusaders, supported by the merchants of Venice, conquered and sacked the Byzantine capital of Constantinople in 1204. This event severely weakened the Byzantine Empire.

Though the quest for the Holy Land was a failure, it led to great economic developments in Europe. It encouraged trade with Muslim merchants and increased the European demand for Asian goods. As a result, Italian merchants from cities such as Venice and Genoa greatly profited, and Europe was reintroduced to the goods, technology, and culture of the other regions.

NOMADIC AND TRAVELING EMPIRES

Nomadic and migrating peoples contributed to the diffusion of technologies, ideas, agricultural techniques, and diseases between 1200 and 1450. The Turkic peoples and the Mongols brought social, cultural, and economic changes to the regions that they encountered. Both of these ethnic groups originated on the Eurasian steppe. Stretching from Eastern Europe to the Pacific Ocean, the Eurasian steppe was home to many nomadic tribes that would periodically invade the settled societies bordering the steppe all throughout history. Prior to the refinement of gunpowder weapons, even small groups of steppe nomads were typically a fierce military force thanks to their expert horsemanship and use of mounted archers with composite bows.

The Turkic Peoples

The Turkic peoples are a collection of various groups sharing the same language family and ethnicity. Generally, the Turkic peoples originated as a pastoral nomadic group from central Asia. They first began to migrate out from the steppe at the end of the first millennium and were often hired by Muslim leaders as mercenaries. The Seljuk Turks, who had converted to Islam, are one such example of nomads hired as mercenaries.

Seljuk Empire and Ottomans

By 1071, the Seljuk Turks had defeated the Byzantine Empire and conquered most of Anatolia (modern-day Turkey) outside of Constantinople. Following the collapse of the Seljuk Empire, a new Turkic body arose at the turn of the fourteenth century, when a tribal leader named Osman founded the Ottoman Empire. The **Ottomans** would conquer Constantinople in 1453, bringing a final end to the Byzantine Empire.

Mamluk Sultanate

The Mamluk Sultanate stretched from Egypt across the Levant. Mamluk comes from the Arabic word for *property*, as Mamluks were slave-soldiers. Mostly but not exclusively Turkic peoples, they overthrew the Ayyubid Dynasty in Egypt following the defeat of a Crusader army in 1250. A decade later, they successfully repulsed a Mongol invasion. However, the Mamluks were eventually conquered by the Ottoman Empire in 1517.

Delhi Sultanate

The Afghan Turks were nomads from Afghanistan. They began a series of raids into India in the tenth century. They looted cities for gold and jewels and destroyed Hindu temples. It wasn't until the twelfth century that they started to govern after invading. This created the Delhi Sultanate, which ruled northern India from 1206 to 1526. The Afghan Turks introduced a strong Muslim presence in India.

The Mongol Empire

High-Yield

The **Mongols** were a pastoral, nomadic group from the central Asian steppe (modern-day Mongolia). These nomadic herders' lives revolved around their camels for transportation; their horses for mobility; and their sheep, goats, and yaks for food, clothing, and shelter. Their clan-based society was organized around bloodlines. The man born Temujin, later renamed **Genghis Khan**, successfully united the various Mongol tribes and created history's largest contiguous land empire.

The Mongols' greatest strength was their mobility. During wartime, every male from 15 years old to 70 years old had to serve. Each soldier was rewarded with captured goods and slaves. The Mongols' military strategy was also extremely effective; they were masters at psychological warfare and at feigning retreats. The Mongols were also skilled at using diplomacy to play enemies against one another and to weaken anti-Mongol alliances.

Once his troops were united, Genghis Khan led them into Central Asia, Tibet, Northern China, and Persia. In 1215, the Mongols attacked and destroyed Zhongdu (modern-day Beijing). The Mongols had relatively few defeats, but they failed to invade the Delhi Sultanate and Japan.

In 1227, Genghis Khan died. While regional control was divided among his four sons in the form of khanates, supreme authority passed to his son, Ögedei. However, by 1259, infighting over succession to the position of Great Khan led to civil war and then fragmentation of the Mongol Empire. In total, the Mongol conquests were the fourth deadliest span of warfare in human history, with conservative estimates placing the death toll at 30 to 40 million people, roughly 10 percent of the world's population at the time.

MONGOL CONQUESTS (1279)

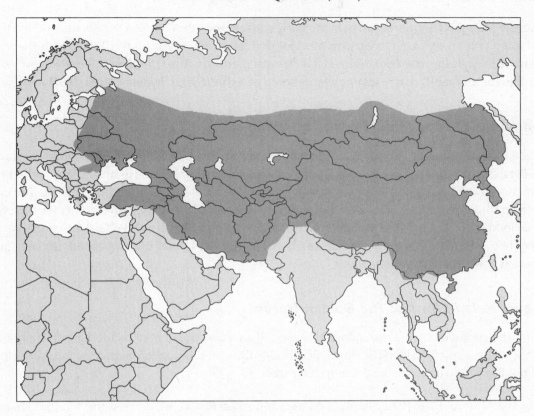

Mongol Rule in China: The Yuan Dynasty

In 1279, Genghis Khan's grandson, Kublai Khan, conquered the Southern Song Dynasty. For the first time, China was under foreign rule. Kublai Khan created a Chinese-style dynasty, taking the name Yuan, and maintained a fixed and regular tax payment system and a strong central government. Foreigners, not Chinese, were employed in most bureaucratic positions, and the civil service exam was no longer used. The Chinese were subject to different laws and were deliberately separated from the Mongols.

In time, overland and maritime trade flourished. Though the Mongols were not directly involved in the trade, they welcomed merchants and foreigners. Merchants converted their foreign currency into paper money when they crossed into China. Under Mongol rule, China prospered and the Mongol capital Khanbaliq developed into a flourishing city.

The Mongol rulers only achieved a limited level of popularity among their Chinese subjects, due to both their discriminatory practices and high taxes. The Red Turban Rebellion (1351–1368) would see the Chinese overthrow their Mongol conquerors. Zhu Yuanzhang, a peasant turned Red Turban commander, would found the Ming Dynasty (1368–1644).

Mongol Rule in Korea

When the Mongols conquered Korea in the thirteenth century, the Goryeo Dynasty maintained their local rule, with Korean kings marrying Mongol princesses. However, by the 1350s, with the Yuan Dynasty destabilizing, the Koreans expelled Mongol garrisons. After the Mongols were overthrown in China, the Goryeo Dynasty lost power in Korea and the Joseon Dynasty (1392–1897) emerged.

Mongol Rule in the Middle East: The Ilkhanate

In 1258, Kublai's brother Hülegü Khan defeated the Abbasid Caliphate, conquered Mesopotamia and Persia, and burned the city of Baghdad, destroying its famed House of Wisdom. Over time, these Mongols converted to Islam and began to mix with their conquered populations. The conquered populations' local rulers were permitted to rule, as long as they delivered tax revenue and maintained order. Though the Mongols did not support agriculture, they did facilitate trade. As the Mongols continued west, they were defeated in 1260 by the armies of the Mamluk Dynasty (also known as the Slave Dynasty) in Egypt.

Mongol Rule in Russia: The Golden Horde

During the centuries before the Mongol invasion, Russia was dominated by feudalism. The princes of Kiev, which also controlled the Russian Orthodox Church, ruled according to the legal principles that the Byzantine emperor Justinian had created.

When the Mongol ruler Batu Khan conquered and ruled Russia, he created the Mongol khanate called the Golden Horde. Batu Khan allowed many local rulers to keep their power, and Russian bureaucrats collected peasants' taxes, which were heavy during this time. Batu Khan's Mongol descendants constituted the upper social classes of the Golden Horde.

The Russian rulers of Muscovy, a territory north of Kiev, gained more control during Mongol rule by closely associating themselves with their Mongol rulers. The Mongols maintained control until Prince Ivan III effectively ended their rule in 1480 and formed the Russian state.

Pax Mongolica

Although Mongol invasions initially interfered with trade and peace, a period called the Mongol Peace (or *Pax Mongolica*) lasted during the thirteenth and fourteenth centuries, when vast areas of Eurasia were under Mongol rule. For about a century, Mongol rule united two continents and eliminated tariffs, which allowed for relatively safe trade and contacts between vastly different cultures.

During this period, the Silk Road trade reached its peak. Paper money—a Chinese innovation—was used in many parts of the Mongol Empire. The Mongols often adopted or converted to local religions or at least maintained religious tolerance.

Mongol Decline

In 1274 and 1281, the Mongols tried to expand their empire again by invading Japan. However, typhoon winds destroyed their fleets both times. The Japanese believed that the kamikaze, or "spirit winds," had protected them.

Despite great military accomplishment, the Mongol Empire lasted for only three or four generations. The Mongols were successful conquerors but poor administrators. Overspending led to inflation in different regions of the empire, and after the death of Kublai Khan, leadership was weak and ineffectual. Rivalry among the great Khan's potential successors further destabilized the empire, and the vast domain was divided among various generals. By 1350, most of the Mongols' vast territory had been reconquered by other armies, and the Mongols had largely assimilated into the societies that they had invaded.

CIVILIZATIONS IN AFRICA

Mali

Sundiata Keita established the Mali Empire in 1230, but it was not until his victory at the Battle of Kirina in 1235 against the rival Sosso that he cemented his nation's place as the strongest West African state during the thirteenth and fourteenth centuries. The poem known as *The Epic of Sundiata* describes how Sundiata Keita founded Mali. This poem exemplifies African oral traditions; it was composed and recited by Mali *griots* (storytellers).

Although most people in Mali were engaged in agriculture, the kingdom of Mali prospered from its participation in the trans-Saharan trade in gold and salt. The kings of Mali controlled and taxed trade within their territories. Local Mali rulers served in religious and economic roles; they honored Islam, provided protection and lodging for merchants, and ensured that the kings of Mali received their tax income. The people of Mali were encouraged, but not forced, to convert to Islam.

Mansa Musa ruled Mali from 1312 to 1337. A devout Muslim, Mansa Musa fulfilled one of the five pillars of faith and went on a pilgrimage, or *hajj*, to Mecca. He brought thousands of soldiers, attendants, subjects, and slaves with him, as well as hundreds of camels carrying satchels of gold. Mansa Musa created a period of inflation, which affected many regions along major trade routes, because he distributed so much gold to other peoples during his journey. Inspired by his travels, Mansa Musa built libraries, Islamic schools, and mosques throughout the kingdom. Timbuktu became Mali's political capital and West Africa's cultural center of Islamic scholarship and art.

Following 1350, after a series of kings that spent lavishly and misruled, provinces began to assert their independence and separate from the Mali Empire, and its power and influence declined.

7

Northeastern African Kingdoms

Many inhabitants of North Africa converted to Islam after 700 as Arab travelers spread their religious beliefs. Christianity also endured, however, especially in Egypt and Ethiopia. Ethiopia evolved into a kingdom with strong Christian traditions. Coptic Christianity stayed popular in Ethiopia, and in Egypt a minority of Coptic Christians remained even after the introduction of Islam. In the medieval period, the Ethiopian Empire spanned the states of present-day Ethiopia and Eritrea. The empire was ruled by the Solomonic Dynasty from 1270 until 1974.

East African City-States

East Africa was populated by peoples who spoke Bantu languages and had migrated centuries earlier from the Niger River territory. These Bantu peoples settled in cities along the East African coast. Although they did not politically unite to form kingdoms, individual city-states such as Mogadishu, Kilwa, and Sofala prospered from participating in Indian Ocean trade with Muslim merchants during the seventh and eighth centuries. In the 900s, Islamic merchants traded gold, slaves, and ivory for pottery, glass, and textiles from Persia, India, and China. As East Africans associated with Arab traders, the Swahili language (which mixes Bantu and Arabic) developed. Because of this, East African city-states are often called **Swahili city-states**. These city-states continued as important hubs of Indian Ocean trade until the monopolization of sea lanes by European imperial powers. For example, Kilwa was visited by Chinese Admiral Zheng He in 1415.

Much like Mali, these powerful city-states were governed by kings. When they converted to Islam for legitimacy and alliances, the kings ruled as caliphs and taxed and controlled trade. They built stone mosques and public buildings in their cities. The ruling elite and wealthy merchants of East Africa often converted to Islam but did not completely separate from their own religious and cultural traditions.

In Southeastern Africa, the kingdom of Zimbabwe prospered from participating in trade with East Africa's city-states. In the eleventh century, its inhabitants created Great Zimbabwe, a city of stone towers, palaces, and public buildings. Zimbabwe prospered between 1300 and 1450.

Hausa Kingdoms

Hausa kingdoms were a collection of states home to the Hausa people. They were located in the northern region of present-day Nigeria. Of these kingdoms, the city-state of Kano rose to greatest prominence for its role in trans-Saharan trade. The various kingdoms exported gold, salt, nuts, and slaves. Muslim clerics and traders filtered into the kingdoms from neighboring Mali, with Kano becoming a beacon of Islamic scholarship.

INTERREGIONAL ECONOMIC AND CULTURAL EXCHANGE

Global trade

The volume of long-distance trade dramatically increased between 1200 and 1450. Luxury items of high value, such as silk and precious stones, were typically transported over land routes. Merchants used sea routes to transport bulkier commodities, such as steel, stone, coral, and building materials.

The Silk Road trade linked the Eurasian land mass. Trans-Saharan trade connected West Africa to the Mediterranean and Islamic Empire. The Indian Ocean trade linked China, Southeast Asia, India, Arabia, and East Africa. The Mediterranean Sea trade linked Europe with goods from the Islamic Empire and Asia.

Because of this global exchange, and because of increased agricultural productivity and slightly warmer global temperatures between 800 and 1300, cities located along trade routes grew substantially. For instance, **Melaka**, a city on the coast of the Malay Peninsula in Southeast Asia, served as an important port city on the Indian Ocean. It became the Sultanate of Melaka, an Islamic state, as Muslim traders settled into the region and spread Islam in the early fifteenth century. Melaka maintained a safe environment for trade, welcomed merchants, and charged reasonable fees. As a result, it thrived in this interconnected world, along with cities like Hangzhou in China, Samarkand in Central Asia, Baghdad in modern-day Iraq, Kilwa in East Africa, Venice in Italy, and Timbuktu in Mali, Africa.

Although cities generally increased in size between 1200 and 1450, military invasions, diseases, and reduced agricultural productivity caused some cities to experience periods of significant economic decline.

Merchants set up their own communities, where they often influenced the dominant culture along trade routes. For example, Muslim merchants in the Indian Ocean region, Chinese merchants in Southeast Asia, and Jewish merchants in the Mediterranean settled in diaspora communities in trade cities. The increase in global interaction led to the spread of agriculture and technology and great changes throughout the world.

Origin	Diffusion	Effect
Magnetic compass from China	Europe via the Indian Ocean trade	Increase in maritime trade and exploration
Sugarcane from Southwest Asia	European Crusaders	Increases in Mediterranean island plantations and increases in slave labor
Gunpowder from China	Persia, the Middle East, and eventually Europe by the Mongols	Advances in weapon technology

Spread of Disease

In addition to religions, technologies, and goods, diseases spread along trade routes. Carried by infected rodents and fleas, the **bubonic plague** (also known as the Black Death) spread from the Yunnan region of southwest China. In the 1340s, Mongols, merchants, and travelers spread the disease even farther along the trade routes west of China. Oasis towns, trading cities of Central Asia, Black Sea ports, the Mediterranean Sea, and Western Europe were all affected. Some scholars estimate that as many as 100 million people, out of a world population of 450 million, died. A third of Europe's population died in the first five years of the plague.

This seemingly apocalyptic event led to many social changes. In Western Europe, for example, the resulting labor shortage led to workers demanding higher wages. Peasants rebelled, weakening the feudal system. Antisemitism led to Jews being scapegoated for the plague, and many Jewish communities were massacred. Christians questioned their faith amid all of the death and seemingly senseless destruction. Self-flagellation (whipping oneself) became popular as a way for people to atone for their apparent sins. The Roman Catholic Church lost much of its seasoned clergy to the plague, and their replacements often lacked proper education and literacy as standards were lowered by necessity.

Travelers

High-Yield

The tremendous amount of long-distance interaction in this period can be illustrated through the travels of three individuals: a Muslim scholar (**Ibn Battuta**), an Italian merchant (**Marco Polo**), and a Nestorian Christian priest (Rabban Sauma). Each traveler recorded his observations during his journeys.

	Ibn Battuta 1304–1369	**Marco Polo 1253–1324**	**Rabban Sauma 1225–1294**
Background	Muslim scholar from Morocco	Italian merchant from Venice	Nestorian Christian priest from Mongol Empire in China
Places traveled	Throughout Dar al-Islam: West Africa, India, Southeast Asia	Throughout the Silk Road to the Mongol Empire in China	Began pilgrimage to Jerusalem in Beijing, but diverted when sent by Mongol Ilkhan of Persia to meet with kings of France and England and the pope to negotiate alliances against Muslims.
Significance	Found government positions as a *qadi*, or judge, throughout the lands he traveled. Demonstrated the widespread influence of Islam and increased European interest in Eastern goods.	Allowed by Kublai Khan to pursue mercantile and domestic missions throughout the empire. Increased European interest in goods from the East.	Did not succeed in attracting the support of Christian Europe to the Mongol cause. Europeans never conquered the Middle East, but instead went around it to reach the Indian Ocean.

Missionaries

Buddhism

Along the Silk Road, Buddhism traveled to Central Asia and adapted into variants, which included polytheism. In Tibet, it became popular as it combined shamanism and the importance of rituals. In East Asia, monks, merchants, and missionaries adapted Buddhism to the political ideas of Confucianism by including Daoist ideas, an emphasis on family, and ancestor worship.

Particularly during chaotic times, Buddhism appealed to people as an avenue toward personal enlightenment. Chinese Buddhism spread to Korea, where it received royal support, and to Japan. In Japan, Shinto leaders initially resisted Buddhism. Eventually, syncretism (the fusion of differing systems of beliefs) occurred after Buddhism blended into the worship of Shinto divinities.

Because Buddhism lacked an organized Church, it could merge with local people's ideas. However, Buddhism was often replaced by more organized religions. In Central Asia, for instance, Islam eventually replaced Buddhism as the dominant religion. In China, the Tang Dynasty stopped supporting Buddhism in the ninth century.

Christianity

Like Buddhism, Christianity emerged as a missionary religion. When the Western Roman Empire was declining, missionary efforts turned toward Northern Europe. The Western Church and the pope sponsored missionary campaigns aimed at converting the Germanic people. The Eastern Orthodox Church also spread Christianity to Eastern Europe and Russia.

Syncretism aided the spread of Christianity. Pagan heroes or holy figures, such as the saints, were seen as mediators between God and his people. Polytheistic holidays were incorporated into Christianity, and Christians placed Christmas on the same day as the pagan winter solstice celebration. In Asia, Nestorian Christianity—the belief that Jesus existed as two distinct entities, mortal man and divine figure—spread to Mesopotamia and Persia, where Islamic conquerors allowed Christians to practice their religion. Merchants also spread Nestorian Christianity as far as India and China, but they received little or no support from local rulers.

Islam

Islam spread through three main avenues: military conquest, trade, and missionary activity. Once Islam was introduced through one of those avenues, the religion spread because of its tolerance for other beliefs, its simple principles, and its emphasis on charity and spiritual equality. Also, Muslim rulers often levied a special tax against non-Muslims, which provided an economic incentive for conversion.

In sub-Saharan Africa, merchants introduced Islam to the ruling class through trade, and syncretism occurred. The kings still held a divine position, and women continued to have a prominent place in society, as was the local custom. In East Africa, Islam arrived via the Indian Ocean, where it mixed Arabic and African languages to create Swahili. In India, Turks brought Islam to the region in the eleventh century when they formed the Delhi Sultanate and used Hindu stories with Muslim characters, attracting both warriors and low-caste Hindus. The Sufis were the most active missionaries after 900, spreading Islam to Southern Europe, sub-Saharan Africa, Central Asia, India, and Southeast Asia.

7

RECOVERY AND RENAISSANCE IN ASIA AND EUROPE

Chinese Developments

In 1368, the Mongol Yuan Dynasty collapsed and Emperor Hongwu started the Ming Dynasty. Hongwu reinstated the Confucian education system and civil service exam and tightened central authority. The Ming relied on mandarins, a class of powerful officials, to implement their policies on the local level. They also conscripted laborers to rebuild irrigation systems; as a result, agricultural production increased. Though the Ming did not actively promote trade, private merchants traded manufactured porcelain, silk, and cotton. Where the Yuan Dynasty had imposed high taxes to support Mongol military efforts, the Ming favored a policy of minimal taxation. This approach facilitated trade but left the Ming state vulnerable to economic disruptions. In the seventeenth century, the Ming finally faced troop defections and rebellions over the state's inability to pay its own soldiers.

The Ming Dynasty strongly promoted Chinese cultural traditions and established Neo-Confucian schools which stressed Confucian values such as self-discipline, filial piety, and obedience to rulers. The Ming Dynasty saw three of the "Four Great Classical Novels" of Chinese literature published: *The Water Margin*, *Romance of the Three Kingdoms*, and *Journey to the West*. Perhaps the most widely read novel in both late imperial and modern China, and culturally influential throughout East Asia, *Romance of the Three Kingdoms* is an 800,000-word epic. The story opens with the Yellow Turban Rebellion at the twilight of the Han Dynasty, and it follows a sprawling cast during the Three Kingdoms period as they battle over whose faction will reunite China. Its opening lines summarize a repeating pattern in Chinese political history: "The world under heaven, after a long period of division, tends to unite; after a long period of union, tends to divide. This has been so since antiquity."

Jesuit missionaries such as Matteo Ricci arrived in China, introducing European science and technology. While the Jesuit goal of converting the Chinese population to Catholicism proved unsuccessful, Ricci's syncretic approach, accepting ancestor veneration while also using Confucian values to "translate" Christian doctrine, demonstrates how religious belief systems adapt to spread between regions.

European Developments

By the 1400s, the regional states in Europe were developing into monarchies. These monarchies were strong enough to tax citizens directly and maintain large standing armies. Milan, Venice, Florence, and other parts of modern-day Italy benefited greatly from increased trade, which increased tax revenues and their governments' authority. This wealth facilitated much of the accomplishments of the **Renaissance**, a period of artistic and scientific self-discovery.

Kings in France and England began to successfully assert their authority over their feudal lords. In Spain, Fernando of Aragon and Isabella of Castile married and united Spain by reconquering the lands formerly controlled by Muslims. The competition among these states led to a refinement and improvement in weapons, ships, and technology, which prepared these regional states for future expansion.

PRACTICE SET

Questions 1–4 refer to the image below.

GRAND CANAL, ZHOUZHUANG, CHINA

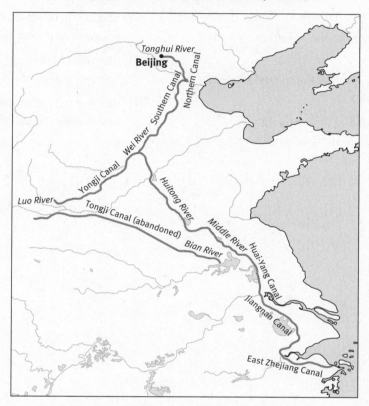

Modern view of the Grand Canal, the construction of which has spanned from 500 B.C.E. to the present

1. The construction of the Grand Canal best illustrates which of the following patterns of the period 1200–1450?

   (A) Commercial growth was facilitated by state-sponsored commercial infrastructures.

   (B) The diffusion of industrial technologies from Europe enabled the construction of public works.

   (C) Confiscation of privately owned land often occurred to benefit political leaders.

   (D) Daoist ideas supported the development of natural waterways.

2. The economic impact of the Grand Canal in China is most similar to the economic impact of which of the following?

   (A) The spread of bubonic plague in Western Europe

   (B) The establishment of the Inca road system in South America

   (C) The construction of the ziggurats in Mesopotamia

   (D) The creation of aqueducts in the Roman Empire

3. Which of the following could best be inferred about the city of Zhouzhuang in the period 1200–1450?

   (A) It was weakened by constant flooding and subsequently abandoned.

   (B) It benefited from access to European technologies.

   (C) It declined as a result of increased susceptibility to invasion.

   (D) It flourished due to the availability of resources from beyond the local area.

4. Which of the following best describes the long-term impact of the Grand Canal on China?

   (A) The region became more economically and politically integrated.

   (B) The northern region became increasingly disconnected from the southern region.

   (C) The cost of building the canal led to an economic depression.

   (D) The rise of an elite merchant class led to social upheaval and rebellion.

Questions 5–7 refer to the passage below.

"We cannot, therefore, point out any definite time and place and say, 'Here is [Bushido's] fountain head.' Only as it attains consciousness in the feudal age, its origin, in respect to time, may be identified with feudalism. . . . As in England the political institutions of feudalism may be said to date from the Norman Conquest, so we may say that in Japan its rise was simultaneous with the ascendency of Yoritomo, late in the twelfth century.

. . . In manifold ways has Bushido filtered down from the social class where it originated, and acted as leaven among the masses, furnishing a moral standard for the whole people. The Precepts of Knighthood, begun at first as the glory of the elite, became in time an aspiration and inspiration to the nation at large; and though the populace could not attain the moral height of those loftier souls, yet *Yamato Damashii*, the Soul of Japan, ultimately came to express the Volksgeist of the Island Realm. If religion is no more than 'Morality touched by emotion,' as Matthew Arnold defines it, few ethical systems are better entitled to the rank of religion than Bushido."

Nitobe Inazō, a Japanese scholar, *Bushido: The Soul of Japan*

5. Which of the following events best explains the governmental structure of Japan in the thirteenth and early fourteenth centuries?

    (A) The removal of the shogun and the restoration of the Japanese emperor to power

    (B) The centralization of authority in a military government run by the shogun

    (C) The invasion and subsequent occupation of Japan by the Mongol Empire

    (D) The government-sponsored codification of a Bushido code for aristocrats and their samurai retainers

6. Nitobe's idealized vision of Bushido in the passage differs most strongly from which of the following aspects of later Japanese history?

    (A) The Tokugawa shogunate requiring *daimyo* to spend every other year in the capital

    (B) The glorification of war expressed by Japanese soldiers and officers during World War II

    (C) The rapid industrialization and modernization of Japan driven partly by family-owned business conglomerates

    (D) The refusal of the Empire of Japan to join the newly formed League of Nations

7. Which of the following contributed most directly to the development of Japanese national identity in the thirteenth century?

    (A) The samurais' adoption of concepts of courtly romance and participation in tournaments due to decreasing warfare

    (B) The destruction of two Mongol fleets during separate attempted invasions of Japan

    (C) The restoration of the emperor to a position of supreme political authority over Japan

    (D) The forced opening of Japanese port cities to foreign trade

Questions 8–10 refer to the following two images.

<u>Image 1</u>

This ceramic star-shaped tile, from Iran (Ilkhanate) in Western Asia, features a raised Chinese dragon. Circa late 1200s.

<u>Image 2</u>

This ceramic star-shaped tile, also from Iran (Ilkhanate) in Western Asia, features a Qur'anic inscription. Circa 1262.

8. The object in <u>Image 1</u> best illustrates which of the following continuities in world history?

    (A) The spread of religious syncretism through global trade networks

    (B) The intensification of social hierarchies including gender hierarchies such as patriarchy

    (C) The cross-cultural interactions fostered by an imperial power and its trade networks

    (D) The development of specialized labor as a result of the demands of social elites

9. The object in <u>Image 2</u> best illustrates which of the following continuities in world history?

    (A) The impact of religious beliefs on cultural development

    (B) Imperial rulers suppressing native religions and practices

    (C) The unifying role of art in diasporic communities

    (D) Artwork legitimizing and celebrating imperial rule

10. Taken together, the two images best support which of the following conclusions?

    (A) The Mongol siege of Baghdad and the destruction of its famous House of Wisdom led to a cultural dark age for Islamic civilizations in the Middle East.

    (B) The conquered populations in the Ilkhanate began to mix with the Mongols over time and adopt Chinese philosophies like Confucianism and Buddhism.

    (C) The Ilkhanate's conquered subjects were influenced via new Eurasian trade routes, but they still largely preserved their own cultures.

    (D) The conquered populations' local rulers were removed from power, and the Mongols directly ruled their new subjects instead.

Questions 11–13 refer to the passage below.

"The Chinese are all infidels: they worship images, and burn their dead just like the Hindoos. The King of China is a Tartar, and one of the descendants of Jengīz Khān, who entered the Mohammedan countries, and desolated many of them. . . .

[The merchants'] transactions are carried on with paper . . . every piece of it is in extent about the measure of the palm of the hand, and is stamped with the King's stamp. . . . But when these papers happen to be torn, or worn out by use, they are carried to their house, which is just like the mint with us, and new ones are given in place of them by the King. This is done without interest; the profit arising from their circulation accruing to the King. When any one goes to the market with a dinar or a dirhem in his band, no one will take it until it has been changed for these notes."

Ibn Battuta, a Moroccan scholar, *Ibn Battuta's Rihla*, 1355, translated by Samuel Lee in *The Travels of Ibn Batūta*

11. The <u>second paragraph</u> in the passage is best understood in the context of which of the following?

   (A) The lingering anger of Islamic societies for their treatment at the hands of the Mongols

   (B) The resurgence of Han cultural identity near the end of the Yuan Dynasty

   (C) The development of a bill of exchange to facilitate a pre-modern economy

   (D) The promotion of both regional and inter-regional trade even after the end of the *Pax Mongolica*

12. The passage can best be used as evidence for which of the following world historical trends that took place during the thirteenth and fourteenth centuries?

   (A) The continuing growth of Mongol political and military power

   (B) The spread of the plague from China to Europe

   (C) The growing interest of Europeans in the Eastern world

   (D) The increasing amount of long-distance interaction in Afro-Eurasia

13. Which of the following best characterizes China under the rule of Genghis Khan's descendants?

   (A) The civil service exam was maintained but foreigners were employed in most bureaucratic positions.

   (B) The people of China disliked both the high taxes and the Mongols' discriminatory practices.

   (C) The Chinese were subject to the same harsh laws as the Mongols, and integration was promoted.

   (D) The Southern Song Dynasty maintained their local rule with Chinese emperors marrying Mongol princesses.

Questions 14–16 refer to the passage below.

"Nor can the violation of the [Hagia Sophia] be listened to with equanimity. For the sacred altar, formed of all kinds of precious materials and admired by the whole world, was broken into bits and distributed among the soldiers, as was all the other sacred wealth of so great and infinite splendor. When the sacred vases and utensils of unsurpassable art and grace and rare material, and the fine silver, wrought with gold, which encircled the screen of the tribunal and the ambo, of admirable workmanship, and the door and many other ornaments, were to be borne away as booty, mules and saddled horses were led to the very sanctuary of the temple. . . . Nay more, a certain harlot, a sharer in their guilt . . . sat in the patriarch's seat*, singing an obscene song and dancing frequently.

No one was without a share in the grief. In the alleys, in the streets, in the temples, complaints, weeping, lamentations, grief, the groaning of men, the shrieks of women. . . ."

*The patriarch was the co-head of the Eastern Orthodox Church alongside the Byzantine emperor. This differed from the Roman Catholic Church, in which the pope was the sole authority.

Niketas Choniates, a Byzantine official and eyewitness to the Sack of Constantinople, *Historia*, early 1200s

14. The events described in the passage are best understood in the context of which of the following?

    (A) The Fall of Constantinople to an invading Ottoman army

    (B) Martin Luther nailing his 95 Theses to the door of Wittenberg Castle church

    (C) Holy wars in which Christians attempted to reclaim the Holy Land from Muslims

    (D) A schism in Christianity formalizing the Eastern Orthodox and Roman Catholic as separate branches

15. The author most likely mentioned the patriarch's seat for which of the following reasons?

    (A) To demonstrate the Crusaders' disdain for the Eastern Orthodox Church

    (B) To criticize the hierarchy of the Eastern Orthodox Church

    (C) To urge his readers to help reinstate the patriarch's authority

    (D) To advocate for a separation of church and state

16. Which of the following was an important long-term effect of the Sack of Constantinople?

    (A) It sparked a formal schism in Christianity, which split into the Roman Catholic Church and the Eastern Orthodox Church.

    (B) It increased the instability and weakness of the Byzantine Empire in the face of growing Islamic rivals.

    (C) It led to the immediate siege and conquest of Constantinople by the forces of the Ottoman Empire.

    (D) It marked the reincorporation of the Eastern Orthodox Church back into the Roman Catholic Church's sphere of influence.

Questions 17–19 refer to the passage below.

"If [the Mongols] were repulsed, and compelled by a superior force to retreat, they would gallop at full speed over the plains, turning at the same time in their saddles, and shooting at their pursuers with their arrows as coolly, and with as correct an aim, almost, as if they were still. While thus retreating the trooper would guide and control his horse by his voice, and by the pressure of his heels upon his sides, so as to have both his arms free for fighting his pursuers. . . .

. . . With a poor bow, or with unskillful management, a great deal of [muscular strength] would be wasted. But with the best possible bow, and with the most consummate skill of the archer, it is the strength of the archer's arm which throws the arrow, after all.

. . . Although the country . . . was now at peace, Temujin . . . made laws to encourage and regulate hunting, especially the hunting of wild beasts among the mountains; and subsequently he organized many hunting excursions himself . . . in order to awaken an interest in the dangers and excitements of the chase among all the khans. He also often employed bodies of troops in these expeditions, which he considered as a sort of substitute for war."

Jacob Abbott, an American writer, *Genghis Khan*, 1901

17. The views described in the passage are best seen as evidence of which of the following in Mongol society?

    (A) Their skill at using diplomacy against enemy alliances

    (B) Their clan-based society organized around bloodlines

    (C) Their mastery of psychological warfare and fighting retreats

    (D) Their martial skill being rooted in rigorous training

18. Ideas similar to those expressed in the passage directly contributed to which of the following aspects of later Mongol imperial history?

    (A) Overspending leading to inflation in different regions of the empire

    (B) Succession crises over the role of Great Khan destabilizing the empire

    (C) Mongol assimilation into the various societies that they had invaded

    (D) Importing foreign advisers to serve as local administrators of conquered peoples

19. All of the following statements are factually accurate. Which most likely explains Temujin's motivation for his actions as described in the third paragraph?

    (A) Temujin aimed to maintain the horseman-ship that allowed the Mongols to outma-neuver enemies.

    (B) The Mongols believed they had a divine mission to conquer the world, so Temujin wished to help future generations succeed.

    (C) The issue of succession after his death concerned Temujin, so he took steps to ensure a smooth transfer of power.

    (D) Women exercised some power and influ-ence even though the Mongols were largely a traditional patriarchal society.

Questions 20–22 refer to the passage below.

". . . [T]he caravan would seem to have pursued the usual road to Egypt, where it camped for a time outside Cairo, and passed on to Mecca and Medina. Here Musa made a profound impression on the peoples of the East, who have left in their annals, says one historian, a record of his voyage, and of their astonishment at the magnificence of his empire. But it appears that he gave only 20,000 gold pieces in alms in each town, and in comparison with the immense extent of the territories he governed, this was not considered munificent. The same author, however, mentions incidentally that throughout his journey, wherever he halted on a Friday, he built a mosque. The funds required for such a purpose, even though some of the mosques were but small, must have been considerable.

. . . Having thus made the complete round of his empire, Mansa Musa re-entered his capital and immediately employed his Spanish architect to design for him a hall of audience, built after the fashion of Egyptian architecture. Abou Ishak, it is said, displayed all the wonders of his genius in the creation of 'an admirable monument' which gave great satisfaction to the king."

Flora Louise Shaw, DBE, a British journalist, *A Tropical Dependency:*
An Outline of the Ancient History of the Western Soudan
with an Account of the Modern Settlement of Northern Nigeria, 1905

20. Mansa Musa's charity in the <u>first paragraph</u> is best understood in the context of which of the following?

   (A) Imperialism

   (B) Religious syncretism

   (C) Missionary work

   (D) Neocolonialism

21. The architectural project described in the <u>second paragraph</u> is evidence of which of the following?

   (A) The Trans-Saharan trade routes flourishing and promoting cross-cultural exchanges

   (B) The spread of Islam along trade routes from the Middle East to East Africa by Muslim merchants

   (C) The exchange of art and architecture between the Islamic portions of sub-Saharan Africa and the Ilkhanate

   (D) The legitimization of a ruler through the building of religious monuments

22. The reference in the <u>second paragraph</u> that "he gave only 20,000 gold pieces" is best understood in the context of which of the following?

   (A) The kingdom of Mali greatly prospered from its participation in the gold and salt trade.

   (B) It was customary for any king making a *hajj* to Mecca to offer far greater in terms of alms.

   (C) Mansa Musa deflated the price of gold along his pilgrimage route by injecting too much gold into regional economies.

   (D) The mosques that Mansa Musa had built were worth this amount of gold on average.

Questions 23–25 refer to the map below.

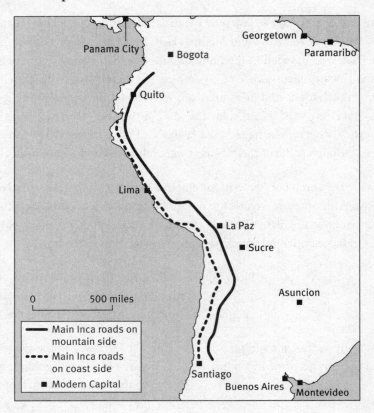

23. Which of the following can most reasonably be inferred from the road network shown on the map?

    (A) The Inca Empire was a Portuguese colony.

    (B) The Inca Empire was a series of city-states.

    (C) The Inca Empire had a centralized government.

    (D) The Inca Empire had a decentralized government.

24. Which of the following systems of coerced labor contributed the most to the ability of the Incas to construct the road network depicted on the map?

    (A) The *encomienda* system

    (B) Indentured servitude

    (C) The *mit'a*

    (D) Chattel slavery

25. Based on the map and your knowledge of world history, which of the following best describes a major purpose of the Inca road network?

    (A) To project military power throughout the empire

    (B) To provide a travel path for the common people

    (C) To promote international trade

    (D) To speed the extraction of natural resources for export

ANSWER KEY

1. A		6. B		11. D		16. B		21. A
2. B		7. B		12. D		17. D		22. A
3. D		8. C		13. B		18. D		23. C
4. A		9. A		14. D		19. B		24. C
5. B		10. C		15. A		20. C		25. A

ANSWERS AND EXPLANATIONS

1. A

The Chinese government sponsored the construction of the Grand Canal. The goal was to improve trade between the northern and southern regions of China since most of China's rivers flowed from west to east. Thus, **(A)** is correct. The canal was built before European industrialization, which began around 1750, making (B) incorrect. (C) is incorrect because, although some land may have been confiscated to build the canal, the building work did not directly benefit leaders; instead, the building of the canal improved commerce throughout the country. (D) is incorrect because a canal is a manmade waterway, not a natural one.

2. B

Both the Grand Canal and Incan roads facilitated trade within the empires by connecting various regions. **(B)** is correct. (A) is incorrect because the Black Death hurt Europe's economy rather than helped it. (C) is incorrect because ziggurats were places of worship, which means they would not have had a strong economic impact. (D) is incorrect because aqueducts carried water and did not necessarily improve trade.

3. D

Zhouzhang's location on the Grand Canal enabled residents to import goods from other cities and regions; the Grand Canal even indirectly connected the city to the Silk Road. **(D)** is correct. (A) is incorrect because canals are not as prone to flooding as are natural waterways, such as rivers. Additionally, the picture is a modern image, which shows that the city was not abandoned. (B) is incorrect because, in this era, Europe was in the Dark Ages and had few technological advances. (C) is incorrect because nomadic invaders mainly attacked northern cities and would most likely have been stopped by the Chinese military from using the Grand Canal to mount attacks.

4. A

The Grand Canal connected Beijing in the north with the rice-growing regions in the south. This allowed for increased commerce and for taxes, in the form of rice, to be sent to the capital. Thus, **(A)** is correct and (B) is incorrect. (C) is incorrect because the canal strengthened China's economy and led to urbanization and more manufacturing. The canal enabled merchants to sell their goods beyond their local area. Due to Confucian ideas, merchants were not viewed as elites; although they were wealthy, they were looked down upon, making (D) incorrect.

5. B

By the dawn of the thirteenth century, Japan was governed by a form of feudal military government known as the Kamakura shogunate. The emperor became a symbolic figurehead. The shogun, the supreme military general, controlled a centralized military government. Thus, **(B)** is correct. (A) is incorrect because it refers to the Meiji Restoration of 1868. While the Mongols twice attempted to invade Japan, both invasions were ultimately failures; (C) is incorrect. As explained in the passage, there is no singular point in time when Bushido was formally made into a clear code. Instead, it developed alongside the rise of the Kamakura shogunate; (D) is incorrect.

6. B

Nitobe's idealized vision of Bushido differs most strongly from the Bushido advocated by Japanese soldiers and officers during World War II. The latter functioned as a militant philosophy that glorified war and death in service to the emperor. Thus, **(B)** is correct. (A) describes part of Japanese feudalism's political structure. As the *daimyo* would be obeying the orders of their superior by spending every other year in the capital, this fits with the description of Bushido as "Precepts of Knighthood" first expressed by

Japanese elites. Because it is consistent with the passage, (A) is incorrect. Likewise, the role of the zaibatsu after the Meiji Restoration was one of elites serving their nation, in this case industrializing Japan to ward off foreign imperialists. Thus, (C) is incorrect. (D) is factually incorrect; the Empire of Japan was, in fact, one of the League of Nation's founding members. The only major power that never joined the League was the United States.

7. B

Typhoons destroying two Mongol invasion fleets, in 1274 and 1281, contributed to a perception that Japan could never be successfully invaded or conquered by foreigners. Thus, **(B)** is correct. (A) is incorrect because it describes hallmarks of chivalry in Europe, not of Bushido in Japan. (C) is incorrect because it references the Meiji Restoration, which took place in the nineteenth century. (D) is incorrect because it references the forced opening of Japan to wider foreign trade by Commodore Perry of the United States Navy in the mid-nineteenth century.

8. C

Image 1 showcases East Asian influence over Iranian art. Its place of origin and date of creation place it firmly amid the *Pax Mongolica*, when the Mongol conquests created a unified Eurasian trade system. This led to cross-cultural interactions that impacted cultural products like artwork. Thus, **(C)** is correct. While religious syncretism can spread through global trade networks, the Mongol Empire was notable for not imposing a religion on its subjects, instead generally respecting local belief systems; (A) is incorrect. The ceramic star-shaped tile with a raised Chinese dragon does not depict anything about gender hierarchies, so (B) is incorrect. While the artful ceramic tiles did require specialized labor, (D) is incorrect because it merely addresses the physical tile itself, not what the tile is displaying.

9. A

Islamic art is characterized by the absence of human figures due to prohibitions against idolatry. Instead, calligraphic and geometric patterns are prolific. Thus, **(A)** is correct. The Mongol Empire was notable for not imposing a religion and respecting local belief systems; (B) is incorrect. Iranian artwork featuring Qur'anic inscription during this time period would not be the product of a diasporic community but of a subject people in a conquered nation. (C) is incorrect. The use of calligraphic and geometric patterns, as well as the lack of East Asian influence that Image 1 showcases, makes (D) incorrect.

10. C

Despite their conquest by the Mongols, the Iranian people largely preserved their own culture even while being influenced by cross-cultural exchanges facilitated by increased Eurasian trade during the *Pax Mongolica*. This is shown by the tiles conforming to the traditional Islamic prohibition against depicting people. Thus, **(C)** is correct. While the destruction of the House of Wisdom during the Siege of Baghdad marked the end of the Islamic Golden Age, (A) is incorrect because it goes too far. Islam did not undergo a significant cultural, demographic, and economic downturn into a dark age. (B) is incorrect because it inverts history; the local Mongols adopted Islamic culture and religion over time. In the Ilkhanate, the conquered populations' local rulers were permitted to continue ruling, as long as they delivered tax revenue and maintained order. (D) is incorrect.

11. D

Though the Mongols ruling China during the Yuan Dynasty were not directly involved in trade, they welcomed merchants and foreigners. Paper money—a Chinese innovation—was used in many parts of the Mongol Empire to facilitate easier trading. Thus, **(D)** is correct. (A) is incorrect because it refers to the context of the first paragraph, not the second, where the narrator describes how the Mongols once "desolated" Islamic states. (B) is incorrect because the use of paper money was authorized by the Yuan Dynasty authorities. The Mongols often adopted practices and innovations of the societies that they conquered. (C) is incorrect because bills of exchange were a Western European innovation, not a Chinese one.

12. D

Ibn Battuta's *Rihla* is an example of the long-distance interaction that took place during this period, as the Mongol invasions sparked awareness of the Eastern world and interest in its peoples, especially as lucrative trade between East and West grew. Ibn Battuta, Marco Polo, and Rabban Sauma are just the most famous examples of individuals who traveled across the Old World during this period. Thus, **(D)** is correct. (A) is incorrect because the Mongol Empire had collapsed and the Yuan Dynasty was near its end by 1355, when *Rihla* was published. While interregional trade and contact spread the plague to Europe, (B) is incorrect because there is no mention of disease in the passage. (C) is incorrect because, while Europeans did have a growing interest in the Eastern world during this period, Ibn Battuta was a Moroccan Muslim writing for his countrymen.

13. B

The high taxes and discriminatory practices of the Mongols inspired little love for them among their Chinese subjects. The Red Turban Rebellion would see the Chinese over-throw their Mongol conquerors and establish the Ming Dynasty; **(B)** is correct. (A) is incorrect because it is only half true. While foreigners were employed in most bureaucratic positions, the civil service exam was abolished. (C) is incorrect because the Chinese were subject to different laws than the Mongols, and integration was discouraged. (D) is incorrect because it describes the circumstances of the Goryeo Dynasty in Korea under Mongol rule.

14. D

The underlying motivation for the Sack of Constantinople in 1204 was religious tensions between the largely Roman Catholic crusaders and the Greek Orthodox inhabitants, as the former saw the latter as heretics. The East-West Schism in Christianity took place in 1054, and laid the groundwork for the events described in this excerpt. Thus, **(D)** is correct. The Fall of Constantinople did not take place until 1453; (A) is incorrect. Likewise, (B) is incorrect because Martin Luther did not nail his 95 Theses to that door until 1517. While the Crusades were the reason why this army of Roman Catholics was close enough to Constantinople to sack it, the underlying motivation for the sack was tension with the Eastern Orthodox Church, not a conflict with Muslims; (C) is incorrect.

15. A

The author describes the extent of the sack of Constantinople, emphasizing the blasphemous way that the crusaders handled and destroyed sacred objects, such as the altar and the patriarch's seat. Furthermore, the patriarch's seat is symbolic of the difference in the way the Eastern Orthodox Church was run versus the way the Roman Catholic Church operated. Thus, **(A)** is correct. This excerpt is an eye-witness account of the events that took place; the author is not espousing views that are critical of the Eastern Orthodox Church, or calling his readers to action, so (B), (C), and (D) are incorrect.

16. B

The Sack of Constantinople severely weakened the Byzantine Empire, leaving it vulnerable to the Seljuk Turks, who had already conquered most of what is modern-day Turkey by 1071. Thus, **(B)** is correct. The East-West Schism in Christianity took place in 1054, while the Sack of Constantinople took place in 1204; (A) is incorrect.

The Ottomans did not arise until around the dawn of the fourteenth century, so (C) is incorrect. The Eastern Orthodox Church was never reincorporated back into Western Christendom, and both factions continue to exist into the present day. (D) is incorrect.

17. D

The passage explains the Mongols' expert use of the bow, and the requirements to achieve such feats. The third paragraph describes how Genghis Khan encouraged hunting in the wilderness, mirroring the conditions of his people's pastoral, nomadic origins to create a comparable form of training. The intention was that the Mongols would not lose the hardiness or training needed to wield their bows during wartime. Therefore, **(D)** is correct. (A) and (B) are incorrect because nothing in the passage touches upon diplomacy or the clan-based structure of their society. While (C) is tempting because the first paragraph discusses Mongol cavalry tactics, the primary focus throughout the whole passage is on the Mongols' usage of bows, the skill required for it, and how the Mongols went about training for it.

18. D

Mongol attempts to maintain the fighting edge of nomadic steppe life were, in essence, attempts to ward off assimilation. Mongols lived apart from their subjects and were governed by different laws. Importing foreign advisers from elsewhere in their empire to serve as local administrators was another attempt to put distance between the Mongols and their subjects. Not only did it draw upon an existing pool of talent in their subjects, but it kept imperial officials from networking and sympathizing with the local residents in their administration area. This helped dampen the odds of a rebellion against Mongol rule. Thus, **(D)** is correct. Inflation primarily impacted the end of the Yuan Dynasty in China, by which point the Mongol Empire had already splintered into rival successor states; (A) is incorrect. While tempting in that succession issues were ultimately fatal to the Mongol Empire, (B) is incorrect because that was a political matter, not a military matter like the focus of the passage. Although (C) is tempting, it is incorrect because assimilation was what Genghis Khan was attempting to avoid.

19. B

A major concern for Temujin, and one that he impressed to varying degrees of success upon his successors, was that as the Mongol Empire grew, the Mongols would lose their nomadic fighting expertise as they assimilated into settled societies. To ward off this assimilation, several steps were taken, including the promotion of traditional hunting. Thus, **(B)** is correct. (A) is incorrect because it only applies to the first paragraph, not the third. (C) and (D) are incorrect because they do not touch on anything discussed in the passage.

20. C

Mansa Musa's gifting of alms and constructing mosques along his pilgrimage route is best understood as a kind of missionary work, encouraging communities along the route to practice Islam, as well as to solidify the Islamic presence in those communities where it already existed. Thus, **(C)** is correct. While Mansa Musa did expand the Mali Empire, he did not do so anywhere near the whole length of his pilgrimage route to Mecca; (A) is incorrect. While the second paragraph alludes to a blending of different regional styles in new Mali buildings under his reign, that is not the same as blending two distinct religious faiths, which is what syncretism is. So (B) is incorrect. Neocolonialism is the indirect control of former colonies by their onetime imperial master through economic influence. This does not apply here, as Mali never had control over most of this pilgrimage route. (D) is incorrect.

21. A

The hall of audience described in the second paragraph was designed by a Spanish architect in the Egyptian style for a West African civilization ruled by a king made famously wealthy by the gold trade. Thus, **(A)** is correct. Mansa Musa ruled the Mali Empire, which was in West Africa. The region of East Africa includes states near or bordering the Indian Ocean or Red Sea. Therefore, (B) is incorrect. Neither Spain nor Egypt were ever part of the Ilkhanate, so the architecture attributed to them cannot also be attributed to the Ilkhanate; (C) is incorrect. The project in the second paragraph was a hall of audience for the king, not a mosque or other religious building; (D) is incorrect.

22. A

The passage describes Mansa Musa's alms of gold in Egypt as somewhat paltry given the sheer size of Mali. For a king of his means, especially one enriched by Mali's position in the sub-Saharan gold and salt trade, the gold coins alone were not thought to be a considerable gift.

Thus, **(A)** is correct. (B) is incorrect because the expectation was greater for Mansa Musa because of Mali's size and economy, not because of an established custom. (C) is tempting because he did depress the regional price of gold in this manner, but it is ultimately incorrect. The author referenced in the passage took issue with the relatively small size of the donation, not with its effect on the larger economy. Finally, (D) is incorrect because the passage notes that the mosques were an additional gift on top of the alms, with no precise indication of how much the mosques cost.

23. C

As can be discerned from the map, the Inca Empire covered a 3,000-mile stretch of land. A roadway running along that length of distance requires a centralized government to coordinate its construction. Thus, **(C)** is correct while (B) and (D) are incorrect. The Inca land was never a Portuguese colony, but it was later conquered by Spain; (A) is incorrect.

24. C

The Inca Empire had a mandatory public service system, called the *mit'a*, which required Incan citizens to participate in various projects, such as constructing the extensive Inca road system. Thus, **(C)** is correct. The *encomienda* was a Spanish system of land grants that allowed colonists in the Americas to exploit the land and indigenous labor; (A) is incorrect. Indentured servitude was a labor system practiced by American colonists and Western Europeans; (B) is incorrect. Chattel slavery is when a person is treated as the personal property of their owner, and slave status is imposed on the children born to slaves. (D) is incorrect.

25. A

As with many states throughout history, the Inca Empire's transportation system served a dual purpose. It facilitated both internal trade and the movement of troops. Thus, **(A)** is correct. The common people were banned from using the road system for personal reasons without special permission; (B) is incorrect. The Inca road system was focused on internal trade within the empire, not with the neighbors of the Inca; (C) is incorrect. The Inca road system predated the European arrival in and colonization of the New World, which subsequently led to the extraction and export of natural resources; (D) is incorrect.

CHAPTER 8

1450 to 1750

THE AGE OF EXPLORATION

Chinese Exploration

After reestablishing authority over China, the Ming decided to refurbish their country's large navy. From 1405 to 1433, they sponsored seven massive naval expeditions in order to reinforce Chinese presence in the Indian Ocean, impose imperial control over trade, and impress foreign peoples with the authority of the Ming Dynasty.

The mariner Zheng He led these expeditions. His first trip alone involved 28,000 troops. Zheng He sailed to Southeast Asia, India, the Persian Gulf, Arabia, and East Africa. Zheng He dispensed and received gifts throughout these travels. However, Confucian officials convinced the Chinese emperor that the voyages were too expensive and unprofitable, especially because of renewed concern over the northern Mongol border. Thus, in 1433, the voyages ended, Zheng He's records were destroyed, and the ships were allowed to rot.

Other Easterners like Muslims, Indians, and Malays continued to use the Indian Ocean for commerce and trade, establishing effective routes and creating a vibrant trade system. When the Europeans did arrive, the world shifted from a primarily Asian-centered economy to a global economy.

European Exploration

Europe emerged from an age of isolation with a desire to explore. In contrast to the Chinese, whose voyages were motivated mainly by a need to bolster their international prestige, European voyages during the Age of Exploration were motivated mainly by financial interests. The Asian goods that Europe purchased, such as pepper, ginger, cloves, and nutmeg, were significantly expensive. Europeans wanted to gain direct access to these goods, increasing supply and lowering prices. Other motives included the spread of Christianity and the desire for adventure.

8

SPAIN AND PORTUGAL IN THE AGE OF EXPLORATION

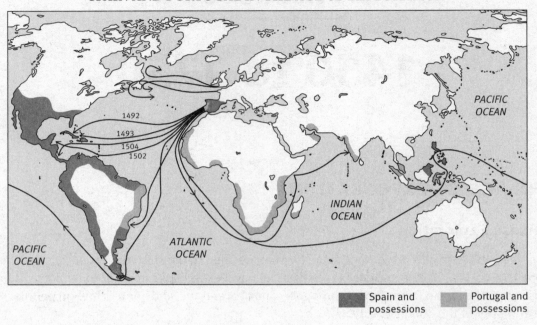

| Spain and possessions | Portugal and possessions |

Portugal

High-Yield

The rough landscape of Portugal was not ideal farmland, and the kingdom was an impoverished one prior to the Age of Exploration. This economic deficiency motivated interest in both accessing luxury goods more cheaply and also in improving Portugal's finances. While the Portuguese nobility was interested in conquering Morocco, its monarchy sought to control the spice trade by finding a sea route to India. There was also interest in locating the kingdom of Prester John, a supposed Christian ruler somewhere in Africa, to form an alliance against Islam.

The Portuguese were early leaders in exploration, under the leadership of Prince Henry the Navigator, who established Portuguese schools and sponsored expeditions along the West African coast. The key innovation of Portuguese navigators was the discovery of the *volta do mar* (literally "turn of the sea"), trade winds that allowed ships to easily sail past the west coast of Africa. This required the counterintuitive step to sail far westward into the open ocean to catch winds that would bring ships back around to the southern tip of Africa, with Bartolomeu Dias rounding the Cape of Good Hope in 1488. The Portuguese first arrived in India in 1498; the first Indian voyage lost a third of its crew but made 60 times a return on the investment of the expedition.

The Portuguese were methodical in their exploration, carefully recording winds, sea currents, tides, port locations, and more. They conducted live trials of their cannons at sea, figuring out how to best sink enemy ships and bombard coastal targets. Despite India hosting a gunpowder empire at the time, Portuguese artillery was superior. Instead of bows, which were still in use in many places throughout Afro-Eurasia, they used crossbows and muskets and had superior armor. All these advantages allowed Portugal to establish a major, lucrative empire.

Spain

It is a myth that **Christopher Columbus** sought to prove that the Earth was round, which was a long-established fact even by 1492. Portuguese mathematicians had calculated the size of the Earth and dismissed the claim of Columbus that one could sail westward to Asia. What they were unaware of was the existence of the Americas. Spain, having just completed the *Reconquista*, sought a way to bypass the Portuguese monopoly on sea routes along West Africa.

While Portugal would build its empire in the Eastern Hemisphere, Spain mainly conquered the Americas. Spain did, however, conquer the Philippines, which had first been explored under Ferdinand Magellan, along with several small islands in the Pacific such as Guam.

COLUMBUS'S FIRST VOYAGE

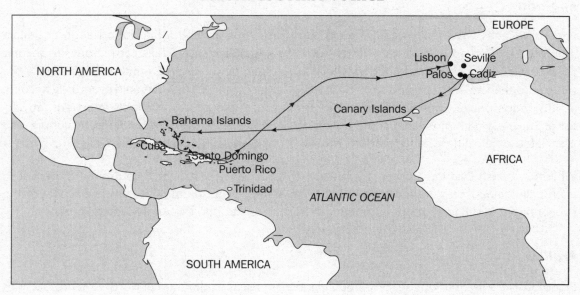

Explorer	Year	Accomplishment
Bartolomeu Dias (Portugal)	1488	Rounded the Cape of Good Hope at the tip of Africa and entered the Indian Ocean
Christopher Columbus (Spain)	1492	Sailed west to reach Asia and instead reached the Bahamas; sailed around the Caribbean, but thought he had reached an island just off the coast of Asia
Vasco da Gama (Portugal)	1497	Reached Calicut, India, in 1498 by rounding Africa
Ferdinand Magellan (Spain)	1519–1522	Sailed around South America to the Philippine Islands where he was killed; his men sailed back through the Indian Ocean and were the first to circumnavigate the globe

The Dutch

Dutch exploration during this period is practically synonymous with the Dutch East India Company, a massive business conglomerate with monopolies in several areas, which served as the right arm of the Dutch Republic. The Dutch East India Company was a model for the British East India Company. The Dutch Empire consisted mainly of its holdings in the East Indies (present-day Indonesia), the Cape Colony (present-day South Africa), and scattered holds in the Americas, India, and China.

As with France, the high standards of living in the Dutch Republic did little to motivate citizens to emigrate abroad to colonial holdings. Some of its outposts like New Amsterdam (present-day New York City) were eventually absorbed by rival, expansionist European powers.

England

English voyages were mainly concentrated on North America and India. John Cabot, an Italian employed by Henry VII, explored coastal North America. Sir Francis Drake carried out the second circumnavigation of the world and was the first captain to survive the entire voyage. Unlike the other European powers, England strongly favored settler colonies. While it would eventually become a global superpower, England at the start of the Age of Exploration was a fairly impoverished sector of Europe, which motivated some people to emigrate to its overseas holdings. Its culture also associated political rights and freedom with land ownership.

While the British East India Company initially struggled against its Dutch counterpart, the British eventually gained a secure foothold in India, expanding over time until it controlled most of the subcontinent and had shut out European rivals, such as through the Anglo-Dutch Wars.

France

France likewise focused on the spice trade in India as well as exploration of North America. Jacques Cartier claimed much of what is present-day Canada for France and was the first European to travel inland in North America. While settlements were made in what was then called New France, the comparative wealth of France itself did not motivate much emigration to rough frontier forts and villages.

THE DEVELOPMENT OF THE GLOBAL ECONOMY

Maritime Technology

The Ottoman **conquest of Constantinople** in 1453 ended the Byzantine Empire, solidifying Muslim influence along the Silk Road and making it less friendly to European traders. The acquisition of technology from China and the Muslim world helped Europeans expand their seagoing capabilities with maritime equipment such as the sternpost rudder, triangular lateen sails, the magnetic compass, and the astrolabe.

Portugal was an early leader in European exploration, aided by the development of the **caravel**, a small, highly maneuverable sailing ship. The **lateen sail** (French for "Latin") dates back to Roman times, but was popularized during the Age of Exploration for its ability to let a boat tack against the wind, increasing maneuverability. This proved useful when sailing out into the Atlantic Ocean to catch the trade winds, but its size was cumbersome, especially during storms. The weaknesses of the lateen sail, and the harsh requirements of long-distance ocean travel, led to the Portuguese developing the **carrack**, a larger and more rugged sailing vessel with three to four masts. However, other nations innovated as well. In the sixteenth century, the Dutch developed the **fluyt**, a dedicated transoceanic cargo vessel that was a key factor in the rise of the Dutch Empire. At their height in the seventeenth century, fluyts carried roughly half of all European cargo.

Trading-Post Empires

The initial goal of European powers in exploring the Indian Ocean was not to conquer, but to control trade. They wanted to force merchant ships to trade in fortified trading sites and to pay duties for the privilege. By the mid 1500s, Portugal had 50 trading posts from West Africa to East Asia, but by the late 1500s its power had started to decline—the country lacked the administrative and military capabilities to keep up with other European powers. The death of King Sebastian I and a large portion of the Portuguese nobility at the Battle of Alcácer Quibir in 1578 in northern Morocco sparked a succession crisis that destabilized the country. Soon, Spain absorbed Portugal and its empire, with Portugal only regaining independence in 1640.

The English and Dutch quickly took Portugal's place as the dominant seafaring powers with faster, cheaper, and more powerful ships. Their imperial expansion was aided by the use of **joint-stock companies**, in which investors, rather than royal governments, funded expeditions.

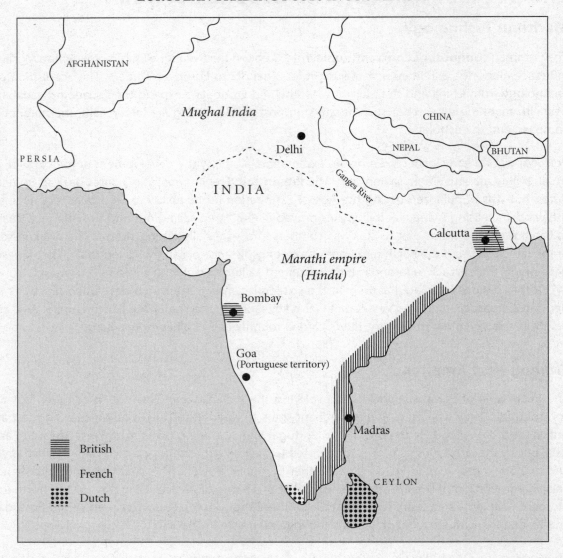

EUROPEAN TRADING POSTS IN SOUTH ASIA

Gujaratis, Javanese, Omanis, and Swahili Arabs continued to enjoy thriving Indian Ocean trade networks even as Europeans began to encroach on the region. In India and elsewhere, however, European powers grew in strength as they blossomed into full-fledged empires. Just as the Mongols once used diplomacy to play their rivals against one another, European states would take sides in local civil wars, sponsoring factions that would weaken a region and leave it indebted.

Reaction to European Expansion

Ming China

Following the voyages of Zheng He, Ming China pursued an isolationist foreign policy. While the Ming restricted European trade to islands like Macau, China still benefited enormously from the Columbian Exchange. New crops like corn and potatoes fueled population growth, offered a cushion against famine, and became staples of regional Chinese cuisine. The influx of New World silver revitalized the Chinese economy, which had suffered from inflation from an oversupply of paper money, but created a trade imbalance that would eventually lead to the Opium Wars. The enactment of the Japanese *sakoku* policy, as well as anti-smuggling efforts by the Spanish, disrupted the flow of silver into China, contributing to the rise of the Qing Dynasty as the Chinese economy collapsed.

Tokugawa Japan

Initially, the shogunate allowed foreign trade, which it monopolized for great financial benefit. However, European influence gradually came to be seen as a threat to the shogunate's power structure, as foreign trade could potentially enrich the *daimyo* enough to allow them to unseat the shogunate. The *sakoku* ("closed country"), a strictly isolationist foreign policy, was enacted in 1633 and would last until 1853. Nevertheless, highly regulated contact was maintained in the city of Nagasaki with the Dutch, while the Koreans had limited contact as well. "Dutch learning" from the West primed Japan for the Meiji Restoration. The then-burgeoning Christian community in Japan was suppressed and all but wiped out.

Kingdom of Kongo

In the fourteenth century, the Kongo emerged as a centralized state along the west coast of central Africa. In this organized state, a powerful king ruled, and officials oversaw military, judicial, and financial affairs. In 1483, a small Portuguese fleet arrived and initiated commercial relations, and within a few years the Portuguese had developed a close political and diplomatic relationship with the king. To improve relations, kings like Affonso I converted to and spread Catholicism across the kingdom, although the local version of Catholicism syncretized local religion practices.

The Portuguese brought great wealth to Kongo, exchanging textiles and weapons for gold, silver, ivory, and slaves. Kongo became a major hub of the transatlantic slave trade and often sourced the slaves it forcibly exported from those captured during Kongo's expansionist wars. Eventually, the Portuguese dealings undermined the king's authority and led to conflict. Moreover, relations with the Portuguese would sour over time, leading to a series of wars with the Portuguese. These wars often tied into dynastic succession issues within the Kingdom of Kongo over which family—and sometimes which member within which family—should rule. The kingdom never fully recovered from these wars.

COLUMBIAN EXCHANGE

Crops, Livestock, and Disease

 High-Yield

The inclusion of the Americas in the global trade network led to what would later be called the **Columbian Exchange**: the transfer of plants, food, crops, animals, humans, and diseases between the Old World and the New. The exchange of food crops and animals revolutionized life around the world.

8

Old World to New World	New World to Old World
Cattle	Avocados
Chickens	Beans
Cotton	Chocolate
Dogs	Maize (Corn)
Goats	Peanuts
Horses	Peppers
Okra	Pineapples
Pigs	Potatoes
Rice	Rubber Tree
Sheep	Tobacco
Sugarcane	Tomatoes
Wheat	Vanilla

New World crops like the potato had a huge impact on food production and population increases from Ireland to China. In the Americas, entire landscapes were stripped to build plantations that grew cash crops like sugarcane, coffee, and tobacco. These agricultural practices degraded the topsoil and reduced vegetative cover, which led to flooding and mudslides. The introduction of horses to the Americas had a significant impact on some American Indian tribes as they adopted more nomadic lifestyles—for example, some tribes used horses to track and hunt the massive buffalo herds which grazed on the Great Plains. This fostered the development of nomadic societies akin to those of the Eurasian steppe. Meanwhile, the raising of cattle and pigs dramatically changed the landscape. Forests were cut to provide grazing land.

However, the Columbian Exchange also led to the spread of disease to the Americas, brought by human carriers, as well as by rats and mosquitoes that Europeans unintentionally brought with them on ships. The introduction of feral pigs to the New World may have contributed to the transmission of diseases in the North American regions initially explored by the Spanish. Smallpox, measles, and other diseases to which the natives of the Americas had no immunity devastated their populations; some estimates of mortality rates for native populations are as high as 90 percent. The loss of life due to disease played a direct role in natives' inability to fend off European advancement. It also led to the importation of enslaved Africans to work on plantations. Relying on dwindling native populations as a labor force became economically unsustainable, and African slaves were used to meet labor demands.

Mercantilism: The Role and Impact of Silver

Silver, the most abundant American precious metal, was responsible for stimulating the global trade network. Spain controlled the two areas richest in silver production, Mexico and the Potosí mines in the Andes, and made use of large numbers of indigenous forced laborers. The Spanish were driven primarily by the economic theory of **mercantilism**. The term *mercantile system* is used to describe the ways in which nation-states enrich themselves by limiting imports and encouraging exports. The goal of mercantilist policies was to achieve a favorable balance of trade that would bring wealth into the country while maintaining domestic employment. The most important objective for mercantilist policies in the sixteenth century was the growth of a nation's economic power relative to competing nation-states. Spain used silver to trade for silk and porcelain in Asia, as China used the precious metal as a primary medium of exchange and to finance a powerful military and bureaucracy.

The Role and Impact of Sugar

Sugar was another important product at this time. Intensive labor and specialized skills were required for **sugar cultivation**. Because smallpox had wiped out so many native peoples in the Americas, enslaved Africans became the main labor force. These slaves worked under excessively harsh conditions—mistreatment, extreme heat, and poor nutrition—which led to a significant number of deaths from disease and abuse.

These sugar plantations were, in many aspects, proto-factories, as they were financed and organized to create a single product in a complex process, foreshadowing the organization of mechanized production in the upcoming Industrial Revolution.

STATE-BUILDING

Ottoman Empire

`High-Yield`

The Ottoman Empire emerged from a group of semi-nomadic Turks who migrated to northwest Anatolia in the thirteenth century. Military might and **gunpowder** weapons drove the Ottomans to power. An elite fighting force of slave troops composed of Christian males, called Janissaries, formed the professional backbone of the Ottoman military. In 1453, the Ottomans conquered Constantinople and brought an end to Byzantine rule. Sultans like Mehmed the Conqueror and Suleiman the Magnificent created an absolute monarchy. Islamic religious scholars and legal experts served administrative functions in the government. As the empire prospered, sultans grew more distant and removed themselves from government administration. The vizier headed the bureaucracy and often had more control and actual power than the sultan. Political succession was often problematic, as many new sultans would execute their brothers to eliminate any challenge to their authority.

In the capital city of Istanbul, formerly Constantinople, the Christian cathedral Hagia Sophia was converted to a grand mosque. The city also had aqueducts, a flourishing marketplace, rest houses, religious schools, and hospitals. A large merchant and artisan class conducted business, but its work was closely regulated by the government.

The sultan's harem, consisting of wives, concubines, and female servants, was influential in Ottoman politics and society. Members of the harem were often of slave origin and non-Muslim, as the enslavement of Muslims was forbidden. Wives and concubines were awarded status when they produced male heirs to the sultan's throne. They were educated in the Quran, reading, sewing, and music. The sultan's mother served as an advisor to the throne, overseeing the imperial household and engaging in diplomacy.

The empire reached its peak in the mid 1600s but became too large to maintain. The effectiveness of the administration declined and was plagued by corruption. In addition, the Ottomans struggled to keep up with ongoing European military and naval advancements. The Ottoman taxation system was also an inefficient patchwork of various approaches, as the empire typically maintained local tax practices of the territories it absorbed into the empire.

EXPANSION OF THE OTTOMAN EMPIRE

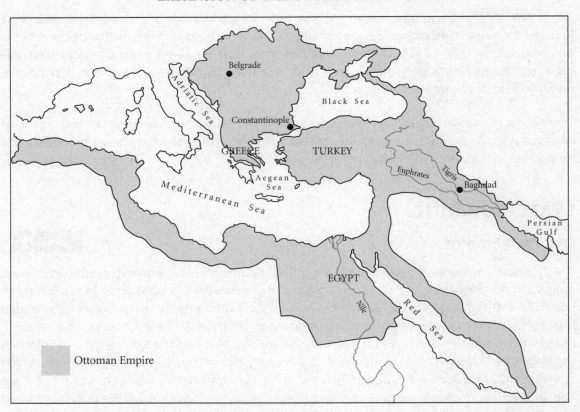

Safavid Dynasty

The formation of the Safavid Dynasty marks the beginning of modern Iranian history. The Safavids replaced the Timurid Empire, a dynasty of Turkicized Mongols, and reunified a politically fragmented Iran, ruling from 1501 to 1736. It was the first native dynasty since the seventh century. At its zenith, its empire stretched from eastern Turkey to western Pakistan and Afghanistan, and it incorporated large portions of Iraq.

The Safavid state was ruled by the Shah, but the system was a blend of royal absolutism mixed with bureaucratic checks and balances to minimize corruption and fraud. The Shah's orders required seconding by the prime minister, who himself was audited by a deputy who reported to the Shah. The economy was agricultural, but Silk Road trade also played an important role. Shah Abbas I forced the Portuguese from the Persian Gulf in 1602 with the aid of the British East India Company, and he was able to negotiate trade agreements with British, Dutch, and French traders. However, the sea routes discovered by Europeans during the Age of Exploration meant that overland Silk Road trade declined, as did the money it brought to the Safavid Dynasty. European merchants also gradually came to monopolize trade routes in the Indian Ocean. By the early eighteenth century, a series of revolts and loss of territory led to the downfall of the Safavid Dynasty.

Mughal India

High-Yield

In 1526, Babur, a descendant of Turkic nomads, began his conquest of India, unifying the subcontinent's regional kingdoms and establishing the **Mughal Empire**. The First Battle of Panipat marked the establishment of the Mughal Empire and also marked its annexation of the Delhi Sultanate. Babur's grandson Akbar continued his legacy and ushered in a period of economic stability and religious harmony. Akbar created a religion called the Divine Faith, which combined elements of Islam and Hinduism together and legitimized his rule as head of state and religion. He initiated a policy of cooperation with Hindu rulers and the Hindu population by encouraging intermarriage. He also abolished the *jizya* (non-Muslim tax) and promoted Hindus to high-ranking government positions. Akbar and his descendants, Jahangir and Shah Jahan, were great patrons of the arts. Emperor Shah Jahan oversaw the construction of the Taj Mahal, built as a tomb for his late wife. The Taj Mahal is perhaps the greatest example of Mughal architecture's unique blend of Islamic domes, arches, and minarets with Hindu-inspired ornamentation.

Aurangzeb, Shah Jahan's son, seized the throne with a neglectful and corrupt bureaucracy and pushed to extend Muslim control of India. He sought to rid India of all Hindu influences, purify Islam, and reinstate the *jizya*. His many wars drained the treasury, and peasant uprisings and revolts by both Muslim and Hindu princes weakened the empire. At this time, India had become a major overseas destination for European traders looking to fulfill demand for cotton. With a weakened empire, those traders were able to increase their influence in the region.

Tax collectors in the Mughal Empire were known as *zamindars* ("intermediaries"). The *zamindars* were aristocratic landowners who collected revenue from the peasants that worked the land. Over time, the title of *zamindar* became more generic and applied to different types of landowners, highborn and lowborn. *Zamindars* also took on more roles, moving from tax collectors to public functionaries, even gaining judicial powers over small-scale issues like petty theft. The *zamindar* system was later adopted, with modifications, by the British when they ruled India.

Songhai

In the 1400s, the West African state of **Songhai** emerged to take power over the weakened Mali Empire. Its leader, Sunni Ali, consolidated his empire by appointing governors to oversee the provinces, building a large army, and creating an imperial navy to patrol the Niger River. The lucrative trans-Saharan trade flowed through the city of Gao, which brought salt, textiles, and metal in exchange for gold and slaves.

Songhai emperors were Muslims who supported the construction of mosques, schools, and an Islamic university at Timbuktu. Though Islam served as the cultural foundation of the empire and a key element in establishing cooperation with Muslim merchants, traditional African religious beliefs were not fully abandoned.

Just as Europeans were making inroads into Africa, the Songhai Empire began to lose control of its subjects. The empire went into decline and was defeated by the Moroccans in 1591, made easier by the use of firearms by the Moroccans.

Spanish and Portuguese Colonies in the New World

Spanish conquistadors led the way in the conquest of the Americas. The primary Spanish settlements, New Spain (Mexico) and New Castile (Peru), were each governed by a viceroy, who reported directly to the Spanish king. In 1494, the Treaty of Tordesillas, an agreement between Spain and Portugal based on an earlier decree by Pope Alexander VI, divided control of any future American territories: the Spanish controlled the land west of the agreed-upon line of demarcation, and the Portuguese controlled the territory east of the line.

Along with its goal of increasing wealth through the creation of an empire, Spain desired to expand the influence of Christianity. Catholic missionaries came to the Americas alongside the conquistadors and built mission churches to convert American Indians, many of whom adopted Christianity but blended it with their indigenous religions. For the most part, however, these Spanish missionaries forcibly imposed European culture on the natives.

The social result of the conquest of this new empire was a multicultural and ethnically mixed population. The *peninsulares*, the highest social class, came directly from the Iberian peninsula, and their American-born descendants were called **Creoles**. Those of mixed European and American Indian descent were called *mestizos*, and those with European and African ancestors were called *mulattos*. At the bottom of the social order were the American Indians, Africans, and the mixed class of *zambos*.

Qing Dynasty

By the 1640s, the Ming Dynasty had declined and been taken over by a peasant army, which established the short-lived Shun Dynasty. The **Manchu**, a community of hunters, fishermen, and farmers from the lands to the northeast of China, soon ousted the Shun and established the Qing Dynasty. Thus, China came under the rule of foreigners for the second time (the first being the Mongol-ruled Yuan Dynasty).

The Manchus established and expanded their rule through military conquest. Like Genghis Khan, who reorganized the Mongol army to diminish the importance of tribal allegiances, the Manchu leader Nurhaci created a large army consisting of units called banners, which were organized on a social basis. Each banner was comprised of a set of military companies, but also included the families and slaves of the soldiers. Banners were led by a hereditary captain, many of whom came from Nurhaci's own lineage. When the Manchu army defeated new groups, they were incorporated into several banners to decrease their potential for insubordination.

The Manchu had adopted elements of Chinese culture generations before the conquest. Unlike the Mongols, they incorporated traditional Chinese practices into government, including using the Confucian civil service exam system to fill government positions. Like the Mongols, however, the Manchu wanted to preserve their own ethnic and cultural identity. They forbade intermarriage between Manchu and Han Chinese, barred Chinese from traveling to Manchuria and learning their language, and forced Chinese men to wear their hair in a braid called a queue as a sign of submission.

The Qing Dynasty created a multiethnic empire that was larger than any earlier Chinese dynasty. It expanded into Taiwan in 1683, increased control of Mongolia throughout the 1690s, and established administrative oversight of Tibet in 1720. The final area to be annexed was Chinese Turkestan in the 1750s. The Manchus ruled Tibet and Turkestan relatively leniently. Local religious leaders, such as the Dalai Lama in Tibet, were allowed to remain in place, and men were not forced to wear the queue. By this time, the expanding Qing and Russian empires were nearing each other, which resulted in Manchu and Russian leaders approving the 1689 Treaty of Nerchinsk, which defined borders and regulated trade.

Russian Empire

After hundreds of years under Mongol tributary rule, Russia emerged as an empire in its own right. The Mongols had forced the Russian princes to submit to their rule and provide them with tribute and slaves. Russian princes collected the khan's taxes and suppressed uprisings, gaining power in the process. Eventually, the Muscovite princes were able to defeat their rivals for power. Ivan III, a grand prince of Moscow, stopped paying tribute to the Mongols and in 1480 began building his own empire. He established a strong central government and ruled as an absolute monarch, a tsar, who was also the head of the Russian Orthodox Church. The tsar claimed that his authority to rule came directly from God. After a series of Muscovite princes, the Romanov family came to power in 1613 and ruled Russia for the next 300 years.

Peter the Great, who reigned from 1682 to 1725, was fascinated with Western technology and instituted a policy of rapid modernization. Needing skilled technicians and industrial experts to carry out his modernization plans, he established schools to produce them. He greatly reformed the military by strengthening the navy and introducing a system of ranks. Peter created an interlocking military-civilian bureaucracy composed of 14 hierarchical ranks which functioned as a quasi-meritocracy; Russian nobles (boyars) started at the bottommost rank and rose up through service to the tsar. Catherine the Great later reformed the system to make promotion automatic after seven years, resulting in the bureaucracy shifting from those striving on merit to those serving out their time. Peter's obsession with westernizing Russia was best demonstrated by his insistence that all Russian men wear Western clothes and shave their beards, imposing heavy taxes on those who refused to comply. His construction of a new capital city, St. Petersburg, provided better access to the West.

> ✔ **AP Expert Note**
>
> **Be sure to know how major countries are categorized geographically**
>
> AP World History: Modern defines the world in five major geographical regions (Africa, the Americas, Asia, Europe, and Oceania) as well as several subregions. Understanding the terminology of the official regions and subregions will help avoid potential confusion on exam questions and prompts. For example, you'll want to know that, for this AP exam, Russia is considered an Asian country, not a European one.

Japan: Tokugawa Shogunate

Tokugawa Ieyasu established the **Tokugawa shogunate** in 1600, after a period of civil war that began in 1467. Fighting had broken out among various *daimyo* (warlords) over succession of the *shogun*, the supreme military leader of Japan. Ieyasu hoped to stabilize the country and end the unrest by increasing his control over the *daimyo*. He required that they spend every other year at the capital, Edo (now Tokyo), where he could more easily monitor them and prevent rebellion.

Relationships with the outside world became closely controlled. Japanese were forbidden from going abroad and from constructing large ships. Europeans were expelled from Japan, and foreign merchants were not allowed to trade in Japanese ports—the only exception was a small number of Chinese and Dutch ships. Despite all these restrictions, the Japanese economy grew, as agricultural production increased and the population grew. In this comparatively peaceful era, the samurai warrior class took on more administrative responsibilities.

Catholicism had made some important inroads in Japan by 1580, with over a hundred thousand Japanese converts, but the government ended these missions and outlawed the religion. The government even went as far as to torture and execute the missionaries who did not leave, as well as the Japanese Catholics who did not renounce their religion. Dutch merchants continued to be the principal source of information about Europe during this time, keeping the Japanese up-to-date with important scientific and technological developments. Knowledge gleaned from the Dutch became termed "Dutch learning" in Japan.

State Conservation of the Environment

This era saw an early awareness of resource conservation. The Tokugawa shogunate's laws restricted timbering operations and mandated that new trees be planted when old ones were cut. Louis XIV's forestry program was intended to manage France's timber resources. Although these programs were economically motivated, the idea that a nation's natural resources be managed by the government would play an important role in the development of environmental management programs in the future. These programs also signaled the growth of state power.

SYSTEMS OF FORCED LABOR

High-Yield

In the New World, burgeoning colonial enterprises relied on various forms of forced or indentured labor to drive lucrative agricultural economies. In the Old World, ancient systems of forced labor persisted in certain places.

Atlantic Slave Trade

Slavery had existed in Africa since ancient times; tribes often took prisoners from neighboring tribes and enslaved them. Many African societies did not recognize private land ownership, so land did not equal wealth in the way that owning slaves did. The spread of Islam established new trade routes across the northern part of the African continent, bringing African slaves to the Middle East as well.

By the time Europeans ventured into sub-Saharan Africa, the slave trade had been well-established on the continent for 500 years. The Portuguese explored the west coast of Africa in the 1500s and began exporting slaves to plantations in Brazil. The slave trade had become transoceanic, and profits from it encouraged other European powers to enter the business.

The forced migration of over 15 million Africans to the New World was one of the most significant components of the Columbian Exchange. By the mid 1600s, thousands of slaves were brought across the ocean each month. This trans-Atlantic journey, known as the Middle Passage, consisted of a four-to six-week trip belowdecks in overcrowded ships. The death toll en route was considerable, with as many as half the enslaved Africans on any one ship dying from disease or brutal mistreatment. Most African slaves were sent to Brazil or sugar plantations in the Caribbean. The **triangular trade** that developed sent European manufactured goods (firearms, in particular) to Africa in exchange for slaves, slaves to the Caribbean and American mainland, and American products back to Europe. Indeed, the Atlantic slave trade and the institution of slavery had an enormous impact on the economies of the Portuguese and Spanish colonies of South America as well as on the Dutch, French, and British colonies of the Caribbean and North America. The labor of enslaved Africans produced huge profits in the extraction of gold and silver from mines, as well as in the production of cash crops such as sugar, cotton, rice, and tobacco.

As more slaves were brought to the coast, African kingdoms reoriented their economies to trade with the Europeans. Some African societies benefited economically from the trade, but several experienced severe population loss and a drastic change in male-female ratio. Also, because many slaves were traded for guns, the addition of firearms led to an increase in violent political conflict in Africa. Though many of the enslaved Africans were Christianized by the Europeans, they retained parts of their language and culture. A unique cultural synthesis occurred, as African music, dress, and mannerisms mixed with Spanish and indigenous cultures in the Americas.

Encomienda System

The early Spanish settlers in the Caribbean needed to recruit a great deal of labor. The *encomienda* system established by the Spanish crown granted colonists the right to demand labor of native peoples in the mines and fields. The laborers were worked hard and punished severely.

Conquistadors like Hernán Cortés and Francisco Pizarro brought this system to the Americas. On the *haciendas* (large estates), natives were often abused; as a result, Spanish officials replaced the *encomienda* system with the *repartimiento* system. *Repartimiento* compelled native communities to supply labor for Spanish mines and farms as *encomienda* had, but it limited work time and mandated that wages be paid to native workers. Many communities, however, were required to send large groups of laborers to work on state projects. In Peru, for instance, the labor system called *mita* mobilized thousands of natives to work in the silver mines. They were paid wages, but there were also many abuses. The *mita* system had disastrous impacts on the indigenous populations of Peru, as it drained them of able-bodied workers at a time when their communities were experiencing huge population losses due to epidemics of Old World diseases. It also led to indigenous people fleeing their communities to avoid being compelled into service. With fewer workers able to work the fields, agricultural production decreased, leading to famine and malnutrition. The demise of these systems led to the establishment of the Atlantic slave trade and widespread use of slave labor in the Americas.

Russian Serfdom

After the Mongol rule of Russia, many free peasants fell into great debt and were forced to become serfs on large estates; serfs were legally bound to the land they worked, with extensive obligations owed to their landlords. The Russian government encouraged this process beginning in the 1500s as a way to satisfy nobility and regulate peasants at the same time. As new territories were added to the empire, serfdom extended along with it.

In 1649, an act proclaimed that serfs were born into their status, with no mechanism by which they could become free. While serfs were not technically slaves, noble landowners had nearly unlimited control of them. This state would largely persist into the twentieth century.

INTELLECTUAL CHANGES

European Renaissance

In the early fifteenth century, beginning on the Italian peninsula, new ways of thinking about the nature of humanity and the world emerged. The Crusades had brought southern Europe into contact with the Arab world, increasing international contact and trade. Scholars uncovered long-lost Roman and Greek literature that had been preserved by Islamic scholars. In reference to this reemergence of ancient knowledge, this intellectual revival became known as the Renaissance, or rebirth. Hallmarks of the Renaissance include: a new view of man as a creative, rational being; a rediscovery of ancient Greco-Roman knowledge; unparalleled accomplishments in literature, music, and art; as well as a celebration of the human individual.

Renaissance Italy was a patchwork of feudal domains, with lands belonging to the Roman Catholic Church, kingdoms, and city-states. Famous noble families such as the Medicis had grown wealthy as merchants, since Italy was ideally located for receiving goods from the Middle East and Asia along Mediterranean trade routes. This lucrative trade with the Islamic and Byzantine cultures allowed wealthy Italians to become patrons of painters, sculptors, and scientists. The period was also a celebration of the Roman past; classical architecture and engineering were reexamined and relearned.

Perhaps the single most important technological and cultural development of the Renaissance was the printing revolution. In 1456, Johann Gutenberg of Germany printed a complete edition of the Bible using the first **printing press** in the West (the Chinese had been using movable type for centuries). This printing revolution brought enormous changes to Europe. Printed books were less expensive and easier to read than copied manuscripts. The increase in the availability of books led to a rapid rise in literacy. European readers gained access to a wide range of knowledge on subjects including medicine, law, mathematics, and philosophy. Along with helping to spread classical knowledge and Renaissance ideas, these new printing presses helped fuel a European religious upheaval during the 1500s: the Protestant Reformation.

Protestant Reformation

Just as the Renaissance inspired an era of exploration, it also created an atmosphere that encouraged debate and criticism of the existing order. The most powerful institution of the day was the Catholic Church, headquartered in Rome. It had held great power over kings and peasants alike for centuries, and it had grown large, wealthy, and corrupt. Practices such as selling forgiveness and salvation began to offend even those in the priesthood.

A movement to reform the Church grew out of these concerns. In 1517, in the German domain of Wittenburg, a then-obscure priest named Martin Luther posted a list of issues that he believed the Church should address. The main issues raised by the **Protestant Reformation** were:

- Divisions within the papacy, in which more than one pope claimed authority ("antipopes")

- Religious traditions and rituals that were not derived from the scriptures (such as purgatory, pilgrimages, and worship of the saints)

- Corrupt practices such as the sale of religious relics and indulgences (forgiveness)

- Mismanagement of Church finances

- Lack of piety in the priesthood

Martin Luther and his fellow reformers unleashed a storm of controversy that eventually split the Catholic Church and divided Europe. Luther was excommunicated from the Church but gained the sympathy of German princes who adhered to his version of Christianity. At the time, German lands were divided into hundreds of small kingdoms and ruled by the Holy Roman Emperor, in this case Charles V of Spain, a staunch Catholic. Many of the northern German princes resented having to support both the Church and a non-German emperor. The German kingdoms became divided into two armed camps: Catholics siding with the Church and Protestants siding with Luther. The resulting conflict devastated German lands, but ended in a treaty (the Peace of Augsburg, 1555) that enabled each prince to decide which religion—Catholic or Lutheran—would be the religion of his domain. Most states in northern Germany chose Lutheranism, while the south remained largely Catholic. This was the doctrine of *Cuius regio, eius religio* ("whose realm, his religion").

The Protestant movement spread from central Europe to the Netherlands, Switzerland, France, and Denmark. The English King Henry VIII, once a strong supporter of the Catholic Church, fell away from the Church after a dispute with the pope regarding his marriage. With the help of Parliament, he created the Church of England, of which the English monarch became the head.

The Thirty Years' War

High-Yield

The religious upheavals of the Protestant Reformation came to a violent conclusion with the Thirty Years' War. The Peace of Augsburg had not resolved the religious tensions between Catholicism and Lutheranism, nor did it account for the rise of other Protestant denominations like Calvinism. Spain sought to expand its hold over the Netherlands into the German states. France likewise sought influence in Germany, and the Catholic kingdom found itself backing Protestant German states. Northern European counties like Sweden sought control over the Baltic Sea.

The result, from 1618 to 1648, was a war that devastated Central Europe and Italy. The Thirty Years' War ranks among the worst catastrophes in European history. Half the male population of Germany died. The Czechs lost a third of their prewar population. Geopolitically, the map of Europe was rewritten. Spain lost control of Portugal and the Netherlands. France enjoyed an upswing in its geopolitical power. The **Peace of Westphalia** in 1648, which ended the war, is notable for establishing the foundation of the modern nation-state. The ruler of a given state was now paramount, with any other religious or secular authority not able to claim control over the people of that state. The widespread, horrific actions taken by mercenary armies during the war, as well as the strengthening of central state authority during and after the war, led to European states favoring professional national armies over mercenaries. The Thirty Years' War was also the last major religious war in continental Europe.

Sunni-Shi'a Split Widens

The Safavid Dynasty was critical in Shi'a Islam becoming the majority religion of present-day Iran. This state-sponsored conversion campaign took place over the sixteenth through eighteenth centuries and resulted in hostilities between Shiites and Sunnis, as centuries of partial accommodation for divergent beliefs in Persia were discarded in favor of state-sponsored conversion. This occasionally brutal process resulted in a great deal of ill-will from Sunnis and contributed to the long-running conflict between Iran (then Persia) and the Ottomans, even after the downfall of the Safavid Dynasty.

While the two major denominations of Islam had existed since the seventh century, the gulf between them widened in this period due to the Ottoman-Iranian Wars. These wars were a series of conflicts that took place between the sixteenth and nineteenth centuries. Not only did the two empires fight over regional power and control of territory, but the conflict was also intensified because the Ottomans were Sunni and the Safavids were Shi'a. In historical terms, the intersection of sectarianism and geopolitics in Ottoman-Safavid tensions is comparable to present-day Saudi-Iranian tensions.

This sectarian division also helped foster odd alliances, as the Safavids sought Christian European aid against a common Ottoman foe, and European powers could rely on the sectarian divide to align the Safavids against their fellow Islamic power. A formal Habsburg-Persian alliance was attempted but existed more as a matter of circumstance than a legally binding agreement. Later Safavid missions to various European courts around the turn of the seventeenth century led to agreements with Britain, and in the eighteenth century diplomatic relations were opened with the French.

The Treaty of Zuhab, signed in 1639, fixed the borders between the Safavid and Ottoman empires, which persist as the present-day Iran-Iraq and Iran-Turkey borders. After 1639, the two empires would not go to war again until 1730.

> ✔ **AP Expert Note**
>
> **Be aware of the complexity of religious wars**
>
> Religious wars are rarely just about theological disputes; typically, they have political and economic dimensions as well. Despite being a Catholic state, France supported Protestant German states in the Thirty Years' War in order to advance its own geopolitical interests. Likewise, while the Sunni-Shi'a split prompted conflicts between the Ottoman and Safavid empires, those two powers also peacefully coexisted for long stretches of time. When examining the impact of religion on world affairs, be sure to consider other factors that might also have had an influence.

Foundation of Sikhism

In the north of the Indian subcontinent, Guru Nanak (1469–1539) founded Sikhism around the the turn of the sixteenth century. Born to Hindu parents of the merchant caste, he is reputed by Sikh tradition to have traveled extensively. Nanak's declaration that "There is no Muslim, and there is no Hindu" captures the essence of Sikhism. An example of syncretism, it bridges Hinduism and Islam, incorporating beliefs from both while maintaining an anti-sectarian stance.

Sikhism would be led by a series of gurus, who would modify its practices. For example, priestesses would be allowed, divorce legalized, and both veils and *sati* banned. Initially a pacifistic faith, it would grow militant in response to violent prosecution under the Mughal Empire from the mid-sixteenth century onward, culminating in the founding of the Sikh Empire (1799–1849). However, Sikhism would maintain its focus on social justice.

SCIENTIFIC REVOLUTION

The Enlightenment

Two English political thinkers, Thomas Hobbes and John Locke, lived through the horrors of the English Civil War. Despite this shared experience, each man came to strikingly different conclusions about human nature and the proper form of government. Their ideas provided the philosophical foundation for the Enlightenment.

Locke believed in self-government. According to Locke, people possess natural rights to life, liberty, and property, and government's purpose is to protect these rights. If government fails at this job,

Locke reasoned, the people had the right to overthrow it. This notion later inspired revolutionary thought in Europe and the Americas.

Hobbes, by contrast, believed a strong ruler was the foundation of any social order. Anything less led to destructive chaos. Unlike Locke, who argued natural rights were intrinsic to humanity, the Hobbesian position was that rights exist because of the state. Only through a strong ruler and the willing submission of the people to the laws of that ruler can rights exist. Otherwise humans enjoyed no rights or freedoms.

Though it started in England with the work of Hobbes, Locke, and the publication of Isaac Newton's *Principia Mathematica* in 1687, the Enlightenment was centered in Paris, where it reached its peak in the mid 1700s. There, intellectuals called *philosophes* gathered to discuss politics and ideas. The *philosophes* believed that reason (one of their primary areas of interest, along with nature, happiness, progress, and liberty) could be applied to both human relationships and the natural world. The Enlightenment emphasis on free thought led to the questioning of traditional authority. Both the Church and the monarchy were challenged, and the political radicalism of the Enlightenment caused great anxiety in the courts of Europe.

However, the Catholic and Protestant churches were not necessarily wholly uninvolved with the development of the Enlightenment. For example, as a result of the Roman Catholic mission to China, Jesuits brought back Chinese knowledge to Europe. The Confucian civil service exams influenced European rulers, and the rational morality of Confucianism appealed to Enlightenment philosophers.

Scientific Revolution

The development of modern science and Enlightenment philosophical ideals had a tremendous impact on the development of the modern world and the modern mentality. Prior to 1500, scholars relied mostly on classical texts and the Bible to answer questions about the natural world. The **Scientific Revolution** began as scientists challenged conventional ideas and used observation to understand the structure and composition of the universe. The Polish cleric and astronomer Nicolaus Copernicus paved the way for modern astronomy when he put forth a heliocentric theory of the universe in 1543, contradicting the Church's belief in an Earth-centered universe. Building on this revolutionary discovery, the Italian scientist Galileo Galilei constructed his own telescope in 1609 and used it to develop new theories about the universe. His findings angered both Catholic and Protestant leaders because they challenged Biblical accounts and the authority of the Christian churches. In fact, Galileo was put on trial before the Inquisition and forced to read a signed confession in which he stated that his ideas were false.

The Scientific Revolution led to the development of the scientific method, a logic-based approach to testing hypotheses through observation and experimentation. Use of the scientific method led to significant advances in the fields of physics, biology, medicine, and chemistry, as well as to the development of the social sciences in the late nineteenth century.

PRACTICE SET

Questions 1–3 refer to the image below.

FAUSTO ZONARO, *SULTAN MEHMED II'S ENTRY INTO CONSTANTINOPLE*

1. The painting is best seen as foreshadowing which of the following events from the fifteenth century?

    (A) The end of the Orthodox Church in Eurasia

    (B) The defeat of the Christian-controlled Byzantine Empire

    (C) The introduction of Shi'a Islam to Eurasia

    (D) The Ottoman Empire's military control of Western Europe

2. Which of the following factors contributed most directly to the Ottoman Empire's ability to conquer new territory?

    (A) Access to cannons and gunpowder weapons

    (B) Superior seafaring and navigational technology

    (C) Its ability to launch surprise attacks

    (D) The disunity between Roman Catholic and Eastern Orthodox churches

8

3. The painting best illustrates which of the following political processes in the period circa 1300 to 1600?

   (A) The emergence of Islam's influence in the Arabian Peninsula

   (B) The Ottoman Empire's focus on creating new city-states

   (C) The ongoing fragmentation of Muslim states

   (D) Sunni Muslim rule expanding into parts of Afro-Eurasia

Questions 4–6 refer to the passage below.

"Papal indulgences for the building of St. Peter's are circulating under your most distinguished name . . . the unhappy souls believe that if they have purchased letters of indulgence they are sure of their salvation; again, that so soon as they cast their contributions into the money-box, souls fly out of purgatory. . . . Works of piety and love are infinitely better than indulgences, and yet these are not preached with such ceremony or such zeal; nay, for the sake of preaching the indulgences they are kept quiet, though it is the first and the sole duty of all bishops that the people should learn the Gospel and the love of Christ, for Christ never taught that indulgences should be preached."

Martin Luther, "Letter to the Archbishop of Mainz," 1517

4. In his letter, Martin Luther is most strongly criticizing which of the following?

   (A) The use of money to build St. Peter's church

   (B) The bishops' interpretation of the Gospel

   (C) The Church's failure to sell indulgences for a fair price

   (D) The promise of salvation through indulgences

5. Based on the passage and your knowledge of world history, which of the following best describes Luther's views?

   (A) Individual believers should be guided more by faith in the Bible than by papal authority.

   (B) Preachers and bishops generally have the highest degree of knowledge on religious matters.

   (C) Neither the Catholic Church nor the Gospel should be considered a primary authority on religious and spiritual matters.

   (D) The Catholic Church should be equal to the state so that Christianity can spread throughout Europe and beyond.

6. Which of the following emerged in Western Europe in the sixteenth century in large part as a reaction to the ideas advocated in the passage?

   (A) King Henry VIII established the Church of England.

   (B) The Holy Roman Empire came to an end.

   (C) Protestantism became the main religion in France.

   (D) The Renaissance was ignited as a major intellectual and artistic movement.

Questions 7–10 refer to the passage below.

"This spring, also, those Indians that lived about their trading house there fell sick of the small poxe, and dyed most miserably; for a sorer disease cannot befall them; they fear it more than the plague; for usually they that have this disease have them in abundance. . . . The condition of this people was so lamentable, and they fell down so generally of this disease, as they were (in the end) not able to help one another; no, not to make a fire, nor to fetch a little water to drink, nor any to bury the dead. . . . But those of the English house, (though at first they were afraid of the infection) yet seeing their woeful and sad condition, and hearing their pitiful cries and lamentations, they had compassion on them, and daily fetched them wood & water, and made them fires, got them victuals whilst they lived, and buried them when they died. For very few of them escaped, notwithstanding they did what they could for them, to the hazard of themselves. The chief Sachem himself now died, & almost all his friends & kindred. But by the marvelous goodness & providence of God not one of the English was so much as sicke, or in the least measure tainted with this disease, though they daily did these offices for them for many weeks together."

William Bradford, *Of Plimoth Plantation,* 1630–1651

7. The passage describes a direct consequence of which of the following?

    (A) The consequences of forced labor in the Americas

    (B) The spreading of disease from the Americas to Europe

    (C) European settlement of territory in the Americas

    (D) Changes in population settlement patterns in the Americas

8. Which of the following agricultural products best represents what indigenous populations primarily raised before the Europeans arrived?

    (A) Bananas and sugarcane

    (B) Wheat and barley

    (C) Beans and squash

    (D) Pigs and cattle

9. Events like those described in the passage most directly led to which of the following labor systems in the Spanish colonies?

    (A) The African slave trade

    (B) The *mita* system

    (C) *Encomienda*

    (D) *Repartimiento*

10. The passage can best be used as direct evidence for which of the following world trends that took place circa 1450 to 1750?

    (A) Global trade networks facilitated the spread of religion.

    (B) The Little Ice Age caused agricultural production to undergo a worldwide decline.

    (C) Economic growth increasingly depended on new forms of manufacturing.

    (D) Trade networks facilitated the exchange of plants, animals, and pathogens.

Questions 11–14 refer to the passage below.

"Until 1700 the national life had remained thoroughly harmonious . . . to his homogenous way of living and regarding things, this uniform roughness and want of culture, an end was put almost at one blow. The nobility whom Peter had forced out of their musings and dreamings . . . into his service—grades in that service and rank went before all privileges of birth—laid aside its native garbs, habits, and language, associated with foreigners, travelled about abroad for years . . . the women deserted the gloomy cells, put on French clothing, learned to dance and play. . . . The old capital of the country was formally deprived of its rights in favour of the new one on the sea."

Aleksandr Brückner, *Literary History of Russia*, 1910

11. According to the passage, Peter the Great implemented reforms that most clearly reflected the principles of a

    (A) merit-based government

    (B) civilian-controlled government

    (C) military-controlled government

    (D) democracy-based government

12. Based on the passage, which of the following could best be inferred about Russia under Peter the Great?

    (A) Russia lacked a sense of culture before Peter's reforms.

    (B) The nobility had long sought to found a new capital near the sea.

    (C) Associating with foreigners was a new concept for most Russians.

    (D) Rejecting isolationism was a key part of Peter's foreign policy.

13. Which of the following describes an accurate similarity between the Russian Empire under Peter the Great and Japan under the Tokugawa shogunate?

    (A) Both successfully resisted trade with the West.

    (B) Both heavily influenced the cultural norms of their people.

    (C) Both accepted and promoted Western European culture.

    (D) Both were expansive land-based empires.

14. The House of Romanov to which Peter the Great belonged would continue to rule Russia until

    (A) the end of the reign of Catherine the Great

    (B) the end of the Crimean War

    (C) the abdication of Tsar Nicholas II

    (D) Joseph Stalin came to power

Questions 15–18 refer to the passage below.

"As trade enrich'd the citizens in England, so it contributed to their Freedom, and this Freedom on the other side extended their Commerce, whence arose the grandeur of the State. Trade rais'd by insensible degrees the naval Power, which gives the English a Superiority over the Seas, and they now are Masters of very near two hundred Ships of War. Posterity will very possibly be surpriz'd to hear that an Island whose only produce is a little Lead, Tin, Fuller's Earth, and Coarse Wool, should become so powerful by its Commerce, as to be able to send, in 1723, three Fleets at the same time to three different and far distanc'd Parts of the Globe."

Voltaire, a French philosopher, "Letters on the English," 1734

15. The passage can best be understood in the context of which of the following in the period from 1450 to 1750?

   (A) The inability of the French to engage in maritime trade in Africa and Asia

   (B) European states establishing trading-post empires in Africa and Asia

   (C) England establishing a large land-based empire along the Indian Ocean region

   (D) England being the only country with a joint-stock company to finance maritime trade

16. Based on the passage and your understanding of world history, which of the following would the English have most likely imported from the Indian Ocean region during the eighteenth century?

   (A) Tea and spices

   (B) Wool, lead, and tin

   (C) Silver and gold

   (D) Manufactured goods

17. By sending fleets to engage in trade throughout the Indian Ocean region, England was able to

   (A) stop exporting manufactured goods and raw ores such as tin and lead

   (B) import much needed tin and lead via the Indian Ocean trade routes

   (C) control the spice trade in the East Indies

   (D) partially bypass trade routes through the Islamic world

18. Along with the British, which other European power made significant use of commercial trading companies to pursue trade in the Indian Ocean region?

   (A) The Dutch

   (B) The French

   (C) The Spanish

   (D) The Portuguese

Questions 19–21 refer to the image below.

MAP OF THE QING EMPIRE, 1820

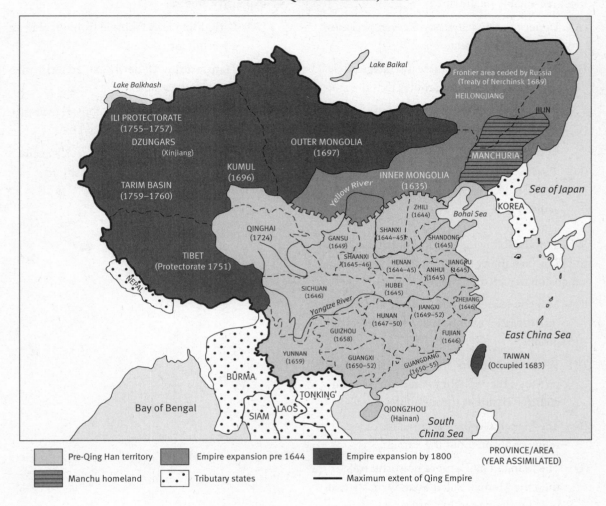

Legend:
- Pre-Qing Han territory
- Manchu homeland
- Empire expansion pre 1644
- Tributary states
- Empire expansion by 1800
- Maximum extent of Qing Empire

PROVINCE/AREA
(YEAR ASSIMILATED)

Map labels:
- Lake Baikal
- Lake Balkhash
- Frontier area ceded by Russia (Treaty of Nerchinsk 1689)
- HEILONGJIANG
- ILI PROTECTORATE (1755–1757)
- DZUNGARS (Xinjiang)
- JILIN
- OUTER MONGOLIA (1697)
- KUMUL (1696)
- MANCHURIA
- TARIM BASIN (1759–1760)
- INNER MONGOLIA (1635)
- Sea of Japan
- Yellow River
- ZHILI (1644)
- KOREA
- QINGHAI (1724)
- GANSU (1649)
- SHANXI (1644–45)
- SHANDONG (1645)
- Bohai Sea
- TIBET (Protectorate 1751)
- SHAANXI (1645–46)
- HENAN (1644–45)
- ANHUI (1645)
- JIANGSU (1645)
- NEPAL
- SICHUAN (1646)
- HUBEI (1645)
- JIANGXI (1649–52)
- ZHEJIANG (1646)
- Yangtze River
- HUNAN (1647–50)
- East China Sea
- GUIZHOU (1658)
- FUJIAN (1646)
- YUNNAN (1659)
- GUANGXI (1650–52)
- GUANGDANG (1650–55)
- TAIWAN (Occupied 1683)
- BURMA
- TONKING'
- QIONGZHOU (Hainan)
- Bay of Bengal
- SIAM
- LAOS
- South China Sea

8

19. Based on the map and your knowledge of world history, which of the following conclusions can most reasonably be drawn?

    (A) Under the Qing Dynasty, Taiwan became an independent state.

    (B) The Manchu homeland was strategically located to access trade routes to India and the South China Sea.

    (C) The Qing Dynasty had no control in Outer Mongolia and Tibet.

    (D) The Russian Empire and the Qing Dynasty competed for territory in the seventeenth century

20. Which of the following factors contributed to the Manchu's ability to undertake the empire expansion depicted on the map?

    (A) Manchu leaders created a large army that incorporated members of newly defeated groups.

    (B) When the Manchu conquered Han Chinese territory, they sought to blend ethnic and cultural identities through intermarriage.

    (C) The Manchu forbade all practice of local religions throughout the empire.

    (D) The Manchu had a more powerful military than the Mongol-ruled Yuan Dynasty that previously reigned in China.

21. Which of the following represents one method that Manchu leaders used to help govern its expansive empire?

    (A) Forbidding Han Chinese from serving as government officials

    (B) Transforming all newly gained territories into tributary states

    (C) Exerting severe military control over protectorate territories such as Tibet

    (D) Using the Confucian civil service exam system to fill government positions

Questions 22–25 refer to the passage below.

"As I saw that they were very friendly to us, and perceived that they could be much more easily converted to our holy faith by gentle means than by force, I presented them with some red caps and strings of beads to wear upon the neck, and many other trifles of small value, wherewith they were much delighted and became greatly attached to us. Afterwards they came swimming to the boats, bringing parrots, balls of cotton thread, javelins, and many other things which they exchanged for glass beads and hawks' bells, which trade was carried on with the utmost good will. But they seemed on the whole a very poor people. They all were completely naked. All whom I saw were young, not above thirty years of age, well made and with fine shapes and faces; their hair short and coarse like that of a horse's tail, combed towards the forehead except a small portion which they suffer to hang down behind and never cut. Some paint themselves with black, others with white, others with red, others with such colors as they can find. Some paint the face, some the whole body. Others only the eyes, others only the nose.

Weapons they have none; nor are they acquainted with them. For I showed them swords which they grasped by the blades and cut themselves through ignorance. They have no iron, their javelins being without it, and nothing more than sticks with fishbones or other things at the ends. I saw some men with scars of wounds upon their bodies and inquired by signs the cause of these. They answered me by signs that other people came from islands in the neighborhood and tried to make prisoners of them and they defended themselves. . . . It appears to me that these people are ingenious and would make very good servants, and I am of the opinion that they would readily become Christians as they appear to have no religion. They very quickly learn such words as are spoken to them. If it please our Lord, I intend at my return to carry home six of them to your Highnesses that they may learn our language."

Christopher Columbus, 1492

22. Which of the following later developments is <u>not</u> prefigured within this passage?

(A) Traditional tribal economies altered in response to new trading opportunities.

(B) American Indian tribes waged wars seeking captives to build their communities.

(C) The Spanish caste system delineated specific roles for American Indians.

(D) American Indian populations declined due to disease.

23. Which of the following systems represented an attempt by the Spanish to reform the harsh treatment of American Indians working in mines and on plantations?

(A) The *encomienda* system

(B) The *repartimiento* system

(C) Debt servitude

(D) The Treaty of Tordesillas

8

24. Columbus's voyages most directly resulted in

   (A) the procurement of gold for European markets

   (B) other explorers ceasing to seek a Western passage to Asian waters

   (C) abundant opportunities for European entrepreneurs

   (D) diplomatic ties between European countries and Caribbean islands

25. Columbus's successful maritime exploration was made possible by

   (A) advances in nautical technology and navigational skills

   (B) support from the Portuguese monarchy

   (C) accurate nautical and geographical calculations

   (D) Ferdinand Magellan's voyages in the Pacific Ocean

ANSWER KEY

1. B	6. A	11. A	16. A	21. D
2. A	7. C	12. D	17. D	22. D
3. D	8. C	13. B	18. A	23. B
4. D	9. A	14. C	19. D	24. C
5. A	10. D	15. B	20. A	25. A

ANSWERS AND EXPLANATIONS

1. B

In 1453, the Ottomans conquered the city of Constantinople, which then led to the defeat of the Christian-controlled Byzantine Empire; **(B)** is correct. While the Orthodox Christian Church suffered a setback with the loss of the Byzantine Empire, which was located in Eurasia, this event did not represent the Church's downfall. In fact, the Ottoman Empire permitted the Church some autonomy. (A) is incorrect. The Ottoman Empire practiced the Sunni version of Islam, not the Shi'a version. Thus, (C) is incorrect. Though expansive in geographical reach, the Ottoman Empire did not control Western Europe. (D) is incorrect.

2. A

While the Ottomans did possess seafaring and navigational capabilities, their success was ultimately due to both their military might and access to gunpowder weapons such as cannons. Thus, **(A)** is correct and (B) is incorrect. Before attacking, the Ottomans repeatedly sought the surrender of the Christian-controlled Byzantine Empire. As such, they did not rely on surprise attacks; (C) is incorrect. While there was a long-standing hostility between the Roman Catholic and Eastern Orthodox churches, this is not a factor that directly contributed to the Ottoman Empire's success in conquering new territory; (D) is incorrect.

3. D

The painting depicts the entry of the Ottoman Empire into Constantinople, which was a Christian-controlled city in the Byzantine Empire. The Ottomans were Sunni Muslims who sought to build an expansive empire during this time period. Thus, **(D)** is correct. (A) is incorrect because the emergence of Islam's influence in the Arabian Peninsula occurred centuries before. (B) is incorrect because the Ottomans were not focused on creating city-states, which typically are small independent states; instead, the Ottomans sought to build an expansive land-based empire. (C) is incorrect because Muslim states, such as the Ottomans and Safavid (in Persia), were not undergoing fragmentation during the specified period. Instead, they were focused on building large, cohesive empires.

4. D

During the Renaissance era, the Catholic Church's practice of selling forgiveness and salvation started to offend many Christians, including Martin Luther. A reform movement, largely led by Luther, grew out of these and other concerns. **(D)** is correct. While Luther did criticize the Church's mismanagement of finances, he is not necessarily opposed to using money for the building of a church, making (A) incorrect. (B) is incorrect because Luther is most strongly criticizing the selling of indulgences in this passage, rather than the bishops' interpretation of the Gospel. (C) is incorrect because Luther is against any selling of indulgences, regardless of price.

5. A

Martin Luther and proponents of the Protestant Reformation encouraged people to read the Bible for themselves. Luther believed that divine salvation was obtained through an individual's faith rather than by papal or church authority. **(A)** is correct. While Luther did recognize that bishops and preachers were capable of vast knowledge on religious matters, he believed that anyone literate enough to read the Bible could obtain such a level of understanding, making (B) incorrect. While Luther was indeed taking issue with the Catholic Church, (C) is incorrect because Luther did believe the Gospel, which is part of the Bible, was authoritative. (D) is incorrect because Luther was criticizing the enormous power

8

of the Catholic Church, arguing that it had become too large and wealthy, leading it to corrupt practices.

6. A

The Protestant Reformation spread from Central Europe to the Netherlands, Switzerland, France, and Denmark. King Henry VIII of England, once a supporter of the Catholic Church, had a fierce disagreement with the Church regarding his marriage. With the help of the English Parliament, he founded the Church of England, which was created as a Protestant church. **(A)** is correct. The Holy Roman Empire did not end until the early nineteenth century; (B) is incorrect. While there were a significant number of Protestants in France, there were more Catholics. Thousands of members of the Protestant minority in France, called the Huguenots, were killed by the Catholics during this time period. Thus, (C) is incorrect. While the Renaissance was a major intellectual and artistic movement, its origins were much earlier, in the fourteenth century, making (D) incorrect.

7. C

One of the consequences of European settlement during the Columbian Exchange was the spread of disease to the Americas. As described in the passage, smallpox devastated native populations. Thus, **(C)** is correct and (B) is incorrect. (A) is incorrect because, while the forced labor systems in the Americas were often brutal, the passage specifically depicts the spread of disease. After the disease epidemic devastated native populations, there were changes in population settlement patterns of the natives. However, this did not cause the disease epidemic, making (D) incorrect.

8. C

Beans and squash were two of the most abundantly grown crops in the Americas, making **(C)** correct. The other plant crops—bananas, sugarcane, wheat, barley— were brought by the Europeans to cultivate in the Americas. (A) and (B) are thus incorrect. The Europeans also brought domesticated animals, such as pigs and cattle, to be raised in the Americas. (D) is incorrect.

9. A

The Columbian Exchange led to the spread of disease to the Americas, devastating native populations. Relying on dwindling native populations as a labor force became economically unsustainable, and African slaves were then brought in to meet the demand for labor. Thus, **(A)** is correct. (B)–(D) are incorrect because they refer to the forced

labor systems the Spanish used on indigenous populations; the systems were not the *result* of population decline due to disease. The first coerced labor system used by the Spanish was *encomienda*, which was a system of land grants that allowed colonists to exploit both the land and indigenous labor. After *encomienda* failed, it was replaced by another compulsory labor system called *repartimiento*, in which natives were given wages and their work time was limited. The *mita* system in Peru forced thousands to work in the silver mines. All of these forced labor systems involved grave abuses and caused many deaths.

10. D

The inclusion of the Americas in the global trade network led to what would be called the Columbian Exchange. While the exchange of food crops and animals revolutionized life around the world, the spread of disease to the Americas greatly affected patterns of settlement and migration there over time. **(D)** is correct. Global trade networks did facilitate the spread of religion, but though God is mentioned in the passage, the spread of religion is not discussed, so (A) is incorrect. (B) is incorrect because, although Europe and North America experienced a colder climate than normal from about the sixteenth through nineteenth centuries, the passage is not describing the effects of this phenomenon. (C) is incorrect because the passage does not provide any evidence about new forms of manufacturing.

11. A

Peter the Great created an interlocking military-civilian bureaucracy composed of 14 hierarchical ranks which functioned as a meritocracy; even people from non-noble origins could rise through the ranks to positions of great authority. Thus, **(A)** is correct and (B) and (C) are incorrect. Peter the Great ruled Russia as an autocrat (a ruler with absolute power). As such, he did not support democracy, making (D) incorrect.

12. D

Peter was fascinated by the West and obsessed with westernizing Russia; as such, he rejected isolationism as a policy. The passage describes effects of this anti-isolationist approach, making **(D)** correct. While the passage describes how Russians adopted new cultural practices, it does not suggest that Russia lacked a sense of culture previously; (A) is incorrect. The passage indicates that a new capital was established, but it was Peter, not the nobility, who desired this; his construction of a new capital city,

St. Petersburg, provided better access to the West. (B) is incorrect. While the passage indicates that under Peter the Russians associated more and more with foreigners, there is no indication that this was entirely new for most Russians, so (C) is also incorrect.

13. B

In Russia under Peter the Great and Japan under the Tokugawa shogunate, the masses were required to follow certain social and cultural norms. Peter's obsession with westernizing Russia was best demonstrated by his insistence that all Russian men wear Western clothes and shave their beards, imposing heavy taxes on those who refused to comply. In Japan, the government did not permit the adoption of certain Western cultural practices. In particular, the practice of Christianity was forbidden. The government went as far as to torture and execute Christian missionaries as well as the Japanese Christians who did not renounce their religion. **(B)** is therefore correct. While Japan limited and highly controlled its trade with the West, it did have some commercial trade activity with the West. Russia also engaged in trade with Europe, making (A) incorrect. While Russia accepted and promoted Western European culture, Tokugawa Japan did not; (C) is incorrect. Russia was considered a large land-based empire under Peter, but Tokugawa Japan was not, making (D) incorrect.

14. C

The Romanov family came to power in 1613 and ruled for the next 300 years. It included both the reigns of Peter the Great and Catherine the Great, lasted well after the Crimean War (1853–1856), and ended with the abdication of Tsar Nicholas II, who was forced out of power by the Bolsheviks in 1917. **(C)** is correct and (A) and (B) are incorrect. Joseph Stalin did not lead Russia until the mid 1920s, several years after the fall of the House of Romanov; (D) is incorrect.

15. B

Voltaire writes that England had "become so powerful by its commerce, as to be able to send, in 1723, three fleets at the same time to three different and far distanced parts of the globe." As such, this passage can be best understood in the broader context of the English as well as the French, Dutch, Portuguese, and other Europeans establishing trading-post empires along the African coast and across the Indian Ocean region in Asia. Thus, **(B)** is correct and (A) incorrect. While England gained much control in Asia, especially in India, it did not establish a large land-based empire there; instead, it developed a maritime and trading-post empire; (C) is incorrect. (D) is incorrect because the Dutch set up the Dutch East India Company in the early seventeenth century, enabling them to develop a robust transoceanic trade network in Asia.

16. A

From the Indian Ocean region—and from India in particular—England imported tea, spices, and other goods that the English considered exotic. **(A)** is correct. It is stated in the passage that wool, lead, and tin are among the goods produced in England, so (B) is incorrect. Silver and gold were not imported by the English from Asia during this time period, making (C) incorrect. (D) is incorrect because England sought primarily to export, rather than import, manufactured goods to Asia and elsewhere.

17. D

Because the Ottoman Empire and others in the Islamic world came to control trade passageways through Eurasia and the Middle East, England and other Western European powers sought another way to access Asia. By developing its maritime trade capabilities throughout the Indian Ocean region, England was able to bypass these land-based trade routes, at least partly. **(D)** is correct. England never ceased exporting manufactured goods, making (A) incorrect. England had tin and lead, according to the passage, so it did not need to import them from Asia, making (B) incorrect. The Dutch controlled much of the spice trade in the East Indies, making (C) incorrect.

18. A

Unlike Spain and Portugal, whose royal governments financed their expeditions, the British and the Dutch relied heavily on commercial trading companies called joint-stock companies, in which prosperous investors—not the crown—funded the expeditions. The Dutch East India Company controlled much of the trade in Indonesia, and the British East India Company set up trading posts in India. Thus, **(A)** is correct, while (C) and (D) are incorrect. While the French pursued trade in the Indian Ocean region, they relied on state support rather than joint-stock trading companies, making (B) incorrect.

19. D

In the seventeenth century, the expanding Qing and Russian empires were nearing each other, which resulted in Manchu and Russian leaders approving the 1689 Treaty of Nerchinsk, which defined borders and regulated trade.

(D) is correct. (A) is incorrect because Taiwan was under the control of the Qing Dynasty. (B) is incorrect because, as the map illustrates, the Manchu homeland was located in the northeast, a far distance from India and the South China Sea. (C) is incorrect because the Qing Dynasty did incorporate Outer Mongolia and Tibet into its empire.

20. A

The Manchus established and expanded their rule through military conquest. Like Genghis Khan, who reorganized the Mongol army to diminish the importance of tribal allegiances, the Manchu created a large army consisting of units called banners, which were organized on a social basis. When the Manchu army defeated new groups, they were incorporated into several banners to decrease their potential for insubordination. Thus, **(A)** is correct. (B) is incorrect because the Manchu wanted to preserve their own ethnic and cultural identity. They forbade intermarriage between Manchu and Han Chinese, barred Han Chinese from traveling to Manchuria and learning their language, and forced Han Chinese men to wear their hair in a braid called a queue as a sign of submission. While Manchu leaders limited the practice of Christianity, some local religious leaders such as the Dalai Lama in Tibet were allowed to remain in place, making (C) incorrect. (D) is incorrect because the Mongol-ruled Yuan Dynasty reigned well before the Manchu came to power in China.

21. D

To enhance its ability to govern China effectively, the Manchu incorporated traditional Chinese practices into their government, including using the Confucian civil service exam system to fill government positions; **(D)** is correct. (A) is incorrect because Han Chinese were allowed to participate in government. As illustrated by the map, (B) is incorrect because not all newly gained territories were classified as tributary states; some became part of the empire. (C) is incorrect because the Manchus ruled Tibet, Turkestan, and some of the annexed territories relatively leniently, exempting them from certain required cultural practices that the Han Chinese had to adopt.

22. D

Although American Indian populations did decrease due to diseases introduced by Spanish conquistadors and other Europeans, this result is not implied by the passage. So, **(D)** is correct. However, this passage does presage other consequences of the Columbian Exchange, such as describing trade with the American Indians that the expedition encountered; (A) is incorrect. The passage also mentions the American Indians' inter-tribal conflict, which would continue into the future; (B) is incorrect. Finally, the passage negatively appraises the worth of the American Indians when the narrator comments that they "would be good servants." This tone exemplifies Europeans' prejudice, which would manifest in the Spanish caste system; (C) is incorrect.

23. B

The *repartimiento* system promised American Indians fair wages for their labor, while the *encomienda* system required American Indians to work for the Spanish as a tribute. Unlike the earlier *encomienda* system, the *repartimiento* system was rarely enforced in practice, and unfair treatment by the Spanish continued until decolonization. Thus, **(B)** is correct and (A) is incorrect. Other forms of coerced labor, such as debt servitude, (C), and slavery, predominated in other colonies, such as the British North American colonies. (D) is incorrect because the Treaty of Tordesillas was the political agreement that divided the newly discovered Americas between Spain and Portugal in the late fifteenth century.

24. C

Columbus's voyages paved the way for the conquest, settlement, and exploitation of the Americas by European entrepreneurs, so **(C)** is correct. (A) is incorrect because Columbus obtained very little gold in the Caribbean. Particularly in the early sixteenth century, many explorers continued to look for a way to sail west to Asia, which makes (B) incorrect. (D) is incorrect because Europeans conquered indigenous peoples and exploited their resources, rather than forging diplomatic relationships.

25. A

Sturdy ships and reliable navigational equipment allowed mariners to make their way across the Atlantic Ocean and back again; thus, **(A)** is correct. It was the Spanish monarchy rather than the Portuguese court that paid for Columbus's expedition; (B) is incorrect. Columbus did not correctly calculate the distance between the Canary Islands and Japan; (C) is incorrect. Magellan sailed in the Pacific Ocean after Columbus sailed to the Americas; (D) is incorrect.

CHAPTER 9

1750 to 1900

REVOLUTIONS AND INDEPENDENCE MOVEMENTS

North America

From 1756 to 1763, the European powers fought the Seven Years' War. As it was fought on three continents—North America, Europe, and the Indian subcontinent—the Seven Years' War can be called the first global war. The North American theater became known as the French and Indian War. This is because the British and their colonists fought an alliance of the French and their Native American allies. Globally, the war proved disastrous for the French. They lost both their Canadian territories in North America and their trade influence in India.

Britain, in debt due to this costly war, enacted a series of laws aimed at raising tax revenues from its North American colonies. The British government felt justified in levying these taxes, as they felt the war had been partially waged in the interest of the colonists. American colonists, however, resented being taxed by a government in which they had no representation. The colonists railed against "taxation without representation" and increasingly wished to govern themselves. Tensions escalated. After the Boston Tea Party, the British government retaliated against Massachusetts by passing the Intolerable Acts, which essentially took away its ability to self-govern. This outraged the other American colonies and led to the formation of the First Continental Congress in 1774.

The Continental Congress organized and coordinated colonial resistance. In 1775, British troops and American militia clashed at Lexington, Massachusetts. On July 4, 1776, the Declaration of Independence—inspired by **Enlightenment** ideas—justified independence. It listed a long list of abuses by the British crown and declared that all men were created equal. Though the British forces possessed many advantages, such as a strong centralized government, stronger military, and colonial loyalists, they were ultimately at a disadvantage. This was due to the war being fought on American soil and to the foreign support the Americans received, most notably from France. In 1781, the **American Revolution** ended with the British surrender at Yorktown to George Washington.

> ✔ **AP Expert Note**
>
> ### Be able to explain how different wars interconnect
>
> The American Revolution wasn't fought in isolation; you can trace its origin to the Seven Years' War. The foreign support offered to the Continental Congress during the American Revolution served as a means for those nations to undermine their rival, Great Britain. Similarly, the debt that France acquired in order to give aid to the United States would later be a major factor contributing to the French Revolution and the subsequent Napoleonic Wars.

In 1783, the Peace of Paris formally recognized American independence. The colonies created a federal republic with 13 states and a written constitution that guaranteed freedom of speech and religion. In reality, only white male property owners enjoyed full rights. Women, landless men, slaves, and indigenous people did not have access to this new freedom. Yet the U.S. Constitution was still an important step in the development of a republic responsible to its people through democratic means.

France

High-Yield

Unlike Americans, who sought independence from British colonial rule, French revolutionaries wanted to replace the existing monarchy and political structure—called the *Ancien Régime*—with a more democratic republic. In order to understand the **French Revolution**, it is important to first understand the social structure of Revolutionary-era France. Society was divided into three classes, or estates. The First Estate was the clergy, the Second Estate was the nobility, and the Third Estate was everyone else. This third class was mostly led by the *bourgeoisie*, which is roughly equivalent to the modern-day middle class. As evidenced by the chart below, the clergy and nobility controlled nearly all the political power.

Estate	Political Leaders	Numbers	% of Population	% of Land Ownership	Taxes Paid
1st Estate	Roman Catholic Clergy	100,000	<1% of pop	10% of land	No taxes
2nd Estate	Nobility	400,000	2% of pop	20% of land	No taxes
3rd Estate	Peasants, townsfolk, merchants	24 million	98% of pop	70% of land	Extensive taxes

Revolutionary sentiment brewed among the Third Estate, inspired by the nobles' refusal to pay taxes, *bourgeois* resentment of the monarchy's power, the incompetence of Louis XVI, entrenched poverty among the peasantry, grain shortages, and the success of the American Revolution.

The Estates General convened in May 1789, the first time it had done so since 1614. However, a dispute over voting created an impasse from the start. Traditionally, each estate met and voted separately. The result from each estate was weighted equally, meaning that the First and Second estates always outvoted the Third Estate 2:1. This time, the Third Estate wanted all the estates to meet as one body and votes to be counted per delegate head. This would make the Third Estate the driving force in politics. After weeks of deadlock, the Third Estate, claiming to represent the interests of all French people, unilaterally declared itself the National Assembly.

Spurred on by the peasants storming the Bastille, a fortress in Paris which symbolized the monarchy, the National Assembly began issuing reforms. These included ending the privileged status of nobles, abolishing feudalism, and issuing the landmark Declaration of the Rights of Man and of the Citizen. The latter, like the Declaration of Independence, reflected Enlightenment-era political ideals. In 1791, the Assembly produced a new constitution that replaced the absolute monarchy with a limited monarchy. However, these reforms were both not enough for French radicals and too much for conservative monarchists. Backed by Paris crowds, the radicals took control of the Assembly and eventually beheaded the king.

The Committee for Public Safety, formed by the extremist Jacobins and led by Maximilien Robespierre, now governed France. It instigated a radical Reign of Terror, executing many aristocrats, dissidents, and critics of the committee. Eventually, the Jacobins were deposed in the Thermidorian Reaction. Napoleon Bonaparte took advantage of the eventual power vacuum in a coup. Later, he named himself First Consul, then Consul for Life, and finally Emperor. In 1804, Napoleon issued his Civil Code, which affirmed the political and legal equality of all adult men, established a merit-based society, and protected private property. However, it also limited free speech and allowed censorship of the newspapers.

Napoleon and his army rapidly defeated many of the European powers and took control of much of the continent. The Napoleonic era lasted from 1803 to 1814, as warfare ranged from Europe to North Africa and the Middle East. At times, France found itself faced with multiple enemies. Taking on Russia in 1812 proved fatal, however, as the army did not survive the winter campaign. A White Terror ensued in France—so called because white was associated with royalists—as the restored monarchy of Louis XVIII imprisoned or killed many associated with Napoleon and the republic. The powers which had defeated Napoleon met at the Congress of Vienna in 1815 to set the terms for a new global balance of power.

The downfall of Napoleonic France left the British Empire as the most powerful state in the international system. From 1815 until the outbreak of World War I in 1914, the *Pax Britannica* period saw British power and influence spread to almost every corner of the globe. Only the Russian Empire rivaled it, and then only in regional terms. This led to conflicts such as the Crimean War and the "Great Game" in Central Asia, and later the Anglo-Japanese Alliance (1902–1923) to contain Russian influence.

> ✔ **AP Expert Note**
>
> ### Be sure to understand the role of anticlericalism
>
> Anticlericalism is opposition to religious authority. Historically, it is associated with opposition to the Roman Catholic Church, although it can be used to refer to opposition to any religious entity. Anticlericalism is a recurring theme throughout many revolutions. Be sure to consider how the relationship between government and religious institutions might influence anticlerical groups to support political revolutions.

Haiti

By the end of the eighteenth century, the Caribbean island of Hispaniola had become a major center of sugar production. The Spanish controlled the east (Santo Domingo), and the French controlled the west (Saint-Domingue). One of the richest of all the European colonies, Saint-Domingue's population consisted of three groups. There were 40,000 white French settlers, 30,000 *gens de couleur* (free people of color) of interracial ancestry, and 500,000 black slaves, most of whom had been born in Africa. These slaves worked under brutal conditions, and the mortality rate was high. Some slaves escaped and formed independent communities in remote areas. These peoples were known as **maroons**. In some cases, maroons directly assisted slave resistance movements.

When the French Revolution began in 1789, the white settlers sought the right to govern themselves, but opposed extending political and legal equality to the *gens de couleur* and slaves. The National Assembly objected to the exclusion of both groups and only allowed the island's whites a third of the seats they sought on the basis of the colony's entire population. The Declaration of the Rights of Man undermined the island's racial hierarchy with its first article: "Men are born and remain free and equal in rights." Both the *gens de couleur* and slaves drew inspiration from that statement.

A slave revolt occurred in August of 1791. As a result, the whites, *gens de couleurs*, and slaves battled each other in a see-sawing multi-sided **Haitian Revolution**. French troops—and later, British and Spanish troops—invaded the island in hopes of gaining control. The slaves, however, were led by Toussaint L'Ouverture, a black military leader who built a strong and disciplined army, and, by 1797, controlled most of Saint-Domingue.

In 1803, independence was declared. By 1804, Haiti was the second independent republic in the Western Hemisphere and the first republic that abolished slavery. However, great economic difficulty followed independence. Many nations, such as the United States, refused to recognize or conduct trade with Haiti due to its emancipation of slaves. Haiti was at a further disadvantage, as the new nation of small farmers was not as economically productive as the former large-scale plantations.

Latin America

In Latin America, the colonies controlled by the Spanish and Portuguese were comprised of a governing class of 30,000 *peninsulares* (Spanish-born Spaniards living in the New World colonies), 3.5 million Creoles (New World–born people of European descent), and 10 million less-privileged classes including black slaves, indigenous people, and those of interracial backgrounds known as *mulattos* and *mestizos*. The Roman Catholic Church also formed a major social and political force in these colonies.

Napoleon's 1807 invasion of Spain and Portugal weakened the authority of those countries in their respective colonies. By 1810, revolts had occurred in Argentina, Venezuela, and Mexico. A crucial document in the history of **Latin American independence movements** is the Jamaica Letter. Written by the Creole leader and revolutionary Simón Bolívar, it expressed his views on the independence movement in his native Venezuela and on the need for a union of the former Spanish colonies. Like the Declaration of Independence and the Declaration of the Rights of Man and of the Citizen, the Jamaica Letter is firmly rooted in Enlightenment political ideals.

In Mexico, Father Miguel de Hidalgo led a peasant rebellion, but conservative Creole forces gained control of the movement. Simón Bolívar led revolts in South America and by 1824 deposed the Spanish armies. His goal was to establish a United States of Latin America, called Gran Colombia, but it did not last. The Portuguese royal family had fled to Brazil after Napoleon's 1807 invasion. When the king returned in 1821, he left his son, Pedro, to rule as regent. Pedro agreed to the demands of Creoles and declared Brazil independent.

As a result of these independence movements, the Creoles became the dominant class, and many *peninsulares* returned to Europe. Latin American society remained economically and racially stratified. Slavery continued. The wealth and power of the Roman Catholic Church persisted. Overall, the lower classes continued to be repressed.

NATIONALISM AND THE NATION-STATE

During the nineteenth century, some groups of people came to identify themselves as part of a community called a nation. The forces that drew these people together were their common language, customs, cultural traditions, values, historical experiences, ethnicity, and sometimes religion. **Nationalism** was often a reaction against foreign rule, as mass politics resulted in the people of a country defining themselves in contrast to their ruling elite. Even in Europe, many kingdoms were ruled by monarchs whose nationality or preferred language differed from those of their subjects. In 1815, the Congress of Vienna sought to stifle nationalist movements in Italy and Germany that had been inspired by the ideas of the French Revolution.

The Revolutions of 1848

Sometimes called the Springtime of the Peoples, the Revolutions of 1848 saw a series of uprisings throughout Europe. Reformers were dissatisfied with rising industrialization and with the conservative consensus that had dominated Europe since the Congress of Vienna. In Italy, Germany, and the Hapsburg Empire, they sought to unify their scattered countrymen under national banners. They also shared the goals of revolutionaries elsewhere in Europe of seeking democratic reforms. The revolutions, however, failed. Rather than reform, many governments increased repression. Many ex-revolutionaries fled to places like the United States, where they would work as activists in their new homelands. For example, one-tenth of the Union Army in the American Civil War consisted of German-born immigrants politically opposed to slavery.

Unification of Italy and Germany

On the Italian peninsula, the Roman Catholic Church still exerted great influence and discouraged the growth of Italian nationalism. The pope himself personally held large estates in central Italy. Under the leadership of Garibaldi in the south, young men pushed for an Italian nation, fighting a military campaign to unite the people behind this idea. In the north, Count Camillo Benso di Cavour, the prime minister to King Victor Emmanuel II of Sardinia, aligned with France and expelled Austria from northern Italy. In 1871, the Kingdom of Italy was proclaimed, and Sardinia's king was chosen as its ruler.

Farther north, the Kingdom of Prussia became more powerful after the defeat of Napoleon. The chancellor of Prussia, Otto von Bismarck, envisioned a united Germany. So he engineered a series of conflicts with Denmark and Austria to consolidate the territory required. Bismarck eventually manipulated France into declaring war on Prussia and used this conflict as a pretext for gathering then-separate German domains together to fight as one. The Franco-Prussian War (1870–1871) was a resounding victory for Prussia, and Bismarck proclaimed the birth of the German nation. He did so in the French palace at Versailles, further humiliating France by taking the territory of Alsace-Lorraine on the Franco-German border. The latter would be an important factor in the outbreak of hostilities between France and Germany in World War I.

The birth of a unified Germany caused a significant shift in the balance of power in Europe. France was in decline, and Germany now rivaled Great Britain as an industrial producer and leader in technology. German military strength and diplomacy contributed to its position in Europe. The new German nation was in many ways deeply conservative in its politics. Bismarck, however, supported a series of reforms that robbed domestic left-wing opponents of causes that might galvanize larger movements. He established state pensions and public health insurance plans that protected the social welfare of the masses.

Zionism

The existence of minority groups conflicted with the nationalist concept of a singular ethnic and religious identity. One such group was the Jewish people. They lived as a minority in many European nations as a result of the Jewish diaspora—the cultural and physical dispersion of Jews since the time of the Roman Empire. Antisemitism increased over the nineteenth century, as burgeoning nationalist identities strengthened traditional prejudice toward Jews and Judaism. In reaction to this antisemitism, the Zionist movement arose. Like other nationalist movements, it sought to establish a state for one people, in this case for the Jews. A Jewish reporter, Theodor Herzl, launched the movement in 1897. Zionism eventually led to the creation of the independent state of Israel in 1948.

Latin America

By the 1830s, most of Latin America was made up of independent nations, which had been established by revolutions against their respective colonial governments. These new nations faced many problems, such as economies that had been disrupted by many years of warfare and large armies loyal to regional commanders (*caudillos*) instead of to the new national governments. Additionally, the role of the Catholic Church remained strong. Few questioned its doctrines, but many wanted to limit its role in civil life. In Mexico, for example, politics was a struggle between conservatives and liberals, and instability and financial difficulty made it a target for foreign intervention by the United States and Europe.

INDUSTRIALIZATION

High-Yield

Scientific discoveries and technological advancements led to the rise of modern industry in the eighteenth and nineteenth centuries. The following factors made rapid industrialization possible:

- Increased agricultural production, to support a large workforce

- Possession of natural resources like coal and iron ore

- Investment capital (money) to build factories

- A stable government that protected private property

- Technical knowledge and communication of discoveries

- Control of sea ports, rivers, and canals

The Industrial Revolution would affect human labor, consumption, family structure, and much more. The following table lists some major economic and social changes that occurred in industrialized nations.

Domestic Impact	Global Impact
Growth of urban centers	Widened gap between industrial and nonindustrial nations
Creation of middle class of merchants and factory owners	Competition for colonial territory to secure natural resources
Unsafe, harsh conditions in factories	Greater economic power in Europe
Loss of traditional artisan guilds	The Revolutions of 1848
Rising standard of living	World trade increased

Preconditions for Industrialization

England was the first modern industrial economy for several reasons. England's geographical position in the Atlantic Ocean gave it access to raw materials from around the globe as well as sea access to markets for its manufactured goods. It also had plentiful natural resources, such as rivers, coal, and iron ore; these provided energy to power factories and other manufacturing. Additionally, England's growing population surpassed the amount of labor needed for agricultural production, thus providing surplus workers for industrial jobs. Finally, England had a business class that had grown wealthy through commerce, especially from the transatlantic slave trade; these people were able to reinvest profits into industry.

Other nations were close behind England in developing industrial capability. The United States and Germany both surpassed England in steel production by 1900, while Russia, Japan, and the Ottoman Empire followed behind. Spain and the rest of continental Europe were largely excluded from industrialization during this period.

An Agricultural Revolution

Though it is counterintuitive, the Industrial Revolution was partially made possible by agricultural advances. The Dutch began this process by erecting earthen walls to reclaim land from the sea and using fertilizer from livestock to renew soil nutrients. In the 1700s, British farmers began experimenting with crop rotation, and Jethro Tull invented a mechanical seed drill that sped up the planting process. Farmers began to share their knowledge and techniques through farm journals. This resulted in higher agricultural output, which in turn created the population growth so key to maintaining an industrial labor force.

Technology

Technological development was the driving force of industrialization. For example, hydropower was used to make mills more efficient. A major advancement was the steam engine, which would become the foundation of this new mechanical age. Coal was vital in the production of iron, which was used to construct machinery and steam engines. New methods for producing iron resulted in a better product produced at lower costs. Iron was a vital material during the Industrial Revolution, especially in railroad construction. Cars, ships, and factories were both products and tools of further industrialization. A second industrial revolution in steel, chemicals, and electricity transformed society in the late nineteenth century. These advancements led to innovations in scientific fields such as engineering and medicine.

Environment

The Industrial Revolution had significant, long-lasting impacts on the environment. Air and water pollution affected the health of people living in the rapidly growing urban areas. Entire landscapes were destroyed as humans cut down timber for railroad ties, stripped hills and mountains for ores, and denuded areas of vegetative cover for farming. This increase in deforestation exacerbated desertification in some areas and flooding and mudslides in others. The invention of dynamite in 1867 opened the way to more effective removal of earth and stone, particularly for mines and tunnels. Mechanical methods of hunting made fishing and whaling more effective, with the result that many areas were significantly depleted even by the early twentieth century. Many whale species were in danger of becoming extinct until the discovery of petroleum products made whale oil less valuable. Improved firearms made hunting easier, often with disastrous results as animals like the bison of the North American plains were hunted almost to extinction.

It was also during this era, however, that concern for the environment, beyond the need to conserve for a nation's resources, first began to assert itself. Many nations formed forestry services, initially based on the French and then the American model. National parks and nature preserves were created to keep areas from being developed. Western curiosity and scientific observations began to note the interconnectedness of nature and man's impact upon it. Scientific methods in medicine and chemistry led to cures and preventative measures like sanitation systems, soaps and disinfectants, and vaccinations for many of the diseases that have plagued mankind throughout the centuries.

Financial Institutions

New financial systems also developed to support the new industrial production. More complex corporate structures, stock markets, and insurance enabled businessmen to raise the capital they needed to begin or expand production as well as to protect their investments from loss.

Large businesses often had a global reach. Transnational corporations such as the United Fruit Company had operations that affected lives in North, Central, and South America. The ideals of laissez-faire capitalism that **Adam Smith** and others had proposed became the inspiration for these changes.

Impact on Gender, Family, and Social Structures

Industrialization greatly affected gender roles and families. It also radically altered the traditional social structures of the day. The family, which previously had been a self-sufficient economic unit, moved economic production outside the home. Working-class women and children entered the industrial workforce as low-paid factory laborers.

A sharp distinction now existed between family life and work life. The status of men increased because industrial work and the wage were considered more important than domestic work, which was largely performed by women. Middle-class values became distinct from those of the industrial working class, which were stereotyped as promiscuous, alcohol-abusing, and immoral. Middle-class women generally did not work outside the home, but instead were pressured to conform to the new models of behavior often referred to as the "cult of domesticity"—the glorification of women as the center of the well-kept home.

The Factory System

The Industrial Revolution led to the establishment of the **factory system** in which factories employed large numbers of workers and power-driven machines to mass-produce goods. In the late 1800s, manufacturers sought to increase productivity and profits by designing products with interchangeable parts: identical components that could be used in place of each other. This process simplified assembly, but also made factory work tedious and repetitive. Factory work was also dangerous and had a negative impact on the health of laborers, both from environmental factors such as dust and chemicals and from accidents with machinery.

Global Effects of Industrialization

As a result of industrialization, a new **global division of labor** emerged. Industrial societies needed raw materials from other lands, and there was a large demand for materials such as raw cotton from India and Egypt and rubber from Brazil and the Congo. Latin America, sub-Saharan Africa, South Asia, and Southeast Asia became dependent on exporting cash crop products to the industrialized nations, but established little or no industrialization themselves. Most of the profits from these cash crops went abroad, and wealth was concentrated among the owners and investors in corporations.

The dependency theory explains the unevenness in development as the result of control by industrial nations. In short, the industrialization of some areas was achieved at the expense of others. Cash crop and colonial economies reinforced dependency on American and European manufactured goods.

Consumer goods became more affordable and plentiful thanks to industrialization. Some basic necessities of life became cheaper, like fabric. Luxuries once available only to aristocrats began to become more available to the middle class.

Improvements in medicine, along with better diets resulting from more food production, led to a dramatic rise in population as well as to an increase in the average life expectancy. The Earth's population in 1750 was 790 million. By 1900, the population had doubled. Urbanization increased even faster than population growth because new methods of transportation (most notably railroads and steamships) led to increases in both internal migration within countries and external migration.

Advances in Transportation and Communication

During the **First Industrial Revolution** (approximately 1760–1820), the development of the steam engine led to creation of steamships and steam-powered locomotives, which rapidly sped up transportation. The creation of canals enabled heavy loads to be transported long distances and linked previously separate waterways. The development of the telegraph revolutionized the speed at which businesses, people, and armies could communicate.

During the **Second Industrial Revolution** (1870–1914), the development of the internal combustion engine transformed how machines operated and initiated the rise of oil as a global commodity. It also saw the beginning of widespread electrification. Economic inequality within industrialized countries, spurred on by the growth of industries like steel and **railroads**, led to a sharp increase in socialist parties and unions.

REACTIONS TO INDUSTRIALIZATION

As the nineteenth century progressed, the Industrial Revolution redefined both society and the economy, stirring new tensions. Enlightenment ideas and sentiments inspired many political movements. Some were revolutionary, while others were reformist. Their impact would be global.

Liberalism

One response to industrialization was the rise of **liberalism**, which resulted from the rapid growth of the middle class. With philosophical roots in the Enlightenment, liberals opposed monarchies and wanted written constitutions based on separation of powers. They were proponents of natural rights. Having greatly benefited from the new capitalist, industrial economy, liberals were staunch supporters of laissez-faire economic ideas. They were lukewarm to unionism and socialism.

Socialism

The appalling conditions experienced by industrial workers in the 1800s inspired revolutionary reformers. Under the broad title of **socialism**, these movements critiqued capitalism and suggested instead an economy that was run by the *proletariat*, the equivalent of the modern-day working class. Socialists opposed the *bourgeoisie*, the class of businessmen and professionals that was becoming ascendant after the decline of the aristocracy.

The most notable expression of socialism in the nineteenth century was the Paris Commune, a revolutionary socialist government that ruled the city of Paris following the collapse of the French Empire in the Franco-Prussian War. It existed from March 18 to May 28 in 1871 and enacted a number of anticlerical and prolabor laws. The Paris Commune inspired many later leftist revolutionaries, like Lenin. It popularized the red flag as a left-wing symbol. The French Army overthrew the Commune, killing approximately 20,000 revolutionaries in the process of retaking Paris.

Unionism

While often tarred as veiled socialism, unionism can be distinguished as reformist rather than revolutionary. The union movement wanted to improve the lives of workers within the constraints of the capitalist economy rather than seeking its overthrow. Unionists advocated the organization of workers so that they could negotiate with their employers for better wages and working conditions. Factory owners fought to stop workers from banding together, resulting in considerable bloodshed. Workers struggled to remain unified against violent oppression.

Communism

Communism, a radical form of socialism, sought to create self-sufficient communities in which property was owned in common. One of the most prominent socialist thinkers was Karl Marx, who, along with Friedrich Engels, wrote *The Communist Manifesto* in 1848. Marx and Engels advocated the overthrow of the moneyed classes which would be followed by a "workers' state." Communism is notable for being an internationalist ideology. It saw workers as a unified class regardless of their outward nationality. Later, after the emergence in the twentieth century of communist states like the Soviet Union and the People's Republic of China, communism came to be associated with central planning of the economy by the government.

Anarchism

Anarchism arose as a revolutionary antiauthoritarian movement. The father of anarchism was the Frenchman Pierre-Joseph Proudhon, who coined the assertion that "property is theft" and defined anarchy as "the absence of a master, of a sovereign." Anarchism sought to replace existing authority structures with decentralized, self-governing cooperatives that rejected hierarchies. Anarchists played a major role in the Paris Commune, and the Commune's decentralized structure reflected that.

In the late nineteenth and early twentieth centuries, anarchists were responsible for a series of high-profile bombings and the assassination of various political leaders. These actions were termed *the propaganda by the deed* and were intended as catalysts for wider revolution.

> ### ✔ AP Expert Note
>
> ### Be aware that political terms can change meaning over time
>
> Source documents on the AP exam will reference terms that might be unfamiliar to you or have a different meaning from what you might expect. For example, *liberalism* in the classical sense differs from present-day American usage; classical liberalism emphasizes laissez-faire economics, whereas modern liberalism promotes social, political, and economic equality. Since political terms can take on different meanings depending on the time period, be sure to check the publication date of source documents on the exam and take into account the historical context in which such terms are used.

Romanticism

Romanticism was a philosophical reaction to both industrialization and the Enlightenment. It manifested itself in the arts, literature, music, and various intellectual outlets. Romanticism emphasized emotion over reason, and glorified individualism over the collective, especially in the form of heroic deeds. Nationalism was a key expression of romanticism. In the twentieth century, it provided a basis for fascism.

Conservatism

Various strains of conservatism developed in response to industrialization and the French Revolution. In England, Edmund Burke favored private property and laissez-faire economics, yet felt that capitalism should serve the traditional social order. In Germany, Otto von Bismarck favored "revolutionary conservatism" where the traditional social hierarchy was strengthened by a welfare state, depriving leftist radicals of modest goals that might organize workers and facilitate revolution. In general, aristocrats saw industrialization and the rise of capitalism as a corrosive threat to their privileges and to the structure of traditional society.

REFORM IN ASIAN STATES

The traditionalist nations of the Ottoman Empire, Russia, China, and Japan were all forced to confront modernization and the social issues accompanying it during this period. Conservative forces resisted these dramatic reforms to varying degrees of success.

Ottoman Empire

By the 1700s, the once-legendary Ottoman armies had fallen behind those of Europe. As the empire's military weakened, its political power weakened too. In addition, nationalist revolts in the Balkans and Greece contributed to the empire's problems.

The Ottomans also experienced economic decline. Europe circumvented them and began to trade directly with India and China. Global trade had shifted to the Atlantic Ocean, where the Ottomans were not involved. European products flowed into the empire, and it began to depend heavily on foreign loans. Europeans were even given capitulations (special rights and privileges), such as being subject to only their own laws, not to those of the Ottomans. All of this was a great blow to the empire's prestige and sovereignty.

The empire did attempt to reform itself, beginning with the rule of Mahmud II. He organized a more effective army and a system of secondary education. The Ottomans built new roads, laid telegraph lines, and created a postal service. These reforms continued into the **Tanzimât** ("Reorganization" in Ottoman Turkish) **Movement** from 1839 to 1879, when the government used the French legal system as a guide to reform its own laws. For example, public trials were instituted.

However, these reforms were met with great opposition, particularly from religious conservatives and the Ottoman bureaucracy. Many saw the concept of civil liberties as a foreign one, a kind of soft imperialism in its spread through Ottoman society. The new sultan, Abdul Hamid II, adopted the first Ottoman constitution in 1876 but suspended it in 1879 and reinstituted absolute monarchy.

The Young Turks, a group of exiled Ottoman subjects, pushed for universal male suffrage, equality before the law, and the emancipation of women and non-Turkish ethnic groups. In 1908, they led a coup that overthrew Abdul Hamid II and set up a "puppet" sultan that they controlled. Though the Ottoman Empire attempted to reform, it was still in a delicate state by 1914. Ultimately, it dissolved in the aftermath of World War I, with large portions colonized by the British and French Empires or ruled by their local allies.

Russia

Much like the Ottoman Empire, the Russian Empire was autocratic, multiethnic, and multilingual. Russian tsars were supported by both the Russian Orthodox Church and the noble class, which owned most of the land. The peasants were the majority of the population, but the feudal institution of serfdom essentially enslaved them. Even at the end of the nineteenth century, the country's literacy rate was below 20 percent, far behind major European nations. Unlike the Ottomans, who were losing territory, the Russian Empire vastly expanded—east to the Pacific, south into the Caucasus and Central Asia, and southwest to the Mediterranean. Its military power and strength could not compete with that of Europe, however, as demonstrated in its defeat in the Crimean War in 1856.

The loss to the Franco-British-Ottoman alliance in the Crimean War (1853–1856) highlighted the comparative weakness of Russia's military and economy, pushing the government to modernize. A first step was the emancipation of the serfs by Tsar Alexander II in 1861. He also created district assemblies (*zemstvos*) in 1864, in which all classes had elected representatives. The government also encouraged industrialization. Policies designed to stimulate economic development were issued, such as the construction of the Trans-Siberian Railroad and the remodeling of the state bank.

Anti-government protests increased through the involvement of the university students and intellectuals known as the *intelligentsia*. The more these groups were repressed by the government, the more radical they became. A member of the revolutionary "People's Will" group, which was organized in 1879 and employed terrorism in its attempt to overthrow Russia's tsarist autocracy, assassinated Tsar Alexander II in 1881, bringing an end to government reform. The new tsars used repression—not gradual political reform—to maintain power, until their overthrow during World War I.

Fast-paced government-sponsored industrialization led to many peasant rebellions and industrial worker strikes. As a response, in 1897 the government limited the maximum workday to 11.5 hours, though it also prohibited trade unions and outlawed strikes. Tsar Nicholas II, in an attempt to deflect attention from the growing opposition, focused on expansion through the Russo-Japanese War in 1904, but the Russians suffered an embarrassing defeat. This loss also sparked an uprising.

In January 1905, a group of workers marched to the Tsar's Winter Palace to petition. They were killed by government troops. The Bloody Sunday massacre set off anger and rebellion across the empire, which as a whole was known as the Revolution of 1905. The government made concessions by creating a legislative body called the Duma, but, in practice, not much changed in Russia until the upheavals of World War I.

China

High-Yield

The Chinese, like the Ottomans and Russians, were forced to confront their own issues of reform and reaction in the nineteenth century. The Qing Dynasty had grown increasingly ineffective as rulers. New World crops, like sweet potatoes and corn, brought about a rapid population increase. During the Qing Dynasty, it is estimated that the Chinese population quadrupled to 420,000,000. This increase created great strains on the nation. Famines were increasingly common, provoking a series of rebellions that further weakened the Qing Dynasty.

The Chinese military also stagnated from the mid-seventeenth century onward, as the evolution of gunpowder weapons finally ended the threat of horse-riding steppe nomads that had troubled China for millennia. The last nomadic confederation to threaten China, the Dzungar Khanate in what is the modern-day Chinese region of Xinjiang, lost a series of conflicts with the Qing Dynasty. These conflicts culminated in organized genocide, as approximately 80 percent of the Dzungar people were killed under the orders of the Qing emperor and ethnic Chinese people were settled on their former lands. Without neighboring threats, China had no reason to innovate its military technology or tactics and its army grew to lack battlefield experience.

With its vast population and resources, China was self-sufficient and, along with its rejection of foreign influence, felt it required nothing that the outsiders produced. However, Europeans, Britain in particular, sought trade with China to acquire silks, lacquerware, and tea, the latter of which was increasing in popularity in their homelands. British merchants paid in silver bullion for Chinese goods. The amount of bullion a nation or company owned determined its wealth and its strength (according to mercantilism). This silver drain from Britain inspired its merchants to find something the Chinese wanted other than bullion. They found it in opium, an addictive narcotic made from the poppy plant. Despite the emperor declaring the opium trade illegal, British merchants smuggled it into the country. Chinese merchants agreed to pay for opium in silver, which the British merchants used to buy Chinese goods, making a profit on both ends of this drug trafficking. This reversed the silver drain from Britain to China, and it also created a large number of Chinese opium addicts.

The **First Opium War** (1839–1842) broke out over a customs dispute, but resentment over British drug trafficking played a major role as well. China suffered a major defeat, and a series of unequal treaties gave Britain and other European nations commercial entry into China. For example, Hong Kong was ceded to the British in 1841, and control over it was only transferred back to China in 1997. This began a period of Chinese history referred to as the Century of Humiliation.

The **Second Opium War** (1856–1860) resulted from the Western European desire to further weaken Chinese sovereignty over trade, to legalize the opium trade, and to expand the export of indentured workers whose situations closely resembled slavery. In October 1860, a Franco-British expeditionary force looted and burned Beijing's Old Summer Palace. British and French museums still feature its stolen art, and the palace ruins are an important landmark for China. Shock over the defeat led to the Qing's **Self-Strengthening Movement**. Drug use also became even more rampant thanks to opium flooding the country.

Rebellions and Revolutions

Uprisings such as the **Taiping Rebellion** (1850–1864) placed further stress on China. An obscure scholar named Hong Xiuquan, who believed he was the brother of Jesus Christ, founded an off-shoot of Christianity. A social reform movement grew from this in the 1850s, which the government suppressed. Hong established the Taiping Tianguo (Taiping Heavenly Kingdom), and his followers created an army that, within two years of fighting, controlled a large territory in central China. Nationalism influenced this rebellion, as the majority Han ethnic group resented rule by the minority Manchus, who had conquered the native Ming Dynasty but now seemed powerless against European imperialism.

Internal disputes within the Taipings finally allowed the Qing Dynasty to defeat them, but it was a long struggle that exhausted the imperial treasury. Between 20 and 30 million people died in the Taiping Rebellion, making it the bloodiest civil war in history. It did, however, lead to greater inclusion of Han Chinese in the Qing Dynasty's government. Both Sun Yat-sen and Mao Zedong viewed Hong Xiuquan as a spiritual predecessor, for both his anti-Manchu and his anti-imperialist stances.

The Qing did implement limited reforms. With government-sponsored grants in the 1860s and 1870s, local leaders promoted military and economic reform in China using the slogan: "Chinese learning at the base, Western learning for use." These leaders built modern shipyards, railroads, and weapon industries, and they founded academies for the study of science. It was a solid foundation, but the Self-Strengthening Movement brought only minimal change. It also experienced resistance from the imperial government.

The Qing's last major reform effort took place in 1898. It was known as the Hundred Days' Reform. This ambitious movement reinterpreted Confucian thought to justify radical changes to the system, with the intent to remake China into a powerful modern industrial society. The Emperor Guangzu instituted a program to change China into a constitutional monarchy, guarantee civil liberties, and build a modern education system. These proposed changes were strongly resisted by conservative officials. Particularly upset was the Empress Dowager Cixi, who cancelled the reforms and imprisoned the emperor in a coup. With that, Qing China's chance for a reformed society ended.

Another rebellion further complicated issues in China. The **Boxer Rebellion** (1899–1901) sought to rid China of foreigners and foreign influence. Empress Cixi supported the movement, hoping to eliminate all foreign influence. A multinational force from countries such as the United States, Russia, and Japan, however, handily defeated the Boxers and forced China to pay a large indemnity in silver for the damages. Afterwards, Cixi belatedly supported modest reforms: the New Policies, also known as the Late Qing Reforms. In Qing China's weakened state, some provinces adopted them, but others did not.

Amid all of these rebellions and attempts at reform, a revolutionary movement was slowly emerging. It was composed of young men and women who had traveled outside China—who had seen the new liberalism and modernization of both the West and Japan. They hoped to import these ideas. Cells were organized in Guangzhou and overseas in Tokyo and Honolulu, where plots to overthrow the Qing were developed.

Under the leadership of Sun Yat-sen (Sun Zhong-shan), after many attempted unsuccessful uprisings, the Qing were forced to abdicate in 1911 and the Republic of China was proclaimed. Sun dreamed of a progressive and democratic China based on his Three Principles of the People: nationalism, democracy, and socialism. His goal would never be achieved due to civil war and the Warlord Era.

Japan—The Meiji Restoration

In its radical response to the challenges of reform and reaction, Japan emerged from this period as a world power. Even as it continued to selectively isolate itself from the rest of world, it was changing from a feudal to a commercial economy.

The Japanese knew of China's humiliation at the hands of the British in the mid 1800s. After the California Gold Rush of 1849, the United States became more interested in Pacific commerce, sending a mission to conclude a trade agreement with Japan. Commodore Matthew Perry, in an example of gunboat diplomacy, arrived in Edo (Tokyo) Bay in 1853 with a modern fleet of armed steamships. For the Japanese, who had restricted their trade from much of the world for over two centuries, this was a troubling sight. Contact with Americans caused tense debate within the ruling Tokugawa shogunate and the samurai class.

Two clans in the south—Satsuma and Choshu—supported a new policy to "revere the emperor and repel the barbarians." This was a veiled critique of the shogun in Edo, as they perceived his inability to ward off the Western "barbarians" as embarrassing. A younger generation of reform-minded samurai far from Edo made bold plans to undermine the *bakufu* (the military government led by the shogun). These "men of spirit" banded together to overthrow the shogun, restore the emperor, and advance the idea of Japanese modernization.

The rebels armed themselves with guns from the West, and a civil war broke out in 1866. When the anti-government forces demonstrated their military superiority, the momentum began to shift in favor of the rebels. The overthrow of the Tokugawa shogunate was complete in 1868, when the victorious reformers pronounced that they had restored the emperor to his throne. His title was

Meiji, or Enlightened One. The nation rallied around the 16-year-old emperor, and plans were made to move the imperial "presence" to the renamed capital of Tokyo (Eastern Capital).

This transition in Japanese history can be seen as both a restoration and a revolution. While the emperor was nominally restored to authority, real power was held by the nobility. A national legislature called the Diet was established, but the aristocratic upper house was in primary control. It reformed Japan in radical ways. Compulsory public schools were introduced. The feudal system was abolished, and the ownership of weapons was no longer restricted to the samurai class.

Some samurai were displeased, not just with the loss of their privileges, but also with the mass adoption of "barbarian" ways by Japan. The resulting Satsuma Rebellion (1877) saw traditionalist samurai launch a brief civil war. Both sides fought with modern weapons, however. In the end, the government's army of peasant conscripts defeated the rebels.

The rapidity of the industrialization and modernization of Japan impressed the rest of the world. This development was driven, in part, by the *zaibatsu* ("financial cliques"), which were family-owned business conglomerates that dominated the economy. Within the first generation of the Meiji period, Japan had built a modern infrastructure and military, had defeated the Chinese and Russians in war, and had begun building an empire in the Pacific. The rise of imperial Japan altered the global balance of power as the twentieth century began.

COMPARATIVE CLOSE-UP: REFORM AND REACTION IN THE NINETEENTH CENTURY		
	Political	**Economic**	**Social**
Ottoman Empire	Institutes French legal code (equality before the law, public trials), but reforms see major opposition. Empire collapses after World War I.	As trade shifts to the Atlantic Ocean, it becomes heavily reliant on loans from Europe.	Young Turks push for greater centralization, universal male suffrage, emancipation of women.
Russia	*Zemstvos* (local assemblies) are created. Duma established after Revolution of 1905, but is subject to whim of tsar. Monarchy overthrown in 1917.	Government sponsors industrialization projects such as the Trans-Siberian Railroad. Unions and strikes banned by law.	Alexander II emancipates the serfs in 1861. Students and intelligentsia spread ideas of change in the countryside.
China	Hundred Days' Reform attempts to create constitutional monarchy, but is halted by Empress Cixi. Rebellions like the Taiping and Boxer weaken the empire. Qing Dynasty overthrown in 1911.	After the Opium Wars, European powers gain economic and territorial concessions under the Unequal Treaties and divide China into spheres of influence.	Peasant-led Taiping Rebellion attempts to create a more egalitarian society, but is eventually defeated.
Japan	Tokugawa shogunate is overthrown by samurai and other elites. The emperor is restored to power. A legislative body, the Diet, is formed.	Government sponsors massive industrialization and trade. Japan rises to economic prominence.	Samurai class loses power, but some transition to roles in industrial leadership. New industrial working class develops.

IMPERIALISM AND ITS IMPACT

At the turn of the twentieth century, large portions of Africa and Asia had been absorbed into foreign empires. The Belgians, British, French, German, Italians, Portuguese, and Spanish, along with the United States and Japan, enthusiastically embraced **imperialism**. Motivations included economic, political, and cultural factors.

Motives for Imperialism

High-Yield

Economically, overseas colonies served as sources of raw materials and as markets for manufactured goods. These colonies were strategic sites with harbors and resupply stations for naval ships, commercial and military. Politically, colonial expansion spurred nationalist sentiment at home, as citizens took pride in military conquest. Lopsided wars against native peoples and second-tier powers were often justified with sensationalist journalism about supposed crimes committed in those foreign countries against Europeans, often missionaries or women.

Culturally, the motivation and justification for imperialism arose in part from the concept of **Social Darwinism**, which attempted to apply the principles of Darwinian evolution to societies and politics. According to proponents of this theory, societies either prospered or failed because, as is the case in nature, only the strong survive as they are able to dominate the weak. Therefore, the imperial powers must be better than those in Asia and Africa and had the right to impose their economic and political will on them.

The theory of scientific racism developed during this period of imperialism to explain differences between nations. These theorists assumed that humans consisted of several distinct racial groups and that European racial groups were intellectually and morally superior. These ideas were often used as justification for the exploitative and cruel treatment of colonized peoples.

James Bruce, the Eighth Earl of Elgin, who fought in the Second Opium War and ordered the looting and burning of the Summer Palace, and later served as Viceroy of India in the British Raj, wrote about the peoples he encountered. His journals were published in the 1872 and reflect the racism that underlined imperialism: "It is a terrible business, however, this living among inferior races. . . . one moves among them with perfect indifference, treating them, not as dogs, because in that case one would whistle to them and pat them, but as machines with which one can have no communion or sympathy."

Additionally, missionaries hoped to convert Asians and Africans to Christianity. While many missionaries served as protectors of native peoples, some saw their mission as one of bringing civilization to the uncivilized. The poem "The White Man's Burden" by Rudyard Kipling, written in 1899, illustrates this mindset well. Kipling intended the poem as an appeal to the American public to embrace a future as an imperial power following the Spanish-American War.

IMPERIALISM CIRCA 1914

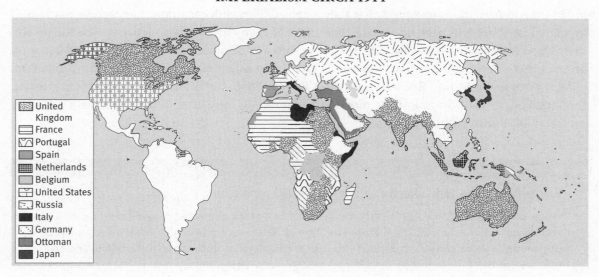

Legend:
- United Kingdom
- France
- Portugal
- Spain
- Netherlands
- Belgium
- United States
- Russia
- Italy
- Germany
- Ottoman
- Japan

India

England's involvement in India began strictly as a business venture. Founded in 1600, the British East India Company enjoyed a monopoly on English trade with India and increasingly took advantage of the Mughal Empire's growing weakness. Expanding its trading posts, the company petitioned the British government to outright conquer areas important to its trade in order to protect its interests. It enforced its rule with a combination of British troops and Indian troops, who were often referred to by the British as *sepoys*.

In the subcontinent's Punjab region, which overlaps modern-day eastern Pakistan and northern India, the previously pacifistic Sikhs grew militant due to persecution under the Mughal Empire. While only 7 percent of the Punjab's population, the Sikh message of religious tolerance and social justice attracted many supporters from other faiths. This eventually led to the founding of the Sikh Empire (1799–1849).

Following the collapse of the Mughals, the Sikh Empire was the last rival power on the subcontinent to the British East India Company. The British sought greater control over Central Asia as part of their "Great Game" with the Russian Empire; they also saw the nonsectarian Sikhs as a potential threat to their control over the rest of India. Indian troops were often used to police areas of the Indian subcontinent that clashed with their own ethnic or religious identity. The British Empire did this to play different native groups against each other, ensuring that they stayed in overall control. Following two Anglo-Sikh wars, the British conquered the Sikhs, cementing imperial control over India.

In 1857, the Indian troops mutinied after they received rifles with cartridges rumored to be greased in animal fat (beef and pork fat violate Hindu and Muslim customs, respectively). The Indian soldiers killed British officers, escalating the conflict into a large-scale rebellion. At least 800,000 Indians would die in the ensuing war. This conflict has been called many names; the most prominent, current term is the **Indian Rebellion of 1857**. By May 1858, the British government had crushed the rebellion. It went on to impose direct imperial rule in India (the "British Raj") with a viceroy representing British authority.

> ✔ **AP Expert Note**
>
> ### Know that one war can have many different names
>
> When studying for AP World History, be aware that a war's name can vary depending on time and context. For example, the Indian Rebellion of 1857 was traditionally referred to as the Sepoy Mutiny, which carries an implicit pro-British perspective since mutiny is a crime, and *sepoy* was a term the British troops used for Indian soldiers. The standpoint of a war's participants also affects naming. For example, the conflict that Americans call the Vietnam War is called the American War by the Vietnamese.

Under British rule, forests were cleared; tea, coffee, and opium were cultivated; and railroads, telegraphs, canals, harbors, and irrigation systems were built. English-style schools were set up for Indian elites, and Indian customs were suppressed. British imperialism had a profound effect on the decline of existing Indian textile production, as British merchants wanted Indian cotton to be shipped to England, made into textiles, and then sold in India. Severe famines became more frequent, as British laissez-faire policies focused on export agriculture rather than domestic food production, and heavy taxes left poorer Indians unable to buy food whenever prices rose. Between the eighteenth and mid-twentieth centuries, areas under British administration would experience 14 major famines. Over 55 million people would die.

Counterintuitively, British rule eventually inspired a sense of Indian national identity. Elite Indians who had been educated in British universities were inspired by Enlightenment values and began to criticize the British colonial regime. They called for political and social reform. As such, with British approval, the Indian National Congress was founded (1885) as a forum for educated Indians to communicate their views on public affairs to colonial officials. It was initially sought to reform rather than end British rule. By the end of the nineteenth century, however, the Congress sought self-rule and joined forces with the All-Indian Muslim League. In 1909, wealthy Indians were given the right to vote, but, by that time, the push for independence had become a mass movement.

Africa

With the exception of coastal colonies and trading posts, Europeans had little presence in Africa in the early nineteenth century. European territorial acquisition occurred rapidly during the imperial "Scramble for Africa." From 1875 to 1914, almost the entire continent was carved up by European empires, with Ethiopia and Liberia the only two African nations to retain their independence.

From 1879 to 1882, the Urabi Revolt (or Revolution) saw Egyptians fight against foreign domination of their country's government, army, and economy. After a naval bombardment of Alexandria, the British launched an invasion that defeated the rebels and took control of the Suez Canal, a key shipping route. In 1885, King Leopold II of Belgium established the **Congo Free State**, ostensibly as a free-trade zone. In reality, the Congo served as his personal colony, with rubber plantations supported by forced labor. The conditions were brutal; infamously, workers who did not meet their quota would have a hand hacked off. As European competition intensified, a world war seemingly loomed. In response to this rising tension, German Chancellor Otto von Bismarck called the Berlin Conference (1884–1885). Delegates—none of whom were African— were invited to establish the ground rules for the colonization of Africa. It was decided that any European state could establish an African colony after notifying the others and establishing a large enough presence.

European colonies in Africa operated under three main types of rule: direct rule, indirect rule, and settler rule. The French, Belgians, Germans, and Portuguese used direct rule. These centralized administrations, usually in urban centers, enforced assimilationist policies by forcing the adoption of Western values and customs. The British mostly used indirect rule to govern their colonies. This system used indigenous African rulers within the colonial administration, although they were often relegated to subordinate roles. Settler rule refers to the type of colonialism in which European settlers imposed direct rule on their colonies. Settler colonies differed from other African colonies in that many immigrants from Europe settled in these colonies. These settlers were not like missionaries or European colonial officials, who often remained attached to their countries of origin. They were more like early European settlers in the United States and Canada, who planned to make the colonies their permanent home and displace the native population.

Japan

Because Japan was so strengthened by government-sponsored industrialization, it was able to compete on the level of the major imperial powers. The First Sino-Japanese War (1894–1895) was sparked by a rebellion in Korea. Japan quickly defeated the Chinese fleet and was ceded Taiwan, the Pescadores Islands, and the Liaodong peninsula. China was forced to sign unequal treaties with Japan as it had with the Western powers. In 1910, Japan annexed Korea.

Japan's victory in the Russo-Japanese War (1904) is, however, the most notable globally. The war solidified Japan's international position. As the first time a non-European people had defeated a major Western power, it inspired anti-colonial activists across the world from Vietnam to Ireland. It also offered inspiration to states under threat of foreign encroachment, such as the Ottoman Empire.

The United States

The expansion of the United States was traditionally limited to the North American continent. However, the late nineteenth century saw a rise in imperialism due to three factors. First, the great powers of the era increasingly competed with one another to gain more colonies as a form of national prestige. Second, U.S. business interests were increasingly dependent on foreign trade and resources. Third, militarism grew increasingly popular, as war was seen as inherently positive.

In 1893, with the support of U.S. government officials, American and European business interests conspired to overthrow the Kingdom of Hawaii's queen and establish a republic. Hawaii was later annexed by the United States in 1898, the same year the Spanish-American War broke out. Ostensibly triggered by the alleged sinking of the *Maine* by Spanish forces, it involved the United States aiding independence efforts in Cuba to protect financial investments there, as well as to safeguard the Gulf Coast from a free Cuba potentially leasing its ports to foreign powers. The United States took control of Cuba, the Philippines, Puerto Rico, and several other islands. The U.S. occupation of the Philippines led to a long-running insurgency there in the Moro Rebellion (1899–1913). The United States also sponsored the secession of Panama from Columbia in this era, in order to secure land for the Panama Canal.

LEGACIES OF IMPERIALISM

Many economic and social changes occurred throughout the world as a result of imperialism. For one, local manufacturers were transformed into suppliers of raw materials and consumers of imported goods. In India, for instance, cotton was cultivated solely for export to England, and English textiles were then imported. India, once the world's leading manufacturer of cotton fabrics, became a consumer of British textiles.

Migration increased as well. Europeans migrated to the United States, Canada, Argentina, Australia, and South Africa in search of cheap land and better economic opportunities. These Europeans often served as a new labor force in industrializing areas. Most traveled as free agents, though some were **indentured servants**.

Migrants from Asia and Africa, on the other hand, were most often indentured servants and went to tropical lands in the Americas, the Caribbean, Africa, and Oceania. With the decrease in slavery, planters still needed laborers to work on their plantations. Because most of the migrant laborers were men, gender roles in the home societies shifted as women took on roles that men had done previously. Indentured servants were offered free passage, food, shelter, clothing, and some compensation, in return for five to seven years of work. As a result, large communities from around the world migrated to new lands, bringing their culture and traditions.

Despite their success at creating supportive ethnic enclaves when they were allowed to immigrate, migrants were often subjected to regulations aimed at blocking their entry into a new nation. For example, the **Chinese Exclusion Act** was passed by the U.S. Congress in 1882. This act placed a 10-year moratorium on Chinese immigration. The rationale for this discriminatory law was that Chinese migrants threatened the social order. Another example would be the "White Australia" policy, which discriminated against Asian and Pacific Islander immigrants. As one Australian prime minister remarked: "This country shall remain forever the home of the descendants of those people who came here in peace in order to establish in the South Seas an outpost of the British race."

EMANCIPATION

Slavery

As Enlightenment ideals of liberty and equality gained traction, many nineteenth-century people in Europe and North America supported the abolition of slavery, since the institution of slavery directly conflicted with these ideals. Additionally, frequent slave revolts in the 1700s and 1800s were making slavery a dangerous business. Economically, slavery became less profitable, as protection from the revolts required an expensive military force.

As the price of sugar decreased, the profitability of sugar declined, but the price for slaves increased. Many plantation owners shifted their investments to manufacturing, where wage labor was more profitable. In turn, those laborers would buy the manufactured goods. Though smuggling of slaves continued through much of the nineteenth century, the slave trade officially ended first in Great Britain in 1807, and then in the United States in 1808. While importing slaves to the United States was illegal after 1808, the institution itself was not. The **emancipation of the slaves** occurred in British colonies in 1833, French colonies in 1848, the United States in 1865, and Brazil in 1888.

Freedom, however, did not bring equality. In the southern United States, for example, property requirements, literacy tests, and poll taxes were implemented to prevent freed slaves from voting, and many freed slaves were trapped in low-paying jobs, such as tenant farming. Throughout the British Empire, colonial peoples, especially from China and India, essentially functioned as a disposable workforce.

The end of the transatlantic slave trade and the eventual emancipation of slaves throughout the Americas led to an increase in indentured servitude. In the mid to late nineteenth century, these indentured servants came from Asian nations like India, Ceylon (modern-day Sri Lanka), the Philippines, Indonesia, and China. This migration led to distinct cultural changes in many Latin American and Caribbean nations.

Serfdom

Eastern Europe and Russia are home to the Slavic peoples, whose ethnic name *slav* is a reference to the Latin word *sclavus* (slave). This is because the Slavic people were often bought and sold as slaves in Byzantium and the Muslim world in medieval times. The formal decline of slavery merely meant that slavs spent centuries toiling as serfs instead.

In Russia, opposition to serfdom had been growing since the 1700s. While some opposed it on moral grounds, most saw it as an obstacle to economic development in Russia, as well as a source of instability due to the possibility of peasant revolt. In 1861, Tsar Alexander II abolished serfdom, and the government compensated landowners for the loss of land and serfs. The serfs gained their freedom and their labor obligations were gradually cancelled.

Nevertheless, ex-serfs won very few political rights and had to pay a redemption tax for most of the land they received. Few former serfs prospered and most were desperately poor and uneducated. Their emancipation led to little increase in agricultural production, as peasants continued to use traditional methods of farming. It did, however, create a large urban labor force for the industrializing empire, providing a large base of revolutionary discontent for a future communist revolution.

Changing Gender Roles

High-Yield

Generally speaking, Enlightenment thinkers were fairly conservative in their views of women's roles in society. In an effort to challenge these widely held beliefs during the French Revolution, Olympe de Gouges's *Declaration of the Rights of Woman and of the Female Citizen* critiqued the inequality inherent in the *Declaration of the Rights of Man*. However, de Gouges was seen as speaking above her station. Suspected of being a royalist due to addressing her document to the queen, she was executed during the Reign of Terror.

Future reformers were influenced by de Gouges. Mary Wollstonecraft published *A Vindication of the Rights of Woman* in 1792, which argued that women should have access to a public education because they possessed the same capacity for reason as men. The writings of de Gouges were paraphrased for the Declaration of Sentiments at the Seneca Falls Conference of 1848. That convention, organized by Elizabeth Cady Stanton and Lucretia Mott, is commonly considered the beginning of the women's suffrage movement in the Western world.

In Britain, Canada, and the United States, a reform and pro-democratic women's movement became active in the nineteenth century. Women began to push for the right to vote in democratic elections. Advocates of **feminism** sought legal and economic gains for women, along with access to professions, education, and the right to vote.

Some feminists, however, were wary of granting women the right to vote, fearing they were too conservative and religious and would thus vote accordingly. The movement continued, however, and New Zealand became the first country to grant women the right to vote (1893). Several others followed after World War I, including Great Britain and Germany (1918), followed soon by the United States (1920).

CULTURAL INFLUENCES

African and Asian Influences on European Art

During this time of seeming Western cultural dominance, European artists took note of the artistic styles of both Africa and Asia. They admired the dramatic, spare style of traditional West African sculpture, wood, and metalwork, as well as the use of color and stylized forms of design found in Japan. Based on those Japanese influences, the Impressionists focused on simple themes in nature, feeling that this type of art liberated them from the rules of classical painting. A new movement of modern art was soon launched, free of traditional constraints.

Cultural Policies of Meiji Japan

As Japan was opening up to the industrialization of the West, it was also heavily influenced by the West's culture. Japanese literature took inspiration from European literature, and writers experimented with Western verse. Architects and artists created large buildings of steel, with Greek columns like those seen in the West, although wooden buildings would continue to predominate throughout the country until their destruction in the Allied firebombings of Japan in World War II.

Leisure and Consumption

The industrial age brought higher wages and shorter work hours. These changes gave people new opportunities. The middle class increased, leading to a new focus on the concept of leisure. The field of advertising communicated to the people the sense of needing things. The bicycle, for instance, became the "must-have item" of the 1880s and a vehicle of women's emancipation. Newspapers, theaters, and professional sports all became popular in this new era of leisure and consumption. The growth of sports spurred changes in fashion. Much as yoga pants became everyday clothing in the twenty-first century, the nineteenth and twentieth centuries saw sports clothing such as tennis shoes, polo shirts, shorts, and sweatshirts become widely adopted.

PRACTICE SET

Questions 1–3 refer to the passage below.

"Moreover, our part has always been a purely passive one; our political existence has always been null, and we find ourselves in greater difficulties in attaining our liberty than we ever had when we lived on a plane lower than servitude, because we had been robbed not only of liberty but also of active and domestic tyranny. . . .

We have been governed more by deception than by force, and we have been degraded more by vice than by superstition. Slavery is the offspring of Darkness; an ignorant people is a blind tool, turned to its own destruction; ambition and intrigue exploit the credulity and inexperience of men foreign to all political, economical or civil knowledge; mere illusions are accepted as reality, license is taken for liberty, treachery for patriotism, revenge for justice. . . . Liberty, says Rousseau, is a succulent food, but difficult to digest. Our feeble fellow-citizens will have to strengthen their mind much before they will be ready to assimilate such wholesome nourishment. Their limbs made numb by their fetters, their eyesight weakened in the darkness of their dungeons and their forces wasted away through their foul servitude, will they be capable of marching with a firm step towards the august temple of Liberty?"

Simón Bolívar, *The Address at the Congress of Angostura*, 1819

1. The passage is best understood as a justification for which of the following positions concerning newly independent Latin American states?

   (A) They should abolish slavery as quickly as possible to demonstrate their commitment to liberty.

   (B) They should establish a strong centralized government to promote stability and order.

   (C) They should establish democratic governments in order to maximize freedoms.

   (D) They should oppose domestic monarchies in order to prevent tyrannical oppression.

2. Which of the following revolutionary figures would be most likely to disagree with the concerns expressed in the passage?

   (A) Toussaint L'Ouverture

   (B) Thomas Jefferson

   (C) Hong Xiuquan

   (D) Napoleon Bonaparte

3. The creation of Gran Colombia at the end of the Congress at Angostura is most representative of which of the following nineteenth-century trends?

   (A) The rapid pace of industrialization

   (B) The abolition of slavery

   (C) The rise of nationalism

   (D) The development of a global economy

Questions 4–7 refer to the graph below.

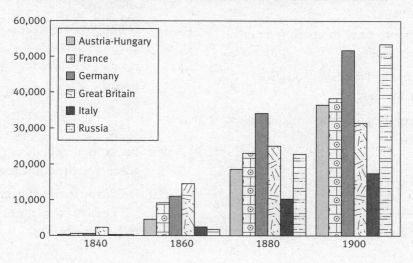

KILOMETERS OF OPEN RAILWAY IN SELECT COUNTRIES

4. A historian would be most likely to use the information depicted in the graph to support which of the following claims?

   (A) The expansion of railroad networks within a country coincided with industrialization within that country.

   (B) Countries of larger geographical size tended to build railroads sooner than countries of smaller geographical size.

   (C) The abolition of slavery in European countries contributed to the growth of railroad networks within those countries.

   (D) The first countries to build railroads tended to have the most kilometers of railroad by 1900.

5. Which of the following best explains the early development of railroads in Great Britain as illustrated by the graph?

   (A) Great Britain had large amounts of natural resources such as coal and iron, and railroads facilitated the transport of these raw materials to factories.

   (B) The size and geography of Great Britain made other forms of transportation difficult, which encouraged the development of railroad networks for travel.

   (C) In response to the threat of war, the British government invested heavily in railroad networks to transport troops and military supplies.

   (D) The urbanization of Great Britain increased the demand for vacation-related travel to rural areas, and railroads made such travel more convenient.

6. Which of the following accurately describes a common function of railroad networks?

   (A) They transported laborers from rural areas to urban areas.

   (B) They transported raw materials from urban areas to rural areas.

   (C) They transported finished goods from rural areas to urban areas.

   (D) They transported food from urban areas to rural areas.

7. The development of railroads in Russia as depicted in the graph was similar to the development of railroads in Japan in which of the following ways?

   (A) In both countries, the government played a significant role in the creation of the first railroad networks.

   (B) Both countries experienced rapid industrialization before building their first railroads.

   (C) Both countries built railroads primarily to advance imperialistic goals.

   (D) In both countries, the railroads were constructed primarily to serve as military transport networks.

Questions 8–10 refer to the image below.

TSUNAJIMA KAMEKICHI, JAPANESE WOODCUT PRINT, 1887

8. The artwork is best viewed as evidence for which of the following characteristics of the Meiji period?

   (A) The elimination of class-based restrictions on employment

   (B) Expanded roles for women in professional and social settings

   (C) A renewed interest in traditional Japanese art forms

   (D) Increased contact between Japan and other countries

9. A historian researching the Meiji period would most likely make which of the following claims about the artwork?

   (A) The grandfather represents the increase in familial devotion that occurred during the Meiji period.

   (B) The painter is indicative of the Meiji government's strong support of Japanese arts and culture.

   (C) The almanac represents the explosion of scientific knowledge that occurred during the Meiji period.

   (D) The gun represents the weakening of the samurai class as well as the military strength of the Meiji government.

10. Which of the following best describes the government of Japan prior to the Meiji period?

    (A) A feudal system that promoted isolationism

    (B) An imperial monarchy with a powerful emperor

    (C) A democracy based on Enlightenment ideals

    (D) A socialist government that promoted industry

Questions 11–15 refer to the maps below.

MAPS OF AFRICA, 1870 (LEFT) AND 1900 (RIGHT)

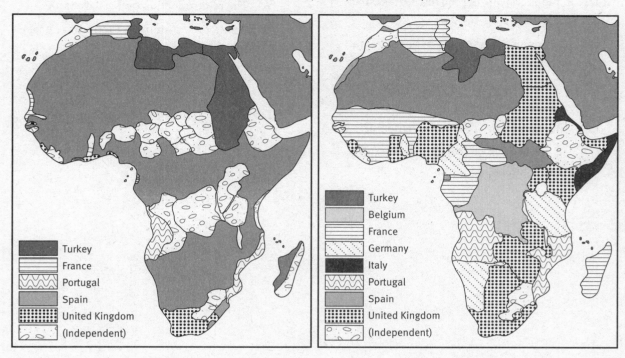

11. The changes reflected in the map of Africa <u>in 1900</u> best illustrate which of the following historical trends?

    (A) Industrialization

    (B) Nationalism

    (C) Decolonization

    (D) Imperialism

12. The expansion of Great Britain's territory as shown in the two maps serves as evidence of British colonizers' desire to

    (A) control a contiguous transportation route between British colonies and Europe

    (B) acquire as much territory as possible on the African continent

    (C) establish and maintain military dominance over indigenous African peoples

    (D) unite diverse African populations into a single British colony

13. Which of the following best explains the timing of the changes observed between the first and second maps?

    (A) Political instability within Africa had concerned European powers, and they believed that colonization would bring order and stability to the African continent.

    (B) Most European countries were suffering from labor shortages, and they established colonies in Africa to make it easier for African laborers to immigrate to Europe.

    (C) Much of Africa had already industrialized, and European powers wanted to colonize those regions in order to usurp their factories and other infrastructure.

    (D) Industrialization had led to higher unemployment in Europe, and European powers believed an influx of raw materials from Africa would alleviate this problem.

14. A proponent of Social Darwinism would have been most likely to express which of the following opinions concerning the territorial expansions depicted by the two maps?

    (A) They are justified on the basis of natural selection.

    (B) They represent an opportunity for rich cultural exchange.

    (C) They should be regarded as temporary.

    (D) They are too large to adequately control and should be reduced.

15. Which of the following was a direct result of the trend depicted in the two maps?

    (A) The reintroduction of the slave trade

    (B) An increase in immigration from Europe to Africa

    (C) An increase in immigration from Africa to Europe

    (D) The creation of African nation-states

Questions 16–19 refer to the passage below.

"But with the development of industry the proletariat not only increases in number; it becomes concentrated in greater masses, its strength grows, and it feels that strength more. The various interests and conditions of life within the ranks of the proletariat are more and more equalized, in proportion as machinery obliterates all distinctions of labor, and nearly everywhere reduces wages to the same low level. The growing competition among the bourgeois, and the resulting commercial crises, make the wages of the workers ever more fluctuating. The increasing improvement of machinery, ever more rapidly developing, makes their livelihood more and more precarious; the collisions between individual workmen and individual bourgeois take more and more the character of collisions between two classes. Thereupon the workers begin to form combinations . . . against the bourgeois; they club together in order to keep up the rate of wages; they found permanent associations in order to make provision beforehand for these occasional revolts. Here and there, the contest breaks out into riots."

Karl Marx and Friedrich Engels, *The Communist Manifesto*, 1888 edition

16. The views expressed in the passage allude to which of the following consequences of industrialization?

    (A) Industrialized countries tend to adopt isolationist foreign policies in order to protect their capital and their technology.

    (B) Manufacturing raises the price of finished goods, making them more difficult for the working class to afford.

    (C) Increased mechanization often leads to reduced wages and fewer jobs for laborers.

    (D) The construction of new factories increases the need for laborers in the industrial sector of the economy.

17. The concerns stated by Marx and Engels are best understood in the context of which of the following?

    (A) Governments seeking to protect workers through the passage of labor reform laws

    (B) Workers forming labor unions to agitate for changes in their working conditions

    (C) Businesses and other employers looking for ways to increase wages by reducing other costs

    (D) Loosely organized social movements promoting antidiscrimination policies in the workplace

18. The relationship between the bourgeoisie and the proletariat as described in the passage is most similar to the relationship between

    (A) the Qing Dynasty and members of the Taiping Heavenly Kingdom in China

    (B) British settlers and the Boers in South Africa

    (C) the Tokugawa shogunate and the Satsuma clan in Japan

    (D) nobles and serfs in the central and southern Russian Empire

19. A proponent of nineteenth-century liberalism would most likely offer which of the following responses to the ideas expressed in the passage?

    (A) Organized attempts to limit productivity or profitability unreasonably interfere with private property rights.

    (B) Governments should take a more active role in the protection of workers' rights.

    (C) Improving the economic circumstances of the poor is more important than promoting industrialization.

    (D) Expanding the role of women in the labor force would remedy some of the adverse economic consequences caused by industrialization.

Questions 20–22 refer to the image below.

PHILIP VEIT, *GERMANIA*, PAINTING, 1848

20. The painting is best understood in which of the following contexts?

   (A) The extension of legal and political rights to German women

   (B) The expansion of the German Empire through African colonization

   (C) The unification of Germany following the Springtime Revolutions

   (D) The passage of legal protections for persecuted religious minorities

21. Which of the following was an eventual result of the goal promoted by the painting?

   (A) Germany split into smaller political subdivisions and did not experience a rise in nationalism until the twentieth century.

   (B) Germany failed to industrialize by the end of the nineteenth century and its economy lagged behind those of other European countries.

   (C) Germany became a major military power and a leader of industrial and technological development by the end of the nineteenth century.

   (D) Germany abandoned its overseas colonies by the end of the nineteenth century in order to focus on democratic reforms and other domestic improvements.

22. Which of the following posed the greatest threat to the success of the goal promoted by the painting?

    (A) The creation of the Zionist movement

    (B) The establishment of German colonies in Africa

    (C) The rise of German nationalism

    (D) The emergence of rival political factions

Questions 23–25 refer to the map below.

PATTERNS OF CHINESE EMIGRATION IN THE LATE NINETEENTH CENTURY

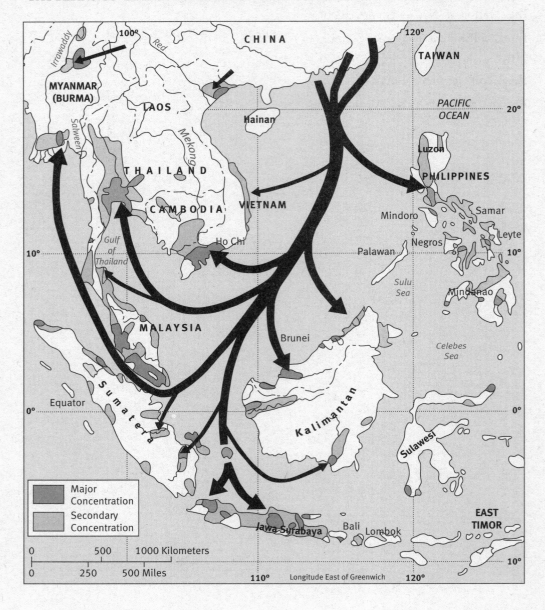

23. Which of the following would be most likely to describe a group of Chinese emigrants whose movements are depicted in the graph?

    (A) Chinese Christians escaping religious persecution

    (B) Political dissidents seeking refuge with friendly governments

    (C) Educators and scientists planning to work for foreign universities

    (D) Unskilled laborers seeking work abroad

24. Which of the following best explains why Chinese immigration to North America was far more limited at the time than the migration indicated in the map?

    (A) High levels of unemployment in the United States and Canada at the time made North America an unattractive destination for Chinese emigrants.

    (B) Rising tensions between China and Japan, culminating in the Sino-Japanese War, made ocean travel to North America difficult during the period depicted.

    (C) The United States and Canada had recently passed laws that severely restricted Chinese immigration into those countries.

    (D) Lingering resentment against the United States for its role in perpetuating the opium trade dissuaded Chinese emigrants from settling there.

25. Which of the following factors outside of China would also have contributed to the emigration pattern depicted in the map?

    (A) The expansion of European imperialism in Africa

    (B) The publication of *The Communist Manifesto*

    (C) The abolition of slavery in industrialized countries

    (D) The end of the Tanzimât reforms in the Ottoman Empire

9

ANSWER KEY

1. B	6. A	11. D	16. C	21. C
2. B	7. A	12. A	17. B	22. D
3. C	8. D	13. D	18. D	23. D
4. A	9. D	14. A	19. A	24. C
5. A	10. A	15. B	20. C	25. C

ANSWERS AND EXPLANATIONS

1. B

In his speech, Bolívar expresses the concern that those living in newly independent states lack experience governing themselves, making it difficult to maintain long-term independence. As a result of this concern, Bolívar advocated for a republican form of government rather than a pure democracy, at least initially, since republicanism would insulate the government from the whims of the majority. Bolívar thought that a strong central authority would help keep the people in check during this period of transition from colony to independent nation-state. Thus, **(B)** is correct. While Bolívar generally endorsed abolition, (A) is incorrect because this passage isn't about slavery; the reference to slavery is a metaphor for the lack of political freedom that could result from the ignorance and inexperience of the people. (C) is incorrect because the passage warns against the notion of maximizing freedoms; Bolívar's concern is that the people will mistake liberty for license to do harm, just as they may mistake patriotism and justice for treachery and vengeance, respectively. (D) is incorrect because the passage does not address the notion of domestic monarchies in its discussion of how the Latin American people will or should respond to their newfound freedom.

2. B

Bolívar endorsed a strong centralized government to promote stability and order during a potentially chaotic transition period. In contrast, Thomas Jefferson, the author of the U.S. Declaration of Independence, advocated for a weaker national government and greater rights for individuals. While both Jefferson and Bolívar were influenced by Enlightenment ideals, they diverged on this key issue. Thus, **(B)** is correct. (A), (C), and (D) are incorrect; Toussaint L'Ouverture, Hong Xiuquan, and Napoleon Bonaparte each endorsed the consolidation of power into a strong central authority in response to the chaos brought about by revolution.

3. C

Gran Colombia was a centralist state that represented Bolívar's vision of a United States of Latin America, uniting Spanish-speaking Creoles into a single nation-state. Thus, Gran Colombia is representative of the rise of nationalism, making **(C)** correct. (A) is incorrect because Gran Colombia was a political entity, not an economic one, so it was not representative of the Industrial Revolution. Similarly, Gran Colombia was not known for participating in the global economy, making (D) incorrect. While Gran Colombia partially abolished slavery in 1821, slavery existed in some form in Gran Colombia until it was dissolved; moreover, Gran Colombia was not created for the purpose of abolishing slavery, so (B) is incorrect.

4. A

Great Britain is notable for being an early industrializer; in fact, many historians would contend that the Industrial Revolution began there. By contrast, Russia is known for its relatively late industrialization when compared to other European countries. Looking at the graph, Great Britain had railroads sooner than the other countries depicted and had the most kilometers of railroad in 1840 and 1860. By 1900, however, after industrialization had taken hold in Russia, that country had more kilometers of railroad than the other countries depicted, including Great Britain. Thus, the graph seems to demonstrate a connection between industrialization and railroad construction; **(A)** is correct. (B) and (D) are incorrect because they contradict information in the graph. Great Britain is a smaller country, but it had the earliest railroads, contradicting (B); similarly, Great Britain had the earliest railroads, but by 1900 it had the second fewest kilometers of railroad among the countries depicted, contradicting (D). (C) is incorrect because the information in the graph does not indicate a relationship between the development of railroads and the abolition of slavery; some countries, like Great Britain, experienced a spike in railroad construction shortly after abolishing slavery, but other countries, like France and Russia, did not experience a significant increase in railroad construction until much later.

5. A

Great Britain was an early industrializer, a fact that is often credited to its great stores of natural resources such as coal and iron that could be used as raw materials for manufacturing. Railroads helped Great Britain utilize these materials more efficiently, so **(A)** is correct. (B) is incorrect because there is nothing about Great Britain's geography that makes other forms of travel particularly difficult; in fact, Great Britain had a system of roads and waterways that long pre-dated the development of train travel. (C) is incorrect because the railroads were not developed for the military, although the British government later used them for that purpose. Similarly, while railroads were eventually used for leisure travel, they were not built for that purpose, making (D) incorrect.

6. A

Railroads served a key role in the Industrial Revolution by transporting raw materials and finished goods between producers and consumers. Railroads also made it easier for laborers in rural areas to travel to cities for work, making **(A)** correct. (B) and (C) incorrectly state the flow of materials and goods; raw materials tended to move from rural areas where mines were located to urban areas where factories were located, while trains then took finished goods from urban factories back to rural areas for sale. Similarly, (D) is incorrect because food would have traveled from farms in rural areas to urban areas rather than the other way around.

7. A

Both Russia and Japan industrialized later in the nineteenth century than other countries such as Great Britain and the United States. Consequently, industrialization in both Russia and Japan was largely driven by their respective governments, which were trying to keep pace with economic and technological advancements elsewhere in the world. In both Russia and Japan, this included the creation of railroads, making **(A)** correct. (B) is incorrect because industrialization happened in tandem with railroad creation, not before. (C) and (D) are incorrect for similar reasons: Russia and Japan built their railroads primarily for economic reasons, even if they may have sometimes been used for other purposes.

8. D

The Meiji period began in response to an internal conflict that arose in Japan after the United States attempted to open trade with the country. The existing Japanese government wanted to maintain its policy of isolation, but a dissenting faction of the ruling class wanted to open up Japan to foreign trade and technological influence. Ultimately, the dissenting faction overthrew the existing government and restored imperial rule under Emperor Meiji, which ultimately led to increased contact between Japan and other countries, especially the United States. The woodcut illustrates this growing relationship between Japan and the West by providing both the Japanese word and the English translation for each object depicted. Thus, **(D)** is correct. (A) is a characteristic of the Meiji period, but it is not depicted in the artwork. (B) and (C) are incorrect because they do not describe characteristics commonly associated with the Meiji period.

9. D

During the Meiji period, Japan underwent rapid industrialization and became a leading military power. In addition, the power of the samurai class was weakened, in part by permitting others to own weapons, such as guns. Thus, **(D)** is correct. (A), (B), and (C) are all incorrect for similar reasons: the Meiji period was not characterized by an increase in familial devotion, (A), government support of the arts, (B), or greater scientific knowledge, (C).

10. A

Prior to the Meiji period, Japan had a feudal system made up of loosely connected clans and was ruled by a military government referred to as the Tokugawa shogunate, which had a long-standing policy of isolationism and permitted very little contact with other countries, especially those outside of Asia. Thus, **(A)** is correct. (B) is incorrect because the Meiji period restored power to the emperor of Japan; prior to this period, the emperor was a figurehead without any significant government authority. (C) and (D) are incorrect for similar reasons: Japan had neither a democratic nor a socialist government prior to the Meiji period.

11. D

The colonization of Africa by Europe in the late 1800s and early 1900s is an example of imperialism; the map of Africa in 1900 shows an increase in colonized land, by multiple imperial powers, as compared to the map of Africa in 1870. Thus, **(D)** is correct and (C) is incorrect. (A) is incorrect because, while colonization provided access to raw materials that ultimately promoted industrialization, the maps do not depict industrialization. (B) is incorrect because nationalism refers to uniting people with a common language or heritage into a single nation-state, while the map shows boundaries imposed by foreigners with little regard for pre-existing cultural or ethnic population groups.

12. A

A primary motivator for Great Britain's colonization efforts in Africa was to build a contiguous railway from South Africa to Egypt to make the transport of raw materials from Africa to Europe more efficient. This is reflected in the two maps; in 1870, Great Britain occupied only the southern tip of Africa and a few small areas in western Africa, but by 1900 Great Britain had acquired additional colonies in the African interior that almost, but not quite, formed a contiguous area from South Africa to Egypt. Thus, **(A)** is correct. (B) is incorrect because British colonial interests were more focused than the choice implies. (C) is incorrect because it states that the purpose of colonization was to establish military dominance over African colonies, but that was more a method of colonization rather than a motivation for colonizing in the first place. In addition, Britain tended to manage its African colonies through indirect rule, rather than through direct military oversight. (D) is incorrect because Great Britain did not intend to create one unified colony; this is evident in the second map, which shows boundary lines between contiguous British colonies, indicating that they were considered separated territories rather than one unified colony.

13. D

In the late nineteenth century, Europe was struggling with high unemployment, a consequence of rapid industrialization and increased mechanization. European powers believed that an influx of new capital in the form of raw materials would help to create more jobs, and they looked to Africa to provide this capital. Thus, **(D)** is correct. Although geopolitical stability was a motivating factor for European colonizers, their concern was about interactions among European powers, not conflicts within Africa, making (A) incorrect. (B) and (C) are incorrect because they describe circumstances that did not exist during the late nineteenth century.

14. A

Proponents of European colonization often used Social Darwinism—the belief that more powerful peoples dominating weaker peoples is a form of natural selection—to justify imperialism. Thus, **(A)** is correct. (B) is incorrect because European colonization was typically motivated by economic considerations, not the potential for cultural exchange. (C) and (D) are incorrect because these views were not held by Social Darwinists; rather, they viewed European expansion of colonized territories as an inevitable and desirable outcome, and they supported increased colonization efforts.

15. B

Many European colonies in Africa operated under settler rule, in which European settlers migrated to Africa and established a permanent homestead there, similar to the early European settlers of North America. Thus, **(B)** is correct. Although working conditions for African laborers in European colonies were often quite harsh, (A) is incorrect because these workers were not considered slaves and the slave trade was not reintroduced during this period. (C) is incorrect because European colonization did not result in any significant immigration from Africa to Europe. (D) is incorrect because the boundary lines of European colonies often did not reflect the geographic distribution of indigenous African ethnic groups, making it more difficult to establish African nation-states in the long run; any nation-states that were created in the twentieth century would not have been a *direct* result of European colonization.

16. C

The passage states that machinery "reduces wages" and that further technological advancement "makes [workers'] livelihood more and more precarious." In other words, Marx and Engels are concerned about the wages and job security of workers after industrialization, making **(C)** correct. (A), (B), and (D) are incorrect because they are not typical consequences of industrialization: usually, industrialized countries participate in the global economy, making (A) incorrect; manufacturing usually decreases labor costs and results in cheaper goods, making (B) incorrect; and new factories often result in a loss of jobs due to increased mechanization, making (D) incorrect.

17. B

The passage mentions that workers have started to form "combinations" and "club together" in response to their class struggles against the bourgeoisie. Thus, **(B)** is correct. (A), (C), and (D) are incorrect because they do not describe trends that coincided with the time period of the passage; government labor reforms and antidiscrimination movements were largely twentieth-century developments, and during the nineteenth century business and industry were more focused on their own profits than on the wages or working conditions of their laborers.

18. D

The relationship between the proletariat and the bourgeoisie is economic; the proletariat are the laborers, and the bourgeoisie control the capital. Of the choices, only Russian serfs and nobles have such an economic relationship. Russian nobles owned the land that the serfs worked, and the nobles profited from the serfs' labor, much in the same way that the bourgeoisie control the capital and profit from the labor of the proletariat. In addition, the larger number of Russian serfs compared to nobles ultimately led to civil and political unrest, just as the passage described. Thus, **(D)** is correct. (A), (B), and (C) are incorrect because they refer to political, not economic, conflicts: the members of the Taiping Heavenly Rebellion fought the Qing Dynasty to reverse ethnic and religious persecution; the Boers and the British fought over political control of land in southern Africa; and the Satsuma clan in Japan was part of the samurai class that challenged the Tokugawa shogunate over its foreign policy.

19. A

Liberalism in the nineteenth century was strongly influenced by the Enlightenment; it was characterized by a belief in natural rights and limited government, especially concerning the economy. Proponents of liberalism tended to promote laissez-faire economic policies and were typically protective of private property rights and skeptical about socialism and labor movements. Thus, **(A)** is correct. (B) and (C) are incorrect because they express positions that are the opposite of nineteenth-century liberalism. (D) is incorrect because, although some proponents of liberalism, particularly those in France, might have endorsed egalitarianism, they would not have viewed an influx of labor as a solution to the problem discussed in the passage; if anything, women entering the workforce would have compounded the problem of a labor surplus and led to even greater unemployment.

20. C

The title indicates that this painting was completed in 1848. Multiple revolutions swept across Europe during the spring of 1848, including a short-lived revolution in Germany known as the March Revolution. Like other revolutions of the same year, the March Revolution aimed to unify disparate German states into one nation and enact democratic reforms. *Germania* is a symbol of this movement; the figure depicted is carrying the German flag and wearing the German crest, and she is larger than the landscape behind her, suggesting the notion of a united Germany that was greater than the sum of its parts. Thus, **(C)** is correct. (A), (B), and (D) are incorrect: in the middle of the nineteenth century, Germany was not experiencing strong movements promoting women's rights, imperialism, or protections for religious minorities, nor does the symbolism in the painting suggest any of these things.

21. C

The painting symbolizes the unification of Germany. Although some Germans' attempt at unification in 1848 was ultimately unsuccessful, a German nation-state eventually emerged in 1871. The unification of Germany led to the consolidation of wealth and power into a single nation, which sparked rapid industrialization and promoted military strength. Thus, **(C)** is correct. (A) is incorrect because the unification of Germany was completed in 1871, an event that both followed and contributed to a rise in German nationalism during the late nineteenth century. (B) is incorrect because it contradicts historical fact; Germany experienced rapid industrialization as a result of unification. (D) is incorrect because Germany maintained its overseas colonies throughout the nineteenth century, losing them only after the First World War.

22. D

When the German Empire was founded in 1871, there had already been several short-lived attempts to create a German nation-state. These previous attempts failed primarily due to competing political factions that could not agree on what type of government a unified Germany should adopt. Thus, **(D)** is correct. (A) is incorrect because the Zionist movement promoted the creation of a Jewish nation-state in the Middle East, not in Germany, so it didn't pose a threat to German unification. (B) and (C) are incorrect because those circumstances had the effect of supporting, rather than threatening, the unification of Germany.

23. D

The map depicts the Chinese diaspora that began during the middle of the nineteenth century. This wave of emigration was primarily driven by economic factors, as uneducated and unskilled workers sought jobs as laborers in foreign countries. Thus, **(D)** is correct. (A) and (B) are incorrect because they describe emigration factors that correspond to later periods in Chinese history: many Christians left China following the Boxer Rebellion in 1900, and both Christians and political dissidents were motived to emigrate later in the twentieth century due to the repressive policies of the communist Chinese government. (C) is incorrect because the emigrants who were part of the wave depicted in the map were mostly uneducated.

24. C

In 1882, the United States passed its Chinese Exclusion Act, which prohibited the immigration of unskilled laborers from China; Canada followed with a similar law a few years later. These laws remained in effect until well into the twentieth century, and they explain why Chinese immigration to North America was limited. Thus, **(C)** is correct. (A) and (B) are incorrect because they make inaccurate statements about the time period: North America was not experiencing high unemployment during the late nineteenth century, and the Sino-Japanese war did not significantly limit ocean travel. (D) is incorrect because lingering resentment, if any, about the opium trade would not have significantly impacted immigration to North America, since Great Britain was the primary foreign participant in the Chinese opium trade.

25. C

The abolition of slavery worldwide by the end of the nineteenth century created a labor shortage in much of the world. Agricultural and industrial employers looked to countries with large populations of unskilled workers, such as China and India, as a new source of labor. Thus, **(C)** is correct. (A) is incorrect because the colonization of Africa would not have had much, if any, impact on Chinese emigration patterns, as European colonizers primarily relied on existing African populations to support their labor force. (B) is incorrect because *The Communist Manifesto* promoted workers' rights, but did not specifically encourage (or discourage) emigration. (D) is incorrect because the end of Tanzimât Movement, which had strengthened the legal system, infrastructure, and military of the Ottoman Empire, would not have had a direct impact on the depicted Chinese emigration.

CHAPTER 10

1900 to the Present

ORIGINS OF WORLD WAR I

The span between 1789 and 1914 is sometimes referred to as "the long nineteenth century." Regardless of one's stance on monarchism and republicanism, capitalism and socialism, European politics was marked by forward-looking optimism, a belief in the perfection of civilization, and a steadfast confidence in European superiority. Then came 1914.

Long-Term Causes of WWI

While Europe had enjoyed a general peace for almost a century after the Battle of Waterloo, long-running issues made a general war more likely. First, tensions stemmed from imperialism both in Europe and in the world at large. As the Ottoman Empire weakened and withdrew from its Balkan lands in southeastern Europe, the Austro-Hungarian and Russian Empires competed to acquire or dominate the area. At the same time, Britain, France, Germany, and Italy engaged in competition for overseas colonies, like those in Africa.

Second, the European balance of power had long depended on **alliances**, defensive plans that would protect a nation in the event that it was attacked. But by 1914, the major powers found themselves committed to supporting their allies even in conflicts that did not threaten their own interests. Germany, Austria-Hungary, and Italy had mutual agreements, and France and Russia were allied if Germany were to attack either one.

Third, nationalism undermined traditional multinational empires. The establishment of Italy and Germany (both in 1871) inspired nationalist movements elsewhere. Poles, Irish, Slavic peoples, Arabs, and others hoped for their own nations. These groups lived within multinational empires that would not agree to their own dissolution.

Fourth, **militarism** was popular in this period. War was seen as an honorable and even purifying aspect of human nature. Militarism led to constant threats, arms races, and ultimatums over minor disputes. For example, the naval arms race between Germany and Britain caused friction between two nations that had previously been allies.

Immediate Causes of WWI

World War I began when all four factors—nationalism, alliances, imperialism, and militarism—violently intersected. During a tour of a Balkan province in the summer of 1914, the heir to the Austro-Hungarian throne and his wife were assassinated by Slav nationalists who wanted the province united with other southern Slavic nations. Austria-Hungary accused Serbia of supporting the terrorists and declared war. Russia sided with its Slavic ally Serbia, while Germany pledged support for Austria-Hungary, its close Germanic ally. When Germany declared war on Russia, France honored its alliance and joined Russia. Great Britain, with no alliances, was the last major European power to enter the war, when German forces violated Belgium's neutrality on their way to attack France.

WORLD WAR I

World War I, originally referred to as the Great War, was largely fought in Europe and the Middle East, but because of European economic and imperial dominion in much of the world at the time, there were secondary fronts in Africa, Asia, and on all the world's oceans. Technologically advanced weapons led to casualties in the millions. The heroic notion of war died in the trenches. In crucial ways that played out over the rest of the century, European civilization lost its self-assured sense of superiority.

While both the Taiping Rebellion and the American Civil War had seen instances of **total war**, World War I applied the doctrine to modern industrialized states. Whole nations were mobilized. Economies were reordered to support the military. As men left for the front, women entered the workforce. The waging of total war has militarized civilian life in countless ways ever since World War I. New media such as posters, radio, and cinema extended governments' ability to propagandize their wars. The logic of total war made the "home front" a legitimate military target. It also made endless sacrifice in the name of national defense an accepted aspect of modern life. Aircraft bombed cities, and navies cut off food shipments to starve whole populations into surrender. From this point forward, no conflict, no matter how small, has excluded civilians from being targets.

> ✔ **AP Expert Note**
>
> **Be aware of the impact of gender and class hierarchies during World War I**
>
> Be sure to keep in mind the completeness of total war. While working class women entered the labor force to support the war effort, middle- and upper-class women were mobilized as a propaganda arm of the state. For example, British women were encouraged to give white feathers symbolizing cowardice to military-age men not in uniform, to shame them into enlisting.

The Treaty of Versailles

`High-Yield`

In the end, the Central Powers were unable to hold out against British, French, and American economic and military pressure, even after Russia had left the war and conceded Eastern Europe to the Germans in the Treaty of Brest-Litovsk. Germany sued for an armistice in November 1918.

The peace conference for World War I was held near Paris at the Palace of Versailles. The leading Allied powers—Italy, Great Britain, France, and the United States—were labeled the Big Four. The

European victors looked to increase their power at the expense of the defeated enemy. In contrast, U.S. president Woodrow Wilson entered the Versailles meetings with his plan, called the Fourteen Points. He called for self-determination of nationalities, peace without victory, disarmament, fair treatment of colonial peoples, and the establishment of the **League of Nations**, a multinational organization for maintaining world peace.

France, supported by Britain, would not allow the generous peace that Wilson had envisioned. Although most of Wilson's ideas were rejected, the League of Nations was approved. Ironically, the U.S. Congress opposed it and the United States did not join the idealistic new international order. The league was established in 1921, but without the great powers of America, Russia, or Germany (before 1926) as members, it struggled to keep the peace when tensions arose.

The Treaty of Versailles laid down harsh terms to which Germany had to agree: accepting sole responsibility for starting the war and paying heavy reparations that would cripple its economy. The map of Europe was redrawn at the expense of the German, Austro-Hungarian, and Russian empires. New nations such as Poland, Czechoslovakia, Hungary, and Yugoslavia were all created in 1919.

Impact on the Allies

The Russian state collapsed. A liberal revolution overthrew the tsar in 1917, but a communist coup seized power months later. The communist government withdrew from the war and signed a desperate peace treaty with Germany in early 1918. A multisided civil war broke out almost immediately. The two biggest factions were leftists led by the Bolsheviks (Reds) and a "big tent" anti-communist alliance (Whites). Over a million Russians died before the final Red victory and the establishment of the Union of Soviet Socialist Republics (USSR) in 1922. Ideologically anti-capitalist and angered by Western intervention in their civil war, the Bolsheviks withdrew from European diplomacy while promoting communist revolution wherever they could, adding to the instability of the postwar world order.

Great Britain lost a significant percentage of its young men. Economically exhausted, it owed billions in loans to the United States. Imperial dominions like Canada and Australia had developed stronger nationalistic identities due to wartime, Ireland revolted and won independence, while independence movements in Africa and Asia grew in strength.

France suffered worse. The Western Front was fought on its territory, with huge casualties and destruction of property. Swaths of the French countryside remain poisoned into the present day. French colonial troops returned to their native countries, with their experiences helping to fuel independence movements. France was also in debt to the United States.

Italy, one of the leading Allied nations, had been promised large portions of the Austro-Hungarian Empire. It received some but not all it had hoped for. Postwar politicians continued to press for more concessions, looking for other imperial projects to distract the nation from its internal divisions.

The United States was elevated to great power status by the war, but the failure of Wilsonian internationalism disillusioned Americans. Its traditional isolationism persisted, as the United States shunned "foreign entanglements" like the League of Nations, which might require it to become involved in foreign conflicts. Conservatives won the White House in 1920, focusing on industrial expansion and retreating from European affairs.

Japan received Germany's Asian territories. At Versailles, it proposed a Racial Equality clause for the League of Nations, hoping to be recognized as an Asian world power fully equal to Europe and America. The Western powers refused, further inflaming Japanese resentment and nationalism.

Impact on the Central Powers

Germany was economically, politically, and socially devastated. It had lost millions of men in the fighting and was now forced to pay huge reparations to the Allies. In addition, it lost its army and navy, all of its overseas empire, and the productive provinces on its eastern and western borders. The Kaiser abdicated and out of the chaos of democratic, socialist, and communist uprisings, a weak parliamentary-style government was assembled in Weimar in 1919. Within a few years, hyperinflation devastated the middle class and angry ex-soldiers promoted the myth that Germany had not been defeated militarily, but had been "stabbed in the back" by traitors on the home front.

Austria-Hungary dissolved as the war ended. The Treaty of Versailles confirmed the independence of new nations like Poland, Czechoslovakia, Yugoslavia, Hungary, and the small new ethnically German state of Austria. Each of these states was individually weaker than the old empire had been, however. The area promised to be the seedbed of future conflicts over nationalism and renewed imperial control by greater powers for the rest of the century.

The Ottoman Empire, which had fought with the Central Powers, was partitioned after the war. Freed from Turkish domination, Arab nationalism rose, inspired partly by Wilson's call for national self-determination and partly by Allied promises made in return for help in defeating the Ottomans. Instead, their land was carved into French and British zones of imperial control, called *mandates*. Palestine was a center of tension, where Arab nationalists competed with Jewish Zionists for control of land they had both been vaguely promised by the British. A rump Ottoman Empire briefly survived, until Turkey declared itself a republic and, under the leadership of Mustafa Kemal Ataturk, instituted a program of modernization and westernization. In the final years of the Ottoman Empire, the Young Turk government undertook the systematic genocide of the Armenian people.

Impact on Other World Powers

Chinese nationalism surged after Japan gained Germany's concessions in China. Beginning with riots and continuing with the cultural and intellectual May Fourth Movement, World War I marked a shift toward a more populist political base and away from the intellectual elites of the former imperial governing class. Both Chinese nationalists in the 1920s and 1930s and Chinese communists in the latter half of the century drew on this growing populism.

India fought loyally as part of the British Empire in World War I, in the hopes of gaining more independence after the war. While Britain introduced some minor reforms and liberalization, it maintained complete control over the Raj. This led to a surge in Indian nationalism under the

10

leadership of the Congress Party as well as the charismatic **Mohandas Gandhi**, who demanded full independence. As with other parts of the colonial world, Indians saw Europeans in a new light after the self-destructive maelstrom of the Great War.

Many colonized peoples complained that Wilson's "self-determination" only applied to nations dominated by the defeated Central Powers. The British and French Empires continued to rule over millions of Africans and Asians, and they would continue to do so until after the next World War.

GLOBAL DEPRESSION

High-Yield

The 1920s saw further modernization of the world economy and concerted efforts by Europeans and Americans to build a future free of war. This changed by the 1930s. One of the greatest causes of the long spiral downwards to **World War II** was the **Great Depression**, which struck in 1929. As the leading creditor nation, the United States was crucial to the health of world markets. After the New York stock market collapsed in October 1929, the American credit-based economy contracted. Existing loans were called in, and new loans were cancelled.

The causes of the Great Depression include:

- Overdependence on American loans and purchasing
- Industrial and farming surpluses leading to deflation
- Poor banking management before and after the market crash
- Increased tariffs and protectionism leading to a trade war

The impact was especially severe in Europe, which had depended on American loans to recover from World War I. A wave of U.S. bank failures had a ripple effect in London, Berlin, Tokyo, and other financial capitals. Global unemployment rose to double-digit levels. Countries tried to protect their economies by cutting public expenditures and limiting imports, which tended to worsen the problems. For example, the United States passed the highest tariff (a tax on imports) in its history, the Smoot-Hawley Tariff Act, sparking a trade war and further limiting its trading partners' abilities to repay their American debts.

CONTRACTION OF WORLD TRADE, 1929–1933

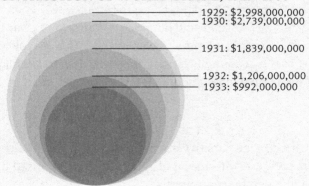

1929: $2,998,000,000
1930: $2,739,000,000
1931: $1,839,000,000
1932: $1,206,000,000
1933: $992,000,000

Economic hardship led to social instability and a rise in political extremism in many nations. On the left, communists criticized the obvious failings of capitalism and advocated Soviet-style collectivism. On the right, fascists sought governmental control and direction of private enterprise to achieve national self-sufficiency. Britain, France, and the United States remained democracies even as they experimented with more state regulation of their economies. Japan, Italy, and Germany looked to dictatorial rule to unify their divided societies, overcome economic hardships, and solidify national power and prestige through aggressions against their neighbors.

RISE OF FASCIST AND TOTALITARIAN STATES

Many countries veered toward increased state power and authoritarian regimes in the 1930s, but a few countries had a large impact on the rest of the world. These large, powerful countries took totalitarian doctrines of state control to the furthest extremes. Fascism and communism were presented as alternatives to the democratic capitalist world order, which seemed to be self-destructing during the Great Depression.

Fascism takes its name from the Italian word *fascio*, literally "a bundle of sticks." It references an old symbol of many thin sticks bound together. Each individual stick was weak, but together they were resilient. Fascists presented themselves as national unifiers, creating one people under one leader. Fascists saw communism as a threat to private property and traditional social structures. So they aimed to destroy labor unions while "balancing" the classes through domination of independent big business. Thus, fascism would dub itself "national socialism" in contrast to Soviet-style "international socialism," even as fascists themselves were hostile to the rights of workers in actual practice.

Fascism centered on the unquestioned rule by a single charismatic leader, with no opposing state institutions. A single political party overrode and dominated all social structures. Fascism embraced ultra-nationalism and glorification of the state. It glorified war as the ultimate expression of power. It rejected liberalism and democracy as weak, failed concepts.

Italy

By 1921, the success of Marxist revolution in Russia led to a growing fear of communism in other nations, especially those that had been destabilized by the war. It was in Italy that the first fully organized reactionary and anti-democratic movement emerged. A small group of men led by **Benito Mussolini** marched on Rome in 1922, demanding to form a government. The king consented, and Italy was soon dominated by Mussolini and his Fascists. Mussolini became the prototypical modern dictator as he accumulated more and more power. By the 1930s, his rule was unquestioned. In light of the tenuous status of the League of Nations, Italy was able to brutally invade Ethiopia in 1935, conquering one of Africa's only independent states.

Germany

The Weimar Republic tried to reestablish Germany's place in the international community. However, the Great Depression, with the withdrawal of American credit, caused a collapse of the economy and rising popularity for German communists.

Opposing the communists with street fighting and uniformed gangs was the National Socialist German Workers' Party, also known as the Nazi Party. Its charismatic leader **Adolf Hitler** railed against communism and used traditional anti-Semitism to suggest that communism was really a global conspiracy organized by the Jewish people. In fact, all of Germany's economic, diplomatic, and social problems were blamed on the nation's Jewish population. Nazism's greatest difference from fascism, on which it was based, was this addition of racial hatred and the promotion of Aryan (Germanic) racial superiority.

In 1933, with a close election victory, Hitler was appointed chancellor. He became dictator, or führer, within months by eliminating his political opponents through terror, intimidation, and forced labor camps. Jews were increasingly persecuted and driven from public life. The Nazi Party and its propaganda of German revival and expansion dominated most areas of national life. Nazi Germany pushed to annul the Versailles treaty's restrictions on German power and to weaken the Western-led alliances among its neighbors. By 1936, the German army moved to reoccupy the demilitarized Rhineland on the French border.

Japan

The "Taishō democracy" of the post-WWI period gave way to repression of communists and labor activists alike. The Great Depression exacerbated existing trends toward an aggressive anti-Western nationalism. A preexisting sense of Japanese racial superiority gained a militant edge. Military officers increasingly replaced civilian politicians in the highest posts of government. One feature of Japanese authoritarianism was an emphasis on collective rule in the name of the divine emperor; Japan was never ruled by a glorified dictator.

Soviet Union

At the same time that Mussolini was consolidating his power in Italy and Hitler was beginning his rise, there was a transfer of power in Moscow. Lenin, the architect of the Bolshevik Revolution, died of a stroke seven years after the revolution. The resulting power struggle within the ruling Bolshevik party ended when **Joseph Stalin** took control in 1927.

Marx's original communism had promoted the idea of a collective leadership, effecting a "dictatorship of the people." Stalin, following Lenin's example but also in line with Russia's tradition of absolute rule, ruthlessly eliminated his colleagues and twisted communism into a one-man dictatorship. His method of rule became associated with modern Soviet-style communism, but it is also referred to as Stalinism.

The ideological attributes of Stalinist communism are:

- Complete state ownership and centralized control of the economy through the use of a Five-Year Plan

- Forced industrialization to modernize the country and military in defense against a hostile capitalist world

- World leadership in the international communist movement to subvert capitalism and imperialism

- Forced collectivism for farming and control of food supply

- Promotion of atheism, forcing organized religion underground

- Complete control of all culture, art, media, and entertainment in service of communism

Drawing from lessons learned during the waging of total war from 1914 to 1918, Stalin, Hitler, and Mussolini represented a new form of political leadership in the twentieth century. Along with the rule of Japan's generals, their dictatorships demonstrated that political ideology, right or left, communist or anti-communist, was in some ways less important than the methods and goals used to mobilize society. Whether in Berlin or Moscow, modern totalitarianism displayed certain distinct features.

ORIGINS OF WORLD WAR II

While the Treaty of Versailles and the societal dysfunction caused by the Great Depression contributed to the outbreak of World War II, those two elements were not the only contributing factors.

The League of Nations

The League of Nations was an organization of mostly European nations but also Japan, Ethiopia, Siam, and many Latin American states. The isolationist United States never joined. The league did have some successes in demonstrating the power of institutional cooperation between nations, notably with combating malaria and other diseases in Europe, stopping labor abuses, controlling the distribution of opium products, and lessening the slave trade in Africa and Asia. However, the league never succeeded with its primary purpose, that of stopping large-scale international conflicts.

Dominated by Britain and France, two powers still war-wary after World War I, the league promoted voluntary cooperation and anti-war policies like trade sanctions rather than creating a global police force. In the 1930s, the league failed to react effectively to the actions of totalitarian regimes: the Japanese invasion of Manchuria, the Italian conquest of Ethiopia, and the German militarization of the Rhineland. The league's final failure was its paralysis during the drawn-out civil war in Spain.

The Spanish Civil War (1936–1939)

Spain had a growing urban population and an impoverished countryside dominated by wealthy families and the Catholic Church. From 1923 to 1931, Spain was run by a military dictatorship. In 1932, the king abdicated and a republic was formed. It introduced liberal reforms such as women's suffrage, legalized divorce, redistribution of land, and anticlerical laws that weakened the Catholic Church's power. Conservative reaction and increasing social discord reached a climax in 1936, when right-wing army officers revolted. Led by General Francisco Franco, the Nationalist faction defeated the Republican faction in 1939. Fascist Spain, shattered by the war, played little part in the Second World War that broke out a few months later. Fascist rule would persist until 1975.

The Spanish Civil War has been called a "dress rehearsal" for the Second World War for two reasons. First, Spanish democracy stood in between two extremes: the fascist-backed Nationalist forces of Franco and the communist-dominated forces supporting the left-wing Republic. The idea of a moderate center holding firm against totalitarianism on the left and right seemed doomed. Second, the war was fought with the active participation of foreign volunteers and soldiers, especially from Italy, Germany, and the Soviet Union. These powers tested new weapons and tactics that would prove effective on the global battlefronts a few years later. Soviet advisers pioneered the use of IEDs. The most famous example, however, was Germany's experimentation with air power. The terror bombing of Guernica inspired Pablo Picasso to produce one of the twentieth century's most famous paintings: *Guernica*. It also served as a model for the daytime bombing of cities in World War II.

Greater East Asia Co-Prosperity Sphere

Japan's goal of economic self-sufficiency necessitated an imperial foreign policy, as the island nation had few natural resources of its own. Japan had already seized Taiwan and Korea in a growing overseas empire, but it now fixed its eye on the rich resources of northeast China. Japan's invasion of Manchuria in 1931 led to protests in the League of Nations but no effective action, so the Japanese kept their new territory and withdrew from the league. Throughout the 1930s, the idea of a Greater East Asia Co-Prosperity Sphere was developed. While rhetorically styled as an anti-imperialist "Asia for the Asiatics" mission, in reality it sought to replace European rule over Asian nations with Japanese rule.

German Domination

Hitler followed his reoccupation of the Rhineland with further claims to German-inhabited territories in Eastern Europe. Britain and France's policy of appeasement (trying to distinguish reasonable from unreasonable demands) allowed Germany to annex Austria, which the Treaty of Versailles had forbidden. In the 1938 Munich Agreement, against Czech protests, Hitler was given the Sudetenland, a German-speaking area in western Czechoslovakia. In exchange, Hitler pledged to make no more territorial demands. However, he invaded and annexed the rest of the country the next spring. With the failure of appeasement, Britain and France reluctantly guaranteed the security of Hitler's next victim, Poland, which separated eastern Prussia from the rest of Germany. The Western allies counted on the Soviet Union to oppose this German threat to its border. However, Hitler and Stalin overcame their ideological differences with a joint agreement to invade Poland in September 1939. Britain and France declared war, and fighting soon consumed the continent, just 25 years after the first World War began. In both cases, the immediate cause was German ambition to dominate Eastern Europe.

WORLD WAR II

World War II featured three main theaters: Europe, the Mediterranean, and the Pacific-Asian theater. Although Germany's 1939 invasion of Poland is usually said to be the beginning of World War II, the war in Asia had been going on since the Japanese invasion of China in 1937. However, neither of these theaters were initially connected to one another. It took until 1941 for the European and Pacific conflicts to merge into one global war, with Japanese offensives against the United States and several European colonies. Events in different regions affected each other. Japan's seizure of Southeast Asian colonies was aided by the preoccupation of Britain, France, and the Netherlands with fighting Germany. The Soviet Union, fighting for its life in the West, did not intervene against Japan in the East until 1945. America's decision to embrace a "Germany first" strategy to relieve Britain and the Soviets likely prolonged the Pacific conflict by several months.

The War in Europe

From 1939 to 1942, Nazi Germany was almost entirely unchecked. They took control of most of Eastern and Northern Europe with few casualties. After the fall of France, only Britain was left to defend itself against invasion, all while fighting to keep open its sea lanes to America and the British Empire. Repelled by British air and sea power, Hitler in 1941 turned his attention elsewhere. After helping their weaker ally Italy to invade the Balkans and North Africa, Germany launched a massive invasion of the USSR, which nearly reached Moscow before winter set in. 1942 was the high tide of Axis power: Germany dominated continental Europe, pushed further into southern Russia and Egypt, and sank ships carrying U.S. reinforcements to Britain and Russia.

The Soviet Union, however, rallied its people and drew on the immense resources provided by Stalin's single-minded industrial development of the 1930s. In a series of huge and brutal battles, notably in the sieges of Stalingrad and Leningrad, the German army was slowly destroyed and pushed back into Eastern Europe. By late 1944, the Allies had effectively crushed Germany on three fronts through successive invasions of North Africa, Italy, and France. With logistical support by American industry, intensive aerial bombing of German cities, and Soviet ground power, the Allies turned the tide in Europe. In 1945, Berlin fell to the Red Army, Hitler committed suicide, and American and Soviet troops shook hands at the Elbe River in the center of Germany.

The War in the Pacific

Japan's invasion of China strained relations with the United States, especially due to popular outrage over massacres such as the Rape of Nanjing. With economic sanctions increasing, Japan gambled that it could seize industrial resources in Southeast Asia from distracted European imperial powers and fend off the United States in a defensive war. Thus, Japanese forces attacked Hawaii and the Philippines in late 1941. By mid 1942, Japan dominated eastern China, Southeast Asia as far west as Burma, and most of the western Pacific Ocean from New Guinea to the Aleutians. It threatened Australia, India, Hawaii, and Alaska.

However, alarmed by totalitarian aggression in the 1930s, the United States had been moving away from its long-standing isolationist policies and had already begun a massive rearmament program. Once it entered the war in 1941, America devoted most of its resources to defeating Germany, which was seen as the greater threat to U.S. allies, but its military presence in Asia was still enough to overwhelm Japan. In a series of fierce naval and air campaigns, American forces advanced on Japan, island by island. By 1944, the United States retook the Philippines, began to bomb the Japanese homeland, used submarines to blockade Japan, and prepared to launch an eventual invasion. By mid 1945, Berlin fell and the Soviet Union soon declared war on Japan, looking to seize Manchuria and Korea. Most of Japan's major cities had been leveled by mass **firebombing**. The United States used the first **atomic bombs** in warfare against the cities of Hiroshima and Nagasaki. Japan's leaders finally surrendered, and Americans occupied the devastated country.

Impact of the War

World War II was the deadliest conflict in human history. Over 70 million people died. Over 50 million of the dead were civilians. In addition to fatalities directly related to military conflict, tens of millions died from famine and war-related diseases. Although all the nations committed war crimes, Germany and Japan adopted the most brutal policies with explicitly racist ideologies of conquest. Millions died in both East Asia and Europe, in work camps set up to detain, torment, and murder political or racial enemies. The noncombatant death toll in Europe is estimated at 17 million, as Jews, communists, labor leaders, prisoners of war, Jehovah's Witnesses, homosexuals, the mentally and physically disabled, and the Romani peoples were shot, gassed, or worked to death. In particular, Hitler targeted the Jewish people, blaming them for all of Germany's problems. Six million of Europe's 9.5 million Jews were murdered in the Holocaust. Even in the present day, the global Jewish population has still not recovered to its pre-Holocaust level. Millions of East Asians, from China and Korea to Indonesia and the Philippines, were murdered as the Japanese exploited and consolidated their imperial conquests. Atomic weapons, chemical weapons, and biological weapons were used. Whole cities on two continents were burnt to ash. Added to this misery were the uncountable wounded, the traumatized, and the separated. Beyond the human cost, the destruction of wealth, by explosives and expenditure, was on the order of a trillion U.S. dollars at the time.

Outcomes of the War

High-Yield

World War II saw no armistice or peace conference. The Allies demanded unconditional surrender to avoid a repeat of the stab-in-the-back myth that fueled the rise of the Nazi Party. Eventually, the Axis nations had no choice but to accept defeat. Both Japan and Germany were occupied by Allied armies. Within the framework of the occupation, the Allies purged the ruling classes, imposed extensive social reforms, and attempted to remake the countries in the image of their own (Western or Soviet) societies. They also held war trials in which top generals and government officials were charged, convicted, and sometimes executed, for crimes against humanity. This set a new precedent in international law, as making war could now be punishable in international courts.

Even more so than after World War I, the victors were in hardly better shape than the losers. France and China, and other countries of Europe and East Asia, had been devastated by their conquerors and occupiers. Britain, although never invaded, was crippled economically and like France was already losing control over its empire.

The clearest "victor" was the United States, which had suffered smaller losses in terms of men killed, had built up its industrial power to supply much of the Allied forces, and, except for the attack

10

on Hawaii in 1941, had not had its homeland touched by actual combat. Also, the United States enjoyed a monopoly on atomic weapons until 1949. While its traditional isolationism would linger until the development of the Truman Doctrine, the United States assumed a strong leadership position in the postwar world. At the Bretton Woods conference in 1944, the United States committed to support the economies of other developed nations by linking its strong domestic currency and undamaged economy to the international gold standard. This enabled a rapid recovery of Europe and Japan over the following decades. The dollar also assumed its position as the world's reserve currency, overtaking the British pound sterling.

On the other side of the world, the Soviet Union had faced annihilation and survived to emerge as a military superpower, dominating large portions of Eurasia. Yet Soviet wartime losses included almost 27 million dead. Immense areas had been occupied and ruined during the "Great Patriotic War." Building on its successful alliance with the Western Allies, it participated in the founding of the **United Nations** and in the war crimes tribunals. However, the Soviets refused to join the American-led postwar international economic system, instead following both ideological and national security imperatives by establishing communist hegemony in Eastern Europe. Like the United States, the Soviet Union took a renewed sense of national greatness from its victory and foresaw opportunities to spread communism across a shattered world.

The United Nations

The victorious Allies resolved to try again with an international organization. The United Nations (UN), headquartered in New York City, attempted to fix the flaws of the failed League of Nations. The Security Council, with permanent membership for the five Allied victors of the war (United States, USSR, Great Britain, France, and the Republic of China), was specifically tasked with keeping the peace by military action if necessary, subject to veto by any of the great powers. The General Assembly of all the member nations is a forum for discussing world problems and potential solutions. It cannot pass laws, but the General Assembly can raise issues and suggest resolutions.

Shortly after its founding, the UN was busy settling disputes in the Middle East and helping the many refugees left by World War II. It made its strongest mark in the Korean War (1950–1953), authorizing an international armed force to resist the communist attack. In later years, as the **Cold War** split the Allies into opposition and many new nations emerged with little stake in a Western-oriented world order, the UN has proved less able to maintain world peace. Just as with the failed League of Nations, without the sovereign power of military enforcement, international organizations must mirror the actual balance of national power at the global level.

REVOLUTIONS

The twentieth century saw several major revolutions of historical importance. Also, ancient regimes and civilizations, which were resistant to imperialism, Western values, and the Cold War ideological binary, set their own terms for modernization in violent and original ways.

Communist Revolutions

Two of the most important revolutions were in Russia and China, in response to exploitation of the laboring classes. This was in contrast to the eighteenth and nineteenth century's revolutions and reform movements. The goals of these communist revolutions were to establish socialist principles of social and economic freedom for the proletariat against aristocrats and the bourgeoisie.

Russia

High-Yield

In 1914, Russia was far behind Western Europe economically, technologically, and politically. It was slowly building an industrial base with foreign capital and increasing agricultural production; however, it was still dominated by a small and wealthy aristocracy, imperial court and bureaucracy, and rigid censorship enforced by the state police. Despite public unrest, Tsar Nicholas II retained all real executive power and had little interest in broadening the base of his government to include the rising middle classes.

The pointless sacrifices of World War I led to social upheaval and riots in March 1917. The tsar, forced to abdicate, ceded power to a provisional republican government. The liberal government decided to stay in the war, resulting in revolts and continued strikes. The leading party of communists, the Bolsheviks, was led by **Vladimir Lenin**. They promised the people exactly what they wanted: "Peace, Land, Bread." In November 1917, Lenin's party seized power and declared Russia the world's first socialist state. In early 1918, it made peace with Germany, ending Russia's part in the war. The Bolshevik government seized all private land, banks, and industries; the former owners were persecuted and their estates looted and burned. Soviets, or popular committees, ruled locally under command of the central party. The Cheka (the secret police) spied on and arrested any who deviated from revolutionary enthusiasm.

Marx had said communism was designed for developed states like Germany and Britain, where the industrial working class would seize and freely share the capital that fueled their production. There was nothing in Marx's writing about how to communize a society like Russia that was largely agricultural and pre-industrial. The Bolsheviks' solution, called Marxism-Leninism, called for dictatorial central direction by a single party until industry, national wealth, and communist thought had developed enough for the state to "wither away."

In 1924, Lenin died, opening space for Joseph Stalin to come to power. Stalin instituted his Five-Year Plans with the goals of increasing industrial and agricultural productivity. Individual farms were collectivized, and over five million who resisted were killed. An intensive program of heavy industrialization was begun. Education and basic health care were universal and free, women were given equal rights under the law, literacy massively increased, and organized religion was suppressed in favor of official atheism. At the same time, civil rights were nonexistent. Until the 1950s, the Communist Party used state terror and purges to enforce submission; hundreds of thousands were tried and executed, and millions were imprisoned in a vast network of deadly labor camps. For several decades, this aspect of communism was denied or minimized; Soviet propaganda seemed to offer a glimpse of a "future that works" to Marxist true believers around the world.

China

At the beginning of the twentieth century, China struggled to reconcile its 2000-year history and imperial traditions with the challenges of the modernizing West. The declining Qing Dynasty finally succumbed in the Xinhai Revolution (the Chinese Revolution of 1911). The last emperor abdicated and China was declared a republic. The new government instituted a program of Western-oriented reforms focused on national independence from foreign control, constitutional democracy, and popular welfare. However, the country soon fragmented into a series of warlord-dominated zones, reflecting China's long history of chaotic regional struggles whenever the strong central government weakened.

The Kuomintang (KMT) was the ruling nationalist party founded by Sun Yixian (Sun Yat-sen) and led after his death in 1925 by Jiang Jieshi (Chiang Kai-shek). They struggled to unify and modernize China in the face of continued Western extraterritorial privileges and increasing Japanese imperialist pressure. Although the new Soviet Union helped build the KMT's military power in the 1920s, by the 1930s the Chinese Communist Party (CCP) had emerged as a major political and military rival, with a program more oriented toward China's huge rural population than its urban middle and working classes. The growing conflict with Japan after 1931 increased national feeling and cooperation among factions, but also weakened or destroyed China's most modern and Westernized sectors. After Japan's surrender in 1945, open civil war broke out. However, military blunders and widespread internal corruption led to the KMT's defeat by 1949; it evacuated to Taiwan.

Due to Cold War politics, the Republic of China's government continued to hold on to its United Nations Security Council seat until 1971, when the People's Republic of China became internationally recognized as the legitimate government of China.

The second Chinese Revolution was launched in 1949 by the communist **Mao Zedong**, who proclaimed the country to be the People's Republic of China. The United States and many other countries refused to recognize the new regime and treated it as a hostile power. Similar to the Russian experience, the Chinese had to adapt the industrial theories of Marx to an almost entirely rural nation. Stalin sent advisors and aid to the newest, largest communist state. Following totalitarian models of the period, the Chinese Communist Party eliminated all opposition by killing and imprisoning millions, completely controlled cultural and political expression, and elevated Mao as the supreme and perfect dictator. Mao expanded the party's existing land reform program, whereby landlords were dispossessed and often killed, and landless peasants were given their own parcels to farm in cooperative groups. This required social adjustment as well as economic. Communist ideology was promoted as a replacement for Confucian ideals, which had enforced traditional class hierarchies for thousands of years. Businesses were nationalized and a Five-Year Plan was begun to develop heavy industry along Soviet lines.

MAO'S INITIAL CHANGES TO CHINA	
Economic	• All businesses were nationalized.
	• Land was distributed to peasants.
	• Peasants were urged to pool their land and work more efficiently on cooperative farms.
Political	• A one-party totalitarian state was established.
	• Communist party became supreme.
	• Government attacked crime and corruption.
Social	• Peasants were encouraged to "speak bitterness" against landlords (10,000 landlords were killed as a result).
	• Communist ideology replaced Confucian beliefs.
	• Schools were opened with emphasis on political education.
	• Health care workers were sent to remote areas.
	• Women won equality (but little opportunity in government and were paid less than men).
	• The extended family was weakened.

Mao's ideological but often impractical focus led to erratic methods of national development. Not satisfied with the technocratic Soviet model, in the late 1950s Mao decreed the **Great Leap Forward**. All life was collectivized, private property was abolished, and ancient social customs were replaced by Communist Party activities. To achieve a modern industrial capacity, backyard steel furnaces were set up, in which farmers made iron and steel from scrap metal. The Great Leap Forward was a failure. To meet state quotas, farmers sometimes melted down their own farming tools. The backyard furnaces produced poor quality iron, and bad weather combined with a drop in agricultural productivity to cause a major famine and the deaths of at least 30 million Chinese.

Mao's second major initiative was the Cultural Revolution of the late 1960s. In an effort to re-revolutionize China, young students known as the Red Guards imposed Maoist orthodoxy on institutions throughout Chinese society. Middle-class and educated people were persecuted or sent to the countryside for reeducation in the ways of the peasantry. As a result, the country lost an entire generation of skilled leaders. The exact death toll is unknown, due to poor record-keeping and the Chinese government's reluctance to relitigate the Cultural Revolution. Estimates range from 700,000 to several million dead. After Mao's death in 1976, the party promoted a more moderate and rational path to modernization.

COMPARATIVE CLOSE-UP: THE ROLE OF WOMEN DURING THE RUSSIAN AND CHINESE REVOLUTIONS	
Russia	**China**
• Women served in the Red Army.	• A new marriage law forbade arranged marriage (was met with resistance).
• 65% of factory workers were women.	• Women worked alongside men in factories.
• The government ordered equal pay (though it was not enforced).	• State-run nurseries were set up to care for children.
• Maternity leave with full pay was established.	• Party leadership remained male.
• Women entered professions.	• Efforts were made to end foot-binding.

Cuba

From 1952 to 1959, the dictatorship of Batista ruled Cuba. A small percentage of people were very wealthy while the masses of peasants were impoverished. **Fidel Castro** organized a guerrilla movement, which, while initially a failure, eventually captured power in 1959. Though he had promised to hold elections, Castro did not do so and at first even denied that he was a communist. His nationalization of foreign-owned land and property alienated the United States and U.S. corporations, and Castro sought closer ties with the Soviet Union for protection.

In 1961, Castro announced his communist plans for Cuba: collectivized farms, centralized control of the economy, and free education and medical services. Tensions with the United States escalated in 1961 when a group of anti-communist Cuban exiles, supported by the United States, launched a failed invasion attempt known as the Bay of Pigs. In 1962, a standoff known as the Cuban Missile Crisis occurred when Soviet missiles were discovered in Cuba. After this tense standoff, the United States and the Soviet Union averted World War III with a compromise.

The Rise and Fall of Communism

China's radical communist revolution took place just as Russia's was moderating. Maoism's apparent success inspired a new generation of communist parties in the developing world. In Cuba and much of Latin America, the economies were primarily based on commodity exports, which made them better suited to the agrarian communism of Mao than the more industrial Soviet-style communist. Cuba's successful revolution, led by Fidel Castro in 1959, introduced communism to the Western Hemisphere. This led to direct nuclear confrontation between the United States and the Soviet Union in the 1962 Cuban Missile Crisis, and to repeated struggles across Latin America and the Caribbean basin between U.S.-supported governments and revolutionaries supported by the USSR and Cuba. Limited communist successes in Peru, Colombia, Venezuela, the Dominican Republic, Nicaragua, and Chile were countered or crushed by the United States and the local governing elites.

Likewise, in Asia and Africa, uprisings, civil wars, and occasionally successful revolutions were based on anti-imperialist or nationalist forms of communism, supported by Soviet and/or Chinese diplomacy, aid, and military supplies. Successful examples include Vietnam and North Korea, which resisted Western military pressure. More isolated communist movements or governments arose in underdeveloped former colonies like Indonesia, Malaya, Angola, Mozambique, and the Republic of the Congo, but these states struggled. At the end of the 1980s and in the early 1990s, the collapse of the Soviet Union and retreat of Chinese communism signaled the failure of Marxism-Leninism and Maoism as world-changing revolutionary ideologies.

Populist and National Revolutions

Early in the twentieth century, before World War I, a number of independent empires on the periphery of the European world order underwent revolutions led by middle-class elites: Russia in 1905, Ottoman Turkey in 1908, and China and Persia in 1911.

Mexico

The Mexican Revolution (1910–1920) involved the common people fighting for increased rights and participation in national affairs. For decades, Mexico had been ruled by the dictator Porfirio Díaz. His approach to modernization was to encourage foreign investment in land and industry, which led to foreign domination of the Mexican economy. In 1910, the people rose up against Díaz in support of the liberal leader Madero. The liberal elites soon discovered they had incited a greater uprising than expected, and events spiraled out of control. Leaders from rural districts such as Pancho Villa and Emiliano Zapata advocated and fought for land reform. Power changed hands continually throughout the civil war, as leaders were assassinated or overthrown. Eventually, conservative forces won out and under Carranza an assembly wrote the historic Constitution of 1917.

The Constitution promised land reform, imposed restrictions on foreign economic control, set minimum salaries and maximum hours for workers, granted workers the right to unionize and strike, and placed restrictions on Church-owned property and schools. Since the concessions to the masses of urban laborers and rural farmers were approved by conservative elites, there was no counterrevolution. Mexico has been relatively stable and slowly developing on its own terms ever since. After its establishment in 1929, the National Revolutionary Party (later named the Party of Institutionalized Revolution, or PRI) dominated politics for the remainder of the century, instituting land redistribution and standing up to foreign companies.

The Islamic World

As the European world order collapsed in this period, Western-style nationalism proved an effective force for anti-imperialist independence movements. At the same time, socialist-inspired economic reforms and nationalization of oil fields were viewed by Western powers, especially Britain and the United States, as communist subterfuge. Over time, Western pushback against Pan-Arab nationalists and leftists created a void filled by Islamists. In contrast to communism's emphasis on radical change, Islamism in the twentieth century focused on traditionalism, including earlier history when the caliphate, established by the Prophet, united all Muslim peoples under one rule.

Turkey

In 1914, the breakup of the Ottoman Empire was already taking place due to European imperial pressure in Eastern Europe and North Africa. In fact, World War I itself was started by competition of two empires, Austria-Hungary and Russia, to control former Ottoman lands in the Balkans. During the Great War, the Allies mobilized Arab resentment of Turkish domination. The Young Turks, progressive modernizers who had already pressed the sultan for reforms before the war, fought to preserve Anatolian Turkey from being carved up by the victorious Allies in 1919. Under Kemal Ataturk, the Caliphate was abolished, with Islam taking a back seat to nationalism and modernization in the new Republic of Turkey. The Kemalist state balanced industrial development, and its strategic position between West and East, against the continuing strength of Islamic faith and practice among its people. In the twentieth century, Turkey was the world's most secular Muslim state.

The Middle East

Pan-Arab nationalists saw the Ottoman Empire cynically replaced by the British and French Empires, which divided the Middle East up into League of Nations mandates that paid no attention to regional demographics or sectarian divides. Iraq, the former Mesopotamian provinces of the Ottomans, rebelled and was gradually given independence by Britain by 1932. The Arabian Peninsula was largely unified by the Saud Dynasty by 1932, becoming Saudi Arabia. Jordan, Palestine, and Syria did not achieve independence until after World War II. Cold War dynamics further complicated Middle Eastern politics.

Iran

Persia, descended from one of the world's oldest civilizations, was still an independent empire in 1914, despite Russian and British incursions. Nationalist elites, allied with the Islamic clergy, had been engaged in a revolution against the dynastic Shahs since 1906. They created a parliament and a constitutional monarchy and removed some of the foreign influence over their government. After World War I, in response to Soviet and British interference to control the nation's oil resources, army leader Reza Pahlavi was declared the new Shah and the country was renamed Iran. Anti-communist and secular, he introduced numerous modern reforms along Western lines. He also followed Turkey's example in demanding that Muslims liberalize their practices to accommodate social progress, wear modern clothing, and give more freedom to women. After he chose to back Nazi Germany in the Second World War, Pahlavi was replaced in 1941 by his son, Mohammed Reza Pahlavi.

In 1953, the United States and Britain sponsored a coup d'état in support of the Shah to protect Western oil interests. In 1963, the Shah launched a massive land reform and industrial program to enlist peasant and working class support against the landlords, clergy, and educated middle classes who resented his authoritarian, antidemocratic rule. Women gained the right to vote, run for elected office, and serve in the judiciary. However, the White Revolution ironically weakened the Shah, as it alienated conservatives and the religious while doing little to win over the peasants and working classes. As a U.S. ally, the Shah also persisted in a strident anti-communist crackdown against leftists.

Fueled by oil revenue, his regime increased in world influence in the 1970s, but he lost touch with the changing social dynamics among his people. Faced with the uncertainties of an industrial revolution, more Iranians from every class saw the traditionalist Shi'ite Muslim clergy, led by exiled Ayatollah Khomeini, as their most faithful representatives. In 1979, increasing civil resistance forced the Shah to leave Iran. Khomeini returned, and within months the nation voted to become an Islamic Republic. The Islamic Revolution put the clergy in charge and imposed a fundamentalist theocracy that was hostile to the secular and Christian West alike, to Israel, and to atheistic communism. Iran remains a regional industrial and military power and an example of the power of religious, rather than political or economic, ideas in modern revolutionary history.

10

THE COLD WAR

Origins of the Cold War

The irony, and tensions, of a grand alliance against Nazi Germany by the two leading capitalist democracies and the first communist totalitarian state were obvious throughout the war. Even before the Battle of Berlin, disputes about the postwar international order threatened the Allies' strategic cooperation. From 1945 on, the Soviet Union sought to control the nations on its western frontier, both to extend communism and to create a buffer to protect itself from future invasions. The United States and Great Britain protested, as the initial cause of the war in 1939 had been to stop Germany from dominating smaller states like Poland and Czechoslovakia. The Red Army's occupation of Eastern Europe, and the Western powers' unwillingness to continue the war, led to a *de facto* division. In the late 1940s, Europe was divided into a capitalist and democratic West and a communist and totalitarian East. In the middle was Germany, split into two states by the Iron Curtain, its capital city divided into West and East sectors by the Berlin Wall. The competition to control Germany, still Europe's greatest industrial and military nation, was a defining feature of the Cold War from beginning to end.

The Superpowers of the Cold War

High-Yield

After two world wars in 30 years, many observers believed World War III was inevitable. However, the United States and the Soviet Union were both nuclear-armed states. Thus, their conflict was one of symbols, threats, imperial influence, trade, and local **proxy wars** between client states. That was why this was called a Cold War.

Military

The Soviets tested their first atomic bomb in 1949, and a far more powerful thermonuclear bomb (H-bomb) was acquired by both nations in the 1950s. However, this meant that nuclear weapons were now impractical. If each side in the Cold War had enough nukes to annihilate the other, then nuclear weapons were primarily useful as deterrents. This doctrine became known as mutual assured destruction (MAD).

The Cuban Missile Crisis of 1962, the closest the two blocs would come to nuclear war, scared both sides into more conservative nuclear policies, including treaties to limit the proliferation and testing of nuclear weapons. In addition, the two countries spent billions on conventional arms in order to develop ever more sophisticated systems for fighting.

Technology

Both nations sought advancements in missile technology in order to deliver nuclear bombs between continents, eventually leading to the launch of the first satellite by the USSR in 1957. This began the Space Race, which culminated in the U.S. moon landing in 1969, countered by a strong Soviet space station program in the 1970s. Soviet engineering and science were world class in state-sponsored sectors like armaments, intelligence gathering, math and physics, and construction, but rigid ideology hampered technological developments in other areas like computers, agriculture, biochemistry, automobiles, and media.

Geopolitics

Both superpowers vied for global influence, especially in the newly independent and developing nations of Asia and Africa. They fought wars in Korea, **Vietnam**, India, Afghanistan, and Angola, and even provided combat troops to the opposing sides. Both superpowers used trade concessions, subsidies, infrastructure investments, cultural and educational exchanges, and diplomatic or military support against local adversaries to maintain and extend geopolitical control. The North Atlantic Treaty Organization (**NATO**) and the **Warsaw Pact** were the main alliances for the Americans and the Soviets respectively. Other American-led treaty organizations and alliances in Latin America, the Middle East, and South and Southeast Asia were less effective.

Ideology

Today, communism is largely extinct. However, in order to properly contextualize the Cold War, it is vital to keep in mind that communism was a popular internationalist ideology. Millions believed it was the economic and political model of the future. The idea that communism would collapse, let alone peacefully without a nuclear exchange, was unfathomable even in the 1980s. Democratic capitalism and dictatorial communism were presented to the world as the only two choices available for political and economic organization.

As many new nations emerged from Western imperial domination in the 1950s and 60s, they perceived that both choices originated in the European historical and cultural tradition from which they had just freed themselves. In 1956, the **Non-Aligned Movement** was founded by the leaders of Yugoslavia, India, Indonesia, Egypt, and Ghana. Its goal was to explore a middle course between East and West for the developing nations of the world.

Progress of the Cold War

Paranoia and existential dread dominated the early Cold War. Western nations became infected with fears about spies and treason. Uprisings in the Soviet states of East Germany, Hungary, and Czechoslovakia were brutally suppressed. China tore itself apart with the Great Leap Forward and the Cultural Revolution. Proxy wars in Korea and Vietnam dogged the United States. Social tensions exploded throughout the West as the postwar baby boom generation came of age in a time of economic prosperity, a stark contrast to the Great Depression that dominated the young lives of their parents.

By the 1970s, the Cold War became more complex. The U.S. took advantage of a Sino-Soviet Split and normalized relations with China in the 1970s, which inspired a détente (diplomatic warming) with the USSR as well. Increased trade, cultural exchanges, arms agreements, and diplomatic settlements in Europe all followed.

> ✔ **AP Expert Note**
>
> ### Be sure to understand the Sino-Soviet Split
>
> The Sino-Soviet Split made the Cold War a tripolar conflict, even as Nixon's diplomacy turned China into a U.S. ally. It was caused by an ideological conflict between the USSR and China over de-Stalinization, peaceful coexistence with the West, and the comparative merits of Maoism and orthodox Marxism-Leninism.

The 1980s saw a resumption of high tension between the superpowers. Détente became tarnished by association with the Nixon Administration after the Watergate scandal. The subsequent Soviet intervention in Angola was seen as the communist world exploiting American weakness in the post-Vietnam stagflation era of the 1970s. Finally, the Soviet invasion of Afghanistan made the idea of peaceful coexistence with the communist world seem foolish to Americans. Only gradually, thanks to Soviet leader Mikhail Gorbachev's reforms, did tension defuse.

The Cold War unexpectedly ended with the resulting implosion of the Soviet Union. In 1989, Gorbachev did not counter attempts by Warsaw Pact members to break away from Soviet domination. The Red Army withdrew peacefully and Soviet support for allies and client states ended; within a few years, the Soviet Union itself broke up into numerous non-communist republics, the largest being the new Russian Federation.

Impact of the Cold War

Although the United States and its allies "won" the Cold War, the result was hardly a peaceful and unified world. America's economy, society, and politics had been distorted by decades of militarization and ideologically driven foreign policy. After a "unipolar moment" in the 1990s, U.S. economic, cultural, and military dominance was challenged by rising powers like China, India, Japan, the **European Union**, and a revived Russia, as well as by a growing number of smaller but influential states like Iran, Brazil, South Africa, Nigeria, and Mexico. Non-state actors and transnational corporations also grew in strength. In the early twenty-first century, the world had shifted back to a multipolar state comparable to the pre–World War I era, with the United States taking the place of the British Empire as the preeminent global power.

INDEPENDENCE AND NATIONALIST MOVEMENTS

Throughout the twentieth century, the decline or defeat of colonial powers inspired independence movements and nationalism. The primary mission of these movements has been to resist and expel foreign occupiers. In some cases, the new nations have been able to negotiate their independence with a relative lack of violence. Factors in the outbreak of colonial warfare included the size of European settler populations, the perceived importance of the colony to the ruling country's economy and national prestige, and the radicalism (real or perceived) of the independence movement's ideology.

Negotiated Independence

India

High-Yield

India's nationalist movement under the British Empire, originating in the late nineteenth century, was led by the upper-class members of the **Indian National Congress**. From the beginning, India's nationalists were divided between Hindu and Muslim factions. The Muslim population was in the minority, overall, and its leaders often deviated from the congress's insistence that British India was destined to be a single independent federated nation. After World War I, Britain's Government of India Act of 1919 granted some domestic power to the congress, but left far more power in British hands compared to "white dominions" such as Canada and Australia, which were also agitating for more independence at this time. Britain balanced its reform effort with increased prosecutions for sedition, arousing popular resentment. At Amritsar, a British general ordered troops to fire on a protest rally, killing hundreds of unarmed civilians. This shocking episode, and the British public's approval of it, began to push Indian opinion away from Dominion status (domestic self-rule within the empire) and toward complete independence.

At this time, Mohandas Gandhi emerged. Gandhi focused on the peasant roots and spiritual traditions of India and helped turn the Congress Party from an elite debating society into a disciplined mass movement. His methods of *satyagraha*, civil disobedience against unjust laws, and *ahimsa*, nonviolence in the face of police action, highlighted the injustice of British rule. In the 1930s, Britain proposed a federal structure for India to protect minority Muslim rights, but the Muslim League, under **Muhammad Ali Jinnah**, countered with a demand that India be divided into two separate states, Muslim and Hindu.

When World War II began, the British offered domestic rule in return for cooperation against Germany and Japan. Despite Gandhi's "Quit India" resistance campaign and Japan's attempts to recruit an Indian liberation army as it approached the Bengali border, the Indian people again generally supported Britain in the war. After the war, the British realized they could no longer count on the Indian bureaucracy for governing and policing, but they could not afford a military campaign of suppression and conquest. On August 15, 1947, independence was granted to India.

However, increasing violence between Hindus and Muslims had persuaded the British to agree to an **India/Pakistan partition**, which led to the creation of Hindu India and Muslim Pakistan. This division led to a mass cross-migration of Muslim and Hindu refugees amid terrible civil slaughter. Hundreds of thousands were killed, which poisoned relations between India and Pakistan going forward. The two nations fought four wars over the next 50 years. Pakistan itself was composed of western and eastern provinces, separated by India. The populations, of different ethnic groups and ancestral history, shared only their Muslim religion. In 1971, East Pakistan fought for its national independence and became Bangladesh.

Africa

By 1914, almost all of Africa had been carved up by European powers. Economically, it had been transformed by the development of monoculture plantations of cash crops for export and mines of precious materials such as gold and diamonds. The ownership of these properties was exclusively in the hands of European merchants. In the period after World War II, the largely left-wing parties running European governments had little interest in subsidizing outright imperial enterprises. In addition, many of the African colonies saw the rise of a democratically minded elite class, eager for independence.

The arbitrary political borders drawn by the European colonial powers created many nations that were comprised of unrelated ethnic groups. These often had a history of conflict that began long before the colonial era, and in the new states they became rivals competing for power. For example, the Republic of the Congo exploded in a five-year civil war in 1960, when Belgium abruptly withdrew in the face of nationalist demands. Secessionist movements, such as Biafra in Nigeria and Shafta in Kenya, and civil conflict, such as in Chad and the Hutu genocide in Burundi, were not uncommon in postcolonial Africa. There were also structural difficulties in development, as the colonial powers had modernized the local economies and societies solely to exploit and export natural resources. More broad-based modernization efforts often stumbled over tensions between unequally developed regions and sectors. Dictatorships and military rule were characteristic aspects of Africa's political culture in the 1960s and 70s.

Zionism and Palestinian Nationalism

Following World War I, the British ruled Palestine under a League of Nations mandate. In the Balfour Declaration of 1917, the British government supported a homeland for Jews in Palestine, in line with the European Zionist movement for Jewish nationalism. However, Arab Palestinians saw both British rule and Jewish settlements as forms of Western imperialism. The British tried to control the violence between communities as the Jewish minority slowly grew in numbers.

At the end of World War II, the regional Pan-Arab movement joined the Palestinians in opposing the creation of a Jewish state, but the Holocaust had motivated the remaining Jewish people to find a secure homeland. By 1947, the weakened British Empire turned the question over to the United Nations, which planned to divide the area into two states. This paralleled India, in that a negotiated end to colonial rule led to violence and mass migrations between rival groups, and a war ensued. Jewish victories over the neighboring Arab nations led to the creation of the state of Israel on May 14, 1948. As Jews were expelled from newly independent Arab states in the region and relocated to Israel, Palestinian refugees from Israel resettled in cities and camps in neighboring Jordan and adjacent lands.

Both sides claim the ancient Holy Land as their national homeland, and fighting continues to plague this region. Israel fought three subsequent wars with its Arab neighbors, including the Six Day War in 1967, which expanded its territory into the Jordanian West Bank and Egypt's Sinai. Israel and the Arab states gradually established a local "Cold War" kind of stability in the 1970s and 80s, and the Palestinian Liberation Organization (PLO) has used terrorism to press for a Palestinian state to replace Israel in the region, as has Hamas. Over time, a détente developed between Israel and Saudi Arabia in order to counter their mutual regional rival, Iran.

Island States

Islands have been important for expanding empires since the Age of Exploration, either as plantation colonies or for their strategic position on the sea lanes. In the twentieth century, a large number of island colonies achieved independence as national movements confronted weakened or restructured empires. The first was Cuba, which rebelled from the decaying Spanish Empire in 1895, only to come under effective political domination by the United States; it took another 60 years until a communist revolution expelled U.S. influence. Ireland, long dominated by nearby Great Britain, waged a guerrilla war after World War I to achieve home rule as the Irish Free State, a Dominion like Canada and Australia. Complete independence as the Republic of Ireland followed soon after in 1937. Britain's rule in Protestant Northern Ireland remained a source of conflict and terrorist violence until the Good Friday Agreement in 1998.

After World War II, independence was conceded to island colonies that were unprofitable, strategically unnecessary, or unsustainable in the face of nationalist resistance. The Philippines, Papua-New Guinea, and many Polynesian island groups in the Pacific; Jamaica and a number of smaller islands in the Caribbean; Cyprus in the Mediterranean; and Madagascar and Sri Lanka in the Indian Ocean all negotiated their national freedom in the postwar period. As with their continental counterparts, these countries were often consumed by factional or ethnic strife that had been suppressed by the colonial powers.

Scotland and Catalonia

The twenty-first century has seen efforts at negotiated independence in Western Europe, as nationalist sentiments remain strong even as a pan-European identity develops in the European Union. In the United Kingdom, Scotland narrowly voted down independence in a 2014 referendum, but separatist sentiments remain strong. In contrast, Spain has so far refused efforts to provide the province of Catalonia with a legal means to determine its relationship with the rest of Spain, frustrating efforts by separatists, who have only been able to organize unofficial referendums that are legally unconstitutional.

Armed Struggles for Independence

Africa

Several European colonies in Africa had developed relatively large white settler communities. Supported by their imperial sponsors, they resisted independence movements by the native majorities, leading to armed conflicts and full-fledged wars. In Kenya, the Mau Mau Uprising was crushed by the British Army, but this accelerated the movement toward full independence in 1963. Similarly, since 1848, coastal **Algeria** had been part of metropolitan France, and a large white settler community had lived there for many generations as a privileged class over the native Algerians. In the 1950s, the National Liberation Front (FLN) began a terrorist campaign to drive out the French. A large French army waged counterinsurgency war for years, and the local French government collapsed as the conflict proved unwinnable. After Algerian independence in 1962, large numbers of colonial whites departed. Algeria was later torn between Islamic and modernizing socialist currents, leading to civil war from 1991 to 2002 that ended with a government victory over Islamists.

Southeast Asia

The peninsulas and archipelagos of Southeast Asia were occupied by Japan during the war. The defeat of the Europeans by an Asian army, as well as the harsher policies of the Japanese themselves, roused a generation of nationalist movements to evict the ruling empires.

In the Dutch East Indies, Sukarno declared independence for Indonesia in 1945, and the Netherlands fought a four-year colonial war before admitting defeat and withdrawing from its 350-year old possessions. Britain was challenged by a communist insurgency in Malaya in the 1950s, which it successfully defeated while preparing the colony for independence. While not directly comparable, the Malayan experience contrasts remarkably with Vietnam. Among other factors, many Malayans knew and trusted the British and were willing to fight with them against the guerrillas, and the British emphasized small-unit jungle tactics rather than massive firepower.

Vietnam

French Indochina was evacuated by Japan in 1945, and immediately a group of Vietnamese nationalists under the leadership of **Ho Chi Minh** began a guerrilla campaign against the returning French. The French-Indochina War lasted nine years before defeat at Dien Bien Phu forced France to quit. Indochina was divided into Vietnam, Laos, and Cambodia. Reflecting the communist ideology of the fighters in the north, Vietnam was split into a communist North and a nationalist South. Cold War dynamics led the United States to support South Vietnam in the name of counterbalancing China. After 1965, the United States committed a massive army to defend South Vietnam, but the North's determination and roots in Vietnamese patriotism eventually won them the war. A negotiated peace preceded full communist victory in 1975, after 30 years of war. Vietnam was devastated by intensive combat and took years to recover. Laos and Cambodia also suffered destruction from civil conflicts, including the Cambodian genocide of the 1970s by the communist Khmer Rouge government. The nationalist character of Vietnamese communism was revealed a few years later when Vietnam fought a war to repel Chinese influence in postwar Indochina.

Failed Struggles

The story of nationalism in the twentieth century would be incomplete without reviewing the many instances of regions or peoples who failed to achieve independence. Some struggles involved violence, terrorism, and guerrilla warfare; others were tied to regional or superpower politics; and others still were expressed more through art and mobilization. Just a few of the most prominent examples were: the Basque region, Catalonia, Northern Ireland, and Turkish Cyprus in Europe; Chiapas, Quebec, and Puerto Rico in the Americas; Biafra and Darfur in Africa; Tibet, Taiwan, Okinawa, Mindanao, East Timor, Kashmir, West Papua, Kurdistan, Palestine, Tamil Sri Lanka, and Chechnya in Asia.

POLITICAL REFORM AND ECONOMIC CHANGES

In the last third of the twentieth century, new trends and patterns emerged in global politics. The developed world's economy had recovered from the global conflicts earlier in the twentieth century. Large sections of the underdeveloped world, freed from imperial influence, were engaged in the industrialization that had once transformed the societies of Europe, America, and Japan. Increasingly efficient technologies and transportation, free trade practices, and liberal monetary policies promoted further globalization, driven by a single world economy backed by the U.S. dollar. This was accompanied by the relative decline of the United States and the growth of other regional world powers. Some of these world powers were derived from the ancient empires of previous eras, such as in Europe, Russia, Western Asia, South Asia, and East Asia. Others were located in new geographies due to changes in resources and populations: Brazil, North America, South Africa, and Australasia.

China

High-Yield

After Mao died in 1976, **Deng Xiaoping** came to power. In contrast to Mao, Deng instituted the Four Modernizations: industry, agriculture, technology, and national defense. Foreign and domestic investment was encouraged; industrialists assembled massive conglomerates and great wealth, and entire cities were redeveloped. Research and development focused on futuristic technologies, and thousands of students were sent abroad to study. As a result of these capitalist-style reforms, the economy boomed, and within a generation China had left behind its developing nation status. It was now on a path to restore, peacefully, its traditional position as a global heavyweight. China also regained the last of its territories held by Europeans: Hong Kong (1997) and Macau (1999).

This new China could not properly be called communist, but the Communist Party still ruled China as a bureaucratic dictatorship. The rising middle class began to push for democratic reforms. In May of 1989, in parallel with the collapse of the Soviet Union, massive student demonstrations occurred in **Tiananmen Square**. Fearing the nationwide chaos that often occurred when an emperor was deposed, as well as a repeat of the political implosion in the Soviet bloc, China's leadership sent troops and tanks to brutally crush the rebellion. Today, the government continues to promote the idea that single-party leadership and political stability are the keys to China's success.

In 2010, China surpassed Japan to become the second largest economy in the world. China has become a lucrative market for businesses all around the world even as Chinese companies become global brands themselves. With its increased stature, China has begun to invest in infrastructure and resource extraction in Asia and Africa as part of its Belt and Road Initiative (BRI), also known as One Belt One Road (OBOR), a modern-day successor to the Silk Road. Economically, China is expected to surpass the United States and become the world's largest economy sometime in the 2020s.

Africa

In the 1970s and 80s, United Nations economic sanctions and international boycotts brought global attention to the fundamental injustice of the apartheid system in South Africa. Finally, in 1989, the government began to institute racial reforms. African National Congress leader Nelson Mandela was released from jail after 26 years, and in 1994 he became the first president elected by all the people of South Africa.

Most African countries, newly independent since the 1960s and 70s, continued to struggle with growing populations, poverty, and resource mismanagement. Some long-term trends include: increasing commitments to democracy, a growing urbanized middle class, suppression of endemic diseases, and new infrastructure to promote intracontinental trade rather than commodity exports to the developed world. Countering these positive developments have been the ongoing epidemic of HIV/AIDS, numerous wars (including a major civil war in the Congo involving most of its neighboring countries), the 1994 genocide in Rwanda, emigration of skilled labor to European and Persian Gulf markets, and ongoing neocolonial economic domination, often by former colonial powers. From 2013 to 2016, a widespread outbreak of the Ebola virus affected several West African countries, killing over ten thousand and debilitating thousands more with lingering long-term health issues.

India and South Asia

After independence in 1948, India adopted a British-style parliamentary political system under the leadership of Nehru. Following congress's socialist orientation, the state took ownership of major industries, resources, transportation, and utilities, but local and retail businesses and farmland remained private.

Unlike Gandhi, Nehru advocated industrialization, which revived Indian business traditions that the British had suppressed. India's foreign policy was one of nonalignment during the Cold War, but in fact it favored relations with the Soviet Union when its rival Pakistan aligned with China. Pakistan's development of nuclear weapons led to India doing the same. The resulting standoff mirrored the Cold War: like the United States and the Soviet Union, each side found it could not realistically destroy the other with atomic weapons, for fear of mutual assured destruction.

Dynastic traditions in the ruling classes of South Asia produced female prime ministers when the wives or daughters of Pakistani, Indian, and Bangladeshi leaders were elected to lead their countries. Nehru's daughter, Indira Gandhi, ruled India on and off from the 1960s until her assassination in 1984; she centralized the government's power, supported the breakup of rival Pakistan, and ruled by decree at one point.

Like Pakistan and Bangladesh, secular India has struggled with fundamentalist radicals who seek to suppress minority religious and ethnic groups within their country. Even so, India remains democratic, and supports a vibrant commercial and media culture that is independent of Western dominance. Later leaders have attempted to liberalize India's bureaucratically inefficient economy, both to modernize and industrialize the peasant countryside and to compete with China in offering cheap manufacturing and outsourced services to Western nations using modern shipping and telecommunications. Like China, India seeks to reestablish itself as a major regional power in production, culture, and military force. In 2014, for example, it became the fourth nation to successfully send a

10

probe to Mars. By 2015, India was the world's seventh largest economy by nominal GDP, up from thirteenth place in 2000.

In the twenty-first century, India's international stature has grown even as old tensions with Pakistan and China linger over border disputes. Since 1997, it has faced a renewed Maoist insurgency that has resulted in the deaths of several thousand Indian civilians.

Soviet Union/Russia

High-Yield

After the death of Stalin, Khrushchev took power in 1953. He publicized and criticized Stalin's faults and crimes in a process called de-Stalinization, shocking communists worldwide. Khrushchev encouraged more freedom of expression in hopes of enlisting a new generation to help rebuild the country in modern ways. He also revitalized communist interest in promoting world revolution, supporting radical factions engaged in colonial liberation struggles. Khrushchev's penchant for long-shot gambles and his apparent losses in Cold War confrontations in Cuba and Berlin led to his removal, making him the first Soviet leader to retire alive.

From 1964 to 1982, Brezhnev focused on keeping the Communist Party in control, with a more restrictive policy toward dissidents and free expression. During this period, industrial growth declined; the primary problems were the absence of economic incentives for individuals and a self-defeating system of production quotas which lowered rather than raised the baselines of acceptable quality and quantity. Communism proved insufficient for Russia's economic needs, while capitalism was better able to promote fair working conditions via government regulation and democratic restrictions on accumulation of wealth. The standard of living in the Warsaw Pact bloc fell behind that in the West. The Soviet Union opened itself to more Western contact in the 1970s, but the resulting ideologies only caused more dissatisfaction. The Soviet Union's involvement in Afghanistan's guerilla war in the 1980s highlighted its own ideological and social weaknesses on the domestic front, as the Afghanistan conflict became its version of the Vietnam War.

When Gorbachev came to power in 1985, he felt that only reform could save the communist system. He introduced his policy of *perestroika* (restructuring), with limited elements of free enterprise and private capital. His parallel policy of *glasnost* (openness) encouraged open discussion of the strengths and weaknesses of the Soviet system. As with some other prerevolutionary settings (France in 1789, Mexico in 1910, Russia in 1917), the attempted reform of a weakening regime only hastened its decline. The most tension existed between the Russian core and the Eastern European nations, as well as the western Soviet republics, like the Baltic states, Belorussia, and Ukraine. From 1989 to 1991, these blocs successively declared their independence from Soviet control, with the discredited Soviet leadership unable to reimpose the old order. The Soviet Union essentially dissolved, succeeded by independent and non-communist republics, including Russia itself.

In the 1990s, Russia's new leader Boris Yeltsin oversaw the liquidation of the state-controlled economy. Massive amounts of capital wealth and natural resources were taken over by oligarchs with connections to the old system, and the common people saw few benefits from the fall of communism. Between 1991 and 1994, the average life expectancy in Russia dropped by five years.

Russia's military forces were weakened, the former Eastern European satellites gravitated toward the European Union and NATO, and terrorists from the Islamic southern provinces of Russia challenged domestic order. Massively unpopular, Yeltsin resigned on New Year's Eve in 1999, handing power to Vladimir Putin.

In the twenty-first century, Russia has become increasingly authoritarian as its democratic institutions have been reduced in power. The oligarchs of the 1990s were either prosecuted or forcibly persuaded to cooperate with the interests of the state. The Russian military has made incursions into neighboring nations Georgia and Ukraine, and Russian forces intervened in the Syrian Civil War.

Eastern Europe

The Soviet Union dominated its satellite states in Eastern Europe following World War II, installing communist leaders and closely monitoring their affairs. Economic hardships, foreign domination, and lack of political liberties led to discontent that erupted at times in rebellion. For example, communist forces had to put down extensive riots in East Germany, which became known as the Uprising of 1953.

In 1956, Hungary rose up, much like it had in 1848 under Austrian domination, but the Red Army crushed the revolt just as the Russian army had done a century earlier. In 1968, the Prague Spring movement for civil and economic freedoms in Czechoslovakia was likewise suppressed by Soviet tanks. As with most communist states in this period, the people did receive more education, the urban working classes grew in size, and the aristocratic classes were dispossessed as industry supplanted agriculture. Eastern Europe's relative success at integrating with the West in recent years indicates that in many ways the two halves of Europe have progressed on separate but parallel tracks.

The decline of the USSR in the 1980s was marked by the rise of Solidarity, a Polish union-led social movement that defied martial law and eventually elected Lech Walesa the first anti-communist president in 1990. In Czechoslovakia, the Velvet Revolution succeeded in 1989 where earlier efforts in 1968 had failed; without Soviet interference, poet Vaclav Havel was elected president. In that same summer, mass demonstrations in East Germany led to the opening of the border to West Germany, including the dramatic televised demolition of the infamous Berlin Wall. Further negotiations solidified the unification of Germany; the country remained in the Western military alliance despite Soviet protests. Memories of Germany's aggressive role in the twentieth century's global conflicts have not faded among its neighbors. While Germany has dominated the European Union through economic, not military, power, resentments still linger.

After two generations of peace, warfare returned to Europe in the 1990s in, once again, the Balkans. The end of the Cold War opened a series of ethnic-based civil wars in Yugoslavia, which split apart into its pre-1919 components of Serbia and Montenegro, Bosnia, Croatia, Slovenia, and Macedonia. Led by Slobodan Milosevic, Serbia revived its nationalist dream of "Greater Serbia" with a genocidal policy of ethnic cleansing in largely Islamic Bosnia and Kosovo. **NATO**, the North Atlantic Treaty Organization, intervened to suppress Serbia, and Milosevic was eventually tried for war crimes at the International War Crimes Tribunal. The international recognition of Kosovo's independence from Serbia led to a souring in relations between the West and Russia.

In the twenty-first century, the expansion of both NATO and the European Union into Eastern Europe, as well as the rise of authoritarianism in Russia, has led to renewed tensions between East and West. Additionally, relations between Western Europe and Eastern Europe have become strained as preexisting issues came to the fore. A half century under communist occupation led to a cultural divergence between the two halves of Europe, resulting in differing approaches to the pressures of modernity and globalization. The dominance of Germany in the European Union has fueled resentment in Eastern and Southern Europe, especially after austerity measures were imposed across the continent during the Great Recession.

Japan and East Asia

For seven years following World War II, Japan was governed by a U.S.-dominated occupation that imposed a liberal constitution, land reforms, and a new education system. The goal was to make Japan more Western-oriented and economically strong, both to prevent a revival of militarism and to defend against communism in East Asia. Rather than allow a rebuilt military capable of new aggression, the United States offered a defensive alliance under its own naval and air forces. At the same time, the European empires in Southeast Asia were disappearing, along with their closed trade systems. America promoted free trade and access to other countries' resources.

With these crucial changes from the prewar world, Japan was able to develop an export economy of manufactured goods, with a strong focus on technology. By the 1970s, Japanese corporations and banks were world-class competitors with European and American enterprises, and Japan had rebuilt itself as a solidly united and wealthy member of the First World, the only country from Asia with such global influence until South Korea gained comparable prominence in the 1990s.

In similar ways, several smaller nations used Japan's approach to build themselves into economic powerhouses. Taiwan, Singapore, Hong Kong, and South Korea lacked natural resources or large territories, but they invested in infrastructure and human capital in order to become advanced industrialized countries or city-states.

In the early 1990s, Japan's economy formed a speculative bubble that, when it burst, caused a contraction that lasted almost 10 years. The "Lost Decade" was made worse by a rapidly aging demographic profile. Other East Asian economies, including not just the four above but also Australia, Thailand, Vietnam, Indonesia, the Philippines, and especially China, grew at faster rates in the 1990s; eventually, though, they too suffered a financial crisis in 1997.

In the twenty-first century, Japan has struggled with lingering economic issues, the lack of inclusion of women in its workforce, and a shrinking population in an aging country. While Japan maintains a position at the forefront of global popular culture, it is increasingly sharing the stage with nations like South Korea and Indonesia. Geopolitically, the key issue for East Asia in the twenty-first century is the great power jockeying between China and the United States, as well as the situation in North Korea, which developed nuclear weapons in 2006.

Latin America

Due to gaining national independence in the nineteenth century, and being distinctly in the United States' area of influence since the beginning of the twentieth century, Latin America's struggle to develop and modernize was less affected by Europe's issues than were the colonies and former empires of Eurasia and Africa. After the Second World War, Latin America's countries began to focus more on internal economic development rather than continue their traditional emphasis on commodity exports.

Growth was slower than in Europe or parts of Asia, and as countries became wealthier, old conflicts arose. Populist or socialist regimes favored more redistribution, while the traditional elites argued for social conservatism, wealth accumulation, and capital reinvestment. Military dictatorships often controlled these conflicts, except in countries like Mexico, Colombia, Venezuela, or Costa Rica, which had achieved a long-term political consensus between the classes and their leaders. Not coincidentally, these countries, along with the continental giant Brazil, also had the highest growth rates and most successful industrial progress. Communism, as promoted by Cuba, challenged many Latin American nations in the 1960s and 1970s, but counterrevolutionary forces supported by the United States prevailed. One example is the U.S.-backed coup that installed Pinochet in power in Chile, ousting the democratically elected socialist government.

In the later decades of the century, regional growth slowed under the impact of high debt incurred during the boom in credit and commodity prices in the 1970s. The world economic crunch in the 1980s led to widespread defaults on loans, negative growth, and instances of hyperinflation in Argentina and Brazil. This, along with the fall of communism, led to a 1990s trend in Latin America toward electoral democracy and neoliberal economics, featuring less regulation, more private investment, the privatization of state enterprises, and freer trade policies. This ideological influence from the United States had mixed results: there were more private enterprise and consumer imports, but also more unemployment and exploitative low-wage jobs.

2008 Financial Crisis

The interconnectedness of the global economy has helped lift hundreds of millions of people out of poverty in recent decades, but that globalized economy suffers from the same potential issues that afflicted the world during the Great Depression. What happens in one major economy can reverberate throughout the rest of the world. When the U.S. housing market collapsed in 2008, more than three million Americans lost their homes, triggering a severe economic downturn. Known as the 2008 Financial Crisis in the United States, it rippled through the global economy, sparking the Great Recession of the late 2000s and early 2010s. This event would have worldwide political implications for many years to come.

Arab Spring

In late 2010, a Tunisian street vendor named Mohamed Bouazizi set himself on fire in response to long-term mistreatment by local police officers, including confiscation of his only means of making a living, his fruit cart. His protest and subsequent death sparked widespread protests in Tunisia, which quickly spread throughout North Africa and the Middle East. Many Arabs viewed Bouazizi as a hero for expressing the frustrations many young people felt over the region's corruption, authoritarianism, poverty, and unemployment. Protestors cited goals such as more equitable government and greater economic opportunity for all.

These protests evolved into what was termed the Arab Spring. While the Tunisian government was overthrown, the results elsewhere were mixed. Egypt saw its longtime dictator, President Mubarak, removed from power only for a democratic interlude to give way to a military coup. Libya descended into a long civil war, and NATO intervention seemed to only further fracture an already unstable state. An uprising in Bahrain was crushed with the aid of Saudi Arabia. However, by far the most visible result was the outbreak of the Syrian Civil War. A sprawling, multisided sectarian conflict that also served as a proxy war for various regional and international powers, the Syrian Civil War resulted in massive loss of life and a refugee crisis that saw over four million Syrians flee abroad.

The Arab Spring also reflects the importance of the Internet and social media in the modern geopolitical landscape. Images and videos shared on social media helped fuel protests, as police crackdowns and personal stories alike illustrated widely shared common causes. Smartphones and texting allowed for youths throughout North Africa and the Middle East to more easily organize. However, Internet censorship was also a factor in the unfolding of the Arab Spring. Egyptians, Libyans, and Syrians all saw their governments shut down the Internet for a length of time, and many governments detained or arrested bloggers. In countries where full-scale civil wars broke out, both pro-democracy rebels and fundamentalist militants used social media to showcase their activities to the world.

TECHNOLOGY, POPULATIONS, AND THE ENVIRONMENT

Developments in Science

The boundaries of scientific knowledge continued to expand in the twentieth century. New theories such as Einstein's Special and General Theories of Relativity, Planck's Quantum Theory, Von Neumann's Game Theory, Shannon's Information Theory, and Wilson's Plate Tectonic Theory led to significant advances in physics and astrophysics, economics, telecommunications and computing, and earth science. Development also continued from earlier theoretical breakthroughs in subjects like genetics, evolution, probability, logic, chemistry, and statistics. This kind of work supported a vast number of more specific discoveries, many of which stemmed from a desire for pure knowledge but eventually resulted in practical technological use. Pure science, in conjunction with more results-oriented research and development, thus became an industry in its own right; governments, corporations, and universities supported sciences in the hope of producing another breakthrough invention or method. The Nobel Prizes, first awarded in 1901, have become a coveted worldwide marker of national and institutional prestige in the sciences.

Developments in Technology

During the early twentieth century, technological inventions stemmed from the nineteenth century's drive to improve devices that ease or replace human labor. Electric motors and internal combustion engines were more practical and portable than steam engines. Automobiles and airplanes supplemented the railroad as transportation. Radio and television continued what the telephone and telegraph had started in communications. Electric appliances in general began to replace servants in households and the workplace. Huge infrastructure investments, like power grids, highways, and communication networks, spread from wealthier areas to other parts of the world.

The second half of the century saw radical breakthroughs; the new field of Information Technology allowed exponential increases in productivity by having machines control other machines. Analog devices like mechanical computers and automated switchboards in the early decades were revolutionized by electronic circuitry developed during World War II. Digital computers and similar equipment exploded onto the technological landscape in the 1960s; these were increasingly miniaturized, and then applied to every form of mechanical device for governments, businesses, and consumers.

No technological development has affected society more in the twenty-first century than the Internet. Although a primitive military computer networking system (ARPANET) had been expanded to the academic community in the 1970s, it was not until 1989 that English scientist Tim Berners-Lee developed the World Wide Web. His system of URLs, HTML, and hyperlinks would establish the framework for what is now a global system, building upon ARPANET's conceptual foundation. By the late 1990s, most Americans used the Internet. With the spread of Internet use came many new challenges: piracy, identity theft, cyberbullying, doxxing, deepfakes, and more. In 2007, the release of the first iPhone ushered in the smartphone era, further entwining the real world and the wired one.

Developments in Energy

Carbon combustion (the burning of oil and coal) remained the basis of the world's power supply throughout the twentieth century. As a result of high-profile incidents at Chernobyl and Three Mile Island, and Cold War fears of nuclear weapons, nuclear power failed to displace fossil fuels. Despite developments in renewable energy (solar, wind, hydropower, geothermal), those technologies would mostly mature only in the twenty-first century. Hydropower saw the earliest widespread adoption but was limited by the number of suitable river locations in a given region. Due to mass carbon combustion, the global climate itself began to change.

The central role of the Middle East in the global petroleum market had profound geopolitical implications in the twentieth century and beyond. The Sykes-Picot Agreement, which concerned the partition of the Ottoman Empire after World War I, largely ensured the security of British and French economic interests, especially access to oil fields necessary to fuel their navies. After World War II, the Soviet Union and United States jockeyed for influence over the oil-producing nations there.

Consequences of Development

Cheap and easily adapted technology compressed the amount of time and money it took to modernize an undeveloped region. Accordingly, the industrial revolutions of the later twentieth century in Asia, Africa, and Latin America were faster and more extensive than Europe's and

North America's revolutions had been a century earlier. The general trend of automated control of mechanized production led to huge shifts in the employment of the working classes in developed countries. Factory work and resource extraction, as well as farm work, now used far fewer workers, while lightweight semi-skilled and service industries expanded to provide more consumer services. Rapid transport and communication, as well as liberalized trade conditions, also allowed these industries to be located in lower-wage world regions, further stressing the prospects of the working class in higher-wage nations. Mass production of goods and energy around the world, however, led to large-scale environmental issues like ecological pollution, threats to public health, and toxic disposal problems.

Population Growth

The human population of the world has grown tremendously in the past century, from approximately 1.6 billion in 1900 to over 7 billion people by 2012. Improved public health was facilitated by the use of sewage systems and new medicines, including vaccines. Technological advances in agriculture, known as the **Green Revolution**, introduced chemical fertilizers and high-producing seeds to the developing world. This postwar phenomenon fed the growing world population and prevented the famines that have cut short earlier eras of peace and prosperity.

Despite increased life expectancy, birth rates actually went down in developed societies. With families investing more resources in each child, and women beginning to enter the workforce full-time, the number of children a family could support decreased. Thus, the population growth in the industrialized West and Japan stabilized by the end of the century. The increase was more dramatic in the poorer, developing regions in Asia and in the Global South. China and India currently have populations over a billion, despite strict family planning policies in China and birth control programs in India.

Diseases

The twentieth century saw two notable pandemics: the 1918 influenza pandemic and HIV/AIDS. The 1918 influenza pandemic ("Spanish flu") is estimated to have killed between 50 to 100 million people. Since the 1970s, HIV/AIDS has killed over 35 million people. Other diseases continue to plague humanity. Traditional killers such as malaria, **cholera**, smallpox, and tuberculosis have come under control due to international public health efforts. However, some of these diseases have persisted in areas of extreme poverty, where treatments are not affordable and public health services are weak. In the wealthier parts of the world, longer lives and changing diets have led to increases in diabetes, heart disease, certain kinds of cancer, and Alzheimer's disease.

Alexander Fleming discovered the world's first antibiotic, penicillin, in 1923, although it would take many years and the research of many others around the world to refine it into a practical medical treatment. In addition to antibiotics, new advances in inoculations have prevented the spread of many diseases. Polio, a worldwide scourge since prehistory, has been all but wiped out since the invention of the Salk vaccine in 1955.

Demographic Shifts

Though migration has been a theme throughout world history, it has increased across the past century. This includes internal migration (such as people moving from rural to urban areas, or fleeing urban areas due to civil strife) and external migration (such as people migrating long distances and across borders, often in search of better economic conditions). The biggest factors have been imperialism, industrialization, and war.

Cause	Effect
Imperialism	In the early twentieth century, colonial empires expanded plantation crops for a growing world market; with slavery no longer an acceptable system, contract labor was imported to work the fields. For instance, British developments in the Caribbean and Indian Ocean basins attracted millions of Chinese and Indian workers.
Industrialization	From its inception, industrialization has depended on a working class drawn from rural areas. The pattern seen in nineteenth-century Europe and America has been repeated across the southern tier (Latin America, Africa, southern Asia) as well as in Soviet Russia and modern China; hundreds of millions have moved to urban areas for work. The resulting explosion of urban areas, industrial slums, and social unrest parallels earlier history in the West.
War	The extensive wars of the twentieth century's global conflicts have produced millions of refugees and displaced persons as borders changed, populations were expelled, workers were summoned to relocated war industries, and people evacuated devastated cities. Similar movements took place in the postcolonial adjustments and wars of liberation that characterized the Cold War era.
Post-Imperialism	Some external migrations have followed from past imperialism. Communities of Algerians and Vietnamese, for example, have settled in Paris; Pakistanis and Jamaicans have settled in London; Filipinos, Cubans, and Iranians have found havens in U.S. cities. This unexpected consequence of imperialism has resulted in new cultural identities for the host nations, as well as anti-immigration movements.

Environmental Issues

The globe's huge population growth, combined with continuing industrialization, has contributed to significant environmental problems in this century that include the overuse of natural resources, contamination by pollution, and losses of plant and animal species. Many oceanic fish species are significantly depleted to the point that governments have had to prohibit commercial fishing. Unique flora and fauna species have disappeared with the destruction of tropical forests for slash-and-burn agriculture and timber operations. Smog has polluted many city areas, causing and exacerbating lung diseases, which can kill vulnerable populations. Water pollution has restricted fresh water access for many, particularly in developing nations. The damming of rivers for power, flood control, or irrigation has also interrupted aquatic species' life cycles; in some cases, so much water is drained off for irrigation projects that the watercourse fails to reach the sea. The increased use of petroleum and heavy metals like mercury in industrial production has also contributed to the pollution of entire ecosystems. Human population growth

10

and prosperity has led to dramatic increases in the amount of trash produced by industrialized societies. Nondegradable and often toxic, this waste ends up in landfills or is transported to less developed countries to be salvaged.

Scientists have established that the industrialized world's massive increase in carbon-based fuels and other greenhouse gases has begun a gradual rise in overall global temperatures. This climate change is projected to have worldwide effects on the ecologies and food supplies of all human habitats, from droughts in some areas to increased precipitation in others. A broadly threatening aspect is rising ocean levels from melting ice caps, which will threaten the viability of most cities that are located on seacoasts.

In reaction to these threats, environmentalism has grown in visibility and political power; this movement to protect and wisely use our natural resources first appeared in the late nineteenth century. Since the 1970s, when postwar development led to visible environmental degradation, most national governments in the West have set up agencies to monitor industrial use of resources and to regulate waste products. The postcommunist states and developing nations have been slower to follow, for fear that excessive regulation will slow national growth. Countries with large natural territories have created regional and national parks and wildlife refuges in order to keep such areas intact for future generations of wildlife and people. International organizations, such as Greenpeace, the Sierra Club, and the World Wildlife Fund, work to protect the environment both through direct action and by lobbying governments for legal action.

GLOBALIZATION

More than ever before, the world in the twentieth century became interconnected through trade, cultural exchange, and political interaction on a mass scale. By century's end, capitalism and free trade stood unrivaled as world-ordering systems. Western nations still dominated in the areas of finance, trade, culture, and technology. However, even this supremacy began to be challenged by rising regional powers like China and India, as well as cultural and technological powerhouses like Japan and South Korea.

The ongoing problem of establishing international law and order did not end with the creation of the United Nations. Regional groups and treaty organizations, with echoes of the ancient tradition of defensive leagues and alliances between nations, do much to channel and direct global exchange.

Trade Organizations

Trade organizations are tasked with regulating trade and investment. The following are some post–World War II trade organizations that are important context for the Cold War and the post–World War II economy.

Organization	Description
World Bank	Created by the United States to ease reconstruction at the end of World War II, the World Bank assembles and distributes loans from wealthier nations to poorer ones. It uses its power to influence development in ways that favor established patterns and parties in the world economy.
International Monetary Fund (IMF)	A postwar U.S. creation that coordinates monetary exchange rates to maintain global financial stability.
Organization for Economic Co-operation and Development (OECD)	An economic group originating in postwar Europe that expanded in 1960 to include other Western-oriented capitalist democracies.
World Trade Organization (WTO)	Replaced the postwar General Agreement on Tariffs and Trade (GATT) in 1995. WTO is a worldwide group that works to promote unrestricted global trade, following the Free Trade theory first put forth by industrial Britain in the nineteenth century. Just as in the past, free trade for competitive industries runs up against the desire for tariff protection for agricultural producers; countries are more willing to depend on trade partners for manufactured goods than they are for their food supply.
Organization of Petroleum Exporting Countries (OPEC)	The first global trade organization that does not represent the institutional dominance of the industrialized West. OPEC was organized in 1960 by four Arab states and Venezuela, as a cartel to raise the price of oil. In 1973, to retaliate against Western support for Israel in the Yom Kippur War, the mostly Muslim OPEC declared an oil embargo against the United States, Britain, and other allies, and raised oil prices worldwide. The short-term effects on the world economy were harsh, but in the long term OPEC lost influence as oil companies found new reserves outside of the group's control.
Asian Infrastructure Investment Bank (AIIB)	Created by China in the 2010s, the AIIB resembles the World Bank in terms of operation, with a particular focus on facilitating infrastructure development in the Asia-Pacific region. It uses its power in ways to advance Chinese influence as a counterweight to the United States in the World Bank.

10

Regional Organizations

Regional organizations have formed to protect local interests. Unlike economic associations, these groups often represent less powerful and formerly colonized areas in opposition to Western pressures.

Organization	Description
Association of Southeast Asian Nations (ASEAN)	Formed in 1967 to accelerate economic progress and promote political stability in the nations of the Southeast Asian archipelago. In recent years, it has expanded relations with neighboring regional superpowers like India, China, Japan, and Australia.
European Union (EU)	Formed from the European Community in 1993 in an effort to strengthen European economic trade relations and balance the influence of the United States. It has worked to smooth the reabsorption of formerly communist Eastern states into a larger but still Western-oriented Europe. Part of its policy has been to form an economic superpower equal to the United States through the adoption of a single multinational currency, the Euro.
Organization of American States (OAS)	The postwar successor of Western Hemisphere conferences that go back to the 1890s. It has been torn between a sense of mutual security in the face of threats from outside the hemisphere and internal conflicts mostly involving Latin American suspicion of U.S. dominance.
North American Free Trade Agreement (NAFTA)	Involved the United States, Canada, and Mexico, and enacted in 1994 to remove trade barriers between these countries. To some degree, it was rooted in the economic reforms of the Reagan Administration, which sought to bolster the North American market.
Arab League	Includes 22 Arabic-speaking Muslim nations from northwest Africa to the Persian Gulf. Since 1945, it has tried to coordinate regional responses to a continual series of crises in the Middle East and northern Africa.
Organization of African Unity (OAU)	Begun in 1963 as sub-Saharan Africa rapidly gained independence from Britain, France, and Belgium. Along with providing coordination and cooperation among member states, the OAU explicitly supported the end of white minority and colonial rule in the continent. With no military force and a policy of noninterference, the OAU was ineffective in stopping wars or human rights violations among its members. In 2002, it was replaced by the African Union (AU), which attempts to emulate the EU with tighter monetary and military bonds among member states.

International Peace and Human Rights

In 1899, European nations set up a permanent Court of Arbitration at the Hague in the Netherlands in order to prevent wars by giving nations a way to settle international differences. This was supplemented in the postwar period by a World Court operated by the League of Nations; the United Nations later restored the World Court. The World Court continues to administer and judge cases of international law between consenting parties, enforced primarily by the UN Security Council.

Before World War I, agreements such as the Hague and Geneva Conventions defined the laws of war and war crimes; after World War II and the Holocaust, the victors set up tribunals at Nuremberg and Tokyo to prosecute war criminals. The Cold War stopped any universal standards from being enforced as each side protected its own interests. The UN did set up tribunals for the genocides committed in former Yugoslavia and Rwanda in the 1990s. The creation of the International Criminal Court (ICC) in 1998 has proven problematic. Major powers such as the United States, China, and Russia do not recognize its authority. African nations have accused the ICC of being a tool of Western imperialism, as it has so far only punished leaders from African states.

Human rights began to gain more attention from international organizations. In 1948, the newly formed United Nations issued a Universal Declaration of Human Rights to set the standard by which totalitarian or other abusive regimes could be judged and sanctioned. The conflict between the West's conceptions of human rights (religious tolerance, political freedom, and women's liberation) and the social and political practices of numerous non-Western member states has yet to be fully resolved. In addition, Western individualism and capitalism continue to conflict with collectivist notions that human rights include basic needs like food, health care, and income.

Finally, nongovernmental organizations (NGOs) such as CARE, Red Cross, Doctors Without Borders, and Greenpeace are rooted in citizen activism and have roots going back to Britain's Anti-Slavery Society in the early 1800s. NGOs work to tackle problems that reach beyond national boundaries and governments. These groups operate like nonprofits, in contrast to influential multinational corporations like Wal-Mart, General Motors, China Petro-Chemical, Hitachi, and Siemens, whose operations are at the heart of globalization, affecting hundreds of millions of people.

Global Conflicts and Terrorism

The increasingly globalized world also saw the rise of non-state threats that transcended traditional borders. In the latter phase of the Cold War, fundamentalist Islamic groups had formed in countries such as Saudi Arabia, Iran, and Afghanistan. In addition to their own sectarian conflicts, many of these groups were opposed to American foreign policy, the U.S. military presence in the Middle East, and the influence of Western culture on their societies. While some of these movements that used violence were established solely for domestic political purposes, others created networks of terrorist cells. Over the next few decades, attacks by various groups would occur throughout the world, from the Philippines to France. Domestic terrorism would also become more common, such as with the Aum Shinrikyo cult's 1995 Tokyo subway sarin gas attack.

The most notable attack was undertaken by a group known as al-Qaeda in 2001. Nearly 3,000 lives were lost in the September 11th attacks, and New York City faced enormous financial and infrastructure damage. The U.S. military and a coalition of allies soon invaded Afghanistan. The Taliban, the Sunni Islamic fundamentalist government that ruled the country and sheltered al-Qaeda, was quickly overthrown. The Taliban persisted as an insurgency, and the Afghanistan War continued into the end of the second decade of the twenty-first century.

In 2003, the United States invaded Iraq in an effort to remove a potentially threatening dictator and his alleged cache of weapons of mass destruction. However, the invasion was not officially sanctioned by the United Nations and was condemned by many U.S. allies around the world. Saddam Hussein was quickly removed from power, but weapons of mass destruction were never located.

A widespread insurgency soon broke out in Iraq. U.S. forces were not entirely removed until 2011. By that point, nearly 4,500 U.S. soldiers had died, mainly during the postwar occupation. Over 100,000 Iraqi civilians are documented as having died during this period. The rise of the Islamic State of Iraq and Syria (ISIS), a quasi-state that never received international recognition, would see the gradual return of U.S. forces to Iraq and their introduction into Syria.

SOCIAL AND CULTURAL CHANGES

Racial Equality Efforts

In 1900, W. E. B. Du Bois declared that "the world problem of the twentieth century is the problem of the color line," and his analysis has stood the test of time. The vast majority of inhabitants in colonies controlled by the white nations of Europe and America were people of color. They received varying degrees of civil and social rights, depending on class and situation, but in almost no cases were they held to be equal in status or ability to the white population. Added to this was the oppression of black and brown minority populations in white settler colonies in the Americas and Australasia. Much of the global fight for independence and national identity can be examined in a racial context, where racial inequality is overthrown along with imperialism. Some important examples of the struggle for racial equality include:

- The negritude movement among Francophone African intellectuals in the 1930s, rejecting assimilation and advocating solidarity among black Africans around the world.

- Afrocentrism among African Americans in the United States during the civil rights era, seeking to correct the Eurocentrism in history, literature, and social studies produced by dominant European and American culture.

- The Civil Rights Act of 1965 in the United States, culminating in a mass movement by American blacks and liberal whites to repeal segregation and white supremacy laws.

- The Brazilian Constitution of 1988, emphasizing civil liberties and criminalizing racial prejudice and speech against minorities, including the large Afro-Brazilian population.

Changing Gender Roles

High-Yield

Before 1914, the Western world held few professional opportunities for women. Most educated women were relegated to childrearing, nursing, or teaching, while working-class women had long been employed in domestic work or light industry. The fight for female suffrage in the West saw its first successes in New Zealand, Australia, and Finland at the turn of the century. Women's participation in the industrial and professional labor forces during World War I changed more minds. In most of Europe and the United States, women became voters between the 1920s and 1940s. In the prosperous 1920s, fashion and popular culture helped create a new image of the modern middle-class woman—free from some of the constraints of traditional gender roles. World War II further advanced women's image as workers, citizens, and even soldiers, but peacetime saw a backlash as women were expected to return to homemaking and low-prestige, part-time jobs in the service economy. In less developed parts of the world, only the most adventurous or high-status women were visible in public life, even as industrialism and urbanization offered up more opportunities to work outside the home.

In the 1960s and 1970s, the Western world experienced a sexual revolution, challenging traditional gender norms, marriage as an institution, and the nuclear family. Related factors included greater access to convenient birth control, liberalized divorce and property laws, countercultural rebellion, and the availability of more lucrative service-sector jobs. Since the 1970s, issues of accessible and affordable child care and equal pay for equal work have been debated but not fully resolved. The realms of politics, law, and medicine have become more open to women in the last half of the twentieth century, while successful female leaders, such as in Israel and Great Britain, have demonstrated that national-level politics is no longer an all-male domain.

The experiences of Western societies should not be considered the sole benchmark to measure the twentieth century. Many communist societies instituted important legal reforms for women, such as the 1950 marriage law in China which granted free choice of partners. The Soviet Union also placed a great deal of emphasis on scientific research, which was facilitated by a push to recruit candidates for technical schools regardless of gender. Even in the postcommunist era, Russian women are far more involved than their Western counterparts in the field of scientific research. In both Eastern Europe and the rest of the former Soviet bloc, feminism in the Western sense of the term is sometimes seen as a foreign ideology, as the former communist world developed socially and politically along different lines than the West. In parts of the developing world, changes to gender roles have varied. However, many traditional customs still prevail there as in other largely rural and preindustrial areas.

Religious Development

Traditional religious devotion declined in much of the developed world during the twentieth century, leading to a rise in secular agnosticism and humanism, as well as liberal Christianity and Judaism. New forms of spirituality also developed from blending Eastern and Western traditions. **Liberation theology in Latin America** reinterpreted Catholicism as an aggressive social reform movement, to the disapproval of the Vatican. However, many communities of faith have turned to fundamentalist forms of religion as a result of globalization, reacting against the changes to traditional beliefs and customs. The shift toward fundamentalism has occurred in factions of all the major religions throughout the world.

Internationalization

As the world becomes more and more connected, distinctions and barriers between cultures have become blurred and weakened. Western entertainment companies (in particular movie and music producers) have spread worldwide, carrying Western cultural ideas along with them. American brands like McDonald's, Coca-Cola, and Kentucky Fried Chicken can be found in most parts of the world today. Western vendors of finance, technology, scholarship, business expertise, architecture, and engineering have helped spread ideas about individualism, consumption, self-fulfillment, and

10

family roles to areas with sometimes radically different approaches to life. This trend has been characterized as cultural imperialism, replacing the political and physical imperialism of the past with something more insidious and invasive.

Globalization, on the other hand, has enabled cultural diffusion to become multidirectional. Tourism, immigration, and the Internet have allowed consumers worldwide to have opportunities to appreciate arts, foods, and other cultural markers from around the world. Latin American soap operas, South Korean K-Pop, and Japanese anime are just some of the products in this global marketplace, popular not just in the West but elsewhere as well. Sports have also become more internationalized, with the Olympics and the World Cup competitions enjoying popularity in all regions of the world. In addition, the rise of social media has made it easier than ever for people all around the world to interact.

PRACTICE SET

Questions 1–4 refer to the passage below.

"I must deal with the question of boycott. . . . In the first place, boycott of British goods has been conceived as a punishment and can have no place in non-co-operation, which is conceived in a spirit of self-sacrifice and is a matter of sacred duty.

Secondly, any measure of punishment must be swift, certain, and adequate for the effect intended to be produced. Resorted to by individuals, therefore, boycott is ineffectual, for, it can give no satisfaction unless it is productive of effect, whereas every act of non-co-operation is its own satisfaction.

Thirdly, boycott of British goods is thoroughly unpractical, for, it involves sacrifice of their millions by millionaires. It is in my opinion infinitely more difficult for a merchant to sacrifice his millions than for a lawyer to suspend his practice or for a title-holder to give up his title or for a parent to sacrifice, if need be, the literary instruction of his children. Add to this the important fact that merchants have only lately begun to interest themselves in politics. They are therefore yet timid and cautious. But the class, to which the first stage of non-co-operation is intended to appeal, is the political class which has devoted years to politics and is not mentally unprepared for communal sacrifice."

Mohandas Gandhi, *The Wheel of Fortune*,
"Boycott of Goods vs. Non-Co-Operation Programme," 1922

1. The recommendations presented in the passage most strongly reflect the tenets of which of the following?

   (A) Socialism

   (B) Nonviolence

   (C) Classical liberalism

   (D) Imperialism

2. This passage by Gandhi is best understood in the context of which of the following world trends in the first half of the twentieth century?

   (A) Workers' protests of the labor conditions and unequal distribution of wealth in capitalist economies

   (B) Colonies' challenges to imperial rule in the midst of social and political upheaval after both world wars

   (C) The economic crises perpetuated by postwar debt, reparations, and the Great Depression

   (D) The emergence of totalitarian states in power vacuums created by the collapse of colonial rule

3. Which of the following was an eventual result of the outcomes advocated by Gandhi?

   (A) The failure of India to secure complete independence and establish itself as an autonomous state

   (B) The economic isolation of India due to its continuation of boycotts and tariffs as part of its economic policy

   (C) The strong political alignment of India with repressive regimes in Southeast Asia

   (D) The displacement of populations when boundaries were established between India and Pakistan

4. Which of the following best characterizes the post–World War II era economic policy pursued by President Nehru?

   (A) He worked to modernize India by involving the government in the development of India's infrastructure and industrial sector.

   (B) He removed all regulations on businesses to promote a domestic economy that functioned purely by the laws of supply and demand.

   (C) He promoted reinstating economic policies that had existed during India's colonial era.

   (D) He adopted highly centralized economic policies similar to those employed by the communist governments in China and the Soviet Union.

Questions 5–8 refer to the passage below.

"Various industries had to be enlisted and many new ones created for the supplies. In order to increase the production of these war commodities day by day, people of the warring countries and even those of the neutral states had to be content with the barest necessities of life and had to give up all former comforts and luxuries.

. . . Furthermore, the unification and nationalization of all the industries, which I might call the Second Industrial Revolution, will be more far-reaching than that of the first one in which Manual Labor was displaced by Machinery. This second industrial revolution will increase the productive power of man many times more than the first one. Consequently, this unification and nationalization of industries on account of the World War will further complicate the readjustment of the post-war industries. . . .

China is the land that still employs manual labor for production and has not yet entered the first stage of industrial evolution, while in Europe and America the second stage is already reached. So China has to begin the two stages of industrial evolution at once by adopting the machinery as well as the nationalization of production. . . . Let us see how this new demand for machinery will help in the readjustment of war industries. All sorts of warring machinery can be converted into peaceful tools for the general development of China's latent wealth. The Chinese people will welcome the development of our country's resources provided that it can be kept out of Mandarin corruption and ensure the mutual benefit of China and of the countries cooperating with us."

Sun Yat-sen, *The International Development of China: A Project to Assist the Readjustment of Post-Bellum Industries*, 1921

5. The reference in the second paragraph to the "unification and nationalization of all the industries" is best understood in the context of which of the following twentieth-century developments?

   (A) The development of improved heavy industrial techniques during a second industrial revolution

   (B) The resistance to foreign influence in the Chinese economy by anti-colonial movements

   (C) The relatively early adoption of machine production in East Asian countries

   (D) The mobilization of resources by states to enable adequate wartime production

6. The reference in the third paragraph to "Mandarin corruption" is best understood in the context of which of the following early twentieth-century developments?

   (A) The world dominance of the Chinese economy

   (B) The spread of Marxism

   (C) The collapse of the Qing Dynasty

   (D) The rebellions against Chinese imperialism

7. Which of the following describes the state of the Chinese economy in the <u>mid-twentieth century</u> under the leadership of Mao Zedong?

   (A) Government control of most economic activity, as guided by Five-Year Plans of the communist leadership

   (B) Land redistributions that seized land from wealthy landowners under a populist government

   (C) Development of a substantial role in international trade and recognition as a wealthy Pacific Rim nation

   (D) Liberalization of formerly restrictive economic policies that led to a flourishing of the middle class

8. Sun Yat-sen's desire referenced in the <u>third paragraph</u> to "ensure the mutual benefit of China and of the countries cooperating with us" differs most strongly from which of the following?

   (A) The development of trade agreements such as ASEAN

   (B) The spread of the Non-Aligned Movement during the Cold War

   (C) The anti-colonial sentiments of the Boxer Rebellion

   (D) The flourishing of the Atlantic system of trade

Questions 9–11 refer to the graph below.

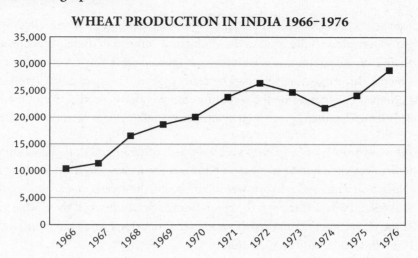

WHEAT PRODUCTION IN INDIA 1966–1976

9. Which of the following best explains the overall trend in the data in the graph?

(A) Communist conflicts in Southeast Asia

(B) The Green Revolution

(C) The heightening of Cold War tensions

(D) The partitioning of Pakistan and India

10. The historical trend represented by the data in the graph is most similar to which of the following?

(A) The impact on the quantity of manufactured goods as a result of the development of new energy sources

(B) The changes in speed of transporting goods as a result of the improvements to transportation afforded by railroads

(C) The change to China's productivity as a result of the government's implementation of economic policies such as the Great Leap Forward

(D) The impacts on domestic economies as a result of the world economic crises sparked by the Great Depression

11. Which of the following was a historical development that enabled the Indian population to adopt policies that led to the results in the graph?

(A) India's new colonial interests had created more markets for wheat.

(B) The official policy of apartheid had been abolished.

(C) India had become an independent country.

(D) India's government had been seized by communist forces.

10

Questions 12–14 refer to the passage below.

"Where are those men on Pancho Villa's payroll, so admirably equipped and mounted, who only get paid in those pure silver pieces Villa coins at the Chihuahua mint? Bah! Barely two dozen mangy men, some of them riding decrepit mares with the coat nibbled off from neck to withers. Can the accounts given by the Government newspapers be really true: are these so-called revolutionists simply bandits grouped together, using the revolution as a wonderful pretext to glut their thirst for gold and blood? Is it all a lie, then? Were their sympathizers talking a lot of exalted nonsense?

If on one hand the Government newspapers vied with each other in noisy proclamation of Federal victory after victory, why then had a paymaster on his way from Guadalajara started the rumor that President Huerta's friends and relatives were abandoning the capital and scuttling away to the nearest port? . . . Well, it looked as though the revolutionists or bandits, call them what you will, were going to depose the Government. Tomorrow would therefore belong wholly to them. A man must consequently be on their side, only on their side."

Mariano Azuela, excerpt from *The Underdogs*, translated by E. Munguia, Jr., 1915

12. The questions the narrator asks in the excerpt are best seen as evidence of which of the following?

   (A) The complicated and conflicting viewpoints that spread through the stages of the Mexican Revolution

   (B) The political upheaval in Mexico and Latin America resulting from heavy casualties in World War I

   (C) The prevalence of an idealized image of the peasant-worker within a country under communist rule

   (D) The impressive wealth of revolutionaries who sided with Pancho Villa during the Mexican Revolution

13. Which of the following best describes the motivations of the "revolutionists" referenced in the passage?

   (A) Advocating the adoption of policies that would increase Mexico's role in international trade and politics

   (B) Securing the independence of Mexico from Spain in light of the democratic ideals of the Enlightenment

   (C) Expressing the need for social relief policies in the midst of the global economic crises of the Great Depression

   (D) Challenging economic policies that had empowered elites and reinforced colonial social hierarchies

14. The policies of the Mexican government <u>begin-</u><u>ning in the 1920s</u> reflect which of the following?

   (A) A commitment to a purely free market economy with essentially no government regulations

   (B) An increased role of governments in national economies after World War I

   (C) A resurgence of land-based economies concentrating wealth with elites who were loyal to the government

   (D) Social and economic restrictions typical of totalitarian states

Questions 15–16 refer to the image below.

WPA POSTER ABOUT COMMUNICABLE DISEASE, 1940

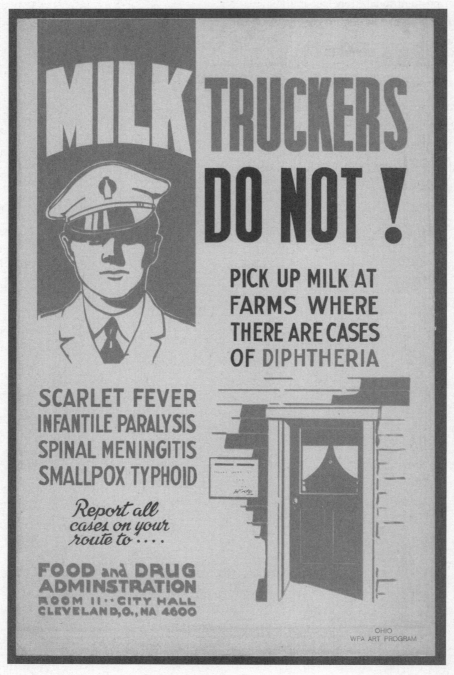

Library of Congress, Prints and Photographs Online Catalog

This poster was created as part of the federal Works Progress Administration Art Program, 1936–1940.

15. The poster reflects which of the following trends in the early twentieth century?

    (A) A tendency of socialist governments to utilize propaganda to maintain the loyalty of their populations

    (B) An increased role for government agencies in regulating economic activities in many nations

    (C) Successful implementation of programs to address postwar health crises by international organizations such as the League of Nations

    (D) A persistence of epidemics despite advances in public health programs that decreased the overall number of fatalities from disease

16. Which of the following is true of epidemics in the late twentieth century?

    (A) New diseases such as Ebola and HIV/AIDS spread throughout both developed and developing countries.

    (B) The occurrence of diseases associated with longer life spans, such as Alzheimer's and heart disease, decreased.

    (C) Widespread epidemics were more common in more developed nations than in less developed nations.

    (D) Medical technology had essentially eliminated most potentially fatal diseases.

10

Questions 17–19 refer to the passage below.

"Treaty of Friendship, Cooperation, and Mutual Assistance Between the People's Republic of Albania, the People's Republic of Bulgaria, the Hungarian People's Republic, the German Democratic Republic, the Polish People's Republic, the Rumanian People's Republic, the Union of Soviet Socialist Republics, and the Czechoslovak Republic.

The Contracting Parties, reaffirming their desire for the establishment of a system of European collective security based on the participation of all European states irrespective of their social and political systems, which would make it possible to unite their efforts in safeguarding the peace of Europe; mindful, at the same time, of the situation created in Europe by the ratification of the Paris agreements, which envisage the formation of a new military alignment in the shape of 'Western European Union,' with the participation of a remilitarized Western Germany and the integration of the latter in the North-Atlantic bloc, which increased the danger of another war and constitutes a threat to the national security of the peaceable states; being persuaded that in these circumstances the peaceable European states must take the necessary measures to safeguard their security and in the interests of preserving peace in Europe."

The Warsaw Security Pact, 1955

17. The passage is best understood in the context of which of the following?

    (A) The military alliances of totalitarian states during World War II

    (B) The outbreak of a land war between NATO and the Warsaw Pact member nations

    (C) The power struggle between capitalist and communist states during the Cold War

    (D) The movement toward a free market economy in the Soviet Union

18. Which of the following developments occurred as a result of the tensions reflected in the passage?

    (A) The maintenance of peace in Central and Eastern European states until the end of the twentieth century

    (B) Involvement by a Warsaw Pact member in proxy wars such as the conflict in Vietnam

    (C) The division of Germany into two states, one influenced by the Soviet Union and one by the other Allied nations

    (D) The fall of the tsar and the establishment of a new government during the socialist Russian Revolution

19. The passage can best be used as evidence for which of the following world historical trends that took place during the twentieth century?

    (A) The establishment of trade agreements to help facilitate free market exchange throughout the world

    (B) The collapse of former empires and the establishment of autonomous governments by former colonies

    (C) The eventual decline of communism in the Soviet Union in light of both foreign and internal political pressures

    (D) The emergence of international organizations in an increasingly interconnected world

Questions 20–23 refer to the map and table below.

<u>Source 1</u>

SIZE OF LAKE CHAD OVER TIME

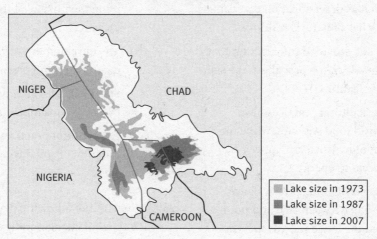

<u>Source 2</u>

Factors Impacting Water Volume in Lake Chad
Damming of tributary rivers
Diversion of water for agriculture irrigation
Strained water resources due to regional population growth
Annual rainfall averaging less than about 12 inches
Semiarid environment at the edge of the Sahara Desert
Climate change

20. The sources best illustrate which of the following trends of the late twentieth century?

    (A) Human activity has led to environmental processes such as desertification that can threaten supplies of natural resources.

    (B) Technology has provided information that was unobtainable in the past about the state of geographic features.

    (C) Improved agricultural practices have increased world food supplies, while the development of hydroelectric power has increased access to energy.

    (D) Repressive governmental policies have widened the gap between rich and poor and restricted the latter's access to basic resources.

21. Which of the following additional pieces of information would be most directly useful in assessing the extent to which the developments reflected in the sources represent a threat to the populations of the states surrounding Lake Chad?

    (A) Satellite images that show the changing shorelines of other African lakes during the same time period

    (B) The average annual rainfall in the Lake Chad Basin for the 30 years prior to 1972

    (C) Data about alternative sources of fresh water accessible to the populations in the Lake Chad Basin

    (D) Schematic drawings of the specific layouts of the irrigation methods used in the Lake Chad Basin

22. The trend represented by the sources is most similar to which of the following?

    (A) The construction of the Panama Canal enabling the linkage of the Atlantic and Pacific Oceans

    (B) The development of vaccines lowering the death rate in nineteenth-century Europe

    (C) Sustainable logging practices helping to preserve Amazonian rain forests

    (D) Agricultural practices leading to the degradation of soil during the American Dust Bowl

23. Which of the following developed in response to the types of changes indicated in the sources?

    (A) The grassroots Green Belt movement that protests inequality in the negative environmental impacts of the world economy

    (B) International finance organizations such as the World Bank to promote economic development in nations in need

    (C) Ideals of liberation theology that emphasize reduction in economic and political oppression

    (D) The spread of the principles of mass production that increased factory output throughout the world

Questions 24–25 refer to the graph below.

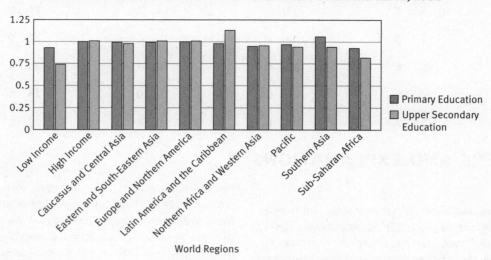

GENDER PARITY INDEX OF EDUCATION ENROLLMENT, 2014

World Regions

Data adapted from UNESCO Institute for Statistics, as reported in UNESCO Education Monitoring Report, 2016

A gender parity index value that is less than 1 indicates higher relative access to education for males than females. A gender parity index value that is greater than 1 indicates higher relative access to education for females than males.

24. Which of the following conclusions is best supported by the data in the graph?

   (A) Some world regions, such as sub-Saharan Africa, have a disparity between female and male access to education.

   (B) In all world regions, females have relatively less access to educational institutions than males.

   (C) Females have the lowest access to upper secondary education in proportion to males in the Latin America region.

   (D) A region's income level has no correlation with the relative access of females and males to education.

25. Based on the graph and your knowledge of world history, which of the following best describes an educational trend of the early twenty-first century?

   (A) Females have increasingly been excluded from access to secondary education in some world regions.

   (B) Europe and North America have adopted identical educational requirements.

   (C) Though full parity has not been achieved, access to education has become more inclusive.

   (D) The idea that access to education is related to a country's economic growth has been rejected.

ANSWER KEY

1. B	6. C	11. C	16. A	21. C
2. B	7. A	12. A	17. C	22. D
3. D	8. C	13. D	18. B	23. A
4. A	9. B	14. B	19. D	24. A
5. D	10. A	15. D	20. A	25. C

ANSWERS AND EXPLANATIONS

1. B

In this passage, Gandhi presents several arguments against the use of boycotts to protest British rule of India, noting throughout that such a strategy conflicts with "non-co-operation." He describes non-co-operation as "conceived in a spirit of self-sacrifice," "its own satisfaction," and involving "communal sacrifice." This description matches the principle of nonviolent protest, used by activists such as Gandhi and Martin Luther King, Jr., to advocate political change; **(B)** is correct. (A) is incorrect because socialism is a political and economic theory that advocates collective control of the means of production; although Gandhi mentions "communal sacrifice," he does not advocate actions based on socialist economic theory. Similarly, (C) is incorrect because Gandhi does not advocate actions based on classical liberalism, an economic theory emphasizing liberty under the rule of law. (D) is incorrect because Gandhi advocates the end of Britain's imperialist control of India.

2. B

Gandhi compares the use of non-co-operation and boycotts to end Britain's imperial rule of India. This goal exemplifies the struggle in many colonies to challenge the rule of foreign countries during the political upheavals of the interwar period and after World War II. **(B)** is correct. (A) and (C) are incorrect because the passage is not concerned with economics, despite its mention of boycotts, but with political freedom and the ideology of protest. (D) is incorrect because Gandhi advocates the end of imperial rule; thus, this passage does not address events *after* colonial rule.

3. D

The outcome Gandhi advocates in his evaluation of the boycott strategy is Indian independence. **(D)** is correct

because it was a result of Indian independence. The separation of India and Pakistan into predominantly Hindu and Muslim regions, respectively, resulted in the displacement of many individuals who found themselves in the religious minority of their region. India became an autonomous nation after World War II, so (A) is incorrect. India entered the world economy after gaining independence, so (B) is incorrect. Independent India did not have strong ties with repressive political regimes, but rather was part of the Non-Aligned Movement, so (C) is incorrect.

4. A

The governments of many former colonies took a large role in economic planning. **(A)** is correct because Nehru's administration took action to build the nation's infrastructure and to promote manufacturing. (B) is incorrect because the government of India advocated a mixed economy, with a strong role for the government, not a pure free market economy. (C) is incorrect because Nehru sought to modernize India, not return India to the economic policies that existed under colonial rule. (D) is incorrect because Nehru established an economy with both government involvement and free enterprise—not a communist system as in China and the Soviet Union.

5. D

In context, "unification and nationalization" refers to wartime production strategies nations imposed on their industries. The first paragraph outlines the need to enlist industries and create new ones "to increase the production of . . . war commodities." The end of the second paragraph mentions that the process will require "readjustment of the post-war industries." Thus, **(D)** is correct because it reflects the wartime practice of governments taking control of industries to devote production to the war effort. (A) misconstrues a key term. While historians typically use the term *second industrial revolution* to refer to the improvements to heavy industry that began in the late nineteenth century, Sun Yat-sen uses the term to describe increased state control of industry. (B) may call to mind earlier economic trends in China, such as those in the late nineteenth century Boxer Rebellion, but the "unification and nationalization" of industry does not refer to foreign control of Chinese industries. (C) is incorrect because the phrase "unification and nationalization" does not refer to the timing of China's adoption of factory production; further, according to Sun, China mechanized its industry relatively late, not early.

6.   C

In the third paragraph, Sun Yat-sen states that China "still employs manual labor for production," reflecting China's feudal past. The reference to "Mandarin corruption" reflects his desire to distance himself from these traditional economic systems that existed under the Qing Dynasty, which collapsed before World War I in favor of industrialization. **(C)** is correct. None of the other choices accurately reflect Sun Yat-sen's motivations. (A) is incorrect because China, not yet a dominant economic power, was trying to increase its economic presence in the postwar world. (B) identifies an early twentieth-century world trend, but Marxism was not relevant to "Mandarin corruption" in China. During this period, China was resisting European imperialism, not engaging in imperialism itself, so (D) is incorrect.

7.   A

By the mid-twentieth century, China was under the communist leadership of Mao Zedong, who enacted highly centralized economic policies. The Five-Year Plans and the Great Leap Forward attempted rapid industrialization and agricultural collectivization through government control of the economy, though all resulted in widespread economic hardship and despair. **(A)** is correct. (B) is incorrect because although the communist economic plans did entail land redistribution, China had a communist, not a populist, government. (C) and (D) are incorrect because they reflect China's economic status in the late twentieth century as it permitted more free market reforms.

8.   C

Sun Yat-sen's topic is the modernization of the Chinese economy and efforts for the "development of China's latent wealth." The "cooperating countries" referenced here are those countries with which Sun Yat-sen hopes China will develop mutually beneficial economic relationships. The correct answer will oppose such relationships. **(C)** is correct because the Boxer Rebellion protested foreign influence in China. (A) and (D) are incorrect because they identify international trade agreements and systems. (B) is incorrect because it does not describe a desire to resist international trade, but a union of countries that wished to remain neutral during the Cold War.

9.   B

The graph shows an overall trend of increased wheat production over time, despite a slight downturn from 1972 to 1974. The correct answer will provide a reason that wheat production would increase during the 1960s and 1970s. **(B)** is correct because the Green Revolution brought improved agricultural practices and chemically and genetically modified agricultural techniques that led to increased production in countries such as India and Mexico. (A) and (C) are incorrect because neither type of conflict would have had a positive impact on India's agricultural production. (D) is incorrect because the partitioning of India and Pakistan resulted in conflict and displacements, not increased agricultural production.

10. A

The graph illustrates the increases in wheat production as a result of improved agricultural technologies and practices. **(A)** is correct because it describes a situation in which improved technology increased the productivity of an economic sector. (B) identifies a technology improvement, but it is incorrect because the choice entails an increase in the *rate of transport*, not the *quantity of creation*, of goods. (C) and (D) are incorrect because both the developments they cite had negative impacts on production.

11. C

Consider the essential difference between the status of India in the early and mid-twentieth century that would make it possible for the Indian people to control decisions about their economy: India became independent from the colonial control of Britain after World War II. **(C)** is correct. (A) is incorrect because it distorts historical details. India was a colony of Britain; India did not have colonies of its own. (B) represents a change in policy in South Africa, not India. (D) is incorrect because India is a parliamentary democratic republic; the government has never been seized by communists.

10

12. A

The narrator's questions express his confusion about the conflicting messages he received during a period of revolution. In the first paragraph, he has heard that Pancho Villa's men are paid in silver, but he sees "barely two dozen mangy men." He wonders whether the government newspapers are correct that the revolutionaries are "simply bandits." In the second paragraph, he questions which is correct: a report that the government's forces are winning "victory after victory" or the rumor that the government leaders are "abandoning the capital." The date of the passage and its references to Pancho Villa and President Huerta identify these conflicting messages as during the Mexican Revolution; **(A)** is correct. (B) is incorrect because while the Mexican Revolution happened at the same time as World War I; Mexico had little involvement in the war. Further, the "political upheavals" described are not the result of turmoil caused by world war casualties, but by the uprisings of the masses against the dictatorial economic policies of the Mexican government. (C) is incorrect because the narrator's questions about the status of the revolution are not related to any views on peasant-workers, idealized or otherwise. (D) is incorrect because it distorts the passage; although the writer has heard reports that Pancho Villa's men are wealthy bandits, he has seen only men in tattered clothes riding shabby-looking horses.

13. D

The passage identifies the "revolutionaries" as about to "depose the Government" of President Huerta during the Mexican Revolution. These "revolutionists" opposed government leadership that was insufficiently supportive of policies that would help Mexico's agrarian class. Farmers had been suffering under neocolonialist policies that concentrated wealth in the hands of European-descended landowners at the expense of members of other classes. **(D)** reflects the nature of the Mexican Revolution and is correct. (A) is incorrect because the primary concern of the "revolutionists" was not increasing Mexico's role in the world. On the contrary, they protested policies that they perceived as favoring foreign interests. (B) is incorrect because Mexican independence from Spain was achieved in the early nineteenth century. (C) is incorrect because the Mexican Revolution occurred before the Great Depression.

14. B

After the Mexican Revolution, Mexico's government, like many of the time, adopted policies to help modernize the economy and address the concerns of the agrarian classes. The government, for instance, established land redistribution policies. These policies reflect **(B)**, making it the correct answer. (A) is incorrect because the Mexican government and those of other countries tended to take a larger role in their nations' economies following the First World War. (C) is incorrect because the post–World War I era saw the dissolution of land-based economies in general; in Mexico specifically, government reforms generally reflected the interests of workers and peasants, not elites. (D) is incorrect because Mexico's policies during the 1920s reflected populist and mildly socialist ideals, not the extreme views of totalitarian states.

15. D

The poster from the late 1930s instructs milk delivery-men to avoid picking up milk at farms where diseases such as diphtheria and smallpox had been reported. This warning indicates that—despite the development of vaccines, the implementation of successful public health programs (such as those enacted by the Food and Drug Administration), and the acceptance of germ theory—concerns about epidemic outbreaks persisted. **(D)** is correct because it reflects organized disease-prevention efforts based on medical understanding of how diseases spread. (A) and (C) are incorrect because, the poster was produced in the United States and is not an example of either socialist propaganda or material created by the League of Nations. (B) is incorrect because, even though the government increased its role in the nation's economy during the Depression, the poster's purpose is to prevent the spread of disease, not to regulate the milk delivery business.

16. A

By the late twentieth century in the United States, vaccinations, better medical practices, and effective public health programs had led to a significant decline in the diseases featured in the poster. Still, in both the United States and the world, new epidemics emerged and impacted millions. **(A)** is correct because it names two newly identified diseases, HIV/AIDS and Ebola, that spread globally in the late twentieth century. (B) is incorrect because medical technology lengthened average life spans, leading to an increase rather than a decrease in age-related conditions. (C) is incorrect because epidemics were more common in locations with high instances of poverty. (D) is too extreme; not all fatal diseases have been eradicated.

17. C

The passage describes a pact, imposed by the Soviet Union, among countries opposed to Western European ideologies: the text cites a "'Western European Union,'" a "remilitarized Western Germany," and a "North-Atlantic bloc" (a reference to NATO) as increasing "the danger of another war." The passage thus reflects the tensions that developed between the communist Soviet Union and its satellite states and the capitalist democracies of Europe and North America during the Cold War, choice (C). (A) is incorrect because the pact was made after World War II. (B) is incorrect because the Cold War did not result in a land war directly between NATO and Warsaw Pact countries. (D) is incorrect because the Soviet Union did not move toward a free market until the late twentieth century.

18. B

The passage lays out the stated reasons for the Soviet-led Warsaw Pact during the Cold War. While the superpowers themselves, the United States and Soviet Union, never had a direct war with each other, they were involved in proxy wars that reflected the clash between their capitalist and communist ideals; (B) is correct because the Soviet Union supported the communist North in the Vietnam conflict. (A) is incorrect because protests and violence broke out in Central and Eastern Europe, especially around the time of the dissolution of the Soviet Union and the former Yugoslavia. (C) and (D) are incorrect because they reflect events that predate the Warsaw Pact. Germany was partitioned immediately after the end of World War II, well before the Warsaw Pact was signed in 1955. The tsar in Russia was overthrown in the 1917 Russian Revolution.

19. D

The passage reflects an agreement among countries for their "Cooperation and Mutual Assistance" in the midst of the global ideological conflict of the Cold War; the correct choice will identify a global trend exemplified by the Warsaw Pact. (D) is correct because the pact exemplifies an increasing interconnectedness among countries and the creation of multi-country organizations during the twentieth century. (A) is incorrect because the pact is not a trade agreement. (B) is incorrect because the Warsaw Pact was a multinational agreement among existing European countries; the pact did not involve any former colonies or provide evidence for the earlier collapse of the tsarist Russian Empire. (C) is incorrect because the pact was created during the spread of communism during the Cold War, not during its later decline in the Soviet Union.

20. A

The map shows the shrinking of Lake Chad over time, and the table lists contributing factors, both human-caused and environmental. The correct answer will relate this phenomenon to a late twentieth-century historical trend. (A) is correct because it identifies the trend of human activity impacting the environment, in this case, by reducing freshwater resources. (B) is incorrect because the sources do not show any geographic information that would have been unattainable in the past, though satellite imagery, as used to generate the maps, has made some information easier to obtain. (C) and (D) are incorrect because the sources do not indicate anything about food and energy supplies or repressive governmental policies.

21. C

The map shows the shrinking size of Lake Chad. The table contains the information that irrigation and damming contributed to this phenomenon. To determine whether the reduction in lake size is a threat to surrounding populations, it would be helpful to know more information about the extent to which the lake is used for agriculture and drinking water, as well as whether the lake provides the only fresh water resource in the region; thus, (C) is correct. (A) is incorrect because information about other African lakes would not clarify whether Lake Chad's changes threaten local populations. While (B) might be useful in understanding the changes to Lake Chad over time, historic rainfall information would not be particularly useful in assessing the current threat. (D) could provide insight into how to improve irrigation practices and lessen their impact on the lake, but it would not help assess the current threat.

22. D

The sources indicate a degradation of a natural environment and reduction in natural resources that can be

10

attributed to both human and natural factors, so look for a comparable situation among the answer choices. **(D)** is correct because it describes a human action (agriculture) leading to the desertification of American farmland. (A) is incorrect because it does not describe a human action that led to a reduction in natural resources; while the construction of the canal undoubtedly impacted local environments, it did not cause a major change such as desertification. (B) is incorrect because it does not describe a change to an environmental feature or a threat to natural resources. (C) is incorrect because it is describes the *opposite* of the trend in the sources.

23. A

Some of the negative environmental changes of recent decades—as exemplified by the shrinking of Lake Chad—have been particularly acute in Africa, where exploitative labor and economic practices have sometimes exacerbated preexisting poverty. **(A)** is correct because groups, such as the Green Belt Movement, have developed to protest the unequal negative impacts of the global economy. (B) is incorrect because the economic work of the World Bank does not necessarily relate to issues of environmental degradation. (C) is incorrect because liberation theology is an ideology that developed in Latin America to protest economic and political oppression, not necessarily environmental issues. (D) is incorrect because the spread of mass production would not be a response to environmental degradation; rather, environmental degradation is a common result of industrialization.

24. A

The note below the graph indicates that the gender parity index means that the closer the value is to 1, the more equity there is in male and female access to education.

Values above 1 indicate more access for females, and values below 1 indicate more access for males. Evaluate the choices in light of these factors. **(A)** is correct because the graph indicates disparities in educational access (bars above or below 1) in several regions and a sizable disparity in access to both primary and higher secondary education (particularly low bars) in sub-Saharan Africa. (B) is incorrect because male and female access to education approaches parity (a value of 1) in world regions such as Eastern and Southeastern Asia. (C) is incorrect because it is the opposite of the data in the graph: the higher the value is above 1, the more relative access *females* have to education. (D) is incorrect because the graph shows that female access to education is relatively low in low income regions, which demonstrates that there is a correlation between income levels and education parity.

25. C

The overall trend in education has been toward increased equality of access for all groups, though the graph shows that actual enrollment is not equal in all world regions, particularly in low-income countries. This assessment matches **(C)**. (A) is incorrect because the historical trend has been toward more female access to all levels of education; though the graph shows a low parity index for secondary education in some regions, such as sub-Saharan Africa, this does not mean that access has been *decreasing*. (B) is incorrect because, while the graph indicates that European and North American countries have similar educational access, it provides no information about their education requirements. (D) is unsupported by the chart and by historical evidence; if anything, the chart supports the inference that parity in access to education correlates positively to income level, and international organizations promote economic growth as a benefit of educational access.

10

CHAPTER 11

The Free-Response Sections

OVERVIEW AND STRATEGY

The free-response questions—which include three required short-answer questions, one document-based question (DBQ), and one long essay question (LEQ)—are worth 60% of your total exam score.

You have 40 minutes to answer three short-answer questions in Section I, Part B of the exam, which gives you about 13 minutes per question. Section II is 100 minutes long, and it's divided into two parts: the first 60 minutes is the suggested writing time for the DBQ (including a recommended 15-minute reading period), and the last 40 minutes is the suggested writing time for the LEQ.

> ✔ **AP Expert Note**
>
> **Treat Section II as a marathon (and train accordingly)**
>
> One hundred minutes can feel like no time at all when you have to write two free-response questions, but it is actually a long time for your brain to maintain sharp focus—especially after you have already spent 95 minutes on Section I. However, if you practice writing, including sticking to the timing and pacing required for Section II, you will build up the necessary stamina and feel much more prepared and confident on the official exam.

Readers will score each individual question according to a rubric. The rubric for the short-answer questions is straightforward: each prompt requires you to complete three tasks, and you can earn one point for successfully completing each task, for a total of three points for each question. The rubrics for the DBQ and long essay question are a bit more complex and relate to demonstrating certain skills, such as thesis development, contextualization, and use of evidence. (Scoring information and sample rubrics will be provided in the following sections about each specific question type.)

The Kaplan Method for Free-Response Questions

While there are three different kinds of free-response questions on the exam, you can and should approach every prompt using the same Kaplan Method. Employing a methodical, strategic approach will help ensure that you effectively address every part of every question. Just follow these four steps (which spell out AP-AP)!

1. **Analyze the prompt.**
2. **Plan your response.**
3. **Action! Write your response.**
4. **Proofread.**

Let's look at the Kaplan Method steps in more detail.

Step 1: Analyze the Prompt

Take the time to understand each and every part of the prompt—or what the question asks you to do. If you don't answer each of the prompt's required tasks, it will be impossible to earn a high score for that question! Analyzing the prompt means thinking carefully about the following components:

- **The content of the question.** Consider exactly what topics the question addresses. Underline key terms and requirements.

- **The action words.** Next, make sure you know exactly what you have to do with the content: *describe, explain,* etc. Consider circling the action words to help you focus on the required tasks. While we often use these action words somewhat interchangeably when speaking, consider carefully how each action word calls for a slightly different treatment of the content. Some examples, from simple to complicated, include:

  - *Identify*: Point out a trend or piece of information; this task does *not* require providing an explanation.

  - *Describe*: Fully lay out the details of something.

  - *Explain*: Analyze the *why* or *how* of something (e.g., what causes it, why it's important) using reasoning or evidence.

  - *Evaluate*: Make a determination about a claim and explain your reasoning.

- **The source stimulus.** Some questions include a primary or secondary source or sources. Analyze each source stimulus thoroughly, noting components such as topic, main idea, author viewpoint, and author background. You must understand the source(s) to effectively answer the prompt.

Step 2: Plan Your Response

This is the *most important* factor in writing a quality response. Planning is never a waste of time; rather, it is a crucial step to creating an effective response that addresses every part of the prompt. The test makers expect you to take time to plan your responses and have built this into the exam timing, so take advantage of it. Ultimately, planning saves you time by helping you write a focused response. You only have time to write each response once, so make it count!

Here are some tips to help you make your plan:

- Think about what you will write for each part of the prompt. Jot down brief notes—phrases and/or examples—for each part.

- Whenever possible, see if you can come up with specific historical examples to help support your response.

- Double-check the prompt to make sure you didn't skip any required tasks.

- Devote an appropriate amount of time to each part, depending on the complexity of the required task. (Tasks that only ask you to *identify* something typically require less time than parts that ask you to *explain* or *describe*.)

Step 3: Action! Write Your Response

After thoroughly completing the pre-writing steps, actually writing the response should be relatively straightforward: just use the notes you jotted down in Step 2 to write your paragraphs. Be sure to write full paragraphs; lists or outline-style notes will not earn you points on the exam.

As you write, keep in mind that your responses should clearly focus on the required tasks, provide full explanations, and firmly assert your claims. Time is limited, so every word you write should help you earn points. The length of your response has nothing to do with your score; the quality of the content and how well it addresses the prompt is what counts.

Finally, make sure you write neatly. Readers can't award points if they can't read what you wrote. Keep in mind that actual people will be reading every word you write, so make them happy by making your responses as easy as possible to read.

> **✔ AP Expert Note**
>
> ### Be strategic with the information you provide
>
> Don't just write as much as you know about the topic of a prompt; rather, respond with information that satisfies each specific requirement. For example, if a free-response prompt asks you to "Identify ONE difference between the impact of the Columbian Exchange on the Americas and its impact on Europe," don't waste time writing out smaller details like long lists of common produce transferred on ships (such as tomatoes, corn, beans, peanuts, bananas, olives, etc.). Instead, it would be more beneficial for you to focus on how the arrival of new animals affected the Americas more than Europe because the new animals, such as horses, changed agricultural styles, diet, and transportation of groups, such as the Plains tribes. Focus your writing on what the question asks for, and move on!

Step 4: Proofread

Try to leave a minute or two to briskly proofread. Your responses need not be perfect, but you should quickly correct any glaring errors that might distract your readers from your content. If you catch a mistake, just neatly cross it out and write the correction above. There's no time for a complete overhaul of the response, but if you made a plan, there won't be any need for one!

A Note on Timing and Pacing

Now that we've established the Kaplan Method (AP-AP) to apply to every free-response question, let's review timing considerations. You should respond to each prompt for an amount of time that is proportional to the work involved. The three short-answer questions in Section I, Part B should each take approximately 13 minutes to analyze, plan, write, and proofread.

For Section II, however, you are working over a long total time span (1 hour and 40 minutes), so pacing yourself among two essays will require some effort and practice. Consider wearing a standard wristwatch to help pace yourself in case there is no clock available in the testing room. And, just as importantly, practice the free-response sections on the practice tests under timed conditions. It's difficult to anticipate how long each section will feel on the day of the exam, so practicing with a watch will greatly increase your familiarity with the required pacing.

> ✔ **AP Expert Note**
>
> **Remember to "AP-AP"**
>
> Recall that the steps of the Kaplan Method for Free-Response Questions spell out AP-AP. Follow all of the steps of this easy-to-remember acronym every time you encounter a free-response prompt, both in practice and on Test Day. By making the Kaplan Method second nature, you won't have to think about what you're doing and can instead focus on the quality of the content you're writing.

SHORT-ANSWER QUESTIONS

Overview

The short-answer part of the test, which appears after the multiple-choice questions, consists of four questions—and you must answer three.

Unlike the DBQ and LEQ later in the exam, your response to each short-answer question will be a brief, to-the-point answer to each question's three required tasks. You should use complete sentences, but there is no need to write a thesis or provide any additional information.

The types of short-answer questions will always be the same:

1. **Question 1** is based on a secondary source or sources. For instance, you might be asked to provide historical evidence to support or refute a historian's argument about a historical trend.

2. **Question 2** is based on a primary source or sources. For instance, you might be asked to explain how a historical image reflects a development in that culture.

3. **Question 3 and Question 4** do not provide sources and include only the three required tasks. You will choose EITHER Question 3 or Question 4. Question 3 will cover the period from 1200–1750. Question 4 will cover the period from 1750–2001.

Strategy

As is the case for every free-response question, you should follow the 4-Step Kaplan Method. Before walking through a sample prompt step-by-step, let's look at some special considerations for short-answer questions:

- Carefully analyze the source stimulus—which could be a passage or image—on questions 1 and 2. Note key details, look for relevant information in the titles and source information, and paraphrase in your own words the main purpose of the source.

- Since each short-answer question consists of three tasks (A, B, and C), read through all three tasks before you begin planning your response. Some tasks may be related to each other (such as providing multiple historical examples), so you want to be sure you have an understanding of all the required tasks before you dive in.

- Short-answer questions do not require a thesis statement or an organized essay response. Directly and concisely address each required task, then move on.

- You will choose EITHER Question 3 or Question 4. Read both questions and consider which one you feel more confident about, keeping in mind that you'll need to be able to explain each part of your response and provide relevant examples. If needed, quickly begin planning one or both questions to help you determine which question to answer in full.

- You may answer the short-answer questions in any order, as long as you write your responses on the corresponding pages of your response booklet. Begin with whichever question you feel most confident about—be sure you give about a third of your time to each question, since each is weighted the same in your score.

The following is a step-by-step walk-through of a sample short-answer question.

Sample Question

Use the passage below to answer all parts of the question that follows.

"Since the decline of Gothic* architecture the ideas which have prevailed respecting it have been for the most part confused and incorrect. Until recently this art has received little serious attention. The very name Gothic originated in a spirit of contempt which has naturally precluded any disposition to study, as it deserves, this splendid manifestation of human genius. The architects and amateurs of the schools in Italy, where the revival of taste for antique art had led to an abandonment of medieval forms of design, could not be expected to admire anything so far removed from the spirit of the art which was in fashion during the sixteenth century. . . .

Finally, it should be considered that the Gothic edifice, with its myriads of sculptured forms, was like a vast open page whereon were written, in imagery which the most illiterate could read, the legends

*Gothic architecture, which first developed in France and was adopted for use in cathedrals throughout Europe from the twelfth through sixteenth centuries, used new architectural techniques that permitted the construction of higher walls and taller stained glass windows.

and traditions of the medieval faith. These legends and traditions must be reckoned among the chief sources of inspiration and stimulus to the imaginations of the Gothic builders. They appealed to the warmest sympathies and quickened the highest aspirations of the people, and filled them with devotion to the fabric which they sought to make, at whatever cost of labour and of treasures, a fitting expression of their beliefs and hopes. . . . Of the greater cathedrals the one in which the Gothic principles were first distinctly and systematically carried out is that of Notre Dame in Paris. Here is a vast nave so admirably roofed with stone that the work has lasted intact for seven hundred years, and will probably, if not wantonly injured, last for centuries to come."

Charles Herbert Moore, *Development and Character of Gothic Architecture,* 1890

a) Identify ONE way in which the author alludes to a historical development in the time period 1450–1750 in the first paragraph.

b) Describe ONE function of large-scale architecture (not specifically mentioned in the passage) in any world region in the period circa 1200–1750.

c) Explain ONE way in which political structures in Afro-Eurasia in the period circa 1200–1750 enabled the construction of large-scale architecture as described in the passage.

Step 1: Analyze the Prompt

Closely read or analyze the source stimulus, marking important details. When finished, briefly paraphrase the purpose of the source in your own words to solidify your understanding. See a high-scoring response writer's notes below. Don't worry about trying to absorb all of the details; focus on the big picture.

¶1: Gothic was held in contempt, author thinks it's "genius"

¶2: Gothic buildings inspired medieval faith

Look for any additional information that may be provided about the source. For this source, note that the footnote provides a description of Gothic architecture. Here you learn when (the 1100s to 1500s) and how (for cathedrals) the style was used. Finally, the source line indicates that the author wrote about Gothic architecture in 1890, so this is a secondary source.

As you did with the source, read the three parts of the prompt carefully, underlining exactly what each requires. Box, underline, or otherwise mark the action words (which, for this sample prompt, are *identify*, *describe*, and *explain*). Make sure to respond in a way that fulfills what each action word requires.

Step 2: Plan Your Response

The paragraphs below describe what a high-scoring writer might notice and think about when planning a response. Samples of what that high-scoring writer might write as notes are provided for each part of the prompt.

This short-answer prompt contains some underlined words and phrases—pay special attention to these hints. Often, underlines are used when parts of a question test different time periods or have other slightly different requirements, so be careful to keep straight what you need to provide for each part of the prompt.

For Part A, the prompt directs you to the first paragraph and asks for a way in which the author alludes to, or indirectly refers to, a historical development between 1450 and 1750. The high-scoring response writer would research the first paragraph, in which Moore states that in sixteenth-century Italy there was a revival of antiquity and a contempt for Gothic style, and think about what historical development this reflects. Note that the writer only has to briefly *identify*, not describe or explain, how the author refers to this historical development.

Part A:

- "antique art" = the spread of Classical, Islamic, and Asian ideas in Europe that led to innovations (Renaissance)

Part B requires a description of a function of big architecture between 1200 and 1750 from any world region. The high-scoring writer would note that the passage already mentions how architecture can inspire religious devotion. The high-scoring writer would brainstorm other functions of architecture, choosing one for which she can write multiple descriptive details. Including a specific example would help support the response.

Part B:

- Architecture can legitimize rule (shows wealth, power, divine approval)
- Example: Cuzco temple of the sun (connected ruler w/ deity and utilized large-scale labor)

Part C asks for an explanation of how a political structure in Afro-Eurasia made large-scale architecture possible. The high-scoring writer would brainstorm political structures in Afro-Eurasia and take notes about how she can describe the relationship between those political structures and architecture.

Part C:

- Describe feudal system in Europe: wealth of emerging kings, manor lords, and clergy enabled construction
- Example: St. Peter's Basilica & Sistine Chapel at Vatican

Step 3: Action! Write Your Response

To form your response, just write out the information, using your planning notes. As you write, remember to label each part of your response (A, B, C) and to keep your writing legible. Refer back to the question's action words to make sure you're doing the correct tasks. See the following sample high-scoring response and scoring explanation at the end of this section. One of the best ways to improve your own free-response answers is to read sample responses, thinking carefully about what makes the responses effective and what features you can copy.

Step 4: Proofread

Leave a minute or so for a quick proofread, neatly correcting any errors you catch.

Sample High-Scoring Response

(a) Moore mentions the "revival of taste for antique art" in the sixteenth century. This reflects the time period during which increased contacts through trade with Islamic and Asian merchants introduced new ideas and technologies into Europe, including the rediscovery of Classical Greek and Roman texts. This infusion of ideas helped spark new art, philosophy, and science.

(b) Large-scale architecture was used by rulers to help legitimize their rule by showcasing their wealth, power, and divine approval. For instance, the impressive temple of the sun in Cuzco demonstrated the power of the Incan ruler, both in his association with the sun god and through his ability to orchestrate the labor and resources required for its construction.

(c) In the 1200s, feudal systems still persisted through much of Europe. In this political and economic framework, serfs could farm portions of the lords' manors in exchange for laboring for the lord. The lords themselves were granted manors by monarchs, who were gradually centralizing their power. Large-scale architecture could thus be funded by the wealth of the lords and monarchs; the wealthiest would construct castles and palaces to signify and defend their power. The Catholic Church also became enmeshed in the feudal system, with some clergy and monasteries controlling manors and amassing political power. In Italy, for example, the wealth of the church enabled the construction of St. Peter's Basilica and the Sistine Chapel at the Vatican.

Sample Response Explanation and Scoring for Question 1: 3 points (1 + 1 + 1)

The following is scoring information an AP reader might use to grade this free-response question. A successful short-answer response accomplishes all three tasks set forth by the prompt. Each part of the prompt is worth 1 point, for a total of 3 possible points.

Part A (1 point)

To earn this point, the response must identify how the first paragraph of the source reflects a historical development. The writer of the sample response does so effectively by accurately identifying a historical trend associated with a short quote from the author.

Part B (1 point)

To earn this point, the response must describe a function of large-scale architecture in the period from 1200–1750. The writer of the sample response goes beyond merely identifying, using details to thoroughly describe how rulers legitimized their power through architecture. The writer effectively supports her claims by identifying the specific example of the sun temple in Cuzco and describing ways in which the temple legitimized the Incan ruler's reign. Since the question stem specifies that the response must use a function that is not mentioned in the passage, the response must describe a function other than inspiring religious devotion.

Additional examples of functions of large-scale architecture include: facilitating religious practice, as in the muezzins in the lofty minarets of Islamic mosques (such as the Great Mosque of Djenné in the Mali Empire) calling believers to prayer; proclaiming rulers' divine right to rule and serving as a means to regulate aristocrats, as in Louis XIV's Palace of Versailles; and providing defense, as in the improvements to the Great Wall of China during the rule of the Ming Dynasty.

Part C (1 point)

To earn this point, the response must explain a way in which political structures in Afro-Eurasia from 1200 to 1750 impacted the building of large-scale architecture. The writer of the sample response effectively explains the role of political structures by first analyzing the relationship between how feudal political structures funded and legitimized architecture, and then by demonstrating how a specific example (the cathedrals at the Vatican) provides evidence of this relationship.

Other examples of political structures include: the incorporation of diverse groups in bureaucracies leading to effective territorial administration, such as the Yuan Dynasty in China being able to fund public works such as the Grand Canal of China; the use of forced labor of subjects to construct architecture, such as the Ming Dynasty in China using forced labor to improve the Great Wall of China; and the development of imperial tax-collection systems to fund imperial projects, such as the zamindar tax collection system of the Mughals in India permitting the funding of the construction of the Taj Mahal.

THE DOCUMENT-BASED QUESTION

Overview

Question 1 in Section II is the document-based question (DBQ). It will always include seven documents offering a variety of perspectives on a historical development or process that took place between the years 1450 and 2001. A high-scoring DBQ response will include the following components:

- **Thesis:** Make a thesis or claim that responds to the prompt. The thesis or claim must be based on historical facts and must establish a line of reasoning.

- **Context:** Provide context relevant to the prompt by describing a broader historical development or process.

- **Evidence:** Use *at least six* of the provided documents to support an argument in response to the prompt.

- **Additional Evidence:** Use a historical example not found in the documents as evidence relevant to an argument about the prompt.

- **Sourcing:** Explain how the context or situation of *at least three* documents is relevant to an argument. This could address the relevance of the document's point of view, purpose, historical situation, and/or audience.

- **Complex Understanding:** Demonstrate a nuanced understanding of an argument that responds to the prompt by using evidence to corroborate, qualify, or modify the argument.

While this may sound like a lot of factors to keep in mind, the strategies below will help you plan your response in such a way to address all the scoring requirements.

Strategy

As always, use the 4-Step Kaplan Method (AP-AP). Also, consider the following special strategies for the DBQ. Scoring requirements are highlighted in bold.

During Step 1: Analyze the Prompt:

- Most prompts will test one of the following historical reasoning skills: causation, continuity and change over time, or comparison. Look for keywords in the prompt that indicate which skill is being tested (for instance, "changes" often indicates continuity and change over time, while phrases such as "transformed" or "led to" often indicate causation); keep the skill in mind as you read the documents and consider organizing your essay according to the skill.

- Use the 15-minute reading period to read the documents and organize them into groups for analysis.

- Feel free to write notes in the test booklet and underline important words in both the source lines and the documents themselves. Nothing in the booklet is read as part of the essay scoring.

- Assume that each document provides only a snapshot of the topic—just one perspective.

- For each document, jot down brief notes to help you solidify your understanding of it. Use your notes to make your plan and write your essay. Take short notes about: the main idea(s) of the source, the purpose of the source (why it was written), and the background of the author and/or the context in which the source was created. Thinking about these factors will help you address several DQB requirements.

- Reread the prompt, thinking about how each of the documents relates to the prompt. Group the documents by their similarities: perhaps they present two or more major viewpoints, causes, or types of changes. When you plan the organization of your essay, each group may correspond with one body paragraph.

- If the 15-minute reading period has passed and you need a few more minutes to review the documents and organize your thoughts, go ahead! The 15 minutes is a suggested amount of time. That said, you will want to give yourself as much time as possible to write a thoughtful response.

During Step 2: Plan Your Response:

- Making a careful plan can help ensure that you address all the scoring requirements.

- Paraphrase your **thesis** statement. Knowing your claim will make it easier for you to plan an effective argument in your essay. In light of the documents, you must make a claim that demonstrates a line of reasoning in response to the prompt. Avoid statements that are vague or general ("The Industrial Revolution was very significant"), and make a specific claim that responds to the prompt using both the documents and your historical knowledge and sets up the rest of your essay ("The Industrial Revolution not only resulted in new capitalist economies but also brought about fundamental changes in social structures by creating new social classes and new roles for women").

- Be sure your thesis or overall plan incorporates a **complex understanding**. You need to demonstrate that you have more than just a basic understanding of the content, so your essay should address the complexity of the historical development—perhaps by including multiple variables, by considering both causes and effects, or by making an insightful connection to another time period.

- Make a note about how you will provide **context** for the topic of the prompt. This may fit well in the introduction or first body paragraph.

- Make a simple outline of your body paragraphs; there will likely be one paragraph for each point you made in your thesis. (For instance, in the above example, there would be a paragraph each about changes in economies, social classes, and roles for women.) For each paragraph, consider these scoring requirements:

  a. List the documents you will use as **evidence**—remember that you must use *six or seven* to earn the maximum number of points for using the documents.

  b. Consider whether the paragraph is a good place to provide **additional evidence**—you must include *one* additional historical example.

  c. Think about when it would be beneficial to explain **sourcing**, or how a document's context or situation is relevant to the argument—you must do so for *three* documents.

- Finally, review your plan and check off each requirement in your test booklet to ensure you addressed all six.

During Step 3: Action! Write Your Response:

- Nothing is more important in the first paragraph than the clear statement of an analytical thesis. The reader is most interested in seeing a strong thesis as soon as possible.

- Your thesis can be more than just one sentence. With the compound questions often asked by the DBQ, two sentences might be needed to complete the idea.

- Each paragraph should address one component of your thesis claim. Begin each paragraph with a clear topic sentence.

- Refer to the authors of the documents, not just the document numbers.

- Including short quotes is an effective way to use the documents to support your claims. However, avoid copying long sentences; use only the words or phrases that are relevant to your essay. The reader is interested in *your* ideas, not those of the documents' authors. See the sample essay later in the chapter for examples of how to incorporate quotes.

- A good idea is to write a concluding paragraph that might extend your original thesis. Think of a way to restate your thesis, adding information from your analysis of the documents.

During Step 4: Proofread:

- Skim for any glaring errors and, if you have time, check again to make sure your response meets each of the DBQ requirements.

A Note about Complex Understanding

Knowing how to earn the complex understanding point can seem elusive. However, incorporating one of the following features into your essay is a tangible way to ensure that your argument demonstrates complexity:

- Analyze multiple variables. Writing a thesis that contains several distinct components (for instance, several changes, causes, effects, differences, etc.) and providing a paragraph of support for each component is a good way to analyze multiple variables.

- Employ complex historical reasoning by explaining both similarities *and* differences, both continuity *and* change, both causes *and* effects, or multiple causes. For example, if the prompt asks you to evaluate the extent to which a change occurred, a thesis that addresses both continuity *and* change might state that "Factor *x* and factor *y* changed, but factor *z* remained the same."

- Explain relevant connections to other world regions or other time periods. Make sure each connection you incorporate is thoroughly explained and demonstrates a strong understanding of historical patterns.

- Corroborate perspectives across multiple course themes (such as environment, cultural developments, governance, economic systems, social organization, and technology). For instance, if a prompt asks about trade patterns, analyzing relevant links to government or technology may make your argument more complex.

- Qualify an argument using other evidence or views. To qualify your argument means to present exceptions to your claim, which may be done using outside evidence or an alternate view from the documents.

Sample Question

Evaluate the extent to which the processes of empire-building affected political structures in the period 1500–1900.

Document 1

Source: Nzinga Mbemba (Afonso I), King of Kongo, letter to the King of Portugal, 1526.

Sir, Your Highness should know that our Kingdom is being lost and it is necessary for you to act, since this is caused by the excessive freedom given to your agents and officials who come to our Kingdom to set up shops that sell goods that have been prohibited by us, and which are spread throughout our Kingdom to our vassals, whom we had in obedience, and who now do not comply because they have things in greater abundance than we ourselves; and it was with these things that we had them content and subjected under our control, so it is doing a great harm not only to the service of God, but the security and peace of our Kingdoms and State as well. . . .

That is why we beg of Your Highness to assist us by commanding your country's traders that they should not send either merchants or wares to Kongo. . . . Pray Our Lord in His mercy to have Your Highness under His guard and let you do forever the things of His service. I kiss your hands many times.

Document 2

Source: Francis Augustus MacNutt, *Fernando Cortes and the Conquest of the Indies, 1485–1547*, 1909. MacNutt based his account on the original letters of Cortes.

While this embassy was absent, Cortes left his camp at the head of his horsemen, one hundred infantry, and some Indian allies, to destroy some neighbouring villages. In reporting the success of this sortie to the Emperor he wrote: "As we carried the banner of the Holy Cross and were fighting for our Faith and in the service of your Sacred Majesty, to your Royal good fortune, God gave us such victory that we slew many people, without ourselves sustaining any injury." . . .

The Tlascalan allies outside the walls were notified that they should hold themselves in readiness on the following morning, and on hearing a musket shot they should make a general assault on the city.

At dawn the next day Cortes mounted his horse and, having placed his heavy guns so as to command the approaches to the temple court or square where his men were encamped and to which there were but three entrances, he awaited the arrival of the caciques and the promised Bearers. . . .

The artillery worked incessantly and the number of Indians killed was never known, but though a hundred fell at each discharge of the guns, a thousand seemed to spring into their places with undiminished courage. . . .

Although the artillery and the arquebusiers worked fearful execution amongst the compact body of Indians, the places of the fallen were immediately filled and the death-dealing volleys seemed to produce no impression whatever, either on the numbers of the enemy or on their courage. Notwithstanding that the [Mexica] had hitherto merely heard salutes fired from the guns, but had never witnessed the deadly efficiency of these engines of warfare, they stormed the very walls of the quarters, seeking to make breaches, while others stationed on the neighbouring house-tops rained arrows, stones, and missiles of all kinds into the midst of the garrison.

Document 3

Source: Gabriel Haslip-Viera, "The Politics of Taíno Revivalism," 2006.

POPULATION ESTIMATES FOR PUERTO RICO BY ETHNICITY

Year	Europeans	Free Blacks	Mulattos*	Black Slaves	Natives
1530	10%	0%	0%	53.6%	36.4%
1600	55.6%	0%	16.6%	27.8%	
1775	40.4%	3.9%	46.7%	9%	
1795	38.4%	8.6%	34.5%	16%	2.5%
1815	47%	6.8%	36.9%	9.3%	
1860	51.5%	41.3%		7.3%	

*people of mixed race

Document 4

Source: François Bernier, physician, *An Account of India and the Great Moghul*, France, 1665.

My Lord, you may have seen before this, by the maps of Asia, how great every way is the extent of the Great Mogul,* which is commonly called India. . . .

[There are] more than an hundred rajahs, or . . . sovereigns, dispersed through the whole empire, some near, some remote, from Agra and Delhi; amongst whom there are about fifteen or sixteen that are very rich and puissant . . . each of them being able in a very short time to raise and bring into the field twenty-five thousand horses, [and] better troops than the Mogul's. . . .

The Mogul is obliged to keep these rajahs in his service for sundry reasons: the first, because the militia of the rajahs is very good (as was said above) and because there are rajahs (as was intimated also) any one of whom can bring into the field above twenty-five thousand men; the second, the better to bridle the other rajahs . . . when they refuse to pay tribute, or when, out of fear or other cause, they will not leave their country to serve in the army when the Mogul requireth it; the third, the better to nourish jealousies . . . that they proceed to fight with one another very frequently.

*Mughal emperor

Document 5

Source: Harry Verelst, Governor of Bengal for Britain's East India Company, letter to the company's Board of Directors in London, written from Delhi, India, 1769.

The ascendancy of the English in the Hindostan [province of India] is in a number of those events which are distinguished by a series of fortunate and unforeseen occurrences, not the result of any fixed or connected plan of policy. A colony of merchants, governed by laws, and influenced by principles of commerce, have acquired a political title and influence over a country, which in size, populousness, and revenue from trade may be compared to many of the most consequential states of Europe. . . . We see, we feel, the increasing poverty of the country from the lack of circulation of money throughout. . . . Since we have become governors here, however, the new policies we have made are designed to restore the equality of commerce, and the spirit of monopoly, promoted by the natives, shall be destroyed.

Document 6

Source: Winston Churchill, excerpt from *The River War: An Account of the Reconquest of the Sudan on the British-Sudanese Battle of Omdurman*, 1899.

The moment was critical. It appeared to our cavalry commander that the [Sudanese fighters] would actually succeed, and their success would involve the total destruction of our corps of Camel cavalry. That could not, of course, be tolerated. . . .

But at the critical moment our gunboat arrived . . . and began suddenly to blaze and flame from [machine] guns, quick-firing guns, and rifles. The range was short, the effect tremendous. . . . The river slopes of the Kerreri Hills, crowded with the advancing thousands [of enemy forces], sprang up into clouds of dust and splinters of rock. The charging [Sudanese fighters] sank down in tangled heaps. Even the masses in rear paused, irresolute. It was too hot even for them. The approach of another gunboat completed their discomfiture. The Camel Corps, hurrying along the shore, slipped past the fatal point of interception, and saw safety.

Document 7

Source: Kisaburō Ohara, student, Keio University Japan, "A Humorous Diplomatic Atlas of Europe and Asia," 1904.

The cartoon was created in the midst of conflict between Japan and Russia over territory in Manchuria and Korea, which led to Russia's defeat in the 1904 Russo-Japanese War. The English text reads in part: "Black Octopus is the name newly given to Russia by a prominent Englishman. For the black octopus is so greedy that it stretches out its eight arms in all directions, and seizes everything that comes within its reach."

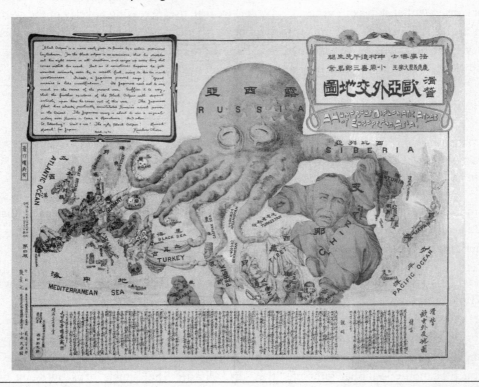

Step 1: Analyze the Prompt

First, read the prompt itself. You'll need to develop an argument using the skill of causation: how did empire-building processes affect political structures in the years from 1500 to 1900? The prompt uses the verb *evaluate*, so you will need to make a claim about the effects on political structures.

Spend the 15-minute reading period analyzing the documents themselves, thinking for each document about its authorship/historical situation, main idea, and why it was written.

Begin grouping the documents into categories that you can use to help organize your essay. A sample high-scoring writer's notes on the documents appear below:

1. King of Kongo asks king of Portugal for help because Portuguese trade is upsetting the vassal system

2. Cortes uses weapons and allies to kill Mexica

3. Puerto Rico population trends: native population ↓, European ↑, mixed ↑

4. French letter describes Mughal use of rajah system in India

5. British governor in India's letter to East India Company says British policies better for economy

6. Churchill describes effectiveness of guns in Sudan

7. Japanese cartoon describes Russian expansion as "black octopus" during time of Russo-Japanese War over territory

Groups of empire-building processes:

- Military: 2, 6, 7

- Colonization: 3

- Economic: 1, 4, 5

Step 2: Plan Your Response

Next, take time to plan your response. Focus on formulating a strong thesis, and check your plan against the six DBQ requirements. See the sample plan that a high-scoring writer might make. Scoring requirements are written in bold for reference; note that the writer includes six of the seven documents and plans to meet the requirement for describing at least three documents' sourcing by noting the viewpoints of two documents and the purpose of one document. Since the prompt asks for how empire-building affected political structures, the writer will organize the essay by explaining multiple causes (processes) that impacted political structures.

¶ intro

- **Context:** Native American governments (villages and empires)

- **Thesis:** causes of empire building: military, colonization, & economics

  - military and colonization destroyed political structures in Americas where disease played a role

  - combination of processes allowed infiltration of political structures in Asia and Africa

  - (**complex understanding:** multiple causes)

Cause ¶1: military conquest → destruction

- **Evidence:** Doc. 2: defeat of Mexica
  - Spanish advantages: horses, guns, local support
  - **Sourcing 1: viewpoint:** Cortes justifies actions by attributing victory to God
- **Additional evidence:** Pizarro defeat of Inca; Spanish set up viceroys and social hierarchy
- **Evidence:** Doc. 6: British defeat of Sudanese
  - **Sourcing 2: viewpoint:** perhaps exaggerated, but shows British expect weapons will win

Cause ¶2: colonization → replace native populations' governments

- **Evidence:** Doc. 3: PR population
  - Stats of native peoples, Europeans
  - Additional factor of disease

Cause ¶3: military + colonization + economic influence → gradual political power

- **Evidence:** Doc. 4: French letter about India
  - Describes political system of rajahs, hints at instability
  - British merchants would gain power
- **Evidence:** Doc. 5: British E. India Company gov.
  - Br. didn't have "fixed plan," but "destroyed" native populations' economic policies
  - Br. gov. made India a colony
- **Evidence:** Doc. 1: King Afonso I letter
  - Port. merchants undermining king's power
  - **Sourcing 3: purpose:** submission may not be genuine

¶ conclusion: 3 processes; when additional factors (disease in Americas) briskly replaced political structures; India more complex interplay of processes

Step 3: Action! Write Your Response

Use your plan to write out your response—if you've taken the time to plan effectively, everything you write should support your thesis.

Step 4: Proofread

Leave a minute at the end to complete a brisk proofread and double-check that you met each of the DBQ requirements.

Sample High-Scoring Response

Before the arrival of Europeans, Native American societies had established diverse political structures. The villages in the northeast of North America practiced a mixture of agriculture and hunter-gathering and sometimes formed alliances among tribes. The large-scale empires of the Mexica and Inca in Central and South America had centralized power in city-states and exacted tribute or labor from subjugated tribes. However, these societies would experience political upheavals when Europeans began their quest for territory in the 1500s. Empire-building typically involved a combination of the processes of military conquest, colonization, and economic influence. Where epidemic disease was also a factor, military and colonization strategies sometimes resulted in the total destruction of previous political structures in the Americas; a combination of the three processes permitted empire-builders to gradually infiltrate, then supersede, the political structures in Asia and Africa.

The extremes of military conquest sometimes resulted in the destruction of the native populations' political structures. Document 2 references the Mexica people's violent devastation at the hands of the Spanish, with a hundred falling "at each discharge of guns." While Cortes attributes his victory to God's favor due to fighting for his faith and king, tangible factors gave him the practical advantage: horses (which were not native to the Americas), guns, the Mexica's unfamiliarity with such weapons, and the support of local allies. Cortes, perhaps seeking to impress the king, likely exaggerates in the claim that the victory was "without ourselves sustaining any injury"; still, the claim indicates both the strength of the Spanish military technology and their attitude of superiority that they used to justify their takeover of the existing Mexica government. Also using military technology and the support of other tribes, the Spanish under Pizarro took control of the Inca empire in the Andes. In both locations, the Spanish essentially destroyed the empires and installed their own political systems, with viceroys who served under the Spanish crown and a hierarchical class system that gave preference to those of European ancestry. The effectiveness of military conquest for destroying political structures is also demonstrated in Document 6, an account of a battle in Sudan that demonstrates the awesome firepower of machine guns to leave the Sudanese fighters in "tangled heaps." Although the document, written by the British Churchill, might provide a glorified account of the battle that exaggerates the British advantage, the fact that Churchill expected their weapon technology would automatically give victory is indicated in the disbelieving sentence: " It appeared to our cavalry commander that the [Sudanese fighters] would actually succeed."

Countries sending large numbers of settlers was another effective method of empire-building. This process enabled European nations to replace native governments in the Americas. For instance, Document 3 indicates that from 1530 to 1795, the proportion of Native Americans in the population of the colony of Puerto Rico dropped dramatically from 36.4 percent of the population to just 2.5 percent. At the same time, Europeans as a share of the population rose from 10 percent to 51.5 percent by 1860. The increase in the proportion of Europeans and blacks corresponds with the Spanish overrunning the native populations and instituting plantations. The spread of diseases among the native populations made it easier for the Spanish to do away with long-standing native governments and establish their own political structures in the Americas.

In India and Africa, Europeans utilized the old strategies of military force and colonization, but unlike in the Americas, newly introduced diseases did not have such a devastating effect on native populations. Thus, the process of empire-building also involved longer-term economic policies that caused a more gradual build-up of political power. European merchants gradually expanded their power in India, aided by the decline of the Mughal empire, as explained in Document 4. A French physician describes the emperor's practice of "nourish[ing] jealousies" among the local rajahs, many of whom commanded armies larger than those of the emperor, to distract the rajahs from ever threatening his power. By describing this potential threat to the emperor, the document hints at the potential for outsiders to take advantage of the political instability, as indeed the British merchants extended their economic influence into political control. Indeed, in Document 5 a governor of the East India Company affirms that British control happened through "fortunate and unforeseen occurrences" rather than a "fixed plan." He also confirms the power of economics in gaining political control, praising the economic policies of the British and celebrating the "destroyed" economic policies of the "natives." Eventually, the British government would take over the East India Company's holdings and rule India as a colony. Document 1 also affirms the potential of economics to provide inroads to political power: King Afonso I of Kongo in Africa appeals to the King of Portugal about the behavior of Portuguese merchants, who are undermining King Afonso's power by enriching his vassals, making them no longer "content and subjected under our control." King Afonso's highly submissive tone ("I kiss your hand many times") may indicate not genuine submission to the King of Portugal, but rather an understanding of the threat that economic power has on his political power. His letter could be part of a calculated approach to get help restoring his political power by appealing to the Europeans' attitude of superiority.

Overall, the empire-building processes of conquest, colonization, and economic influence allowed empire-builders to exert power over territories. When additional factors, such as epidemic disease, also played a role, as they did in the Americas, the empire-builders could sometimes briskly overthrow and replace the original political structures. In locations such as India, empire-building involved a more complex interplay of economics with the pre-existing political structures, though the Europeans were still able to eventually gain control.

Scoring for Sample Question: 7 Points (1 + 1 + 3 + 2)

Category	Scoring Criteria	Notes
Thesis/Claim (0–1 points)	Historically defensible thesis/claim with a logical line of reasoning. The response must make a thesis or claim without restating the prompt itself. The thesis must consist of one or more sentences located in one place, either in the introduction or the conclusion.	**Thesis** This question is assessing the historical reasoning skill of causation. The thesis should make a claim about the impact of empire-building processes on political structures. The thesis is in the last two sentences of the first paragraph. The writer of the sample response claims that three main processes—conquest, colonization, and economic policies—were involved in empire-building and that the effects of these processes included destruction or infiltration of existing political structures. The writer will add complexity to the argument by analyzing multiple causes throughout the essay: the three identified empire-building processes and the added factor of epidemic disease.
Contextualization (0–1 points)	Broader historical context related to the prompt. The response must connect the topic to historical developments, events, or processes; these can occur before, during, or after the time frame of the prompt itself.	**Context** Contextualization for this prompt should explain, not merely mention, broader factors related to empire-building. The writer of the sample response does not just briefly mention another historical detail, but rather in the first paragraph provides background context about the political structures in the Americas before European empire-building.

(continued)

Category	Scoring Criteria	Notes
Evidence (0–3 points)	Use of evidence to support the thesis. The response must utilize the content from at least *three* documents to address the *topic* of the prompt. (1 point) OR The response must use at least *six* documents to support an *argument* based on the prompt. (2 points)	**Evidence** Evidence from the documents must be paraphrased, not merely quoted. The writer of the sample response specifically relates the content of six sources to the claims about processes of empire-building and their impact on political structures. If the writer had time, using document 7 to explore an Asian perspective on European empire-building would provide further analysis.
	The response must use at least one additional piece of historical evidence, beyond what is found in the documents, to support an argument. This additional evidence must be different from what was used for contextualization. (1 point)	**Additional Evidence** The writer offers evidence beyond the documents to support the thesis when describing in the second paragraph how the defeat of the Inca Empire and the political structures established by the Spanish support the claim that military conquest destroyed native societies' political structures.
Analysis and Reasoning (0–2 points)	Complexity of understanding and reasoning. The response must explain, for at least *three* of the documents, how or why the document's purpose, historical basis, point of view, and/ or audience are relevant to an argument. (1 point)	**Sourcing** Factors' relevance to the argument about methods of empire-building should be explained, not just identified. The writer of the sample response relates the role of the viewpoints of documents 2 and 6 to the claim that military conquest could destroy political structures, and the purpose of document 1 to the claim that economic policies were used to infiltrate political structures.
	The response must show a complex understanding of the content of the prompt, using evidence to support, qualify, or modify an argument about the prompt. (1 point)	**Complex Understanding** A complex understanding should be incorporated into the overall argument about the impact of empire-building processes on political structures. The writer of the sample response analyzes how multiple variables impacted empire-building, explaining how combinations of the processes of conquest, colonization, and economics— along with the additional factor of disease— led to either destruction or infiltration of existing political structures.

LONG ESSAY QUESTIONS

Overview

The second part of Section II of the AP World History exam contains three long essay questions—you must respond to one. The long essay question assesses your ability to apply knowledge of history in a complex, analytical manner. In other words, you are expected to treat history and historical questions as a historian would. This process is called historiography—the skills and strategies historians use to analyze and interpret historical evidence to reach a conclusion. Thus, when writing an effective essay, you must be able to write a strong, clearly developed thesis and supply a substantial amount of relevant evidence to support your thesis and develop a complex argument.

The College Board's characteristics of a high-scoring long essay question response are listed below. Note that the requirements are very similar to those of the DBQ; the primary difference is that any requirements related to use of the documents are removed from the scoring requirements for the LEQ.

- **Thesis:** Make a thesis or claim that responds to the prompt. The thesis or claim must be historically defensible and establish a line of reasoning.

- **Context:** Provide context relevant to the prompt by describing a broader historical development or process.

- **Evidence:** Use specific and relevant examples as evidence to support an argument in response to the prompt.

- **Historical Skill:** Use a historical reasoning skill (causation, comparison, or continuity and change) to develop an argument in response to the prompt.

- **Complex Understanding:** Demonstrate a complex understanding of an argument that responds to the prompt by using evidence to corroborate, qualify, or modify the argument.

Strategy

The LEQ may be the most abstract prompt you encounter on the free-response section. It is therefore extra important to use the Kaplan Method in order to organize your ideas and logically think through your response. You must select one of the three LEQ prompts. While each question will focus on the same reasoning process (for instance, all three questions may test causation), the questions will address different time periods: Question 2 will focus on the time period from 1200 to 1750, Question 3 will focus on the time period from 1450 to 1900, and Question 4 will focus on the time period from 1750 to 2001. Choose the option that will best showcase your ability to construct a historically defensible thesis and provide specific, relevant evidence.

As with every free-response question, follow the 4-Step Kaplan Method (AP-AP). Consider the following special strategies for the long essay question. Scoring requirements are highlighted in bold.

During Step 1: Analyze the Prompt:

- Each long essay question begins with a general statement that provides context about the tested time period, and then the second sentence identifies your task, which will always entail developing an evaluative argument. Make sure to read all three prompts carefully. Think of the evidence you could use and the argument you could develop in response to each one, then choose the question you feel most confident about.

- Begin crafting your **thesis** statement. You must have a thesis that takes a stand, answers the entire question, and shows the reader the path you will take in your essay answer. It is not enough to merely restate the task as your thesis. One of the most important things to do is to take a position. Don't be afraid of taking a strong stand for or against a prompt as long as you can provide proper and relevant evidence to support your assertions. Each prompt will lend itself to building a thesis that employs a **historical skill**, such as causation, continuity and change, or comparison.

- Part of developing your thesis should be considering how your essay's argument will demonstrate a **complex understanding**. As for the DBQ, your argument should address the complexity of the historical development or process—perhaps by including multiple variables, by considering both causes and effects, or by making an insightful connection to another time period. See the DBQ section of this chapter for a complete list of ways to demonstrate complex understanding.

During Step 2: Plan Your Response:

- Make short notes that outline each paragraph of your essay, including the points you will make and the evidence you will use to support your points.

- The first paragraph of your essay will likely contain your thesis statement; the thesis may also appear in the conclusion, but placing it in the introduction will make it easier for your readers to follow your essay.

- Consider how you will provide **context** for the essay topic. The context you provide must be more detailed than a brief reference and should situate the topic of the prompt in relation to developments before, during, or after the time period from the prompt. The introduction paragraph or first body paragraph may be good places to include contextualization.

- In general, each body paragraph should address one part of your claim or one category of evidence you are providing in support of your thesis. Organizing your essay according to the historical skill being tested is an easy and effective way to structure your essay; each paragraph of an essay responding to a prompt about causation could address one cause, for instance. Jot down the **evidence** you will include in each body paragraph. To earn the maximum points for use of evidence, you must use examples that support your overall argument—merely listing relevant examples but not explaining how they support your claim will only earn 1 instead of 2 possible points for evidence.

- Confirm that your plan addresses all the essay requirements before moving into the writing step.

During Step 3: Action! Write Your Response:

- There is no "standard" number of paragraphs you must have. AP readers look for quality, not quantity.

- The first paragraph of your essay should include your thesis and any other organizational cues you can give your reader. There is no need to spend time creating a "hook" or flashy statement for your first sentence or using rhetorical questions. AP graders are reading for the items that are listed in the rubric. You will notice that creativity in language is not a listed item. However, a well-written and developed argument is a desired item.

- Your body paragraphs should follow the "road map" you set in your introduction and thesis. Don't stray from your plan, or you will find yourself straying from the prompt. You have taken the time to make a plan, so follow it! Do not merely list facts and events in a "laundry list" fashion. You must have some element of analysis between each set of evidence you provide. Using transition words, such as *however*, *therefore*, and *thus*, to show shifts in thought can make creating analytical sentences quick and easy. You should practice stringing facts and thoughts together using these "qualifying transitions" in your sentences.

- Beware of telling a story rather than answering the question. Readers are looking for analysis, not a revised version of your textbook. Do not attempt to shower the reader with extra factoids and showy language; focus on developing a well-crafted argument.

- Because this is a formal essay, you should avoid using personal pronouns, such as *you*, *I*, or *we*, and slang words. Because your essay is about history, write your essay in the past tense.

- You should end each body paragraph with a mini-conclusion that ties the paragraph back to the thesis. It can serve as a transition sentence into the next paragraph or stand alone. In either case, the reader should be able to tell easily that you are shifting gears into another part of the essay.

- Lastly, write your conclusion. Restate your thesis, but in a new way. Instead of rewriting your thesis word for word, explain why your thesis is significant to the question. Do not introduce new evidence in your conclusion. The conclusion should tie all of the mini-conclusion sentences together and leave the reader with a sense of completion. If you are running out of time when you reach the conclusion, you may leave it off without incurring a specific penalty. However, the conclusion can help solidify your entire argument in the minds of your readers, so practice writing timed essays so you can learn the proper timing it takes to write a complete essay (conclusion included).

During Step 4: Proofread:

- Neatly correct any obvious errors.

Sample Question

In the period 1850 to 2001, new technologies emerged that had significant social, political, and economic effects.

Develop an argument that evaluates the extent to which changes in the spread of ideas/information before and after World War I impacted societies.

Step 1: Analyze the Prompt

On the actual exam, you will read three questions and determine which you can answer most confidently. For this sample question, note that you will be evaluating how changes in the spread of ideas impacted societies. The words "changes," "impacted," and "the extent" indicate that this prompt is testing the historical skill of continuity and change.

As you choose which question you will answer, begin thinking about what your thesis will entail and how your essay will demonstrate a complex understanding. The notes of a sample high-scoring writer are below. Note that the writer plans to develop a complex argument by addressing not only changes, as required by the prompt, but also continuities in societies before and after World War I.

> **Thesis:** changes: faster spread of ideas made news, politics, and war more immersive and fast-paced; continuity: cross-cultural interactions transform all cultures (complex understanding, historical skill)

Step 2: Plan Your Response

Next, take time to plan your response. Check your plan against the long essay question requirements. See the following sample plan that a high-scoring writer might make; scoring requirements are written in bold for reference.

- ¶ intro
  - **Context:** Gutenberg → 2nd industrial revolution (steamship, train, telegraph) → digital revolution (radio, TV, Internet)
  - **Thesis:** changes: faster spread of ideas made news, politics, and war more immersive and fast-paced; continuity: cross-cultural interactions transform all cultures (**complex understanding, historical skill**)
- Body ¶1: change: impact of news quicker and more significant
  - **Evidence:** War of 1812 versus WWII, Vietnam, Gulf War
- Body ¶2: change: wars became more ideological, propaganda-based
  - **Evidence:** American Revolution versus Cold War

- Body ¶3: continuity: interactions still change cultures, though intensified today
  - **Evidence:** language: Arab traders & Swahili, and modern business & English
- ¶ conclusion: impacts of tech on society have become more pervasive, though tendency towards cross-cultural influence has persisted

Step 3: Action! Write Your Response & Step 4: Proofread

Use your plan to write each part of the response, and briskly skim for errors when finished.

See the following high-scoring response, and be sure to read the rubric to help you identify what makes this response effective. Think about what features you can incorporate into your own free-response answers.

Sample High-Scoring Response

Several landmark new technologies dramatically changed the speed of communication before and after the First World War. For most of history, faster communication was necessarily related to physical factors, such as a horse's speed or the condition of trails between locations. Gutenberg's printing press helped lower the cost of written material and thus democratized the spread of ideas beginning in the fifteenth century. By the nineteenth century, improvements to transportation technology during the second industrial revolution (the steamship and train) enabled ideas to spread across continents in days instead of weeks, and the telegraph made communication, at least that of short messages, nearly instantaneous. Remarkably, this process of change intensified after the communication and digital revolutions following WWI, as the radio and eventually television and the Internet brought instant news and ideas into nearly every home in industrialized nations. This accelerated pace of news has made societies more immersed in global politics and conflicts, while intensifying the historic tendency of cross-cultural interactions to transform societies.

A key change between these eras of communication is how the speed of ideas' dissemination impacts their force of impact and makes news more pervasive in civilians' lives. In the distant past, the slow rate of communication caused reactions that were often months, or even years, after the initial communication. For instance, the final battle of the War of 1812 was fought after the signing of the war's peace treaty because news had not yet traveled by ship across the Atlantic Ocean. In contrast, the peace treaties of WWII were celebrated in cities around the world mere minutes after news of their signing was shared by telegram and radio signals. The quick spread of images and video from the Vietnam conflict helped intensify Americans' resistance to the war. In recent decades, 24-hour live coverage of conflicts, as in CNN's being the first to provide constant coverage of a war during the Gulf War, allowed policymakers and civilians to respond instantly to developments. As news became quicker, so its impact became more significant and more immediate.

Another change is that the quick and pervasive spread of ideas has made political conflicts more ideological and propaganda-based, further drawing societies into global disputes. Political rebellions of the eighteenth century, such as the American and French Revolutions, were based on Enlightenment ideals such as equality and representative government; they made use of propaganda in the form of printed political cartoons, tracts, and engravings to spread their ideals among the populace. However, the news communication made possible by radio and television after World War II helped propel the ideological conflict between the communist Soivet Union and the democratic United States into a worldwide phenomenon that intensely impacted both nations' citizens. Technology was able to so effectively spread this war of ideas that the two major superpowers never engaged in direct battle themselves; still, citizens were drawn into a culture of propaganda that demonized the other side, made bomb shelters and bomb drills a part of daily life due to fear of nuclear warfare, and saw governments pour millions of dollars into the space race. Technology thus made it possible for conflicts to become all-immersive, even if they were based on ideas rather than physical confrontations.

Despite changes in communication, constants about its impacts remain. Cross-cultural communications still transform societies as they borrow and adapt ideas from others. For instance, from the eighth century onward, Arab traders who traveled throughout West Africa and along the eastern and northern coasts not only enriched communities economically but also spread Islam. Further, the necessity for communication among traders led to the rise of Swahili, a language that combined Arabic and African words and is still the lingua franca in much of East Africa today. Similarly, in modern times, as Britain and then the United States dominated world trade, English became a kind of worldwide lingua franca of modern business. Just as Arab traders spread their religion, American culture also diffused to other societies: almost every nation in modern times, for instance, built American-style fast food restaurants. Mirroring the trends related to the spread of news and politics, cultural diffusions in recent decades occurred at a faster rate and to a more pervasive extent than in the past. Whereas primarily traders would have adopted Swahili as it developed over generations, today English is taught in grade schools throughout the world.

Cultures that interact always influence each other. In the past century, however, technology has made the impact of this spread of ideas more pervasive and significant as news and political ideas travel at a faster pace. As they have in the past, societies will continue to transform as they encounter ideas from other cultures, but with this increased intensity of communication, the impacts of ideas will continue to escalate.

Scoring for Sample Question: 6 Points (1 + 1 + 2 + 2)

Category	Scoring Criteria	Notes
Thesis/Claim (0–1 points)	Historically defensible thesis/claim with a logical line of reasoning. The response must make a thesis or claim without restating the prompt itself. The thesis must consist of one or more sentences located in one place, either in the introduction or the conclusion.	**Thesis** This question assesses the skill of continuity and change. A strong thesis should make a claim about the extent to which societies were impacted by changes in how ideas spread. The thesis is the last sentence of the first paragraph. The writer of the sample response claims that the quickened spread of news has increased societies' immersion in global politics and conflicts. The writer adds complexity to the argument by making the claim that there were also continuities in the impact of the spread of ideas: the continuation of cross-cultural influences.
Contextualization (0–1 points)	Broader historical context related to the prompt. The response must connect the topic to historical developments, events, or processes; these can occur before, during, or after the time frame of the prompt itself.	**Context** Contextualization for this prompt should explain, not merely mention, broader factors relevant to the spread of ideas. The writer of the sample response does not just briefly mention another historical development, but rather in the first paragraph situates the spread of ideas in the context of the invention of the printing press, the second industrial revolution, and the digital revolution. This summary enables a relevant background for comparison of the spread of ideas before and after World War I.
Evidence (0–2 points)	Use of evidence to support the thesis. The response identifies specific examples *relevant to the topic* of the prompt. (1 point) OR The response uses examples to *support an argument* about the prompt. (2 points)	**Evidence** Evidence must be paraphrased, not merely quoted. To earn 2 points, the evidence must be used to support an argument about the spread of ideas. The writer of the sample response uses specific historical examples to support each part of the thesis. For instance, in the third paragraph the writer uses the characteristics of the American/French Revolutions and the Cold War to support the claim that changes in the spread of ideas impacted the nature and scope of political conflicts.

(continued)

Category	Scoring Criteria	Notes
Analysis and Reasoning (0–2 points)	Complexity of understanding and reasoning. The response shows historical reasoning to make an argument about the prompt. (1 point) AND The response demonstrates complex understanding, using evidence to support, qualify, or modify an argument about the prompt. (2 points)	**Complex Understanding** Comparison, causation, or continuity and change over time should be incorporated into the overall argument about the spread of ideas. The writer of the sample response addresses changes in the spread of ideas before and after World War I as directed by the prompt. AND A complex understanding should be incorporated into the overall argument about the spread of ideas. The writer of the sample response develops an argument that addresses not only changes, but also continuities before and after World War I, devoting the second and third paragraphs of the response to changes and the fourth paragraph to continuity.

PART 4

Practice Exams

HOW TO TAKE THE PRACTICE EXAMS

The final section of this book consists of five full-length practice exams. Taking a practice AP exam gives you an idea of what it's like to answer AP questions under conditions that approximate those of the real exam. You'll find out which areas you're strong in and where additional review may be required. Any mistakes you make now are ones you won't make on the actual exam, as long as you take the time to learn where you went wrong.

Our full-length practice exams each include 55 multiple-choice questions, three short-answer questions (including your choice of two prompts for the third question), one document-based question, and one long essay question (your choice from three prompts). Before taking a practice exam, find a quiet place where you can work uninterrupted, and bring blank lined paper for the free-response questions. (The proctor will provide lined paper when you take the official exam.) Time yourself according to the time limit given at the beginning of each section: 55 minutes for the multiple-choice questions, 40 minutes for the short-answer questions, 60 minutes for the document-based question, and 40 minutes for the long essay question. It's okay to take a short break between sections, but for the most accurate results, you should approximate real test conditions as much as possible.

As you take the practice exams, remember to pace yourself. Train yourself to be aware of the time you are spending on each question. Try to be aware of the general types of questions you encounter, and be mindful of the particular strategies and approaches that help you handle those questions more effectively.

After taking each practice exam, complete the following steps.

1. Self-score your multiple-choice section using the answer key immediately following each exam.
2. Read the full answers and explanations that follow each exam. These detailed explanations will help you identify areas that could use additional study. Even when you have answered a question correctly, you can learn additional information by looking at the explanation.
3. Self-score your free-response questions using the rubrics in the answers and explanations section.
4. Navigate to the scoring section of your online resources (kaptest.com/moreonline) to input all of these raw scores and see what your overall score would be with a similar performance on Test Day.

Finally, it's important to approach the exam with the right attitude. Trust that you're going to get a great score because you've reviewed the material and learned the strategies in this book.

Good luck!

Practice Exam 1

Practice Exam 1 Answer Grid

1. Ⓐ Ⓑ Ⓒ Ⓓ
2. Ⓐ Ⓑ Ⓒ Ⓓ
3. Ⓐ Ⓑ Ⓒ Ⓓ
4. Ⓐ Ⓑ Ⓒ Ⓓ
5. Ⓐ Ⓑ Ⓒ Ⓓ
6. Ⓐ Ⓑ Ⓒ Ⓓ
7. Ⓐ Ⓑ Ⓒ Ⓓ
8. Ⓐ Ⓑ Ⓒ Ⓓ
9. Ⓐ Ⓑ Ⓒ Ⓓ
10. Ⓐ Ⓑ Ⓒ Ⓓ
11. Ⓐ Ⓑ Ⓒ Ⓓ
12. Ⓐ Ⓑ Ⓒ Ⓓ
13. Ⓐ Ⓑ Ⓒ Ⓓ
14. Ⓐ Ⓑ Ⓒ Ⓓ

15. Ⓐ Ⓑ Ⓒ Ⓓ
16. Ⓐ Ⓑ Ⓒ Ⓓ
17. Ⓐ Ⓑ Ⓒ Ⓓ
18. Ⓐ Ⓑ Ⓒ Ⓓ
19. Ⓐ Ⓑ Ⓒ Ⓓ
20. Ⓐ Ⓑ Ⓒ Ⓓ
21. Ⓐ Ⓑ Ⓒ Ⓓ
22. Ⓐ Ⓑ Ⓒ Ⓓ
23. Ⓐ Ⓑ Ⓒ Ⓓ
24. Ⓐ Ⓑ Ⓒ Ⓓ
25. Ⓐ Ⓑ Ⓒ Ⓓ
26. Ⓐ Ⓑ Ⓒ Ⓓ
27. Ⓐ Ⓑ Ⓒ Ⓓ
28. Ⓐ Ⓑ Ⓒ Ⓓ

29. Ⓐ Ⓑ Ⓒ Ⓓ
30. Ⓐ Ⓑ Ⓒ Ⓓ
31. Ⓐ Ⓑ Ⓒ Ⓓ
32. Ⓐ Ⓑ Ⓒ Ⓓ
33. Ⓐ Ⓑ Ⓒ Ⓓ
34. Ⓐ Ⓑ Ⓒ Ⓓ
35. Ⓐ Ⓑ Ⓒ Ⓓ
36. Ⓐ Ⓑ Ⓒ Ⓓ
37. Ⓐ Ⓑ Ⓒ Ⓓ
38. Ⓐ Ⓑ Ⓒ Ⓓ
39. Ⓐ Ⓑ Ⓒ Ⓓ
40. Ⓐ Ⓑ Ⓒ Ⓓ
41. Ⓐ Ⓑ Ⓒ Ⓓ
42. Ⓐ Ⓑ Ⓒ Ⓓ

43. Ⓐ Ⓑ Ⓒ Ⓓ
44. Ⓐ Ⓑ Ⓒ Ⓓ
45. Ⓐ Ⓑ Ⓒ Ⓓ
46. Ⓐ Ⓑ Ⓒ Ⓓ
47. Ⓐ Ⓑ Ⓒ Ⓓ
48. Ⓐ Ⓑ Ⓒ Ⓓ
49. Ⓐ Ⓑ Ⓒ Ⓓ
50. Ⓐ Ⓑ Ⓒ Ⓓ
51. Ⓐ Ⓑ Ⓒ Ⓓ
52. Ⓐ Ⓑ Ⓒ Ⓓ
53. Ⓐ Ⓑ Ⓒ Ⓓ
54. Ⓐ Ⓑ Ⓒ Ⓓ
55. Ⓐ Ⓑ Ⓒ Ⓓ

SECTION I, PART A
Time—55 minutes
55 Questions

Directions: Section I, Part A of this exam contains 55 multiple-choice questions, organized into sets with corresponding historical sources. Each of the questions or incomplete statements is followed by four suggested answers or completions. Using both the provided sources and your own historical knowledge, select the best answer choice.

Questions 1–4 refer to the following two maps.

<u>Map 1</u>

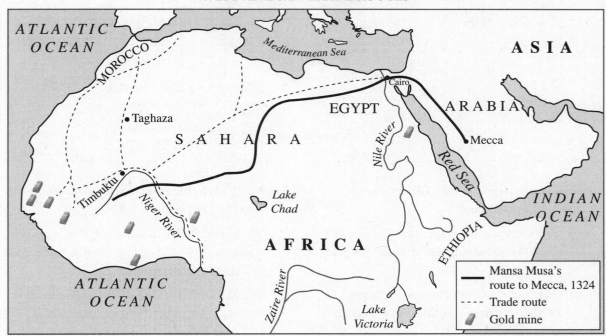

WEST AFRICAN TRADE ROUTES

GO ON TO THE NEXT PAGE

Map 2

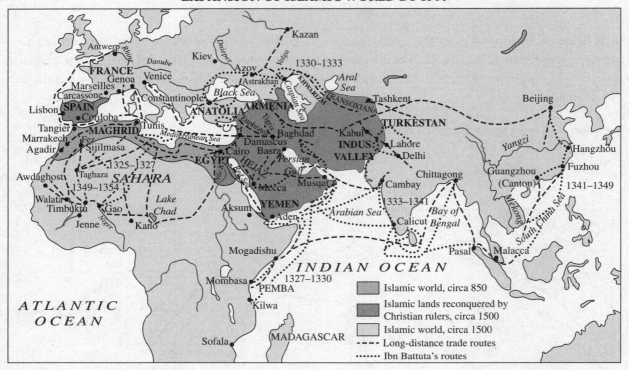

EXPANSION OF ISLAMIC WORLD BY 1500

1. Which of the following conclusions is best supported by the maps?

   (A) Timbuktu and the kingdoms of Mali and Ghana were the singular producers of gold in the world.

   (B) People moved throughout western and northern Africa to work in the gold trade.

   (C) The expansion of trade in West Africa helped spread the influence of Islam into those territories.

   (D) The spread of Islam caused the expansion of gold trade routes in West Africa.

2. Which of the following historical developments is most strongly illustrated in Map 1?

   (A) Use of the Silk Road across the Asian continent declined as trans-Saharan trade routes rose in prominence.

   (B) The wealth generated by the Empire of Mali contributed to trade networks in Afro-Eurasia.

   (C) The development of new maritime technology expanded the spread of innovations between cultures.

   (D) Timbuktu's influence sharply declined after Mansa Musa returned from his journey to Mecca.

GO ON TO THE NEXT PAGE ⟶

3. Which of the following developments in the period 1200–1450 is most similar to the trends of cultural exchange depicted in the maps?

   (A) Ibn Battuta's writings about his travels in Asia resulting in his readers converting to new religions

   (B) The spread of Confucianism and Buddhism throughout East Asia solidifying a cultural identity

   (C) Christianity spreading along the Silk Road during the Mongol Yuan Dynasty

   (D) China's voluntary isolation from foreign trade in an attempt to bolster its economy internally

4. Which of the following was a lasting impact of the Islamic world?

   (A) The creation of a single, unified empire that lasted for many centuries

   (B) Technological and scientific advancements that were used by other cultures

   (C) A unique system of government that provided the foundation for future societies

   (D) Advancements in agriculture and livestock farming

GO ON TO THE NEXT PAGE

Questions 5–7 refer to the passage below.

"Although the mass of the people lived in the open country with their flocks and herds, there were, notwithstanding, a great many towns and villages, though such centres of population were much fewer and less important among them than they are in countries the inhabitants of which live by tilling the ground. Some of these towns were the residences of the khans and of the heads of tribes. Others were places of manufacture or centres of commerce, and many of them were fortified with embankments of earth or walls of stone.

The habitations of the common people, even those built in the towns, were rude huts made so as to be easily taken down and removed. The tents were made by means of poles set in a circle in the ground, and brought nearly together at the top, so as to form a frame similar to that of an Indian wigwam. A hoop was placed near the top of these poles, so as to preserve a round opening there for the smoke to go out."

Jacob Abbott, *Genghis Khan, Makers of History*, 1880

5. A historian could use the passage to support which of the following conclusions?

   (A) The Mongols were able to build their empire under Genghis Khan because they were nomadic.

   (B) While nomadic in nature, the Mongols often interacted with settled peoples.

   (C) Mongol khans always settled their people close to other towns or cities.

   (D) The nomadic Mongol dwellings described in the passage were inspired by Amerindian dwellings.

6. How did the Mongols and the Turks exemplify the concept of peripheral peoples from 1200 to 1450?

   (A) They were semi-organized and often lived at the edges of more settled civilizations.

   (B) They were nomadic cultures.

   (C) They had large bureaucratic governments.

   (D) They were known for being skilled horsemen.

7. Which of the following best describes why Central Asia was the source of repeated nomadic incursions on Eurasian civilizations to the east, south, and west?

   (A) The Silk Road trade routes gave nomadic peoples timely information on the military weaknesses of adjacent empires.

   (B) The Turks and Mongols desired to live in urban civilizations, whether Chinese, Persian, or Islamic.

   (C) The nomadic peoples were mobile, used to raiding, and lived on the open steppes, which gave them access to the entire continent.

   (D) The expanding empires pressured the nomadic peoples, fenced in the pasture lands, and imposed heavy taxation.

GO ON TO THE NEXT PAGE

Questions 8–10 refer to the object shown in the image below.

WOODEN GILDED STATUE OF THE BODHISATTVA AVALOKITEŚVARA, CHINESE SONG DYNASTY, 960–1279

The bodhisattva Avalokiteśvara, who represents the compassion of all Buddhas.

8. The object in the image above best demonstrates which of the following cultural trends from 1200 to 1450?

    (A) The increased popularity of Neo-Confucianism in response to Buddhism and Daoism

    (B) The emergence of foot binding as a standard of beauty

    (C) The rise of decentralized empires such as the Song Dynasty

    (D) The spread and increasing influence of Buddhism in much of Asia

9. The political organization of the Song Dynasty was most similar to which of the following groups from the period 1200–1450?

    (A) The Arab caliphates

    (B) The Turks

    (C) The Kamakura shogunate

    (D) The Hanseatic League

10. Which of the following most accurately describes how Buddhism shaped societies in Asia in the period 1200–1450?

    (A) Buddhism created a unified culture that transcended political boundaries.

    (B) Buddhism spread due to the Mongols' protection of trade routes.

    (C) Buddhism became the official religion in China and Japan.

    (D) Buddhism's spread relied primarily on regional, cultural, and ethnic commonalities.

GO ON TO THE NEXT PAGE

Questions 11–14 refer to the following two passages.

Passage 1

"Its population [Dhofar*] consists of merchants who live entirely on trade. When a vessel arrives they take the master, captain and writer in procession to the sultan's palace and entertain the entire ship's company for three days in order to gain the goodwill of the shipmasters. Another curious thing is that its people closely resemble the people of Northwest Africa in their customs. . . .

In the neighbourhood of the town there are orchards with many banana trees. The bananas are of immense size; one which was weighed in my presence scaled twelve ounces and was pleasant to the taste and very sweet. They grow also betel-trees and coco-palms, which are found only in India and the town of Dhafari. Since we have mentioned these trees, we shall describe them and their properties here."

*Dhofar is located in modern-day Oman, near Saudi Arabia.

Ibn Battuta, account of his travels in Asia and Africa, 1325–1354

Passage 2

"Taianfu is a place of great trade and great industry, for here they manufacture a large quantity of the most necessary equipments for the army of the Emperor. There grow here many excellent vines, supplying great plenty of wine; and in all Cathay this is the only place where wine is produced. It is carried hence all over the country. There is also a great deal of silk here, for the people have great quantities of mulberry-trees and silk-worms.

From this city of Taianfu you ride westward again for seven days, through fine districts with plenty of towns and boroughs, all enjoying much trade and practising various kinds of industry. Out of these districts go forth not a few great merchants, who travel to India and other foreign regions, buying and selling and getting gain. After those seven days' journey you arrive at a city called PIANFU, a large and important place, with a number of traders living by commerce and industry. It is a place too where silk is largely produced.

So we will leave it and tell you of a great city called Cachanfu. But stay—first let us tell you about the noble castle called Caichu."

Marco Polo and Rustichello of Pisa, *The Travels of Marco Polo, Volume 2*, circa 1300

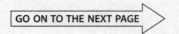
GO ON TO THE NEXT PAGE

11. Based on <u>Passage 1</u> and your knowledge of world history, how were the travels of Ibn Battuta significant during the fourteenth century?

    (A) His journeys through the Mongol Empire demonstrated the dangers of long-distance travel.

    (B) His travelogues provided readers with detailed accounts of locations, but he lacked the experience to compare different cultures.

    (C) His writings fueled a growing European interest in foreign trade goods.

    (D) The purely economic nature of his journeys reflected the refusal of travelers of the time period to spread their religions.

12. The details in the two passages most directly reflect which of the following trends in the time period 1200–1450?

    (A) An increased demand in Afro-Eurasia for luxury goods that strengthened trade networks

    (B) The decline of traditional sea ports as overland travel on emerging trade routes became more lucrative

    (C) The inability of countries that produced specialty goods to sell those goods in foreign markets

    (D) The importance of imperial armies in establishing and maintaining long-distance trade routes

13. Based on <u>Passage 2</u> and your knowledge of world history, which of the following was a significant impact of the Silk Road?

    (A) The use of paper money in Europe

    (B) The spread and use of gunpowder in Europe

    (C) The elevated social status of merchants in China

    (D) The spread of Islam into East Africa

14. A historian could use these passages to illustrate which of the following later historical developments?

    (A) The way in which the Hanseatic League created rules for fair trade

    (B) The way in which the Columbian Exchange developed between Europe and the Americas

    (C) The way in which the international trade policies of the Tokugawa shogunate spread to other regions

    (D) The way in which European mercantilism grew from international trade and the rise of state building

GO ON TO THE NEXT PAGE

Questions 15–17 refer to the passage below.

"The crimes committed by these men during a long series of years in promoting the Christian faith contrary to the decrees of the Shogun are very numerous, and exceedingly serious; last year [1639] the Shogun has, under the gravest penalties, forbidden anyone to sail from Macao to Japan, and he has decreed that if any vessel disregard this prohibition, the said vessel shall be burned and passengers put to death without exception. All the points have been foreseen, provided for, and drawn up in Articles which have been published in due form. Yet, by coming in this ship, these men have flouted the Edict."*

*This refers to the Closed Country Edict of 1635, by which the Tokugawa shogunate enforced strict isolationist policies.

James Murdoch, *A History of Japan, Vol. 2*, 1903

15. Based on the passage and your knowledge of world history, how did the policies of the Tokugawa shogunate differ from the policies of other governments in Asia in this time period?

    (A) In an era of increasing global interconnection, Japan successfully countered this trend.

    (B) The shoguns deliberately imitated Chinese and Korean responses to Western pressure.

    (C) Japan was the first East Asian country to adopt Western modes of production and warfare.

    (D) Japan's policies of agricultural and industrial expansion used wage labor rather than slavery or other forced systems.

16. The viewpoint expressed in the passage differs most directly from which of the following historical developments in Japan?

    (A) Its feudal political structure of *daimyo* and samurai classes

    (B) Its adherence to principles of traditional Shintoism

    (C) Its policies towards U.S. and European influence during the Meiji Era

    (D) Its rapid territorial expansion between the world wars

17. The development of the Russian Empire under Peter the Great was most different from the Tokugawa shogunate in which of the following ways?

    (A) The Russian people were encouraged to adopt foreign customs and practices.

    (B) The Russian Empire was relatively stable under Peter the Great.

    (C) The Russian Empire lacked military governance in favor of bureaucratic systems.

    (D) The economy of the Russian Empire flourished.

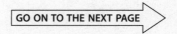

GO ON TO THE NEXT PAGE

Questions 18–20 refer to the passage below.

"The last message of the Byzantine Emperor to the Turkish Sultan had been somewhat in these words: 'As it is plain thou desirest war more than peace, as I cannot satisfy thee by my vows of sincerity or by my readiness to swear allegiance, so let it be according to thy will. I turn now and look above to God. If it be His will that the city should become thine, where is he who can oppose His will? If He should inspire thee with a wish for peace, I shall indeed be happy. Nevertheless I release thee from all thy oaths and treaties to me, I close the gates of my city, I will defend my people to the last drop of my blood. And so, reign in happiness till the Righteous and Supreme Judge shall call us both before the seat of His judgment.'"

William Holden Hutton, *Constantinople: The Story of the Old Capital of the Empire*, 1900

18. The passage is best understood in the context of which of the following events?

    (A) The destruction of the Christian cathedral Hagia Sophia

    (B) The conquest of Constantinople by the Mughal Empire

    (C) The fall of the Byzantine Empire to the Ottoman Empire

    (D) The destruction of Constantinople by the Seljuk Turks

19. Which of the following best describes the significance of Constantinople?

    (A) Constantinople directly facilitated global trade and commerce prior to 1453.

    (B) Constantinople advanced the emergence of Protestantism in the fifteenth century.

    (C) Constantinople promoted the exclusive observance of Muslim beliefs after 1453.

    (D) Constantinople simplified Roman laws during the fifteenth century.

20. Present-day historians might view the conquest of Constantinople as illustrative of which of the following?

    (A) The creation of the Delhi Sultanate

    (B) The development of the caravel

    (C) The spread of Christianity

    (D) The use of gunpowder in warfare

GO ON TO THE NEXT PAGE

Questions 21–23 refer to the image below.

ENGRAVING FROM *HARMONIA MACROCOSMICA*,
A STAR ATLAS COMPILED BY ANDREAS CELLARIUS, 1660

The engraving depicts the Copernican System. Earth's hemispheres and the planets are shown encircled by zodiac symbols. A royal figure, wearing a blindfold, sits next to a globe depicting Ptolemy's geocentric theory.

21. A historian could use this image as evidence for which of the following statements?

    (A) The heliocentric theory challenged mainstream thought and religion.

    (B) The scientific method inspired the development of the Copernican System.

    (C) The laws of planetary motion supported the heliocentric theory.

    (D) The invention of the telescope was instrumental to the Copernican System.

22. Copernicus's heliocentric theory had which of the following effects?

    (A) Scientists began to reject the use of observation to understand the structure and composition of the universe.

    (B) Scientists began to question the Catholic Church's belief in a geocentric universe.

    (C) Scholars increasingly relied on their own knowledge traditions rather than incorporating scientific knowledge of other cultures.

    (D) Scholars began to rely mostly on classical texts and the Bible to explain the natural world.

GO ON TO THE NEXT PAGE

23. The development of the Copernican System is most comparable to which of the following?

    (A) Reformation changes to the religious map of Europe, with Protestants in the north and Catholics in the south

    (B) Renaissance accomplishments in literature, music, and art

    (C) Sikhism emerging as a bridge between Hinduism and Islam

    (D) Enlightenment ideals emphasizing free thought and questioning traditional authority

GO ON TO THE NEXT PAGE

Questions 24–26 refer to the passage below.

"Although a Kingdom may be enriched by gifts received, or by purchase taken from some other Nations, yet these are things uncertain and of small consideration when they happen. The ordinary means therefore to encrease our wealth and treasure is by Forraign Trade, wherein wee must ever observe this rule; to sell more to strangers yearly than wee consume of theirs in value. For suppose that when theis Kingdom is plentifully served with the Cloth, Lead, Tinn, Iron, Fish and other native commodities, we doe yearly export the overplus to forraign Countries to the value of twenty two hundred thousand pounds; by which means we are enabled beyond the Seas to buy and bring in forraign wares for our use and Consumption, to the value of twenty hundred thousand pounds; By this order duly kept in our trading, we may rest assured that the Kingdom shall be enriched yearly two hundred thousand pounds, which must be brought to us in so much Treasure; because that part of our stock which is not returned to us in wares must necessarily be brought home in treasure."

Thomas Mun, *England's Treasure by Forraign Trade or the Balance of our Forraign Trade is The Rule of Our Treasure*, 1664

24. A historian would most likely use this passage to illustrate which of the following economic practices?

   (A) The specialization in specific goods by different states

   (B) A critical need to increase trade with the Americas

   (C) An economy based on mercantilist policies

   (D) The avoidance of coerced labor and the slave trade

25. The economic practices espoused in the passage were upheld in part by which of the following?

   (A) The spread of disease in the Americas due to the Columbian Exchange

   (B) A shift toward imperialism as a means to acquire goods

   (C) The forced conversion of Amerindians by Catholic missionaries

   (D) John Locke's philosophy on the natural rights of human beings

26. Which of the following accurately describes Spanish economic practices that significantly influenced international trade?

   (A) Spanish merchants had a monopoly on the sugar trade primarily cultivated in Mexico and the Potosí mines.

   (B) Spanish merchants cornered the market of slaves using the trans-Saharan trade routes.

   (C) Spanish merchants used gold they obtained in the Americas to trade for salt in West Africa.

   (D) Spanish merchants used the silver they obtained in the Americas to trade for silk in Asia.

GO ON TO THE NEXT PAGE

Questions 27–29 refer to the passage below.

"The poverty of the incapable, the distresses that come upon the imprudent, the starvation of the idle, and those shoulderings aside of the weak by the strong, which leave so many 'in shallows and in miseries,' are the decrees of a large, farseeing benevolence."

Herbert Spencer, *Social Statics*, 1851

27. Spencer's vision of society could be used as an argument for which of the following statements?

    (A) Scientific processes can address all issues formerly only answered through religion.

    (B) Industrialization will lead to the eventual revolution of the working class, resulting in a natural reordering of society.

    (C) The domination of Europeans over subject peoples is an inevitable result of innate superiority.

    (D) A ruler has an obligation to protect the natural rights of his citizens.

28. Present-day historians would likely agree that writings such as Spencer's were used to justify which of the following?

    (A) The American Revolution

    (B) The First Opium War

    (C) The Second Industrial Revolution

    (D) Imperialism in Africa and Asia

29. A proponent of Spencer's view would most likely agree with which of the following theories?

    (A) The theory of communism as presented by Karl Marx

    (B) The theory of liberalism as presented by John Locke

    (C) The theory of nationalism as presented by Zionists

    (D) The theory of capitalism as presented by Adam Smith

GO ON TO THE NEXT PAGE

Questions 30–32 refer to the passage below.

"It is my humble opinion that this seizing of Oudh filled the minds of the sepoys* with distrust and led them to plot against the Government. Agents . . . worked upon the feelings of the sepoys, telling them how treacherously the foreigners had behaved towards their king. They invented ten thousand lies and promises to persuade the soldiers to mutiny and turn against their masters, the English, with the object of restoring the Emperor of Delhi to the throne. They maintained that this was wholly within the army's powers if the soldiers would only act together and do as they were advised.

It chanced that about this time the Sirkar sent parties of men . . . for instruction in the use of the new rifle. These men performed the new drill for some time until a report got about . . . that the cartridges used for these new rifles were greased with the fat of cows and pigs.

The men from our regiment wrote to others in the regiment telling them of this, and there was soon excitement in every regiment. Some men pointed out that . . . nothing had ever been done by the Sirkar to insult their religion, but . . . [i]nterested parties were quick to point out that the great aim of the English was to turn us all into Christians, and they had therefore introduced the cartridge in order to bring this about, since both Muslims and Hindus would be defiled by using it."

*The word *sepoy* was originally used to describe an Indian infantryman in the armies of the Mughal Empire. The term was later used in the 1800s for the locally recruited Indian soldiers in Britain's service.

Sita Ram, excerpt about the Indian Rebellion of 1857 from his memoir "From Sepoy to Subedar," written in 1873

30. This excerpt from Sita Ram's memoirs is best understood in the context of which of the following prior events?

(A) The British had achieved imperial control over India after two Anglo-Sikh wars.

(B) Severe famines had plagued the Indian soldiers as a result of British laissez-faire policies that focused on export agriculture.

(C) Heavy taxes to support the British Empire had left poorer Indians unable to buy food.

(D) The existence of British rule had inspired a sense of Indian national identity.

31. A historian researching the processes of state-building in the nineteenth century would most likely use this passage to illustrate which of the following?

(A) A religiously influenced reaction of multiple groups against imperial rule

(B) An ideological disagreement that turned into a military conflict between two religious groups

(C) A military confrontation over territory among several competing imperialist powers

(D) A technological innovation sparking resistance among practitioners of traditional cultures

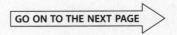
GO ON TO THE NEXT PAGE

32. Present-day historians would most likely agree that the Indian Rebellion of 1857 was most similar to which of the following armed conflicts?

   (A) The clashes between the Dutch-descended Boers and the British during the Boer Wars

   (B) The uprising against the Díaz regime during the Mexican Revolution

   (C) The forcible establishment of a communist government in Russia in the Bolshevik Revolution

   (D) The protest against Western spheres of influence in China during the Boxer Rebellion

GO ON TO THE NEXT PAGE

Questions 33–35 refer to the image below.

ENGRAVER ABRAHAM GOOS AND CARTOGRAPHER JOHN SPEED,
ENGRAVING OF THE AMERICAS, 1627

The map of the Americas above depicts indigenous towns on its top border and indigenous peoples on its side borders. Original caption: "America with those known parts in that unknowne worlde both people and manner of buildings discribed."

GO ON TO THE NEXT PAGE

33. Which of the following systems contributed the most to the map's depiction of the Americas?

    (A) Patriarchy

    (B) The *encomienda* system

    (C) Imperialism

    (D) Globalization

34. Based on the engraving and your knowledge of world history, which of the following historical developments most directly enabled the cartographers to map locations "in that unknowne worlde"?

    (A) Increased understanding of ocean wind patterns

    (B) The technology of the second industrial revolution

    (C) The security of trade networks afforded by the Mongol Empire

    (D) The Spanish casta system

35. Based on the map and your knowledge of world history, which of the following best describes indigenous societies in the Americas prior to the arrival of Europeans?

    (A) Indigenous peoples lacked the resources necessary to expand and protect their societies.

    (B) Indigenous peoples participated in the Columbian Exchange, cultivating maize, potatoes, and beans.

    (C) Indigenous peoples were decentralized and lacked clear rulers to govern their societies.

    (D) Indigenous peoples had their own trade systems and experienced commercial growth.

GO ON TO THE NEXT PAGE

Questions 36–38 refer to the passage below.

"It appears from all this that the person of the king is sacred, and that to attack him in any way is sacrilege. God has the kings anointed by his prophets with the holy unction in like manner as he has bishops and altars anointed. . . . Without this absolute authority the king could neither do good nor repress evil. It is necessary that his power be such that no one can hope to escape him, and, finally, the only protection of individuals against the public authority should be their innocence. This conforms with the teaching of St. Paul: 'Wilt thou then not be afraid of the power? Do that which is good.'

. . . God is infinite, God is all. The prince, as prince, is not regarded as a private person: he is a public personage, all the state is in him; the will of all the people is included in his. As all perfection and all strength are united in God, so all the power of individuals is united in the person of the prince. What grandeur that a single man should embody so much!"

Jacques-Bénigne Bossuet, *Politics Drawn from the Very Words of Holy Scripture*, 1707

36. According to the passage, Bossuet was advancing an approach to European politics that most clearly reflected which of the following?

   (A) Democratic and republican forms of government

   (B) Increasingly decentralized governments

   (C) Strong, centralized governments in the form of monarchies

   (D) Diplomatic rather than military resolutions to conflict

37. The assertions in the passage <u>differ</u> most strongly from the principles of which of the following events?

   (A) The triumph of Parliament in England's Civil War

   (B) Peter the Great's modernization of the Russian state

   (C) Louis XIV's enormous expansion of the Palace of Versailles

   (D) The refortification of the Great Wall by Ming emperors

38. The granting of divine, absolute power to a state ruler, as espoused in the passage, is most similar to the customs in which of the following early eighteenth-century areas?

   (A) Japan

   (B) Safavid Dynasty

   (C) Poland-Lithuania

   (D) Scotland

GO ON TO THE NEXT PAGE

Questions 39–41 refer to the passage below.

"Freeman and slave, patrician and plebeian, lord and serf, guild-master and journeyman, in a word, oppressor and oppressed, stood in constant opposition to one another, carried on an uninterrupted, now hidden, now open fight, a fight that each time ended, either in a revolutionary reconstitution of society at large, or in the common ruin of the contending classes.

The modern bourgeois society that has sprouted from the ruins of feudal society has not done away with class antagonisms. It has but established new classes, new conditions of oppression, new forms of struggle in place of the old ones."

Karl Marx, *The Communist Manifesto*, 1848

39. Marx's writing is best understood in the context of which of the following?

    (A) The middle class had begun to rapidly grow in response to the new industrial economy.

    (B) Industrialization had resulted in poor conditions for the working class.

    (C) Following industrialization, middle-class women generally did not work outside of the home.

    (D) Manufacturers sought to increase productivity and profits by designing products with interchangeable parts.

40. Marx's view of society as expressed in the passage most directly influenced which of the following historical developments?

    (A) The Second Industrial Revolution

    (B) The Meiji Era in Japan

    (C) The Russian Revolution

    (D) The Revolutions of 1848 in France and Germany

41. Proponents of Marxist ideals would likely attribute a political revolution within a state to which of the following?

    (A) A political corruption scandal involving the leader of a country

    (B) A cycle of inflation and deflation

    (C) An increase in monopolization of private businesses

    (D) A significant increase in government regulation of business

GO ON TO THE NEXT PAGE

Questions 42–44 refer to the passage below.

"Moreover, our part has always been a purely passive one; our political existence has always been null, and we find ourselves in greater difficulties in attaining our liberty than we ever had when we lived on a plane lower than servitude, because we had been robbed not only of liberty but also of active and domestic tyranny. . . .

Our fundamental laws would not be altered in the least should we adopt a legislative power similar to the British Parliament. We have divided, as Americans did, national representation into two Chambers, the Representatives and the Senate. . . . If the Senate, instead of being elective were hereditary, it would be, in my opinion, the foundation, the binding tie, the very soul of our republic. . . . The hereditary Senate, as a part of the people, shares in its interests, in its sentiments, in its spirit. For this reason it is not to be presumed that a hereditary Senate would disregard the popular interests or forget its legislative duties. . . . The creation of a hereditary Senate would be in nowise a violation of political equality; I do not pretend to establish a nobility because, as a famous republican has said, it would be to destroy at the same time equality and liberty. It [being a Senator] is a calling for which candidates must be prepared; it is an office requiring much knowledge and the proper means to become learned in it."

Simón Bolívar, *The Address at the Congress of Angostura*, 1819

42. According to the passage, Bolívar sought to shape a society that most directly mirrored the ideals of

(A) the Enlightenment

(B) industrialization

(C) imperialism

(D) communism

43. In the second half of the nineteenth century, which of the following most directly resulted from colonization of Latin America?

(A) Hyperinflation

(B) Uneven distribution of wealth

(C) Agricultural exports

(D) Military control of government

44. Which of the following best explains why the political visions of Bolívar and other Latin American liberators in the nineteenth century were not fully realized?

(A) The new nations failed to establish trade relations.

(B) The *peninsulares* and Creoles had ongoing power struggles.

(C) Latin American Catholics opposed these ideologies.

(D) The new nations lacked a democratic tradition.

GO ON TO THE NEXT PAGE

Questions 45–47 refer to the passage below.

"Much laughter has been indulged in at my expense for having told the Congress audience at Calcutta that if there was sufficient response to my programme of non-co-operation Swaraj* would be attained in one year. . . . Swaraj means a state such that we can maintain our separate existence without the presence of the English. If it is to be a partnership, it must be partnership at will. There can be no Swaraj without our feeling and being the equals of Englishmen. To-day we feel that we are dependent upon them for our internal and external security, for an armed peace between the Hindus and the Mussulmans**, for our education and for the supply of daily wants, nay, even for the settlement of our religious squabbles. The Rajahs are dependent upon the British for their powers and the millionaires for their millions. The British know our helplessness . . . To get Swaraj then is to get rid of our helplessness. . . .

India cannot cease to be one nation because people belonging to different religions live in it. The introduction of foreigners does not necessarily destroy the nation; they merge in it. A country is one nation only when such a condition obtains in it. That country must have a faculty for assimilation. India has ever been such a country. In reality, there are as many religions as there are individuals, but those who are conscious of the spirit of nationality do not interfere with one another's religion. If they do, they are not fit to be considered a nation."

*Indian self-rule

**an archaic term for followers of Islam

Mahatma Gandhi, *Freedom's Battle*, 1922

45. Which of the following best explains Gandhi's approach to gaining Indian independence?

   (A) The use of political action

   (B) The imposition of economic sanctions on Britain

   (C) The combination of Hindu and Islamic beliefs

   (D) The encouragement of nonviolent civil disobedience

46. Based on the passage and your knowledge of world history, which of the following events represented a divergence from Gandhi's vision of an independent India?

   (A) The 1931 Round Table Conference

   (B) The creation of India and Pakistan

   (C) The Amritsar Massacre

   (D) Nehru's post-independence reforms

47. Which of the following would best explain the context of Gandhi's words in the passage?

   (A) The people of India were dissatisfied that Britain had maintained complete control of the country after World War I.

   (B) The British East India Company had solidified its political control over a large portion of India.

   (C) India had recently gained its independence from Britain and now ruled itself.

   (D) India's economy had been strengthened through the Green Revolution, which increased the domestic food supply.

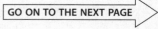
GO ON TO THE NEXT PAGE

Questions 48–49 refer to the image below.

Тов. Ленин ОЧИЩАЕТ
землю от нечисти.

The image above, from the twentieth century, shows Lenin sweeping away kings and the wealthy. The caption reads, "Comrade Lenin cleans impurities from the Earth."

48. The image is best understood in the context of which of the following?

   (A) The Russian Revolution led to a new form of liberal government.

   (B) Imperialism had edged its way into Russian politics as a result of the revolution.

   (C) Communism was beginning to take root within many world powers.

   (D) Communist ideology was considered an adequate replacement for Confucian ideals.

49. Which of the following is a commonality between the aftermaths of the Russian Revolution and the Chinese Revolution?

   (A) Communist China and the Soviet Union broke from their founders' intents by introducing capitalist reforms.

   (B) The leaders of the Russian Revolution and the Chinese Revolution both favored Five-Year Plans to restore devastated economies.

   (C) The Russian Revolution and the Chinese Revolution resulted in the replacement of corrupt monarchies.

   (D) The revolutions in Russia and China benefited from national military-industrial complexes.

GO ON TO THE NEXT PAGE

Questions 50–52 refer to the passage below.

"We invoke, we give notice: that [regarding] the fields, timber, and water which the landlords, scientists, or bosses have usurped, the pueblos or citizens who have the titles corresponding to those properties will immediately enter into possession of that real estate of which they have been despoiled by the bad faith of our oppressors, maintain at any cost with arms in hand the mentioned possession; and the usurpers who consider themselves with a right to them [those properties] will deduce it before the special tribunals which will be established on the triumph of the revolution. . . .

[T]he immense majority of Mexican pueblos and citizens are owners of no more than the land they walk on, suffering the horrors of poverty without being able to improve their social condition in any way or to dedicate themselves to Industry or Agriculture, because lands, timber, and water are monopolized in a few hands."

Emiliano Zapata, Mexican revolutionary, Plan of Ayala, 1911

50. Which of the following most directly contributed to the outbreak of the revolution mentioned in the passage?

 (A) Communist policies granting the Mexican government control of all land and businesses

 (B) Neocolonialism and economic imperialism practiced by the United States and European powers

 (C) Resistance to Spanish imperial rule following the conquest of the Mexica Empire

 (D) Modernized sects of Catholicism promoting social justice and political reform

51. The ideas expressed by the author of the passage are most closely associated with which of the following?

 (A) Religious movements that embrace liberation theology

 (B) Political movements that reject the Enlightenment notion of natural rights

 (C) Land reform movements fighting the unequal distribution of resources

 (D) Political movements that seek to strengthen the relationship between church and state

52. Which of the following best describes a similarity between the Mexican Revolution of 1910 and the Russian Revolution of 1917?

 (A) Both were prompted by the desire to overthrow autocratic monarchs.

 (B) Both gained the support of bureaucrats within the existing governments.

 (C) Both were initiated in response to invasions by foreign powers.

 (D) Both gained the support of peasants with the promise of property redistribution.

GO ON TO THE NEXT PAGE

Questions 53–55 refer to the following two passages.

Source 1

"One of the beneficial results of the Great War has been the teaching of thrift to the American housewife. For patriotic reasons and for reasons of economy, more attention has been bestowed upon the preparing and cooking of food that is to be at once palatable, nourishing and economical. . . .

It has therefore been thought that a book of PRACTICAL RECIPES OF THE ITALIAN CUISINE could be offered to the American public with hope of success. It is not a pretentious book, and the recipes have been made as clear and simple as possible. Some of the dishes described are not peculiar to Italy. All, however, are representative of the Cucina Casalinga of the peninsular Kingdom, which is not the least product of a lovable and simple people, among whom the art of living well and getting the most out of life at a moderate expense has been attained to a very high degree."

Maria Gentile, *The Italian Cookbook*, 1919

Source 2

"This let me say to the middlemen of every sort, whether they are handling our food-stuffs or our raw materials of manufacture or the products of our mills and factories: The eyes of the country will be especially upon you. This is your opportunity for signal service, efficient and disinterested. The country expects you, as it expects all others, to forego unusual profits, to organize and expedite shipments of supplies of every kind, but especially of food, with an eye to the service you are rendering and in the spirit of those who enlist in the ranks, for their people, not for themselves. I shall confidently expect you to deserve and win the confidence of people of every sort and station."

Woodrow Wilson, speech on World War I, April 1917

53. Source 1 most directly alludes to which of the following in the early twentieth century?

    (A) The use of propaganda to stir anti-foreign sentiments

    (B) The pull toward frugality as a national value

    (C) The use of analog devices to improve communication

    (D) The continued friendly relations among the Allied Powers

54. Which of the following best explains the ideals portrayed in Source 2?

    (A) Ideals of patriotism and national mobilization surrounding World War I took precedence over the ideal of individualism.

    (B) Ideals of individualism and capitalism continued to shape the United States throughout World War I.

    (C) The ideal of individualism replaced the previous ideal of isolationism leading up to World War I.

    (D) Ideals of conservation and capitalism replaced the previous ideal of national mobilization around World War I.

GO ON TO THE NEXT PAGE

55. The two passages are best understood in the context of which of the following?

    (A) World War I disproportionately affected the United States.

    (B) The United States mobilized its citizens in ways that other countries did not.

    (C) World War I was a total war that mobilized entire nations to provide for armies.

    (D) The United States used propaganda during the war, while other countries did not.

GO ON TO THE NEXT PAGE

END OF PART A

**IF YOU FINISH BEFORE TIME IS CALLED,
YOU MAY CHECK YOUR WORK ON THIS SECTION.**

DO NOT GO ON TO PART B UNTIL YOU ARE TOLD TO DO SO.

SECTION I, PART B
Time—40 minutes
3 Questions

Directions: Section I, Part B of this exam consists of short-answer questions. You must respond to Questions 1 *and* 2. For your final response, you must choose to answer Question 3 *or* Question 4. In your responses, be sure to address all parts of the questions, using complete sentences.

1. Use the passage below to answer all parts of the question that follows.

   "The British Empire helped not only to create many of the nation-states of the contemporary world, it was also instrumental in forging many of the transnational economic and cultural links that bound them together in complex and often unstable ways, and therefore the study of the British empire can enable historians to transcend the boundaries of the nation-state which have proven to be such a constraint on the historical imagination. . . . This is not to say that imperial history is necessarily any less Eurocentric than other forms of history: in fact, in its earliest iterations imperial history was excessively preoccupied with Europe at the expense of non-European forces and factors. Imperial territories in such instances were often little more than an exotic field upon which European superiority could be displayed in sharp relief."

   Douglas M. Peers, "Is Humpty Dumpty Back Together Again?:
   The Revival of Imperial History and the 'Oxford History of the British Empire,'" 2002

   (a) Explain ONE piece of evidence that would <u>support</u> Peers's argument regarding the influence of the British Empire on transnational cultural or economic links.
   (b) Explain ONE piece of evidence that would <u>challenge</u> Peers's argument regarding the influence of the British Empire on transnational cultural or economic links.
   (c) Identify ONE reason why the early imperial history described in the passage was typically Eurocentric.

GO ON TO THE NEXT PAGE

2. Use the image below to answer all parts of the question that follows.

**IMAGE OF SULTANHANI CARAVANSERAI, KONYA, TURKEY,
ORIGINALLY CONSTRUCTED IN THE THIRTEENTH CENTURY**

Caravanserai were roadside inns in Asia, North Africa and Southeast Europe where travelers, often merchants, could stop and rest.

   (a) Identify ONE <u>change</u> that occurred in trade between 1200 and 1450 that contributed to the need for the building shown in the image.

   (b) Explain ONE way the image reflects a <u>continuity</u> in economic patterns in the period 1200–1450.

   (c) Explain ONE way interregional trade changed as a result of the rise of the Mongol Empire.

GO ON TO THE NEXT PAGE

Choose EITHER Question 3 OR Question 4.

3. Answer all parts of the question that follows.

   (a) Identify ONE <u>change</u> that occurred in agricultural production in the period 1200–1450.
   (b) Explain ONE factor that contributed to changes in agricultural production in the period 1200–1450.
   (c) Identify ONE <u>continuity</u> that occurred in agricultural production in the period 1200–1450.

4. Answer all parts of the question that follows.

   (a) Identify ONE way in which ideas developed by Enlightenment philosophers transformed European views on government between 1750 and 1900.
   (b) Explain ONE way in which ideas developed by Enlightenment philosophers reflected <u>continuity</u> with previous patterns of thinking.
   (c) Explain ONE way in which political movements outside of Europe were influenced by Enlightenment ideas from circa 1800 to the present.

GO ON TO THE NEXT PAGE

END OF SECTION I

**IF YOU FINISH BEFORE TIME IS CALLED,
YOU MAY CHECK YOUR WORK ON THIS SECTION.**

DO NOT GO ON TO SECTION II UNTIL YOU ARE TOLD TO DO SO.

SECTION II
Time—100 minutes

Question 1: Document-Based Question

Suggested reading period: 15 minutes

Suggested writing time: 45 minutes

Directions: Question 1 is based on the accompanying documents. The documents have been edited for the purpose of this exercise.

In your response you should do the following:

- Make a thesis or claim that responds to the prompt. The thesis or claim must be historically defensible and establish a line of reasoning.

- Provide context relevant to the prompt by describing a broader historical development or process.

- Use at least six of the provided documents to support an argument in response to the prompt.

- Use a historical example not found in the documents as evidence relevant to an argument about the prompt.

- Explain how the context or situation of at least three documents is relevant to an argument. This could address the relevance of the document's point of view, purpose, historical situation, and/or audience.

- Demonstrate a complex understanding of an argument that responds to the prompt by using evidence to corroborate, qualify, or modify the argument.

GO ON TO THE NEXT PAGE

1. Evaluate the factors that enabled Eurasian rulers to consolidate power in the period 1450–1750.

Document 1

Source: Examples of laws issued by Tokugawa Shogun to regulate *daimyo*, seventeenth century.

Personal Life	Governance
Marriages had to be approved by the shogunate.	If reported to the shogunate, castles could be repaired, but new construction was not permitted.
Clothing had to match one's social station; purple silk, for instance, could only be worn by the highest classes.	*Daimyo* could not bring large groups of their soldiers when visiting the capital city.
Samurai were not permitted to overtly display their wealth.	*Daimyo* were required to appoint skilled, non-corrupt administrators.

GO ON TO THE NEXT PAGE

Document 2

Source: Edicts of Russian Emperor Peter I (the Great) of Russia, reigned 1682–1725.

Decree on the Invitation of Foreigners, 1702

Since our accession to the throne all our efforts and intentions have tended to govern this realm in such a way that all of our subjects should, through our care for the general good, become more and more prosperous. For this end we have always tried to maintain internal order, to defend the state against invasion, and in every possible way to improve and to extend trade. With this purpose we have been compelled to make some necessary and salutary changes in the administration, in order that our subjects might more easily gain a knowledge of matters of which they were before ignorant, and become more skillful in their commercial relations. We have therefore given orders, made dispositions, and founded institutions indispensable for increasing our trade with foreigners, and shall do the same in the future.

Decree on Promotion to Officer's Rank, 1714

Since there are many who promote to officer rank their relatives and friends—young men who do not know the fundamentals of soldiering, not having served in the lower ranks—and since even those who serve [in the ranks] do so for a few weeks or months only, as a formality; therefore . . . let a decree be promulgated that henceforth there shall be no promotion [to officer rank] of men of noble extraction or of any others who have not first served as privates in the Guards.

GO ON TO THE NEXT PAGE

Document 3

Source: Henry Martyn Baird, *The Huguenots and the Revocation of the Edict of Nantes*, 1895.

The recognized existence of Huguenots in France ceases at the publication of the law recalling the Edict of Nantes. Louis the Fourteenth had willed that there should be no more adherents of the Reformed religion in his dominions, and the law, regarding the king's will as supreme and of ultimate authority, not only refused to accord them any of the rights of men, but denied the very fact that they lived and breathed. The signature Louis affixed to the Edict of Fontainebleau was credited with having had the magical effect of transmuting all the Huguenots of the realm into 'New Converts,' or 'New Catholics,' as they were indifferently called . . . For the first few years, the clergy, and that large part of the population which seemed to have given itself up to the clergy's inspiration, appeared to entertain the serious belief that the conversion of the 'Calvinists' of France had either been accomplished, or would be fully accomplished before long.

GO ON TO THE NEXT PAGE

Document 4

Source: Jacques Bossuet, French Bishop, court preacher to Louis XIV of France, seventeenth century.

It appears from all this that the person of the king is sacred, and that to attack him in any way is sacrilege. God has the kings anointed by his prophets . . . as he has bishops and altars anointed.

Document 5

Source: Ogier Ghiselin de Busbecq, Austrian diplomat to the Ottoman Empire, letters to a friend, 1555–1562.

No distinction is attached to birth among the Turks; the deference [respect] to be paid to a man is measured by the position he holds in the public service. There is no fighting for precedence; a man's place is marked out by the duties he discharges. In making his appointments the Sultan pays no regard to any pretensions on the score of wealth or rank, nor does he take into consideration recommendations or popularity; he considers each case on its own merits, and examines carefully into the character, ability, and disposition of the man whose promotion is in question. It is by merit that men rise in the service, a system which ensures that posts should only be assigned to the competent. Each man in Turkey carries in his own hand his ancestry and his position in life, which he may make or mar as he will.

GO ON TO THE NEXT PAGE

Document 6

Source: Voltaire, *The History of Peter the Great, Emperor of Russia*, 1759.
Translated to English by T. Smollett, 1845.

The tsar was willing to accustom his people to the manners and customs of the
nations which he had visited in his travels, and from whence he had taken the
masters who were now instructing them.

It appeared necessary that the Russians should not be dressed in a different manner
from those who were teaching them the arts and sciences . . . In general, the robe
was formerly the dress of all nations, as being a garment that required the least
trouble and art; and, for the same reason, the beard was suffered to grow. The tsar
met with but little difficulty in introducing our mode of dress, and the custom of
shaving among his courtiers; but the people were more obstinate, he found himself
obliged to lay a tax on long coats and beards . . . and whoever refused to pay the tax
were obliged to suffer their robes and their beards to be curtailed. . . .

The tsar, therefore, introduced those assemblies which the Italians call *ridotti*. To
these assemblies he invited all the ladies of his court, with their daughters; and they
were to appear dressed after the fashions of the southern nations of Europe. He
was even himself at the pains of drawing up rules for all the little decorums to be
observed at these social entertainments. Thus, even to good breeding among his
subjects, all was his own work, and that of time.

To make his people relish these innovations the better, he abolished the word
golut, *slave*, always made use of by the Russians when they addressed their tsar, or
presented any petition to him; and ordered, that, for the future, they should make
use of the word *raab*, which signifies *subject*. This alteration in no wise diminished
the obedience due to the sovereign, and yet was the most ready means of
conciliating their affections. Every month produced some new change or institution.

GO ON TO THE NEXT PAGE

Document 7

Source: King James I, English monarch, address to Parliament, 1609.

The state of monarchy is the supremest thing upon earth; for kings are not only God's lieutenants upon earth, and sit upon God's throne, but even by God himself are called gods. . . .

Kings are justly called gods, for that they exercise a manner or resemblance of divine power upon earth: for if you will consider the attributes of God, you shall see how they agree in the person of a king. God hath power to create or destroy, make or unmake at his pleasure, to give life or send death, to judge all and to be judged nor accountable to none; to raise low things and to make high things low at his pleasure, and to God are both souls and body due. And the like power have kings: they make and unmake their subjects, they have power of raising and casting down, of life and of death, judges over all their subjects and in all causes and yet accountable to none but God only.

GO ON TO THE NEXT PAGE

END OF DOCUMENTS FOR QUESTION 1

Question 2, Question 3, OR Question 4: Long Essay Question
Suggested writing time: 40 minutes

Directions: Choose Question 2, Question 3, OR Question 4 to answer.

In your response you should do the following:

- Make a thesis or claim that responds to the prompt. The thesis or claim must be historically defensible and establish a line of reasoning.
- Provide context relevant to the prompt by describing a broader historical development or process.
- Use specific and relevant examples as evidence to support an argument in response to the prompt.
- Use a historical reasoning skill (causation, comparison, or continuity and change) to develop an argument in response to the prompt.
- Demonstrate a complex understanding of an argument that responds to the prompt by using evidence to corroborate, qualify, or modify the argument.

2. In the period 1200–1450, new states and empires demonstrated continuity, innovation, and diversity as they developed in various regions such as western Africa, the Middle East, and East Asia.

   Develop an argument that evaluates how one or more new states or empires administered their territory in this time period.

3. In the period 1450–1750, new connections between the Eastern and Western Hemispheres resulted in the Columbian Exchange.

   Develop an argument that evaluates how the Columbian Exchange changed one or more regions in this time period.

4. In the period 1750–1900, increasing discontent with imperial rule propelled reformist and revolutionary movements around the world.

   Develop an argument that evaluates the similarities of two reformist and/or revolutionary movements in this time period.

END OF SECTION II

STOP

END OF EXAM

ANSWER KEY

Section I, Part A

1. C	15. A	29. D	43. B
2. B	16. C	30. A	44. D
3. C	17. A	31. A	45. D
4. B	18. C	32. D	46. B
5. B	19. A	33. C	47. A
6. A	20. D	34. A	48. C
7. C	21. A	35. D	49. A
8. D	22. B	36. C	50. A
9. A	23. D	37. A	51. C
10. B	24. C	38. B	52. C
11. C	25. B	39. B	53. B
12. A	26. D	40. C	54. A
13. B	27. C	41. C	55. C
14. D	28. D	42. A	

Section I, Part B and Section II

See Answers and Explanations, and self-score free-response questions.

Section I, Part A Number Correct: _____

Section I, Part B Points Earned: _____

Section II Points Earned: _____

Sign into your online account at kaptest.com and enter your results in the scoring section to see your 1–5 score.

Haven't registered your book yet? Go to kaptest.com/moreonline to begin.

ANSWERS AND EXPLANATIONS

Section I, Part A

1.   C

Map 1 shows the gold-salt trade, one of the key trade networks of the postclassical period, and Map 2 shows the expansion of Islamic lands. A historian would likely note the overlap between the areas depicted in these two maps showing the cultural exchanges that occurred along the trade routes. Thus, **(C)** is correct. Gold deposits were discovered elsewhere in the world, so (A) is incorrect. (B) is incorrect because the routes depicted by black lines on Map 1 are trade routes for goods, not migration patterns of people. (D) is incorrect because the relationship is reversed.

2.   B

Map 1 depicts West African trade routes and the journey of Mansa Musa to Mecca. As reflected by the presence of gold mines in West Africa, the kingdom of Mali increased in wealth and expanded into an empire, thereby further increasing its wealth through profitable trade routes. Even if unfamiliar with Mansa Musa as a ruler of Mali who completed a pilgrimage, famously showering gold on those he visited, the map indicates the concurrent growth of trade and wealth in Mali, so **(B)** is correct. (A) and (C) are incorrect because Map 1 does not indicate anything about the Silk Road or maritime trade; further, use of the Silk Road did not decline during this time period, but rather trade across all of Afro-Eurasia flourished. (D) is incorrect because the map indicates no such decline; Mali actually continued to flourish as a trade empire after Mansa Musa's journey.

3.   C

The titles of the maps indicate their content: the maps depict trade routes and the expansion of Islam. The correct answer should also reflect a connection between trade and the diffusion of religion. Like the spread of Islam in western Africa by way of salt and gold trade routes as shown in the maps, Western religions like Christianity spread and flourished at the same time in China along the Silk Road; **(C)** is correct. (A) is incorrect because, although Map 2 does show Ibn Battuta's travel routes, few travel writers attempted to convert their readers, nor is such a trend depicted in the maps. Although it is true that the widespread adoption of Confucianism and

Buddhism solidified a cultural identity through much of East Asia, this trend was not the result of trade routes; (B) is incorrect. (D) is incorrect because China's isolation from world trade occurred in later centuries, during the Ming Dynasty; further, Map 2 indicates international trade routes to locations in China.

4.   B

The greatest developments made in the Islamic world concerned mathematics (such as algebra and the concept of zero), medicine, and astronomy, in addition to the promotion of Greek literature and historical writings; **(B)** is correct. (A) is incorrect because the various empires that became part of the Islamic world (the kingdoms of West Africa, city-states in East Africa, etc.) were not unified by one common ruler. (C) is incorrect because Islam did not dictate one common structure for government. The Islamic world is not known for significant developments in agriculture or livestock; therefore, (D) is incorrect.

5.   B

Nomadic groups like the Mongols interacted with settled people, often because of settled people's technology, as is evidenced by the passage's reference to "places of manufacture or centres of commerce"; **(B)** is correct. While there are many contributing reasons why the Mongols conquered large portions of the Asian continent, the primary reason was Genghis Khan's ability to unite the clans under a single leader; (A) is incorrect. Although it is true that the Mongols sometimes resided close to towns and cities, as a nomadic people they moved often and also lived in the countryside; (C) is incorrect. (D) is also incorrect, because the Mongol people never came into contact with Amerindian people and thereby had no way of having knowledge of the wigwam structure. The reference to the "Indian wigwam" by the author is used to help the reader understand and picture the structure based on an assumed previous knowledge of the Amerindian dwelling.

6.   A

As "peripheral" groups, both the Mongols and Turks were semi-organized peoples who lived at the edges of more urban or settled civilizations, making **(A)** correct. Typically, they pressured or even occupied adjacent imperial realms when environmental, economic, or political conditions allowed. Although the Mongols and Turks were nomadic and known for being skilled horsemen, this does not make them peripheral peoples; (B) and (D) are incorrect. Only the Turks later developed an organized bureaucracy in the Ottoman Empire, making (C) incorrect.

7. C

Central Asia's relatively harsh climate and topography, containing thousands of miles of open steppe land, facilitated both trade and conquest, and was better suited to nomadic herding than intensive agriculture. Therefore, **(C)** is correct. While the Silk Road fostered communication, the information exchange did not provide a tactical advantage, making (A) incorrect. The Turks, Mongols, and other such groups appreciated the luxuries of the neighboring empires but typically did not find urban living attractive, so (B) is incorrect. Finally, these conflicts were multifaceted, with the nomads often under military or economic pressure from their adversaries, but the imperial armies did not have the ability to fence or tax the nomadic homelands; (D) is incorrect.

8. D

The spread of Buddhism solidified a cultural identity throughout East Asia, including the Song Dynasty during the period 1200–1450; **(D)** is correct. Although Neo-Confucianism did develop and spread in response to Buddhism and Daoism, this was predominantly prior to 1200. Further, the image depicted is Buddhist art, making (A) incorrect. While foot binding was a cultural practice that emerged and grew in popularity during the Song Dynasty, it was not a religious practice and has no connection to the Buddhist figure in the image; (B) is incorrect. The Song Dynasty did rise through the late thirteenth century but was a centralized empire in China, making (C) incorrect.

9. A

Like the Song Dynasty, the Arab caliphates were centralized states built on the successful models of past empires that would later decline and end with the Mongol invasions; **(A)** is correct. Although the Turks would later form the Ottoman Empire, contemporary Turks were decentralized and nomadic, making (B) incorrect. (C) is also incorrect; while the Song Dynasty had a weak military, the Kamakura shogunate controlled a centralized military government based on feudalism. The Hanseatic League was not a form of centralized government, but an organization of trade guilds founded in Germany in the 1200s; (D) is incorrect.

10. B

As the Mongol Empire grew into East Asia, trade routes were largely protected, which facilitated the spread of Buddhism; **(B)** is correct. (A) is incorrect because it describes the effects of Islam, not Buddhism, during this period. (C) is incorrect because, although Buddhism spread and was adopted by the Song Dynasty and other parts of East Asia, it was not made an official religion. Furthermore, Buddhism was initially resisted in Japan in preference for the Shinto religion and only later became part of the Japanese faith as a blend with Shinto. (D) is incorrect because Buddhism primarily spread as a missionary religion, going beyond regional and ethnic identity.

11. C

As illustrated in Passage 1, Ibn Battuta described the trade and goods of the places he traveled. Like other travel narratives of the time, these writings sparked European interest in African and Asian cultures and products; **(C)** is correct. (A) is incorrect, as travelling through the Mongol Empire is not described in the passage; further, Mongol rule made the Silk Road safer, not more dangerous. (B) is incorrect because the passage contains a comparison between Dhofar and Northwest Africa. (D) is incorrect because religion spread along long-distance trade routes during the time period.

12. A

Both passages describe the various goods, such as produce in Passage 1 and silk in Passage 2, which were specific to particular locations and considered luxury items, driving the expansion of trade networks; **(A)** is correct. (B) is incorrect because sea travel was an integral part of long-distance trade during this time period; Passage 1 mentions how the sultan welcomed foreign ships to the city. (C) is incorrect because both passages describe the activity of merchants traveling to other locations. Passage 2 mentions that "go forth not a few great merchants"; the phrase "not a few" means that many merchants traveled, indicating that foreign markets were purchasing their goods. (D) is incorrect because, although armies could help maintain safer trade routes, the passages do not reflect this development, only mentioning in Passage 2 that Taianfu manufactured equipment for the army.

13. B

The Silk Road facilitated European trade in Asian goods; among these goods was gunpowder (invented in China circa 900), which Europeans used to create gunpowder weapons; **(B)** is correct. Although paper money was invented at the peak of the Silk Road and used throughout parts of the Mongol Empire, it would not be used in Europe until the seventeenth century, making (A) incorrect. (C) is incorrect; the Chinese did not value merchants during this period because they did not make anything themselves and instead profited off of the work of others. (D) is incorrect because, while Islam did spread through the Silk Trade, specifically into Central Asia and China, it was through the Indian Ocean trade routes that Islam spread to East Africa.

14. D

Mercantilism is a national economic policy that was designed to maximize the exports of a nation. While mercantilism did not arise until the 16th century, it grew out of the rise of nationalism through state building and the spread of international trade, which is illustrated in both passages. **(D)** is correct. Although the Hanseatic League did emerge in order to promote fair trade among merchant guilds, the trade described in the passage is centralized with the state rather than groups of independent merchants, making (A) incorrect. Although Africa would become a part of the Columbian Exchange through further expansion of the slave trade in the Americas, this is not what is described in either passage; (B) is incorrect. The Tokugawa shogunate ruled Japan under isolationist policies that heavily restricted international trade, which is opposed to the trade that is described in both passages. Thus, (C) is also incorrect.

15. A

A major theme of world history in the early modern era (1450–1750) is the increase in global interaction. **(A)** correctly notes that the Japanese policy of isolation was remarkable, not because it was attempted, but because it succeeded. Reasons for the success were Japan's island setting, its isolated location at the edge of East Asia on the vast northern Pacific Ocean, and its advanced social and economic institutions after centuries of interaction with China and other neighbors. Japan did not respond to Western advances, making (B) incorrect. (C) is incorrect because it is out of period; it looks ahead to the next era

of Japanese history, after the Meiji Restoration in the 1860s. (D) is incorrect because Japan did not introduce wage labor or factory-system industry at this time, nor did its peasantry work under more coercion than in any other feudal-style system.

16. C

The viewpoint in the passage describes strict Japanese government policies that prohibit spreading Christianity or sailing from Macau to Japan. The correct answer should contrast with the policy of having restrictions on foreign influence, especially Western influences, in Japan. **(C)** is correct because Japan welcomed Western industrialization and other modernization practices during the Meiji Era. (A) is incorrect because the passage implies the power of the shogun, but does not indicate anything else about its feudal structure. (B) is incorrect because adherence to Shintoism would not directly differ from restricting another religion, Christianity, as described in the passage. (D) is incorrect because the passage does not discuss territorial expansion.

17. A

Peter the Great sought to rapidly modernize Russia through policy and practices, such as mandating that his people shave their beards and wear Western clothing, and constructing a new capital closer to the West in St. Petersburg. Conversely, the Tokugawa period saw an emphasis on unified Japanese culture without outside influences. Thus, **(A)** is correct because it describes Russia's differing approach. (B) is incorrect because, like Russia, Japan was comparatively peaceful and stable during the Tokugawa period. (C) is incorrect because, during this period, both Russia and Japan had a thriving military situated within the bureaucratic system. Their economies both flourished due to internal trade and progressive policies, making the turn to a Western industrial system in the nineteenth century both possible and successful; (D) is incorrect.

18. C

The passage discusses the Ottoman Turks and their attack on the city of Constantinople in 1453, leading to its eventual takeover and the end of Byzantine rule; **(C)** is correct. The Hagia Sophia was not destroyed but was transformed into a mosque under Ottoman rule following the fall of Constantinople, making (A) incorrect.

(B) is incorrect because the Mughal Empire, established in 1526, extended across the Indian subcontinent and did not include Constantinople. (D) is incorrect because, although the Seljuk Turks had defeated much of the Byzantine Empire in Anatolia centuries earlier, their dynasty collapsed and gave rise to the Ottomans, who conquered Constantinople in 1453.

19. A

Constantinople was the center of the Byzantine Empire, which replaced the Eastern Roman Empire and lasted until 1453. At Constantinople, traders from Western and Eastern kingdoms converged and exchanged goods as well as cultural ideas; thus, **(A)** is correct. The Byzantine Empire was Christian, but its church was the Eastern Orthodox Church, which preceded the emergence of Protestantism in Germany in 1517; (B) is incorrect. Although Constantinople fell to the Ottoman Empire in 1453, and the famous cathedral (Hagia Sophia) was transformed into a mosque, many subjects remained Christian and thus Constantinople (renamed Istanbul) did not exclusively promote Islam; (C) is incorrect. (D) is incorrect because, although the Byzantine ruler Justinian did simplify Roman law (in the sixth century), that is not the reason that Constantinople was so significant.

20. D

The conquest of Constantinople in 1453 by the Ottoman Empire was representative of the growing use of gunpowder weapons by emerging empires to conquer lands such as the Mughal Empire. Therefore, **(D)** is correct. The Delhi Sultanate was a culmination of invasions by the nomadic Afghan Turks, which began much earlier than the conquest of Constantinople, making (A) incorrect. (B) is incorrect because a caravel is a small, highly maneuverable sailing ship used by the Portuguese in exploration. (C) is incorrect because the Ottoman conquest of Constantinople and the end of the Byzantine Empire marked a move away from Christianity; the Ottoman Turks were Muslim, and thus transformed churches and cathedrals into mosques.

21. A

Geocentricism was a widely accepted ancient idea proposed as early as the third century B.C.E. that persisted into the sixteenth century. It posited that the Earth was the center of the universe. The Copernican System

features the heliocentric theory, which positions the sun at the center of the solar system in which the Earth and planets revolve. The image shows a royal figure, who remains blindfolded to this new theory and still adheres to the old way of thinking. **(A)** is correct. The scientific method was developed as an empirical way to obtain knowledge through inductive reasoning during the Scientific Revolution. However, it was the work of Copernicus that inspired the development of the scientific method, not the other way around, making (B) incorrect. Kepler developed three scientific laws of planetary motion that describe the motion of planets around the sun. While Kepler's work improved on Copernicus's heliocentric theory by describing the motion of the planets around the sun, there is no indication of this in the image, making (C) incorrect. Although the invention of the telescope in 1608 was an effort to better understand the cosmos using mathematics that were in development during the Scientific Revolution, and Galileo used it to develop new theories about the universe, this occurred after Copernicus developed his heliocentric theory; thus, (D) is incorrect.

22. B

Copernicus's heliocentric theory emerged at a time when Europeans, due to increased trade with Islamic and Asian cultures, were increasingly exposed to and adopted other cultures' scientific developments and knowledge of classical texts. Scientific advances based on observation and the scientific method (such as the heliocentric theory) began to contradict the Church's traditional beliefs (such as the geocentric theory); **(B)** is correct. The other choices are incorrect because they reflect the opposite of the scientific mindset and cross-cultural exchanges of knowledge that were happening in Europe in this time period.

23. D

Critical to the Scientific Revolution was the promotion of rational thinking that encouraged scholars and scientists to challenge conventional ideas, particularly those held by authorities like the Catholic Church. Like the Enlightenment *philosophes*, scientists like Copernicus challenged previous theories through critical reasoning and empirical observation. Thus, **(D)** is correct. (A) and (C) are incorrect because, while the Copernican System challenged the Church's ideas, it didn't cause such widespread religious changes. (B) is incorrect because the development of the Copernican System was situated in scientific advances of the time, not developments in the arts.

24. C

The author of the passage states that the way to "encrease our wealth and treasure is by Forraign Trade, wherein wee must ever observe this rule; to sell more to strangers yearly than wee consume of theirs in value." This reflects the economic theory of mercantilism that was prevalent in European nations in the sixteenth, seventeenth, and eighteenth centuries: that countries should enrich themselves by limiting imports and encouraging exports; **(C)** is correct. (A) is incorrect because, while the passage discusses trade, it does not focus on specialization in certain goods. While trade with the Americas could benefit nations, it is not a mercantile idea, making (B) incorrect. (D) is incorrect because the mercantile ideas expressed in the passage do not include a moral position on coerced labor or the slave trade.

25. B

The economic practices of mercantilism were based upon extreme competition between nation states for goods; several nations, including England, utilized imperialism as a way to more easily obtain certain goods, such as sugar in the West Indies and gold in Mexico. **(B)** is correct. (A) is incorrect because the spread of disease, while an effect of international trade, did not help to support it. Although Catholic missionaries often came alongside European conquerors, conversion was not directly related to mercantilism or the imperialism that supported it, making (C) incorrect. (D) is incorrect because the philosophies of Locke and other Enlightenment philosophers did not uphold mercantilism.

26. D

The demand for silk, which inspired one of the most important trade routes in the medieval era, is reflected in Spain's mercantile imperialism of the silver trade. Thus, **(D)** is correct and (C) is incorrect. (A) is incorrect because the Spanish did not have a monopoly on the sugar trade; this trade also primarily occurred in the West Indies, not Mexico and the Andes. Although Spain was a major player in the slave trade, it was one of many European nations

doing so, and it was primarily involved in the Atlantic Slave trade; (B) is incorrect.

27. C

Spencer's notion of "survival of the fittest" is similar to the theory of Social Darwinism, in which the conquest and subjugation of people viewed as "less civilized" reflects the laws of nature. **(C)** is correct. While scientific progress was seen as an indicator of superiority, Spencer's philosophy does not specifically advocate for science replacing religion, so (A) is incorrect. In Spencer's view, social classes emerged from natural order, so he would not be concerned with the working-class upheavals in (B) or supportive of the concept of natural rights in (D).

28. D

The concept of Social Darwinism, as discussed by Spencer in this passage, served as motivation and justification for imperialism. According to proponents of this theory, societies either prospered or failed because, as is the case in nature, only the strong survive as they are able to dominate the weak. In this line of thought, "a large, farseeing benevolence" decreed that strong nations were destined to dominate lands and resources occupied by those considered weaker (indigenous peoples in Asia and Africa). Thus, **(D)** is correct. Both (A) and (B) are incorrect because the American Revolution and the First Opium War were underpinned by conflicts with imperial powers, not by a belief that those nations should be in power. While ideologies such as Spencer's had links to industrialization, they did not directly serve as motivation for the Second Industrial Revolution; thus, (C) is incorrect.

29. D

Someone who believes that poverty stems from people being "incapable," "imprudent," and "idle" would likely disagree with any government assistance or intervention designed to benefit the poor. This resonates with Adam Smith's laissez-faire capitalism, which promoted minimal government interference; **(D)** is correct. (A) is incorrect because communism promotes governments making economic decisions for the people, which is the opposite of Spencer's perspective. (B) is incorrect because John Locke was an English philosopher who believed that the government is meant to serve the people. A proponent of Spencer's view would not support a separate state created to support a marginalized group; (C) is incorrect.

30. A

The excerpt describes the events and growing dissatisfaction leading up to the Indian Rebellion of 1857. Important context for this rebellion is the fact that the British had established imperial control over India after conquering the Sikhs. Indian soldiers termed *sepoys* were often used to police areas of the Indian subcontinent that clashed with their own ethnic or religious identity. The British Empire intentionally played different native groups against each other, ensuring that they stayed in overall control; **(A)** is correct. (B), (C), and (D) are incorrect because these events occurred after the Indian Rebellion of 1857, once Britain had cemented its direct imperial rule.

31. A

The passage describes how a report spread among Muslim and Hindu soldiers that the English "masters" were trying to "defile" the Indian soldiers and make them Christian. The writer of the passage explains that these reports occurred in the midst of attempts to spread "distrust" among the soldiers and persuade them to "mutiny" against the English, "with the object of restoring the Emperor of Delhi to the throne." Since India was under the imperial rule of the British at this time, the passage thus illustrates how religious concerns intermingled with resistance against imperial rule; **(A)** is correct. (B) is incorrect because the conflict between the English and the Indian soldiers was not a purely "ideological" one, but was rooted in the imperial system. (C) is incorrect because India was not itself an imperial power, but under the imperial rule of the British. Although the passage mentions "instruction in the use of the new rifle," the conflict described was not primarily about technology, but about imperial governance and religion.

32. D

As indicated in the passage, the Indian Rebellion of 1857 occurred shortly after Indian soldiers heard that beef and pork fat were used to seal ammunition cartridges (meaning that Hindu and Muslim soldiers would have to bite the seals, thereby consuming taboo foods). While this incident was a major catalyst, the rebellion was also fueled by resentment of British rule, including heavy taxation and invasive social policies. The correct answer should reflect another rebellion against foreign influence or occupation. **(D)** describes an uprising against foreign influence in China and is correct. (A) is incorrect because the Boer Wars were fought between rival groups of non-native settlers of South Africa. (B) is incorrect because the Mexican Revolution was a civil war involving the democratic supporters of Francisco Madero and the authoritarian supporters of Porfirio Díaz. (C) is incorrect because the Bolshevik Revolution replaced the post-tsarist provisional government with the communist government that would transform Russia into the Soviet Union.

33. C

The map of the "unknowne worlde" of the Americas most directly reflects imperialism, the system of European countries extending their authority in other regions and establishing global empires. With an underpinning of imperialistic goals, maps such as this one depicted the land and native peoples as exotic and the resources as lush and ripe for the taking. Thus, **(C)** is correct. Although patriarchy pervaded most civilizations in this time period, it is not directly suggested by the map, so (A) is incorrect. Similarly, the map does not directly reflect the *encomienda* system (a specific system in which indigenous peoples provided labor for Spanish settlements); (B) is incorrect. Globalization (the worldwide diffusion of ideas, cultures, technologies, and other phenomena) did not emerge until the twentieth century as technological advances further facilitated global exchange, making (D) incorrect.

34. A

The map indicates that by 1627, Europeans were familiar with the coasts of the Americas and, as shown by the illustrations of ships, that sea vessels were a primary means of transportation and exploration. Transoceanic travel was facilitated by the development of new maritime technologies, informed by contact with other Afro-Eurasian cultures and initially led by the Portuguese. One of these developments was increasing knowledge of ocean currents and wind patterns; **(A)** is correct. (B) is incorrect because the technologies of the second industrial revolution, such as electricity and more efficient steel production, occurred in the nineteenth century; these developments helped spur nineteenth-century imperialism, but are not relevant to this map. (C) is incorrect because it relates to safer travel on Afro-Eurasian trade networks, such as the Silk Road, not to travel in the Americas. (D) describes the Spanish social hierarchy in the Americas, but is not directly related to cartographers' improved geographic knowledge.

35. D

Indigenous peoples in the Americas cultivated their own systems of trade prior to the arrival of Europeans, including transportation routes, such as the Inca road system. The top border of the map contains detailed illustrations of indigenous towns that appear to be prosperous, and the indigenous peoples in the side borders seem to reflect various social statuses and occupations. Thus, **(D)** is correct. (A) is incorrect because the Incas conquered a large territory and absorbed many groups in central and western South America. In 90 years, the Inca Empire grew into a stretch of land that covered over 3,000 miles. (B) is incorrect because the Columbian Exchange began following Columbus's arrival in 1492. The Inca Empire was centralized, led by a king and a privileged class of nobles, and the Mexica were led by a single monarch, who exerted power over local rulers, making (C) incorrect.

36. C

In the passage, Bossuet writes that "the person of the king is sacred" and that kings must have "absolute authority," which suggests the rise of absolute monarchs in early modern Europe. Most famously epitomized by the Sun King, Louis XIV of France, these European kings and queens united their bureaucratic and mercantilist states by modernizing their armies, reforming feudal-era laws and customs, weakening the regional nobles, and justifying it all with their "divine right" to rule. **(C)** is correct. Although republics and early forms of democracy were emerging in peripheral states like England and the Netherlands, this was not the major political trend throughout Europe during this period; (A) is incorrect. Likewise, (B) is incorrect because decentralized government was seen in only a few ill-fated states like Poland and supra-states like the Holy Roman Empire. (D) is incorrect because it overlooks that the new absolute monarchs were driven by power dynamics and sought to increase their influence by conquering neighboring territories; diplomacy and treaties followed wars but did not replace them.

37. A

Bossuet was writing in the context of a French regime that was trying to establish absolute rule against the wishes of both local and regional nobles and institutions, as well as in opposition to theoretical arguments for limited monarchy from England and the Netherlands. Only **(A)** correctly makes this connection clear: after its recent civil war, the English Parliament of nobles and commoners had tried and executed the king for treason against the state, which Bossuet argued would now be an impossibility. The remaining choices are incorrect because they are actions of absolutist rulers exercising their power by utilizing their subjects' labor; thus, they are examples that support Bossuet's argument as opposed to differing from it.

38. B

The Safavid Dynasty represents a similar example of the trend toward centralization during this period; the shahs imposed Shi'a Islam and imported foreign clergy to preach their legitimate descent from the Prophet, which conveys divine authority according to Islam. **(B)** is correct. (A), (C), and (D) are incorrect because in those states the monarch at the time had limited political or religious authority: Japan's emperor had the status of divine ancestry, but under the Tokugawa shogunate he had almost no political power. The king of Poland-Lithuania was an elected monarch, subject to the power of the nobles' assembly. The Presbyterians of Scotland, in the wake of the English Civil War, feared a too-powerful king would threaten their Protestant religious independence.

39. B

On the heels of industrialization, socialism and communism emerged in response to the poor conditions for industrial workers; **(B)** is correct. Liberalism, not communism, resulted from the rapid growth of the middle class in conjunction with industrialization, making (A) incorrect. (C) is incorrect because Marx was concerned with working conditions rather than the fact that middle-class women rarely worked outside of the home following industrialization. While manufacturers sought to increase productivity and profits, Marx wrote *The Communist Manifesto* in response to the declining working conditions that resulted from this new focus, making (D) incorrect.

40. C

In the passage, Marx describes forms of class struggle that he claims still persist in "modern bourgeois society." In the early twentieth century, Russia was still transitioning from its historic feudalism to an industrial economy; many farmers and laborers, facing economic struggle and opposing Russia's role in World War I, supported first the overthrow of the tsar and then the establishment of a government based on communist principles.

(C) is correct. Communism and socialism developed as reactions against the type of industrialization evident in the second industrial revolution, making (A) incorrect. (B) is incorrect because the Meiji Era was a period favoring Western-style modernization and the restoration of an emperor, at least symbolically, in Japan. While the Revolutions of 1848 were also a reaction to industrialization, most revolutionaries at that time sought democratic reforms, not socialist or communist reforms; (D) is incorrect.

41. C

According to Marxism, when the capitalist class controls too much of private enterprise, working class people are further removed, or alienated, from their work. This will eventually lead to a revolution of workers against the owner classes, making **(C)** correct. (A) and (B) are incorrect because neither would be enough to ignite a revolution; Marx attributed political revolution to an oppressive ruling class, not scandal or economic uncertainty. (D) is incorrect because additional government regulation may or may not favor the working class.

42. A

In the passage, Bolívar makes reference to "attaining our liberty," "our republic," having a legislative body that regards the "popular interest," and the idea that a nobility would "destroy at the same time equality and liberty." These statements mirror the Enlightenment ideas of equality, liberty, and independence; **(A)** is correct. Industrialization catalyzed economic transformation with an emphasis on production and profits rather than on equality and liberty; (B) is incorrect. The passage expresses Bolívar's views on how to set up the government of an independent Venezuela, so it does not reflect imperialism; (C) is incorrect. (D) is incorrect because, while communism is rooted in the idea of economic equality and shared ownership, Bolívar's passage is focused on the equality of rights and liberty.

43. B

During the Age of Exploration, the Spanish Crown granted land to new settlers of Latin America through the *encomienda* system. Consequently, a new social order emerged, in which *peninsulares* (Spanish-descended and Spanish-born people) were the most prominent members of society, followed by the Creoles (Spanish-descended, but Latin American-born), then people with mixed heritage, then Africans and Indians. This class system led to uneven distribution of wealth, an issue which persists in present-day Latin America; **(B)** is correct. (A) is incorrect because hyperinflation began to plague many Latin American nations after World War II, not in the nineteenth century. (C) is incorrect because the Spanish colonizers of Latin America were interested in mining silver; exportation of agricultural goods began much later. (D) is incorrect because military rule only began in many Latin American nations after World War II.

44. D

Although Bolívar and the other Latin American liberators were educated in democratic ideals, the majority of Latin Americans only knew rule by the landed elite. Often, nations would transition from being ruled by the elite class to being governed by military dictators called *caudillos*. **(D)** is correct. (A) is incorrect because the war-torn new nations quickly established trade relations, especially with the United States. (B) is incorrect because the Creoles emerged as the dominant powers in Latin America; in fact, many *peninsulares* were loyal to the Spanish king and had much to lose from the wars for independence, so they fled to Spain. The liberators themselves were largely Catholic, making (C) incorrect.

45. D

The core tenet of Gandhi's independence movement was the idea of satyagraha ("holding onto truth"), which involved a determined commitment to nonviolence in the face of evil. Through such acts as the Salt March, repeated hunger strikes, and the creation of homespun cloth, Gandhi and his followers sought independence and inspired generations of nonviolent protests. Therefore, **(D)** is correct. (A) is incorrect because Gandhi, who had been a key leader of the Indian National Congress, felt that the Congress was using his beliefs for political gain, and he therefore resigned in 1934. Although Gandhi's campaigns did hurt Britain's economy, particularly after he urged his followers to weave their own cloth, he never issued economic sanctions on Britain itself, making (B) incorrect. (C) is incorrect because Gandhi drew his ideas from not just Hindu and Muslim beliefs, but several religions, especially the Jain principle of ahimsa, or nonviolence.

46. B

In August of 1947, in the midst of rising tensions between Hindus and Muslims, the countries of India and Pakistan declared their independence from Britain. Gandhi, who had envisioned a single state in which Hindus and Muslims governed and lived jointly, opposed the separation of South Asia into a Hindu-led India and a Muslim-led Pakistan. This view led to his assassination by a Hindu extremist just five months later. Thus, **(B)** is correct. (A) is incorrect because Ghandi volunteered to represent the Indian National Congress at the 1931 Round Table Conference in London, hoping to represent all people of India. While the division among delegates limited the results of the conference, it did not directly contradict Gandhi's vision of an independent India. (C) is incorrect because the Amritsar Massacre, in which British soldiers killed over 400 Hindus and Muslims protesting the Rowlatt Acts, was the spark for the larger independence movement. (D) is incorrect because Jawaharlal Nehru, India's first prime minister, initiated reforms that helped India modernize on its own terms; most of these reforms were in line with Gandhi's views of social equality, education, and economic self-reliance.

47. A

India had fought loyally as part of the British Empire in World War I, in the hopes of gaining more independence after the war. When the fighting ended, Britain introduced some minor reforms and liberalization but maintained complete control. This led to a surge in Indian nationalism under the leadership of the Congress Party and Gandhi; **(A)** is correct. The Salt March began in March 1930, which was before Gandhi delivered his "Quit India" speech, making (B) incorrect. India achieved its independence in August 1947, which occurred after Gandhi's speech; (C) is incorrect. Gandhi's longest fast lasted 21 days in February 1943, which took place after the speech, making (D) incorrect.

48. C

The losses and fruitless sacrifices of World War I led to disorder and riots in March 1917. The Russian tsar was forced to abdicate, and a provisional republican government took power. The leading party of communists, the Bolsheviks, was led by Vladimir Lenin. They promised the people exactly what they wanted: "Peace, Land, Bread." As alluded to in the image, the Bolshevik government seized all private land, banks, and industries; the former owners were persecuted and their estates looted and burned. Thus, **(C)** is correct. (A) is incorrect because Lenin's party seized power and declared Russia the world's first socialist state in November 1917. The Russian Revolution led to a communist state, not an imperialistic one, making (B) incorrect. (D) is incorrect because this describes the Chinese Revolution, not the Russian Revolution.

49. A

With Mikhail Gorbachev's *perestroika* and Deng Xiaoping's Four Modernizations, capitalist reforms were gradually introduced into the Soviet Union and China, respectively, in the 1980s. Among other reforms, Soviets and Chinese were allowed to own small businesses and sell select goods on the open market. Thus, **(A)** is correct. Although both the Soviet Union and communist China used the Five-Year Plan, (B) is incorrect because Joseph Stalin was the first Soviet leader to use the Five-Year Plan. The Russian Revolution overthrew the corrupt Tsar Nicholas, but in China, the unpopular Qing monarch had been overthrown 38 years prior to the Chinese Revolution, making (C) incorrect. (D) is incorrect because neither leader used the promise of a strong military to garner support.

50. A

Like many industrial nations, Japan suffered economically during the Global Depression of the 1930s. Consequently, to keep its economy afloat, Japan acquired new territory in Korea, China, and Southeast Asia to obtain natural resources. **(A)** is correct. (B) is incorrect because Japan wanted to cooperate and coexist with the other industrial powers. (C) is incorrect because the invasion of Manchuria in 1931 actually weakened the League of Nations' prestige when the Japanese military defied the league's orders to withdraw. Although the expansion in the 1930s was a way for Japan to draw on militaristic traditions, (D) is incorrect because Japan had already asserted its military might in 1905 when it defeated the superior Russian military in the Russo-Japanese War.

51. C

Ryūtarō referenced the Monroe Doctrine, the policy devised by the United States in 1823 to protect the new nations of Latin America from European colonization;

in effect, this created "an America for all Americans." Because Japan desired to create "an Asia for all Asians" through the Greater East Asia Co-Prosperity Sphere, **(C)** is correct. (A) is incorrect because the Open Door Policy was the American policy, issued in 1899, that allowed equal trading privileges in China among the industrial powers, including Japan. (B) is incorrect because Manifest Destiny was the idea that America was destined to expand from coast to coast. The Roosevelt Corollary, issued in 1904, was an addition to the Monroe Doctrine that justified U.S. intervention in Latin America when American interests in the area were threatened; (D) is incorrect.

52. C

Japan, emboldened by France's early defeat in World War II, invaded French Indochina in 1941, which matches **(C)**. (A) and (B) are incorrect because, while both events transpired as part of Japan's quest for empire, Japan would not have chosen to invade French Indochina if France's defeat in World War II had not made it so vulnerable. (D) is incorrect because U.S. President Franklin D. Roosevelt issued an oil embargo against Japan in response to Japan's invasion of Indochina. In retaliation to the oil embargo, Japan bombed the U.S. Navy base at Pearl Harbor, drawing the United States into World War II.

53. B

World War I, also called the Great War, was the first total war; politics, media, and the arts were interconnected in unprecedented ways toward the goal of greater nationalism. In the first source, the author emphasizes how some women in World War I learned "thrift" and assisted in the efforts by stating, ". . . for patriotic reasons and for reasons of economy, more attention has been bestowed upon the preparing and cooking of food that is to be at once palatable, nourishing and economical." Thus, **(B)** is correct. (A) is incorrect because, while a cookbook could be used as a means of political mobilization, this source does not indicate anti-foreign sentiments, but rather emphasizes sharing the author's Italian culture. (C) is incorrect because these technologies appeared after the publication of this 1919 cookbook. (D) is incorrect because, while both Italy and the United States were part of the Allied Powers, this passage is written by a civilian and does not necessarily indicate that the Allied Powers continued their friendly relations.

54. A

In Source 2, Wilson speaks to the civilians who served as "middlemen" preparing food and other items for the military, explaining that they should "forego unusual profits." Prior to World War I, America had industrialized and embraced capitalism and individualism, which could logically have led to maximizing profit in the midst of high demand for goods. Thus, Source 2 reflects a shift in ideals away from traditional capitalism and toward patriotism and national mobilization; **(A)** is correct and (B) is incorrect. While isolationism was a key ideal before World War I, individualism was as well. These two ideals were replaced by patriotism and national mobilization; (C) is incorrect. (D) is incorrect because the motivation to mobilize as a nation reduced the focus on capitalism.

55. C

During World War I, civilians were crucial to the war effort, as industrial workers labored to provide armies with supplies. With so many men on the front lines, many women entered the workforce, and everyone was expected to cut back on luxuries. Thus, **(C)** is correct. (A) and (B) are incorrect because other countries, such as Great Britain, France, and Germany, were heavily involved in war efforts and experienced great losses as a result of World War I. All countries involved engaged in total war efforts that linked the government, soldiers, and citizens in unprecedented ways. (D) is incorrect because the United States was not the only nation to create propaganda to unite its citizens during World War I.

Section I, Part B

1. A successful short-answer response accomplishes all three tasks set forth by the prompt. Each part of the prompt is worth 1 point, for a total of 3 possible points.

(a) To earn the point, the response must explain how a specific fact supports the author's claim that the British Empire created strong links among many modern nations. Examples include the use of the English language as a global business language, the popularity of parliamentary forms of government resulting from the mimicking of British government structure by former colonies (such as Canada, India, and Australia), and the use of capitalist economic systems and free trade in many former colonies.

(b) To earn the point, the response must explain a link between countries that is present despite British rule. Examples include the prevalence of Islam in South and Southeast Asia despite British attempts at conversion; regional organizations, such as the African Union and ASEAN, which were formed to promote cooperation in the period after British rule; and the persistence of local languages despite the use of English.

(c) To earn the point, the response must explain why much of history was Eurocentric. One example is the idea that Europeans were often those who studied history and dominated the field, so they promoted their own culture. Another example is the economic and political control by European powers until relatively recent history, which created instability among non-Europeans and reinforced the idea that Europeans were superior.

2. A successful short-answer response accomplishes all three tasks set forth by the prompt. Each part of the prompt is worth 1 point, for a total of 3 possible points.

(a) To earn this point, the response must show an understanding of the reasons for expansion of trade that led to the flourishing of trading cities and caravanserai, which served as rest stops for merchant caravans. For example, trade routes contributed to a greater volume of trade by connecting larger empires and more people. Also, the expansion of the Mongol Empire facilitated trade by protecting trade routes and drawing conquered peoples into a larger empire-wide economy.

(b) To earn this point, the response must identify a pattern of trade in this era. For example, throughout this period, the goods traded by merchants who utilized the caravanserai were mainly luxury items, such as silk, porcelain, ivory, and spices that were in demand in Afro-Eurasia. This was due to the expense of trading across long distances.

(c) To earn this point, the response must explain the increase in trade that resulted from Mongol expansion. For example, the Mongols controlled the Silk Road trading networks, which made it safer for merchants to travel longer distances and led to the thriving of powerful cities along trade routes. In addition, the Mongols had a courier system that improved communication.

3. A successful short-answer response accomplishes all three tasks set forth by the prompt. Each part of the prompt is worth 1 point, for a total of 3 possible points.

(a) To earn this point, the response must explain how agricultural production expanded in volume, providing food surpluses and larger-scale production of cash crops.

(b) To earn this point, the response must explain how new technologies contributed to increased agricultural production, such as terrace farming by the Inca, the three-yield system in Europe, the draining of swamps in China, or the cultivation of *chinampas* by the Aztecs (Mexica).

(c) To earn this point, the response must identify a specific continuity. One example is the focus on the production of food crops rather than cash crops to support a growing population. Another example is agricultural labor consisting of a variety of free peasants and coerced labor.

4. A successful short-answer response accomplishes all three tasks set forth by the prompt. Each part of the prompt is worth 1 point, for a total of 3 possible points.

(a) To earn this point, the response must provide a specific idea about how Enlightenment ideas caused changes in government. Examples could include: the questioning of divine right and absolutism and the support for more representative governments rather than the rule of a single monarch; the idea that governments should protect rights rather than oppress subjects; the questioning of the role of religion in public life and advocating for the separation of religion and government; the idea that natural rights lead to the desire for greater participation in government; and the idea that the people have the right to overthrow oppressive governments, such as France's monarchy, which led to the French Revolution.

(b) To earn this point, the response must explain continuity in political theory. An example could include continued views of gender roles that led to the idea that women should not participate in government, reflected in the fact that women did not gain the right to vote until the early twentieth century. Another example could explain how the continued dominance of elites in government led to the lack of universal male suffrage until the end of the period.

(c) To earn this point, the response must explain how Enlightenment ideas spread outside Europe and brought change to other regions. Examples could include: anti-colonial movements that used Enlightenment ideas of representative government, natural rights, and liberty to call for independence from European control, such as those in Africa, India, or Latin America; the push for the extension of rights in Latin American and African societies ruled by oppressive regimes after independence; and the extension of rights to groups such as women, ethnic minorities, and religious minorities.

Section II

1. *Evaluate the factors that enabled Eurasian rulers to consolidate power in the period 1450–1750.*

Category	Scoring Criteria	Notes
Thesis/Claim (0–1 points)	Historically defensible thesis/claim with a logical line of reasoning. The response must make a thesis or claim without restating the prompt itself. The thesis must consist of one or more sentences located in one place, either in the introduction or the conclusion.	This question is assessing the historical reasoning skill of causation. The thesis should make a claim about two to three main factors that led to increased control by rulers during this time. Examples: The use of religion to justify one's rule; steps taken to limit corruption and control bureaucrats; limiting the power of landowning elites.
Contextualization (0–1 points)	Broader historical context related to the prompt. The response must connect the topic to historical developments, events, or processes; these can occur before, during, or after the time frame of the prompt itself.	Contextualization for this prompt should explain, not merely mention, broader factors that contributed to increased control by rulers. Examples: The rise of European maritime empires due to exploration and increased participation in global trade; the rise of Asian land empires due to the use of gunpowder weapons and the conquering of weak empires of previously decentralized regions.
Evidence (0–3 points)	Use of evidence to support the thesis. The response must utilize the content from at least *three* documents to address the *topic* of the prompt. (1 point) OR The response must use at least *six* documents to support an *argument* based on the prompt. (2 points)	Evidence from the documents must be paraphrased, not merely quoted. Examples: Documents 4 and 7 to support rulers' use of religion to justify one's rule; document 3 to support rulers' use of the law and enforcement of religious conformity; document 5 to support rulers' limiting corruption and controlling bureaucrats; documents 1, 2, and 6 to support rulers limiting the power of elites.
	The response must use at least *one* additional piece of historical evidence, beyond what is found in the documents, to support an argument. This additional evidence must be different from what was used for contextualization. (1 point)	Examples: The use of the Mandate of Heaven in China when discussing the use of religion to legitimize one's rule; the use of the civil service exam by Chinese emperors to limit the influence of landowning families.

Category	Scoring Criteria	Notes
Analysis and Reasoning (0–2 points)	Complexity of understanding and reasoning. The response must explain, for at least *three* of the documents, how or why the document's purpose, historical basis, point of view, and/or audience are relevant to an argument. (1 point)	Factors' relevance to the argument about rulers consolidating power should be explained, not just identified. Example: The role of audience in document 7, in which King James I is addressing Parliament, the law-making body of his kingdom; he is likely trying to claim he has to answer only to God in order to persuade Parliament that he is not subject to its laws.
	The response must show a complex understanding of the content of the prompt, using evidence to support, qualify, or modify an argument about the prompt. (1 point)	A complex understanding should be incorporated into the overall argument about rulers consolidating power. Examples: An examination of distinctions among different factors, such as the reasons for limiting corruption; an analysis of both the reasons for and the effects of these policies; a comparison with rulers' policies in another time period.

2. *In the period 1200–1450, new states and empires demonstrated continuity, innovation, and diversity as they developed in various regions such as western Africa, the Middle East, and East Asia.*

   Develop an argument that evaluates how one or more new states or empires administered their territory in this time period.

Category	Scoring Criteria	Notes
Thesis/Claim (0–1 points)	Historically defensible thesis/claim with a logical line of reasoning. The response must make a thesis or claim without restating the prompt itself. The thesis must consist of one or more sentences located in one place, either in the introduction or the conclusion.	This question assesses the skill of causation. A strong thesis should make a claim about at least two ways one or more states governed in this period. For this question, focusing on one empire may be best, or focusing on two that are similar. Example: "In the period from 1200 to 1450, the Yuan and Ming Dynasties built upon the administration of previous dynasties but implemented new ideas in national integration and more extensive foreign trade."
Contextualization (0–1 points)	Broader historical context related to the prompt. The response must connect the topic to historical developments, events, or processes; these can occur before, during, or after the time frame of the prompt itself.	Contextualization for this prompt should explain, not merely mention, broader factors relevant to how states administered their territories. Examples: A description of the decline of civilizations that preceded the Yuan and Ming, such as the Tang and Song Dynasties; an explanation of the reasons for the resurgence of the later dynasties.

(continued)

Category	Scoring Criteria	Notes
Evidence (0–2 points)	Use of evidence to support the thesis. The response identifies specific examples *relevant to the topic* of the prompt. (1 point) OR The response uses specific examples to *support an argument* about the prompt. (2 points)	Evidence must be paraphrased, not merely quoted. To earn 2 points, the evidence must be used to support an argument about how states administered their territories. Examples: The bureaucratic structure of the Han Dynasty, the Yuan Dynasty's unification of the entire territory of China.
Analysis and Reasoning (0–2 points)	Complexity of understanding and reasoning. The response shows historical reasoning to make an argument about the prompt. (1 point) OR The response demonstrates complex understanding, using evidence to support, qualify, or modify an argument about the prompt. (2 points)	Comparison, causation, or continuity and change over time should be incorporated into the overall argument about how states administered their territories. Example: An explanation of how the Yuan and Ming Dynasties borrowed ideas from previous governments to establish their rule (continuity and change). OR A complex understanding should be incorporated into the overall argument about how states administered their territories. Examples: An explanation of how the Yuan and Ming both borrowed from previous governments *and* developed new policies; an examination of multiple variables that impacted governance of the Yuan and Ming Dynasties, such as the expansion of foreign trade and interaction, scientific developments such as the first accurate calendar, and the construction of the majority of the Great Wall of China.

3. *In the period 1450–1750, new connections between the Eastern and Western Hemispheres resulted in the Columbian Exchange.*

Develop an argument that evaluates how the Columbian Exchange changed one or more regions in this time period.

Category	Scoring Criteria	Notes
Thesis/Claim (0–1 points)	Historically defensible thesis/claim with a logical line of reasoning. The response must make a thesis or claim without restating the prompt itself. The thesis must consist of one or more sentences located in one place, either in the introduction or the conclusion.	This question assesses the skill of change and continuity over time. A strong thesis should make a claim about at least two major changes that occurred in one or more regions. Example: "The Columbian Exchange positively impacted the Americas and Europe by introducing new crops and livestock, but it negatively impacted American populations by introducing disease and new exploitative labor systems."
Contextualization (0–1 points)	Broader historical context related to the prompt. The response must connect the topic to historical developments, events, or processes; these can occur before, during, or after the time frame of the prompt itself.	Contextualization for this prompt should explain, not merely mention, broader factors relevant to changes brought by the Columbian Exchange. Examples: A description of European motivations for exploration, such as the invention of new navigational tools and access to technologies gained from Arab merchants through the Crusades, the sponsorship of voyages of exploration by European powers due to the desire to profit from Asian trade, and the desire to circumvent the Ottomans to by finding a direct route to Asia.
Evidence (0–2 points)	Use of evidence to support the thesis. The response identifies specific examples *relevant to the topic* of the prompt. (1 point) OR The response uses specific examples to *support an argument* about the prompt. (2 points)	Evidence must be paraphrased, not merely quoted. To earn 2 points, the evidence must be used to support an argument about changes brought by the Columbian Exchange. Examples: Changes in the Americas include the introduction of pathogens; the introduction of European animals, such as horses, pigs, and cattle, that led to new lifestyles and diets; the introduction of crops such as sugarcane that led to the clearing of land for plantations and soil depletion due to the continued cultivation of one crop in the same area (monoculture); the introduction of African slaves as a result of the demand for labor on plantations. Changes in Europe include the introduction of new crops from the Americas, such as beans and potatoes, that led to more nutritious diets and growing populations; the introduction of corn to feed livestock.

(continued)

Category	Scoring Criteria	Notes
Analysis and Reasoning (0–2 points)	Complexity of understanding and reasoning. The response shows historical reasoning to make an argument about the prompt. (1 point) OR The response demonstrates complex understanding, using evidence to support, qualify, or modify an argument about the prompt. (2 points)	Comparison, causation, or continuity and change over time should be incorporated into the overall argument about changes brought by the Columbian Exchange. Examples: A detailed explanation of changes such as those listed above (continuity and change); an explanation that new pathogens were particularity fatal to populations native to the Americas due to lack of immunity and the sometimes purposeful spread of disease by colonists (causation). OR A complex understanding should be incorporated into the overall argument about changes brought by the Columbian Exchange. Examples: A description of both changes *and* continuities in the Americas, such as the continued cultivation of traditional crops, and in Europe, such as the continued importance of wheat in diets despite the introduction of new crops; an explanation of both causes *and* effects of new pathogens on native populations, such as the devastation of entire tribes and the facilitation of continued European conquest; an analysis of multiple perspectives on the Columbian Exchange based on the positive economic results for Europeans but the exploitative conditions for native populations and Africans, who were imported as slaves.

4. *In the period 1750–1900, increasing discontent with imperial rule propelled reformist and revolutionary movements around the world.*

   Develop an argument that evaluates the similarities of two reformist and/or revolutionary movements in this time period.

Category	Scoring Criteria	Notes
Thesis/Claim (0–1 points)	Historically defensible thesis/claim with a logical line of reasoning. The response must make a thesis or claim without restating the prompt itself. The thesis must consist of one or more sentences located in one place, either in the introduction or the conclusion.	This essay is assessing the skill of comparison. An acceptable thesis will address at least two specific similarities in the causes, events, or results of the movements. Examples: Comparing any two revolutions of the time period: the French Revolution against absolute monarchy, the American Revolution against British colonial rule, the Haitian Revolution against French rule, or the Latin American revolutions against Spanish rule. Reform movements include the abolitionist and feminist movements.

Category	Scoring Criteria	Notes
Contextual-ization (0–1 points)	Broader historical context related to the prompt. The response must connect the topic to historical developments, events, or processes; these can occur before, during, or after the time frame of the prompt itself.	Contextualization for this prompt should explain, not merely mention, broader factors relevant to the two movements discussed. Examples: Depending on the movements compared, could include a discussion of the rise of Enlightenment ideas in response to the consolidation of power by European absolute monarchs, the economic situation that led to control of colonies in the Americas, or the role of the Seven Years' War in the American and French Revolutions.
Evidence (0–2 points)	Use of evidence to support the thesis. The response identifies specific examples *relevant to the topic* of the prompt. (1 point) OR The response uses specific examples to *support an argument* about the prompt. (2 points)	Evidence must be paraphrased, not merely quoted. To earn 2 points, the evidence must be used to support an argument about the similarities between the movements. Examples: A comparison of the role of Enlightenment ideas in the American and French revolutions; the similar constitutional governments created after revolutions.
Analysis and Reasoning (0–2 points)	Complexity of understanding and reasoning. The response shows historical reasoning to make an argument about the prompt. (1 point) OR The response demonstrates complex understanding, using evidence to support, qualify, or modify an argument about the prompt. (2 points)	Comparison, causation, or continuity and change over time should be incorporated into the overall argument about the similarities between the movements. Examples: A description of the changes sought by feminist and abolitionist movements (continuity and change); an explanation of causes of the Haitian and Latin American independence movements (causation). OR A complex understanding should be incorporated into the overall argument about the similarities between the movements. Examples: A description of the changes sought *and* the continuities of traditional thinking by feminist and abolitionist movements; an explanation of causes *and* results of the Haitian and Latin American independence movements; a discussion of multiple perspectives of revolutions or reform movements.

Practice Exam 2

Practice Exam 2 Answer Grid

1. Ⓐ Ⓑ Ⓒ Ⓓ	15. Ⓐ Ⓑ Ⓒ Ⓓ	29. Ⓐ Ⓑ Ⓒ Ⓓ	43. Ⓐ Ⓑ Ⓒ Ⓓ
2. Ⓐ Ⓑ Ⓒ Ⓓ	16. Ⓐ Ⓑ Ⓒ Ⓓ	30. Ⓐ Ⓑ Ⓒ Ⓓ	44. Ⓐ Ⓑ Ⓒ Ⓓ
3. Ⓐ Ⓑ Ⓒ Ⓓ	17. Ⓐ Ⓑ Ⓒ Ⓓ	31. Ⓐ Ⓑ Ⓒ Ⓓ	45. Ⓐ Ⓑ Ⓒ Ⓓ
4. Ⓐ Ⓑ Ⓒ Ⓓ	18. Ⓐ Ⓑ Ⓒ Ⓓ	32. Ⓐ Ⓑ Ⓒ Ⓓ	46. Ⓐ Ⓑ Ⓒ Ⓓ
5. Ⓐ Ⓑ Ⓒ Ⓓ	19. Ⓐ Ⓑ Ⓒ Ⓓ	33. Ⓐ Ⓑ Ⓒ Ⓓ	47. Ⓐ Ⓑ Ⓒ Ⓓ
6. Ⓐ Ⓑ Ⓒ Ⓓ	20. Ⓐ Ⓑ Ⓒ Ⓓ	34. Ⓐ Ⓑ Ⓒ Ⓓ	48. Ⓐ Ⓑ Ⓒ Ⓓ
7. Ⓐ Ⓑ Ⓒ Ⓓ	21. Ⓐ Ⓑ Ⓒ Ⓓ	35. Ⓐ Ⓑ Ⓒ Ⓓ	49. Ⓐ Ⓑ Ⓒ Ⓓ
8. Ⓐ Ⓑ Ⓒ Ⓓ	22. Ⓐ Ⓑ Ⓒ Ⓓ	36. Ⓐ Ⓑ Ⓒ Ⓓ	50. Ⓐ Ⓑ Ⓒ Ⓓ
9. Ⓐ Ⓑ Ⓒ Ⓓ	23. Ⓐ Ⓑ Ⓒ Ⓓ	37. Ⓐ Ⓑ Ⓒ Ⓓ	51. Ⓐ Ⓑ Ⓒ Ⓓ
10. Ⓐ Ⓑ Ⓒ Ⓓ	24. Ⓐ Ⓑ Ⓒ Ⓓ	38. Ⓐ Ⓑ Ⓒ Ⓓ	52. Ⓐ Ⓑ Ⓒ Ⓓ
11. Ⓐ Ⓑ Ⓒ Ⓓ	25. Ⓐ Ⓑ Ⓒ Ⓓ	39. Ⓐ Ⓑ Ⓒ Ⓓ	53. Ⓐ Ⓑ Ⓒ Ⓓ
12. Ⓐ Ⓑ Ⓒ Ⓓ	26. Ⓐ Ⓑ Ⓒ Ⓓ	40. Ⓐ Ⓑ Ⓒ Ⓓ	54. Ⓐ Ⓑ Ⓒ Ⓓ
13. Ⓐ Ⓑ Ⓒ Ⓓ	27. Ⓐ Ⓑ Ⓒ Ⓓ	41. Ⓐ Ⓑ Ⓒ Ⓓ	55. Ⓐ Ⓑ Ⓒ Ⓓ
14. Ⓐ Ⓑ Ⓒ Ⓓ	28. Ⓐ Ⓑ Ⓒ Ⓓ	42. Ⓐ Ⓑ Ⓒ Ⓓ	

SECTION I, PART A

Time—55 minutes

55 Questions

Directions: Section I, Part A of this exam contains 55 multiple-choice questions, organized into sets with corresponding historical sources. Each of the questions or incomplete statements is followed by four suggested answers or completions. Using both the provided sources and your own historical knowledge, select the best answer choice.

Questions 1–3 refer to the following two images.

Image 1

ASTROLABE OF ʿUMAR IBN YUSUF, YEMENI PRINCE, 1291

GO ON TO THE NEXT PAGE

Image 2

"PREPARING MEDICINE FROM HONEY," FROM AN ARABIC TRANSLATION OF A FIRST-CENTURY C.E. GREEK MEDICAL ENCYCLOPEDIA, 1224

GO ON TO THE NEXT PAGE

1. The details depicted in <u>Image 1</u> best reflect which of the following characteristics of Islamic scholars in the period circa 1200 to 1450?

   (A) Their reliance on the earlier works of astronomers Copernicus and Galileo

   (B) Their belief that observation and record-keeping aid scientific investigation

   (C) Their development of intellectual fields such as mathematics and navigation

   (D) Their interest in spreading the Islamic faith throughout Southeast Asia

2. <u>Image 2</u> best illustrates which of the following long-term continuities in world history?

   (A) The spread of Islamic cultural and religious traditions throughout Europe and Asia

   (B) The development of medical science to enable humans to live healthier lives

   (C) The influence of global economic factors on the spread of medical knowledge

   (D) The interactions of Muslims and Christians in Europe and Asia

3. The two images demonstrate which of the following regarding the history of technological and cultural transfers in the period 1200 to 1450?

   (A) The origins of Islam and how it spread as a result of expanding exchange networks

   (B) The transfer of science and technological innovation from Western Europe to the rest of the world

   (C) The advancement of astronomy, science, and medicine in China and throughout East Asia

   (D) The diffusion of medical and scientific knowledge from the Islamic world to Western Europe

GO ON TO THE NEXT PAGE

Questions 4–6 refer to the passage below.

"I say, then, that the years [of the era] of the fruitful Incarnation of the Son of God had attained to the number of one thousand three hundred and forty-eight, when into the notable city of Florence, fair over every other of Italy, there came the death-dealing pestilence, which, through the operation of the heavenly bodies or of our own iniquitous dealings, being sent down upon us mortals by God . . . [It] had its origin some years before in the East, whence, after destroying an innumerable multitude of living beings, it had propagated itself without respite from place to place, and so calamitously, had spread into the West."

Giovanni Boccaccio, *Decameron*, 1353

4. Which of the following best explains the overall demographic trend that resulted from the event described in the passage?

   (A) Mortality rates increased due to the forced migrations of people from the East.

   (B) Invasions by peoples from Asia into Italy led to a population decline.

   (C) The unintentional spread of disease by European colonists to the Americas devastated native populations.

   (D) The diffusion of disease resulted in massive population changes in Europe.

5. Which of the following is most clearly reflected in Boccaccio's views as expressed in the passage?

   (A) Catholicism

   (B) Nationalism

   (C) Secularism

   (D) Protestantism

6. The passage is best understood in the context of which of the following?

   (A) How religious traditions can be transformed as a result of epidemic disease

   (B) How trade across extensive exchange networks can affect different types of societies

   (C) How environmental and geographical factors have influenced the dissolution of states

   (D) How travel and trade networks developed in Europe and Asia

GO ON TO THE NEXT PAGE

Questions 7–9 refer to the following two sources.

<u>Source 1</u>

MAP OF THE LANDHOLDINGS OF THE DAIMYO, CIRCA 1570

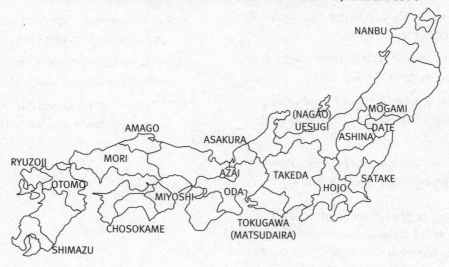

<u>Source 2</u>

SOCIAL HIERARCHY DURING THE TOKUGAWA SHOGUNATE, 1600–1867

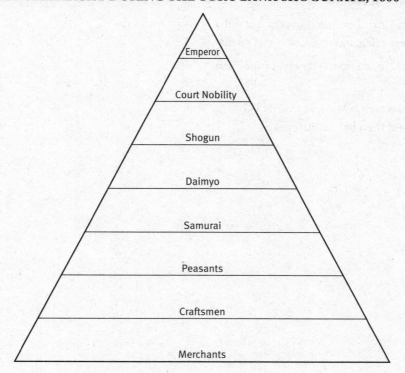

GO ON TO THE NEXT PAGE

7. Based on the map in <u>Source 1</u> and your knowledge of world history, which of the following could best be inferred about sixteenth-century Japan?

    (A) Japan was politically fragmented under the authority of feudal lords.

    (B) Japan's emperor evolved from a figurehead role to a dictatorial role.

    (C) Japan was governed under a policy of isolationism, closing off most trade with Europe.

    (D) Japanese clans were able to unify Japan through a century-long era of peace.

8. Based on <u>Source 2</u>, a historian interested in world cultures of the seventeenth and eighteen centuries would most reasonably conclude that

    (A) the Japanese emperor who was both the figurehead and military leader commanded the shogun and *daimyo*

    (B) the samurai lost their previous respectability and were relegated to a low social status

    (C) the samurai made up the largest proportion of society

    (D) merchants were viewed less favorably by the Japanese than by the Europeans

9. Taken together, the images best illustrate which of the following?

    (A) The way in which the power of political elites can fluctuate over time

    (B) The economic dependence of lower social classes on the ruling class

    (C) The widening of economic opportunities due to ending isolationism

    (D) The way in which a stable political system can challenge social hierarchies

GO ON TO THE NEXT PAGE

Questions 10–13 refer to the passage below.

"Some years ago, as Your Serene Highness well knows, I discovered in the heavens many things that had not been seen before our own age. The novelty of these things, as well as some consequences which followed from them in contradiction to the physical notions commonly held among academic philosophers, stirred up against me no small number of professors—as if I had placed these things in the sky with my own hands in order to upset nature and overturn the sciences. They seemed to forget that the increase of known truths stimulates the investigation, establishment, and growth of the arts; not their diminution or destruction.

Persisting in their original resolve to destroy me, . . . these men are aware of my views in astronomy and philosophy. They know that as to the arrangement of the parts of the universe, I hold the sun to be situated motionless in the center of the revolution of the celestial orbs while the earth revolves about the sun. They know also that I support this position not only by refuting the arguments of Ptolemy and Aristotle, but by producing many counter-arguments . . . they have endeavored to spread the opinion that such propositions in general are contrary to the Bible and are consequently heretical."

Galileo Galilei, letter to Grand Duchess Christina, 1615

10. The discoveries such as those described in the passage were most directly facilitated by which of the following developments in Europe?

   (A) The emergence of large-scale industrial economies

   (B) The break with the Catholic Church during the Protestant Reformation

   (C) The decline of significant bouts of epidemic disease

   (D) The diffusion of Greco-Islamic science knowledge

11. Based the passage and your understanding of world history, those who opposed Galileo's views would most likely have advocated for an approach to science that reflected

   (A) a reconciliation between the teachings of the Church and the teachings of classical scholars

   (B) an acceptance that the sun is a motionless celestial orb around which the Earth revolves

   (C) the Church's counterarguments to the work of Ptolemy and Aristotle

   (D) an observation-based inquiry method that relied on collecting, organizing, and measuring data

GO ON TO THE NEXT PAGE

12. Which of the following best characterizes the Roman Catholic Church's view of Galileo's work?

   (A) Fear that new scientific understanding would stimulate a renewed interest in classical learning

   (B) Concern that most devout Catholics would stop accepting the Church's interpretation of the Bible

   (C) Worry that newly formed Protestant churches would embrace Galileo's scientific discoveries

   (D) Resistance to any notion that would potentially undermine Church teachings

13. The revelations that Galileo says "stirred up against me no small number of professors" can best be understood in the context of which of the following?

   (A) An era in which scientific understanding was advanced primarily through argument and counterargument

   (B) A departure from some of the previous Greco-Roman classical teachings

   (C) The gradual acceptance of the views of Ptolemy and Aristotle by Church leadership

   (D) The Church's reluctance to accept the geocentric theory

GO ON TO THE NEXT PAGE

Questions 14–17 refer to the passage below.

"Thus the barbarians from beyond the seas, though their countries are truly distant, have come to audience bearing precious objects and presents.

The Emperor, approving of their loyalty and sincerity, has ordered us [Zheng] He and others at the head of several tens of thousands of officers and flag-troops to [use] more than one hundred large ships to go and confer presents on them in order to make manifest the transforming power of the imperial virtue and to treat distant people with kindness."

Zheng He, Fujian province temple inscription, 1431

14. Based on the passage, the voyages of Zheng He illustrate which of the following continuities in world history?

    (A) How environmental factors can shape transportation methods

    (B) How diverse technology can affect maritime activity

    (C) How maritime and trade activity can encourage cultural transfers

    (D) How interregional contact and conflict can discourage exchange

15. The events described in the passage represent a reaction most directly against which of the following beliefs?

    (A) Capitalism

    (B) Colonialism

    (C) Imperialism

    (D) Isolationism

16. Which of the following best explains why the Ming Dynasty halted the voyages of Zheng He?

    (A) The Chinese had a difficult time competing with European technology.

    (B) The Chinese had an unfavorable balance of trade with foreign powers.

    (C) The voyages were expensive and the world beyond China was deemed of little value.

    (D) Many of Zheng He's ships had been greatly damaged during his earlier expeditions.

17. The Emperor's order in the second paragraph can be best understood in context of which of the following?

    (A) State policies contributing to the development of exchange networks

    (B) Existing trade routes along the Silk Road through Central Asia to Europe enabling China to flourish

    (C) State policies to abandon overland trade routes from China to Europe

    (D) Internal political factors influencing state expansion

GO ON TO THE NEXT PAGE

Questions 18–20 refer to the map below.

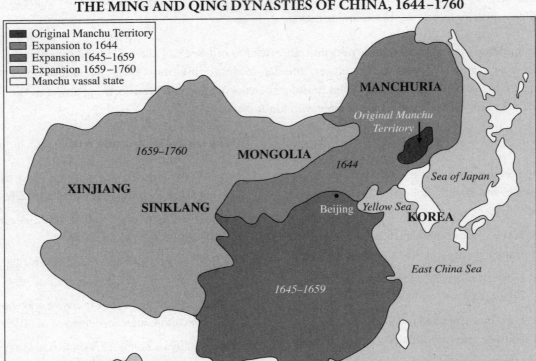

THE MING AND QING DYNASTIES OF CHINA, 1644–1760

Original Manchu Territory
Expansion to 1644
Expansion 1645–1659
Expansion 1659–1760
Manchu vassal state

1659–1760

MANCHURIA

Original Manchu Territory

MONGOLIA

1644

XINJIANG

Sea of Japan

SINKLANG

Beijing *Yellow Sea*

KOREA

East China Sea

1645–1659

SIAM

18. China's control of Korea during the time period mentioned in the map can most likely be attributed to which of the following?

   (A) China's goal to regain original Manchu territory that was lost prior to 1644

   (B) China's desire to set up a trading post empire in Korea

   (C) China's active resistance of the spread of Islam in East Asia

   (D) China's efforts to establish tributary relationships with neighboring states

19. Based on the map, which of the following factors contributed most strongly to the downfall of the Ming Dynasty and transition to rule by the Qing Dynasty, founded by the Manchus, in the seventeenth century?

   (A) The Ming's inability to slow Islam's expansion in Central Asia

   (B) The lack of modern ships to compete for trade throughout the Indian Ocean region

   (C) The lack of a taxation system to fund its military

   (D) The growing military aggression of northern people

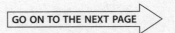

GO ON TO THE NEXT PAGE

20. Which of the following represents a similarity in the way the Mongol Empire and the Man-chu Empire interacted with the Chinese?

    (A) Each encouraged intermarriage with ethnic Han Chinese

    (B) Each sought to preserve its own ethnic and cultural identity

    (C) Each forced the ethnic Han Chinese to learn its language

    (D) Each adopted the Confucian civil service examination system

GO ON TO THE NEXT PAGE

Questions 21–23 refer to the map below.

SLAVE TRADE OUT OF AFRICA

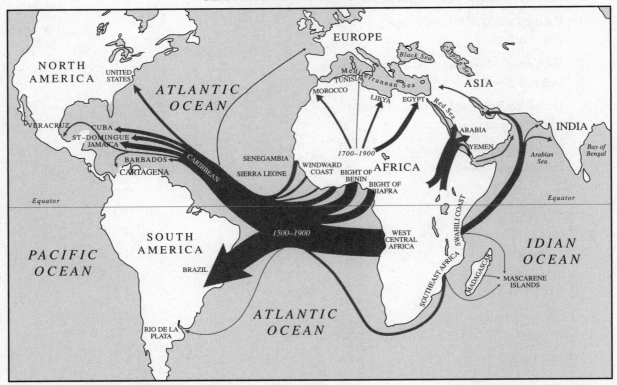

21. Based on the map and your knowledge of world history, the forced migration of enslaved Africans to the Americas in the seventeenth and eighteenth centuries resulted in

    (A) a higher number of enslaved Africans going to the United States than to South America

    (B) a decline in the slave trade to Western Asia and the Mediterranean

    (C) lower agricultural yields in the Caribbean and Latin America

    (D) altered male-to-female ratios in sub-Saharan Africa

22. Based on the map, which of the following could best be inferred about the African slave trade?

    (A) It was under the direct political control of Europe.

    (B) The demand for slaves from eastern Africa was greater than for slaves from western Africa.

    (C) It produced the primary source of labor in Europe.

    (D) Both Christian and Islamic states demanded slaves.

GO ON TO THE NEXT PAGE

23. More slaves were transported to Brazil than to any other country because

    (A) it was the shortest sea voyage from west central Africa to a large area of cultivable land

    (B) North and Central America had relatively few slave-owning European colonies

    (C) Portugal's laws allowed slavery with no interference by royal or church authorities

    (D) slaves needed to be replaced more often due to high mortality rates from disease and the labor-intensive sugar production process

GO ON TO THE NEXT PAGE

Questions 24–27 refer to the passage below.

"We stayed one night in this island [Mombasa], and then pursued our journey to Kulwa [Kilwa], which is a large town on the coast. The majority of its inhabitants are Zanj, jet-black in colour, and with tattoo marks on their faces. I was told by a merchant that the town of Sufala lies a fortnight's journey [south] from Kulwa [Kilwa] and that gold dust is brought to Sufala from Yufi in the country of the Limis, which is a month's journey distant from it. Kulwa [Kilwa] is a very fine and substantially built town, and all its buildings are of wood. Its inhabitants are constantly engaged in military expeditions, for their country is contiguous to the heathen Zanj.

The sultan at the time of my visit was Abu'l-Muzaffar Hasan, who was noted for his gifts and generosity. He used to devote the fifth part of the booty made on his expeditions to pious and charitable purposes, as is prescribed in the Koran, and I have seen him give the clothes off his back to a mendicant who asked him for them. When this liberal and virtuous sultan died, he was succeeded by his brother Dawud, who was at the opposite pole from him in this respect. Whenever a petitioner came to him, he would say, 'He who gave is dead, and left nothing behind him to be given.' Visitors would stay at his court for months on end, and finally he would make them some small gift, so that at last people gave up going to his gate."

Ibn Battuta, describing his visit to port city of Kilwa in Eastern Africa, *Travels in Asia and Africa*, circa 1330

24. All of the following statements are factually accurate. Which best explains the actions of Sultan Abu'l-Muzaffar Hasan described in the <u>second paragraph</u>?

   (A) One of the Five Pillars of Islam is to pray five times a day facing Mecca.

   (B) According to the Quran, a Muslim should fast during the holy month of Ramadan.

   (C) In the Islamic faith, it is a duty to give alms or charity to the poor.

   (D) The Quran provides guidance on inheritance.

25. Which of the following can be inferred about the East African society described in the <u>first paragraph</u> of the passage?

   (A) Islam failed to spread to East African cities along trading networks.

   (B) The majority of Zanj people from the neighboring country converted to Islam.

   (C) English was a commonly spoken language in eastern Africa.

   (D) Some merchants prospered through trade and the gold exchange.

GO ON TO THE NEXT PAGE

26. Which of the following describes a significant transformation that occurred in Kilwa and in other East African locations on the Indian Ocean in the <u>sixteenth century</u>?

   (A) The Swahili mixture of African and Arabian culture weakened the region's cultural unity and caused an economic collapse.

   (B) Portuguese traders used military force to take control of East Africa in order to advance their trade with the East.

   (C) Trade along the Indian Ocean routes diminished after the Silk Road was created, leading to economic ruin.

   (D) Natural disasters such as volcanic eruptions and drought severely diminished East Africa's population.

27. Which of the following is true of trade in Kilwa as well as throughout the Indian Ocean region during the period circa 1200 to 1450?

   (A) Europeans played a dominant role as ship builders and maritime traders.

   (B) Due to nomadic invasions from groups in Central Asia, economic activity slowed considerably.

   (C) Chinese merchants were the only major participants from Asia in the trade.

   (D) Trade flourished with a mix of African, South Asian, and Middle Eastern merchants.

GO ON TO THE NEXT PAGE

Questions 28–30 refer to the passage below.

"Legislatures and other agencies of government directly representative of the people did not exist in Spanish or Portuguese America. The Spanish cabildo, or town council, however, afforded an opportunity for the expression of the popular will and often proved intractable. Its membership was appointive, elective, hereditary, and even purchasable, but the form did not affect the substance. The Spanish Americans had an instinct for politics. 'Here all men govern,' declared one of the viceroys; 'the people have more part in political discussions than in any other provinces in the world; a council of war sits in every house.'

The movement which led eventually to the emancipation of the colonies differed from the local uprisings which had occurred in various parts of South America during the eighteenth century. Either the arbitrary conduct of individual governors or excessive taxation had caused the earlier revolts. To the final revolution foreign nations and foreign ideas gave the necessary impulse. A few members of the intellectual class had read in secret the writings of French and English philosophers."

William R. Shepherd, *Hispanic Nations of the New World*, 1919

28. The reference in the <u>first paragraph</u> to the hereditary nature of membership in the cabildos is best understood in the context of which of the following?

    (A) The development of hierarchical social structures with new political elites

    (B) The monarchical rule that predominated in Europe in the fifteenth through eighteenth centuries

    (C) The eventual decline of Spanish dominance among European nations in overseas colonial empires

    (D) The merit-based economic systems that predominated in other European colonial holdings

29. In the <u>second paragraph</u>, Shepherd is claiming that the "final revolution" was influenced by ideas from which of the following?

    (A) Marxism

    (B) The Enlightenment

    (C) Mercantilism

    (D) Industrial capitalism

30. A present-day historian would most likely link the historical interpretation advanced in the passage to which of the following early twentieth-century developments in Latin America?

    (A) Attempts to make Latin American countries successful in the world economy by industrializing

    (B) The interruption of continued colonial independence uprisings due to World War I

    (C) Resistance movements against neocolonialist economic and political policies

    (D) Export-led economic growth dependent on transportation and communication advances originating in Europe and North America

GO ON TO THE NEXT PAGE

Questions 31–34 refer to the following two tables.

Table 1

RAW COTTON CONSUMPTION IN GREAT BRITAIN, SELECTED YEARS

Year	Cotton in Millions of Pounds
1787	22
1800	52
1850	588

Table 2

COKE IRON PRODUCTION IN GREAT BRITAIN, SELECTED YEARS

Year	Coke Iron Produced in Tons
1720	400
1750	2,500
1788	54,000
1806	250,000

31. The two tables serve best as evidence for which of the following in the eighteenth and nineteenth centuries?

    (A) The dominance of Great Britain as an exporter

    (B) The growth of industrial production

    (C) The concentration of populations in urban areas

    (D) The high demand for iron for military purposes

32. Which of the following was a result of the trend illustrated by the tables?

    (A) The decrease in demand for agricultural products

    (B) The typical family unit ceasing to serve as the center of economic production

    (C) The improvement of sanitation in urban worker neighborhoods over that in agricultural dwellings

    (D) The decline of the middle class that had been developing during the period of mercantilism

GO ON TO THE NEXT PAGE

33. Which of the following was a factor that impacted Great Britain's capacity to produce coke iron during the years depicted in <u>Table 2</u>?

    (A) The development of electric-powered engines and new processes for steel production

    (B) An overuse of resources that forced agricultural workers to find jobs in factories

    (C) Britain's economy being more regulated than other countries' economies

    (D) Rivers that supplied water power and material transportation for early factories

34. Which of the following describes an impact of the trends depicted in the tables on other parts of the world?

    (A) The beginning of the transatlantic slave trade

    (B) Increased demand for commodities

    (C) A massive influx of migrants into Europe

    (D) The abolition of slavery in British colonial holdings

GO ON TO THE NEXT PAGE

Questions 35–38 refer to the passage below.

"It used to take ten days to get the twenty baskets of rubber—we were always in the forest to find the rubber vines, to go without food, and our women had to give up cultivating the fields and gardens. Then we starved. Leopards killed some of us while we were working away in the forest and others got lost or died from exposure and starvation. We begged the white man to leave us alone, saying we could get no more rubber, but the white men and their soldiers said: 'Go. You are only beasts yourselves, you are only nyama (meat).' We tried, always going further into the forest, and when we failed and our rubber was short, the soldiers came to our towns and killed us. Many were shot, some had their ears cut off; others were tied up with ropes round their necks and taken away."

Joseph Conrad, description of conditions in Congo Free State
under Belgium rule, *Heart of Darkness*, 1899

35. Which of the following historical developments is reflected in the conditions described in the passage?

   (A) The partitioning of Africa among European imperial powers

   (B) The outbreak of regional proxy wars in African territories

   (C) The attempts to redistribute land among native Africans

   (D) The raiding of Africa for plantation slave labor

36. Which of the following factors most directly enabled European actions such as those described in the passage?

   (A) The expansion of the slave trade under the Atlantic network of trade among Africa, Europe, and the Americas

   (B) Decreasing populations in Europe, which forced European nations to turn to other world regions for labor

   (C) The development of steamships, which improved the speed and navigation capabilities of European naval vessels

   (D) The weakening of the power of monarchs and land-holding aristocrats throughout Europe

37. Which of the following was an eventual outcome of the actions of European nations as reflected in the passage?

   (A) Continued competition for resources and land-holdings helped instigate World War I.

   (B) Although initially exploited, most African colonies took control over their economic resources in the early twentieth century.

   (C) The United States loosened its protectionism in Latin America, and European colonization resumed.

   (D) The economic drain created in Europe as a result of imperialism led to the Great Depression.

38. The passage reflects which of the following justifications for imperialism?

   (A) The struggle and toil required during the Industrial Revolution

   (B) The duty of European people to bring order and enlightenment to distant lands

   (C) The responsibility of men to take care of their wives and children

   (D) The guilt faced by Western civilizations for their role in creating systems of slavery

GO ON TO THE NEXT PAGE

 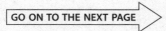

Questions 39–41 refer to the passage below.

"Our relations with socialist countries, including the allies of the Warsaw Treaty Organization, entered a difficult, critical stage. . . . Perestroika, the development of democratization, [and] glasnost, confirmed the role of the Soviet Union as the leader in the process of socialist renewal. . . .

The European socialist countries found themselves in a powerful magnetic field of the economic growth and social well-being of the Western European states. . . . The constant comparing and contrasting of the two worlds, of their ways of life, production, intellectual cultures, entered our daily life thanks to the mass media, and there is no way around it. . . .

As a consequence, in a number of socialist countries, the process of rejection of the existing political institutions and the ideological values by the societies is already underway now."

> Central Committee of the Communist Party of the Soviet Union, communication
> with Alexander Yakovlev, *Strategy of Relations with European Socialist Countries*, February 1989

39. The passage is best understood in the context of which of the following?

    (A) The use of propaganda by totalitarian regimes to influence the ideologies of their citizens

    (B) Russia's tumultuous transition from a traditional tsarist land empire to a socialist state

    (C) Governments seeking policies of economic and political liberalization at the end of the Cold War era

    (D) The emergence of influential international organizations after World War II

40. The "rejection of the existing political institutions" referenced in the passage was most likely the result of which of the following?

    (A) The prevalent economic deprivation and lack of consumer goods that resulted from the Soviet government's planned economy

    (B) The concentration of land holdings in the hands of a few wealthy Soviet communist elites

    (C) The widely unpopular moves by the Soviet government to borrow democratic principles from foreign governments

    (D) The pressure from former Soviet republics to be permitted to rejoin the Union of Soviet Socialist Republics

GO ON TO THE NEXT PAGE

41. The passage implies that the policies of *glasnost* and *perestroika* contributed to the collapse of the Soviet Union by

    (A) stabilizing the economy, allowing citizens to abandon socialist theory

    (B) exposing citizens to ethnic tensions that ultimately caused the USSR's division

    (C) allowing citizens to voice dissent and undermine the Communist Party's power

    (D) acquiescing to growing anti-communist rhetoric coming from the United States

GO ON TO THE NEXT PAGE

Questions 42–44 refer to the image below.

JAPANESE PERIOD PRINT, 1861

GO ON TO THE NEXT PAGE

42. The scene depicted in the print best illustrates which significant development in Japan in the mid-nineteenth century?

    (A) The Japanese military's first defeat of a Western power

    (B) The first wave of migration of Americans to Japan

    (C) The arrival of the first Christian missionaries in Japan

    (D) The end of isolationism and start of modernization

43. The policies begun in Japan during the Meiji Era are most similar to policies begun in the late nineteenth century in which of the following states?

    (A) The United States

    (B) China

    (C) India

    (D) Great Britain

44. The changes in Japan that are reflected in the scene in the print most directly resulted in which of the following?

    (A) Japan's socialist movements resulting in the overthrow of the emperor

    (B) A resurgence of conservatism resulting in the reinstatement of isolationism

    (C) Japan's need for raw materials resulting in imperialist expansion

    (D) A rebellion against foreign influence resulting in an international military response

GO ON TO THE NEXT PAGE

Questions 45–47 refer to the passage below.

"The peace conditions imposed upon Germany are so hard, so humiliating, that even those who have the smallest expectation of a 'peace of justice' are bound to be deeply disappointed. . . .

The financial burden is so heavy that it is no exaggeration to say that Germany is reduced to economic bondage. The Germans will have to work hard and incessantly for foreign masters, without any chance of personal gain, or any prospect of regaining liberty or economic independence. . . .

These conditions will never give peace. All Germans must feel that they wish to shake off the heavy yoke imposed by the cajoling Entente, and we fear very much that that opportunity will soon present itself. For has not the Entente recognized in the proposed so-called 'League of Nations' the evident right to conquer and possess countries for economic and imperialistic purposes? Fettered and enslaved, Germany will always remain a menace to Europe."

Dutch editorial on Treaty of Versailles, *Algemeen Handelsblad*, June 1919

45. According to the passage, the Treaty of Versailles would contribute to which of the following factors that led to World War II?

(A) International alliances

(B) Containment policies

(C) Conflicting ideologies

(D) Financial hardships

46. After the Treaty of Versailles was signed in 1919, the most imminent threat to peace in Europe was

(A) colonial independence in Africa and Asia

(B) unrest among veterans returning from war

(C) the lack of stable governments in war-torn nations

(D) the rise of ideological tension between world superpowers

47. A present-day historian would most likely use the claims in the third paragraph as evidence that some contemporaries of the treaty anticipated which of the following?

(A) The relative ease with which countries displaying extreme nationalism could translate those motivations into territorial expansion

(B) The eventual rise of a new international organization, the United Nations, to replace the relatively weak League of Nations

(C) European states' use of the principles of the League of Nations to justify their territorial acquisitions in Africa

(D) The crash of the United States' stock market that would contribute to a global economic depression

GO ON TO THE NEXT PAGE ⇒

Questions 48–51 refer to the following two passages.

Passage 1

"Ghana over the past few years has been able to finance the major portion of its development from its own resources. . . . However, this was accomplished mainly as a result of inflated world prices for cocoa in the period 1951–1955; those prices fell sharply thereafter. Thus Ghana's economic position is heavily dependent on an export commodity which is vulnerable to severely fluctuating prices and to limitation of production by various diseases. Over half of the country's export earnings were derived from cocoa in 1956. Timber, diamonds, gold, and manganese each accounted for roughly 10 percent of those earnings. But future prospects for greater yields of those commodities are not bright. . . . [The Volta River project]'s primary purpose is to provide electric power sufficient for production of over 20,000 tons of aluminum annually. . . .

Nkrumah has an interest in promoting a West African federation initially composed of Ghana and the several British colonies in the region as they achieve independence. However, most Ghanaians are now preoccupied with domestic questions. Nkrumah will be further inhibited from any action in this realm by the present need to avoid conflict with the UK for economic reasons. . . ."

The Outlook for Ghana, CIA report, 1957

Passage 2

"A great part of Tanzania's land is fertile and gets sufficient rain. Our country can produce various crops for home consumption and for export. . . . From now on we shall stand upright and walk forward on our feet rather than look at this problem upside down. Industries will come and money will come, but their foundation is the people and their hard work, especially in agriculture. This is the meaning of self-reliance."

Julius Nyerere, *Arusha Declaration,* 1967

Kwame Nkrumah of Ghana and Julius Nyerere of Tanzania were leaders in their countries' independence movements, and they served terms as prime minister and president of their respective countries after independence from Britain.

48. What did both the CIA and Nyerere identify as necessary in postcolonial African countries?

   (A) The utilization of Africa's abundant natural resources

   (B) An alliance of African countries and their former colonial powers

   (C) The development of a union of African countries

   (D) The rise of strong military leaders in Africa

49. Nkrumah's goals for Africa as stated in Passage 1 are most similar to the goals of which of the following?

   (A) The Declaration of Independence

   (B) The "I Have a Dream" speech of Martin Luther King, Jr.

   (C) Adam Smith's *The Wealth of Nations*

   (D) The Jamaica Letter

GO ON TO THE NEXT PAGE

50. Which of the following was a challenge faced by African countries in the postcolonial period?

(A) Pressure from the United States to disband their development of nuclear weapons

(B) Constant disagreement between the Organization of African Unity and the United Nations

(C) The outbreak of proxy wars associated with conflict between ideologies in the Cold War

(D) A lack of foreign activity in the economies of most independent African states

51. The discussion of water power in the first paragraph of Passage 1 reflects which of the following characteristics of industry in the twentieth century?

(A) Water power's use of fossil fuels made the energy source a controversial industrial power supply.

(B) Water power became the most commonly used energy source in industrial production.

(C) Improvements to energy technologies enabled increased industrial production.

(D) Renewable energy sources supplanted nonrenewable energy sources in industrial production.

GO ON TO THE NEXT PAGE

Questions 52–55 refer to the following two tables.

Table 1

INVENTIONS OF THE FIRST INDUSTRIAL REVOLUTION

Innovation	Year
Steam engine	1775
Puddling process for iron production	1784
Cotton gin	1793
Locomotive	1804

Table 2

INVENTIONS OF THE SECOND INDUSTRIAL REVOLUTION

Innovation	Year
Bessemer process for steel production	1856
Electrical current (DC)	1882
Automobile	1885
Diesel engine	1892

52. Which of the following contributed to the rise of the innovations of the First Industrial Revolution as shown in Table 1?

    (A) The abandonment of rural areas and resulting urbanization

    (B) The backing of monarchs and new navigation technologies

    (C) The decline in population and access to iron and coal from the Americas

    (D) The accumulation of capital and the rise of the factory system

53. Which of the following was an effect of the development of the innovations of the Second Industrial Revolution shown in Table 2?

    (A) Overseas migration declined due to greater access to domestic jobs.

    (B) Global population fell with the use of new technologies in food production.

    (C) The global economy grew rapidly due to innovations in transportation.

    (D) European policy became increasingly driven by nationalist ideologies.

GO ON TO THE NEXT PAGE

54. A historian might argue that the inventions described in <u>Table 2</u> reflected a turning point in world history primarily because the diesel engine and the automobile

    (A) were signs of the growing influence of Marxism on the European and American proletariat

    (B) made control of Middle East resources a matter of global geopolitical importance

    (C) freed factories from relying on naturally occurring energy sources like rivers and wind

    (D) directly led to the use of tanks throughout World War I

55. Which of the following occurred in response to the expansion of industrializing states as a result of the innovations shown in both tables?

    (A) The governments of the Ottoman Empire and Qing China sought to modernize their economies.

    (B) Factory workers and peasants in Western Europe overthrew existing governments.

    (C) Nationalist leaders in colonized areas adopted European economic and political methods.

    (D) Reform movements in industrialized states failed to gain the support of government.

GO ON TO THE NEXT PAGE

END OF PART A

**IF YOU FINISH BEFORE TIME IS CALLED,
YOU MAY CHECK YOUR WORK ON THIS SECTION.**

DO NOT GO ON TO PART B UNTIL YOU ARE TOLD TO DO SO.

SECTION I, PART B

Time—40 minutes

3 Questions

Directions: Section I, Part B of this exam consists of short-answer questions. You must respond to Questions 1 *and* 2. For your final response, you must choose to answer Question 3 *or* Question 4. In your responses, be sure to address all parts of the questions, using complete sentences.

1. Use the passage below to answer all parts of the question that follows.

    "Europe's Dutch and English East India Companies are often viewed as prototypes of modern multinational corporations. The scholarly literature recognizes that huge quantities of silver flowed to Asia, but this phenomenon is considered a reflection of Europe's balance-of-trade deficit with east Asia; Europeans developed a far greater taste for Asian finery than the other way around, according to conventional wisdom, so treasure had to flow from west to east to pay for Europe's trade deficit. In short, all the key issues are normally framed in terms of European perspectives. Acceptance of a global perspective instead of the predominant Eurocentric view outlined above yields a startlingly different view. It becomes clear that Europeans did indeed play an important role in the birth of world trade, but their role was as middlemen in the vast silver trade; they were prime movers on neither the supply side (except Spain in America) nor the demand side of the worldwide silver market. Europeans were intermediaries in the trade between the New World and China. Massive amounts of silver traversed the Atlantic. After it had reached European soil, the Portuguese in the sixteenth century and Dutch in the seventeenth century became dominant distributors of silver by a multitude of routes into Asia."

    Dennis O. Flynn and Arturo Giráldez, *Born with a "Silver Spoon": The Origin of World Trade in 1571*, 1994

    (a) Explain ONE specific historical example of Europeans' role in global trade in the period 1450–1750 that would <u>support</u> the authors' argument in the passage.
    (b) Explain ANOTHER specific historical example of Europeans' role in global trade in the period 1450–1750 that would <u>support</u> the authors' argument in the passage.
    (c) Explain ONE piece of evidence about global trade in the period 1450–1750 that would <u>challenge</u> the authors' argument regarding the role of Europe in world trade.

GO ON TO THE NEXT PAGE

2. Use the map below to answer all parts of the question that follows.

ZHENG HE'S VOYAGES, 1405–1433

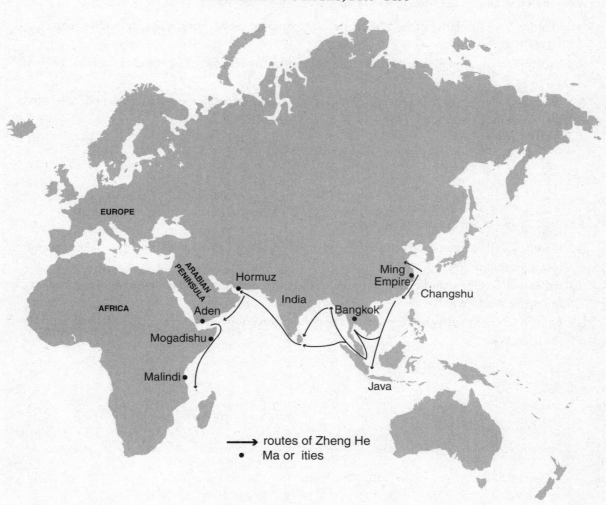

(a) Describe ONE <u>change</u> that resulted from the voyages depicted on the map.

(b) Describe ONE <u>continuity</u> in the Indian Ocean basin from 1200–1450.

(c) Describe ONE way the decision to end voyages like the one depicted in the map impacted China in the period 1450–1900.

GO ON TO THE NEXT PAGE

Choose EITHER Question 3 OR Question 4.

3. Answer all parts of the question that follows.

    (a) Identify ONE <u>similarity</u> in the administrative techniques used by imperial states in the period 1200–1450.

    (b) Explain ONE reason for the use of similar administrative techniques of imperial states in the period 1200–1450.

    (c) Identify ONE <u>difference</u> between the political systems of imperial states and those of decentralized regions in the period 1200–1450.

4. Answer all parts of the question that follows.

    (a) Identify ONE economic challenge of the twentieth century that led governments to take a more active role in economic life.

    (b) Explain ONE <u>difference</u> between economic policies of communist states and newly independent states following World War II.

    (c) Explain ONE <u>similarity</u> in the economic policies of governments in the period following the end of the Cold War.

GO ON TO THE NEXT PAGE

END OF SECTION I

IF YOU FINISH BEFORE TIME IS CALLED,
YOU MAY CHECK YOUR WORK ON THIS SECTION.

DO NOT GO ON TO SECTION II UNTIL YOU ARE TOLD TO DO SO.

SECTION II

Time—100 minutes

Question 1: Document-Based Question

Suggested reading period: 15 minutes

Suggested writing time: 45 minutes

Directions: Question 1 is based on the accompanying documents. The documents have been edited for the purpose of this exercise.

In your response you should do the following:

- Make a thesis or claim that responds to the prompt. The thesis or claim must be historically defensible and establish a line of reasoning.

- Provide context relevant to the prompt by describing a broader historical development or process.

- Use at least six of the provided documents to support an argument in response to the prompt.

- Use a historical example not found in the documents as evidence relevant to an argument about the prompt.

- Explain how the context or situation of at least three documents is relevant to an argument. This could address the relevance of the document's point of view, purpose, historical situation, and/or audience.

- Demonstrate a complex understanding of an argument that responds to the prompt by using evidence to corroborate, qualify, or modify the argument.

GO ON TO THE NEXT PAGE

1. Evaluate the extent to which European conquest and colonization changed societies in Latin America from 1492 to circa 1750.

Document 1

Source: Letter from Amerigo Vespucci to Lorenzo Pietro Francesco di Medici, 1503, translated by Clements R. Markham in *The Letters of Amerigo Vespucci*, 1894.

As regards the people: we have found such a multitude in those countries that no one could enumerate them, as we read in the Apocalypse. They are people gentle and tractable, and all of both sexes go naked, not covering any part of their bodies . . . They have no cloth, either of wool, flax, or cotton, because they have no need of it; nor have they any private property, everything being in common. They live amongst themselves without a king or ruler, each man being his own master, and having as many wives as they please. . . . They have no temples and no laws, nor are they idolaters. What more can I say! They live according to nature, and are more inclined to be Epicurean than Stoic. They have no commerce among each other, and they wage war without art or order. The old men make the youths do what they please, and incite them to fights, in which they mutually kill with great cruelty. . . . We did all we could to persuade them to desist from their evil habits, and they promised us to leave off. . . .

They live for 150 years, and are rarely sick. If they are attacked by a disease they cure themselves with the roots of some herbs. These are the most noteworthy things I know about them. The air in this country is temperate and good, as we were able to learn from their accounts that there are never any pestilences or epidemics caused by bad air. Unless they meet with violent deaths, their lives are long.

GO ON TO THE NEXT PAGE

Document 2

Source: Christopher Columbus letter to Luis de Santangel, 1493, printed in *Columbus and the New World of His Discovery*, 1906.

Again, for new silver coin they [the indigenous populations] would give everything they possessed, whether it was worth two or three doubloons or one or two balls of cotton. Even for pieces of broken pipe-tubes they would take them and give anything for them, until, when I thought it wrong, I prevented it. And I made them presents of thousands of things which I had, that I might win their esteem, and also that they might be made good Christians and be disposed to the service of Your Majesties and the whole Spanish nation, and help us to obtain the things which we require and of which there is abundance in their country. They do not carry arms nor know what they are, because I showed them swords and they took them by the edge and ignorantly cut themselves. They have no iron: their spears are sticks without iron, and some of them have a fish's tooth at the end and others have other things. They are all generally of good height, of pleasing appearance and well built . . . They must be good servants and intelligent, as I see that they very quickly say all that is said to them, and I believe that they would easily become Christians, as it appeared to me that they had no sect. If it please our Lord, at the time of my departure, I will take six of them from here to your Highnesses that they may learn to speak. I saw no beast of any kind except parrots on this island.

GO ON TO THE NEXT PAGE

Document 3

Source: Guamán Poma de Ayala, descendant of royal Inca, illustrated letter to the Spanish king, circa 1601. A portion of the text says: "The Execution of Atahualpa Inka in Cajamarca." The Royal Danish Library, Copenhagen, *El primer nueva corónica y buen gobierno conpuesto por Don Phelipe Guaman Poma de Ayala, señor y príncipe.* Cover.

GO ON TO THE NEXT PAGE

Document 4

Source: Bartolomé de Las Casas, a Spanish priest, account addressed to the king of Spain hoping for new laws to prevent the brutal exploitation of Native Americans, 1542.

Now this infinite multitude of Men are by the Creation of God innocently simple, altogether void of and averse to all manner of Craft, Subtlety and Malice, and most Obedient and Loyal Subjects to their Native Sovereigns; and behave themselves very patiently, submissively and quietly towards the Spaniards, to whom they are subservient and subject; so that finally they live without the least thirst after revenge, laying aside all litigiousness, commotion, and hatred . . .

The natives are capable of Morality or Goodness and very apt to receive the principles of Catholic Religion; nor are they averse to Civility and good Manners . . . I myself have heard the Spaniards themselves (who dare not assume the Confidence to deny the good Nature in them) declare, that there was nothing wanting in them for the acquisition of eternal grace, but the sole Knowledge and Understanding of the Deity.

GO ON TO THE NEXT PAGE

Document 5

Source: Pedro Cieza de Leon, *The War of Quito*, circa 1550, translated by Clements R. Markham, 1913.

They [the Viceroy and Judges of the Court] required that all the men and women of Peru should be sent to their native homes at the cost of those who possessed them, it being the will of the King that they should be free, as his subjects and vassals. Notwithstanding that the order was just and righteous, some of the Indians evaded it because they were married, others because they liked their masters and were tolerably instructed in the matters of our Holy Catholic Faith. Even of those who were ordered to depart many merely went to hide in secret places so as not to go whither they were sent, and others went to the churches, whence they were taken by order of the Viceroy, and put on board ships, where many died. So that very few returned to their native places, and those that did went back to the rites and idolatries they had formerly been accustomed to. There was thus no benefit derived from compliance with this ordinance. Some Spanish conquerors, who returned to Spain, had lived with Indian women for many years, and had children by them. These were to be sent to the native places of the mothers at the cost of their masters. If they disputed or complained they had to pay double for freight and passage. . . .

There was no less commotion in Tierra Firme than in Peru on hearing that the Viceroy intended to enforce the ordinances . . . the Indians had been informed that they were vassals of the Emperor our Lord, and that the *Encomenderos* had no authority over them except for the collection of tribute which the Indians were bound to pay: also that the ordinances would be enforced as the King had ordered.

GO ON TO THE NEXT PAGE

Document 6

Source: Hernan Cortés, Spanish conquistador, letter to the Spanish king Charles V, describing Mexico City, 1520.

Three halls are in this grand temple, which contain the principal idols; these are of wonderful extent and height, and admirable workmanship, adorned with figures sculptured in stone and wood; leading from the halls are chapels with very small doors, to which the light is not admitted, nor are any persons except the priests, and not all of them. In these chapels are the images of idols, although, as I have before said, many of them are also found on the outside; the principal ones, in which the people have greatest faith and confidence, I precipitated from their pedestals, and cast them down the steps of the temple, purifying the chapels in which they had stood, as they were all polluted with human blood, shed ill the sacrifices. In the place of these I put images of Our Lady and the Saints, which excited not a little feeling in Moctezuma and the inhabitants, who at first remonstrated, declaring that if my proceedings were known throughout the country, the people would rise against me; for they believed that their idols bestowed on them all temporal good, and if they permitted them to be ill-treated, they would be angry and without their gifts, and by this means the people would be deprived of the fruits of the earth and perish with famine. I answered, through the interpreters, that they were deceived in expecting any favors from idols, the work of their own hands, formed of unclean things; and that they must learn there was but one God, the universal Lord of all, who had created the heavens and earth, and all things else, and had made them and us; that He was without beginning and immortal, and they were bound to adore and believe Him, and no other creature or thing.

GO ON TO THE NEXT PAGE

Document 7

Source: Antonio Vázquez de Espinosa, Spanish monk, *Compendium and Description of the West Indies*, circa 1620.

The ore was very rich black flint, and the excavation so extensive that it held more than 3,000 Indians working away hard with picks and hammers, breaking up that flint ore; and when they have filled their little sacks, the poor fellows, loaded down with ore, climb up those ladders or rigging, some like masts and others like cables, and so trying and distressing that a man empty-handed can hardly get up them. That is the way they work in this mine, with many lights and the loud noise of the pounding and great confusion. Nor is that the greatest evil and difficulty; that is due to the thievish and undisciplined superintendents. . . .

These Indians are sent out every year under a captain whom they choose in each village or tribe, for him to take them and oversee them for the year each has to serve; every year they have a new election, for as some go out, others come in. This works out very badly, with great losses and gaps in the quotas of Indians, the villages being depopulated; and this gives rise to great extortions and abuses on the part of the inspectors toward the poor Indians, ruining them and thus depriving the chief Indians of their property and carrying them off in chains because they do not fill out the mit'a assignment, which they cannot do, for the reason given and for others which I do not bring forward.

GO ON TO THE NEXT PAGE

END OF DOCUMENTS FOR QUESTION 1

Question 2, Question 3, OR Question 4: Long Essay Question
Suggested writing time: 40 minutes

Directions: Choose Question 2, Question 3, OR Question 4 to answer.

In your response, you should do the following:

- Make a thesis or claim that responds to the prompt. The thesis or claim must be historically defensible and establish a line of reasoning.
- Provide context relevant to the prompt by describing a broader historical development or process.
- Use specific and relevant examples as evidence to support an argument in response to the prompt.
- Use a historical reasoning skill (causation, comparison, or continuity and change) to develop an argument in response to the prompt.
- Demonstrate a complex understanding of an argument that responds to the prompt by using evidence to corroborate, qualify, or modify the argument.

2. In the period circa 1200–1450, the reconstitution of empires affected the expansion or decline of cities across Afro-Eurasia.

   Develop an argument that evaluates how the growth of empires led to change in urban growth in Afro-Eurasia in the period circa 1200–1450.

3. In the period 1450–1750, imperial expansion relied on the increased use of gunpowder, cannons, and armed trade to establish large empires in both hemispheres.

   Develop an argument that evaluates the extent to which empire-building among European powers was different from empire-building by the Ottoman Empire in this time period.

4. In the period 1750–1900, the process of industrialization changed the way in which goods were produced and consumed, with far-reaching effects on the global economy.

   Develop an argument that evaluates how the process of industrialization transformed the global economy in this time period.

GO ON TO THE NEXT PAGE

 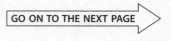

END OF SECTION II

STOP

END OF EXAM

ANSWER KEY

Section I, Part A

1. C	15. D	29. B	43. B
2. B	16. C	30. C	44. C
3. D	17. A	31. B	45. D
4. D	18. D	32. B	46. C
5. A	19. D	33. D	47. A
6. B	20. B	34. B	48. A
7. A	21. D	35. A	49. D
8. D	22. D	36. C	50. C
9. A	23. D	37. A	51. C
10. D	24. C	38. B	52. D
11. A	25. D	39. C	53. C
12. D	26. B	40. A	54. B
13. B	27. D	41. C	55. A
14. C	28. A	42. D	

Section I, Part B and Section II

See Answers and Explanations, and self-score free-response questions.

Section I, Part A Number Correct: _____

Section I, Part B Points Earned: _____

Section II Points Earned: _____

Sign into your online account at kaptest.com and enter your results in the scoring section to see your 1–5 score.

Haven't registered your book yet? Go to kaptest.com/moreonline to begin.

ANSWERS AND EXPLANATIONS

Section I, Part A

1. C

For centuries, Islamic scholars were at the forefront of developing advanced mathematics. That knowledge can be seen in such developments as the astrolabe and the concepts of latitude and longitude. Thus, **(C)** is correct. (A) is incorrect because Image 1 depicts the work of a scholar who lived before Galileo and Copernicus. (B) is incorrect because, while observation and record-keeping were important to Islamic scholars during this time period, it does not specifically reflect characteristics of the astrolabe, which was the product of advanced mathematics and used extensively in navigation. (D) is incorrect because, while some Islamic scholars wanted to spread Islam throughout Southeast Asia, there is no indication of this in Image 1. Islamic navigators used the astrolabe for many purposes, not just proselytizing in Southeast Asia.

2. B

The early transfer of medical knowledge from the Middle East, as well as from the Greeks and the Chinese, to Western Europe was one of the most important exchanges in human history. Image 2 is an example of the early study of medicine that would lay the foundations for centuries of advancements, enabling humans to live longer, healthier lives. **(B)** is correct. While (A), (C), and (D) do accurately represent continuities in world history, they do not directly relate to Image 2, making those choices incorrect.

3. D

The two images depict advancements in scientific and medical knowledge in the Islamic world. The Islamic Golden Age saw many new advancements from Islamic scholars, as well as the translation and preservation of classical Greek knowledge. All of this would eventually flow to Europe and the rest of the world, making **(D)** correct. (A) is incorrect because the images have no direct connection to Islam's origins. Islam was founded in 622 by the Prophet Muhammad. (B) is incorrect because, while Image 2 deals with Islamic scholars preserving and spreading European medical knowledge, Image 1 depicts the product of mathematical research

by Islamic scholars. (C) is incorrect because the images reflect advancements in science and medicine in the Middle East rather than in East Asia.

4. D

Carried by infected rodents and fleas, the Black Death (bubonic plague) spread from China to mainland Europe in the 1340s. Mongols, merchants, and travelers passed the disease along trade routes, and cities from Central Asia to Western Europe were all affected. Some scholars estimate that a third of Europe's population died within five years of the plague's arrival in mainland Europe. **(D)** is correct. (A) and (B) are incorrect because the Black Death was spread by merchants and traders; it was not caused by diseased people invading Europe or by forced migrations. While the Black Death was unintentionally spread among Europeans, it occurred well before the Europeans colonized parts of America, making (C) incorrect.

5. A

In explaining the outbreak of the pandemic, Boccaccio says the disease was "sent down upon us mortals by God." Such a view would have been associated with Catholicism during Boccaccio's time. Therefore, **(A)** is correct and (C) is incorrect. While Boccaccio praises Florence and Italy, there is no clear indication that he is expressing views associated with nationalism, so (B) is incorrect. (D) is incorrect because Protestantism would not emerge until the sixteenth century.

6. B

The passage deals with the spread of disease due to extensive international trade networks; this matches **(B)**. There is no indication from the passage that the disease pandemic changed religious traditions or influenced the dissolution of states, so (A) and (C) can be eliminated. While (D) may be tempting, it is incorrect because the passage is not directly related to how travel and trade networks were actually developed in Europe and Asia. Instead, the spread of the bubonic plague was a consequence of cross-cultural contact.

7. A

In sixteenth-century Japan, which was before the Tokugawa shogunate came to power, the *daimyo* (lords) controlled much of Japan under a feudal system. The system centered on the relationship between lord and warrior or peasant; the *daimyo* controlled his land and his peasants. In exchange, the warriors, or samurai, provided the *daimyo* protection. **(A)** reflects this political scenario and is correct. (B) is incorrect because the emperor remained a mostly ceremonial position throughout the feudal and shogun eras of Japanese history. It was not until increasing European attempts to trade in later centuries that Japan become isolationist, making (C) incorrect. (D) is incorrect because Japan still experienced internal as well as external conflict in the sixteenth century; the map indicates a fragmented rather than a strongly unified nation.

8. D

According to Source 2, merchants had the lowest social standing under the Tokugawa shogunate. In Europe, merchants were generally viewed favorably by society and by governments. As such, **(D)** is correct. (A) is incorrect because under the Tokugawa shogun, the emperor was just a figurehead. The shogun truly ruled Japan. While in some areas of Japan the samurai lost some of their former reverence and respectability, they were not generally relegated to a low social status; (B) is incorrect. The pyramid in Source 2 does not indicate population size but instead indicates social standing. While the samurai formed a sizable proportion of society at this time, they were outnumbered by other groups, such as the peasants. (C) is thus incorrect.

9. A

Source 1 illustrates how Japanese territory was controlled by different clans in 1570. Each clan would have been led by a *daimyo* during the sixteenth century. In 1600, the Tokugawa shogunate came to power in Japan and would take some of the power away from the *daimyo*, which is illustrated by their lower social standing in Source 2. **(A)** is therefore correct. While (B) may be tempting, it is incorrect because the images do not convey a sense that the lower social classes depended on the ruling class for their economic well-being. (C) is incorrect because, under the Tokugawa shogunate, Japan would become more isolationist. (D) is incorrect because, during this time period, Japan experienced some instability as it was undergoing a political transformation.

10. D

In Europe in the time of Galileo, philosophers and scientists made significant advances in fields such as astronomy, medicine, and chemistry. Many of these developments were informed by the use of the emerging scientific method, a logic-based approach to testing hypotheses through observation and experimentation. These advances came after increasing contacts between Europeans and other cultures; the knowledge of Asian and Islamic scholars, as well as that of preserved Classical texts, sparked new discoveries in Europe. **(D)** is correct. (A) is incorrect because industrial economies developed after this period of seventeenth-century scientific advances. While (B) and (C) both occurred slightly before the time period described in the passage, neither had as direct an impact on the increase in scientific advances.

11. A

Church leaders and many scholars during Galileo's time relied on the works of classical scholars such as Aristotle and Ptolemy who claimed that the Earth was the center of the universe. This belief was reconciled with the Church's teachings and beliefs. Galileo's work contradicted Aristotle and Ptolemy and as such angered both Catholic and Protestant leaders. Thus, **(A)** is correct, and (B) and (C) are incorrect. (D) is incorrect because the Church was more concerned with whether or not scientific findings agreed with Church teaching, not necessarily with the exact methods used by scientists.

12. D

The Roman Catholic Church vehemently opposed any scientific findings that contradicted or undermined Church doctrine. Because his work went against the Church's teaching, Galileo was put on trial before the Inquisition and forced to read a signed confession in which he stated that his ideas were false. **(D)** is correct. (A) is incorrect because the Church supported some of the classical learning that was passed down from the Greeks and Romans. (B) is incorrect because it is too extreme to conclude that the Church believed that most of its devout followers would stop accepting the Church's teachings. (C) is incorrect because, along with Catholic Church leaders, many Protestant leaders were opposed to Galileo's work.

13. B

As the passage indicates, Galileo opposed important arguments from Aristotle and Ptolemy. One point of contention was whether the universe was centered around the Earth (claimed by Aristotle and Ptolemy) or the sun (claimed by Galileo). As such, his letter is best understood as a departure from some of the previous Greco-Roman classical teachings. **(B)** is correct and (C) is incorrect. It would be misleading to say that scientific understanding is advanced primarily through argument and counterargument, so (A) is incorrect. (D) is incorrect because the Church was reluctant to accept the heliocentric theory, which says that the sun rather than the Earth is the center of the solar system.

14. C

Paragraph 1 of the passage indicates that people from distant lands traveled to China and gave the Chinese "precious objects and presents." Paragraph 2 then says that the Chinese, led by Zheng He, were to undertake a voyage to offer presents to the "distant people." As such, this passage illustrates how maritime and trade activity can encourage cultural transfers; thus, **(C)** is correct and (D) is incorrect. There is no support in the passage for environmental factors shaping transportation methods, or for the effects of technology, so (A) and (B) are incorrect.

15. D

The passage indicates that the Chinese approved of the foreigners who came to China giving gifts. Further, the passage says that the Chinese were to undertake a voyage to bestow gifts to foreigners. As such, it can be concluded that the events are a reaction against isolationism; **(D)** is correct. Capitalism was not yet a defined economic system at the time of this passage, so (A) is incorrect. While Zheng He gives a positive account to the cross-cultural exchange, there is no indication that the events represent a reaction against colonialism or imperialism, making (B) and (C) incorrect.

16. C

The Ming voyages were the policy of just one emperor who wished to impress China's Indian Ocean trade partners with his power and glory. More traditional Confucian factions in the government disapproved of the fleet's expense and did not value the trade income. Thus, **(C)** is correct. China and Europe were not in direct competition at this time, so (A) is incorrect. (B) is incorrect because it confuses balance of trade with the government's internal tax income, which was indeed strained by the expense of the voyages. There is no evidence that damage had weakened the fleet, making (D) incorrect.

17. A

In the second paragraph, the emperor orders a maritime expedition to deliver gifts to distant people. This is an example of a state policy contributing to the development of an exchange network, which makes **(A)** correct. While China did flourish due to trade routes along the Silk Road through Central Asia to Europe, the passage is discussing a sea voyage, making (B) incorrect. (C) is incorrect because there is no evidence to suggest China was looking to abandon overland trade routes. (D) is incorrect because the passage concerns cross-cultural exchange and trade—not how internal politics influence state expansion.

18. D

China dealt with its neighboring areas by establishing tributary relationships in which the tributary states would have to recognize China's superiority. China had invaded Korea under the Tang and Song Dynasties, and Korea became part of China's sphere of influence. Thus, **(D)** is correct. (A) is incorrect because Korea was not part of the original Manchu territory. Although China was involved in trade, it did not seek Korea in order to set up a trading post empire, making (B) incorrect. Lastly, Islam did not spread to East Asia to any significant degree, so (C) is incorrect.

19. D

As indicated on the map by the increase in the Manchu territory, the Ming Dynasty was repeatedly attacked by Manchu raiders from the north, weakening its army until the Qing eventually superseded the Ming. **(D)** is correct. Though Islam did spread into Central Asia during this time, this was not a factor that affected the Ming Dynasty's ability to govern, nor is such a trend indicated on the map; (A) is incorrect. China's lack of silver was partly due to trade in the Indian Ocean region, but lacking modern ships was not a factor causing the Ming's downfall; Admiral Zheng He completed his voyages under Ming rule, so (B) is incorrect. While the depletion of silver coinage did negatively impact the Ming's ability to collect some tax payments, (C) is incorrect because, reflecting the sophisticated bureaucracy typical of Chinese empires, the Ming had a highly structured taxation system.

20. B

Both the Mongols and the Manchu wanted to protect and preserve their own ethnic and cultural identity; **(B)** is correct. (A) is incorrect because neither the Mongols nor the Manchu encouraged the intermarriage between their respective groups and the ethnic Han Chinese. In fact, the Manchu strictly forbade such intermarriages. (C) is incorrect because neither the Mongols nor the Manchu forced the Han Chinese to learn another language. (D) is incorrect because while the Manchu did adopt the Confucian civil service examination system, the Mongols did not.

21. D

During the Atlantic slave trade, more men than women were enslaved in Africa. As a result, the male-to-female ratio in sub-Saharan Africa was skewed; **(D)** is correct. More enslaved Africans went to South America than to the United States, so (A) is incorrect. While it is true that the Muslim lands in Western Asia and the Mediterranean bought far fewer slaves than the highly profitable American colonies, (B) is incorrect because it mistakenly says the trade was actually declining in these years. Agricultural productivity under slavery increased in this period as the system proved brutally efficient; (C) is incorrect.

22. D

The map shows that enslaved Africans were transported not only to Christian states in the Americas but also to Islamic states in the Middle East and Asia. **(D)** is correct. While Europe had a major role in the African slave trade, states in Asia, the Americas, and even Africa also had direct control of the trade, so (A) is incorrect. (B) is incorrect because more slaves were taken from West Africa than East Africa, as the map indicates. While enslaved Africans were forced to work in Europe, they never constituted the primary source of labor in Europe, making (C) incorrect.

23. D

The brutal nature of the sugar production work in Brazil, along with its climate and the proliferation of disease, led to increased deaths among slaves. This, in turn, led to labor shortages, which required more new slaves to be transported; **(D)** is correct. While South America's Brazilian coast is significantly closer to equatorial Africa than any other region of the New World, it was the not the primary reason for increased voyages there, making (A) incorrect. (B) is incorrect because there were many colonies farther north that had slavery. (C) is incorrect because it does not account for the huge volume of slaves brought to Brazil

compared to the Spanish and American colonies, which also had laws promoting slavery.

24. C

The second paragraph says that the Sultan gave "the fifth part of the booty made on his expeditions to pious and charitable purposes." The passage then explains that the Sultan was acting according to instruction from the Quran. Therefore, **(C)** is correct. While (A), (B), and (D) are accurate statements about Islam, they do not directly relate to what is described in the second paragraph.

25. D

According to the first paragraph, it can reasonably be inferred that, through trade and access to gold, some merchants in eastern African society prospered. The passage says that "Kulwa was a very fine and substantially built town," which gives further evidence that **(D)** is correct. (A) is incorrect because Islam did indeed spread to East Africa, as indicated by the passage. (B) is incorrect because the passage does not provide any indication that a majority of Zanj people converted to Islam. While English would later become a commonly used language in eastern Africa, it was not common during the time period of this passage, so (C) is incorrect.

26. B

Portuguese explorers arrived in East Africa at the end of the fifteenth century. They destroyed many buildings in Kilwa and other cities when they invaded, which permanently weakened Kilwa. **(B)** is correct. Although Swahili culture did emerge in regions of East Africa, this cultural development did not economically weaken Kilwa; (A) is incorrect. The Silk Road was established centuries before Kilwa was established, and natural disasters such as volcanic eruptions did not significantly weaken Kilwa, making (C) and (D) incorrect.

27. D

During the period 1200 to 1450, Indian Ocean trade linked China, Southeast Asia, India, Arabia, and East Africa. This newly created interregional trade network led to the growth of new trading cities, enabling merchants and traders to flourish; thus, **(D)** is correct and (C) is incorrect. (A) is incorrect because it would be the sixteenth century before Europeans would play a dominant role in Indian Ocean maritime trade. Economic activity along the Indian Ocean did not slow due to nomadic invasions, which would largely occur on land instead of by sea; (B) is incorrect.

28. A

Although the author claims the cabildos "afforded an opportunity for the expression of the popular will," the often exclusive nature of cabildo membership and the reference to the "*Spanish* Americans" indicates that the author is primarily describing the power of those born in Europe (*peninsulares*) or descendants of Europeans (Creoles)—a power structure that excluded native-born and African populations. The reference to hereditary membership in cabildos thus reflects the hierarchical social structures in Latin America during the colonial period, so **(A)** is correct. (B) is incorrect because the author is describing "hereditary" political power in Latin America, not Europe. Although Spanish predominance of colonial possessions was eventually eclipsed by other European nations, particularly Britain, (C) is incorrect because the passage is referring to power structures within Spanish colonies, not the eventual decline of Spanish influence. (D) is incorrect because European colonies did not have purely merit-based economic systems; in fact, many relied on class-based or slave labor.

29. B

By "the final revolution," Shepherd is referring to "the movement which led eventually to the emancipation of the colonies"—the Latin American independence movements against Spanish and Portuguese rule. Independence movements throughout the colonies were inspired by Enlightenment ideas that advocated more democratic governments and natural rights; **(B)** is correct. (A) is incorrect because Marxism had not yet developed during the initial Latin American independence movements, though these ideas would impact twentieth-century protests against Latin American governments. (C) is incorrect because the revolution discussed in the passage is political, not economic; *mercantilism* refers to the economic goal during the period of exploration and colonization of establishing a favorable balance of trade. (D) is incorrect because the author makes no reference to economic systems, and the "French and English philosophers" to which the author refers are those associated with the Enlightenment, not economic theory, since the author claims their writings helped motivate independence movements.

30. C

The author discusses various aspects of Latin American colonies leading up to their independence movements: the lack of direct political representation, the exclusive nature of town councils, and the revolutions' roots in political ideals rather than reactions to specific events as in earlier revolts. The early twentieth century also saw political uprisings in Latin America. Many of these uprisings were populist in nature, protesting government policies that favored elites and foreigners, and advocating reforms and land redistribution. **(C)** is correct because it reflects the nature of the twentieth-century resistance movements. (A) and (D) are incorrect because the passage describes political movements, not economic development. (B) is incorrect because most Latin American countries had achieved their independence by World War I.

31. B

The first table shows that the consumption of raw cotton, which would have been used in textile production, grew significantly over the indicated time period. The second table shows that the amount of coke iron produced also increased substantially. Both data sets directly support **(B)**. Although (A) and (C) describe trends that accompanied the industrialization of Great Britain, neither is directly supported by the tables, which provide no data comparing British industrial exports with those of other countries or chronicling the growth of cities. Similarly, the tables do not indicate anything about how the coke iron produced was being used, so (D) is incorrect.

32. B

In preindustrial societies, the family had been the basic productive unit. Industrialization changed this dynamic by moving economic production outside the home, making **(B)** correct. Although fewer people were employed in agriculture, (A) is incorrect because the demand for foodstuffs increased as populations increased. (C) is incorrect because living conditions in urban tenements were notoriously disease-ridden, overcrowded, and unsanitary. (D) is incorrect because a middle class of factory managers, merchants, and service workers continued to grow.

33. D

One of the factors that was important for early factories was having a source of energy—moving rivers—in the days before electricity. Additionally, rivers made it possible to cheaply ship raw materials to factories and send finished products to markets. Thus, **(D)** is correct. (A) is incorrect because it lists changes that occurred during the second wave of industrialization, which began in the late nineteenth century. (B) is incorrect because Britain had an abundance of natural resources, which enabled it to industrialize. Former farmers did provide labor, but they had often left their farms for economic opportunities and due to the enclosure movement, not because they had overused natural resources. (C) is incorrect because the opposite is true: Britain placed few restraints on the country's economy, thus creating opportunities for new businesses.

34. B

As indicated by the increase in consumption and production in the tables, the Industrial Revolution created demand for cheap raw materials, such as raw cotton, palm oil, and rubber, making **(B)** correct. Supply of these products relied heavily on slave labor from distant tropical regions of the world. (A) is incorrect because the start of the transatlantic slave trade dates to the fifteenth century, while the Industrial Revolution began in the eighteenth century. (C) is incorrect because, in the second half of the nineteenth century, tens of millions of Europeans *emigrated from* Europe to the United States in search of employment and better living standards. Although Britain did outlaw slavery before the United States, this policy was not a result of increased industrial production; in fact, slavery had helped supply raw materials that Britain needed in its factories. (D) is thus incorrect.

35. A

As established by the principles at the Berlin Conference, European powers colonized most of the African continent. The conditions described in the passage reflect the exploitative economic practices established by many European powers in their African colonies, so **(A)** is correct. (B) is incorrect because it reflects Cold War conflict in Africa, not events during Africa's colonization. (C) is incorrect because land redistribution was attempted in some African nations in the twentieth century. (D) reflects conditions in Africa primarily in the seventeenth and eighteenth centuries.

36. C

The correct answer will be a factor that enabled European powers to colonize other world regions. One significant factor was European industrialization, which brought about technological improvements in transportation and communication and boosted European military strength. Thus, **(C)** is correct because steamships are an example of these new industrial technologies; specifically, steamships reduced the cost and time of ocean travel and made possible the navigation of inland rivers. (A) is incorrect because the slave trade and Atlantic system had ended prior to the period of African colonization described in the passage. (B) is incorrect because, while imperialism was driven by economic motives, the European nations were in need of raw materials, not a labor force, for industrial products. (D) is incorrect because the weakening of traditional authority was not universal throughout Europe (King Leopold II of Belgium had direct control over the Congo Free State, for instance), nor would this scenario lead to increased state imperialism.

37. A

Imperialism at its core was a competition among more industrialized nations to expand political control over other regions, benefiting from their colonies' raw materials and labor. Nations were also driven by nationalistic tendencies to expand their power and influence. These motivations helped create the political climate that led to World War I, so **(A)** is correct. (B) is incorrect because most of the decolonization of Africa did not take place until after World War II. (C), which reflects the 1823 Monroe Doctrine, is incorrect because Europe did not resume colonizing Latin America. (D) is incorrect because Europe benefited financially from imperialism.

38. B

Nineteenth-century Europeans believed it was their responsibility to bring civilization to African and Asian lands, often using Social Darwinism to justify their actions. In addition to the mistreatment described in the passage, the soldiers call the Africans "beasts" and "nyama (meat)," confirming these Social Darwinist ideas. Thus, **(B)** is correct and (D) is incorrect. While the passage does describe struggle and hard work, it is not used as a justification, making (A) incorrect. (C) is incorrect because the passage does not discuss family duty as a reason for imperialism.

39. C

The passage, written by the Communist Party in the Soviet Union a couple of years before the dissolution of the Soviet Union and months before the fall of the Berlin Wall, reports that Eastern Europeans are rejecting communist authoritarian institutions in favor of *perestroika* and *glasnost*. These policies, introduced by Gorbachev, increased political, economic, and press freedoms. The passage thus reflects the move toward liberalization as the Cold War era came to a close; **(C)** is correct. (A) is incorrect because, although the Soviet Union utilized propaganda, the "mass media" referenced in the passage is from democratic Western European states. (B) is incorrect because it reflects changes in Russia at the beginning of the twentieth century. The passage references the Warsaw Pact, but the topic of the excerpt is the liberalization of the Soviet Union and Eastern Europe, not international organizations, so (D) is incorrect.

40. A

The first paragraph mentions the trend toward democratization (*perestroika*) in the Soviet Union, in light of the population's growing awareness of the "economic growth and social well-being of the Western European states." The "existing political institutions" must contrast with these values. Indeed, the communist government promoted initial rapid industrialization and collectivization under a planned economy, eventually stagnating in an inefficient, non-market based economy. **(A)** is correct. (B) is incorrect because land was collectivized during the communist era. (C) is incorrect because many Soviet citizens faced economic hardship under communism and favored liberal reforms. Most Soviet republics were demanding independence at the time the passage was written, making (D) incorrect.

41. C

The passage claims that Soviet citizens were now, in the midst of *perestroika* and *glasnost*, constantly exposed to the "comparing and contrasting of the two worlds, of their ways of life, production, intellectual cultures." Having been denied freedom of speech and a free press for decades, Soviet citizens finally had a chance to hear alternate worldviews through the media and to voice their opinions on the failures of communism when Mikhail Gorbachev introduced *glasnost* (the policy of openness that unintentionally allowed a significant anti-communist

movement to emerge). Gorbachev's further reforms, combined with a weakened economy, led to his resignation in 1991, ending communism and the Soviet Union. Therefore, **(C)** is correct. (A) is incorrect because the economy continued to suffer from price fluctuations, shortages, and inflation under *perestroika*. Although ethnic tensions caused Estonia, Latvia, and Lithuania to declare independence in 1990, the ethnic violence was not caused by *glasnost* and *perestroika*, so (B) is incorrect. (D) is incorrect because U.S. president Ronald Reagan actually softened his anti-communist views when Gorbachev came to power.

42. D

The scene depicts the arrival of Americans (led by Commodore Matthew Perry) to Japan on a new technology, the steamship. Such contacts influenced a movement to industrialize Japan. A group of young progressive samurai demanded that the Tokugawa shogun open Japan to foreign trade and ideas. These demands led to a civil war, in which Western technology aided the samurai in overthrowing the shogun and installing Emperor Meiji in 1868, allowing Japan to build a modern infrastructure and rapidly industrialize. Therefore, **(D)** is correct. (A) and (C) are both incorrect because these events involved European, not American, powers; Japan asserted itself as a dominant military power by defeating Russia in the Russo-Japanese War in 1905, and the first Christian missionaries to Japan arrived in the sixteenth century. (B) is incorrect because few Americans actually settled in industrialized Japan.

43. B

The Meiji Restoration entailed Japan's rapid industrialization, made possible through the sponsorship of Emperor Meiji, whose pro-business leadership introduced Western ideas to Japan. Although there was more resistance to foreign influence in China (as demonstrated in the Boxer Rebellion) and internal conflict frustrated progress, the late Qing government also adopted modernization policies, so **(B)** is correct. (A) and (D) are incorrect because both the United States and Great Britain had begun industrializing before this period. (C) is incorrect because India was still under Britain's imperial control during this period and was thus not undergoing rapid state-led modernization; rather, India supplied raw materials for Britain's industry.

44. C

Japan underwent rapid industrialization after the scene depicted in the print. However, as an island nation, Japan lacks many of the basic natural resources needed for industry, such as coal, iron ore, and oil. The quest for raw materials, combined with nationalist sentiments, inspired imperialism; **(C)** is correct. (A) is incorrect because there was no socialist uprising in Japan, and Japan continues to have at least a figurehead emperor today. (B) is incorrect because Japan did not embrace isolationism, but rather welcomed foreign modernization. (D) is incorrect because it describes the Boxer Rebellion in China; no such event occurred in Japan.

45. D

The passage mentions several factors that contributed to the conditions in Germany that prompted the rise of fascism and led to the eventual outbreak of World War II. The author cites the "humiliating" conditions of the peace settlement, in which Germany was forced to accept full responsibility for the war. The treaty also placed Germany in a state of "economic bondage" without "any prospect of regaining liberty." These factors would contribute to resentment, economic crises, and nationalism. **(D)** reflects one of these factors, and is therefore correct. Although the passage mentions the international *organization* of the League of Nations, the passage does not mention any particular *alliances* that contributed to conflict, so (A) is incorrect. (B) is incorrect because it reflects the democratic powers' goal of containing the spread of communism during the Cold War and thus refers to a later era. (C) is incorrect because conflicting ideologies are not mentioned in the passage.

46. C

The end of World War I saw the fall of autocratic regimes in Germany, Italy, and Russia. Having no democratic tradition upon which to draw, and facing economic devastation, citizens of these countries sought stability. A totalitarian regime emerged under Stalin in the Soviet Union, and fascist states arose in Italy under Mussolini and in Germany under Hitler, whose territorial ambitions directly led to World War II. Therefore, **(C)** is correct. Although Germany and Italy lost overseas colonies after World War I, the British and French empires lasted through World War II, making (A) incorrect. (B) is incorrect because, while there were isolated incidents of veteran unrest, especially among those who struggled to find employment after the war, this generally led to the development of veterans' organizations, not to direct threats to political stability. (D) is incorrect because it reflects international conditions after World War II.

47. A

The author claims in the third paragraph that the conditions of the treaty "will never give peace" since Germany will "wish to shake off the heavy yoke imposed." The author thinks that the "evident right to conquer and possess countries for economic and imperialistic purposes," likely as reflected in Germany being forced to cede territory after the war, will provide Germany a justification, or "opportunity," to claim territories itself in the future—as indeed Hitler would later take over the Rhineland and Austria. **(A)** summarizes these insights and is therefore correct. (B) is incorrect because, even though the author holds a low opinion of the League of Nations, labeling it "so-called," he never anticipates the rise of a new international organization. (C) is incorrect because the principles of the League of Nations, which sought to maintain world peace, did not actually justify imperialism. (D) is incorrect because the passage anticipates economic problems in Germany, not in the United States or the rest of the world.

48. A

While the Central Intelligence Agency and Julius Nyerere held different opinions about how successful postcolonial Africa would be, they agreed that Africa's vast wealth in agricultural and mineral resources was necessary for future development. Thus, **(A)** is correct. (B) is incorrect because the leaders of Africa's independence movements sought to distance themselves as much as possible from their countries' former colonizers, whose continuing economic influence was seen as neocolonialism. (C) is incorrect because only Nkrumah advocates this policy in the passages. Although military regimes did arise, (D) is incorrect because most African independence leaders advocated for a more democratic approach in an attempt to ease ethnic tensions.

49. D

Nkrumah's vision of postcolonial Africa was to promote pan-Africanism, as noted by his desire to create a West African federation that would expand outward. This was most similar to the goals articulated in Simón Bolívar's Jamaica

Letter, which expressed a desire to unite the newly independent Latin American countries. Thus, **(D)** is correct. Although the Declaration of Independence was the joint statement of diverse colonies, (A) is incorrect because the document concerns natural rights and political theories justifying independence from Britain, not a call for the political bodies to unite. (B) is incorrect because King's speech advocates civil rights and equality among diverse races and is not a call for separate nations to unite. (C) is incorrect because it describes the economic theory of capitalism and is not a call to international unity.

50. C

Similar to what occurred throughout Asia and Latin America, Africa experienced interventions during the Cold War as the West and the Communist Bloc attempted to increase their spheres of influence. A relatively weak colonial presence after World War II made many African regions particularly prone to outside interference, including proxy wars between the Soviet Union and the United States; **(C)** is correct. (A) is incorrect because most African countries were not politically or economically equipped to develop nuclear weapons during the postcolonial period. (B) is incorrect because the Organization of African Unity (OAU), which embraced the ideals of pan-Africanism, had an effective working relationship with the UN, especially concerning refugees and the elimination of colonialism. (D) is incorrect because foreign nations often created exploitative neocolonial economic relationships with African states; as the CIA report notes, the newly independent Ghana must take care to maintain its economic ties with its former colonizer, the United Kingdom.

51. C

The CIA report describes the dependence of Ghana on export commodities. The construction of a major hydroelectric dam on the Volta River is meant to boost production of aluminum, an export commodity. Thus, **(C)** is correct. (A) is incorrect because while the use of fossil fuels is controversial due to its impact on the environment, water power does not much involve fossil fuels. (B) and (D) are incorrect because they distort the characteristics of industrial energy sources; while use of renewable energy sources has expanded, nonrenewable fossil fuels continue to provide a large portion of industrial energy.

52. D

Industries producing products in greater quantities drove demand for more efficient processes, and as those new processes were instituted they prompted further change. Industrialists were able to invest capital into new technologies, and the increase in raw materials was absorbed into the expanded production capacity of factories; **(D)** is correct. Urbanization was an effect of industrialization, not a cause, and it would not be true to say rural areas were abandoned; (A) is incorrect. Royal backing and navigation technologies were important in the age of exploration in the fifteenth and sixteenth centuries, not the nineteenth century; (B) is incorrect. Iron and coal were abundantly available in Europe, and the most common imports from the Americas were food crops, fibers such as cotton, and precious metals. Population grew in this time with the availability of new food sources. Thus, (C) is incorrect.

53. C

Innovations in transportation, combined with increased demand for manufactured goods and an expanding population, caused global economic growth in the late nineteenth century; **(C)** is correct. The increasing population outstripped the available jobs and combined with other factors such as famine to contribute to a rise in European emigration to countries such as the United States; (A) is incorrect. The use of the technologies in the chart, especially diesel engines, led to further increases in agricultural production and a greater availability of agricultural imports thanks to advances in transportation; (B) is incorrect. (D) is not supported by the chart; while European politics began to show explicit nationalism in this period, that cannot be inferred from the inventions listed.

54. B

The diesel engine and the automobile were both powered by petroleum products, and their development reflects the rising importance of petroleum at the turn of the twentieth century. Access to Middle Eastern oil was of critical importance for empires like the British and French, as they shifted from coal-fueled ships to ones that burned oil. This need for secure access to petroleum is what, in part, led to the partition of the Ottoman Empire after World War I. Thus, **(B)** is correct. (A) is incorrect; the economic and social forces resulting from the Second

Industrial Revolution led to Marxism's growth in popularity in the late nineteenth century, but this was unrelated to these particular inventions. (C) is incorrect because it better describes how the steam engine, not the diesel engine or the automobile, was a turning point in world history. (D) is incorrect because tanks were developed during World War I in response to trench warfare and were not a direct result of the invention of the diesel engine and the automobile.

55. A

As European economies thrived and European political and military influence grew, the Ottoman and Chinese governments experimented with reforms to help improve their economies in an attempt to keep up. **(A)** is correct. Peasant rebellions did not occur in Western Europe; (B) is incorrect. Nationalist leaders sought to emphasize native traditions and drew contrasts with the European colonizers; (C) is incorrect. After decolonization, many governments did adopt capitalist market policies, but that is not supported by these tables. (D) is incorrect, as many reform movements did gain official support and recognition at the end of the nineteenth century, both in Europe and the United States.

Section I, Part B

1. A successful short-answer response accomplishes all three tasks set forth by the prompt. Each part of the prompt is worth 1 point, for a total of 3 possible points.

(a) and **(b)** To earn the points, the response must explain how two specific pieces of evidence support the authors' claim that the role of Europeans was primarily as middlemen in the silver trade. Examples include the use of silver to purchase goods throughout trading posts in the Indian Ocean, the transportation of silver from the Americas to the Philippines to buy goods from China, the role of silver as a new global currency, the role of the Dutch in the spice trade, and the establishment of trading posts by the Portuguese in the Indian Ocean basin and coastal West Africa. The response should not simply summarize the author's claims.

(c) To earn the point, the response must explain how evidence refutes the claim that silver flowed from West to East. Possible evidence includes China's demand for silver as a payment for goods such as silk, porcelain, and tea and the lack of demand for European goods by Asian markets that led to trade deficits or an unfavorable balance of trade.

2. A successful short-answer response accomplishes all three tasks set forth by the prompt. Each part of the prompt is worth 1 point, for a total of 3 possible points.

(a) To earn the point, the response must explain a specific change that resulted from increased contact between the Chinese navy and ports in the Indian Ocean basin. For example, the voyages established new trade relationships between Chinese merchants and merchants in the ports that were visited. These relationships lasted beyond the voyages and expanded commerce in the region. Another change that resulted was how the Chinese government projected military authority to new areas such as South Asia and East Africa through the use of a large navy.

(b) To earn the point, the response must explain a continuity in the Indian Ocean basin, such as the trade in specific luxury goods like spices from Southeast Asia and cotton from India, the diffusion of Islam through merchant and missionary activity, and the dominance of Arab merchants in conducting trade.

(c) To earn the point, the response must describe a long-term impact of the decision to end the voyages on China. For example, the lack of the presence of the Chinese navy in the Indian Ocean basin enabled European merchants to expand their influence in the region. It created competition for private Chinese merchants. Another impact was that the rise of European maritime empires eventually fueled industrialization and economic imperialism in China in the nineteenth century.

3. A successful short-answer response accomplishes all three tasks set forth by the prompt. Each part of the prompt is worth 1 point, for a total of 3 possible points.

(a) To earn the point, the response must identify a similarity used to govern imperial states, such as the use of merit-based bureaucracies by the Chinese and Mongol empires, the collection of tribute by the central authority in the Mexica and Songhai empires, and the permission of local religious and government practices as long as they did not interfere with the security of the empire by the Songhai and Mongol empires and the Delhi Sultanate.

(b) To earn the point, the response must explain a reason why multiple empires used these techniques. For example, bureaucracies were used in China by both Chinese and Mongol rulers because they were an effective way to manage a large empire and preserved an important Confucian tradition.

(c) To earn the point, the response must identify a difference between the government structures of an empire and decentralized region. For example, the Swahili city-states of East Africa were governed independently and controlled the surrounding countryside. In contrast, the kingdoms of Ghana and Mali in West Africa used tax revenues to expand their military and protect trade routes and gold mines.

4. A successful short-answer response accomplishes all three tasks set forth by the prompt. Each part of the prompt is worth 1 point, for a total of 3 possible points.

(a) To earn the point, the response must identify a challenge or issue that governments were attempting to address. Examples include: the Great Depression, which led to unemployment and a decline in production that devastated national economies; the world wars, which required the mobilization of resources and the investment of capital into the war effort; and the need of newly independent countries to industrialize in the aftermath of independence.

(b) To earn the point, the response must explain a difference in policies of communist and newly independent states in the twentieth century. For example, communist states, such as the Soviet Union and China, controlled all aspects of the economy through policies such as the Five-Year Plans to promote industrialization and the Great Leap Forward in China, intended to promote increased agricultural yields to support industrial workers. Newly independent states often promoted industrialization through government investment in business, such as the government-run factories in India following independence.

(c) To earn the point, the response must explain how, in the period following the end of the Cold War in 1991, global economic trends have reflected liberalization and/or cooperation. For example, formerly communist economies in Russia and China allowed more free market conditions, and many governments reduced trade barriers, such as tariffs, and promoted participation in regional trade agreements, such as the European Union.

Section II

1. *Evaluate the extent to which European conquest and colonization changed societies in Latin America from 1492 to circa 1750.*

Category	Scoring Criteria	Notes
Thesis/Claim (0–1 points)	Historically defensible thesis/claim with a logical line of reasoning. The response must make a thesis or claim without restating the prompt itself. The thesis must consist of one or more sentences located in one place, either in the introduction or the conclusion.	This question is assessing the historical reasoning skill of change and continuity over time. The thesis should make a claim about at least two major changes in the Americas as a result of the arrival of Europeans. Examples: The subjugation of Native Americans; violent conquest; spread of disease; the introduction of European cultural/religious elements; the establishment of European rather than indigenous governments.
Contextualization (0–1 points)	Broader historical context related to the prompt. The response must connect the topic to historical developments, events, or processes; these can occur before, during, or after the time frame of the prompt itself.	Contextualization for this prompt should explain, not merely mention, broader factors that impacted the interactions in Latin America. Examples: An explanation of factors prompting European expeditions, such as the desire for trade routes; the characteristics of the existing native empires; the economic, imperial, and religious motivations of Spanish settlers after initial contact.
Evidence (0–3 points)	Use of evidence to support the thesis. The response must utilize the content from at least *three* documents to address the *topic* of the prompt. (1 point) OR The response must use at least *six* documents to support an *argument* based on the prompt. (2 points)	Evidence from the documents must be paraphrased, not merely quoted. Examples: Documents 1, 2, 4, and 7 to support that Europeans subjugated Native Americans; document 3 to support that empires were violently conquered; document 1 to support that indigenous societies were impacted by new diseases; documents 1, 2, 4, 5, and 6 to support that European cultural/religious elements were introduced; documents 5 and 7 to support that Europeans created new government systems.
	The response must use at least *one* additional piece of historical evidence, beyond what is found in the documents, to support an argument. This additional evidence must be different from what was used for contextualization. (1 point)	Examples: The religious beliefs or political structure of indigenous societies before European contact; the use of forced labor on Caribbean plantations; the eventual development of a social hierarchy based on race.

(continued)

Category	Scoring Criteria	Notes
Analysis and Reasoning (0–2 points)	Complexity of understanding and reasoning. The response must explain, for at least *three* of the documents, how or why the document's purpose, historical basis, point of view, and/or audience are relevant to an argument. (1 point)	Factors' relevance to the argument about impacts on Latin America should be explained, not just identified. Example: The role of point of view in document 7, in which the Spanish monk clearly feels sympathetic toward the natives based on his description of the labor. He even calls the native inhabitants "poor fellows," which is likely due to his close relationship with the natives when attempting to convert them.
	The response must show a complex understanding of the content of the prompt, using evidence to support, qualify, or modify an argument about the prompt. (1 point)	A complex understanding should be incorporated into the overall argument about impacts on Latin America. Examples: Using documents 2, 4, 6, and 7 to explain multiple factors, such as economic and religious, that motivated Europeans; using documents 2, 4, and 7 to analyze multiple European perspectives about treatment of native populations; using documents 1, 2, 4 to analyze multiple European views about the indigenous populations.

2. *In the period circa 1200–1450, the reconstitution of empires affected the expansion or decline of cities across Afro-Eurasia.*

Develop an argument that evaluates how the growth of empires led to change in urban growth in Afro-Eurasia in the period circa 1200–1450.

Category	Scoring Criteria	Notes
Thesis/Claim (0–1 points)	Historically defensible thesis/claim with a logical line of reasoning. The response must make a thesis or claim without restating the prompt itself. The thesis must consist of one or more sentences located in one place, either in the introduction or the conclusion.	This question assesses the skill of causation. A strong thesis should make a claim about at least two ways that empires impacted urban growth. Example: "The growth of empires from 1200 to 1450 stimulated the growth of cities by creating government support for economies, facilitating trade, and expanding agriculture."
Contextualization (0–1 points)	Broader historical context related to the prompt. The response must connect the topic to historical developments, events, or processes; these can occur before, during, or after the time frame of the prompt itself.	Contextualization for this prompt should explain, not merely mention, broader factors relevant to the changes to empires and/or cities. Examples: An explanation of circumstances that led to the fall of previous empires, such as the Roman, Han, Persian, or Gupta empires; a description of factors that enabled the rise of new empires, such as bureaucracies that were effective at governing large territories.

Category	Scoring Criteria	Notes
Evidence (0–2 points)	Use of evidence to support the thesis. The response identifies specific examples *relevant to the topic* of the prompt. (1 point) OR The response uses specific examples to *support an argument* about the prompt. (2 points)	Evidence must be paraphrased, not merely quoted. To earn 2 points, the evidence must be used to support an argument about how empires impacted urban growth. Examples: The pattern of urbanization during the Ming Dynasty due to government support of the economy and renovation of the Grand Canal after moving the capital to Beijing; the revival of trading cities across Central Asia due to trade under the Mongol Empire; the flourishing of trade cities in West African kingdoms such as the Empire of Mali; agricultural expansion resulting from new technologies supporting urban populations in consolidating European states.
Analysis and Reasoning (0–2 points)	Complexity of understanding and reasoning. The response shows historical reasoning to make an argument about the prompt. (1 point) OR The response demonstrates complex understanding, using evidence to support, qualify, or modify an argument about the prompt. (2 points)	Comparison, causation, or continuity and change over time should be incorporated into the overall argument about how empires impacted urban growth. Examples: An explanation of how the evidence described led to the growth of cities (causation); a description of the similarities in how both the Mongol Empire and the Empire of Mali facilitated trade, stimulating the growth of trade cities along the Silk Road and the city of Timbuktu (comparison). OR A complex understanding should be incorporated into the overall argument about how empires impacted urban growth. Examples: An explanation of both the causes of urban growth *and* the effects of such growth, such as the spread of culture along trade routes and the flourishing of arts and learning in cities in the Empire of Mali and the Abbasid Caliphates; qualifying the argument about empires causing urban growth by discussing the flourishing of cities that were not part of an empire, such as the East African city-states.

3. *In the period 1450–1750, imperial expansion relied on the increased use of gunpowder, cannons, and armed trade to establish large empires in both hemispheres.*

Develop an argument that evaluates the extent to which empire-building among European powers was different from empire-building by the Ottoman Empire in this time period.

Category	Scoring Criteria	Notes
Thesis/Claim (0–1 points)	Historically defensible thesis/claim with a logical line of reasoning. The response must make a thesis or claim without restating the prompt itself. The thesis must consist of one or more sentences located in one place, either in the introduction or the conclusion.	This question assesses the skill of comparison. A strong thesis should make a claim about two to three major differences between European empires and the Ottoman Empire. Example: "Between 1450 and 1750, European and Ottoman powers differed both in their methods of initial conquest and in their political and economic policies for administering conquered groups."
Contextualization (0–1 points)	Broader historical context related to the prompt. The response must connect the topic to historical developments, events, or processes; these can occur before, during, or after the time frame of the prompt itself.	Contextualization for this prompt should explain, not merely mention, broader factors relevant to European or Ottoman empire-building. Examples: An explanation of factors that motivated empire expansion, such as Ottoman influence in the Mediterranean causing European merchants to search for alternate routes to Asia, leading to the conquest and colonization of the Americas; an explanation of the Ottomans' ability to increase influence by taking advantage of Byzantine weaknesses.
Evidence (0–2 points)	Use of evidence to support the thesis. The response identifies specific examples *relevant to the topic* of the prompt. (1 point) OR The response uses specific examples to *support an argument* about the prompt. (2 points)	Evidence must be paraphrased, not merely quoted. To earn 2 points, the evidence must be used to support an argument about the differences in European and Ottoman empire-building. Examples: This treatment of conquered groups, with the Ottomans showing more tolerance through the millet system, while the Spanish forced Native Americans to convert to Christianity; different methods of conquest, with the Ottomans using naval power and advanced gunpowder technology, and the Europeans benefiting from the Native Americans' lack of access to gunpowder weapons; different economic policies, with the Europeans using coerced labor such as the *encomienda* system and African slavery, and the Ottomans taxing peasant laborers but not making extensive use of coerced labor.

Category	Scoring Criteria	Notes
Analysis and Reasoning (0–2 points)	Complexity of understanding and reasoning. The response shows historical reasoning to make an argument about the prompt. (1 point) OR The response demonstrates complex understanding, using evidence to support, qualify, or modify an argument about the prompt. (2 points)	Comparison, causation, or continuity and change over time should be incorporated into the overall argument about the differences between European and Ottoman empire-building. Examples: A description of the continuities in the empires after 1750, such as the continued impacts of neocolonialism in Latin America and the persistence of the Ottoman Empire until the early twentieth century (continuity and change); a detailed explanation of the differences in the military and administrative policies of both empires (comparison). OR A complex understanding should be incorporated into the overall argument about the differences between European and Ottoman empire-building. Examples: A description of continuities *and* changes in the empires after 1750, such as the outbreak of independence movements in Latin America and uprisings in the Ottoman Empire before and during World War I; an explanation of differences *and* similarities between the empires, such as the use of military conquest by both empires.

4. *In the period 1750–1900, the process of industrialization changed the way in which goods were produced and consumed, with far-reaching effects on the global economy.*

Develop an argument that evaluates how the process of industrialization transformed the global economy in this time period.

Category	Scoring Criteria	Notes
Thesis/Claim (0–1 points)	Historically defensible thesis/claim with a logical line of reasoning. The response must make a thesis or claim without restating the prompt itself. The thesis must consist of one or more sentences located in one place, either in the introduction or the conclusion.	This question assesses the skill of continuity and change over time. A strong thesis should make a claim about two to three major changes in the global economy due to industrialization. Example: "Between 1750 and 1900, industrialization in Europe prompted the increasing interdependence of the global economy as industrialized nations sought colonies for raw materials and markets, leading to economically exploitative relationships."
Contextualization (0–1 points)	Broader historical context related to the prompt. The response must connect the topic to historical developments, events, or processes; these can occur before, during, or after the time frame of the prompt itself.	Contextualization for this prompt should explain, not merely mention, broader factors relevant to how industrialization impacted the global economy. Examples: A description of the factors that enabled industrialization; an explanation of the motivations for European imperialism and how this impacted global markets.
Evidence (0–2 points)	Use of evidence to support the thesis. The response identifies specific examples *relevant to the topic* of the prompt. (1 point) OR The response uses specific examples to *support an argument* about the prompt. (2 points)	Evidence must be paraphrased, not merely quoted. To earn 2 points, the evidence must be used to support an argument about how industrialization impacted the global economy. Examples: The increase in Europe's share of manufacturing and growing demand for raw materials; the desire for materials and markets driving the spread of mercantilist policies and prompting imperialism; the greater interdependence of economies around the world.

Category	Scoring Criteria	Notes
Analysis and Reasoning (0–2 points)	Complexity of understanding and reasoning. The response shows historical reasoning to make an argument about the prompt. (1 point) OR The response demonstrates complex understanding, using evidence to support, qualify, or modify an argument about the prompt. (2 points)	Comparison, causation, or continuity and change over time should be incorporated into the overall argument about how industrialization impacted the global economy. Examples: An explanation of how mercantilist policies were continued from the previous period of colonial expansion in the Americas (continuity and change); an explanation of why improvements in industrialization would lead to new types of global economic relationships (causation). OR A complex understanding should be incorporated into the overall argument about how industrialization impacted the global economy. Examples: An explanation of both the continuities *and* changes in mercantilist policies, such as the growing need for colonies' increasing manufacturing output spurring demand for both supplies and markets; a description of multiple perspectives about the global economy, such as the exploitative working conditions that developed on plantations in the Americas, the expansion of slave labor, and the economic imperialism in African colonies.

Practice Exam 3

Practice Exam 3 Answer Grid

1. Ⓐ Ⓑ Ⓒ Ⓓ
2. Ⓐ Ⓑ Ⓒ Ⓓ
3. Ⓐ Ⓑ Ⓒ Ⓓ
4. Ⓐ Ⓑ Ⓒ Ⓓ
5. Ⓐ Ⓑ Ⓒ Ⓓ
6. Ⓐ Ⓑ Ⓒ Ⓓ
7. Ⓐ Ⓑ Ⓒ Ⓓ
8. Ⓐ Ⓑ Ⓒ Ⓓ
9. Ⓐ Ⓑ Ⓒ Ⓓ
10. Ⓐ Ⓑ Ⓒ Ⓓ
11. Ⓐ Ⓑ Ⓒ Ⓓ
12. Ⓐ Ⓑ Ⓒ Ⓓ
13. Ⓐ Ⓑ Ⓒ Ⓓ
14. Ⓐ Ⓑ Ⓒ Ⓓ

15. Ⓐ Ⓑ Ⓒ Ⓓ
16. Ⓐ Ⓑ Ⓒ Ⓓ
17. Ⓐ Ⓑ Ⓒ Ⓓ
18. Ⓐ Ⓑ Ⓒ Ⓓ
19. Ⓐ Ⓑ Ⓒ Ⓓ
20. Ⓐ Ⓑ Ⓒ Ⓓ
21. Ⓐ Ⓑ Ⓒ Ⓓ
22. Ⓐ Ⓑ Ⓒ Ⓓ
23. Ⓐ Ⓑ Ⓒ Ⓓ
24. Ⓐ Ⓑ Ⓒ Ⓓ
25. Ⓐ Ⓑ Ⓒ Ⓓ
26. Ⓐ Ⓑ Ⓒ Ⓓ
27. Ⓐ Ⓑ Ⓒ Ⓓ
28. Ⓐ Ⓑ Ⓒ Ⓓ

29. Ⓐ Ⓑ Ⓒ Ⓓ
30. Ⓐ Ⓑ Ⓒ Ⓓ
31. Ⓐ Ⓑ Ⓒ Ⓓ
32. Ⓐ Ⓑ Ⓒ Ⓓ
33. Ⓐ Ⓑ Ⓒ Ⓓ
34. Ⓐ Ⓑ Ⓒ Ⓓ
35. Ⓐ Ⓑ Ⓒ Ⓓ
36. Ⓐ Ⓑ Ⓒ Ⓓ
37. Ⓐ Ⓑ Ⓒ Ⓓ
38. Ⓐ Ⓑ Ⓒ Ⓓ
39. Ⓐ Ⓑ Ⓒ Ⓓ
40. Ⓐ Ⓑ Ⓒ Ⓓ
41. Ⓐ Ⓑ Ⓒ Ⓓ
42. Ⓐ Ⓑ Ⓒ Ⓓ

43. Ⓐ Ⓑ Ⓒ Ⓓ
44. Ⓐ Ⓑ Ⓒ Ⓓ
45. Ⓐ Ⓑ Ⓒ Ⓓ
46. Ⓐ Ⓑ Ⓒ Ⓓ
47. Ⓐ Ⓑ Ⓒ Ⓓ
48. Ⓐ Ⓑ Ⓒ Ⓓ
49. Ⓐ Ⓑ Ⓒ Ⓓ
50. Ⓐ Ⓑ Ⓒ Ⓓ
51. Ⓐ Ⓑ Ⓒ Ⓓ
52. Ⓐ Ⓑ Ⓒ Ⓓ
53. Ⓐ Ⓑ Ⓒ Ⓓ
54. Ⓐ Ⓑ Ⓒ Ⓓ
55. Ⓐ Ⓑ Ⓒ Ⓓ

SECTION I, PART A

Time—55 minutes

55 Questions

Directions: Section I, Part A of this exam contains 55 multiple-choice questions, organized into sets with corresponding historical sources. Each of the questions or incomplete statements is followed by four suggested answers or completions. Using both the provided sources and your own historical knowledge, select the best answer choice.

Questions 1–4 refer to the map below.

MAIN ROUTES OF THE SILK ROAD

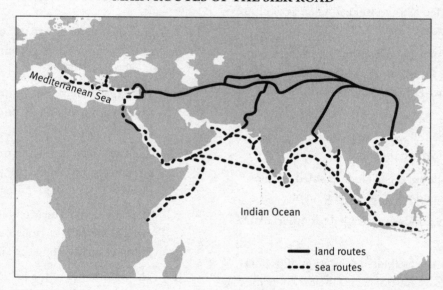

GO ON TO THE NEXT PAGE

1. Based on the map and your knowledge of history, which of the following statements best explains the increase in Silk Road trade in the period circa 1200 to 1450?

   (A) The expansion of the Mali Empire connected the West African gold and salt trade into the wider Afro-Eurasian trade network.

   (B) The expansion of the Mongol Empire facilitated communication and secured overland routes.

   (C) The expansion of the Grand Canal in China facilitated a boom in East Asian agriculture and trade.

   (D) The expansion of Indian Ocean trade connected the Swahili Coast and Malacca into the Afro-Eurasian trade network.

2. Which of the following was a major effect of the network shown on the map?

   (A) Cross-cultural exchange enabled technological and political development.

   (B) Luxury goods were traded for other luxury goods.

   (C) The routes facilitated migration of populations from East Asia and the Mediterranean

   (D) The cities and kingdoms located along the network were weakened.

3. Based on the map and your knowledge of history, which of the following is most similar to the Silk Road?

   (A) The migration of Indian populations as indentured servants in British colonies

   (B) The Inca Empire's use of its vast network of roadways to facilitate troop movements

   (C) The United Nations' fostering of international cooperation among diverse states

   (D) The Internet's facilitation of worldwide exchange of information and goods

4. Which of the following events contributed to the decline of the routes depicted on the map in the period 1450 to 1750?

   (A) The expansion of the Ottoman Empire led to an Islamic monopoly on Silk Road trade between Europe and Asia.

   (B) The Little Ice Age altered monsoon patterns in the Indian Ocean, which negatively impacted traditional sailing routes.

   (C) The downfall of the Mongol Empire led to a general increase in violence and the restoration of tariffs along the Silk Road.

   (D) The dominance of the British East India Company and rise of British imperialism led to a general decline in Silk Road trade.

GO ON TO THE NEXT PAGE

Questions 5–7 refer to the passage below.

"You wonder I did not tell you of [the Ninety-five Theses]. But I did not wish to have them widely circulated. I only intended submitting them to a few learned men for examination, and if they disapproved of them, to suppress them; or make them known through their publications, in the event of their meeting with your approval. But now they are being spread abroad and translated everywhere, which I never could have credited, so that I regret having given birth to them—not that I am unwilling to proclaim the truth manfully, for there is nothing I more ardently desire, but because this way of instructing the people is of little avail. As yet I am still uncertain as to some points, and would have gone into others more particularly, leaving some out entirely, had I foreseen all this. . . . Yes, when the Lord grants me leisure, I purpose issuing a book on the use and misuse of the Indulgences*, in order to suppress the before-mentioned points. I have no longer any doubt that the people are deceived, not through the Indulgences, but through their use."

*Luther discussed the commercialization of indulgences, which the Catholic Church taught lessened the punishment for forgiven sins, in the Ninety-five Theses.

Martin Luther, a German theologian, 1518

5. Which of the following conclusions is best supported by the passage?

   (A) The printing press facilitated the dissemination of new philosophies and belief systems.

   (B) The Black Death weakened the institutional authority of the Catholic Church.

   (C) The Hanseatic League facilitated a regional network of exchange among its members.

   (D) The monarchies of Europe sought to weaken the Pope's political power over their kingdoms.

6. Which of the following was an important long-term effect of the movement spurred by the publication of the Ninety-five Theses?

   (A) The diffusion of new astronomical understandings of the universe

   (B) The cementing of the Pope's political supremacy over monarchs in Catholic kingdoms

   (C) Transformations within Catholicism and the emergence of new Protestant groups

   (D) The end of the Catholic Church's influence in central and western European countries

7. Luther's view of indulgences, as alluded to in the passage, is most similar to the views associated with which of the following historical developments in the period from 1750 to 1900?

   (A) The development of the religion of Sikhism

   (B) The collapse of a centralized Abbasid caliphate in Dar al-Islam

   (C) The arguments in the Declaration of the Rights of Man and of the Citizen

   (D) The resurgence of conservatism in Europe after the Revolutions of 1848

GO ON TO THE NEXT PAGE

Questions 8–10 refer to the following two images.

Image 1

ETCHING OF COLUMBUS ARRIVING IN THE AMERICAS, 1594

Image 2

ETCHING OF COLUMBUS ARRIVING IN THE AMERICAS, 1788

GO ON TO THE NEXT PAGE →

8. The depiction of Columbus and his expedition in <u>Image 1</u> best illustrates which of the following continuities in world history?

   (A) The growth of networks of exchange leading to the creation of syncretic belief systems

   (B) Technological innovations leading to increases in agricultural production

   (C) The expansion of trade networks facilitating cultural and demographic change

   (D) Rulers using works of art to legitimize their rule in the eyes of their subjects

9. The depiction of Christian symbolism in <u>Image 2</u> best illustrates which of the following cultural processes in the period circa 1450–1750?

   (A) The importance of major financial backing for naval expeditions to the Americas

   (B) The interconnection of missionary efforts and colonial expansion

   (C) The political and religious rivalries between European states expressed through their competing maritime empires

   (D) The tensions between Protestants and Catholics in Europe

10. Taken together, the two images best illustrate which of the following cultural processes?

   (A) The practice of neocolonialism by industrial powers

   (B) The use of Social Darwinism to rationalize imperialism

   (C) The influence of European religious practices in the Americas

   (D) The development of racial hierarchies to justify colonialism

GO ON TO THE NEXT PAGE

Questions 11–13 refer to the following two tables.

Table 1

COMPOSITION OF ENGLISH GUNPOWDER, SIXTEENTH AND SEVENTEENTH CENTURIES

	1569	1578	1588	1595	1695
Saltpeter	50.0%	66.6%	71.4%	75.0%	75%
Charcoal	33.3%	16.6%	14.3%	12.5%	15%
Sulfur	16.6%	16.6%	14.3%	12.5%	10%

Table 2

COMPOSITION OF CONTINENTAL EUROPEAN GUNPOWDER, SIXTEENTH AND SEVENTEENTH CENTURIES

	Sweden 1560	Germany 1595	Denmark 1608	France 1650	Sweden 1697
Saltpeter	66.6%	52.5%	68.3%	76.5%	73%
Charcoal	16.6%	26.1%	23.2%	13.6%	17%
Sulfur	16.6%	21.7%	8.5%	10.8%	10%

Note: The most effective composition for gunpowder is 75% saltpeter, 15% charcoal, and 10% sulfur.

11. Which of the following factors most contributed to Europeans' ability to undertake the refinement of gunpowder depicted in the tables?

   (A) Noninterference in the internal affairs of sovereign states

   (B) The Islamic world reintroducing Greek texts to Europe

   (C) Interregional diffusion of technology along trade routes

   (D) Establishment of joint-stock companies

12. The improvements in the refining of gunpowder, presented in the tables, are best understood in the context of which of the following?

   (A) Competition between European states over Indian Ocean trade routes

   (B) Religious conflicts between Protestant and Catholic states

   (C) European crusades into the Middle East

   (D) Enlightenment thinking reviving republican principles of government

GO ON TO THE NEXT PAGE

13. Which of the following was an important <u>direct</u> effect of the refinement of gunpowder depicted in the tables on Eurasia?

(A) The decline of horse-riding steppe nomads as a threat to settled agricultural societies

(B) The conquest of the indigenous peoples of the Americas and their assimilation into transoceanic empires

(C) The decline in the need for states to build fortifications and other defensive walls

(D) The strengthening of feudalism in order to support large standing armies wielding firearms

GO ON TO THE NEXT PAGE

Questions 14–16 refer to the passage below.

"During this period [the fifteenth century], the whole of the Swahili Coast enjoyed a revival of fortunes due to a combination of factors. The overland route to the east had been cut by the Mongols, leaving the sea route via the east African coast as the alternative. Several large trading fleets were sent by the Chinese to Africa, and an insatiable demand for eastern spices, particularly in Europe, helped put the city-states of the Swahili Coast, which acted as middlemen, back in the centre of international trade."

"The Wealth of Africa: The Swahili Coast," notes prepared for educators by The British Museum

14. The passage can best be used as evidence for which of the following world historical trends that took place during the period 1450 to 1750?

   (A) The growing interconnectedness of the Eastern and Western hemispheres

   (B) The expansion of empires around the world as they incorporated diverse subjects

   (C) The impact of religion on interregional travel and connectedness

   (D) The growth of the transatlantic slave trade which saw millions of Africans forcibly transported to the Americas

15. Based on the passage and your knowledge of world history, which of the following best describes the reason for the the final decline of the Swahili city-states?

   (A) Waning demand for eastern spices in Europe

   (B) Government mismanagement of income from trade

   (C) Religious tension between local and foreign merchants

   (D) Competition from European trading post empires

16. The passage mentions a "revival of fortunes" for the Swahili city-states in the fifteenth century. Which of the following historical developments had previously had the most direct negative impact on the economic power of these city-states?

   (A) The improvements in Portuguese maritime technologies

   (B) The spread of the plague known as the Black Death

   (C) The development of caravan technology along trans-Saharan trade routes

   (D) The voyages of the Chinese admiral Zheng He

GO ON TO THE NEXT PAGE

Questions 17–19 refer to the image below.

TAJ MAHAL

Commissioned by the Mughal emperor Shah Jahan

17. The building depicted in the image illustrates which of the following consequences of Mughal rule?

   (A) The widespread artistic integration of Indian and Persian architectural styles

   (B) The religious strife created as the Mughals sought to rid India of Hindu influences

   (C) The increasing dominance of British imperial authority over the Indian subcontinent

   (D) The imposition of foreign cultural practices to ensure the subjugation of a conquered people

18. The building depicted in the image illustrates which of the following continuities in world history?

   (A) Rulers claiming divine connections in order to justify their authority

   (B) Rulers developing syncretic belief systems and practices due to the varying religious and ethnic sects under their authority

   (C) Rulers utilizing tax collection to fuel efforts for territorial expansion

   (D) Rulers using public displays of art and monumental architecture to legitimize their authority

GO ON TO THE NEXT PAGE

19. Which of the following was a policy under many Mughal rulers that helped stabilize their empire?

   (A) The abolition of an imperial taxation system in order to inject capital into the economy

   (B) The replication of the British parliamentary system in Mughal imperial administration

   (C) The inclusion of followers of diverse religions into the empire's bureaucracy

   (D) The restriction of international trade shutting out influences from cultures that bordered the Indian Ocean

GO ON TO THE NEXT PAGE

Questions 20–22 refer to the passage below.

"War dominated much of Peter's reign. At first Peter attempted to secure the principality's southern borders against the Tatars and the Ottoman Turks. His campaign against a fort on the Sea of Azov failed initially, but after he created Russia's first navy, Peter was able to take the port of Azov in 1696. To continue the war with the Ottoman Empire, Peter traveled to Europe to seek allies. The first tsar to make such a trip, Peter visited Brandenburg, Holland, England, and the Holy Roman Empire during his so-called Grand Embassy. Peter learned a great deal and enlisted into his service hundreds of West European technical specialists. The embassy was cut short by the attempt to place Sofia on the throne instead of Peter, a revolt that was crushed by Peter's followers. As a result, Peter had hundreds of the participants tortured and killed, and he publicly displayed their bodies as a warning to others. . . . Through his victories, Peter acquired a direct link with Western Europe. In celebration, Peter assumed the title of emperor as well as tsar, and Muscovy officially became the Russian Empire in 1721."

Glenn E. Curtis, *Russia: A Country Study*, 1991

20. The actions of Peter the Great, as described in the passage, most clearly exemplify which of the following?

    (A) Divine right of kings

    (B) Consolidation of power

    (C) Inflation

    (D) Nationalism

21. The events recounted in the passage are best seen as evidence of which of the following about the Russian state?

    (A) Its rejection of foreign alliances against regional rivals

    (B) Its negative reaction to the introduction of Western fashions

    (C) Its focus on developing technological innovations domestically

    (D) Its rejection of Enlightenment political concepts

22. Based on the passage and your knowledge of world history, which of the following was an important long-term development of Peter the Great's reign?

    (A) Rulers became known as tsars.

    (B) Protestants such as Huguenots emigrated.

    (C) Aristocratic women participated more in society.

    (D) Enlightenment ideals spread throughout government.

GO ON TO THE NEXT PAGE

Questions 23–26 refer to the passage below.

"[I]t is not so familiar to some persons as it ought to be that a Tartar and not a Chinese sovereign is now seated on the throne in China. For some time after the accession of the first Manchu emperor, there was considerable friction between the two races. The subjugation of the empire by the Manchus was followed by a military occupation of the country, which survived the original necessity, and has remained part of the system of government until the present day. The dynasty . . . has remained in power through the entire period of intercourse with western nations. The title adopted by the first emperor of the line was Shun-che. It was during the reign of this sovereign that Adam Schaal, a German Jesuit, took up his residence at Peking and that the first Russian embassy, 1656, visited the capital. But in those days the Chinese had not learned to tolerate the idea that a foreigner should enter the presence of the Son of Heaven unless he were willing to perform the prostration known as the Ko-t'ow, and the Russians not being inclined to humor any such presumptuous folly left the capital without opening negotiations."

Trumbull White, an American journalist, *The War in the East*, 1895

23. All of the following statements are factually accurate. Which most likely explains White's reference to the subjugation of the Chinese by the Manchus?

   (A) The eunuchs lost influence over the imperial government and were severely reduced in number.

   (B) The long-standing civil service examination system was abolished.

   (C) The practice of foot binding was common during the Qing Dynasty.

   (D) The Manchus forced Han Chinese men to adopt the braided hairstyle known as the queue during the Qing Dynasty.

24. The particular demands placed upon foreign diplomats most strongly support which of the following statements about Qing Dynasty China?

   (A) The Chinese state's Confucian values caused it to view Christian Europeans negatively.

   (B) The Chinese viewed themselves as sitting atop a global social hierarchy.

   (C) The established elites resisted reform efforts that seemingly threatened their own influence.

   (D) The ongoing maintenance of the Qing Dynasty's regional dominance was a key Chinese priority.

GO ON TO THE NEXT PAGE

25. Which of the following additional pieces of information about the time period described in the passage would have been most directly useful to the author in assessing whether China's treatment of the Russian diplomatic mission could have had a potentially negative impact on China?

    (A) Information on Russia's ability to project military force into East Asia

    (B) Information on the specific goods that Russia was offering to trade

    (C) Information on whether the Russia mission was in communication with the German Jesuit

    (D) Information on any trade agreements Russia made with neighboring Japan

26. The reference to "considerable friction between the two races" is best understood in the context of which of the following nineteenth-century developments that contributed to the decline of the Qing Empire?

    (A) The Opium Wars between China and European powers, particularly the British

    (B) The increasing influence of communist groups in China that culminated in communists seizing power

    (C) The rise in tensions between supporters of a traditional agrarian economy and reformers who advocated for modernization

    (D) The civil war between the Manchu-Qing rulers and supporters of the Taiping Heavenly Kingdom

GO ON TO THE NEXT PAGE

Questions 27–30 refer to the passage below.

"To the German workman, for example, it seems plain that English proletarians will not gain *his* salvation; he must gain it himself. The German wage-earner must be better fed, clothed, housed, educated, organised, and all these needs translate themselves into more regular work, better paid. But if German industry is defeated by English industry, the German workman will suffer unemployment, reduction of wages, lockouts, unsuccessful strikes, and a decline in trade union membership. Such a retrogression means a delaying of the ultimate working class victory as well as a worse situation in the present. And, parenthetically, workingmen and Socialists, being ordinary men with the ambitions and appetites of ordinary men, do not spend seven evenings in the week in contemplation of a Co-operative Commonwealth any more than the average church-goer devotes his entire mind to the Day of Judgment. . . . If imperialism appears to raise wages as well as profits, he is not likely to oppose it on sentimental grounds, especially as there are theorists who stand ready to prove that Imperialism is merely the last phase of Capitalism and will bring Socialism all the sooner."

Walter E. Weyl, an American economist, in *American World Policies*, 1917

27. Weyl's analysis is best understood in the context of which of the following?

   (A) The outbreak of warfare between democratic nations with large socialist parties

   (B) The organization of workers into labor unions and political parties

   (C) The expansion of the global economy in the nineteenth century

   (D) The establishment of settler colonies in imperial possessions

28. The reference to "Imperialism is merely the last phase of Capitalism" is best understood in the context of which of the following <u>nineteenth-century</u> developments?

   (A) Napoleon's loss at Waterloo ushering in a century-long Pax Britannica

   (B) Adam Smith outlining the idea of economic self-interest in *The Wealth of Nations*

   (C) Industrialization promoting the population growth and geographical expansion of urban areas

   (D) The development of the Marxist idea that human history is the history of class conflict

29. Present-day historians would most likely agree with which of the following aspects of the passage's historical interpretations?

   (A) Imperialism is the final historical phase of capitalism.

   (B) Workers can achieve class solidarity at a national level but not at an international level.

   (C) European nations are inherently economic competitors with one another.

   (D) Empire is a requirement to maintain an industrialized economy.

30. The historical trend described in the passage is most similar to which of the following?

   (A) The spread of Pan-Africanism in the twentieth century

   (B) The rise of neocolonialism after the Second World War

   (C) The role of republicanism in the French Revolutionary Wars

   (D) The failure of the Tanzimât Movement in the nineteenth century

GO ON TO THE NEXT PAGE

Questions 31–32 refer to the passage below.

"There is a most stately temple to be seen, the walls made of stone and lime, and a princely palace. . . . Here are many shops of artificers, and merchants, and especially those who weave linen and cotton cloth. And here do the Barbarie merchants bring cloth of Europe. All the women of this region except maidservants go with their faces covered . . . The inhabitants, and especially strangers there residing, are exceeding rich, insomuch that the king that now is, married both his daughters unto two rich merchants. . . . Corn, cattle, milk, and butter this region yields in great abundance: but salt is very scarce here; for it is brought hither by land from Tagaza, which is five hundred miles distant. When I my self was here, I saw one camel's load of salt sold for 80 ducats. The rich king of Tombuto (Timbuktu) hath many plates and scepters of gold, some whereof weigh 1300 pounds. . . . Here are great store of doctors, judges, priests, and other learned men, that are bountifully maintained at the king's cost and charges. And hither are brought diverse manuscripts or written books out of Barbarie, which are sold for more money than any other merchandise."

Leo Africanus, "The history and description of Africa and of the notable things therein contained," c. 1550

31. The passage most strongly reflects which of the following sixteenth-century trends?

   (A) Nations that participated in the slave trade experienced an economic boom followed by a long-term decline.

   (B) Communities that amassed great wealth tended to do so in isolation from other communities.

   (C) Travelers who wrote about their experiences in foreign lands had little impact on globalization.

   (D) Societies that acted as trade centers often valued the gathering of information as well as goods.

32. Which of the following provides the best explanation for Timbuktu's prosperity as described in the passage?

   (A) Christian pilgrims frequently visited Timbuktu on their way to Jerusalem.

   (B) Timbuktu occupied an advantageous location on regional trade routes.

   (C) The economy of Timbuktu was not dependent on foreign exports.

   (D) Timbuktu had a thriving agricultural economy due to its favorable weather conditions.

GO ON TO THE NEXT PAGE

Questions 33–35 refer to the image below.

UNKNOWN ARTIST, *EL LIBERTADOR SIMÓN BOLÍVAR*, PAINTING

33. The painting is best understood in the context of which of the following nineteenth-century developments?

 (A) The Latin American independence movements

 (B) The worldwide abolition of slavery

 (C) European colonization of Africa and Asia

 (D) Advancements in military technology

34. A historian researching the period would most likely make which of the following claims about the painting's symbolism?

 (A) It emphasizes Bolívar's imperialistic motivations.

 (B) It likens Bolívar's devotion to nonviolent civil disobedience to the passion of a war hero.

 (C) It highlights Bolívar's achievements as a military leader.

 (D) It represents Bolívar's appreciation for traditional European styles of dress.

35. The subject of the painting was most strongly influenced by which of the following?

 (A) The principles of mercantilism

 (B) The ideals of the Enlightenment

 (C) The theories of classical liberalism

 (D) The tenets of Marxism

GO ON TO THE NEXT PAGE

Questions 36–38 refer to the passage below.

"1. The basis for the Constitution will be respect for the predominance of the national will. One of the consequences of this principle will be to require without delay the responsibility of the minister before the Chamber, and, consequently, to consider the minister as having resigned, when he does not have a majority of the votes of the Chamber.

2. Provided that the number of senators does not exceed one-third the number of deputies, the Senate will be named as follows: one-third by the Sultan and two-thirds by the nation, and the term of senators will be of limited duration.

. . .

14. Provided that the property rights of landholders are not infringed upon (for such rights must be respected and must remain intact, according to law), it will be proposed that peasants be permitted to acquire land, and they will be accorded means to borrow money at a moderate rate.

. . .

17. All schools will operate under the surveillance of the state. In order to obtain for Ottoman citizens an education of a homogeneous and uniform character, the official schools will be open, their instruction will be free, and all nationalities will be admitted. . . . Schools of commerce, agriculture and industry will be opened with the goal of developing the resources of the country."

Ottoman Young Turks, a proclamation, 1908

36. The passage is best understood in the context of which of the following global trends?

(A) Long-standing empires experiencing reform movements that promoted democratic reforms and modernization

(B) Former colonies seeking to establish their own governments after achieving independence

(C) Countries with feudal economies seeking to implement Marxist reforms

(D) Democratic societies attempting to eliminate discrimination against women and minorities

37. The structure for the senate outlined in the second paragraph most closely reflects which of the following goals of the group that issued the proclamation?

(A) To promote a theocratic government rooted in Islamic law

(B) To restore power to the monarchy following an attempt at democracy

(C) To concentrate power in the hands of landowners

(D) To shift the balance of power from the monarch to the people

GO ON TO THE NEXT PAGE

38. The statements concerning property rights in the <u>third paragraph</u> are most consistent with which of the following political ideologies?

    (A) Classical liberalism

    (B) Socialism

    (C) Anti-imperialism

    (D) Anarchism

GO ON TO THE NEXT PAGE

Questions 39–41 refer to the following two charts.

Chart 1

EARNINGS OF MARRIED WOMEN IN GREAT BRITAIN, 1787–1865

	1787–1815	*1816–1820*	*1821–1840*	*1841–1845*	*1846–1865*	*All time periods*
High-wage agriculture						
% family income	9.2	16.7	13.5	12.5	12.5	11.4
% husband's earnings	11.7	22.3	35.2	16.2	14.3	17.2
Sample size	(22)	(7)	(5)	(2)	(1)	(37)
Low-wage agriculture						
% family income	11.4		15.6	10.0	13.4	13.1
% husband's earnings	15.7	n.a.	27.5	27.6	15.9	20.8
Sample size	(83)		(60)	(5)	(5)	(153)
Mining						
% family income	40.9	13.9	9.1	8.5		14.2
% husband's earnings	69.2	26.4	16.7	10.3	n.a.	26.0
Sample size	(1)	(15)	(2)	(2)		(20)
Factory						
% family income	23.1	17.6	15.6		24.3	18.2
% husband's earnings	48.2	21.4	22.6	n.a.	37.5	29.9
Sample size	(4)	(1)	(10)		(1)	(16)
Outwork						
% family income	14.7	20.9	24.8	18.9	18.3	20.9
% husband's earnings	24.1	41.6	55.3	32.5	23.9	41.1
Sample size	(7)	(65)	(33)	(27)	(9)	(141)
Trades						
% family income	5.2	18.0			8.0	11.2
% husband's earnings	7.2	24.3	n.a.	n.a.	10.9	15.3
Sample size	(4)	(5)			(3)	(12)

Chart 2

WAGES OF FACTORY WORKERS IN GREAT BRITAIN, 1833

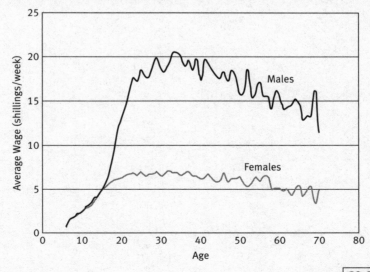

GO ON TO THE NEXT PAGE ⟶

39. Which of the following circumstances best accounts for the data presented in Chart 1?

    (A) An influx of foreign workers following decolonization

    (B) The abolition of slavery within the British Empire

    (C) A decline in the gender-based division of labor

    (D) Increased political rights for women due to early feminism

40. Which of the following best explains why the data in Chart 1 most likely reflects working-class families rather than middle-class families?

    (A) Middle-class women were subject to the pressures of the cult of domesticity and were unlikely to work outside the home.

    (B) Working-class women generally earned a smaller percentage of their family's total income than did middle-class women.

    (C) Middle-class women tended to be employed in jobs such as teaching and nursing, which are not reflected in the table.

    (D) Working-class women were more likely to be married than middle-class women, and the table provides data only about married women.

41. A historian researching economic developments during the Industrial Revolution could use the information in Chart 2 to learn more about which of the following?

    (A) The effects of a large-scale international conflict on the wage gap between men and women

    (B) The relationship between women's suffrage and their income relative to that of men

    (C) The influence of Marx's *Communist Manifesto* on factory workers in the British economy

    (D) The economic impact of child laborers in the industrialized workforce of Great Britain

GO ON TO THE NEXT PAGE

Questions 42–45 refer to the passage below.

"Having acknowledged the gravity of the economic problem, Gorbachev exudes an optimism that he and his team can . . . accelerate economic growth. . . .

Beyond this, he has been less specific on other economic initiatives, but his statements suggest he may intend to press even more controversial policies touching on the powers of the bureaucracy:

. . . He would like to see greater autonomy for [factory] plant managers and will probably push for reduction of centrally dictated indicators.

He has criticized intermediate management bodies that choke off initiative, hinting that they should be streamlined or eliminated. His aim is to eliminate some of the massive bureaucratic apparatus that, as he complained in this speech to the S&T conference, implements Central Committee decisions in such a manner that after they are finished 'nothing is left of these principles.'

He may advocate legalizing some parts of the 'second economy' and allow a limited expansion of the role of private agriculture, despite potential ideological opposition. . . ."

> CIA Directorate of Intelligence, "Gorbachev, the New Broom," June 1985

42. The statements in the passage are best understood in the context of which of the following?

(A) The deescalation of the Cold War arms race between the Soviet Union and the United States

(B) The economic liberalization experienced by some communist countries in the late twentieth century

(C) The increase in civil disobedience by Soviet dissidents advocating for the Soviet military's withdrawal from foreign conflicts

(D) The failure of neocolonial capitalist practices to sustain the global economy

43. The changes described in the <u>third and fourth paragraphs</u> most strongly reflect which of the following?

(A) The redistribution of wealth advocated by Karl Marx and Friedrich Engels in *The Communist Manifesto*

(B) The capitalist economic principles advanced by Adam Smith in *The Wealth of Nations*

(C) The democratic ideals championed by Thomas Jefferson in the Declaration of Independence

(D) The philosophy of social justice promoted by Gustavo Gutierrez in *A Theology of Liberation*

GO ON TO THE NEXT PAGE

44. A present-day historian would likely claim that the implementation of changes like those mentioned in the passage most directly contributed to which of the following?

    (A) The eventual collapse of the Soviet Union

    (B) An escalation in Cold War tensions

    (C) Improved relations among Soviet republics

    (D) The withdrawal of Soviet forces from Afghanistan

45. The ideas expressed in the passage most closely parallel which of the following developments in Chinese history?

    (A) The implementation of market reforms by Deng Xiaoping

    (B) The advancement of communism under Mao Zedong's Five-Year Plans

    (C) The inclusion of Han Chinese in bureaucratic positions after the Taiping Rebellion

    (D) The effects of the Opium Wars on China's position in the global economy

GO ON TO THE NEXT PAGE

Questions 46–48 refer to the image below.

LEONARD RAVEN-HILL, "GAP IN THE BRIDGE," 1919

THE GAP IN THE BRIDGE.

46. The cartoon is best understood in the context of which of the following twentieth-century developments?

(A) The proliferation of public works projects in Europe and the United States designed to improve infrastructure and strengthen national economies

(B) The creation of multinational organizations aimed at maintaining peace and fostering international cooperation

(C) Technological advances that increased the speed of travel between countries in Europe and North America

(D) The spread of transnational movements, such as communism, that united like-minded people living in different countries

47. The symbolism in the cartoon most likely represents which of the following criticisms of the League of Nations?

(A) It lacked the ability to enforce its mandates through military action.

(B) It consisted of two rival factions that struggled to form a consensus.

(C) It focused too heavily on economic reforms and not enough on political reforms.

(D) It failed to establish an internal hierarchy to govern its decision-making process.

48. The decision of the United States to refrain from joining the League of Nations most closely reflects which of the following foreign policies?

(A) Disarmament

(B) Isolationism

(C) Containment

(D) Multilateralism

GO ON TO THE NEXT PAGE

Questions 49–52 refer to the following two maps.

<u>Map 1</u>

BRITISH EMPIRE, 1919

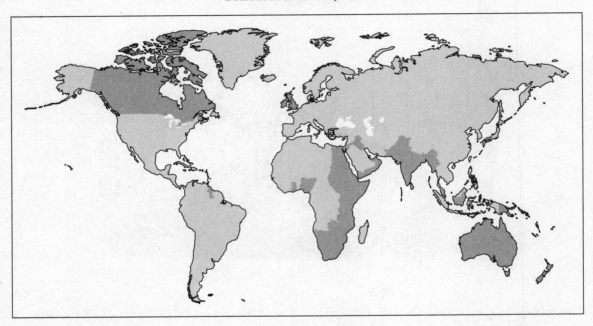

<u>Map 2</u>

BRITISH EMPIRE, 1959

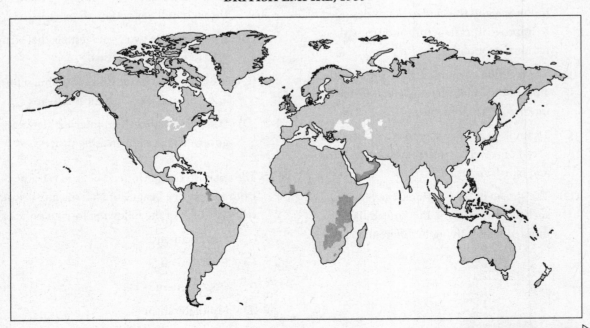

GO ON TO THE NEXT PAGE →

49. The differences between the first and second maps best illustrate which of the following global trends?

    (A) Neocolonialism

    (B) Decolonization

    (C) Abolitionism

    (D) Social Darwinism

50. Which of the following best explains the information depicted in <u>Map 1</u>?

    (A) British imperial power had diminished due to economic and social unrest in its overseas colonies.

    (B) The continued success of British manufacturing depended on raw materials imported from overseas.

    (C) Manufactured goods from Great Britain were in high demand in developing regions overseas.

    (D) Concern about the spread of Islam motivated Christian missionaries to establish colonies overseas.

51. Which of the following factors most directly contributed to the changes reflected in <u>Map 2</u>?

    (A) The spread of communism throughout the developing world

    (B) Rising concern for the environmental effects of industrialization

    (C) The global shift from an industrial to a service-based economy

    (D) The expansion of nationalist movements in Africa and Asia

52. Which of the following identifies a consequence that can most likely be attributed to the changes indicated in <u>Map 2</u>?

    (A) The disappearance of traditional art forms in former African colonies due to cultural imperialism

    (B) Decreased ethnic tensions in East Africa resulting from political and economic unification

    (C) The emergence of destructive environmental changes within Africa such as deforestation and desertification

    (D) African civil wars, such as the one fought between the Nigerian government and Biafra secessionists

GO ON TO THE NEXT PAGE

Questions 53–55 refer to the passage below.

"We should approach these problems, whether domestic or international problems, in our own way. If by any chance we align ourselves definitely with one Power group, we may perhaps from one point of view do some good, but I have not the shadow of a doubt that from a larger point of view, not only of India but of world peace, it will do harm. Because we then lose that tremendous vantage ground that we have of using such influence as we possess (and that influence is going to grow from year to year) in the cause of world peace. What are we interested in world affairs for? We seek no domination over any country. We do not wish to interfere in the affairs of any country, domestic or other. . . . We do not desire to interfere in world affairs and we do not desire that other people should interfere in our affairs. If, however, there is interference, whether military, political or economic, we shall resist it."

Jawaharlal Nehru, speech to the Constituent Assembly, 1949

53. The ideas expressed in the passage are best understood in the context of which of the following twentieth-century developments?

(A) The Cold War between the United States and the Soviet Union

(B) The dissolution of the Ottoman Empire

(C) The rise in tensions between Shi'a and Sunni Muslims

(D) The modernization of former British colonies

54. Which of the following best describes a type of country that was likely to adopt Nehru's stance of nonalignment?

(A) A country seeking to resolve internal conflicts between ethnic or religious groups

(B) A former colonizing country seeking to redress the harms caused by colonization

(C) A newly formed nation-state seeking to govern itself following decolonization

(D) A developing nation seeking to modernize its infrastructure and educational system

55. The ideas expressed in the passage differ most strongly from those associated with which of the following ideologies?

(A) Isolationism

(B) Social Darwinism

(C) Neutrality

(D) Liberation theology

GO ON TO THE NEXT PAGE

END OF PART A

**IF YOU FINISH BEFORE TIME IS CALLED,
YOU MAY CHECK YOUR WORK ON THIS SECTION.**

DO NOT GO ON TO PART B UNTIL YOU ARE TOLD TO DO SO.

SECTION I, PART B
Time—40 minutes
3 Questions

Directions: Section I, Part B of this exam consists of short-answer questions. You must respond to Questions 1 *and* 2. For your final response, you must choose to answer Question 3 *or* Question 4. In your responses, be sure to address all parts of the questions, using complete sentences.

1. Use the passage below to answer all parts of the question that follows.

   "The peace conditions imposed upon Germany are so hard, so humiliating, that even those who have the smallest expectation of a 'peace of justice' are bound to be deeply disappointed. . . .

   These conditions will never give peace. All Germans must feel that they wish to shake off the heavy yoke imposed by the cajoling Entente, and we fear very much that that opportunity will soon present itself. For has not the Entente recognized in the proposed so-called 'League of Nations' the evident right to conquer and possess countries for economic and imperialistic purposes? Fettered and enslaved, Germany will always remain a menace to Europe."

   Dutch editorial on Treaty of Versailles, Algemeen Handelsblad, June 1919

   (a) Provide ONE piece of historical evidence that would support one of the reasons the author identifies as causing German discontent after the Treaty of Versailles.
   (b) Explain ONE additional factor (not specifically mentioned in the passage) that contributed to the outbreak of World War II.
   (c) Explain ONE way in which the international situation created by the end of World War II <u>differed</u> from the international situation created by the end of World War I.

GO ON TO THE NEXT PAGE

2. Use the image below to answer all parts of the question that follows.

FIRST THANKSGIVING IN 1621, 1932

(a) Explain ONE <u>similarity</u> between the impact of the Columbian Exchange on the Americas and its impact on Europe.

(b) Explain ONE <u>difference</u> between the impact of the Columbian Exchange on the Americas and its impact on Europe.

(c) Describe ONE way in which the content of the painting reflects the artist's likely viewpoint about the Columbian Exchange.

GO ON TO THE NEXT PAGE

Choose EITHER Question 3 OR Question 4.

3. Answer all parts of the question that follows.

   (a) Identify ONE factor that facilitated the growth of empires in the period 1200–1750.

   (b) Explain ONE way in which empire-building among European maritime empires was <u>similar</u> to empire-building among Asian land empires in the period 1200–1750.

   (c) Explain ONE way empire-building among European maritime empires was <u>different</u> from empire-building among Asian land empires in the period 1200–1750.

4. Answer all parts of the question that follows:

   (a) Identify ONE way the development and spread of industrial technology changed patterns of global trade in the period 1750–1900.

   (b) Explain ONE <u>change</u> that occurred in the social structure of industrialized states of Western Europe in the period 1750–1900.

   (c) Describe ONE significant <u>continuity</u> that persisted in the social structure of industrialized states of Western Europe in the period 1750–1900.

GO ON TO THE NEXT PAGE

END OF SECTION I

**IF YOU FINISH BEFORE TIME IS CALLED,
YOU MAY CHECK YOUR WORK ON THIS SECTION.**

DO NOT GO ON TO PART B UNTIL YOU ARE TOLD TO DO SO.

SECTION II
Time—100 minutes

Question 1: Document-Based Question

Suggested reading period: 15 minutes

Suggested writing time: 45 minutes

Directions: Question 1 is based on the accompanying documents. The documents have been edited for the purpose of this exercise.

In your response you should do the following:

- Make a thesis or claim that responds to the prompt. The thesis or claim must be historically defensible and establish a line of reasoning.

- Provide context relevant to the prompt by describing a broader historical development or process.

- Use at least six of the provided documents to support an argument in response to the prompt.

- Use a historical example not found in the documents as evidence relevant to an argument about the prompt.

- Explain how the context or situation of at least three documents is relevant to an argument. This could address the relevance of the document's point of view, purpose, historical situation, and/or audience.

- Demonstrate a complex understanding of an argument that responds to the prompt by using evidence to corroborate, qualify, or modify the argument.

GO ON TO THE NEXT PAGE

1. Evaluate the extent to which Enlightenment ideas caused rebellions against existing governments in the period 1750–1900.

Document 1

Source: John Locke, *Second Treatise on Civil Government*, 1690.

Of the State of Nature

. . . (W)e must consider, what state all men are naturally in, and that is, a state of perfect freedom to order their actions, and dispose of their possessions and persons, as they think fit, within the bounds of the law of nature. . . .

There [is] nothing more evident, than that creatures of the same species and rank . . . should also be equal one amongst another without subordination or subjection.

Of the Dissolution of Government

(W)hen the government is dissolved, the people are at liberty to provide for themselves, by erecting a new legislative, . . . for the society can never, . . . lose the native and original right it has to preserve itself, which can only be done by a settled legislative, and a fair and impartial execution of the laws made by it. But the state of mankind is not so miserable that they are not capable of using this remedy, . . . they have not only a right to get out of [a failed government], but to prevent it.

Document 2

Source: Montesquieu, French Enlightenment philosopher, *The Spirit of the Laws*, 1748.

The political liberty of the subject is a tranquillity of mind arising from the opinion each person has of his safety. In order to have this liberty, it is requisite the government be so constituted as one man need not be afraid of another.

When the legislative and executive powers are united in the same person, or in the same body of magistrates, there can be no liberty, because apprehensions may arise, lest the same monarch or senate should enact tyrannical laws, to execute them in a tyrannical manner. Again, there is no liberty if the judiciary power be not separated from the legislative and executive. . . .

There would be an end of everything, were the same man, or the same body, whether of the nobles or of the people, to exercise those three powers, that of enacting laws, that of executing the public resolutions, and of trying the causes of individuals.

GO ON TO THE NEXT PAGE

Document 3

Source: Thomas Jefferson, Declaration of Independence, signed by 56 members of the Continental Congress, 1776.

IN CONGRESS, July 4, 1776.

The unanimous Declaration of the thirteen united States of America: We hold these truths to be self-evident, that all men are created equal, that they are endowed by their Creator with certain unalienable Rights, that among these are Life, Liberty and the pursuit of Happiness.—That to secure these rights, Governments are instituted among Men, deriving their just powers from the consent of the governed . . .

When a long train of abuses and usurpations, pursuing invariably the same Object evinces a design to reduce them under absolute Despotism, it is their right, it is their duty, to throw off such Government, and to provide new Guards for their future security.

Such has been the patient sufferance of these Colonies; and such is now the necessity which constrains them to alter their former Systems of Government. The history of the present King of Great Britain is a history of repeated injuries and usurpations, all having in direct object the establishment of an absolute Tyranny over these States. To prove this, let Facts be submitted to a candid world. . . .

He has refused his Assent to Laws, the most wholesome and necessary for the public good. . . .

For cutting off our Trade with all parts of the world. . . .

For imposing Taxes on us without our Consent. . . .

For depriving us in many cases, of the benefits of Trial by Jury. . . .

For suspending our own Legislatures, and declaring themselves invested with power to legislate for us in all cases whatsoever. . . .

GO ON TO THE NEXT PAGE

Document 4

Source: National Assembly of France, Declaration of the Rights of Man and of the Citizen, statement of rights, August 26, 1789.

The representatives of the French people, constituted as a National Assembly, and considering that ignorance, neglect, or contempt of the rights of man are the sole causes of public misfortunes and governmental corruption, have resolved to set forth in a solemn declaration the natural, inalienable, and sacred rights of man: so that by being constantly present to all the members of the social body this declaration may always remind them of their rights and duties; so that by being liable at every moment to comparison with the aim of any and all political institutions the acts of the legislative and executive powers may be the more fully respected; and so that by being founded henceforward on simple and incontestable principles the demands of the citizens may always tend toward maintaining the constitution and the general welfare.

In consequence, the National Assembly recognizes and declares, in the presence and under the auspices of the Supreme Being, the following rights of man and the citizen:

1. Men are born and remain free and equal in rights. Social distinctions may be based only on common utility.

2. The purpose of all political association is the preservation of the natural and imprescriptible rights of man. These rights are liberty, property, security, and resistance to oppression.

3. The principle of all sovereignty rests essentially in the nation. No body and no individual may exercise authority which does not emanate expressly from the nation. . . .

GO ON TO THE NEXT PAGE

Document 5

Source: Governor General Toussaint L'Ouverture, leader of the slave rebellion against the French government, Haitian Constitution of 1801, July 8th, 1801.

Art. 3.—There cannot exist slaves on this territory; servitude is therein forever abolished. All men are born, live, and die free and French.

Art. 4.—All men, regardless of color, are eligible to all employment. . . .

Art. 5.—The law is the same for all whether in punishment or in protection. . . .

Art. 12.—The Constitution guarantees freedom and individual security. No one shall be arrested unless a formally expressed mandate is issued from a functionary to whom the law grants the right to order arrest and detention in a publicly designated location.

Art. 13.—Property is sacred and inviolable. All people, either by himself, or by his representatives, have the free right to dispose and to administer property that is recognized as belonging to him. Anyone who attempts to deny this right shall become guilty of crime towards society and responsible towards the person troubled in his property. . . .

Document 6

Source: Emanuel Leutze, "Washington Crossing the Delaware," 1851.

This image depicts George Washington, American revolutionary leader, crossing the Delaware River to face British troops in battle.

GO ON TO THE NEXT PAGE

Document 7

Source: Simón Bolívar, South American revolutionary leader, "Letter from Jamaica," 1815.

But we . . . are neither Indians nor Europeans, but a mixture of the legitimate owners of the country and the usurping Spaniards; in short, we, being Americans by birth and with rights equal to those of Europe, have to dispute these rights with the men of [Spain]. . . .

Americans, under the Spanish system now in action, have in society no other place than that of serfs fit for work, and, at the most, that of simple consumers. And even this is limited by absurd restrictions, such as: prohibition of the cultivation of European products; the monopoly of certain goods by the king; the prevention of America factories not owned by Spain; the exclusive privileges of trade, even regarding the necessities of life; the obstacles placed in the way of the American provinces so that they may not deal with each other . . . nor trade. In short, do you want to know what was our lot? The fields in which to cultivate indigo, cochineal, coffee, sugar cane, cocoa, cotton; the solitary plains to breed cattle; the deserts to hunt the wild beasts; the bosom of the earth to extract gold, with which that avaricious country was never satisfied. . . .

We were never viceroys or governors except by very extraordinary reasons; archbishops and bishops, seldom; ambassadors, never; military men, only as subordinates; nobles, without privileges; lastly, we were neither magistrates nor financiers, and hardly merchants. All this we had to accept in direct opposition to our institutions.

GO ON TO THE NEXT PAGE

END OF DOCUMENTS FOR QUESTION 1

Question 2, Question 3, or Question 4: Long Essay Question
Suggested writing time: 40 minutes

Directions: Choose Question 2, Question 3, OR Question 4 to answer.

In your response you should do the following:

- Make a thesis or claim that responds to the prompt. The thesis or claim must be historically defensible and establish a line of reasoning.

- Provide context relevant to the prompt by describing a broader historical development or process.

- Use specific and relevant examples as evidence to support an argument in response to the prompt.

- Use a historical reasoning skill (causation, comparison, or continuity and change) to develop an argument in response to the prompt.

- Demonstrate a complex understanding of an argument that responds to the prompt by using evidence to corroborate, qualify, or modify the argument.

2. In the period 1200–1450, changes in trade networks resulted from and stimulated an increase in productive capacity, with important implications for social and gender structures.

   Develop an argument that evaluates the changes in social and gender structures in the period 1200–1450.

3. In the period 1450–1750, rulers used a variety of methods to legitimize and consolidate their power.

   Develop an argument that evaluates how one or more rulers consolidated and legitimized their power in this time period.

4. In the period 1750–1900, the process of industrialization changed the way in which goods were produced and consumed, with far-reaching effects on the global economy, social relations, and culture.

   Develop an argument that evaluates the factors that contributed to the rise of industrialization in Europe in this time period.

GO ON TO THE NEXT PAGE

 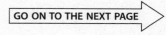

END OF SECTION II

STOP

END OF EXAM

ANSWER KEY

Section I, Part A

1. B	15. D	29. B	43. B
2. A	16. B	30. C	44. A
3. D	17. A	31. D	45. A
4. A	18. D	32. B	46. B
5. A	19. C	33. A	47. A
6. C	20. B	34. C	48. B
7. C	21. D	35. B	49. B
8. C	22. C	36. A	50. B
9. B	23. D	37. D	51. D
10. D	24. B	38. A	52. D
11. C	25. A	39. C	53. A
12. B	26. D	40. A	54. C
13. A	27. A	41. D	55. B
14. A	28. D	42. B	

Section I, Part B and Section II

See Answers and Explanations, and self-score free-response questions.

Section I, Part A Number Correct: _____

Section I, Part B Points Earned: _____

Section II Points Earned: _____

Sign into your online account at kaptest.com and enter your results in the scoring section to see your 1–5 score.

Haven't registered your book yet? Go to kaptest.com/moreonline to begin.

ANSWERS AND EXPLANATIONS

Section I, Part A

1. B

The expansion of the Mongol Empire most strongly contributed to the growth of Silk Road trade in the period circa 1200 to 1450. Not only did the Mongols politically unify formerly separate states, thus eliminating tariffs and other trade barriers, but the Pax Mongolica was based upon Mongol military dominance. Caravans could travel the Silk Road with little fear of bandits, boosting profitability and thus the amount of caravans. So, **(B)** is correct. While tempting in that the Mali Empire did connect the West African gold and salt trade into the wider Afro-Eurasian trade network, (A) is incorrect because the Mongols had a far larger effect on spurring an increase in Silk Road trade. The Mongol Empire controlled vast amounts of territory in Eurasia, from Korea in the West to the Middle East, while the Mali Empire only controlled a chunk of West Africa. Likewise, (C) is incorrect because the continuing expansion of the Grand Canal only facilitated trade in China, which, while important, was dwarfed in scale by the Mongol Empire. (D) is incorrect because it is an example of the increase in Silk Road trade, not a cause that explains why that trade increased in the first place.

2. A

The widespread network of the Silk Road facilitated cultural exchange, along with the act of moving goods from one empire to the next; **(A)** is correct. (B) is incorrect, as it does not describe an effect of the Silk Road, but rather just states one purpose of the nework. (C) is incorrect because these trade routes mainly transported goods and disseminated culture; the Silk Road was not primarily a migration route for people. Though passage along the Silk Road was dangerous and vulnerable to bandits, trade enhanced the economies of the cities along the way, turning them into major trading ports. Therefore, (D) is incorrect.

3. D

The Internet facilitates cultural exchanges as well as the exchange of goods, both within particular regions and between different regions. It is also an international system that it not wholly under the control of any one state.

Thus, **(D)** is correct. None of the other choices describe systems of international trade that also fostered cross-cultural interactions.

4. A

The Ottomans demanded a high price from Europeans for Asian spices and other goods. This fact encouraged the Age of Exploration, as Europeans sought an alternate sea route to India in order to undercut the Ottomans on the price of Asian spices and luxury goods. Thus, **(A)** is correct. The Little Ice Age strongly affected the Northern Hemisphere's higher latitudes, not places nearer the equator like India; (B) is incorrect. (C) is incorrect because the Mongol Empire had essentially disintegrated by the early fourteenth century, before the period in question. Likewise, British domination of East Asian trade came in a later period, from 1750 to 1900, so (D) is incorrect.

5. A

While the beliefs of previous Church protesters had been suppressed, such as those of the Czech theologian Jan Hus a century earlier, Martin Luther's ideas could spread more rapidly because of the invention of the printing press. The press allowed for the production and distribution of documents that had once been copied by hand, often by Catholic monks. Thus, **(A)** is correct. While the Black Death did weaken the institutional authority of the Catholic Church, it was the printing press that allowed Martin Luther's ideas to spread instead of being suppressed; (B) is incorrect. While networks of exchange such as the Hanseatic League facilitated the spread of Luther's work, copies of his papers only existed in mass quantities thanks to the printing press. (C) is incorrect because, although some monarchs, such as in England, took advantage of Protestantism to undermine the Pope's political power in their kingdoms, those developments only came later. The passage originates from 1518, only one year after Martin Luther posted his Ninety-five Theses, widely regarded as the beginning of the Protestant Reformation. (D) is incorrect.

6. C

The publication of the Ninety-five Theses initiated the Protestant Reformation, which led to over a century of various religious wars. The most notable conflict, the Thirty Years' War, saw approximately 20 percent of the overall population of the German states killed. **(C)** is correct. (A) is incorrect because, while the heliocentric theory of the universe did spread during the period from 1450 to 1750, that was as a result of the Scientific Revolution; both Catholic and Protestant leaders initially opposed the heliocentric theory. Even before the Reformation, the papacy's influence had weakened in Catholic kingdoms. For example, the Avignon Papacy (1309 to 1376) saw the French monarchy gain substantial influence over the Catholic Church. Thus, (B) is incorrect. The last crusades ended at the turn of the sixteenth century, with only the Reconquista of major note, which involved Catholics warring against Muslims; (D) is incorrect.

7. C

The Protestant Reformation is most similar to the growth of anticlericalism during the French Revolution. Both movements began with intellectual critiques of corruption in a religious institution, critiques which then gained widespread public support. Attempts at peaceful reform gradually spiraled into violence, as both sides eventually tried to purge one another. The French Revolution saw an attempt to foster the Cult of Reason, a state-sponsored atheistic religion, in a manner similar to how some German princes sponsored Lutheran churches. Thus, **(C)** is correct. Sikhism was a new religion born from the interaction of two other competing religions, while Protestantism was born from a religious schism; (A) is incorrect. The Islamic Revolution in Iran involved a transition to a theocracy, one based on an existing and long-entrenched Shi'a Islam. While some kingdoms during the Protestant Reformation could be argued to be theocracies, their adoption of Lutheranism was a break from long-established Catholicism. Thus, (B) is incorrect. While (D) is tempting in that the Taiping Rebellion could be said to represent a new faction of Christianity, it is incorrect. Luther did not claim divine revelation, as Hong Xiuquan did when he claimed to be the brother of Jesus Christ. The Taiping lost their religious war, and their faith never gained wider traction as Protestantism did.

8. C

Image 1 best illustrates how the expansion of trade networks facilitates cultural and demographic change. The arrival of Columbus heralded the beginning of the Columbian Exchange, which in the Americas saw indigenous peoples suffer massive demographic losses due to Old World diseases. Also, European colonialism led to massive cultural shifts even within the surviving Native American groups. Thus, **(C)** is correct. While the image does feature a Christian cross, there are no elements to suggest syncretism with Native American belief systems, so (A) is incorrect. The Columbian Exchange did result in the transfer of crops between the Americas and Eurasia, but agricultural activity is not depicted in the image; (B) is incorrect. The publication date of the etching, 1594, is over a century after Columbus first arrived in the Americas, ruling out Columbus being alive and using the etching to justify any authority of his. (D) is incorrect.

9. B

The looming presence of a Christian cross over the shoulder of Christopher Columbus, as well as the kneeling of the Spaniards and the submissive portrayal of Native Americans, illustrates the interconnection of missionary efforts and colonial expansion. Note that Columbus wields a long dagger in this etching, portraying Columbus as a conqueror for Spain. Both Columbus and the Christian cross are given prominent positions, especially in comparison to the first image, highlighting their symbolic importance. Thus, **(B)** is correct. While early expeditions to the Americas required backing from wealthy nobles or joint-stock companies, there is nothing in the image that alludes to the issue of funding or that praises the wealthy. So, (A) is incorrect. Likewise, the image is fixed solely on Columbus, the Spaniards, and the Native Americans, with no allusions to other European states; (C) is incorrect. Although Spain was a notable Catholic power, there is nothing suggestive in the image of tensions between the Protestant and Catholic branches of Christianity. Moreover, the Protestant Reformation did not really commence until after Columbus's voyages. (D) is incorrect.

10. D

In Image 1, Spain is glorified through the background display of the three ships in Columbus's expedition, and Image 2 illustrates Native Americans in a clearly inferior position to the taller Columbus. This illustrates the conquest of indigenous people, and the glorification surrounding it. Thus, **(D)** is correct. (A) is incorrect because neocolonialism was a development of the twentieth century and because Spain was not an industrialized power during the period depicted. Social Darwinism as a concept did not exist until the late nineteenth century, making (B) incorrect. While both images depict the Spanish raising a Christian cross, in both cases it is a secondary visual element placed off to the side. The focus is on Columbus and the Native Americans; (C) is incorrect.

11. C

Gunpowder was originally developed in China and spread to Europe along the Silk Road. Without this technological diffusion, the refinement of gunpowder's composition as depicted in the tables would not have taken place. Thus, **(C)** is correct. Noninterference in the internal affairs of sovereign states is termed Westphalian sovereignty, after the Peace of Westphalia in 1648; this occurred after the innovations illustrated in the tables, so (A) is incorrect. Although the contributions of the Islamic world in the field of chemistry aided the development of gunpowder depicted in the tables, that was a purely Islamic innovation; the ancient Greek texts were primarily works of philosophy and mathematics, not chemistry. (B) is incorrect. (D) is incorrect because the establishment of joint-stock companies contributed little to gunpowder's refinement.

12. B

The period identified in the tables occurred after the Protestant Reformation and during a period of conflict that involved Catholic and Protestant powers, during the Thirty Years' War (1618–1648); **(B)** is correct. Although the time period identified in the tables occurred during a time of competition between European states, it was not over Indian Ocean trade routes; (A) is incorrect. The last crusades into the Middle East concluded by the late thirteenth century; the developments in gunpowder depicted in the tables occurred much later, so (C) is incorrect. Republican principles of government were mainly revived in England, not Europe at large, and then mainly only in the seventeenth century. (D) is incorrect. On the contrary, the ease of training and equipping infantrymen with gunpowder weapons led to the empowerment of monarchies and the growth of centralized states in Europe.

13. A

Prior to the refinement of gunpowder weapons, even small groups of steppe nomads were typically a fierce military force thanks to their expert horsemanship abilities and use of mounted archers with composite bows. The Mongols are the most notable example. However, firearms gradually lessened the importance of bows as a weapon and made cavalry-focused armies a liability. Thus, **(A)** is correct. (B) is incorrect because it discusses a direct effect on the Americas, not on Eurasia. (C) is incorrect because fortifications remained a vital part of militaries around the world through the First World War. (D) is incorrect because feudalism was mainly a European system of government, not one found throughout Eurasia. Also, gunpowder weapons contributed to the decline of feudalism as large, quickly trained and equipped armies required a powerful centralized state to support them.

14. A

The Swahili city-states were plugged into a growing global trade network, especially after the Columbian Exchange began, as silver from the Americas rippled eastward through global trade networks all the way to China. Thus, **(A)** is correct. Although the Swahili city-states largely fell under Portuguese domination, (B) is incorrect because nothing in the passage hints at the Swahili Coast's future. Likewise, (C) is incorrect; while the spread of Islam to the Swahili city-states allowed disparate peoples and rulers to find common ground in their shared faith, it did not share a common faith with the Chinese or Europeans plugged into its trade routes. Also, the passage does not describe the interregional travel of religion. (D) is incorrect because the passage rightfully describes the Swahili city-states as being in East Africa. In other words, they are on the Indian Ocean, not the Atlantic.

15. D

The Swahili city-states, with access to trade routes linking Asia, the Middle East, and Europe, were in a highly advantageous position to prosper economically. However, European trading post empires increased and eventually overtook the region economically; thus, **(D)** is correct. The passage mentions an "insatiable demand for eastern spices," so (A) is incorrect. (B) and (C) are incorrect because neither played a role in the decline.

16. B

The Black Death killed approximately one-third of the population of Europe in the fourteenth century. This had far-reaching implications for global commerce, lowering European demand for gold and other commodities traded by the Swahili city-states. Thus, **(B)** is correct. The other choices are incorrect because each had the impact of strengthening trade relationships, which would have benefited the Swahili city-states.

17. A

The Taj Mahal, a famous mausoleum, symbolizes how Persian and Indian architectural and artistic styles were successfully integrated during the Mughal Empire. **(A)** is correct. The Mughal Empire only sought to purge India of Hindu influences in favor of a purified Islam later in its history; (B) is incorrect. Built in the mid-seventeenth century, the Taj Mahal and this culturally integrationist phase of the Mughal Empire predate British imperial dominance in India, making (C) incorrect. (D) is incorrect because it better describes the Mughal Empire near the beginning and the end of its life span, when it imposed such things as the *jizya* (non-Muslim tax) on its subjects.

18. D

The Taj Mahal represents the use of a public display of monumental architecture to legitimize a ruler's authority. While intended as a mausoleum for Emperor Shah Jahan's wife, the great expense and effort required for its construction served as an overt demonstration of the Mughal emperor's wealth and power. Thus, **(D)** is correct. The Mughals were an Islamic empire, and thus would not claim their bloodline was divine since that would be heretical; (A) is incorrect. (B) is incorrect because the Taj Mahal represented a blend of Persian and Indian artistic and architectural styles, not a blending of Islam and Hinduism. Sikhism, a syncretic blending of those two religions, was practice by the Sikh Empire, not the Mughal Empire. (C) is incorrect because, while it was built using tax funds, the Taj Mahal was a memorial, not any sort of launching pad for territorial expansion.

19. C

As Mughal rulers expanded their territories, they generally adopted policies of toleration towards the groups they absorbed, permitting practices such as religious tolerance and intermarriage. The Muslim Mughal rulers often incorporated Hindus into their bureaucratic structures; **(C)** is correct. (A) is incorrect because the Mughal rulers employed a sophisticated taxation system, and some rulers instituted a special tax on non-Muslims. (B) is incorrect because India did not adopt a parliamentary government until after it gained independence in the mid-twentieth century. (D) is incorrect because during this time period India flourished due to the Indian Ocean trade.

20. B

Peter the Great was the Romanov monarch who ruled Russia in the late seventeenth and early eighteenth century. As numerous actions cited in the passage demonstrate, Peter the Great was an absolute monarch—a ruler who held complete, consolidated power over his empire. Thus, **(B)** is correct. The passage does not mention any connection between political and religious traditions, making (A) incorrect. *Inflation* is an economic term, describing a sustained ongoing increase in prices, which does not apply to the events described in the passage; (C) is incorrect. While tempting in that nationalism involves the prioritization of one's country, (D) is incorrect because the passage emphasizes Peter's reliance upon foreign European nations to cement his rule.

21. D

Peter was an absolute monarch who sought to introduce French culture and Western technology to Russia. He did not, however, seek to incorporate Enlightenment political ideas into the Russian state. He ruled absolutely and made public displays of the bodies of his enemies to scare off his remaining rivals. The absolutism of the Russian state would persist until the Russian Revolutions of 1917. **(D)** is correct. (A) is incorrect because the passage describes Peter seeking foreign alliances against the Ottomans, a long-time regional adversary for the Russian state. (B) is incorrect because nothing in the passage touches on the subject of Western fashions in Russia. While tempting because Peter is described as being focused on developing Russia on the technical front, (C) is incorrect because Peter is described as consulting Western European specialists. He did not focus on developing domestically within Russia the technical skills those specialists offered.

22. C

Peter the Great successfully integrated Western cultural traditions into Russian society; for instance, he promoted Western styles of dress, which allowed Russian women to participate in social events without veils. This enhanced the influence of women, particularly aristocrats, on Russian society, making **(C)** correct. Russian rulers had been called tsars since the sixteenth century, making (A) incorrect. Louis XIV was an absolute monarch in France in the seventeenth century and early eighteenth century, and he promoted Catholicism, causing Protestants such as Huguenots to leave France. Therefore, (B) is incorrect, as it refers to French events and not Russian events. In addition, Peter the Great ruled according to absolutist ideals, not Enlightenment ideals, which makes (D) incorrect.

23. D

The Manchus forced Han Chinese men to adopt the queue hair braid as a sign of submission to Qing rule. Thus, **(D)** is correct. Eunuchs were unpopular in the Ming Dynasty, and many Chinese saw them as corrupt. The Qing reducing their numbers and influence in the imperial government was thus not a cause of friction; (A) is incorrect. The imperial examination system was abolished in 1905, and by that point, the examination system was widely seen within China as insufficient to the country's needs. Its demise was not unpopular, and was not a means of subjugation. (B) is incorrect. The Qing actually attempted to ban foot binding at the start of Manchu rule, but bound feet remained both common and fashionable in China for centuries afterward. This practice was therefore not something the Manchus implemented to subjugate the people, making (C) incorrect.

24. B

As it was largely self-sufficient in terms of natural resources and traditionally the greatest power in its world region, China viewed itself as sitting atop a global social hierarchy. Thus, foreign diplomats were expected to bow before the emperor as a sign of respect; **(B)** is correct. While Confucianism strongly influenced Qing Dynasty China, it had no animus toward either Europeans or Christians in particular. Foreigners were simply lower on the global social hierarchy. So, (A) is incorrect. While established elites in Qing Dynasty China did resist reform and modernization efforts, that fact is not directly connected to the treatment of diplomats described in the passage; (C)

is incorrect. China's regional dominance was considered a self-apparent fact in this period, and not something that required upkeep. This attitude left them vulnerable to European, American, and Japanese encroachment over time. (D) is incorrect.

25. A

Trumbull White, the passage's author, wrote his analysis at a time when Chinese power was at a historic low point while Russian power was considerable. The publication date, 1895, is a decade before the Russo-Japanese War, which was the first time in modern history that an Asian power defeated a Western power militarily, an event which was shocking to contemporary observers. Also, in the mid-seventeenth century, Russia's eastern border was still confined to near the Ural Mountains. Its long conquest of Siberia had only just begun in the era referenced in this passage. Thus, **(A)** is correct. In order to judge the merits of the Chinese treatment of the Russians, the goods themselves were not as important as the possible actions Russians could have taken in reaction to their treatment, which included military action. (B) is incorrect. The German Jesuit mentioned in the passage was only referenced as a sign of the Qing Dynasty being in contact with Western people in the early modern era. (C) is incorrect. By 1656, Japan had entered its isolation period under the Tokugawa shogunate's *sakoku* policy. The Dutch were the only foreigners allowed to trade with Japan. (D) is incorrect.

26. D

The phrase "considerable friction between the two races" is in reference to tension between the Han Chinese and their Manchu rulers. The most famous uprising against the Qing Dynasty was the Taiping Rebellion, one of the deadliest wars of the modern era. Thus, **(D)** is correct. The Opium Wars were conflicts between Qing Dynasty China as a whole and Western powers, principally the British Empire. (A) is incorrect. (B) and (C) are incorrect because they represent conflicts based on ideologies, political and economic, rather than conflict based on race; further, the Chinese government did not become communist until the twentieth century.

27. A

Weyl's analysis highlights how everyday needs undermine the class solidarity of German workers and English workers. While the two groups shared similar interests in virtue of being part of the working class, their livelihoods and families depended on the success of their respective states, which included imperial ventures. Given that Weyl's book was published in 1917, when German and English workers were engaged in fighting the First World War against one another, he was most likely attempting to explain how that situation came to be. Thus, **(A)** is correct. While (B) is tempting in that Weyl discusses socialist aims, his analysis focuses on how those aims are subservient in practice to nationalistic and imperialist goals. (C) is incorrect because it provides too broad a context; Weyl is focusing on the process of nations competing to dominate the global economy, not the characteristics of the global economy itself. Weyl does not discuss settler colonies, which are only one form of imperialism; (D) is incorrect.

28. D

Weyl's reference to theorists who "stand ready" to prove that imperialism "will bring Socialism all the sooner" is best understood in the context of Marxist historiography. Essentially, Marxism holds that human history is the history of class conflict and that the end state of history will be a classless communist society. Thus, **(D)** is correct. (A) is incorrect because Weyl discusses imperialism in general terms, not the specific case of the British. (B) is incorrect because Adam Smith published *The Wealth of Nations* in the eighteenth century. (C) is incorrect because it does not explain why theorists would justify imperialism.

29. B

Present-day historians would most likely agree with the passage's historical interpretation of workers organizing at the national level but being incapable of doing so at the international one. Political parties advocating for workers' rights are commonplace in twentieth and twenty-first century democracies, and they have created many new laws and programs. International solidarity of labor has become increasingly rare over time and never overcame nationalist enterprises like the First World War. Thus, **(B)** is correct. Many present-day historians do not endorse the Marxist interpretation of history as a class struggle and would be reluctant to view imperialism as the last phase of capitalism, particularly since more recent history includes mass decolonization without weakening the grip of capitalism on the global economy; (A) is incorrect. The rise of the European Union illustrates that European

nations are not necessarily economic competitors but can cooperate and integrate; many modern historians would thus disagree with (C). (D) is incorrect because present-day historians could point to examples of non-imperialist industrialized economies in Eurasia and other parts of the world. For example, despite extensive decolonization in the twentieth century that weakened the imperialist ambitions of several Western European nations, Western Europe has continued to maintain a relatively strong industrialized economy.

30. C

Weyl describes a situation where the claimed ideological goals of a movement came into conflict with the everyday needs of its members. Of the available options, this situation is most similar to the role of republicanism in the French Revolutionary Wars. While the French championed political freedom and rule by the people, their expanding war efforts required territory "liberated" from monarchies and nobles be placed under French rule. This action was rationalized as being for the greater good of spreading republicanism throughout Europe, just as Weyl alludes to socialists rationalizing the benefits of imperialism. Thus, **(C)** is correct. Although tempting, as Pan-Africanism like socialism is an internationalist ideology, (A) is incorrect because Pan-Africanism has not been used to justify imperialism (like republicanism did during the Napoleonic Wars). (B) is incorrect because neocolonialism is a form of imperialism, as the former imperial overlord of a colonized country continues to exert influence through economic domination of that country's postcolonial economy. (D) is incorrect because the Tanzimât Movement in the Ottoman Empire failed in a more straightforward fashion. Its reforms were put forward, and some were enacted, but entrenched interests managed to defeat them.

31. D

The passage mentions that Timbuktu has a "great store of doctors, judges, priests, and other learned men" who were paid by the king, and that books were more valuable there than any other commodity. In fact, Timbuktu was a center for learning as much as for trade, with informal "universities" and libraries of Islamic and secular studies operated by three local mosques. **(D)** is correct. (A) is incorrect because it is contrary to fact; the slave trade tended to provide sustained benefits to participating societies. (B) is incorrect because during the sixteenth century trade was a key factor in many nations' prosperity; trade is alluded to in this passage with multiple mentions of "merchants" as well as products from Tagaza and Barbarie. (C) is incorrect because travel writing flourished during this time period, and these authors' influence was strong, contributing to map-making, trade, and further travel and exploration.

32. B

Timbuktu became an important city because of its location on the Niger River at the edge of the fertile savanna to the south and the Sahara Desert to the north. As such, it was a natural transfer point for the gold and salt trade among the humid forests of the Gold Coast, the salt mines of the central desert, and the rich Mediterranean civilizations further north. Thus, **(B)** is correct. (A) is incorrect because Timbuktu was not known as a stopping point for Christian pilgrims. (C) is incorrect because Timbuktu was a trading center, so its economy relied heavily on exports (and imports). (D) is incorrect because Timbuktu has a hot, dry desert climate that is not particularly well suited for agriculture.

33. A

Símon Bolívar was a leader of the Latin American independence movement in the early nineteenth century, making **(A)** correct. (B) is incorrect because, while Bolívar was an abolitionist, his independence movement failed to abolish slavery within Latin America; thus, Bolívar is not strongly associated with the abolition movement. (C) is incorrect because Bolívar fought for Latin American independence from Europe; he is not associated with colonization efforts in Asia or Africa. (D) is incorrect because, although Bolívar was a military leader, he is not known for developing or even using the most advanced military technology of the period.

34. C

Bolívar is considered a war hero in Latin America, where he fought for independence from European colonialism. The painting shows Bolívar in his military regalia, emphasizing his military achievements. Thus, **(C)** is correct. (A) is incorrect because Bolívar opposed imperialism. (B) is incorrect because Bolívar was a military leader who used warfare to achieve independence; he was not committed to nonviolent civil disobedience. (D) is incorrect because Bolívar wanted to create an independent Latin American nation-state that celebrated the unique culture

of the Latin American people; while his uniform includes some features of European military attire, appreciation for European styles of dress or culture in general did not figure prominently in his life.

35. B

Bolívar was strongly influenced by Enlightenment thinkers, such as John Locke, Thomas Paine, and Thomas Jefferson; **(B)** is correct. (A), (B), and (D) are all incorrect for similar reasons: each represents an economic (rather than a political) ideology, and Bolívar was a political revolutionary, not an economic one. In addition, classical liberalism and Marxism developed largely after Bolívar's lifetime.

36. A

The proclamation was issued during a revolution in the Ottoman Empire that began when a group of political dissidents known as the Young Turks were able to gain control of the government through a series of popular uprisings. The Young Turks primarily wanted to enact democratic reforms and modernize the Ottoman Empire, making **(A)** correct. (B) is incorrect because the Ottoman Empire was a colonizer itself, not a former colony. (C) is incorrect because the Young Turks were seeking to implement democratic, not socialist, reforms. (D) is incorrect because the Ottoman Empire was a monarchy, not a democracy, when the Young Turks' revolution began.

37. D

The Young Turks wanted to enact democratic reforms, which included reducing the power of the sultan, who was the monarch of the Ottoman Empire. In the proclamation, the Young Turks planned for the sultan to choose only one-third of the senate, while the people would choose the other two-thirds. This plan would have shifted the balance of power from the monarch to the people. Thus, **(D)** is correct. (A), (B), and (C) are incorrect for similar reasons; each describes a motivation that is the opposite of the Young Turks' actual goal, which was to initiate democratic reforms.

38. A

The protection of property rights is most closely associated with classical liberalism; **(A)** is correct. (B) is incorrect because socialism is generally associated with a forced redistribution of wealth, not the protection of private property rights. (C) is incorrect because the protection of property rights is unrelated to an anti-imperialist (or an imperialist) ideology. (D) is incorrect because anarchism would involve a lack of organized government and, therefore, a lack of protection for property rights.

39. C

The data in Chart 1 show that, during the period from 1787 to 1865, married women in most industries earned an increasing proportion of their family's income; for example, married women working in high-wage agriculture earned 9.2 percent of their family's income between 1787 and 1815 and earned 12.5 percent of their family's income between 1846 and 1865. These changes reflect the fact that economic roles for women increased due to industrialization, which coincided with a decline in the gender-based division of labor. Thus, **(C)** is correct. (A) is incorrect because Britain did not experience an influx of foreign workers during the period; in addition, although some decolonization occurred between 1787 and 1865, most British colonies did not gain independence until the twentieth century. (B) is incorrect because, while the British Empire did abolish slavery in 1833, the vast majority of former slaves worked in British colonies in the Americas, the Caribbean, and Africa; the abolition of slavery would have had little impact on the economic opportunities of women living and working in Great Britain. Finally, (D) is incorrect because political rights for women were still very limited between 1787 and 1865; for example, women's suffrage was not achieved until the twentieth century. Instead, the increase in economic opportunities for women was primarily attributable to industrialization and other economic changes that occurred during the period.

40. A

During the Industrial Revolution, middle-class women tended to be supported by their husband's wages and, thus, did not have an economic need to work. In addition, there was a growing pressure on middle-class women to conform to the cult of domesticity, which was the idea that a married woman's sphere of influence was properly in the home, where it was her responsibility to raise children and manage household affairs. Thus, **(A)** is correct. (B) is incorrect because middle-class women typically did not have paying jobs at all, so working-class women were likely earning a higher percentage of their family's income than were middle-class women. (C) is

also incorrect as middle-class women were unlikely to work outside the home during the time periods reported in the table. (D) is incorrect because it does not describe a demographic trend observed during the Industrial Revolution.

41. D

The graph shows that, in 1833, wages were earned by factory workers (both male and female) between the ages of approximately 6 and 15. Thus, a historian could use this data to learn more about the economic impact of child laborers in industrialized Britain, making **(D)** correct. (A) is incorrect because Britain was not involved in any large-scale international conflicts in 1833. (B) and (C) are incorrect because they reference events that happened later in history: women's suffrage was not achieved in Britain until the twentieth century, and *The Communist Manifesto* was not published until 1848.

42. B

In this passage, the CIA is reporting on Soviet leader Mikhail Gorbachev's plans for the economy. The measures such as seeking "greater autonomy for [factory] plant managers," reducing "centrally dictated indicators," and expanding "the role of private agriculture" indicate a shift from the centrally planned economy of communism to a market-based economy. These recommendations were in response to an economic decline experienced by the Soviet Union and other communist countries in the late twentieth century. **(B)** is correct. (A) is incorrect because, even though the Soviet Union and the United States negotiated arms reduction treaties during the 1980s, Soviet weapons production actually increased during the decade; in addition, the passage reflects Gorbachev's plans for the economy rather than for foreign or military policy. (C) is incorrect because Gorbachev's measures in this passage were economic in nature and were not influenced by war protesters. (D) is incorrect because Gorbachev's plans included capitalist principles; they were a response to a failure of communism, not capitalism.

43. B

Gorbachev's intended changes in these paragraphs include "greater autonomy" for managers, fewer "centrally dictated indicators," and possible removal of management bodies "that choke off initiative." This move away from a planned economy reflects the laissez-faire, free-market principles advanced by Adam Smith, making **(B)** correct. (A) is incorrect because the reforms suggested in these paragraphs are contrary to a communist ideology. (C) and (D) are incorrect because they refer to political and social reforms, respectively, whereas the passage discusses only economic reforms.

44. A

Gorbachev's pursuit of market reforms was controversial in the Soviet Union, particularly, as mentioned in the passage, when reforms involved "policies touching on the powers of the bureaucracy." The last paragraph also acknowledges that changes would be made "despite potential ideological opposition." The resulting internal tensions weakened the Soviet Union's political system, ultimately leading to its collapse. Thus, **(A)** is correct. (B) is incorrect because the changes described in the passage represent a move away from communism and toward capitalism, which ultimately reduced tensions between the Soviet Union and the United States. (C) and (D) are factually incorrect. Economic reforms did not increase unity among the Soviet republics, many of which began advocating for independence in the mid-1980s and continued until the dissolution of the Soviet Union in 1991. The withdrawal of Soviet forces from Afghanistan was motivated by political and military concerns.

45. A

China, another communist country, also experienced an economic decline in the late twentieth century. Like Gorbachev, Deng Xiaoping, China's head of state at the time, implemented a series of market reforms designed to introduce elements of capitalism into the Chinese economic system. Thus, **(A)** is correct. (B) is incorrect because the Five-Year Plans were designed to promote communist economic principles. (C) and (D) are incorrect because neither describes the results of a shift from a socialist to a market economy.

46. B

The cartoon depicts a bridge symbolizing the League of Nations, which was an international organization created to promote global peace following the First World War. **(B)** is correct. (A), (C), and (D) are incorrect because they each describe developments that are unrelated to the League of Nations.

47. A

The cartoon depicts Uncle Sam sleeping next to the bridge representing the League of Nations, and the bridge is missing its keystone. This imagery reflects the refusal of the United States to join the League of Nations, which is often cited as a key reason for the league's failure; without the United States, it lacked the resources and the desire to enforce its mandates through military action. Thus, **(A)** is correct. (B), (C), and (D) are incorrect because they do not describe criticisms of the League of Nations.

48. B

During the early twentieth century, the United States practiced a policy of isolationism; that is, the United States generally refrained from interjecting itself into global affairs. This stance explains the reluctance of the United States to enter World War I, as well as its decision not to join the League of Nations, making **(B)** correct. (A) refers to a reduction in weapons, usually undertaken as part of an agreement with another country or countries, which is inconsistent with isolationism. (C) refers to a United States foreign policy developed later in the twentieth century designed to stop the spread of communism. Finally, (D) is incorrect because organizations like the League of Nations were multilateral; that is, they were formed through the agreement of more than two nations. Thus, the United States' decision not to join the League of Nations would be the opposite of multilateralism.

49. B

The British Empire reached its height in the early twentieth century, with territory on every inhabited continent. However, by the middle of the twentieth century, many of these colonies had gained independence, making **(B)** correct. (A) is incorrect because neocolonialism refers to economic, social, and cultural influence, whereas the maps depict actual physical control of territories. (C) is incorrect because the British Empire had abolished slavery during the nineteenth century; many workers in Britain's twentieth-century colonies were paid low wages and worked in deplorable conditions, but they were not slaves, and the changes in the second map do not reflect the abolition of slavery. (D) is incorrect because Social

Darwinism was used as a justification for imperialism, not decolonization.

50. B

Britain maintained its colonies primarily to ensure a supply of raw materials for manufacturing or to aid in the transportation of such raw materials to Great Britain. Thus, **(B)** is correct. (A) is incorrect because British imperialism was at its height around 1919, not declining. (C) is incorrect because there was not a high demand for manufactured goods in developing regions at that time. (D) is incorrect because, though religious conversion was often used as a justification for colonization, it was not a prime motivator for maintaining a colonial empire.

51. D

The rise of nationalism in African and Asian colonies was a significant factor leading to decolonization, making **(D)** correct. (A) is incorrect because communism had little, if any, positive impact on decolonization within the British Empire; if anything, Britain's concerns about the spread of communism in the early years of the Cold War might have impeded the process of decolonization rather than encouraged it. (B) is incorrect because decolonization was not influenced by environmentalism, which was still a fledgling movement in 1959. (C) is incorrect because it describes economic changes that took place after 1959.

52. D

When former colonies gained independence, their political or geographic borders often did not align with traditional religious or ethnic identities, an incongruity that frequently led to internal strife. The civil war in Nigeria is an example of this problem, making **(D)** correct. (A) is incorrect because the disappearance of traditional art forms is not associated with decolonization; if anything, decolonization allowed such art forms to flourish. (B) is incorrect because the postcolonial political boundaries in East Africa often led to increased, rather than decreased, ethnic tensions. (C) is incorrect because, although parts of Africa have been experiencing deforestation and other detrimental environmental changes, these changes are not the result of decolonization; instead, they are largely the result of human economic activity that likely would have occurred with or without decolonization.

53. A

After India gained independence, its prime minister, Jawaharlal Nehru, advocated taking a neutral position in the Cold War between the United States and the Soviet Union; **(A)** is correct. (B) and (C) are incorrect because these events had minimal influence on India's nonalignment stance, and (D) is incorrect because modernization refers to an economic process, not a foreign policy position.

54. C

Nehru's justification for nonalignment was that India had just gained its independence and needed to focus on its own internal affairs. Many other former colonies agreed with this reasoning and joined the organized Non-Alignment Movement, making **(C)** correct. (A) and (D) are incorrect because many countries seeking to impose domestic order or to improve their infrastructure ultimately aligned with either the United States or the Soviet Union in order to gain support for their objectives. (B) is incorrect because former colonizers were not in the same position as former colonies like India; former colonizing countries were relatively stable, politically speaking, and tended to align with one side or the other in the Cold War in order to protect their domestic and international interests.

55. B

Nehru advocated for India to refrain from interjecting itself into world affairs. This differs from the ideology of Social Darwinism, which was often used to justify intervention into the internal affairs of other nations. Thus, **(B)** is correct. (A), (C), and (D) are incorrect because isolationism, neutrality, and liberation theology are consistent with Nehru's policy of nonalignment.

Section I, Part B

1. A successful short-answer response accomplishes all three tasks set forth by the prompt. Each part of the prompt is worth 1 point, for a total of 3 possible points.

(a) To earn this point, the response must identify a historical example that illustrates one of the reasons the author identifies as causing German discontent. To support the claim about the inadequacies of the League of Nations (referred to as "so-called" by the author), examples include the lack of participation of Germany (until 1926) and the United States, and the inability of the league to prevent actions such as German remilitarization of the Rhineland and occupation of the Sudetenland. To support the claim about the Versailles treaty being "humiliating" to Germany, examples include the heavy reparations and war guilt clause forced upon Germany.

(b) To earn this point, the response must explain a factor not mentioned in the passage that also contributed to World War II. Examples include: the worldwide economic depression, the charisma of Hitler, the militarism of Japan, the development of fascism in Italy, and European appeasement of Germany's occupation of the Sudetenland at the Munich Conference.

(c) To earn this point, the response must explain a way in which the international situation after World War II differed from the situation after World War I. Examples of differences after World War II include: the Allied occupation of Japan and more extensive Allied occupation of Germany, the lack of imposition of a war guilt clause on Germany, the establishment of the more powerful United Nations rather than the League of Nations, the efforts to rebuild the economy of Japan, and the development of Cold War conflicts that eased remaining tensions between non-Soviet Allied powers and Germany and Japan.

2. A successful short-answer response accomplishes all three tasks set forth by the prompt. Each part of the prompt is worth 1 point, for a total of 3 possible points.

(a) To earn this point, the response must explain a way in which the impact of the Columbian Exchange was similar in the Americas and Europe. Examples include how new agricultural crops impacted the lifestyles of the indigenous peoples in both locations, such as potatoes eventually supporting the population of Ireland due to the crop producing a high number of calories per acre, and wheat and rice being introduced in the Americas.

(b) To earn this point, the response must explain a way in which the impact of the Columbian Exchange was different in the Americas and Europe. Examples include the more significant impact of new animal species such as cattle and horses on the Americas due to the previous scarcity of draft animals and domesticated livestock, leading to new agricultural styles and greater mobility

for Plains tribes hunting buffalo. Another example is the greater impact of newly introduced pathogens on the populations in the Americas, which were sometimes devastated by diseases such as smallpox.

(c) To earn this point, the response must describe a way in which the painting reflects a likely attitude of the artist about the Columbian Exchange. Examples that the artist thinks the exchange was good for the indigenous American populations include the European settlers offering food to the native tribe members and the presence of a friendly looking domesticated dog. Examples that the artist thinks the Europeans held a superior position in the exchange include the depiction of native tribe members sitting in a lower position and the visible display of European weapons.

3. A successful short-answer response accomplishes all three tasks set forth by the prompt. Each part of the prompt is worth 1 point, for a total of 3 possible points.

(a) To earn the point, the response must identify a specific cause of imperial expansion. Examples include navigational innovations, such as improved ship designs and use of the compass. Such technologies enabled Europeans to build overseas empires, and larger navies allowed European powers to conquer trading posts. Use of gunpowder technology enabled Muslim empires (Ottoman and Mughal) to conquer weaker states.

(b) To earn the point, the response must explain a similarity among these empires. Examples include: the incorporation of diverse ethnic or religious groups (Spanish, Ottoman, Mughal, Russian); the use of a merit-based bureaucracy to administer the empire (Ming/Qing and Ottoman); the conquest of weaker groups (Spanish conquest of Native Americans); and decentralized regions (Mughals in India, British in North America).

(c) To earn the point, the response must explain a difference beyond the fact that Asian empires were land-based and European empires were sea-based, as already stated in the question stem. Examples include European empires having outposts (colonies and trading posts) around the world, whereas Asian land empires only expanded in one region. European empires developed mercantilist policies, while Asian land empires imposed taxes on conquered groups. Asian land empires were often tolerant of religious beliefs (Ottoman, Mughal, Qing), while some European empires forced Christianity on the Native Americans (Spanish).

4. A successful short-answer response accomplishes all three tasks set forth by the prompt. Each part of the prompt is worth 1 point, for a total of 3 possible points.

(a) To earn the point, the response must identify one change in global trade as a result of industrialization. Examples include: the growth of export economies and demand for raw materials needed for production, such as rubber, oil, cotton, iron, and copper; the increase in the trade of European manufactured goods as a result of mass production; the expansion of mercantilist policies to new areas, such as Asia and Africa, due to European imperialism; and the increased involvement of the United States and Japan in the global economy due to industrialization.

(b) To earn the point, the response must explain why a change in social structure occurred. Examples include: the formation of the working class due to the demand for unskilled labor in urban factories; the emergence of new elites in the upper class, such as factory owners, due to the profits from industrialization; the decline in demand for farmers due to agricultural innovations and machines; the increase of unmarried women, especially in the work force outside the home; and the growth of the middle class due to jobs in management and professional services.

(c) To earn the point, the response must describe a specific continuity, such as the continued domestic role for women after marriage, the privileges of the landholding elites and nobility, and the difficult living conditions of rural farmers and factory workers.

Section II

1. *Evaluate the extent to which Enlightenment ideas caused rebellions against existing governments in the period 1750–1900.*

Category	Scoring Criteria	Notes
Thesis/Claim (0–1 points)	Historically defensible thesis/claim with a logical line of reasoning. The response must make a thesis or claim without restating the prompt itself. The thesis must consist of one or more sentences located in one place, either in the introduction or the conclusion.	This question is assessing the historical reasoning skill of causation. The thesis should make a claim about two to three ways Enlightenment ideas were used in the American, French, Haitian, or Spanish-American revolutions. Example: "Enlightenment ideas regarding natural rights, the right to overthrow oppressive governments, and the participation of citizens in government inspired revolutionaries in the New World to overthrow their imperial rulers and incorporate these principles into new representative governments."
Contextualization (0–1 points)	Broader historical context related to the prompt. The response must connect the topic to historical developments, events, or processes; these can occur before, during, or after the time frame of the prompt itself.	Contextualization for this prompt should explain, not merely mention, broader factors that contributed to the development of Enlightenment ideas or the political environment before revolutions. Examples: The development of Enlightenment ideas in response to the English Civil War and the estate system and centralization of power in France by monarchs, such as Louis XIV; how the Scientific Revolution inspired Enlightenment philosophers to embrace the use of reason and examine human relationships.
Evidence (0–3 points)	Use of evidence to support the thesis. The response must utilize the content from at least *three* documents to address the *topic* of the prompt. (1 point) OR The response must use at least *six* documents to support an *argument* based on the prompt. (2 points)	Evidence from the documents must be paraphrased, not merely quoted. Examples: Explaining how the Enlightenment concepts that the people have the right to a non-tyrannical government (document 2) and the right to overthrow an oppressive government (document 1) were used to justify the American (documents 3 and 6), French (document 4), and Spanish-American (document 7) revolutions; explaining how the concept of natural rights was incorporated into new governments, as shown in the Haitian Constitution (document 5) and Declaration of the Rights of Man and of the Citizen (document 4).
	The response must use at least *one* additional piece of historical evidence, beyond what is found in the documents, to support an argument. This additional evidence must be different from what was used for contextualization. (1 point)	Examples: The use of the United States Constitution or the example of republics forming after Spanish-American Revolutions when discussing new governments based on Enlightenment ideas; the use of mid-nineteenth-century revolutions against monarchs in Austria, Germany, and Italy when discussing the impact of Enlightenment ideas.

Category	Scoring Criteria	Notes
Analysis and Reasoning (0–2 points)	Complexity of understanding and reasoning. The response must explain, for at least *three* of the documents, how or why the document's purpose, historical basis, point of view, and/or audience are relevant to an argument. (1 point)	Factors' relevance to the argument about the impact of the Enlightenment should be explained, not just identified. Example: The role of purpose in document 3, in which the colonists were trying to justify their right to rebel by depicting the king of England as a tyrant, listing ways in which he had violated their rights.
	The response must show a complex understanding of the content of the prompt, using evidence to support, qualify, or modify an argument about the prompt. (1 point)	A complex understanding should be incorporated into the overall argument about the impact of the Enlightenment. Example: A discussion of the nuances of the application of Enlightenment ideas, such as how the revolutionaries sought equality and liberty, yet they did not apply those ideas to women, and most newly independent states did not abolish slavery (except Haiti).

2. *In the period 1200–1450, changes in trade networks resulted from and stimulated an increase in productive capacity, with important implications for social and gender structures.*

Develop an argument that evaluates the changes in social and gender structures in the period 1200–1450.

Category	Scoring Criteria	Notes
Thesis/Claim (0–1 points)	Historically defensible thesis/claim with a logical line of reasoning. The response must make a thesis or claim without restating the prompt itself. The thesis must consist of one or more sentences located in one place, either in the introduction or the conclusion.	This question assesses the skill of change and continuity over time. A strong thesis should make a claim about at least two major changes in social structures. Example: "The increases in both agricultural production and the extent of trade networks during the period from 1200 to 1450 led to changes such as the rise of merchant classes and the entrenchment of the practice of limiting women's social status."
Contextualization (0–1 points)	Broader historical context related to the prompt. The response must connect the topic to historical developments, events, or processes; these can occur before, during, or after the time frame of the prompt itself.	Contextualization for this prompt should explain, not merely mention, broader factors relevant to changes in social structures. Examples: A description of wider political and economic trends of the period that would impact social structures, such as the expansion of long-distance trade networks, the consolidation of power by monarchs and empires, and the increases in agricultural production and urbanization.

(continued)

Category	Scoring Criteria	Notes
Evidence (0–2 points)	Use of evidence to support the thesis. The response identifies specific examples *relevant to the topic* of the prompt. (1 point) OR The response uses specific examples to *support an argument* about the prompt. (2 points)	Evidence must be paraphrased, not merely quoted. To earn 2 points, the evidence must be used to support an argument about changes in social structures. Examples: The increasing complexity of social hierarchies as the growth of cities and the expansion of long-distance trade led to increased specialization, guilds, and a growing role for merchants; the increase in excluding women from public life in the midst of the growth of power of guilds in Europe, such as curtailing property rights and barring women from guild membership.
Analysis and Reasoning (0–2 points)	Complexity of understanding and reasoning. The response shows historical reasoning to make an argument about the prompt. (1 point) OR The response demonstrates complex understanding, using evidence to support, qualify, or modify an argument about the prompt. (2 points)	Comparison, causation, or continuity and change over time should be incorporated into the overall argument about changes in social structures. Example: An explanation of how increases in trade and agricultural production led to the development of merchant and trade classes (causation). OR A complex understanding should be incorporated into the overall argument about changes in social structures. Examples: A discussion of varying attitudes among civilizations, such as the thriving of merchant classes in European cities in contrast with the prejudice against merchants in China based on Confucian beliefs, or the increasing limits on women in the trade-based economic structures in Europe in contrast with women's roles in China continuing to be defined by kinship rules based on Confucian relationships; a description of both changes in European social structures *and* the continuity of rulers and landowning elites continuing to dominate the social hierarchy.

3. *In the period 1450–1750, rulers used a variety of methods to legitimize and consolidate their power.*

   Develop an argument that evaluates how one or more rulers consolidated and legitimized their power in this time period.

Category	Scoring Criteria	Notes
Thesis/Claim (0–1 points)	Historically defensible thesis/claim with a logical line of reasoning. The response must make a thesis or claim without restating the prompt itself. The thesis must consist of one or more sentences located in one place, either in the introduction or the conclusion.	This question assesses the skill of causation. A strong response should make a claim about two to three specific ways that rulers gained more power. Example: "In the period 1450–1750, rulers consolidated power through the use of religion to justify their right to rule, limiting the power of landholding elites, and recruiting bureaucrats who were trained to be loyal."
Contextualization (0–1 points)	Broader historical context related to the prompt. The response must connect the topic to historical developments, events, or processes; these can occur before, during, or after the time frame of the prompt itself.	Contextualization for this prompt should explain, not merely mention, broader factors relevant to how rulers legitimized and consolidated power. Examples: An explanation of how the European Age of Exploration enabled European monarchs to increase revenues; a discussion of how gunpowder technologies were used by Ottomans and Mughals to conquer larger territories.
Evidence (0–2 points)	Use of evidence to support the thesis. The response identifies specific examples *relevant to the topic* of the prompt. (1 point) OR The response uses specific examples to *support an argument* about the prompt. (2 points)	Evidence must be paraphrased, not merely quoted. To earn 2 points, the evidence must be used to support an argument about how rulers legitimized and consolidated power. Examples: The use of divine right by European leaders and the Mandate of Heaven by the Chinese; the restrictions placed on *daimyo* by the Tokugawa shoguns; the tsars in Russia appointing boyars rather than basing positions on inheritance; the civil service exam in China; the *devshirme* system in the Ottoman Empire.

(continued)

Category	Scoring Criteria	Notes
Analysis and Reasoning (0–2 points)	Complexity of understanding and reasoning. The response shows historical reasoning to make an argument about the prompt. (1 point) OR The response demonstrates complex understanding, using evidence to support, qualify, or modify an argument about the prompt. (2 points)	Comparison, causation, or continuity and change over time should be incorporated into the overall argument about how rulers legitimized and consolidated power. Example: An explanation of the similarities between the concepts of divine right in Europe and the Mandate of Heaven in China (comparison). OR A complex understanding should be incorporated into the overall argument about how rulers legitimized and consolidated power. Examples: An explanation of the similarities *and* differences between the concepts of divine right in Europe and the Mandate of Heaven in China; an examination of both the need for rulers' policies to legitimize and consolidate power and the effects of these policies.

4. *In the period 1750–1900, the process of industrialization changed the way in which goods were produced and consumed, with far-reaching effects on the global economy, social relations, and culture.*

Develop an argument that evaluates the factors that contributed to the rise of industrialization in Europe in this time period.

Category	Scoring Criteria	Notes
Thesis/Claim (0–1 points)	Historically defensible thesis/claim with a logical line of reasoning. The response must make a thesis or claim without restating the prompt itself. The thesis must consist of one or more sentences located in one place, either in the introduction or the conclusion.	This question assesses the skill of causation. A strong thesis should make a claim about two or more specific causes of industrialization. Examples: The Agricultural Revolution; the Enlightenment; European participation in global trade in the early modern period; geographic, political, and economic factors in Great Britain.
Contextualization (0–1 points)	Broader historical context related to the prompt. The response must connect the topic to historical developments, events, or processes; these can occur before, during, or after the time frame of the prompt itself.	Contextualization for this prompt should explain, not merely mention, broader factors relevant to the rise of industrialization. Examples: A description of how the Age of Exploration contributed to the growth of European empires and global economies; an explanation of how increases in agricultural production led to labor surpluses and urbanization.

Category	Scoring Criteria	Notes
Evidence (0–2 points)	Use of evidence to support the thesis. The response identifies specific examples *relevant to the topic* of the prompt. (1 point) OR The response uses specific examples to *support an argument* about the prompt. (2 points)	Evidence must be paraphrased, not merely quoted. To earn 2 points, the evidence must be used to support an argument about the rise of industrialization. Examples: The spread of Enlightenment ideas leading to changes in law that protected private property, giving an incentive to business owners to invest in machines; the innovations of the Agricultural Revolution (crop rotation, seed drill, fertilizers, new plows) increasing yields that provided food for urban factory workers; European economic policies enabling manufacturers to acquire cheap raw materials, such as cotton for textiles, from overseas colonies.
Analysis and Reasoning (0-2 points)	Complexity of understanding and reasoning. The response shows historical reasoning to make an argument about the prompt. (1 point) OR The response demonstrates complex understanding, using evidence to support, qualify, or modify an argument about the prompt. (2 points)	Comparison, causation, or continuity and change over time should be incorporated into the overall argument about the rise of industrialization. Example: A detailed explanation of how the factors listed above contributed to the rise of industrialization (causation). OR A complex understanding should be incorporated into the overall argument about the rise of industrialization. Examples: An explanation of both the causes *and* the effects of industrialization, such as the impact on social structures and a new wave of imperialism in Africa and Asia; an analysis of both the similarities *and* differences among European nations that facilitated or limited industrialization, such as Germany's delayed industrialization due to its less open political climate and lack of overseas territories.

Practice Exam 4

Practice Exam 4 Answer Grid

1. Ⓐ Ⓑ Ⓒ Ⓓ
2. Ⓐ Ⓑ Ⓒ Ⓓ
3. Ⓐ Ⓑ Ⓒ Ⓓ
4. Ⓐ Ⓑ Ⓒ Ⓓ
5. Ⓐ Ⓑ Ⓒ Ⓓ
6. Ⓐ Ⓑ Ⓒ Ⓓ
7. Ⓐ Ⓑ Ⓒ Ⓓ
8. Ⓐ Ⓑ Ⓒ Ⓓ
9. Ⓐ Ⓑ Ⓒ Ⓓ
10. Ⓐ Ⓑ Ⓒ Ⓓ
11. Ⓐ Ⓑ Ⓒ Ⓓ
12. Ⓐ Ⓑ Ⓒ Ⓓ
13. Ⓐ Ⓑ Ⓒ Ⓓ
14. Ⓐ Ⓑ Ⓒ Ⓓ

15. Ⓐ Ⓑ Ⓒ Ⓓ
16. Ⓐ Ⓑ Ⓒ Ⓓ
17. Ⓐ Ⓑ Ⓒ Ⓓ
18. Ⓐ Ⓑ Ⓒ Ⓓ
19. Ⓐ Ⓑ Ⓒ Ⓓ
20. Ⓐ Ⓑ Ⓒ Ⓓ
21. Ⓐ Ⓑ Ⓒ Ⓓ
22. Ⓐ Ⓑ Ⓒ Ⓓ
23. Ⓐ Ⓑ Ⓒ Ⓓ
24. Ⓐ Ⓑ Ⓒ Ⓓ
25. Ⓐ Ⓑ Ⓒ Ⓓ
26. Ⓐ Ⓑ Ⓒ Ⓓ
27. Ⓐ Ⓑ Ⓒ Ⓓ
28. Ⓐ Ⓑ Ⓒ Ⓓ

29. Ⓐ Ⓑ Ⓒ Ⓓ
30. Ⓐ Ⓑ Ⓒ Ⓓ
31. Ⓐ Ⓑ Ⓒ Ⓓ
32. Ⓐ Ⓑ Ⓒ Ⓓ
33. Ⓐ Ⓑ Ⓒ Ⓓ
34. Ⓐ Ⓑ Ⓒ Ⓓ
35. Ⓐ Ⓑ Ⓒ Ⓓ
36. Ⓐ Ⓑ Ⓒ Ⓓ
37. Ⓐ Ⓑ Ⓒ Ⓓ
38. Ⓐ Ⓑ Ⓒ Ⓓ
39. Ⓐ Ⓑ Ⓒ Ⓓ
40. Ⓐ Ⓑ Ⓒ Ⓓ
41. Ⓐ Ⓑ Ⓒ Ⓓ
42. Ⓐ Ⓑ Ⓒ Ⓓ

43. Ⓐ Ⓑ Ⓒ Ⓓ
44. Ⓐ Ⓑ Ⓒ Ⓓ
45. Ⓐ Ⓑ Ⓒ Ⓓ
46. Ⓐ Ⓑ Ⓒ Ⓓ
47. Ⓐ Ⓑ Ⓒ Ⓓ
48. Ⓐ Ⓑ Ⓒ Ⓓ
49. Ⓐ Ⓑ Ⓒ Ⓓ
50. Ⓐ Ⓑ Ⓒ Ⓓ
51. Ⓐ Ⓑ Ⓒ Ⓓ
52. Ⓐ Ⓑ Ⓒ Ⓓ
53. Ⓐ Ⓑ Ⓒ Ⓓ
54. Ⓐ Ⓑ Ⓒ Ⓓ
55. Ⓐ Ⓑ Ⓒ Ⓓ

SECTION I, PART A
Time—55 minutes
55 Questions

Directions: Section I, Part A of this exam contains 55 multiple-choice questions, organized into sets with corresponding historical sources. Each of the questions or incomplete statements is followed by four suggested answers or completions. Using both the provided sources and your own historical knowledge, select the best answer choice.

Questions 1–3 refer to the passage below.

> "The king, the officers, the people, the Buddhists, and Daoist priests etc. came long distances out of the city to meet the master [Qiu Chuji]. . . . The master asked what they reckoned the distance to the place where the [Mongol] emperor then was. All agreed in estimating it at ten thousand *li** and more to the south-west.
>
> . . . . It must be observed that the country from this place to the east belonged to China at the time of the Tang dynasty. West of it are neither Buddhists nor Daoists. The Hui only worship the west.
>
> . . . we arrived at the encampment of the emperor, who had sent one of his high officers to meet the master. After having been installed in his lodging, the master presented himself to the emperor; who greeted him and said: "You were invited by the other courts (the Song and the Jin), but you refused. Now you have come to see me having traversed a road of ten thousand *li*, I am much gratified." The master answered: "The wild man of the mountains came to see the emperor by order of your Majesty; it was the will of Heaven." Genghis Khan invited him to sit down, and ordered a meal to be set before him. After this he asked him: "Sainted man, you have come from a great distance. Have you a medicine of immortality?" The master replied: "There are means for preserving life, but no medicines for immortality." Genghis Khan lauded him for his sincerity and candor. By imperial order two tents were pitched for the master, to the east of the emperor's tents. The emperor gave him the title of *shen-sien* (the immortal)."

*roughly 3,100 miles

Qiu Chuji's Travels to the West, by Li Zhichang, a Daoist disciple (1228)

GO ON TO THE NEXT PAGE

1. Which of the following characteristics of the Mongol Empire enabled Qiu Chuji's audience with Genghis Khan, as described in the third paragraph?

   (A) The Mongol Empire adopted the trappings of Chinese civilization following its conquest of the Southern Song Dynasty.

   (B) Succession issues over who would fill the Mongol Empire's leadership role eventually led to the destabilization and fragmentation of the empire.

   (C) Mongol rule resulted in vast areas of the Eurasian continent being safe for even small groups of travelers.

   (D) The spread of the bubonic plague along the trade routes west of China led to people questioning their faith.

2. All of the following statements are factually accurate. Which would best explain the description of the Hui as people who "only worship the west," as described in the second paragraph?

   (A) The Mongol Empire displaced China as the greatest geopolitical power in East Asia.

   (B) Muslims are expected to pray five times a day facing Mecca.

   (C) The Mongol Empire did not impose a particular religion on its conquered subjects.

   (D) China is a state with ethnic and religious diversity.

3. Qiu Chuji's interactions with Ghengis Khan best illustrate the fact that the Mongol Empire

   (A) strengthened itself by utilizing the talented people of those areas it conquered

   (B) emphasized the idea that the ruler should treat his subjects with compassion

   (C) appointed people to high rank based on merit rather than on bloodline or ancestry

   (D) was skilled at using diplomacy to play enemies off one another

GO ON TO THE NEXT PAGE

Questions 4–7 refer to the following two passages.

Source 1

"'The Delhi Sultanate was founded by a slave.'

So runs the well-known jibe. And it is true. . . . [India's] conquest belongs by rights to Aibak . . . who took the name of Qutb al-Din Aibak, or Pole-star of the Faith.

To those who know India the name conjures up one of the most marvelous sights . . . the Qutb Minar, the finest [minaret] in the world. It was built by the Turkic slave Aibak, and one can forgive him much in that he left the world such a thing of beauty to be a joy for ever. And yet as one . . . looks round on the dismantled ruins of still more ancient temples, the mind suddenly ceases to give the glory . . . and turns almost with amaze to the thought of the Hindu architects who built it to order out of their dishonored shrines."

Flora Annie Steel, *India Through the Ages: A Popular and Picturesque History of Hindustan*, 1911

Source 2

"When Kublai permanently established himself at Beijing . . . he was thus able to deal wisely and also vigorously with a society with which he was only imperfectly acquainted. . . . At first he treated with equal consideration Buddhism, Mohammedanism, Christianity, and even Judaism, and he said that he treated them all with equal consideration because he hoped that the greatest among them would help him in heaven. If some doubt may be felt as to the sincerity of this statement, there can be none as to Kublai's effort to turn all religions to a political use, and to make them serve his turn. . . . He insisted on the proper prayers being offered to himself and the extreme reverence of the kow-tow."

Demetrius Charles Boulger, *China*, 1893

4. The views expressed in the two passages best describe what difference between nomadic conquest in South Asia and in East Asia?

   (A) Nomads in Central and East Asia were more tolerant of existing beliefs.

   (B) Nomads in South and West Asia were more tolerant of existing beliefs.

   (C) Nomads in India and Anatolia often incorporated existing beliefs into their empires.

   (D) Nomads in China discouraged the practices of Buddhism and Daoism.

5. The cross-cultural interactions described in the two passages most directly contributed to which of the following?

   (A) The start of a civil war between Hindus and Muslims in India

   (B) The adoption of Mongol spiritual practices by the Chinese

   (C) The spread of the Turkish language to Asia Minor

   (D) The conversion to Islam by Chinese peasants

GO ON TO THE NEXT PAGE

6. The philosophy reflected in Source 1 most directly contributed to the founding of which of the following empires?

   (A) The Mali Empire

   (B) The Russian Empire

   (C) The Yuan Dynasty

   (D) The Ottoman Empire

7. A historian might argue that the conquests described in both passages reflected a turning point in world history primarily because the Delhi Sultanate and the Yuan Dynasty

   (A) spread pastoralism to cultivators in South and East Asia

   (B) facilitated an intensification of Eurasian trade and expansion of trade networks

   (C) suffered collapse within a century due to revolts by their conquered subjects

   (D) popularized the concept of religious toleration as a human right

GO ON TO THE NEXT PAGE ⟹

Questions 8–12 refer to the table below.

EDICTS OF THE TOKUGAWA SHOGUNATE FOR MILITARY HOUSEHOLDS

Edict Number	Rule
8	Marriages must be approved by the shogun and must not be performed in private. To form a factional alliance through marriage is treason.
10	Lords and vassals must observe proper clothing and dress materials. They may not wear fine white clothing, silk garments, kimono sleeves without a family crest, etc.
12	Samurai must practice frugality and not display any wealth, in order to help balance the differences between rich and poor.
13	The lords of the domains must choose officials who have administrative abilities. This is the way the domain can flourish.

8. The edicts issued by the Tokugawa shogunate are best seen as evidence for which of the following?

    (A) Landowning classes caused significant challenges to state consolidation and expansion.

    (B) Peasant labor intensified in many regions as a result of growing demand for raw materials.

    (C) Widening global economic opportunities contributed to the formation of new economic elites.

    (D) The power of existing elites fluctuated in response to increasingly powerful leaders.

9. Which of the following can best be inferred about the purpose in issuing the edicts for the military households?

    (A) The shogun wanted to justify the creation of an imperial examination system.

    (B) The samurai strained resources in a time of economic depression.

    (C) The shogun wanted to consolidate power and lessen attempts at rebellion.

    (D) The *daimyo* refused to pledge loyalty to the Tokugawa shogun.

GO ON TO THE NEXT PAGE

10. The edicts by the Tokugawa shogunate are best understood in the context of which of the following?

   (A) The period of civil war among *daimyo* prior to the rise of the shogunate

   (B) The arrival of European merchants in Japanese ports

   (C) The trading agreements forcibly imposed by Western powers

   (D) The spread of Neo-Confucian values as a result of a tributary relationship with China

11. Which of the following was the most immediate effect of the edicts issued by the Tokugawa shogun?

   (A) The power of the shogun was threatened by the supporters of the emperor.

   (B) Japan became dominated by European merchants wishing to control the silver trade.

   (C) The government of Japan was overthrown by resentful *daimyo*.

   (D) Japan experienced a period of relative peace and political stability.

12. The rule of the Tokugawa shogunate in Japan was disrupted by which of the following during the nineteenth century?

   (A) The conquest of the Tokugawa shogunate by Western imperial powers

   (B) The emergence of Meiji Japan as a result of U.S. and European influence

   (C) The defeat of Japan in a series of wars with Chinese naval forces

   (D) The collapse of Japan's economy as a result of regulations on construction and commerce

GO ON TO THE NEXT PAGE

Questions 13–15 refer to the map below.

EMPIRES IN THE AMERICAS, CIRCA 1750

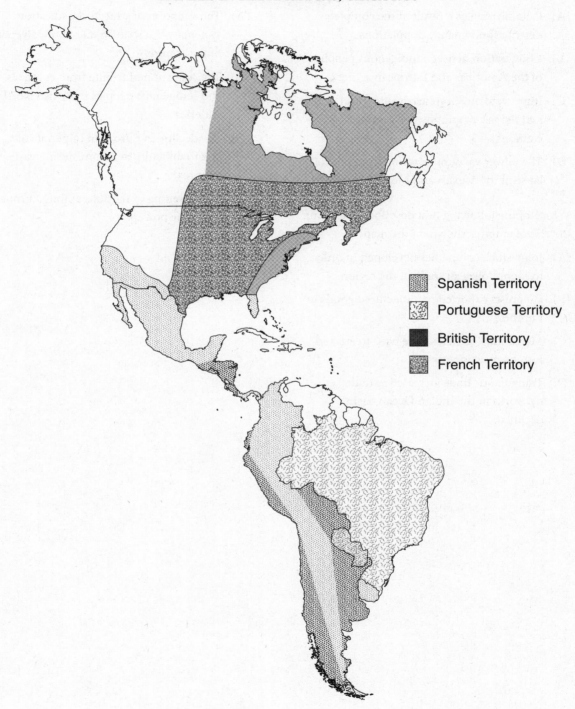

Spanish Territory

Portuguese Territory

British Territory

French Territory

GO ON TO THE NEXT PAGE

13. Which of the following most directly contributed to the establishment of empires shown on the map?

    (A) Colonization as a result of the complete destruction of native populations

    (B) Cooperation between indigenous peoples of the Americas and European settlers

    (C) Improvements in transoceanic travel and the use of gunpowder weapons and cannons

    (D) The power vacuum resulting from the collapse of the Mexica and Inca Empires

14. Which of the following best describes a result of the rise of empires shown on the map?

    (A) Joint-stock companies developed in order to monopolize all trade in the region.

    (B) Colonists exported manufactured goods to Europe.

    (C) Mercantilist policies were used to expand European economies.

    (D) Transatlantic trade increased as trade networks in the Indian Ocean basin declined.

15. The establishment of empires shown on the map led to the development of which of the following?

    (A) The adoption of a racial classification system by the Spanish due to the diversity of the empire

    (B) The collection of tribute from colonists and indigenous peoples in British North America

    (C) The decline in European imperial rule due to difficulty in administering vast empires

    (D) The lessening of tensions among European maritime powers

GO ON TO THE NEXT PAGE

Questions 16–17 refer to the following image.

TAJ MAHAL, CONSTRUCTED IN THE SEVENTEENTH CENTURY IN AGRA, INDIA

16. The image best illustrates which of the following political developments in the period 1450–1750?

   (A) The development of military professionals to increase centralized control over populations

   (B) The contraction of empires as a result of challenges to imperial authority

   (C) The increase in tax revenues as a result of the establishment of Eurasian empires

   (D) The rise of European land empires due to access to gunpowder weapons

17. The image best illustrates which of the following continuities in world history?

   (A) The construction of fortifications for defensive purposes

   (B) The use of monumental architecture by rulers

   (C) The universal adoption of Greco-Roman architectural features

   (D) The use of religious ideas to legitimize the rule of monarchs

GO ON TO THE NEXT PAGE

Questions 18–21 refer to the passage below.

"Europe's Dutch and English East India Companies are often viewed as prototypes of modern multinational corporations. The scholarly literature recognizes that huge quantities of silver flowed to Asia, but this phenomenon is considered a reflection of Europe's balance-of-trade deficit with east Asia; Europeans developed a far greater taste for Asian finery than the other way around, according to conventional wisdom, so treasure had to flow from west to east to pay for Europe's trade deficit. In short, all the key issues are normally framed in terms of European perspectives. Acceptance of a global perspective instead of the predominant Eurocentric view outlined above yields a startlingly different view. It becomes clear that Europeans did indeed play an important role in the birth of world trade, but their role was as middlemen in the vast silver trade; they were prime movers on neither the supply side (except Spain in America) nor the demand side of the worldwide silver market. Europeans were intermediaries in the trade between the New World and China. Massive amounts of silver traversed the Atlantic. After it had reached European soil, the Portuguese in the sixteenth century and Dutch in the seventeenth century became dominant distributors of silver by a multitude of routes into Asia."

Dennis O. Flynn & Arturo Giráldez, *Born with a "Silver Spoon":*
The Origin of World Trade in 1571, 1995

18. Which of the following most directly led to the increased presence of Europeans in Asian trade?

(A) European maritime reconnaissance in the Indian Ocean basin

(B) British conquest of India

(C) European colonization of North America

(D) The establishment of trading posts in coastal West Africa

19. Which of the following would best support the author's assertion that Europeans were "middlemen" in the global silver trade?

(A) Silver mined in South America was transported to Spain.

(B) Europeans had a great demand for Asian luxury items.

(C) Chinese goods were purchased by Europeans with silver mined in South America.

(D) European monarchies required silver to finance large building projects in their home countries.

20. What was an important effect of the process described in the passage?

(A) Imperial rule in China weakened as European interference in China's economy strengthened.

(B) Europeans conquered and colonized indigenous peoples of Latin America.

(C) Demand for European manufactured goods in Asia increased.

(D) Europeans established trading post empires in Africa and Asia.

21. The contact between Europeans and Asians described in the passage contributed most directly to which of the following?

(A) The complete adoption of Western culture by Asian peoples

(B) The diffusion of existing religions, such as Christianity

(C) Chinese sponsorship of the voyages of Zheng He

(D) European conquest of Africa in order to acquire slaves

GO ON TO THE NEXT PAGE

Questions 22–24 are based on the following two images.

<u>Image 1</u>

CARAVEL SHIP, CIRCA 1500

<u>Image 2</u>

**COMPASS USED BY EUROPEAN EXPLORERS IN
THE FIFTEENTH AND SIXTEENTH CENTURIES**

GO ON TO THE NEXT PAGE

22. The object in <u>Image 1</u> contributed to which of the following developments in the period 1450–1750?

    (A) The creation of the first trade link between Europe and Asia

    (B) The disappearance of previously established trade networks

    (C) The creation of a global economy and the rise of mercantilism

    (D) The diffusion of Chinese technology to Europeans as a result of the Crusades

23. The object in <u>Image 2</u> best illustrates which of the following developments in the period 1450–1750?

    (A) The diffusion of knowledge from Islamic and Asian Empires to European navigators

    (B) The development of new syncretic cultural traditions

    (C) The intensification of existing trade networks

    (D) The influence of the Columbian Exchange on technological knowledge

24. When taken together, the two images best support which of the following conclusions?

    (A) Europeans developed entirely new technologies to begin maritime expeditions.

    (B) Improved technology enabled Europeans to undertake transoceanic voyages.

    (C) European technology in this era was completely adopted from other regions.

    (D) Improved technology was the result of new contact between Europeans and the Americas.

GO ON TO THE NEXT PAGE

Questions 25–28 refer to the passage below.

"The religion of the Hindoos, who form a great part of the natives of India, teaches many things which seem very strange to Englishmen. Among other things they are taught that they will be defiled if they eat any part of a cow. By this defilement they will meet with much contempt from their fellows, and will suffer much after their death in another world. The bulk of the army in India was composed of Hindoos, and it happened that an improved rifle had lately been invented for the use of the soldiers, and that the cartridges used in this rifle required to be greased, in order that they might be rammed down easily into the barrel. The men believed that the grease used was made of the fat of cows, though this was not really the case. There was, therefore, much suspicion and angry feeling among the native soldiers, and when ignorant men are suspicious and angry they are apt to break out into deeds of unreasoning fury. The danger was the greater because a great many of the native princes were also discontented. These princes governed states scattered about over India, though they were not allowed to make war with one another. Many of them had governed very badly, had ruined their subjects by hard taxation, and had spent the money they thus obtained in vicious and riotous living. The English Government in India had interfered with some of these, and had dethroned them, annexing their territories to its own, and ruling the people who had been their subjects by means of its own officers. The consequence was that some of the princes who had been left in possession of authority thought that their turn would come next, and that they too would be dethroned before long. These men were therefore ready to help against the English, if they thought that they had a chance of succeeding."

Account of the Indian Revolt of 1857 (found in an English textbook edited for American students), *Gardiner's English History for Schools*, 1881

25. The anger of Indian soldiers described in the passage resulted from which of the following?

    (A) Legislation enacted by the British to suppress India's agricultural production

    (B) British attitudes of superiority and lack of respect for native religious traditions

    (C) Policies which forced native peoples to adopt Christianity and abandon traditional belief systems

    (D) Enlightenment ideas incorporated into colonial governments

26. The actions of Indian princes described in the passage are best seen as evidence of which of the following?

    (A) The cooperation between native rulers and colonial authorities

    (B) The stable positions of colonial governors as a result of imperial policies

    (C) The rise of anti-colonial movements due to questions about political authority

    (D) The economic benefits of cooperation with imperial governments

GO ON TO THE NEXT PAGE

27. The presence of the British government in India was the result of which of the following broader historical developments in the period 1750–1900?

    (A) States with existing colonies strengthened their control over those colonies.

    (B) Maritime reconnaissance in the Indian Ocean basin led to the establishment of trading posts.

    (C) In some parts of their empires, Europeans established settler colonies.

    (D) Industrializing powers practiced economic imperialism and neocolonialism in some areas.

28. Which of the following early twentieth century developments was an effect of the conflict described in the passage?

    (A) The rise of nationalist leaders and groups seeking autonomy from imperial rule

    (B) The loosening of economic and political restrictions by imperial rulers

    (C) The unification of British and Indian government officials due to transnational movements

    (D) The abandonment of resistance movements by colonists

GO ON TO THE NEXT PAGE

Questions 29–31 refer to the passage below.

"In republishing at this period the Life of Toussaint Louverture, I am induced to dedicate it to your Imperial Majesty, by feelings which those who know how to appreciate true elevation of character cannot fail to understand.

That illustrious African well deserved the exalted names of Christian, Patriot, and Hero. He was a devout worshipper of his God, and a successful defender of his invaded country. He was the victorious enemy, at once, and the contrast of Napoleon Bonaparte, whose arms he repelled, and whose pride he humbled, not more by the strength of his military genius, than by the moral influence of his amiable and virtuous character: by how many ties, then, of kindred merit and generous sympathy must he not be endeared to the magnanimous Liberator of Europe!

In nothing, however, will your Imperial Majesty more sympathize with the brave Toussaint, than in his attachment to the great cause in which he fell—the cause, not of his country only, but of his race; not merely of St. Domingo, but of the African continent."

James Stephen, British abolitionist, dedication to Tsar Alexander of Russia,
History of Toussaint Louverture, 1814

29. Which of the following most likely explains the author's attitude toward Toussaint L'Ouverture?

    (A) His audience, the Russian tsar

    (B) His point of view as an abolitionist

    (C) His goal of defeating Napoleon

    (D) His British national heritage

30. The author's stance as an abolitionist is likely the result of which of the following?

    (A) The successful Haitian Revolution

    (B) The independence of the United States

    (C) The violence of the Napoleonic wars

    (D) The diffusion of Enlightenment ideas

31. The Haitian Revolution is best understood in the context of which of the following?

    (A) The Atlantic Revolutions

    (B) The Enlightenment

    (C) The Industrial Revolution

    (D) The Russian Revolution

GO ON TO THE NEXT PAGE

Questions 32–34 refer to the passage below.

"Steam-engines furnish the means not only of their support but of their multiplication. They create a vast demand for fuel; and, while they lend their powerful arms to drain the pits and to raise the coals, they call into employment multitudes of miners, engineers, shipbuilders, and sailors, and cause the construction of canals and railways. Thus therefore, in enabling these rich fields of industry to be cultivated to the utmost, they leave thousands of fine arable fields free for the production of food to man, which must have been otherwise allotted to the food of horses. Steam-engines moreover, by the cheapness and steadiness of their action, fabricate cheap goods, and procure in their exchange a liberal supply of the necessaries and comforts of life produced in foreign lands."

Andrew Ure, London publication, *Philosophy of Manufactures*, 1835

32. The passage is best seen as evidence for which of the following?

   (A) The implementation of the factory system led to increased demand for skilled laborers.

   (B) The limited supply of fossil fuels led to innovations in transportation.

   (C) The rise of industrial technology improved living conditions for all members of society.

   (D) The development of machines led to increased agricultural production and population growth.

33. Which of the following groups in industrial societies of the nineteenth century would be most likely to <u>disagree</u> with the author's view of machines?

   (A) Industrial capitalists

   (B) Government officials

   (C) Landholding elites

   (D) Industrial workers

34. Which of the following factors contributed to the rise of industrial production described in the passage?

   (A) The accumulation of capital and the protection of private property

   (B) The conquest of overseas colonies in Africa and access to slaves

   (C) The reduction of Europe's population and the need for labor-saving devices

   (D) The decline in agricultural productivity and a lack of skilled workers

GO ON TO THE NEXT PAGE

Questions 35–37 refer to the passage below.

"1. The establishment of a university at Peking.

2. The sending of imperial clansmen to foreign countries to study the forms and conditions of European and American government.

3. The encouragement of the arts, sciences and modern agriculture. . . .

7. Urged that the Lu-Han railway should be prosecuted with more vigour and expedition.

8. Advised the adoption of Western arms and drill for all the Tartar troops.

9. Ordered the establishment of agricultural schools in all the provinces to teach the farmers improved methods of agriculture. . . .

12. Special rewards were offered to inventors and authors.

13. The officials were ordered to encourage trade and assist merchants. . . .

15. Bureaus of Mines and Railroads were established.

16. Journalists were encouraged to write on all political subjects.

17. Naval academies and training-ships were ordered. . . .

20. Commercial bureaus were ordered in Shanghai for the encouragement of trade."

Issac Taylor Headland, summary of reforms proposed by Guangxu
(Chinese emperor in the late nineteenth century), 1909

35. The proposed reforms shown in the passage were most likely issued in reaction to which of the following?

(A) Colonization by Western powers and the desire for Chinese independence

(B) The spread of Enlightenment ideas and the willingness of the emperor to abdicate

(C) The collapse of the Qing Dynasty and the resulting period of disorder

(D) Encroachment by industrializing states and subsequent economic imperialism

36. The reforms outlined in the passage were most similar to which of the following?

(A) The Russian Revolution

(B) The Meiji Restoration

(C) The Mexican Revolution

(D) The Second Industrial Revolution

37. The conditions in the early twentieth century in China that these reforms attempted to address led to which of the following later developments?

(A) Industrialization and the establishment of a stable democracy

(B) The fall of the existing monarchy and rise of a new dynasty

(C) A civil war and communist revolution under Mao Zedong

(D) The rise of a foreign-ruled totalitarian state government

GO ON TO THE NEXT PAGE

Questions 38–41 refer to the poem below.

"Take up the White Man's burden—
Send forth the best ye breed—
Go bind your sons to exile
To serve your captives' need;
To wait in heavy harness
On fluttered folk and wild—
Your new-caught, sullen peoples,
Half devil and half child.

. . .

Take up the White Man's burden—
And reap his old reward:
The blame of those ye better,
The hate of those ye guard—
The cry of hosts ye humour
(Ah, slowly!) toward the light: —
'Why brought ye us from bondage,
Our loved Egyptian night?'"

Rudyard Kipling, British novelist and poet, "White Man's Burden," 1899

38. The attitudes reflected in the poem are most similar to which of the following?

    (A) Spanish missionaries in the New World during the fifteenth and sixteenth centuries

    (B) Religious conflict between Protestants and Catholics in the sixteenth century

    (C) Ideological conflict behind proxy wars in the twentieth century

    (D) Genocides in the twentieth century, like the Holocaust and the Hutu/Tutsi in the 1990s

39. The description of the colonized peoples in the poem is best understood in the context of which of the following?

    (A) Racial ideologies in Europe

    (B) The rise of fascist governments

    (C) Democratic revolutions in Latin America

    (D) The spread of Enlightenment ideas

GO ON TO THE NEXT PAGE

40. A counter viewpoint to the poem comes from one of Kipling's contemporaries, Mohandas Gandhi, who worked for Indian independence using which of the following strategies?

    (A) Aggressive Hindu nationalism

    (B) Internal political reforms

    (C) Nonviolent civil disobedience

    (D) Ethnic separatist movements

41. An historian doing a comparative cultural analysis of this poem would benefit most from which of the following?

    (A) A piece of fiction from a colonial subject who supported independence

    (B) A political white paper from a European group opposing colonialism

    (C) Economic records from the British Imperial Service regarding India

    (D) Contemporaneous newspaper accounts of life in the British colonies

GO ON TO THE NEXT PAGE

Questions 42–44 refer to the table below.

ITALIAN EMIGRANTS BY DESTINATION, 1876–1905

Years	Africa	Americas	Asia	Europe	Oceania	Total
1876–1885	39,488	425,588	404	850,219	990	1,314,689
1886–1895	31,082	1,386,057	1,516	970,133	2,261	2,391,049
1896–1905	82,107	2,340,519	3,108	1,890,943	5,748	4,322,425
Total	152,677	4,150,164	5,028	3,711,295	8,999	8,028,163

42. A modern historian might use the data in the table to best support which of the following arguments?

(A) A large portion of the Italian population emigrated between the years 1896–1905 due to financial concerns

(B) The increase in immigrants from Southern Europe caused political unrest among Northern and Western European countries

(C) Advances in transportation technology allowed diasporic communities to form far from their countries of origin

(D) Italian migrants came from high-skilled urban areas and displaced skilled workers in their new countries

43. Given your knowledge of world history, which of the following best explains the patterns shown in the table?

(A) The availability of economic opportunities in the Americas and Europe

(B) The decades of peace in Europe at the end of the nineteenth century

(C) The sponsorship of immigrants by governments in the Americas and Europe

(D) The resistance to foreign immigrants by governments in Asia and Oceania

44. Which of the following best describes a likely effect of the patterns shown in the table during the time period covered?

(A) Italian migrants abandoned cultural elements from their home societies and adopted new practices.

(B) Italian migrants formed ethnic enclaves to transplant their culture into new environments.

(C) Italian migrants created a syncretic form of Christianity in their new society based on local practice.

(D) Italian migrants rejected all cultural elements of the regions to which they migrated.

GO ON TO THE NEXT PAGE

Questions 45–48 refer to the map below.

MILITARY ALLIANCES AND POLITICAL MOVEMENTS, CIRCA 1955

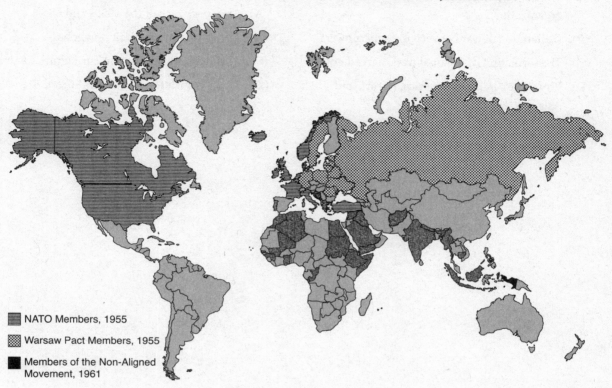

▤ NATO Members, 1955

▨ Warsaw Pact Members, 1955

■ Members of the Non-Aligned
Movement, 1961

45. The military alliances shown on the map were
developed as a result of which of the following?

(A) The economic crisis engendered by the
Great Depression

(B) Religious and ethnic movements that challenged colonial rule

(C) Ideological struggle between communist
and capitalist powers

(D) Extremist movements that annihilated
specific populations

46. The Non-Aligned Movement shown on the map
developed for which of the following reasons?

(A) To create a military alliance to counter
NATO and the Warsaw Pact

(B) To oppose the existing global political and
economic order

(C) To unite colonies in fighting for independence from imperial rulers

(D) To remove economic barriers and promote
free trade

GO ON TO THE NEXT PAGE

47. Which of the following was the most direct effect of the alliances shown on the map?

    (A) The development of environmental organizations

    (B) Declaration of war between the superpowers

    (C) The formation of regional trade agreements

    (D) Proxy wars in Latin America, Africa, and Asia

48. Conflict between the alliance blocs shown on the map most directly led to which of the following?

    (A) The space race of the 1950s and 60s

    (B) Development of atomic weapons

    (C) The Green Revolution in agriculture

    (D) Democratization in Eastern Europe

GO ON TO THE NEXT PAGE

Questions 49–51 refer to the table below.

GDP PER CAPITA IN CURRENT US$

Year	South Korea	Singapore	Hong Kong
1960	158	428	429
1970	279	926	960
1980	1,704	4,928	5,700
1990	6,516	11,862	13,486
2000	11,948	23,852	25,757
2010	22,087	47,237	32,550
2018	31,363	64,582	48,717

49. The table best illustrates which of the following economic changes in the late twentieth century?

    (A) The shift in industrial production from China and Japan to Singapore, Hong Kong, and South Korea

    (B) The decline in consumption by the United States and the new role of Asian consumerism

    (C) The shift in manufacturing from Europe and the United States to the Pacific Rim

    (D) The decline in European participation in the global economy as a result of self-sufficiency

50. The changes shown on the table have been facilitated most by which of the following?

    (A) New international organizations that were formed to maintain world peace

    (B) New economic institutions and regional trade agreements

    (C) Movements that protested the economic consequences of global integration

    (D) Greater control of national economies by governments that enacted isolationist policies

51. The trend shown in the table is most similar to the trend in which of the following?

    (A) Western Europe in the twentieth century

    (B) Sub-Saharan Africa in the twentieth century

    (C) India and China in the nineteenth century

    (D) Western Europe in the nineteenth century

GO ON TO THE NEXT PAGE

Questions 52–55 refer to the passage below.

"Twenty years ago, the first genetically modified (GM) crops were planted in the USA, alongside dazzling promises about this new technology. Two decades on, the promises are getting bigger and bigger, but GM crops are not delivering any of them. Not only was this technology supposed to make food and agriculture systems simpler, safer and more efficient, but GM crops are increasingly being touted as the key to 'feeding the world' and 'fighting climate change.' The promises may be growing, but the popularity of GM crops is not. . . .

Why have GM crops failed to be the popular success the industry claims them to be? As the promises have expanded, so too has the evidence that GM crops are ill adapted to the challenges facing global food and agriculture systems. These promises have proved to be myths: some of these benefits have failed to materialize outside the lab, and others have unraveled when faced with the real-world complexities of agricultural ecosystems, and the real-world needs of farmers. In reality, GM crops have reinforced the broken model of industrial agriculture, with its biodiversity-reducing monocultures, its huge carbon footprint, its economic pressures on small-scale farmers, and its failure to deliver safe, healthy and nutritious food to those who need it."

Greenpeace International, "Twenty Years of Failure:
Why GM Crops Have Failed to Deliver on Their Promises," 2015

52. The passage is a reaction to which of the following developments?

(A) The end of the Cold War

(B) The Green Revolution

(C) The rise of the European Union

(D) New international organizations

53. Based on the passage, it can be inferred that the organization might also support which of the following assertions?

(A) Government intervention in farming will lead to better alternatives to genetically modified crops.

(B) The rise of multinational corporations in food production will be beneficial to the environment.

(C) Scientific advances will eventually lead to a solution for global poverty and famine relief.

(D) Regulatory agencies should be more concerned with broader human outcomes from scientific products.

54. The passage reflects which of the following developments in the twentieth century?

(A) The rise of groups that protested the environmental consequences of global integration

(B) The spread of free-market economic principles that led to regional trade agreements

(C) The growth of religious movements to redefine the relationship between the individual and the state

(D) Transnational ideological movements that sought to unite people across state borders

55. The author of the passage is responding to the arguments of which of the following?

(A) Supporters of small and organic local farming

(B) International organizations for famine relief

(C) Neoliberal supporters of industrial agriculture

(D) Supporters of American food export businesses

GO ON TO THE NEXT PAGE

END OF PART A

**IF YOU FINISH BEFORE TIME IS CALLED,
YOU MAY CHECK YOUR WORK ON THIS SECTION.**

DO NOT GO ON TO PART B UNTIL YOU ARE TOLD TO DO SO.

SECTION I, PART B
Time—40 minutes
3 Questions

Directions: Section I, Part B of this exam consists of short-answer questions. You must respond to Questions 1 *and* 2. For your final response, you must choose to answer Question 3 *or* Question 4. In your responses, be sure to address all parts of the questions, using complete sentences.

1. Use the passage below to answer all parts of the question that follows.

   "In the northern states of America, where the means of subsistence have been more ample, the manners of the people more pure, and the checks to early marriages fewer than in any of the modern states of Europe, the population was found to double itself for some successive periods every twenty-five years. . . .

   It may safely be pronounced therefore, that population when unchecked goes on doubling itself every twenty-five years, or increases in a geometrical ratio. . . .

   Let us call the population of this island [England] eleven millions, and suppose the present produce equal to the easy support of such a number. In the first twenty-five years the population would be twenty-two millions . . ."

   Thomas Malthus, *An Essay on the Principle of Population*, 1798

   (a) Identify ONE cause of the population trends reported or predicted by Malthus.
   (b) Explain ONE cause of changes in world population trends in the period <u>1900 to the present</u>.
   (c) Explain ONE change in the relationship between humans and the environment as a result of population trends in the period from <u>1750 to the present</u>.

GO ON TO THE NEXT PAGE

2. Use the following image to answer all parts of the question that follows.

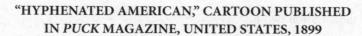

"HYPHENATED AMERICAN," CARTOON PUBLISHED IN *PUCK* MAGAZINE, UNITED STATES, 1899

In the cartoon above, Uncle Sam sees Americans with hyphenated names and asks, "Why should I let them cast whole ballots when they are only half-Americans?"

(a) Explain ONE way the cartoon illustrates a continuity in the attitudes toward immigrants between <u>1750 and 2001</u>.

(b) Identify ONE change in world migration patterns between <u>1750 and 1900</u>.

(c) Explain ONE economic change that led to new migration patterns in the period <u>1750–1900</u>.

GO ON TO THE NEXT PAGE

Choose EITHER Question 3 OR Question 4.

3. Answer all parts of the question that follows.

   (a) Explain ONE demographic change that occurred as a result of the Columbian Exchange.

   (b) Explain ONE environmental change that occurred as a result of the Columbian Exchange.

   (c) Explain ONE economic change that occurred as a result of the Columbian Exchange.

4. Answer all parts of the question that follows.

   (a) Identify ONE way Enlightenment ideas impacted the Haitian Revolution.

   (b) Explain ONE difference between the causes of the Haitian Revolution and the American Revolution.

   (c) Explain ONE similarity in how Enlightenment ideas affected governments in Haiti and the United States after independence.

GO ON TO THE NEXT PAGE

END OF SECTION I

**IF YOU FINISH BEFORE TIME IS CALLED,
YOU MAY CHECK YOUR WORK ON THIS SECTION.**

DO NOT GO ON TO SECTION II UNTIL YOU ARE TOLD TO DO SO.

SECTION II
Time—100 minutes

Question 1: Document-Based Question
Suggested reading period: 15 minutes
Suggesting writing time: 45 minutes

Directions: Question 1 is based on the accompanying documents. The documents have been edited for the purpose of this exercise.

In your response, you should do the following:

- Make a thesis or claim that responds to the prompt. The thesis or claim must be historically defensible and establish a line of reasoning.

- Provide context relevant to the prompt by describing a broader historical development or process.

- Use at least six of the provided documents to support an argument in response to the prompt.

- Use a historical example not found in the documents as evidence relevant to an argument about the prompt.

- Explain how the context or situation of at least three documents is relevant to an argument. This could address the relevance of the document's point of view, purpose, historical situation, and/or audience.

- Demonstrate a complex understanding of an argument that responds to the prompt by using evidence to corroborate, qualify, or modify the argument.

GO ON TO THE NEXT PAGE

1. Evaluate the differences in responses to the negative effects of industrialization on European workers in the period 1750–1900.

Document 1

Source: Thomas Malthus, English economist, *An Essay on the Principle of Population*, second edition, 1803.

The principal and most permanent cause of poverty has little or no relation to forms of government, or the unequal division of property; and as the rich do not in reality possess the power of finding employment and maintenance for [all] the poor, the poor cannot, in the nature of things, possess the right to demand them; [these] are important truths flowing from the principle of population. . . . And it is evident that every man in the lower classes of society, who became acquainted with these truths, would be disposed to bear the distresses in which he might be involved with more patience.

Document 2

Source: Karl Marx and Friedrich Engels, *The Communist Manifesto*, 1848.

. . . The Communists everywhere support every revolutionary movement against the existing social and political order of things.

In all these movements, they bring to the front, as the leading question in each, the property question, no matter what its degree of development at the time. . . .

The Communists disdain to conceal their views and aims. They openly declare that their ends can be attained only by the forcible overthrow of all existing social conditions. Let the ruling classes tremble at a Communistic revolution. The proletarians have nothing to lose but their chains. They have a world to win.

Working Men of All Countries, Unite!

GO ON TO THE NEXT PAGE

Document 3

Source: David Ricardo, English economist, *Principles of Political Economy and Taxation*, 1817.

Like all other contracts, wages should be left to the fair and free competition of the market, and should never be controlled by the interference of the legislature. The clear and direct tendency of the Poor Laws* is in direct opposition to these obvious principles: . . . instead of making the poor rich, they are calculated to make the rich poor. . . . The comforts and well-being of the poor cannot be permanently secured without some regard on their part, or some effort on the part of the legislature, to regulate the increase of their numbers.

*British laws that provided a government subsidy to workers who received less than a certain amount of wages

Document 4

Source: G. A. Henty, *Through the Fray: A Tale of the Luddite Riots*, 1880.

"'I don't suppose they would,' the nurse said, 'but there is never no saying. Poor fellows! . . . What with the machines, and the low price of labor, and the high price of bread, they are having a terrible time of it. And no wonder that we hear of frame breaking in Nottingham, and Lancashire, and other places. How men can be wicked enough to make machines, to take the bread out of poor men's mouths, beats me altogether.'

'Father says the machinery will do good in the long run, Abijah—that it will largely increase trade, and so give employment to a great many more people than at present. But it certainly is hard on those who have learned to work in one way to see their living taken away from them.' . . .

The weavers were affected even more than the croppers, for strength and skill were not so needed to tend the power looms as to work the hand looms. Women and boys could do the work previously performed by men, and the tendency of wages was everywhere to fall.

For years a deep spirit of discontent had been seething among the operatives in the cotton and woolen manufactures, and there had been riots more or less serious in Derbyshire, Nottingham, Lancashire and Yorkshire, which in those days were the headquarters of these trades. Factories had been burned, employers threatened and attacked, and the obnoxious machines smashed."

GO ON TO THE NEXT PAGE

Document 5

Source: British Factory Act of 1833.

. . . no person under eighteen years of age shall [work] between half-past eight in the evening and half-past five in the morning, in any cotton, woolen, worsted, hemp, flax, tow, linen or silk mill. . . .

. . . no person under the age of eighteen shall be employed in any such mill . . . more than twelve hours in . . . one day, nor more than sixty-nine hours in . . . one week. . . .

It shall be lawful for His Majesty to appoint four Inspectors of factories where . . . children and young persons under eighteen years of age [are] employed, empowered to enter any . . . mill, and any school . . . belonging thereto, at all times . . . by day or by night, when such . . . factories are at work.

The Inspectors shall have power to make such rules as may be necessary for the execution of this act, binding on all persons subject to the provisions of this act; and are authorised to enforce the attendance at school of children employed in factories according to the provisions of this act.

Every child restricted to the performance of forty-eight hours of labour in any one week shall attend some school.

Document 6

Source: Label from The American Federation of Labor (AFL), a group of labor unions, circa 1900. *Labor omnia vincit* is a Latin phrase meaning "work conquers all" and was used as a slogan for the labor movement.

GO ON TO THE NEXT PAGE

Document 7

Source: Robert Owen, utopian socialist, *Observations on the Effect of the Manufacturing System: With Hints for the Improvement of Those Parts of It Which Are Most Injurious to Health and Morals*, 1817.

It is thence evident that human nature can be improved and formed into the character which it is for the interest and happiness of all it should possess, solely by directing the attention of mankind to the adoption of legislative measures judiciously calculated to give the best habits, and most just and useful sentiments to the rising generation—and in an especial manner to those who are placed in situations, which, without such measures, render them liable to be taught the worst habits, and the most useless and injurious sentiments.

GO ON TO THE NEXT PAGE

END OF DOCUMENTS FOR QUESTION 1

Question 2, Question 3, or Question 4: Long Essay Question
Suggested writing time: 40 minutes

Directions: Choose Question 2, Question 3, OR Question 4 to answer.

In your response, you should do the following:

- Make a thesis or claim that responds to the prompt. The thesis or claim must be historically defensible and establish a line of reasoning.
- Provide context relevant to the prompt by describing a broader historical development or process.
- Use specific and relevant examples as evidence to support an argument in response to the prompt.
- Use a historical reasoning skill (causation, comparison, or continuity and change) to develop an argument in response to the prompt.
- Demonstrate a complex understanding of an argument that responds to the prompt by using evidence to corroborate, qualify, or modify the argument.

2. In the period 1200–1750, along with alterations in social structures and in methods of production, there were also some important changes in labor management.

   Develop an argument that evaluates the changes in labor systems in the period 1200–1750.

3. In the period 1450–1750, existing regional patterns of trade intensified in the context of the new global circulation of goods.

   Develop an argument that evaluates how one or more trade networks changed as a result of the new global circulation of goods in this time period.

4. In the period 1750–1900, industrializing powers established transoceanic empires.

   Develop an argument explaining the factors that contributed to the rise of transoceanic empires by industrializing powers in the period 1750–1900.

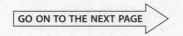 GO ON TO THE NEXT PAGE

END OF SECTION II

STOP

END OF EXAM

ANSWER KEY

Section I, Part A

1. C	15. A	29. B	43. A
2. B	16. C	30. D	44. B
3. A	17. B	31. A	45. C
4. A	18. A	32. D	46. B
5. C	19. C	33. D	47. D
6. D	20. D	34. A	48. A
7. B	21. B	35. D	49. C
8. D	22. C	36. B	50. B
9. C	23. A	37. C	51. D
10. A	24. B	38. A	52. B
11. D	25. B	39. A	53. D
12. B	26. C	40. C	54. A
13. C	27. A	41. A	55. C
14. C	28. A	42. C	

Section I, Part B and Section II

See Answers and Explanations, and self-score free-response questions.

Section I, Part A Number Correct: _____

Section I, Part B Points Earned: _____

Section II Points Earned: _____

Sign into your online account at kaptest.com and enter your results in the scoring section to see your 1–5 score.

Haven't registered your book yet? Go to kaptest.com/moreonline to begin.

ANSWERS AND EXPLANATIONS

Section I, Part A

1. C

The Pax Mongolica is what enabled Qiu Chuji to travel westward to meet with Genghis Khan. Prior to the rise of the Mongol Empire, trade and travel across Eurasia was difficult due to multiple border crossings and banditry. However, the Mongols enforced strict control over the areas they conquered, enabling increased traffic along routes like the Silk Road. Thus, **(C)** is correct. (A) is incorrect because the Southern Song Dynasty was not conquered until the 1270s, after the Mongol Empire had fragmented. The faction that formed the Yuan Dynasty adopted the trappings of Chinese civilization, while other factions such as the Ilkhanate did not. (B) is incorrect because it explains why Qiu Chuji was invited to speak with Genghis Khan, to discuss the secret of immortality, but not how the audience was able to take place at all. (D) is incorrect because there is nothing in the passage to indicate that any disease is rampant; furthermore, the Black Death did not spread until the fourteenth century, while this passage is dated as 1228.

2. B

The passage describes the Hui people of northwestern China as practicing neither Buddhism nor Daoism, suggesting they practice some other religion. Recall that one of the five duties of Islam is to pray five times a day facing Mecca. From the perspective of someone in China, Mecca, located in present-day Saudi Arabia, would be to the west. Thus, **(B)** is correct because the author is alluding to the Hui people being Muslims when he says that they "only worship the west." (A) is incorrect because it does not address the religious aspect of the quotation, which is clear from the author previously stating that the Hui were neither Buddhists nor Daoists. (C) is incorrect because it only explains why the Hui were allowed to continue following their religion, not what that religion was nor what "only worship the west" meant. While tempting because China is diverse, (D) is incorrect because the passage suggests that only land to the east of the narrator's location historically belonged to China, while the land to the west, where the Hui were, did not.

3. A

The passage concerns a Daoist master, Qiu Chuji, accepting the invitation of Ghengis Khan. Their interactions are an example of the Mongol Empire utilizing the talents of conquered peoples; in this case, Ghengis Khan's efforts were initially focused on discovering the secret of immortality, and later he sought to dine with Qiu Chuji to speak with the Daoist master further. Thus, **(A)** is correct. (B) is incorrect because the Mongols were anything but compassionate to many of their subjects, gaining a reputation for wholesale slaughter. (C) is incorrect because, even though Genghis Khan awards the master an ironic title after his honest response, there is no indication that the master is being appointed to a position of high rank that is warranted based on merit. While the Mongols were skilled at diplomacy, as demonstrated in part by the way Ghengis Khan easily accepted Qiu Chuji giving him an undesired answer to his question about the secret to immortality, the excerpt does not mention Ghengis Khan playing his enemies off one another. Qiu Chuji is merely an expert he is consulting. (D) is incorrect.

4. A

In Source 1, Steel describes how the Empire of Delhi had a minaret constructed out of the remnants of Hindu temples. In Source 2, Boulger describes how Kublai Khan, leader of the Mongol Empire and founder of the Yuan Dynasty, showed tolerance for existing beliefs among his conquered subjects. No particular religion was discouraged under Kublai Khan. Thus, **(A)** is correct and (D) is incorrect. The Empire of Delhi is shown to disregard existing beliefs among its conquered subjects and impose its own religion. (C) and (D) are incorrect.

5. C

As the Turks conquered Asia Minor, which is modern-day Turkey, they imposed their language on the region, making **(C)** correct. Eliminate (A) because, although there were religious tensions between Hindus and Muslims, a civil war did not break out in this period. (B) is incorrect because the Chinese retained their belief systems even under Mongol rule; in fact, the Mongols often adopted the religions of the groups they conquered. Eliminate (D), too, because the Mongols who attacked China did not spread Islam.

6. D

The first source describes an empire founded by a nomadic Turkic group. Following the collapse of the Seljuk Dynasty, a new Turkic body arose at the turn of the fourteenth century, when a tribal leader named Osman founded the Ottoman Empire. Thus, **(D)** is correct. While an Islamic empire, (A) is incorrect because Mali was not based on nomads conquering a settled society. (B) is incorrect because the Russian Empire arose as a result of Muscovite princes resisting Mongol conquest. In the context of Source 1, this would be akin to an Indian empire arising after resisting Turkic conquest. (C) is incorrect because the Yuan Dynasty practiced religious toleration, unlike what was described in Source 1.

7. B

Nomadic expansion, especially that of the Mongols, increased trade connections. This occurred because the nomads controlled the entire length of the Silk Road, making it safer to travel; **(B)** is correct. (A) is incorrect because farmers rarely became herders or pastoralists; they lived in areas ideal for agriculture and were used to a sedentary way of life. (C) is incorrect because, while the Yuan Dynasty was short-lived, the Delhi Sultanate lasted some 300 years. (D) is incorrect because the Delhi Sultanate did not practice religious toleration; Hindu and Buddhist temples were often targeted for destruction.

8. D

In this era, rulers attempted to centralize power by limiting the power of existing elites. These elites were typically large, landowning families (in this case, the *daimyo*). By implementing these regulations, the ruler was eliminating threats to his power. **(D)** is correct. (A) is incorrect because landowning classes often worked in cooperation with central rulers. In most cases, they were still responsible for carrying out regulations. They also benefited from expansion of the empire, so they would likely not resist expansion efforts. (B) is incorrect because, although this is true of the time period, the document was addressing the upper-class *daimyo* and samurai warriors, rather than the peasantry. (C) is incorrect because, in spite of widening global economic opportunities during this time period that raised many merchants to positions in a new economic elite, Japanese merchants did not benefit due to restrictions on trade.

9. C

These regulations served to limit the power of the *daimyo*, who ruled locally. To that end, these regulations prevented the *daimyo* from forming alliances and displaying their wealth, thus ensuring stability throughout Japan and limiting the possibility of rebellion. **(C)** is correct. (A) is incorrect because an imperial examination system would be merit-based to select members of the bureaucracy. In contrast, this system used existing large landowners as local governors. (B) is incorrect because the economy flourished in the Tokugawa period. The shogun encouraged frugality to limit threats to his power. (D) is incorrect because the *daimyo* were already under the control of the shogun. If they were not, these edicts would be meaningless and would not do anything to help the shogun gain the loyalty of the *daimyo*.

10. A

The Tokugawa shoguns feared rebellion due to the prior period of civil war, in which several leaders claimed to be shogun. During that prior period, wars occurred and the *daimyo* changed their allegiances. The Tokugawa shoguns implemented these regulations to limit threats to their power. **(A)** is correct. (B) is incorrect because, although European merchants began to arrive in Japan in the sixteenth century, the edicts did not discuss regulations regarding trade or interactions with foreigners. (C) is incorrect because Western merchants arrived to engage in trade in this period. However, trade agreements were not forced on Japan by the West until after Matthew Perry's voyage in the mid-nineteenth century. (D) is incorrect because, even though Neo-Confucian values were embraced by the Tokugawa shoguns, the shoguns did not have a tributary relationship with China.

11. D

Tokugawa Ieyasu established the Tokugawa shogunate in 1600, after a period of civil war that began in 1467. Ieyasu hoped to stabilize the country and end the unrest by increasing his control over the *daimyo*. The unification of Japan under the Tokugawa family began a period of peace and prosperity that lasted over 250 years. **(D)** is correct. (A) is incorrect because the emperor remained a figurehead in the Tokugawa era and was not a threat to the shogun's power. In fact, emperors were typically ceremonial rulers prior to the Meiji period that began in the mid-nineteenth century. (B) is incorrect because the Tokugawa implemented a series of regulations that are often called the "closed country edicts." They strictly regulated trade with Westerners and banned Christianity. (C) is incorrect because the shogun was not overthrown until the Meiji Restoration in the mid-nineteenth century.

12. B

Western encroachment in the nineteenth century forced Japan to open up trade with Europe and the United States. This led to rebellions against the Tokugawa shoguns and the restoration of the emperor to power, known as the Meiji Restoration. **(B)** is correct. (A) is incorrect because, even though the Western powers influenced Japan's economy, they did not conquer or colonize Japan. Japan did not have any conflicts with China at this time, making (C) incorrect. (D) is incorrect because, despite these regulations, there was strong economic growth within Japan due to the period of peace fostered by the Tokugawa shogunate.

13. C

Indigenous tribes and empires, such as the Mexica and Inca, were conquered by Europeans who used new ships and navigational tools to reach their land. These tribes and empires lacked gunpowder weapons that were used by Europeans to subdue them. **(C)** is therefore correct. (A) is incorrect because, although indigenous populations eventually declined by approximately 90 percent, they were not completely destroyed. Colonization occurred shortly after initial contact due to superior weapons technology. Even though in some cases indigenous peoples provided assistance to the Spanish, such as enemies of the Mexica, most resisted subjugation, so (B) is correct. (D) is incorrect because the Mexica and Inca empires collapsed as a result of conquest by Europeans, not before European arrival.

14. C

Mercantilist economic policies were embraced by European monarchs in order to increase revenues. One goal of mercantilism was to have a favorable balance of trade in which the kingdom exported more than it imported. Another goal was for the kingdom to have a monopoly on trade with its colonies. This allowed a kingdom to pay relatively low prices to the colonies for raw materials and to charge high prices for selling finished goods to the colonies. **(C)** is correct. (A) is incorrect because joint-stock companies were mainly used in the Indian Ocean basin network to engage in trade. In contrast, the governments of the European mother countries controlled trade in the Americas. The colonies were the source of cash crops, such as cotton, sugar, tobacco, coffee, and indigo, and of raw materials, such as furs, whale oil, and lumber, making (B) incorrect. (D) is incorrect because Atlantic trade developed and increased in this era. Indian Ocean trade was thriving and intensifying as well due to a European presence and the use of silver from the Americas.

15. A

As the Spanish conquered indigenous peoples and colonized much of Latin America, they developed a hierarchy of racial classifications often referred to as the *casta* system. In this system, those of European descent had higher status than mixed-race groups (e.g., *mestizos*) and those without European ancestry. Thus, **(A)** is correct. (B) is incorrect because colonists paid taxes to the British government in North America. This later led to a revolution against British imperial rule. European governments used a variety of administrative techniques to manage their overseas colonies. In addition, European control was not overthrown until revolutions occurred in the late eighteenth and early nineteenth centuries, making (C) incorrect. (D) is incorrect because tensions among European maritime powers increased due to competition over claiming land. These powers also competed to dominate global maritime trade.

16. C

The building of monumental architecture like that shown was financed using money generated from taxing trade and mercantilist policies. Note that mercantilism is the belief that a nation's power was based on its material wealth, particularly in gold and silver. Therefore, **(C)** is correct. (A) is incorrect because, although militaries were used to centralize power, the Taj Mahal does not reflect that. Empires at this time were expanding due to the use of gunpowder weapons, as opposed to contracting or losing territory; (B) is incorrect. (D) is incorrect because the Taj Mahal was from an Asian empire.

17. B

Throughout history, empires have sponsored the construction of buildings to display their power and wealth. The Taj Mahal is an excellent example of such prominent construction. **(B)** is correct. The Taj Mahal was a tomb, not a defense fortification, making (A) incorrect. (C) is incorrect because architecture throughout the world has not used Greco-Roman features, such as domes, columns, and arches, so it has not been universally adopted. (D) is incorrect because, although the Taj Mahal was a tomb, it was not built as a religious building or place of worship.

18. A

European involvement in Asian trade was due to maritime *reconnaissance*, which is another term for *exploration*. The initial goal of European powers in exploring the Indian Ocean was not to conquer, but to control trade. By the mid-1500s, Portugal had 50 trading posts from West Africa to East Asia. The English and Dutch later became the dominant seafaring powers with faster, cheaper, and more powerful ships. Their imperial expansion was aided by the use of joint-stock companies, in which investors, rather than royal governments, funded expeditions. **(A)** is correct. (B) is incorrect because British imperialism in India occurred much later, in the nineteenth century. Although Europeans did conquer North America, silver was mined in Latin America (mainly in Mexico and Peru), making (C) incorrect. (D) is incorrect because, while trading posts were established in West Africa, their purpose was mainly to acquire slaves to bring to the Americas rather than to acquire goods to trade with Asia.

19. C

Silver, the most abundant American precious metal, was responsible for stimulating the global trade network. Spain, for example, used silver to trade for silk and porcelain in Asia. China used the precious metal as a primary medium of exchange and to finance a powerful military and bureaucracy. Europeans had a large role in the global circulation of silver because they brought it from its source (Latin America) to China. **(C)** is correct. (A) and (D) are incorrect because these choices represent Europeans using silver themselves rather than serving as "middlemen" in trade. Although (B) is a true statement, it does not discuss the role of silver.

20. D

Due to the silver trade, Europeans set up trading posts in the Indian Ocean basin in order to get the goods they desired. As a result, Europeans became intermediaries in global trade. **(D)** is correct. (A) is incorrect because the Ming and Qing Dynasties ruled in this period. The imperial government remained strong until the nineteenth century. The conquest of American Indians happened in the decades after Columbus's arrival, and silver was mined once colonial rule was established, making (B) incorrect. (C) is incorrect because goods from Europe were not highly valued by those in Asia because Europeans had very few products that Asian civilizations were not already producing.

21. B

Missionaries, such as the Jesuits, traveled to Asia to spread Christianity in this period. In Japan, for example, Christianity made some important inroads by 1580, with 150,000 Japanese Christian converts, but the government ended these missions and outlawed the religion. Jesuit missionaries such as Matteo Ricci arrived in China, introducing European science and technology. The Jesuit goal of converting the Chinese population to Christianity proved to be unsuccessful, but the missionaries were able to bring back Chinese knowledge to Europe. **(B)** is correct. (A) is incorrect because, although some Asians may have adopted some Western cultural aspects, it was not typical. Additionally, one group rarely ever completely adopted all the elements of another group. Zheng He's voyages took place before Europeans arrived in Asia (early in the fifteenth century), making (C) incorrect. (D) is incorrect because Africa was not conquered in this period. The slave trade was due to the demand for labor on plantations in the Americas.

22. C

Improved ship designs led to the discovery and conquest of the Americas. This caused trade to be truly global and led to mercantilist policies. Mercantilism is an economic theory that describes the ways in which nation-states enrich themselves by limiting imports and encouraging exports. **(C)** is correct. (A) is incorrect because the first trade links between Europe and Asia were via the Silk Road. (B) is incorrect because, although the caravel led to the establishment of new trade networks, existing ones remained and intensified. (D) is incorrect because, while Chinese navigational technology diffused to Europe indirectly through the Crusades, the caravel was a European design.

23. A

The compass was invented in China but was adopted by merchants in the Indian Ocean basin in the previous time period and spread to Europeans as a result of the contact with Arabs during the Crusades. **(A)** is correct. (B) is incorrect because the technology spread rather than blended with existing technologies. Although the intensification of existing trade networks did occur in this period, it was not due to the compass but, rather, the arrival of Europeans; (C) is incorrect. (D) is incorrect because the technology spread from China, not from the Americas due to Columbus's voyages.

24. B

Major technological developments such as the compass and improved shipbuilding technology shaped the development of the world by facilitating exploration and cross-cultural contact. This in turn led to the development of trade routes, especially through the Indian Ocean region, and the growth of trading cities. **(B)** is correct. (A) is incorrect because these technologies were not new. Although technologies diffused from other regions, some were adapted by the Europeans, making (C) incorrect. (D) is incorrect because the Americas did not have any of these inventions prior to the arrival of Europeans.

25. B

In 1857, the Indian troops mutinied after they received rifles with cartridges rumored to be greased in animal fat; consuming beef and pork fat violates Hindu and Muslim customs, respectively. The troops killed British officers, escalating the conflict into a large-scale rebellion, which is referred to as the Indian Rebellion of 1857. At least 800,000 Indians would die. British racial ideologies led to the treatment of native peoples as inferior while viewing their cultural traditions as barbaric, which caused the Indian soldiers to be angry. **(B)** is correct. (A) is incorrect because agricultural production was not limited by the British since they relied on cheap cash crops from India, such as cotton. (C) is incorrect because, while Christian missionaries attempted conversions, Indians were not forced to convert and most retained their Hindu or Muslim beliefs. (D) is incorrect because the British did not incorporate Enlightenment ideas, such as representative government and legal equality, into the colonial government.

26. C

Elite Indians who had been educated in British universities were inspired by Enlightenment values and began to criticize the British colonial regime. They called for political and social reform. This passage describes how Indian princes were afraid of losing power due to British interference, so they joined the rebellion to preserve their power. **(C)** is correct, and (A) is therefore incorrect. (B) is incorrect because positions were not stable, as shown by the description of English actions. The passage focuses on rebellion and political aspects, rather than economic conditions, so (D) is incorrect.

27. A

England's involvement in India began strictly as a business venture. Founded in 1600, the British East India Company enjoyed a monopoly on English trade with India and increasingly took advantage of the Mughal Empire's growing weakness. Expanding its trading posts, the company petitioned the British government to outright conquer areas important to its trade in order to protect its interests. It enforced its rule with a combination of British troops and Indian troops. In 1857–1858, the British government had crushed the Indian rebellion referenced in the passage. It went on to impose direct imperial rule on India (the "British Raj") with a viceroy representing British authority. **(A)** is correct. (B) is incorrect because exploration (maritime reconnaissance) took place in the previous era. India was not a settler colony, like Australia or South Africa. Settler colonies were often in temperate climates and there were large-scale migrations of Europeans that settled in these areas permanently. Thus, (C) is incorrect. (D) is incorrect because imperialism was beyond economic—there was political control too.

28. A

India fought loyally as part of the British Empire in World War I, in the hopes of gaining more independence after the war. When the fighting ended, Britain introduced some minor reforms and liberalization but maintained complete control. This led to a surge in Indian nationalism under the leadership of the Congress Party as well as the charismatic Mohandas Gandhi, who demanded full independence. **(A)** is correct. Fearing losing one of their most lucrative colonies in response to nationalist movements, the British sought to maintain complete control.

(B) is therefore incorrect. (C) is incorrect because British and Indian leaders were in opposition to one another. The British wanted to maintain control of India, while the Indians wanted independence. The Indian colonists continued to resist until they were successful in achieving independence shortly after World War II, so (D) is incorrect.

29. B

Toussaint L'Ouverture fought in the Haitian Revolution in the French colony of Saint-Domingue and helped end the practice of slavery there, which accords with the author's views as an abolitionist; **(B)** is correct. (A) is incorrect because the tsar was conservative, and coerced labor continued in Russia until the emancipation of the serfs in 1861. Therefore, it would not explain why the author glorifies L'Ouverture. (C) is incorrect because, while L'Ouverture fought the French in the Haitian Revolution, that explanation does not jibe with the final sentence of the passage. (D) is incorrect because the fact that he is British would not necessarily demonstrate why he would support a former slave who rebelled against the French. His position as an abolitionist is more important in understanding that support.

30. D

As Enlightenment ideas of human equality and liberty spread throughout the eighteenth and nineteenth centuries, abolition became an important political cause in several Western countries; **(D)** is correct. The Haitian Revolution was interpreted through preexisting ideology; those who opposed colonialism supported it, those who supported colonialism opposed it. The revolution alone would be unlikely as a cause for the author's pro-abolition stance; (A) is incorrect. The creation of the United States did not result in the emancipation of slaves; this was the cause of the American Civil War from 1861–1865. (B) is incorrect. While the Napoleonic wars were certainly violent, slavery was not a central issue in them; (C) is incorrect.

31. A

The Haitian Revolution was inspired by the American Revolution and took place during the French Revolution. Saint-Domingue was a lucrative French colony based on a system of plantation labor, and those slave laborers were at the forefront of the uprising against French rule; **(A)** is correct. While Enlightenment ideas influenced all three revolutions, they were not as relevant as the revolutions themselves; (B) is incorrect. The Industrial

Revolution changed production and working conditions on the European continent, but the colonies were not industrialized themselves; (C) is incorrect. The Russian Revolution happened in 1918; thus, (D) is anachronistic and incorrect.

32. D

The passage claims that advances in transportation and mechanical production allowed for more intensive agricultural cultivation; **(D)** is correct. The workers listed in the passage (with the exception of engineers) are unskilled laborers like miners and construction workers; (A) is incorrect. The supply of fossil fuels was seemingly unlimited, and it was the steady demand for those fuels that spurred developments in transportation; (B) is incorrect. The argument of (C) is not directly addressed by the passage, but inequality between laborers and owners increased during the Industrial Revolution period. There were waves of emigration from Europe to the United States, suggesting that things were not perfect for the whole society. (C) is incorrect.

33. D

Often, workers in the industrial era did not see the benefits that accrued to the owners of factories, child labor was widespread, wages were low, and conditions were generally poor. Thus, it is likely that industrial workers would not have as positive an opinion about the advent of machine labor; **(D)** is correct. Capitalists typically owned the factories or made money trading their products, and they would likely agree with the author of the passage; (A) is incorrect. Governments during this period were practicing a laissez-faire type of capitalist oversight and would likely agree with the author of the passage. Later in the nineteenth century, reform movements arose that were concerned with the living and working conditions of the lower classes, but that had not yet occurred when the passage was written; (B) is incorrect. Landholding elites often benefited by industrial production, either by direct investment or increased utilization and value of their land; (C) is incorrect.

34. A

European participation in global trade in the early modern period provided profits that were used to invest in factories and other ventures. In addition, changes in government caused by Enlightenment ideas led to laws protecting private property. **(A)** is correct. (B) is incorrect because the colonization of Africa occurred as an effect of industrial production due to the increased demand for raw materials, not the other way around. Europe's population was increasing due to the introduction of American food crops and new agricultural methods; (C) is incorrect. (D) is incorrect because agricultural surpluses were necessary before industrialization in order to feed urban factory workers.

35. D

The reforms were an attempt to modernize China in response to Western economic imperialism that occurred following the Opium Wars, particularly the creation of European spheres of influence in Asia; **(D)** is correct. (A) is incorrect; China was not colonized and the Qing Dynasty retained control of the government. While Enlightenment ideals can be seen in points 1, 3, and 16, the bulk of the edicts are clearly economic in nature; (B) is incorrect. As noted above, the Qing Dynasty retained control of the government during this time period; (C) is incorrect.

36. B

In Japan during the Meiji Restoration, the government actively sought to modernize the country and promote reforms that would improve technology and the economy, which is what China was attempting to do; **(B)** is correct. (A) is incorrect because the Russian Revolution was a movement that sought to overthrow the existing political and social order and found a new government, not reform what was there. (C) is incorrect because the Mexican Revolution was focused on land reform and other social changes rather than on technological and economic reforms. The Second Industrial Revolution was a private set of changes, not something guided and driven by government policy; (D) is incorrect.

37. C

The weak government and failure to modernize led to the overthrow of the Qing Dynasty and eventually to a civil war between Chinese communists and nationalists, which then led to the Chinese Communist Revolution. **(C)** is correct. While China is an industrial power now, that happened in the late twentieth century, and it is not a democracy; (A) is incorrect. The Qing Dynasty fell but was replaced by a short-lived republican form of government; (B) is incorrect. China was never controlled by a foreign power other than the brief occupation by Japan in the Second World War; (D) is incorrect.

38. A

The "White Man's Burden" is popularly understood to mean that Europeans had a mission to bring "civilization" to their colonial possessions, particularly in the areas of hygiene, social organization, religion, and technology. This is the particular ideology behind the Spanish missions in the New World, which were designed to convert the indigenous population to the Catholicism of the Spanish crown. **(A)** is correct. While Protestants and Catholics experienced severe conflict, it was not based on a desire to civilize either group, but rather on sectarian religious disagreement between otherwise similarly situated groups of people; (B) is incorrect. Similarly, the proxy wars during the Cold War were justified as halting the expansionist aggression of the communist (or capitalist, from the Soviet viewpoint) powers, but neither group considered themselves to have a civilizing mission. They were concerned with their own geopolitical conflict, not the well-being or status of their proxies. (C) is incorrect. Genocides do not target groups for conversion or reeducation, but annihilation, which was the purpose of the Holocaust. The poem evinces a paternalistic attitude toward non-Western peoples, but not a genocidal one. (D) is incorrect.

39. A

Particularly in the first stanza, there is infantilizing language used to describe colonized peoples, and the phrase "half devil" especially reflects scientific racism. **(A)** is correct. Fascist governments did not arise until the 1920s and 30s, and were mainly a reaction to global economic instability, not colonialism; (B) is incorrect. The revolutions of the nineteenth century in Latin America affected Spanish and Portuguese colonies, and while they dealt with issues of racism and colonialism, this is less specific than the racial ideologies mentioned in **(A)**; (C) is incorrect. Enlightenment ideas were used by opponents of colonization to justify their independence movements, but they are not reflected in the poem; (D) is incorrect.

40. C

Gandhi famously followed the concept of ahimsa, or nonviolence, in his struggle against British rule in India. This inspired other civil rights leaders of the twentieth century, like Dr. Martin Luther King, Jr., in the United States and Nelson Mandela in South Africa. **(C)** is correct. Gandhi was not a Hindu nationalist, and he wanted to create a unified Indian state. (A) and (D) are incorrect. However, examples of both of these things would appear in Indian politics in later decades. After experiences in South Africa, Gandhi did not believe in working for reform within the British system, but rather pushed for total independence; (B) is incorrect.

41. A

When doing a comparative historical analysis, it is best to compare like items, so the analysis can focus on the meaning, not differences in style or structure. All of the items listed would be of interest to a historian of the era, but **(A)** provides a directly contrasting viewpoint in a similarly fictional and allegorical mode; thus, **(A)** is correct. A white paper from a European group would give more of the European understanding of the issue but would not illuminate the other side of the poem; (B) is incorrect. The poem deals with cultural and social factors, and while economic records might provide some limited information about those subjects, they would not be as useful in a cultural analysis as contemporaneous fiction; (C) is incorrect. Similarly the newspaper accounts would be interesting for context, but not comparison; (D) is incorrect.

42. C

As transit options like steamships and railways became larger and faster, more migrants were able to take advantage of the lower costs and undertake voyages to other countries like the United States; **(C)** is correct. A historian would be able to look at the chart and connect the rise in Italian emigration to the expansion of the U.S. economy, the rise of the steamship era, and the acceleration of a globally connected economic system that would eventually result in the Great Depression of the 1930s. Because the table only gives us absolute numbers of emigrants and not relative numbers, there is no way to know from the data presented what portion of the population emigrated, large or small. The reasons for emigration cannot be inferred from the number of migrants alone; (A) is incorrect. As above, all we can see in the chart are raw totals, and we do not know the countries to which the Italian migrants went in Europe. Without further data, this conclusion cannot be supported; (B) is incorrect. The premise that the workers were high-skilled cannot be supported by the data in the table, as it does not address the nature, but rather the numbers, of the immigrant experience. (D) is incorrect.

43. A

Italian migrants came to the Americas looking for jobs as the region industrialized; Italy was economically behind Northern and Western Europe. **(A)** is correct. While there were decades of peace after the Franco-Prussian War in the 1870s, typically peacetime is not a driver of migration, so this explanation is not the best. (B) is incorrect. Governments in the destination countries accepted immigrants with varying degrees of welcome, but none of them sponsored immigrants or immigrant voyages; (C) is incorrect. Governments in the less frequented regions like Asia and Oceania did not restrict Italian immigration, but they did not have as many available jobs as the Americas or Europe; (D) is incorrect.

44. B

Often, immigrants were viewed with suspicion by native residents in their new countries, and there were typically language barriers, as immigrants seldom spoke the native tongue. As a consequence, they often formed ethnic neighborhoods in the areas where landlords would rent to them, keeping traditional cultural forms alive in a new setting; **(B)** is correct. While many children of immigrants abandon traditional practices in favor of assimilation into the majority, this is a process that takes generations; (A) is incorrect. The majority of Italian immigrants were Roman Catholic and moved to other Christian areas where Catholic practice was accepted, so there was no need to form a syncretic religion; (C) is incorrect. Migrants typically adopt pieces of their new home culture, and Italians were no different—there was no wholesale rejection of new cultural forms in their diaspora; (D) is incorrect.

45. C

NATO and the Warsaw Pact were alliances during the Cold War that developed due to tensions between the United States (and its capitalist allies) and the Soviet Union (and its communist allies). Non-Aligned Movement members wished to remain neutral in the conflict between the United States and the Soviet Union. **(C)** is correct. (A) is incorrect as the world economy had recovered from the Great Depression by the mid-1950s, due to extensive war spending in World War II, and there was no economic crisis. While decolonization was happening during the period, it did not lead to the alliance system. The Non-Aligned Movement was mostly comprised of newly independent states attempting to avoid being slotted into the preexisting NATO/Warsaw Pact framework; (B) is incorrect. While genocidal practices had been present in the Nazi state during World War II, they did not lead to the creation of the postwar alliance system; (D) is incorrect.

46. B

The Non-Aligned Movement was meant to reject the polarization of the world into communist and capitalist spheres. During the Cold War, NATO and the Warsaw Pact attempted to bring newly independent states into their orbit, and leaders feared this would lessen their ability to create their own path in the postcolonial world; **(B)** is correct. (A) is incorrect; the Non-Aligned Movement was not a military alliance, but more of a cooperative of nations, similar to the United Nations. (C) is incorrect because these nations were already independent. If they had been colonies, they would have been subject to control of their mother country. (D) is incorrect; while the Non-Aligned Movement touched economic concerns due to the nature of the Cold War, that was not its reason for being.

47. D

There never was a direct outbreak of war between the United States and the Soviet Union, but there was indirect fighting in proxy wars, particularly in Southeast Asia in countries like Korea and Vietnam. **(D)** is correct. The Soviet Union provided weapons and intelligence for the communist groups while the United States provided aid to those fighting communism. (A) is incorrect because environmental organizations tend to be nongovernmental organizations, such as Greenpeace, and did not arise out of military alliances. As mentioned, war between the United States and the Soviet Union did not occur; (B) is incorrect. While one could argue that trade agreements like the North American Free Trade Agreement stem from the jockeying for position in the Cold War, they are not a direct result; (C) is incorrect.

48. A

The space race developed directly out of conflict between the Soviet Union and the United States, beginning with the launch of the first Sputnik satellite in 1957 and culminating in the United States landing on the moon in 1969. **(A)** is correct. While they were an important part of the Cold War conflict, atomic weapons were first developed during the Second World War; (B) is incorrect. The Green Revolution happened in the 1960s and 70s and is not

directly tied to the Cold War; (C) is incorrect. Democratization in Eastern Europe occurred after the fall of the Soviet Union, not during the height of its power, as represented on the map. (D) is incorrect.

49. C

As the United States and Western Europe moved toward knowledge-based jobs and service industries, manufacturing shifted away from the West toward Asia and the Pacific Rim, resulting in rapid economic growth there. **(C)** is correct. (A) is incorrect because China began rapid industrialization in the 1970s and Japan continued to manufacture items such as computers and cars. The United States still has very high levels of consumption and strong demand for imported goods; (B) is incorrect. Europe is fully integrated into the global economy, and no area of the modern world is "self-sufficient"; (D) is incorrect.

50. B

Economic institutions, such as the World Bank and International Monetary Fund, as well as regional agreements, such as the European Union, have facilitated economic growth and stimulated demand, as well as allowed states to modernize their industrial capacity; **(B)** is correct. (A) is incorrect because, while international organizations such as the United Nations lay a foundation for economic growth, they do not directly or necessarily lead to it. (C) is incorrect because countries that grow their economies often violate human rights by providing few protections for workers; most protest movements against globalism, if effective, would decrease economic activity rather than increase it. (D) is incorrect because economic isolation would not result in rising per capita GDP in the modern global economy.

51. D

The rapid economic growth among Asian Tigers, caused by a fundamental shift in economic basis, mimics the growth of Europe's economy during the Industrial Revolution; **(D)** is correct. (A) is incorrect because Western Europe in the twentieth century generally did not experience rapid economic growth, due to the world wars and the Great Depression. (B) is incorrect because industrial growth has occurred slowly in sub-Saharan Africa, which remains one of the least industrialized areas in the world. (C) is incorrect because in the nineteenth century, India and China were economically dominated by Western powers seeking to extract resources.

52. B

Genetically modified crops were developed by private companies beginning in the 1970s during the Green Revolution, aimed at increasing agricultural yields; **(B)** is correct. (A) is incorrect because the end of the Cold War did not impact food production or farming methods. (C) is incorrect because the European Union reduced trade barriers and promoted economic integration, but this did not lead to the production of GM crops, and the EU has opposed some of their use. (D) is incorrect because new international organizations, such as the United Nations, did not directly impact scientific advances in agriculture.

53. D

The problems identified in the Greenpeace statement reflect a consideration beyond economics and toward broader human well-being, apart from whether or not the genetically modified seeds "work." **(D)** is correct. While the passage clearly does not support industry, it also does not mention government intervention, so we cannot infer the author's position on that issue; (A) and (B) are incorrect. While scientific advances may move us toward the goals identified in (C), the statement is focused on economic and social structures and their control on technology, not the technology itself; (C) is incorrect.

54. A

Nongovernmental organizations, like Greenpeace, developed to bring attention to environmental issues that have arisen due to globalization and population growth, **(A)** is correct. While neoliberal economic policies can be inferred from the references to "industrial agriculture," regional trade agreements are not implicated in the passage; (B) is incorrect. Greenpeace is a secular organization and its stated concerns are political and economic, not religious; (C) is incorrect. The environmental movement is a global movement, but it is not an ideology, like capitalism, communism, or fascism; (D) is incorrect.

55. C

The production of genetically modified seed crops is often done by private companies like Monsanto and Bayer, which make large profits and charge high prices for their seeds, and we can see the opposition to this in the second paragraph. **(C)** is correct. Small farms and organic farming are not implicated in the statement, other

than as an example of the failures of genetically modified crops; (A) is incorrect. Organizations dedicated to famine relief presumably support higher crop yields and are less concerned with economic issues; (B) is incorrect. Similarly, food exports have risen as a result of industrial agriculture, but this is not why Greenpeace opposes the use of GMOs, as we can see in the second paragraph. (D) is incorrect.

Section I, Part B

1. A successful short-answer response accomplishes all three tasks set forth by the prompt. Each part of the prompt is worth 1 point, for a total of 3 possible points.

(a) To earn the point, the response must identify a specific factor that led to population growth in the United States or England in the late eighteenth or early nineteenth centuries. Examples include: increases in agricultural yields due to practices such as enclosure and crop rotation; the invention of new farm tools that improved productivity such as the seed drill and steel plow; and the development of the smallpox vaccine by Edward Jenner.

(b) To earn the point, the response must identify a population trend in the period since 1900 and explain a cause of that population trend. One example is the rapid growth of overall world population due to factors including advances in agricultural production such as the Green Revolution and the use of fertilizers, and the development of new vaccines and medical treatments. Other examples of population trends include the stagnating of population growth in more developed countries in comparison with less developed countries due to factors including availability of contraceptives, and lower worldwide infant mortality rates due to availability of food and improved diets.

(c) To earn the point, the response must explain a way in which population trends led to changes in the environment. Examples of the impact of increased world populations include: the depletion of resources such as fossil fuels, clean water, and timber due to more people using limited resources; the increased release of greenhouse gases due to increased industrial production resulting from greater demand for consumer goods; and agriculture causing the degradation of land and ecosystems, as in the processes of soil erosion, mineral depletion, and fertilizer runoff.

2. A successful short-answer response accomplishes all three tasks set forth by the prompt. Each part of the prompt is worth 1 point, for a total of 3 possible points.

(a) To earn the point, the response must explain a specific continuity in views of immigrants. Examples can include: the negative attitudes toward new minority groups in the United States that led to restrictions such as the Chinese Exclusion Act and quotas that limited migrants from certain European countries; the persistence of the idea that immigrants are less loyal to the government than native peoples, such as suspicions in democratic countries of foreigners being communists during the Cold War; and the formation of anti-immigrant groups, such as the Know-Nothings in the nineteenth-century United States.

(b) To earn the point, the response must identify a change in patterns of migrations. In North and South America, examples include: the shift in migrations from Western European countries, such as England, France, and Germany, to migrations from Southern and Eastern European countries, such as Italy, Poland, and Russia; the shift from forced labor migrations from Africa to voluntary labor migrations from Europe and Asia; and the shift in migrants seeking factory jobs rather than agricultural work. Other examples of world migration patterns include the migration of Europeans and indentured workers from China and India to European colonies.

(c) To earn the point, the response must explain an economic reason for changes in migration patterns. Examples include: how the Industrial Revolution led to poor working and living conditions in European cities, resulting in migrations to the Americas; the global economy created by the Industrial Revolution creating demand for raw materials and laborers; and the mechanization of farming in Europe resulting in more unskilled laborers who were seeking jobs.

3. A successful short-answer response accomplishes all three tasks set forth by the prompt. Each part of the prompt is worth 1 point, for a total of 3 possible points.

(a) To earn the point, the response must explain a demographic (population) change that occurred as a result of the contact between the Eastern and Western Hemispheres following Columbus's initial voyage. Examples include: the decline of native populations as a result of diseases; the increase in populations in Afro-Eurasia as a result of new food crops from the Americas; the mixing of populations in the Americas; the emergence of *mestizo* and *mulatto* populations; and the disruptions in African societies due to the slave trade.

(b) To earn the point, the response must explain an environmental change. Examples include: deforestation and soil depletion due to the clearing of land for plantation agriculture; the impacts of monocultures on plantations; the introduction of new species of plants, such as wheat and rice, and animals, such as horses, cattle, and pigs, into the ecosystems of the Americas and Europe; and the mining boom in the Americas due to the demand for silver.

(c) To earn the point, the response must explain a specific economic change. Examples include: the rise of the Atlantic trading system, the global silver trade, the trade of cash crops grown in the Americas, the development of mercantilist policies, and the integration of the Americas into global trade.

4. A successful short-answer response accomplishes all three tasks set forth by the prompt. Each part of the prompt is worth 1 point, for a total of 3 possible points.

(a) To earn the point, the response must identify a major Enlightenment idea used by Haitian revolutionaries. Examples could include the use of the ideas of equality and natural rights to advocate for the emancipation of slaves held by French colonists and the use of the ideas of liberty and consent of the governed to justify the overthrow of French rule.

(b) To earn the point, the response must explain a difference in the motivations or causes of the Haitian and American Revolutions. For example, the French colonists in Haiti were advocating for the emancipation of slaves, while British colonists in North America were agitated by taxation policies and lack of political representation. The leaders of North American revolutions were mainly against emancipation of slaves, whereas most Haitian revolutionaries were slaves themselves. The Haitians were protesting coerced labor systems, while American colonists were protesting mercantilist policies that restricted trade.

(c) To earn the point, the response must explain the impact of Enlightenment ideas following the revolutions. Examples include: the establishment of constitutions that protected natural rights, the implementation of representative governments, and the abolition of slavery based on Enlightenment ideas (although delayed in the United States).

Section II

1. *Evaluate the differences in responses to the negative effects of industrialization on European workers in the period 1750–1900.*

Category	Scoring Criteria	Notes
Thesis/Claim (0–1 points)	Historically defensible thesis/claim with a logical line of reasoning. The response must make a thesis or claim without restating the prompt itself. The thesis must consist of one or more sentences located in one place, either in the introduction or the conclusion.	This question is assessing the historical reasoning skill of comparison. The thesis should identify two to three major responses to the negative effects of industrialization and summarize how these responses differ. Examples: Advocating that the government should be hands-off in the economy and the poor should help themselves; advocating for political reform; workers organizing themselves through violent or nonviolent means.
Contextualization (0–1 points)	Broader historical context related to the prompt. The response must connect the topic to historical developments, events, or processes; these can occur before, during, or after the time frame of the prompt itself.	Contextualization for this prompt should explain, not merely mention, broader factors that influenced worker conditions. Examples: Factors contributing to the Industrial Revolution; descriptions of typical conditions for the working poor and how conditions differed from agricultural work of the past.
Evidence (0–3 points)	Use of evidence to support the thesis. The response must utilize the content from at least *three* documents to address the *topic* of the prompt. (1 point) OR The response must use at least *six* documents to support an *argument* based on the prompt. (2 points)	Evidence from the documents must be paraphrased, not merely quoted. Examples: Documents 1 and 3 as examples of those who advocated a purely free market economy; documents 5 and 7 as examples of those who supported government legislation to address working conditions; documents 2, 4, and 6 as examples of workers organizing.
	The response must use at least *one* additional piece of historical evidence, beyond what is found in the documents, to support an argument. This additional evidence must be different from what was used for contextualization. (1 point)	Example: Additional legislation passed, such as universal male suffrage and compulsory education, which allowed the lower class the opportunity to voice their opinions and improve their jobs.

Category	Scoring Criteria	Notes
Analysis and Reasoning (0–2 points)	Complexity of understanding and reasoning. The response must explain, for at least *three* of the documents, how or why the document's purpose, historical basis, point of view, and/or audience are relevant to an argument. (1 point)	Factors' relevance to the argument about responses to industrialization should be explained, not just identified. Example: The role of purpose in document 4, in which the author presents different responses to the increasing use of machinery in the textile industry.
	The response must show a complex understanding of the content of the prompt, using evidence to support, qualify, or modify an argument about the prompt. (1 point)	A complex understanding should be incorporated into the overall argument about responses to industrialization. Examples: Qualifying the responses to industrialization based on individuals' situations, as the philosophers in the documents, who were not in the position of the workers, advocated a lack of government intervention (with the exception of Owens), while the workers themselves advocated change; connecting the development of communism to the later socialist and Marxist revolutions of the twentieth century.

2. *In the period 1200–1750, along with alterations in social structures and in methods of production, there were also some important changes in labor management.*

Develop an argument that evaluates the changes in labor systems in the period 1200–1750.

Category	Scoring Criteria	Notes
Thesis/Claim (0–1 points)	Historically defensible thesis/claim with a logical line of reasoning. The response must make a thesis or claim without restating the prompt itself. The thesis must consist of one or more sentences located in one place, either in the introduction or the conclusion.	This essay question assesses the skill of continuity and change over time. A strong essay examines at least two major changes in labor systems. Examples: The development of serfdom in Japan and Eastern Europe; the decline of serfdom in Western Europe; the Inca development of the *mit'a* system; the coerced labor systems employed by the Spanish and other European colonizers of the Americas.
Contextual-ization (0–1 points)	Broader historical context related to the prompt. The response must connect the topic to historical developments, events, or processes; these can occur before, during, or after the time frame of the prompt itself.	Contextualization for this prompt should explain, not merely mention, broader factors relevant to changes to labor systems. Examples: Explanations of why these labor systems developed or declined during this time, such as the impact of the shogun rule in Japan; agricultural, economic, and industrial developments in Europe; the exploration and colonization of the Americas by Europeans.
Evidence (0–2 points)	Use of evidence to support the thesis. The response identifies specific examples *relevant to the topic* of the prompt. (1 point) OR The response uses specific examples to *support an argument* about the prompt. (2 points)	Evidence must be paraphrased, not merely quoted. To earn 2 points, the evidence must be used to support an argument about changes to labor systems. Examples: The rise of feudalism in Japan as a result of warfare under the rule of the shogunate; the decline of serfdom in Western Europe as the economy diversified through trade; agricultural innovations increased output and made serfdom less profitable for landowners; the enclosure movement and the eventual start of the Industrial Revolution; the development of the *mit'a* system in the Inca Empire to redistribute agricultural surplus and create/maintain infrastructure; the introduction of *encomienda*; the reconstitution of *mit'a*; and the institution of slave plantation labor by the Spanish in American colonies.

Category	Scoring Criteria	Notes
Analysis and Reasoning (0–2 points)	Complexity of understanding and reasoning. The response shows historical reasoning to make an argument about the prompt. (1 point) OR The response demonstrates complex understanding, using evidence to support, qualify, or modify an argument about the prompt. (2 points)	Comparison, causation, or continuity and change over time should be incorporated into the overall argument about changes to labor systems. Examples: A detailed description of one or more of the changes to labor systems listed above (continuity and change over time); an explanation of the factors that led to one of the changes to labor systems (causation). OR A complex understanding should be incorporated into the overall argument about changes to labor systems. Examples: Explaining both causes *and* effects of changes to labor systems, such as the freeing up of laborers for industrial work in Western Europe, the delaying of industrial development in Eastern Europe, and the devastation to native populations in the Americas and importation of African slaves; corroborating the argument about changes in labor systems due to European colonization by discussing it in terms of multiple course themes, such as the cultural, economic, political, religious, and environmental impacts on native populations and landscapes.

3. *In the period 1450–1750, existing regional patterns of trade intensified in the context of the new global circulation of goods.*

Develop an argument that evaluates how one or more trade networks changed as a result of the new global circulation of goods in this time period.

Category	Scoring Criteria	Notes
Thesis/Claim (0–1 points)	Historically defensible thesis/claim with a logical line of reasoning. The response must make a thesis or claim without restating the prompt itself. The thesis must consist of one or more sentences located in one place, either in the introduction or the conclusion.	This question assesses the skill of continuity and change over time. A strong thesis should make a claim about at least two major changes in trade networks due to the rise of truly global trade systems. Example: "New trade networks emerged and old ones declined as the Americas were incorporated into a system of global trade from 1450–1750. Europeans profited from trade in precious metals and cash crops from the Americas, eventually developing the Atlantic system, while some traditional trade routes such as the Silk Road declined in importance."
Contextualization (0–1 points)	Broader historical context related to the prompt. The response must connect the topic to historical developments, events, or processes; these can occur before, during, or after the time frame of the prompt itself.	Contextualization for this prompt should explain, not merely mention, broader factors relevant to changes to trade networks. Examples: A summary of European motivations for sea exploration; a description of the voyage of Vasco da Gama and Portuguese expansion in the Indian Ocean basin.
Evidence (0–2 points)	Use of evidence to support the thesis. The response identifies specific examples *relevant to the topic* of the prompt. (1 point) OR The response uses specific examples to *support an argument* about the prompt. (2 points)	Evidence must be paraphrased, not merely quoted. To earn 2 points, the evidence must be used to support an argument about changes to trade networks. Examples: The rise of transatlantic trade due to the establishment of plantations in the Caribbean and Brazil; the widespread use of silver from the Americas as a global currency; the spread of Christianity; the shift from the dominance of Arab merchants in the Indian Ocean basin due to the new role of Europeans as middlemen in trade; the establishment of trading posts by Europeans; the colonization of Indonesia by the Dutch and the Philippines by the Spanish; the decline in Silk Road trade due to the rise of direct sea routes from Europe to Asia and the increased risk of overland travel in Central Asia after the fall of the Mongol Empire.

Category	Scoring Criteria	Notes
Analysis and Reasoning (0–2 points)	Complexity of understanding and reasoning. The response shows historical reasoning to make an argument about the prompt. (1 point) OR The response demonstrates complex understanding, using evidence to support, qualify, or modify an argument about the prompt. (2 points)	Comparison, causation, or continuity and change over time should be incorporated into the overall argument about changes to trade networks. Examples: A detailed description of one or more of the changes to trade networks listed above (continuity and change over time); an explanation of the factors that led to one of the changes to trade networks, such as reasons that silver became a world currency, including its abundance in South American mines and Europeans' desire to trade it for goods from China and Japan (causation). OR A complex understanding should be incorporated into the overall argument about changes to trade networks. Examples: Describing both changes *and* continuities of trade networks, such as the integral role of Arab, Indian, and African merchants and the continuance of trade in luxury goods (silk, porcelain, tea, spices) in Indian Ocean trade systems; explaining both causes *and* effects of changes to trade networks, such as the use of silver causing exploitation of native workers who were forced to mine it, the enrichment of China, and the eventual economic downturn in Spain due to its outflow of silver to purchase goods from other countries.

4. *In the period 1750–1900, industrializing powers established transoceanic empires.*

   Develop an argument explaining the factors that contributed to the rise of transoceanic empires by industrializing powers in the period 1750–1900.

Category	Scoring Criteria	Notes
Thesis/Claim (0–1 points)	Historically defensible thesis/claim with a logical line of reasoning. The response must make a thesis or claim without restating the prompt itself. The thesis must consist of one or more sentences located in one place, either in the introduction or the conclusion.	This question assesses the skill of causation. A strong thesis should make a claim about two or three specific factors that led to transoceanic empires. Example: "The establishment of European empires around the world between 1750 and 1900 was due to industrial technology, the demand for resources and markets for European products, and ideologies that justified conquest."

(continued)

Category	Scoring Criteria	Notes
Contextual-ization (0–1 points)	Broader historical context related to the prompt. The response must connect the topic to historical developments, events, or processes; these can occur before, during, or after the time frame of the prompt itself.	Contextualization for this prompt should explain, not merely mention, broader factors relevant to the development of empires. Examples: A description of the Industrial Revolution and its impact on global capitalism; a description of the Age of Exploration, which enabled Europeans to begin dominating global trade.
Evidence (0–2 points)	Use of evidence to support the thesis. The response identifies specific examples *relevant to the topic* of the prompt. (1 point) OR The response uses specific examples to *support an argument* about the prompt. (2 points)	Evidence must be paraphrased, not merely quoted. To earn 2 points, the evidence must be used to support an argument about the development of empires. Examples: To support the argument that industrial technology helped Europeans establish empires, the invention of steamships that provided an advantage over sail-powered ships, such as in the Opium Wars; the use of accurate, mass-produced weapons that enabled Europeans to put down rebellions by native populations. To support the argument about increased demand for resources, the mass production of manufactured goods, such as textiles, that increased demand for raw materials, such as cotton. To support the argument about justifying ideologies, the roles of nationalism, religious conversion, and the concept of Social Darwinism.
Analysis and Reasoning (0–2 points)	Complexity of understanding and reasoning. The response shows historical reasoning to make an argument about the prompt. (1 point) OR The response demonstrates complex understanding, using evidence to support, qualify, or modify an argument about the prompt. (2 points)	Comparison, causation, or continuity and change over time should be incorporated into the overall argument about the development of empires. Example: A detailed explanation of one or more of the factors listed above that led to the development of empires (causation). OR A complex understanding should be incorporated into the overall argument about the development of empires. Examples: Describing both causes *and* effects of transoceanic empires, such as the exploitation of people and resources, and the lasting impacts of neocolonialism and independence movements in the twentieth century; incorporating multiple perspectives on empires, such as the nonviolent protests of Mohandas Gandhi against British rule in India and Nelson Mandela against the legacy of European supremacy and apartheid in South Africa.

Practice Exam 5

Practice Exam 5 Answer Grid

1. Ⓐ Ⓑ Ⓒ Ⓓ
2. Ⓐ Ⓑ Ⓒ Ⓓ
3. Ⓐ Ⓑ Ⓒ Ⓓ
4. Ⓐ Ⓑ Ⓒ Ⓓ
5. Ⓐ Ⓑ Ⓒ Ⓓ
6. Ⓐ Ⓑ Ⓒ Ⓓ
7. Ⓐ Ⓑ Ⓒ Ⓓ
8. Ⓐ Ⓑ Ⓒ Ⓓ
9. Ⓐ Ⓑ Ⓒ Ⓓ
10. Ⓐ Ⓑ Ⓒ Ⓓ
11. Ⓐ Ⓑ Ⓒ Ⓓ
12. Ⓐ Ⓑ Ⓒ Ⓓ
13. Ⓐ Ⓑ Ⓒ Ⓓ
14. Ⓐ Ⓑ Ⓒ Ⓓ

15. Ⓐ Ⓑ Ⓒ Ⓓ
16. Ⓐ Ⓑ Ⓒ Ⓓ
17. Ⓐ Ⓑ Ⓒ Ⓓ
18. Ⓐ Ⓑ Ⓒ Ⓓ
19. Ⓐ Ⓑ Ⓒ Ⓓ
20. Ⓐ Ⓑ Ⓒ Ⓓ
21. Ⓐ Ⓑ Ⓒ Ⓓ
22. Ⓐ Ⓑ Ⓒ Ⓓ
23. Ⓐ Ⓑ Ⓒ Ⓓ
24. Ⓐ Ⓑ Ⓒ Ⓓ
25. Ⓐ Ⓑ Ⓒ Ⓓ
26. Ⓐ Ⓑ Ⓒ Ⓓ
27. Ⓐ Ⓑ Ⓒ Ⓓ
28. Ⓐ Ⓑ Ⓒ Ⓓ

29. Ⓐ Ⓑ Ⓒ Ⓓ
30. Ⓐ Ⓑ Ⓒ Ⓓ
31. Ⓐ Ⓑ Ⓒ Ⓓ
32. Ⓐ Ⓑ Ⓒ Ⓓ
33. Ⓐ Ⓑ Ⓒ Ⓓ
34. Ⓐ Ⓑ Ⓒ Ⓓ
35. Ⓐ Ⓑ Ⓒ Ⓓ
36. Ⓐ Ⓑ Ⓒ Ⓓ
37. Ⓐ Ⓑ Ⓒ Ⓓ
38. Ⓐ Ⓑ Ⓒ Ⓓ
39. Ⓐ Ⓑ Ⓒ Ⓓ
40. Ⓐ Ⓑ Ⓒ Ⓓ
41. Ⓐ Ⓑ Ⓒ Ⓓ
42. Ⓐ Ⓑ Ⓒ Ⓓ

43. Ⓐ Ⓑ Ⓒ Ⓓ
44. Ⓐ Ⓑ Ⓒ Ⓓ
45. Ⓐ Ⓑ Ⓒ Ⓓ
46. Ⓐ Ⓑ Ⓒ Ⓓ
47. Ⓐ Ⓑ Ⓒ Ⓓ
48. Ⓐ Ⓑ Ⓒ Ⓓ
49. Ⓐ Ⓑ Ⓒ Ⓓ
50. Ⓐ Ⓑ Ⓒ Ⓓ
51. Ⓐ Ⓑ Ⓒ Ⓓ
52. Ⓐ Ⓑ Ⓒ Ⓓ
53. Ⓐ Ⓑ Ⓒ Ⓓ
54. Ⓐ Ⓑ Ⓒ Ⓓ
55. Ⓐ Ⓑ Ⓒ Ⓓ

SECTION I, PART A
Time—55 minutes
55 Questions

Directions: Section I, Part A of this exam contains 55 multiple-choice questions, organized into sets with corresponding historical sources. Each of the questions or incomplete statements is followed by four suggested answers or completions. Using both the provided sources and your own historical knowledge, select the best answer choice.

Questions 1–3 refer to the following two images.

Japanese Feudal System

European Feudal System

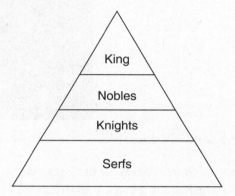

1. The diagrams best support which of the following comparative statements about Japan and Europe in the period 1200–1450?

   (A) Elites in Japan were relatively wealthier than elites in Europe.

   (B) Warrior classes in both Europe and Japan were subjugated.

   (C) European nobles were more influential than Japanese *daimyo*.

   (D) Landowning classes in both Europe and Japan enjoyed a relatively high social status.

2. Which of the following factors led to the rise of the feudal system in Europe?

   (A) The fall of the Roman Empire

   (B) The prominence of the Roman Catholic Church

   (C) The notion of divine right of kings

   (D) The Crusades

3. Which of the following most directly led to the end of Japan's feudal system in the nineteenth century?

   (A) The arrival of foreigners following the Treaty of Kanagawa

   (B) The rise of the Tokugawa shogunate

   (C) The restoration of the Meiji emperor

   (D) The imperial rule by Western Europeans

GO ON TO THE NEXT PAGE

Questions 4–6 refer to the image below.

ADMIRAL ZHENG HE STATUE IN THE QUANZHOU MARITIME MUSEUM*

*Quanzhou Maritime Museum is the only museum in China that specializes in overseas relations.

4. A historian would most likely use the image as support for which of the following assertions?

(A) Zheng He's voyage to Malacca furthered trade relations between China and the Malay Peninsula.

(B) The Malaysian government benefited from contact with China via Zheng He's voyages.

(C) Malaysian artists often incorporated elements of Chinese history into their works.

(D) Zheng He's voyage was inconsequential in the history of Malacca.

5. Which of the following was an effect of the event shown in the image?

(A) The spread of Chinese ideas to West Africa

(B) The complete adoption of Chinese traditions by Malaysians

(C) The transfer of Malaysian religious beliefs to China

(D) The diffusion of Chinese knowledge to Southeast Asia

6. The end of China's expeditions in the Indian Ocean, as depicted in the image, led to which of the following in the period 1450–1750?

(A) China's naval expeditions focused on maritime reconnaissance of the Pacific Ocean.

(B) European navies established trading posts in the Indian Ocean basin.

(C) China became completely isolated from Indian Ocean trade.

(D) Europeans adopted Chinese shipbuilding techniques.

GO ON TO THE NEXT PAGE

Questions 7–9 refer to the passage below.

"There came the death-dealing pestilence [to Florence, Italy] through the operation of the heavenly bodies or of our own sinful dealings, being sent down upon us mortals by God . . . [It] had its origin some years before in the East, whence, after destroying an innumerable multitude of living beings, it had propagated itself without respite from place to place, and so calamitously, had spread into the West. And there against no wisdom or human foresight, nor yet humble supplications made unto God by devout persons . . . could halt its dolorous effects. To the cure of these maladies no physician or virtue of any medicine appeared to avail . . . not only did few recover thereof, but well nigh all died within the third day from the appearance of signs of sickness."

Giovanni Boccaccio, *Decameron*, 1353

7. The deaths described in the passage were due to which of the following?

   (A) New military technologies introduced by merchants

   (B) Physicians' refusal to provide medicine to commoners

   (C) The diffusion of epidemic diseases as a result of trade contacts

   (D) The unsanitary conditions in urban areas

8. A historian would most likely use this passage to illustrate which of the following?

   (A) Political responses to the spread of pathogens

   (B) Burial practices of the early Renaissance era

   (C) The link between religious beliefs and epidemics

   (D) Italian trade relations with Eastern countries

9. Which of the following was a direct effect of the situation described in the passage?

   (A) The Catholic Church grew more powerful.

   (B) Overseas trade between Europe and Asia was created.

   (C) Antibiotics were developed to counter epidemics.

   (D) Labor shortages weakened serfdom.

GO ON TO THE NEXT PAGE

Questions 10–12 refer to the following two sources.

Source 1

OTTOMAN EMPIRE AT ITS GREATEST EXTENT IN 1683

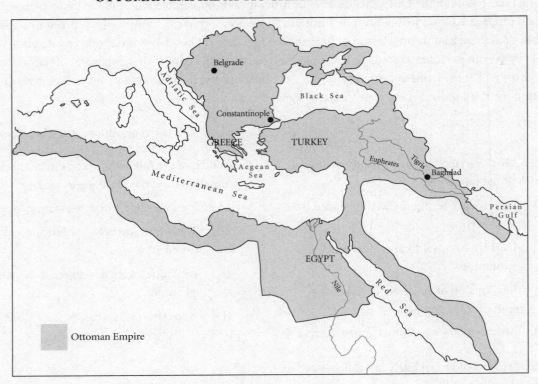

Source 2

"No distinction is attached to birth among the Turks; the deference [respect] to be paid to a man is measured by the position he holds in the public service. There is no fighting for precedence; a man's place is marked out by the duties he discharges. In making his appointments the *Sultan* pays no regard to any pretensions on the score of wealth or rank, nor does he take into consideration recommendations or popularity; he considers each case on its own merits, and examines carefully into the character, ability, and disposition of the man whose promotion is in question. It is by merit that men rise in the service, a system which ensures that posts should only be assigned to the competent. Each man in Turkey carries in his own hand his ancestry and his position in life, which he may make or mar as he will."

Ogier Ghiselin de Busbecq, Austrian diplomat to the Ottoman Empire,
letters to a friend, 1555–1562

10. Which of the following factors most directly contributed to the expansion shown in <u>Source 1</u>?

    (A) The power vacuum that resulted from the collapse of the Mongol Empire

    (B) The Ottoman Empire's use of gunpowder technologies and superior naval forces

    (C) The alliance between the Ottomans and Russians against Western European powers

    (D) The decline of European maritime empires as a result of competition and state rivalries

11. The system described in <u>Source 2</u> had which of the following purposes?

    (A) To prevent the political influence of individuals who were not related to the sultan

    (B) To reinforce the existing social hierarchy to ensure stability

    (C) To ensure that landowning elites maintained political influence

    (D) To recruit bureaucratic elites in order to maintain centralized control

12. The political structure described in <u>Source 2</u> is most similar to which of the following?

    (A) The Chinese imperial examination system

    (B) The bureaucracy of the Spanish Empire in the Americas

    (C) The use of boyars in imperial Russia

    (D) The tribute system of the Mongol Empire

GO ON TO THE NEXT PAGE

Questions 13–16 refer to the passage below.

"Espanola is a wonderful island, with mountains, groves, plains, and the country generally beautiful and rich for planting and sowing, for rearing sheep and cattle of all kinds, and ready for towns and cities. The harbours must be seen to be appreciated; rivers are plentiful and large and of excellent water; the greater part of them contain gold. . . .

Again, for new silver coin they [the indigenous populations] would give everything they possessed, whether it was worth two or three doubloons or one or two balls of cotton. Even for pieces of broken pipe-tubes they would take them and give anything for them, until, when I thought it wrong, I prevented it. And I made them presents of thousands of things which I had, that I might win their esteem, and also that they might be made good Christians and be disposed to the service of Your Majesties and the whole Spanish nation, and help us to obtain the things which we require and of which there is abundance in their country. They do not carry arms nor know what they are, because I showed them swords and they took them by the edge and ignorantly cut themselves. They have no iron: their spears are sticks without iron, and some of them have a fish's tooth at the end and others have other things. They are all generally of good height, of pleasing appearance and well built . . . They must be good servants and intelligent, as I see that they very quickly say all that is said to them, and I believe that they would easily become Christians, as it appeared to me that they had no sect. If it please our Lord, at the time of my departure, I will take six of them from here to your Highnesses that they may learn to speak. I saw no beast of any kind except parrots on this island."

> Christopher Columbus letter to Luis de Santangel, 1493, printed in
> *Columbus and the New World of His Discovery* by Filson Young, 1906

13. The contact described in the passage led most directly to which of the following?

    (A) The decline of American Indian populations due to exposure to European diseases

    (B) The growth of the African slave trade and the rise of capitalism

    (C) The establishment of European trading posts in the Indian Ocean basin

    (D) The rise in the global silver trade and the establishment of European maritime empires

14. The author's description of the indigenous peoples he encountered most directly reflects the influence of which of the following?

    (A) His desire to find a direct route to Asia by sailing across the Atlantic

    (B) His considerable understanding of the culture of Native Americans

    (C) His beliefs, based in Christianity, about the ethics of fair economic policies

    (D) His desire to please the monarchs who sponsored his voyages

GO ON TO THE NEXT PAGE

15. Which of the following best explains the author's description of the technology of indigenous peoples?

    (A) His desire to study the cultural heritage of the people of the Caribbean

    (B) His desire to teach indigenous peoples how to use European-style weapons

    (C) His desire to profit from the expedition he led by subjugating the indigenous population

    (D) His desire to teach the indigenous population the Spanish language

16. Which of the following was the most direct effect of the contact described in the passage?

    (A) The growth of European cities

    (B) The mixing of American and European cultures

    (C) The establishment of colonies in Africa

    (D) The development of European joint-stock companies

GO ON TO THE NEXT PAGE

Questions 17–20 refer to the following two passages.

Passage 1

"Since our accession to the throne all our efforts and intentions have tended to govern this realm in such a way that all of our subjects should, through our care for the general good, become more and more prosperous. For this end we have always tried to maintain internal order, to defend the state against invasion, and in every possible way to improve and to extend trade. With this purpose we have been compelled to make some necessary and salutary changes in the administration, in order that our subjects might more easily gain a knowledge of matters of which they were before ignorant, and become more skillful in their commercial relations. We have therefore given orders, made dispositions, and founded institutions indispensable for increasing our trade with foreigners, and shall do the same in the future. . . ."

Edict of Emperor Peter I (Peter the Great) of Russia
(reigned 1682–1725), *Decree on the Invitation of Foreigners*, 1702

Passage 2

"Since there are many who promote to officer rank their relatives and friends—young men who do not know the fundamentals of soldiering, not having served in the lower ranks—and since even those who serve [in the ranks] do so for a few weeks or months only, as a formality; therefore . . . let a decree be promulgated that henceforth there shall be no promotion [to officer rank] of men of noble extraction or of any others who have not first served as privates in the Guards. This decree does not apply to soldiers of lowly origin who, after long service in the ranks, have received their commissions through honest service or to those who are promoted on the basis of merit, now or in the future. . . ."

Edict of Emperor Peter I (Peter the Great) of Russia
(reigned 1682–1725), *Decree on Promotion to Officer's Rank*, 1714

17. Based on <u>Passage 1</u>, Peter the Great's policy on trade had which of the following purposes?

   (A) To establish trade links after a period of isolation

   (B) To encourage exploration to establish a sea route to Asia

   (C) To obtain colonies in the Americas for plantation agriculture

   (D) To promote trade in order to increase tax revenues

18. <u>Passage 1</u> is best understood in the context of which of the following?

   (A) The intensification of trade due to the creation of a global economy

   (B) The isolation of Russia as a result of continued Mongol control

   (C) The competition between Russia and the Ottoman Empire for control of Mediterranean trade

   (D) The collapse of the Silk Road network ending overland Eurasian trade

GO ON TO THE NEXT PAGE

19. Based on <u>Passage 2</u>, the Russian Empire exhibited which of the following characteristics common to empires in the period 1450–1750?

    (A) The supremacy of landholding elites in political and military affairs continued despite the increasing power of hereditary leaders.

    (B) The power of existing political elites fluctuated as they confronted challenges to their ability to affect the policies of increasingly powerful monarchs.

    (C) The weakening of militaries occurred due to the use of gunpowder weaponry, and a period of relative peace resulted from fewer rivalries.

    (D) Practices were adopted to incorporate diverse ethnic and religious groups into the expanding empire.

20. The economic and military policies described in both passages resulted in which of the following?

    (A) Increased influence of the Russian nobility

    (B) Less control over trade and a lack of centralized rule

    (C) Consolidation of power by Russian rulers

    (D) The decline of serfdom and economic liberalization

GO ON TO THE NEXT PAGE

Questions 21–23 refer to the passage below.

"We have fire-arms, bows and arrows, broad two-edged swords and javelins: we have shields also which cover a man from head to foot. All are taught the use of these weapons; even our women are warriors, and march boldly out to fight along with the men. Our whole district is a kind of militia: on a certain signal given, such as the firing of a gun at night, they all rise in arms and rush upon their enemy. . . . I was once a witness to a battle in our common. We had been all at work in it one day as usual, when our people were suddenly attacked. I climbed a tree at some distance, from which I beheld the fight. There were many women as well as men on both sides; among others my mother was there, and armed with a broad sword. After fighting for a considerable time with great fury, and after many had been killed our people obtained the victory, and took their enemy's Chief prisoner. He was carried off in great triumph, and, though he offered a large ransom for his life, he was put to death. . . . Those prisoners which were not sold or redeemed we kept as slaves: but how different was their condition from that of the slaves in the West Indies! With us they do no more work than other members of the community, even their masters; their food, clothing and lodging were nearly the same as theirs, (except that they were not permitted to eat with those who were free-born); and there was scarce any other difference between them, than a superior degree of importance which the head of a family possesses in our state, and that authority which, as such, he exercises over every part of his household. Some of these slaves have even slaves under them as their own property, and for their own use."

> Olaudah Equiano, describing life in Africa, *Interesting Narrative of the Life of Olaudah Equiano, or Gustavus Vassa*, 1789

21. The passage is best used as evidence for which of the following?

    (A) Warfare and social stratification on African plantations

    (B) Weapons and family relationships in the West Indies

    (C) Gender roles among European slaveholders

    (D) Military strategies and labor systems of West Africa

22. The passage best illustrates which of the following continuities in the period 1200–1450?

    (A) The use of gunpowder weapons by West African tribes

    (B) The exchange of African slaves within sub-Saharan Africa and the Indian Ocean basin

    (C) The transatlantic slave trade and commerce with European merchants

    (D) The egalitarian nature of sub-Saharan African tribal groups

GO ON TO THE NEXT PAGE

23. The passage is best understood in the context of which of the following?

(A) The increased demand for slaves by Europeans, which led to slave raids in West Africa

(B) The initial development of slavery in Africa due to the establishment of European trading posts

(C) The establishment of social stratification in Africa due to the wealth from the slave trade

(D) The increase in slave raids as a result of the spread of European diseases in West Africa

GO ON TO THE NEXT PAGE

Questions 24–27 refer to the passage below.

"1. Men are born and remain free and equal in rights. Social distinctions may be founded only upon the general good.

2. The aim of all political association is the preservation of the natural and imprescriptible rights of man. These rights are liberty, property, security, and resistance to oppression.

3. The principle of all sovereignty resides essentially in the nation. No body nor individual may exercise any authority which does not proceed directly from the nation.

4. Liberty consists in the freedom to do everything which injures no one else; hence the exercise of the natural rights of each man has no limits except those which assure to the other members of the society the enjoyment of the same rights. These limits can only be determined by law.

5. Law can only prohibit such actions as are hurtful to society. Nothing may be prevented which is not forbidden by law, and no one may be forced to do anything not provided for by law."

Excerpt from the *Declaration of the Rights of Man and of the Citizen*,
approved by the National Assembly of France, August 26, 1789

24. The declaration is best understood in the context of which of the following?

   (A) The conquest of France by neighboring powers

   (B) The establishment of slavery and serfdom in France

   (C) The spread of anti-colonial movements

   (D) The rise and diffusion of Enlightenment ideas

25. The passage best illustrates which of the following processes occurring in the Atlantic world in the late eighteenth century?

   (A) Slave resistance challenged existing authorities.

   (B) Subjects challenged centralized imperial governments.

   (C) Rebellions were influenced by diverse religious ideas.

   (D) Authority of rulers became increasingly centralized.

26. Ideas expressed in the declaration would have the most significant influence on which of the following?

   (A) The development of representative governments

   (B) The unification of diverse populations through nationalism

   (C) The rise of communist ideologies

   (D) The increasing influence of religion on political affairs

27. Which of the following groups would most likely <u>disagree</u> with the ideas expressed in the excerpt?

   (A) French landowning elites

   (B) Slaves in French colonies

   (C) European monarchs

   (D) Peasants and serfs

GO ON TO THE NEXT PAGE

Questions 28–30 refer to the following image.

"AUTHENTIC AND IMPARTIAL NARRATIVE OF THE TRAGICAL SCENE WHICH WAS WITNESSED IN SOUTHAMPTON COUNTY," 1831

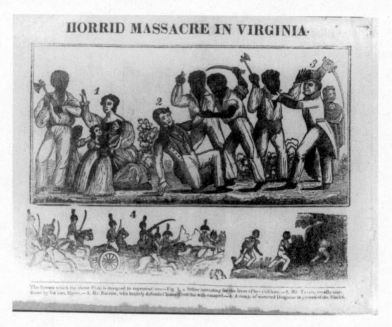

This political cartoon was published after Nat Turner's Rebellion. The caption states, "The Scenes which the above Plate is designed to represent are— Fig. 1. A Mother intreating for the lives of her Children.—2. Mr. Travis, cruelly murdered by his own Slaves.—3. Mr. Barrow, who bravely defended himself until his wife escaped.—4. A comp. of mounted Dragoons in pursuit of the Blacks."

28. The image best reflects which of the following processes in the period 1750–1900?

   (A) Plantations were established primarily for the production of cash crops.

   (B) A result of Enlightenment ideas was the emancipation of slaves.

   (C) Slave rebellions were successful in ending the practice of slavery.

   (D) Slave resistance challenged existing authorities in the Americas.

29. Developments such as the one depicted in the image most directly contributed to which of the following?

   (A) Immediate emancipation of slaves throughout the Americas

   (B) Reform movements advocating for the abolition of slavery

   (C) Continuous slave rebellions throughout the American South

   (D) Expansion of suffrage to former slaves

GO ON TO THE NEXT PAGE

30. Which of the following was most likely the purpose of the image?

    (A) To justify the actions of the rebels

    (B) To promote abolitionist movements

    (C) To vilify slaves that engaged in rebellions

    (D) To support slave resistance movements

GO ON TO THE NEXT PAGE

Questions 31–34 refer to the passage below.

"You are horrified at our intending to do away with private property. But in your existing society, private property is already done away with for nine-tenths of the population; its existence for the few is solely due to its non-existence in the hands of those nine-tenths. You reproach us, therefore, with intending to do away with a form of property, the necessary condition for whose existence is the non-existence of any property for the immense majority of society.

In one word, you reproach us with intending to do away with your property. Precisely so; that is just what we intend.

From the moment when labor can no longer be converted into capital, money, or rent, into a social power capable of being monopolized, i.e., from the moment when individual property can no longer be transformed into bourgeois property, into capital, from that moment, you say individuality vanishes.

You must, therefore, confess that by 'individual' you mean no other person than the bourgeois, than the middle-class owner of property. This person must, indeed, be swept out of the way, and made impossible.

Communism deprives no man of the power to appropriate the products of society; all that it does is to deprive him of the power to subjugate the labor of others by means of such appropriation."

Friedrich Engels & Karl Marx, *The Communist Manifesto*, 1848

31. The views expressed in the passage best illustrate which of the following processes?

    (A) The development of alternative visions of society in response to the spread of global capitalism

    (B) The spread of ideologies similar to those of John Stuart Mill and Adam Smith

    (C) The rise of the middle class as a result of the spread of industrial technology

    (D) The organization of workers into labor unions to improve working conditions

32. Which of the following occurred in the late nineteenth and early twentieth centuries in Western Europe that diminished the appeal of ideas such as those expressed in the passage?

    (A) Marxist revolutions led to government control of the means of production.

    (B) Labor unions and government reforms improved living and working conditions.

    (C) Migration to overseas colonies alleviated crowded conditions and created job opportunities.

    (D) State-sponsored industrialization improved working conditions in factories and mines.

GO ON TO THE NEXT PAGE

33. The authors' point of view regarding private property was likely influenced by which of the following developments?

    (A) The rise of government-owned factories as a result of state-sponsored industrialization

    (B) Government reforms to improve living conditions and make elementary education compulsory

    (C) The increase in the United States' share of global manufacturing

    (D) The unequal distribution of wealth as a result of laissez-faire capitalism

34. Ideas similar to those expressed in the passage led to which of the following in the early twentieth century?

    (A) The overthrow of the Russian monarchy

    (B) The abolition of private property in Germany

    (C) World War I beginning in order to combat Marxist ideas

    (D) Revolutions led by those prohibited from owning property

GO ON TO THE NEXT PAGE

Questions 35–37 refer to the graph below.

PER CAPITA AMOUNT OF INDUSTRIALIZATION, 1750–1900

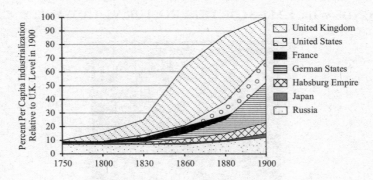

35. Which of the following explains the change in Europe's per capita level of industrialization between 1750 and 1900?

    (A) The availability in Europe of raw materials such as oil and cotton

    (B) The concentration of labor in factories and the fossil fuels revolution

    (C) The organization of workers into labor unions and the rise of Marxism

    (D) The rise of new social classes and the onset of changing family dynamics

36. Which of the following was the most immediate effect of the trend shown on the graph?

    (A) The proliferation of large-scale transnational businesses

    (B) The spread of industrial technology to South and East Asia

    (C) The creation of colonies in the Americas and the Caribbean

    (D) The contraction of the global economy

37. How did the expansion of Japanese and Russian manufacturing differ from manufacturing by Western European powers?

    (A) Japanese and Russian manufacturing was hindered by strict regulations that discouraged production.

    (B) Japanese and Russian manufacturing was focused mainly on the production of food instead of on consumer goods.

    (C) Japanese and Russian industrialization was funded by private investors rather than by the state.

    (D) Japanese and Russian industrialization was sponsored by the government rather than by private investors.

GO ON TO THE NEXT PAGE

Questions 38–41 refer to the following two images.

Image 1

"VICTORY BONDS WILL HELP STOP THIS. KULTUR VS. HUMANITY," CANADA, 1918

A Canadian soldier holds a drowned Red Cross worker in front of the sinking Llandovery Castle, a Canadian Red Cross ship attacked by a German submarine.

Image 2

"WHEN YOU RIDE ALONE YOU RIDE WITH HITLER! JOIN A CAR-SHARING CLUB TODAY!" UNITED STATES, EARLY 1940s

GO ON TO THE NEXT PAGE

38. <u>Image 1</u> best illustrates which of the following?

    (A) The importance of naval battles in ending the war

    (B) Increased wartime casualties due to the waging of "total war"

    (C) The use of fascist ideologies to mobilize resources for war

    (D) Diminished importance of military strategies in warfare

39. The conflict referred to in <u>Image 2</u> was a result of which of the following developments in the first half of the twentieth century?

    (A) The collapse of the land-based Ottoman and Qing empires

    (B) The complete dissolution of European transoceanic empires

    (C) The global economic crisis caused by the Great Depression

    (D) The rise of the United States and the Soviet Union as superpowers

40. A historian would most likely use these images to study which of the following developments in the 1900s?

    (A) The use of propaganda to inspire citizens to support the war

    (B) The factors contributing to the start of global military conflicts

    (C) The response of civilians to propaganda campaigns

    (D) The impact of industrialization on global military conflicts

41. Which of the following was created as a direct reaction to the conflicts shown in the images?

    (A) Groups that promoted alternatives to the existing order, such as the Non-Aligned Movement

    (B) The formation of military alliances, including NATO and the Warsaw Pact

    (C) Movements that used violence against civilians to achieve political aims, such as al-Qaeda

    (D) International organizations to facilitate international cooperation, such as the United Nations

GO ON TO THE NEXT PAGE

Questions 42–44 refer to the table below.

POPULATION MOVEMENTS, 1947–1951

		Migrated To			
		West Pakistan	East Pakistan	India	Total Out Migration
Migrated From	India	6.5*	0.7*	-	7.2
	West Pakistan	-	-	4.7**	4.7
	East Pakistan	-	-	2.6**	2.6
	Total In Migration	6.5	0.7	7.3	

*primarily Muslim populations
**primarily Hindu or Sikh populations

42. The movement of people depicted in the table most directly emerged from which of the following developments in the early twentieth century?

   (A) The end of British policies promoting cooperation between Hindus and Muslims

   (B) The desire of nationalist leaders to transform an independent India into a Hindu theocracy

   (C) British colonial policies that furthered existing religious tensions in the region

   (D) The Hindu majority's view of many Mughal policies as intolerant

43. The movements shown in the table reflect which of the following historical processes?

   (A) The migration of former colonial subjects to cities in the former colonizing country

   (B) The development of ethnic enclaves as migrants moved to seek work opportunities

   (C) The migration patterns associated with male seasonal laborers

   (D) The population resettlement caused by redrawing former colonial boundaries

44. The circumstances surrounding migrations shown in the table are most similar to which of the following?

   (A) Population displacements following the creation of Israel

   (B) Migrations after the collapse of communism in Eastern Europe

   (C) Population resettlements after the American Civil War

   (D) Migrations following the collapse of the Ottoman Empire

GO ON TO THE NEXT PAGE

Questions 45–47 refer to the table below.

MEMBER NATIONS OF THE EUROPEAN UNION

Country	Date Joined	Country	Date Joined
Austria	1995	Italy	1957
Belgium	1957	Latvia	2004
Bulgaria	2007	Lithuania	2004
Croatia	2013	Luxembourg	1957
Cyprus	2004	Malta	2004
Czech Republic	2004	Netherlands	1957
Denmark	1973	Poland	2004
Estonia	2004	Portugal	1986
Finland	1995	Romania	2007
France	1957	Slovakia	2004
Germany	1957	Slovenia	2004
Greece	1981	Spain	1986
Hungary	2004	Sweden	1995
Ireland	1973	United Kingdom	1973

The table shows when each member nation joined the European Union (EU), which was created to reduce trade barriers among member nations. The 1993 Maastricht Treaty founded the EU from its predecessor organization, the European Communities.

45. The formation of the organization shown in the table best illustrates which of the following processes of the twentieth century?

(A) Regional trade agreements that reflected the spread of free-market principles and practices

(B) Popular movements that promoted regional trade and rejected participation in global trade

(C) Economic nationalism and government intervention in national economies

(D) Military alliances created in response to the rivalries that developed during the Cold War

46. Which of the following best explains why countries of Eastern Europe were admitted later than other European Union members?

(A) Support of these countries' agrarian populations for protectionist trade policies

(B) Control of those countries by the Soviet Union until the end of the Cold War

(C) Resistance to the West by fascist governments in those countries

(D) The greater effect on those countries of the Great Depression and world wars

GO ON TO THE NEXT PAGE

47. Which of the following most directly contributed to the creation of the European Union?

    (A) A desire to strengthen European economic trade relations and balance the influence of the United States

    (B) A motivation to accelerate economic progress and promote political stability

    (C) A drive to propel Great Britain to become a superpower that could rival the United States

    (D) An intention to promote unrestricted global trade as a means to create friendly relations among all countries

GO ON TO THE NEXT PAGE

Questions 48–52 refer to the following two images.

Image 1

SOVIET POSTER, 1931

The text reads, "The arithmetic of an industrial-financial counter-plan: 2 + 2 plus the enthusiasm of the workers = 5."

GO ON TO THE NEXT PAGE

Image 2

A SCENE FROM *THE RED DETACHMENT OF WOMEN* (BALLET), 1972

Scene from a ballet performed at the Great Hall of the People and attended by President and Mrs. Nixon during their trip to Peking, China.

48. Which of the following directly enabled the establishment of the government that produced Image 1?

(A) The failure of the existing monarchy to abolish serfdom and other forms of coerced labor

(B) Redrawn national boundaries as a result of peace treaties at the end of World War I

(C) Increased rebellion by ethnic minorities due to imperial expansion in the nineteenth century

(D) Discontent with the monarchy and financial pressures of World War I

49. The ideology reflected in Image 2 is most directly the result of which of the following developments of the nineteenth century?

(A) Growing discontent with the unequal distribution of wealth and lack of women's suffrage

(B) Enlightenment ideas that challenged monarchies and viewed global capitalism with skepticism

(C) Demands for women's rights and empowerment of the proletariat

(D) Rebellions throughout China against European and Japanese settler colonies

GO ON TO THE NEXT PAGE

50. The images reflect which of the following responses to economic challenges of the twentieth century?

    (A) Governments controlled national economies in communist states through repressive policies.

    (B) Governments often played a strong role in guiding economic life in newly independent states.

    (C) Governments expanded free-market economic policies and promoted economic liberalization.

    (D) Governments began to take a more active role in economic life as a result of the Great Depression.

51. Which of the following best describes the likely purpose of the images?

    (A) To build support for anti-imperialist movements in Asia and Africa

    (B) To promote support for the prevailing political order and ward off alternatives

    (C) To build support for centrally directed economic programs

    (D) To promote participation in international organizations and trade agreements

52. Which of the following differs most strongly from the purpose of the images shown?

    (A) To encourage citizens to adopt Western popular culture

    (B) To mobilize support for proxy wars during the Cold War

    (C) To promote support for alliances, such as the Warsaw Pact

    (D) To demonize capitalist countries and economic policies

GO ON TO THE NEXT PAGE

Questions 53–55 refer to the graph below.

WHEAT YIELDS IN SELECTED COUNTRIES, 1950–2004

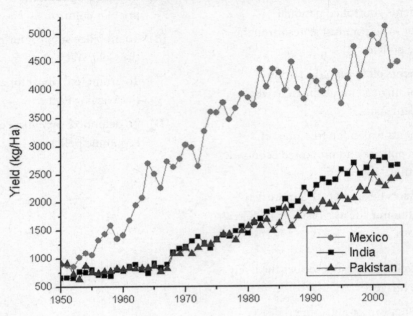

53. The trend shown on the graph is most directly due to which of the following?

(A) The redistribution of land to create a more equitable social system

(B) The spread of chemically and genetically modified forms of agriculture

(C) The increased use of fossil fuels and nuclear power as energy sources

(D) The control of farm production by the governments of these nations

54. Which of the following most directly resulted from the trend shown on the graph?

(A) Increased agricultural production led to the eradication of poverty in these nations.

(B) Increased yields in these nations led to economic collapse in other wheat producing nations.

(C) Increased population led to longer life spans and fewer epidemics.

(D) Increased population led to competition for resources more intensely than before.

GO ON TO THE NEXT PAGE

55. The trend shown on the graph is most similar to which of the following?

    (A) Sub-Saharan Africa in the period 1450–1750

    (B) Europe in the period 1200–1450

    (C) China in the period 1200–1450

    (D) India in the period 1750–1900

GO ON TO THE NEXT PAGE

END OF PART A

**IF YOU FINISH BEFORE TIME IS CALLED,
YOU MAY CHECK YOUR WORK ON THIS SECTION.**

DO NOT GO ON TO PART B UNTIL YOU ARE TOLD TO DO SO.

SECTION I, PART B
Time—40 minutes
3 Questions

Directions: Section I, Part B of this exam consists of short-answer questions. You must respond to Questions 1 *and* 2. For your final response, you must choose to answer Question 3 *or* Question 4. In your responses, be sure to address all parts of the questions, using complete sentences.

1. Use the passage below to answer all parts of the question that follows.

"The Green Revolution also contributed to better nutrition by raising incomes and reducing prices, which permitted people to consume more calories and a more diversified diet. Big increases occurred in per capita consumption of vegetable oils, fruits, vegetables, and livestock products in Asia. . . .

Critics of the Green Revolution argued that owners of large farms were the main adopters of the new technologies because of their better access to irrigation water, fertilizers, seeds, and credit. Small farmers were either unaffected or harmed because the Green Revolution resulted in lower product prices, higher input prices, and efforts by landlords to increase rents or force tenants off the land. Critics also argued that the Green Revolution encouraged unnecessary mechanization, thereby pushing down rural wages and employment. Although a number of village and household studies conducted soon after the release of Green Revolution technologies lent some support to early critics, more recent evidence shows mixed outcomes. Small farmers did lag behind large farmers in adopting Green Revolution technologies, yet many of them eventually did so. Many of these small-farm adopters benefited from increased production, greater employment opportunities, and higher wages in the agricultural and nonfarm sectors. Moreover, most smallholders were able to keep their land and experienced significant increases in total production. In some cases, small farmers and landless laborers actually ended up gaining proportionally more income than larger farmers, resulting in a net improvement in the distribution of village income."

International Food Policy Research Institute, "Green Revolution: Blessing or Curse?" 2002

(a) Identify ONE reason why the institute was most likely evaluating the effects of the Green Revolution at the time indicated by the passage.
(b) Identify ONE additional piece of information that would be most directly useful in assessing the author's conclusions about the effects of the Green Revolution.
(c) Explain ONE specific example from the period 1450–1750 that had results similar to those indicated in the passage.

GO ON TO THE NEXT PAGE

2. Use the image below to answer all parts of the question that follows.

BRITISH IMPERIAL MARITIME LEAGUE POSTER, 1914

The poster shows women and a child watching soldiers march away.

(a) Describe ONE way in which the perspective expressed in the image shows a <u>continuity</u> with the nineteenth century in views about the roles of women.

(b) Explain how ONE specific historical development led to <u>change</u> in views about the roles of women in the nineteenth or early twentieth centuries.

(c) Explain ONE way in which images such as this can be considered examples of the political uses of art in the twentieth century.

GO ON TO THE NEXT PAGE

Choose EITHER Question 3 OR Question 4.

3. Answer all parts of the question that follows.

    (a) Explain ONE <u>cultural</u> change that occurred in African societies as a result of their encounters with Arab travelers in the period 1200–1750.

    (b) Explain ONE <u>economic</u> change that occurred in African societies as a result of their encounters with Arab travelers in the period 1200–1750.

    (c) Explain ONE area of <u>continuity</u> in African societies as they encountered Arab travelers during the period 1200–1750.

4. Answer all parts of the question that follows.

    (a) Identify ONE economic effect of the spread of industrial technology in Europe in the period 1750–1900.

    (b) Explain ONE <u>similarity</u> between the responses of governments and the responses of workers to the development and spread of industrialization in the period 1750–1900.

    (c) Explain ONE <u>difference</u> between the responses of governments and the responses of workers to the development and spread of industrialization in the period 1750–1900.

GO ON TO THE NEXT PAGE

END OF SECTION I

**IF YOU FINISH BEFORE TIME IS CALLED,
YOU MAY CHECK YOUR WORK ON THIS SECTION.**

DO NOT GO ON TO SECTION II UNTIL YOU ARE TOLD TO DO SO.

SECTION II

Time—100 minutes

Question 1: Document-Based Question

Suggested reading period: 15 minutes

Suggesting writing time: 45 minutes

Directions: Question 1 is based on the accompanying documents. The documents have been edited for the purpose of this exercise.

In your response, you should do the following:

- Make a thesis or claim that responds to the prompt. The thesis or claim must be historically defensible and establish a line of reasoning.

- Provide context relevant to the prompt by describing a broader historical development or process.

- Use at least six of the provided documents to support an argument in response to the prompt.

- Use a historical example not found in the documents as evidence relevant to an argument about the prompt.

- Explain how the context or situation of at least three documents is relevant to an argument. This could address the relevance of the document's point of view, purpose, historical situation, and/or audience.

- Demonstrate a complex understanding of an argument that responds to the prompt by using evidence to corroborate, qualify, or modify the argument.

GO ON TO THE NEXT PAGE

1. Evaluate the responses of native populations to the expansion of overseas empires by industrializing states in the nineteenth century.

Document 1

Source: John Maynard Keynes, English Economist, *The Economic Consequences of the Peace*, 1920.

The [Versailles] Treaty includes no provisions for the economic rehabilitation of Europe,—nothing to make the defeated Central Empires into good neighbors, nothing to stabilize the new States of Europe, nothing to reclaim Russia; nor does it promote in any way a compact of economic solidarity amongst the Allies themselves; no arrangement was reached at Paris for restoring the disordered finances of France and Italy, or to adjust the systems of the Old World and the New. . . .

Europe consists of the densest aggregation of population in the history of the world. This population is accustomed to a relatively high standard of life, in which, even now, some sections of it anticipate improvement rather than deterioration. In relation to other continents Europe is not self-sufficient; in particular it cannot feed Itself. Internally the population is not evenly distributed, but much of it is crowded into a relatively small number of dense industrial centers. . . .

The danger confronting us, therefore, is the rapid depression of the standard of life of the European populations to a point which will mean actual starvation for some (a point already reached in Russia and approximately reached in Austria). Men will not always die quietly. For starvation, which brings to some lethargy and a helpless despair, drives other temperaments to the nervous instability of hysteria and to a mad despair. And these in their distress may overturn the remnants of organization, and submerge civilization itself in their attempts to satisfy desperately the overwhelming needs of the individual. This is the danger against which all our resources and courage and idealism must now co-operate.

GO ON TO THE NEXT PAGE

Document 2

Source: Excerpt from the Washington Naval Treaty, signed by the United States, the United Kingdom, France, Italy, and Japan in Washington, D.C., February 6, 1922.

Article VII

The total tonnage for aircraft carriers of each of the Contracting Powers shall not exceed in standard displacement, for the United States 135,000 tons (137,160 metric tons); for the British Empire 135,000 tons (137,160 metric tons); for France 60,000 tons (60,960 metric tons); for Italy 60,000 tons (60,960 metric tons); for Japan 81,000 tons (82,296 metric tons).

GO ON TO THE NEXT PAGE

Document 3

Source: Hon. Philander Chase Knox, "Treaty of Versailles speech," delivered before the U.S. Senate, August 1919.

Think you Germany—smarting and staggering under the terms of this, the hardest treaty of modern times—will, even if we were to set up the league and she should join it, supinely rest content with the dole of grade and sufrance we are vouchsafing her, the crumbs from her victors' table? . . .

There can, of course, be no question as to the propriety of compelling Germany to disgorge the loot which she seized and which she still has, nor in requiring her to replace that which she seized and has since consumed or otherwise used or destroyed. No matter what this may mean to Germany, no matter how it may leave her, this must be done. . . . But when we get away from this and go beyond this, it behooves us to proceed with care, lest we go beyond the bounds of wise statesmanship . . .

Thus, we take practically all of Germany's means of conducting commerce through her own vessels with overseas countries. . . . Thus seemingly under a theory of replacement the treaty likewise strips Germany of much of her island shipping. . . . The effect of all this upon Germany's future and upon her ability to meet the other requirements of this treaty are well worthy of deep and mature reflection. . . .

Mr. President, the more I consider this treaty the more I am convinced that the only safe way for us to deal with it is to decline to be a party to it at all. I think we should renounce in favor of Germany any and all claims for indemnity because of the war and see that she gets credit for what we renounce . . . I see no reason why we should be parties to imposing upon Germany a treaty whose terms, our negotiators say, she will not be able to meet.

GO ON TO THE NEXT PAGE

Document 4

Source: Agreement among Germany, the United Kingdom, France, and Italy, commonly referred to as the Munich Pact, concluded September 29, 1938, following the German invasion of the Sudeten region of Czechoslovakia.

GERMANY, the United Kingdom, France and Italy, taking into consideration the agreement, which has been already reached in principle for the cession to Germany of the Sudeten German territory, have agreed on the following terms and conditions governing the said cession and the measures consequent thereon, and by this agreement they each hold themselves responsible for the steps necessary to secure its fulfillment: . . .

(4) The occupation by stages of the predominantly German territory by German troops will begin on 1st October . . .

(8) The Czechoslovak Government will within a period of four weeks from the date of this agreement release from their military and police forces any Sudeten Germans who may wish to be released, and the Czechoslovak Government will within the same period release Sudeten German prisoners who are serving terms of imprisonment for political offences. . . .

Document 5

Source: Table of selected countries national debt as a percentage of national GDP.

	1921	1924	1929
Germany*	305%	155%	134%
France	258%	196%	140%
United Kingdom	154%	175%	160%
Italy	153%	141%	98%
United States	33%	24%	16%

*debt including reparations

GO ON TO THE NEXT PAGE

Document 6

Source: President Franklin Delano Roosevelt, telegram to Adolph Hitler, April 1939.

Three nations in Europe and one in Africa have seen their independent existence terminated. A vast territory in another independent nation of the Far East has been occupied by a neighboring state. Reports, which we trust are not true, insist that further acts of aggression are contemplated against still other independent nations. Plainly the world is moving toward the moment when this situation must end in catastrophe unless a more rational way of guiding events is found.

. . . The discussions which I have in mind relate to the most effective and immediate manner through which the peoples of the world can obtain progressive relief from the crushing burden of armament which is each day bringing them more closely to the brink of economic disaster. Simultaneously the Government of the United States would be prepared to take part in discussions looking towards the most practical manner of opening up avenues of international trade to the end that every nation of the earth may be enabled to buy and sell on equal terms in the world market as well as to possess assurance of obtaining the materials and products of peaceful economic life.

. . . We recognize complex world problems which affect all humanity but we know that study and discussion of them must be held in an atmosphere of peace. Such an atmosphere of peace cannot exist if negotiations are overshadowed by the fear of war.

GO ON TO THE NEXT PAGE

Document 7

Source: Treaty of Versailles, selected articles, 1919.

80. Germany will respect the independence of Austria.

81. Germany recognizes the complete independence of Czechoslovakia.

87. Germany recognizes the complete independence of Poland.

119. Germany surrenders all her rights and titles over her overseas countries.

159. The German military forces shall be demobilized and reduced not to exceed 100,000 men.

181. The German navy must not exceed 6 battleships, 6 light cruisers, 12 destroyers, and 12 torpedo boats. No submarines are to be included.

198. The Armed Forces of Germany must not include any military or naval air forces.

231. Germany and her Allies accept the responsibility for causing all the loss and damage to the Allied Powers.

233. Germany will pay for all damages done to the civilian population and property of the Allied Governments.

428. To guarantee the execution of the Treaty, the German territory situated to the west of the Rhine River will be occupied by Allied troops for fifteen years.

431. The occupation forces will be withdrawn as soon as Germany complies with the Treaty.

GO ON TO THE NEXT PAGE

END OF DOCUMENTS FOR QUESTION 1

Question 2, Question 3, or Question 4: Long Essay Question
Suggested writing time: 40 minutes

Directions: Choose Question 2, Question 3, OR Question 4 to answer.

In your response you should do the following:

- Make a thesis or claim that responds to the prompt. The thesis or claim must be historically defensible and establish a line of reasoning.
- Provide context relevant to the prompt by describing a broader historical development or process.
- Use specific and relevant examples as evidence to support an argument in response to the prompt.
- Use a historical reasoning skill (causation, comparison, or continuity and change) to develop an argument in response to the prompt.
- Demonstrate a complex understanding of an argument that responds to the prompt by using evidence to corroborate, qualify, or modify the argument.

2. In the period 1200–1450, improved transportation technologies and commercial practices led to the intensification of trade.

   Develop an argument that evaluates how improved technologies and commercial practices led to changes in Afro-Eurasian trade networks during this time period.

3. In the period 1450–1900, significant economic changes in the areas of agriculture and industry occurred throughout the world, impacting demand for labor.

   Develop an argument that evaluates how labor systems changed as a result of increased demand for labor in this time period.

4. In the period 1750–1900, revolutions and rebellions began against existing governments, leading to the establishment of new nation-states around the world.

   Develop an argument that evaluates how Enlightenment ideas contributed to revolutions against imperial or monarchical rule in one or more regions in this time period.

GO ON TO THE NEXT PAGE

 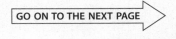

END OF SECTION II

STOP

END OF EXAM

ANSWER KEY

Section I, Part A

1. D	15. C	29. B	43. D
2. A	16. B	30. C	44. A
3. C	17. D	31. A	45. A
4. A	18. A	32. B	46. B
5. D	19. B	33. D	47. A
6. B	20. C	34. A	48. D
7. C	21. D	35. B	49. C
8. C	22. B	36. A	50. A
9. D	23. A	37. D	51. B
10. B	24. D	38. B	52. A
11. D	25. B	39. C	53. B
12. A	26. A	40. A	54. D
13. A	27. C	41. D	55. C
14. D	28. D	42. C	

Section I, Part B and Section II

See Answers and Explanations, and self-score free-response questions.

Section I, Part A Number Correct: _____

Section I, Part B Points Earned: _____

Section II Points Earned: _____

Sign into your online account at kaptest.com and enter your results in the scoring section to see your 1–5 score.

Haven't registered your book yet? Go to kaptest.com/moreonline to begin.

ANSWERS AND EXPLANATIONS

Section I, Part A

1. D

The landowning classes (the *daimyo* in Japan and nobles in Europe) were both considered the upper class in their respective societies; **(D)** is correct. (A) is incorrect because we cannot determine the level of wealth based on these diagrams. In addition, the elites were the wealthiest in each society. The warrior classes—samurai and knights—had some status and were not at the bottom of the social hierarchy, making (B) incorrect. (C) is incorrect because nobles and *daimyo* had a similar position in their respective societies.

2. A

The fall of the Roman Empire due to Germanic invasions led people to flee the cities and to agree to provide service to a landowner in exchange for protection; **(A)** is correct. Even though the Catholic Church was prominent in the absence of a central government, it did not cause the feudal system to develop, making (B) incorrect. (C) is incorrect because divine right is an idea absolute monarchs embraced to justify their power in the later period of 1450–1750. (D) is incorrect because the Crusades arose toward the end of the feudal period and actually weakened feudalism by exposing Western Europeans to new ideas and providing them with opportunities to leave the manor.

3. C

The Meiji Restoration was the establishment of a centralized government under the rule of the emperor in the late nineteenth century. This led to the end of the feudal system, making **(C)** correct. The Treaty of Kanagawa led to the opening of ports for trade with Westerners but did not change the government directly, making (A) incorrect. Discontent with this treaty led to the overthrow of the Tokugawa shogunate. (B) is incorrect because the Tokugawa shogunate arose around 1600. Although the political system became more centralized, the social structure remained relatively similar. (D) is incorrect because Europeans never colonized Japan.

4. A

Zheng was a Chinese mariner and commander of expeditionary voyages throughout much of southern Asia and East Africa from 1405 to 1433. **(A)** is correct as the primary purpose of He's voyages was to establish trade relations. (B) is incorrect because it is unclear whether the Malaysian government commissioned the mural. Further, there is no evidence from the mural that the Malaysian government benefited from contact with China. (C) is incorrect because Zheng He voyaged to Malacca and would thus be in a mural of Malaysia's history. Moreover, it is not the norm for artists to depict historical events from other regions. Zheng's voyage to Malacca promoted the relationship between Malacca and China, making (D) incorrect. Also, if the voyage were not important to Malacca, it most likely would not have been commemorated in art.

5. D

The impetus for Chinese voyages were in large part to assert Chinese presence in the Indian Ocean and impose imperial control over trade in South and Southeast Asia. These expeditions resulted in the spread of knowledge into Southeast Asia, making **(D)** correct. (A) is incorrect because Zheng He's voyages were in the Indian Ocean basin, which includes East Africa but not West Africa. Although some Chinese traditions were likely adopted, Malaysians would not have abandoned their own traditions, making (B) incorrect. (C) is incorrect because China retained its core belief systems throughout its history, while Malaysians adopted Islam and Buddhism due to trade relationships and missionary activity.

6. B

The lack of the presence of the Chinese navy enabled European merchants to establish trading posts throughout the Indian Ocean basin; thus, **(B)** is correct. (A) is incorrect because China's fleet was destroyed, so the Chinese could not explore in the Pacific. Chinese merchants continued to participate in existing trade routes despite the destruction of the navy, making (C) incorrect. (D) is incorrect because shipbuilding techniques were lost when the fleet was destroyed.

7. C

The passage describes disease that began in the East and spread through the West. The bubonic plague, or

Black Death, spread along the Silk Road in this period, leading to the loss of approximately one-third of Europe's population; thus, **(C)** is correct. (A) is incorrect because the passage refers to disease, not new military technologies. (B) is incorrect because the passage describes how no medicine would work against this disease. While the plague often spread through crowded areas with unsanitary conditions, these conditions were not the primary cause of death; (D) is incorrect.

8. C

The passage indicates that the spread of disease was "sent down upon us mortals by God"; in other words, it was considered a punishment from God, making **(C)** correct. (A) is incorrect because the passage does not indicate anything about the government's response. While the passage mentions many deaths, it does not provide detail about burial, so (B) is incorrect. (D) is incorrect because, while the passage states that disease came from trade with the East, there are no further specifics about trade relations.

9. D

The sudden death of roughly one-third of the population of Europe due to plague led to fewer workers. Since the survivors were able to negotiate for lower dues or move off of manors to take city jobs, serfdom was weakened, making **(D)** correct. (A) is incorrect because the Catholic Church could not help stop the spread of the disease and had no other direct effect resulting in power. Additionally, the ideas of humanism and secularism arose in this period. Trade between Europe and Asia was a cause of the spread of disease described in the passage, not an effect, making (B) incorrect. (C) is incorrect because antibiotics were not developed until the twentieth century.

10. B

The Ottomans were able to conquer the remains of the Byzantine Empire and the city of Constantinople by using superior gunpowder weapons and siege tactics. The Ottoman Empire thus was able to expand in the eastern Mediterranean using its navy, making **(B)** correct. Although the Mongols controlled the Middle Eastern area known today as Iran, they never conquered Eastern Europe or North Africa. So even though the Mongols had fallen by this time, the power vacuum did not factor into the rise of the Ottomans, making (A) incorrect. (C) is incorrect

because the Ottomans and Russians were often enemies rather than allies. They were competing for control of the Black Sea. (D) is incorrect because European maritime empires were expanding and thriving at this time, rather than declining, which is what prevented the Ottomans from expanding to Western Europe.

11. D

The Ottomans used the *devshirme* system of recruitment in which Christian boys from the Balkans were enslaved, converted to Islam, and trained as either bureaucrats or janissaries (soldiers). This enabled the sultans to create a loyal bureaucracy that was merit-based rather than related to family ties; thus, **(D)** is correct. Although the sultan's position was hereditary, the bureaucracy was not. The officials were not relatives of the sultan but were recruited through the *devshirme* system, making (A) incorrect. (B) is incorrect because this system was merit-based rather than dependent on social class, family connections, or wealth. (C) is incorrect because the influence of landowning elites was limited in this system because recruitment occurred through *devshirme*.

12. A

Like the bureaucratic system described in the passage, the Chinese civil service exam was merit-based, making **(A)** correct. It served to recruit bureaucrats who were capable and to limit the influence of landowning families. (B) is incorrect because the viceroys who governed Spanish colonies were often from noble families who were deemed loyal to the king. (C) is incorrect because boyars were noble landowners who ruled over their lands and managed serfs bound to the land. The Mongols did not have an elaborate bureaucracy in areas from which they collected tribute; instead, they used local rulers, making (D) incorrect.

13. A

Contact between indigenous peoples of the Americas and Europeans led to a dramatic population decline among the Amerindians due to their lack of immunity; thus, **(A)** is correct. Although the African slave trade eventually came about as a result of Columbus's voyages, it was not a direct effect; because the focus of this passage is on the people of the Caribbean, (B) is incorrect. (C) is incorrect because trading posts were established due to exploration but not due to Columbus's voyages. (D) is incorrect because the increase in silver trade was another indirect effect that eventually came about many years after the conquest of the native peoples.

14. D

In describing the land as plentiful and the indigenous peoples—who were willing to trade, unfamiliar with weapons, and ready to learn the Spanish language—as people who would make good servants, Columbus wanted to show the king and queen of Spain, who had sponsored his voyage, how their investment would pay off, making **(D)** correct. Although Columbus was searching for a direct route to Asia, the description in the passage is not based on this desire, so (A) is incorrect. (B) is incorrect because Columbus described the indigenous peoples based on his observations as seen through a European lens. He had no understanding of their customs because this was his first encounter with them. Even though Columbus claims he stopped the unfair trading because he "thought it wrong," (C) is incorrect because this statement was likely made to make himself look good to his readers; further, the focus of the letter was not Columbus's concern for the indigenous peoples but for convincing his readers the land would be valuable.

15. C

The passage describes how amenable the author believed the indigenous people would be to subjugation, saying that they could potentially be good servants. The author most likely notes that the indigenous peoples did not have iron weapons because he wanted to conquer them and profit from their labor, making **(C)** correct. (A) is incorrect because the author wanted to subjugate the indigenous population rather than learn about their history or culture. His observations are specific to their suitability as servants and their lack of weapons. Although the author mentions showing the native peoples his sword, he did not do so out of a desire to teach them about weapons. Instead, he includes this detail to indicate how ignorant they were about weaponry, making (B) incorrect. While the author mentions teaching the indigenous peoples his language, that is not why he describes their lack of weapons; instead he is citing evidence for the idea that they would be good servants; thus, (D) is incorrect.

16. B

As a result of Columbus's voyage, Europeans migrated to the Americas and conquered the indigenous populations. In doing so, aspects of American Indian and European cultures merged; these included religion, food, dress, and property ownership. **(B)** is correct. Although cities in Europe did eventually grow due to increased trade, that phenomenon was not as directly related to the Americas, making (A) incorrect. (C) is incorrect because Africa was not colonized on a large scale until the nineteenth century and, at any rate, Columbus journeyed to the Western Hemisphere. (D) is incorrect because joint-stock companies arose primarily to lessen the risks to merchants of long-distance trade, which was not specific to the Americas.

17. D

If Russia had been involved in global trade, the government would have benefited from taxing trade and using the revenue to fund the military, infrastructure, and monumental architecture. This sentiment is articulated in Passage 1 through the discussion of trade alongside the assertion that all of the subjects are part of the movement to help the whole become more prosperous, making **(D)** correct. Although Russia was not directly involved in maritime trade prior to Peter the Great's rule due to lack of warm water ports, the empire was involved in overland trade. Thus, the edict in the passage would not establish the first trade links, making (A) incorrect. (B) is incorrect because Peter the Great sought to increase trade with Western powers and had access to Asian trade due to expansion to the Pacific in this period. (C) is incorrect because, by the time of Peter the Great's reign, much of the Americas was claimed by European powers. Russia was seeking to export its products, such as iron, timber, and furs, rather than produce cash crops.

18. A

Russia's interest in increased participation in global trade was the result of greater connections among world regions due to the incorporation of the Americas and the rise of the silver trade; thus, **(A)** is correct. Even though Russia failed to engage in maritime trade partly because it was under Mongol control for a long period, by the time of the decree the Mongols no longer controlled Russia, so (B) is incorrect. In addition, Mongol rule helped involve Russia in overland Asian trade, so Russians were not isolated. While the Ottomans were expanding in the eastern Mediterranean in this period, competition with Russia was over access to the Black Sea rather than the Mediterranean, making (C) incorrect. In fact, this competition was just beginning in this period. (D) is incorrect because, in spite of trade via the Silk Road declining in this period because it was riskier than sea trade, it did not collapse.

19. B

The edict in Passage 2 required nobles, who were the existing political elites, to serve in the lower ranks of the military before being promoted based on merit. This was designed to limit the influence of nobles by forcing them to earn their positions rather than inherit them. This decree issued by a monarch demonstrated how the power of the nobles changed as monarchs consolidated power; thus, **(B)** is correct. (A) is incorrect because the decree imposed by the monarch was attempting to limit the influence of nobles. This was typical during this time period as monarchs around the world attempted to centralize control. (C) is incorrect because militaries grew stronger in this era due to the use of gunpowder weapons, which led to larger armies. In addition, rivalries among European maritime empires increased as each claimed territory and control of trade routes. Although the decline of serfdom and economic liberalization occurred as empires expanded in this era, this edict was not attempting to be more inclusive of ethnic or religious minorities. Instead, the purpose of the edict was to make positions in the military more merit-based; thus, (D) is incorrect.

20. C

Increased participation in global trade by Russia and military reforms helped to increase the power of Russian tsars; thus, **(C)** is correct. (A) is incorrect because the influence of the nobility on Russia's government decreased due to edicts passed by Russian rulers. (B) is incorrect because the edict in Passage 1, in particular, was designed to increase trade and because a stronger military increased centralized rule. Restrictions on peasants were strengthened, leading to increased serfdom, making (D) incorrect.

21. D

The passage describes Equiano's tribe in West Africa in terms of defense from attacks and the roles of slaves;

thus, **(D)** is correct. Although the passage describes warfare, it does not discuss divisions among social classes, making (A) incorrect. (B) is incorrect because the author mentions how the slavery discussed was different from that in the West Indies, so we can infer that it is not describing the West Indies. (C) is incorrect because the passage examines gender roles of slaves from West Africa, not the slaveholders.

22. B

Prior to the Atlantic slave trade, which arose in the sixteenth century, African slaves were transported within sub-Saharan Africa and in the Indian Ocean basin trade networks. This passage illustrates the continuity of this trade to a new location in the world map during this time period; thus, **(B)** is correct. European merchants did not bring gunpowder weapons to trade until the fifteenth century and is thereby not a continuity throughout this period. Further, the focus of this passage is not the use of gunpowder weaponry, but slavery; so (A) is incorrect. (C) is incorrect because the transatlantic slave trade did not exist prior to 1492 since Europeans did not know the Americas existed. (D) is incorrect because the passage shows that heads of families had the greatest authority, so tribes were not totally egalitarian, or equal.

23. A

Slave raids increased greatly due to the transatlantic slave trade in which Europeans brought manufactured goods to coastal tribes in exchange for slaves, who were captured by Africans, making **(A)** correct. (B) is incorrect because slavery existed in Africa before the arrival of the Europeans. (C) is incorrect because social stratification existed before the Atlantic slave trade, although the tribes tended to be less stratified than other regions. Contact with European merchants did not lead to the spread of disease on a large scale, making (D) incorrect. There was previous indirect contact between Europe and Africa in the postclassical age.

24. D

This document includes Enlightenment ideas such as equality under the law, natural rights, popular sovereignty, and liberty, which had been circulating in France and inspired the French Revolution to overthrow the absolute monarchy; thus, **(D)** is correct. Although France fought its neighbors, it was not conquered by them, making (A) incorrect. (B) is incorrect because slavery and serfdom had been well established in the French Empire by this point. (C) is incorrect because the French were rejecting their oppressive government, not declaring independence from an imperial ruler.

25. B

The source was written during the French Revolution to restructure the government so that citizens' rights would be protected. Thus, during the French Revolution the ideas held by citizens challenged the power of the absolute monarchy, making **(B)** correct. (A) is incorrect because the French Revolution was not a slave rebellion, but a rebellion against the monarchy. (C) is incorrect because the rebellions were not religious in nature. Rulers consolidated their power in the previous period and rebellions rejected oppressive governments, making (D) incorrect.

26. A

Enlightenment ideas led to a greater participation in government by citizens through representatives; thus, **(A)** is correct. (B) is incorrect because the document focuses on rights rather than national symbols. Communist ideologies arose in response to the social inequalities that were increased by the Industrial Revolution, making (C) incorrect. (D) is incorrect because Enlightenment ideas promoted the separation of church and state.

27. C

European monarchs would lose power if governments that protected rights and encouraged participation by citizens were implemented; thus, **(C)** is correct. Some French nobles participated in the revolution because they resented the power of the absolute monarch and wanted to have a say in government, making (A) incorrect. (B) is incorrect because slaves in French colonies wanted the ideas of liberty to apply to them. (D) is incorrect because peasants and serfs would typically support ideas like equality under the law.

28. D

Image 1 features a maroon community, which is a settlement of runaway slaves. This suggests that there were resistance movements because slaves had escaped; **(D)** is correct. (A) is incorrect because, even though plantations were indeed created to exploit cash crops, the image shows a maroon community rather than a plantation. (B) is incorrect because the slaves in the image ran away and were not actually freed legally by abolitionist movements inspired by Enlightenment ideas. The image does not show evidence of a rebellion, making (C) incorrect.

29. B

Reform movements called for the abolition of slavery on humanitarian grounds, but also took into consideration that rebellions were disruptive to society and preventing them was costly. This led some to question the economic benefits of coerced labor; **(B)** is correct. (A) is incorrect because slavery was not immediately ended throughout the Americas, persisting until the middle of the nineteenth century, for instance, in the United States until the Civil War. (C) is incorrect because "continuous" implies that they occurred constantly. In fact, major rebellions occurred rarely. (D) is incorrect because the right to vote was not granted to slaves in response to rebellions, even after emancipation. There still were restrictions designed to limit voting by freed slaves, such as property requirements.

30. C

The caption of the image shows anger toward the slaves by calling the depicted events a "horrid massacre" and using the phrase "cruelly murdered." The image was designed to enrage those who viewed it; **(C)** is correct. Even supporters of abolition would typically not advocate the use of violence, making (A) incorrect. (B) is incorrect because, while some claimed that slavery should be abolished before slaves freed themselves, most viewed rebellions as evidence that slaves were inferior and deserved their treatment. (D) is incorrect because the image is not condoning the rebellion.

31. A

Communism developed as a reaction to the inequalities created by the capitalist system, offering the elimination of private property as a solution. Thus, **(A)** is correct. (B) is incorrect because John Stuart Mill is known for liberalism, not communism, and Adam Smith is referred to as the father of capitalism because of his ideas regarding the forces of the market. Neither man's ideas call for the drastic social change proposed by Marx and Engels.

Although the middle class expanded, the passage focuses on the inequities of capitalist society, particularly when looking at wealthy elites compared to the working class; (C) is incorrect. (D) is incorrect because communism called for a dramatic overhaul of the system through revolution rather than the organization of workers into unions.

32. B

In the late nineteenth and twentieth centuries in Western Europe, laws were passed to address poor working conditions and limit hours. Workers organized themselves into unions in order to push for improved wages. This led to less support for communism since the existing system helped improve conditions; **(B)** is correct. (A) is incorrect because Western Europe did not undergo communist revolutions; however, some Marxist political parties developed. Although migration occurred, it was not enough to improve living conditions, making (C) incorrect. (D) is incorrect because state-sponsored industrialization was common in Russia and Japan to jump-start the industrial process. In addition, Western European factories were typically privately owned but became subject to more regulations.

33. D

In the excerpt, Marx and Engels promote communism in response to unequal distribution of wealth. Laissez-faire capitalism rejected government intervention in the economy, leading to social inequalities due to the desire of factory owners to maximize profits at the expense of the workers. Thus, **(D)** is correct. (A) is incorrect because state-sponsored industrialization was not typical in Germany, which is where Marx was from. (B) is incorrect because government reforms were not common until later in the nineteenth century in much of Western Europe. While the United States was industrializing and increasing its share in global manufacturing, it did not directly prompt Marx and Engels to propose the abolition of private property since they were from Western Europe; (C) is incorrect.

34. A

Marxist ideas led to the Russian Revolution of 1917, which overthrew tsarist rule and led to the establishment of the communist Soviet Union. Thus, **(A)** is correct. (B) is incorrect because Germany never had a communist revolution. (C) is incorrect because no powers were communist at the onset of World War I. That war was fought due to militarism, competition among nationalist European powers, and alliances. The capitalist system did not prevent anyone from owning property; instead, it just made property ownership difficult for lower-class workers, making (D) incorrect.

35. B

Europe's per capita level of industrialization increased as a result of the invention of coal-powered machines and the factory system, both of which increased the output of finished goods; **(B)** is correct. (A) is incorrect because oil is not naturally found in Europe and the combustion engine was developed fairly late in the nineteenth century. In addition, cotton requires a warm climate and does not grow well in Europe. Although unions formed and Marxist ideology developed, those did not increase Europe's industrialization, making (C) incorrect. (D) is incorrect because new social classes and family life developed as a result of changes in production but did not impact industry.

36. A

The profits generated and technology developed from industrialization in Europe led to the rise of large companies, such as banks and shipping companies, that operated around the world. Thus, **(A)** is correct. (B) is incorrect because Europeans wanted people in South and East Asia to purchase mass-produced consumer goods and thus practiced imperialism here. As a result, countries in these areas did not industrialize until after they gained independence. (C) is incorrect because the conquest and colonization of the Americas occurred before this period. The global economy expanded as global capitalism led to increased demand for raw materials and markets for European manufactured goods, making (D) incorrect.

37. D

The governments of Russia and Japan actively tried to promote industrialization by financing factories, railroads, and mines. In contrast, Western European industrialization was due mainly to investments by individuals or private corporations. Thus, **(D)** is correct. (A) is incorrect because both the Russian and Japanese governments tried to promote industrialization rather than restrict it. Food was not routinely mass produced in this era and was not as profitable as the production of consumer goods, making (B) incorrect. (C) is incorrect because industrialization was state sponsored in these countries.

38. B

The caption explains how the Germans sunk a Red Cross ship, which was not a military vessel, but one providing humanitarian aid. This illustrates the concept of "total war," in which civilians mobilize in the war effort, but are also considered potential targets. Thus, **(B)** is correct. (A) is incorrect because the war ultimately ended due to Russia's withdrawal and the United States' entry. (C) is incorrect because fascism arose in the period after World War I. Military strategies are usually key to wars, so although strategies change, they do not become less important, making (D) incorrect.

39. C

Hitler rose to power in the aftermath of World War I partly due to the economic crisis in Germany that was caused by the Treaty of Versailles and worsened by the Great Depression. Additionally, the Great Depression contributed to World War II because Western powers were more focused on their economic situation than international affairs and responding to German aggression. Thus, **(C)** is correct. (A) is incorrect because the Ottoman and Qing empires collapsed in the early twentieth century (1918 and 1911, respectively) as a result of their failure to industrialize and internal unrest. (B) is incorrect because European empires did not completely dissolve until the period after World War II, when most colonies achieved independence. The United States and the Soviet Union developed as superpowers in the aftermath of World War II, not before, making (D) incorrect.

40. A

Both posters served to encourage civilians to support the war by buying war bonds (Image 1) and carpooling (Image 2), reflecting the significance of propaganda in mobilizing populations to support the war effort; **(A)** is correct. (B) is incorrect because the posters were created during the war and were seeking support. They do not clearly indicate the reasons why the war began. (C) is incorrect because we cannot tell from the posters alone whether these campaigns were successful. Industrialization made the war deadly, and the effects of industrialization on warfare are not clearly shown in the posters; (D) is incorrect.

41. D

After World War I and World War II, international organizations, such as the League of Nations and the United Nations, were created in order to resolve conflict diplomatically; **(D)** is correct. (A) is incorrect because the Non-Aligned Movement was a response to the polarization of the world during the Cold War, when countries pledged to remain neutral in the conflict. NATO and the Warsaw Pact were military alliances formed during the Cold War, making (B) incorrect. While movements using violence against civilians developed after World War II, they were not in response to it; (C) is incorrect.

42. C

When India became independent from Great Britain, the region was partitioned into mostly Hindu India and mostly Muslim Pakistan. Tension between the groups, fueled by British rule, caused violence to break out. Also, Hindus in Pakistan and Muslims in India feared being minorities in the new countries, so many emigrated to the country where they would be in the majority. Thus, **(C)** is correct. (A) is incorrect because the British did not promote cooperation between Hindus and Muslims. Instead, they exploited tensions between the populations to make them easier to control. (B) is incorrect because India became a parliamentary democracy upon independence; today it is the world's largest democracy in terms of population. Additionally, it is a secular government rather than a theocracy. While some policies under the former Mughal Empire were viewed as intolerant, British rule most directly caused the tensions that led to migrations in the twentieth century, making (D) incorrect.

43. D

The migrations depicted in the table occurred due to the partitioning of India, which split the former British colony into two states: India and Pakistan (which later split into Pakistan and Bangladesh). **(D)** is correct. (A) is incorrect because the former colonizer of India was Great Britain, which is not shown in the table. These migrations were for political and religious reasons, not economic reasons; (B) is incorrect. (C) is incorrect because these migrations were not seasonal, like farmwork, but were permanent relocations.

44. A

The creation of Israel led mainly Muslim Palestinian Arab refugees to flee to neighboring countries. Religious affiliation also motivated most of the migration depicted in the table, making **(A)** correct. (B) is incorrect because migrations from Eastern Europe occurred because people sought economic opportunity, not because they feared becoming a religious minority. Neither the American Civil War nor the collapse of the Ottoman Empire resulted immediately in large-scale migrations; (C) and (D) are incorrect.

45. A

The European Union (EU) reduced economic barriers to trade, such as tariffs, in order to promote economic growth; **(A)** is correct. (B) is incorrect because the EU member nations participate in global trade as well as regional trade. Economic nationalism protects individual economies and often raises taxes on exports to protect domestic products; in contrast, the EU promotes free trade among member nations, making (C) incorrect. NATO, not the EU, was the alliance that formed originally in response to the Soviet threat in Europe; (D) is incorrect.

46. B

After revolutions occurred in Eastern Europe and the Soviet Union collapsed in 1991, Eastern European nations could liberalize their economies and participate in trade agreements. This allowed them to be admitted to the EU, making **(B)** correct. While protectionist policies did restrict international trade in Eastern Europe, these were not in place primarily due to popular support; (A) is incorrect. (C) is incorrect because fascist governments arose between the world wars, not after, and are not associated with these countries. The Great Depression and world wars occurred in the first half of the century, making (D) incorrect.

47. A

The European Union (EU) was formed from the European Communities in 1993 in an effort to strengthen European economic trade relations and balance the influence of the United States. Thus, **(A)** is correct and (D) is incorrect. (B) is incorrect because this was a contributor to the formation of the Association of Southeast Asian Nations, not the European Union; the Association of Southeast Asian Nations was created to accelerate economic progress and promote political stability in the nations of the Southeast Asian archipelago. (C) is incorrect because the EU was created so the member countries could form an economic superpower equal to the United States through the adoption of a single multinational currency, the euro, not to make Great Britain alone a superpower.

48. D

Image 1 is a poster from the Soviet Union. Unhappiness with the tsar and economic troubles stemming from World War I caused the Russian Revolution, which led to the Soviet Union's establishment. Thus, **(D)** is correct. Serfdom was abolished in the mid-nineteenth century, prior to the revolution in 1917; (A) is incorrect. The revolution occurred during World War I, not after its conclusion; (B) is incorrect. Ethnic minorities did not try to break free from Russian rule until after the revolution; (C) is incorrect.

49. C

Image 2 shows a dramatic fictional representation of female soldiers from the People's Republic of China. Communist political theory often stressed the rights of women alongside the emancipation of the oppressed proletariat. Thus, **(C)** is correct. While communists reacted to the economic inequality of the nineteenth century, the right of women, or indeed anyone, to vote was not important to communists; (A) is incorrect. The Communist Revolution in China developed after the fall of the Qing Dynasty (monarchy) and the establishment of the Republic of China; (B) is incorrect. While the Empire of Japan briefly established settlements in Manchuria and the Second Sino-Japanese War fatally weakened the Republic of China, the European powers focused on establishing preferential treaties and a sphere of influence in China rather than founding large-scale settler colonies as they had in Africa. (D) is incorrect.

50. A

Image 1 emphasizes the positive impacts of industrialization in the Soviet Union. Image 2 underlines the strong military image that the People's Republic of China wished to project, especially during a visit by a foreign leader like Richard Nixon. Together, these images show the economic control that communist governments fostered and the violent means by which they maintained that control. Thus, **(A)** is correct. While portions of China were briefly colonized by Japan, Russia was never colonized by a foreign power; (B) is incorrect. Communist governments dealt with economic challenges by controlling the economy rather than allowing the forces of supply and demand to shape production; (C) is incorrect. The Soviet Union rose to power before the Great Depression, and communist governments went beyond simply playing "an active role" and controlled nearly all aspects of the economy. (D) is incorrect.

51. B

Both images are propaganda aiming to convince the masses that the communist rule was beneficial, fostering industrialization, military strength, and women's liberation. Thus, **(B)** is correct. These images focus on content for domestic consumption; the ballet in Image 2, for example, would not have been widely exported at the time, given the Cultural Revolution and China's general isolation from the outside world. So, (A) is incorrect. Only Image 1 is propaganda specifically for a centrally directed economic program; (C) is incorrect. These governments wanted to spread communist ideologies but did not need to persuade their people that their country's participation in international organizations was beneficial; (D) is incorrect.

52. A

During this time, the communist nations of the Soviet Union and China were in an ideological struggle with Western capitalist nations and did not encourage the adoption of Western culture; **(A)** is correct. Proxy wars fought indirectly between the Communist Bloc and the West, such as the Korean War, required internal popular support, so propaganda was used; (B) is incorrect. Governments used propaganda to promote government policies, just as Image 1 promotes industrial policy; (C) is incorrect. Communist nations viewed capitalist nations as the enemy during the Cold War; (D) is incorrect.

53. B

The chart depicts the impact of the Green Revolution on wheat yields. During this time period, people began using chemical fertilizers and experimenting with crop strains that were more resistant to fungi and weather patterns, contributing to higher wheat yields, making **(B)** correct. (A) is incorrect because land redistribution did not occur on a large scale in these nations, and land reform would not necessarily lead to increased

production. (C) is incorrect because these sources of energy are not directly correlated with agricultural production. The economies of these countries were mainly capitalist, so government control would be minimal; (D) is incorrect.

54. D

As food production increases, population generally tends to increase as well, leading to greater competition for resources such as clean air, fresh water, and oil. Thus, **(D)** is correct. (A) is incorrect because poverty has not been completely eliminated in these nations due to other economic factors, such as low wages in factories. (B) is incorrect because increased wheat yields would not lead to economic collapse; instead, the grain market globally would benefit from these technologies, and wheat is a relatively low-priced crop. (C) is incorrect because epidemics have still occurred despite increased food supply because of the spread of contagious diseases. In addition, longer life spans are not directly related to more wheat.

55. C

For the nations listed on the chart, wheat production increased dramatically. In a similar way, China doubled its rice yields from 600 to 1450 after being introduced to a new rice strain, referred to as *champa* rice, or fast-ripening rice; **(C)** is correct. (A) is incorrect because sub-Saharan Africa's population rose only slightly due to the forced removal of slaves by Europeans. In the period after the fall of Rome, Europe was in the Dark Ages, or Middle Ages, and agricultural production was suppressed due to few technological innovations, making (B) incorrect. (D) is incorrect because India did not experience rapid population growth due to widespread famines that occurred as more land was put into use for the production of cash crops. These cash crops included cotton rather than food crops.

Section I, Part B

1. A successful short-answer response accomplishes all three tasks set forth by the prompt. Each part of the prompt is worth 1 point, for a total of 3 possible points.

(a) To earn this point, the response must identify one reason why the institute was most likely evaluating the Green Revolution in 2002. Examples include: the rise of organizations that raised concerns about possible environmental impacts of agricultural practices; debates about the causes of climate change; and, as mentioned by the author, the fact that previous research about the Green Revolution's results was outdated and long-term impacts had not been studied.

(b) To earn this point, the response must identify a piece of information not already mentioned in the passage that would be useful in assessing the author's conclusion that small farmers benefited from the Green Revolution. Examples include: specific data about small farmers' average earnings before and after they had implemented Green Revolution techniques, comparisons of small farmers' earnings in different world regions, and data about conditions of small farmers who were not able to adopt Green Revolution techniques.

(c) To earn this point, the response must explain an agricultural development between 1450 and 1750 that also resulted in increased agricultural yields and/or had varying effects on small and large farmers. Examples include: improvements in farming techniques as a result of scientific advances, such as crop rotation and the seed drill; the enclosure movement in Europe that displaced small farmers as large farms successfully employed new agricultural techniques; and the effects of the Columbian Exchange in introducing new plants and animals to regions, thus diversifying diets and impacting lifestyles.

2. A successful short-answer response accomplishes all three tasks set forth by the prompt. Each part of the prompt is worth 1 point, for a total of 3 possible points.

(a) To earn this point, the response must describe a way in which the perspective in the image shows continuity about the roles of women. Although women's rights movements began in the nineteenth century, many still maintained that women should fill traditional roles of homemaker and child-rearer. Examples of ways in which the image reflects continuity include: the depiction of women remaining in the home while the men leave for war, reflecting traditional homemaker roles, and the depiction of a child holding on to the garment of a woman, reflecting traditional child-rearing roles.

(b) To earn this point, the response must explain how a historical development led to changes in views about the roles of women. The response must not just identify a development, but must connect the development to

changing views about women. Examples include: the Industrial Revolution causing more women to work outside the home and thus weakening the role of women as homemaker, the ideas of the Enlightenment (and resulting revolutions) about equality being applied to women in the nineteenth and twentieth centuries, the significant participation of women in non-combat roles in World War I challenging the traditional ideas about women and warfare, and the women's rights movement advocating for suffrage and equal rights legitimizing the idea of changing roles for women.

(c) To earn this point, the response must explain a use of political art. Examples include: the use of propaganda during times of war, such as during the world wars to engage civilians in the war effort; the mobilization of all citizens in environments of total war, such as encouraging men to enlist and women to support soldiers; and the use of art for political purposes by governments in order to promote nationalist feelings.

3. A successful short-answer response accomplishes all three tasks set forth by the prompt. Each part of the prompt is worth 1 point, for a total of 3 possible points.

(a) To earn this point, the response must explain a cultural change that occurred in African societies that resulted from their contact with Arab travelers. Examples include: the spread of Islam; the adoption of Arab architectural styles; and the development of the Swahili language, a mixture of traditional Bantu speech with Arabic words, to help facilitate trade along the East African Indian Ocean coast.

(b) To earn this point, the response must explain an economic change that occurred in African societies that resulted from their contact with Arab travelers. Examples include the flourishing of African ports such as Kilwa and Mombasa and the strengthening of West African kingdoms such as Mali that prospered due to the trans-Saharan gold and salt trade.

(c) To earn this point, the response must explain a continuity in African societies. Examples include the persistence of traditional languages for noncommercial activity and the integration of elements of indigenous African religions with Islam.

4. A successful short-answer response accomplishes all three tasks set forth by the prompt. Each part of the prompt is worth 1 point, for a total of 3 possible points.

(a) To earn this point, the response must identify an economic effect of industrial technology. Examples include: the mass production of consumer goods, such as textiles; lower prices of manufactured goods because labor was less expensive and goods were produced quickly; changes to labor systems as fewer workers were employed in agriculture; the emergence of reform movements and ideologies such as communism in response to workers' conditions; and the development of new financial instruments, such as the stock market and insurance.

(b) To earn this point, the response must explain a similarity between governments' and workers' responses to industrialization. Examples include: the shared desire to address issues created for workers by industrialization, including alleviating poor living conditions, such as overcrowding and unsanitary cities; improving working conditions, such as providing better wages, hours, and safety; and extending suffrage to all men in society.

(c) To earn this point, the response must explain a difference between governments' and workers' responses to industrialization. Examples include: that government action tended to involve a mixture of maintaining a hands-off approach to the economy or passing laws to regulate working conditions, such as limiting child labor; and workers' most common responses were to organize themselves into unions, advocate for themselves, or embrace new ideologies such as Marxism.

Section II

1. *Evaluate the extent to which the international situation following World War I contributed to World War II.*

Category	Scoring Criteria	Notes
Thesis/Claim (0–1 points)	Historically defensible thesis/claim with a logical line of reasoning. The response must make a thesis or claim without restating the prompt itself. The thesis must consist of one or more sentences located in one place, either in the introduction or the conclusion.	This question is assessing the historical reasoning skill of causation. The thesis should identify two or more international conditions after the end of World War I and make an assessment as to how much those conditions led to World War II. Example: "World War II mainly resulted from the treaties signed after World War I. Germany and Japan viewed these agreements as unfair, leading to the rise of nationalist and extremist groups that were allowed to pursue aggressive policies by major world powers."
Contextualization (0–1 points)	Broader historical context related to the prompt. The response must connect the topic to historical developments, events, or processes; these can occur before, during, or after the time frame of the prompt itself.	Contextualization for this prompt should explain, not merely mention, broader factors relevant to World War I or the interwar period. Examples: The factors leading to World War I; the ways the war itself impacted the provisions of international agreements, such as the fighting occurring on French soil impacting France's support for requiring reparations from Germany.
Evidence (0–3 points)	Use of evidence to support the thesis. The response must utilize the content from at least *three* documents to address the *topic* of the prompt. (1 point) OR The response must use at least *six* documents to support an *argument* based on the prompt. (2 points)	Evidence from the documents must be paraphrased, not merely quoted. Examples: Documents 1, 3, and 7 to analyze the impacts and perceptions of the Treaty of Versailles; documents 2 and 4 to analyze the impact of international agreements in the interwar period; document 2 to support the argument that Japan considered itself slighted by Western powers in the interwar period; documents 1, 3, 5, and 6 to describe interwar international economic crises; documents 4 and 6 to analyze the responses of other countries to German aggression.
	The response must use at least *one* additional piece of historical evidence, beyond what is found in the documents, to support an argument. This additional evidence must be different from what was used for contextualization. (1 point)	Example: An explanation of how the Great Depression exacerbated economic conditions in Germany and caused other countries to focus on their domestic economies rather than on German or Japanese expansion.

(continued)

Category	Scoring Criteria	Notes
Analysis and Reasoning (0–2 points)	Complexity of understanding and reasoning. The response must explain, for at least *three* of the documents, how or why the document's purpose, historical basis, point of view, and/or audience are relevant to an argument. (1 point)	Factors' relevance to the argument about the international situation after World War I should be explained, not just identified. Example: The role of purpose in document 6, in which FDR is attempting to appeal to Hitler to curtail German aggression by referring passively to Germany taking over European countries, speaking as though he gives German intentions the benefit of the doubt ("Reports, which we trust are not true"), and advocating disarmament and economic solutions.
	The response must show a complex understanding of the content of the prompt, using evidence to support, qualify, or modify an argument about the prompt. (1 point)	A complex understanding should be incorporated into the overall argument about how the international situation after World War I led to World War II. Examples: An explanation of how multiple variables, such as the Treaty of Versailles, international agreements, and the world economic depression, all contributed to instigating World War II; an analysis of how the international situation after World War I connects with the international situation in a different time period, for instance, how appeasement of Germany after World War I relates to Allies' interactions with the Soviet Union after World War II.

2. *In the period 1200–1450, improved transportation technologies and commercial practices led to the intensification of trade.*

Develop an argument that evaluates how improved technologies and commercial practices led to changes in Afro-Eurasian trade networks during this time period.

Category	Scoring Criteria	Notes
Thesis/Claim (0–1 points)	Historically defensible thesis/claim with a logical line of reasoning. The response must make a thesis or claim without restating the prompt itself. The thesis must consist of one or more sentences located in one place, either in the introduction or the conclusion.	This question is assessing the skill of continuity and change over time. A strong thesis should make a claim about at least two changes in trade networks that resulted from technologies and commercial practices. Example: "In the period 1200–1450, improved ship designs and navigational tools increased the reach of Indian Ocean trade, while the development of money economies intensified trade networks across Afro-Eurasia."
Contextualization (0–1 points)	Broader historical context related to the prompt. The response must connect the topic to historical developments, events, or processes; these can occur before, during, or after the time frame of the prompt itself.	Contextualization for this prompt should explain, not merely mention, broader factors relevant to Afro-Eurasian trade networks. Examples: The rise of Islam, which provided a common cultural background for merchants, particularly in the Indian Ocean basin; the Golden Age of Islam, which provided the cultural climate in which scholars and scientists could invent, reinvent, and spread maritime technologies; the extent of the Mongol Empire, in which trade along the Silk Road prospered.
Evidence (0–2 points)	Use of evidence to support the thesis. The response identifies specific examples *relevant to the topic* of the prompt. (1 point) OR The response uses specific examples to *support an argument* about the prompt. (2 points)	Evidence must be paraphrased, not merely quoted. To earn 2 points, the evidence must be used to support an argument about Afro-Eurasian trade networks. Examples: The increased knowledge of the patterns of the monsoon winds contributed to safer, more reliable transportation in the Indian Ocean; the use of new tools, such as the compass and astrolabe, made navigation more accurate and therefore less risky; the development of new commercial practices, such as the extension of credit and the use of currencies, facilitated trade; the practice in the Mongol Empire of providing protection along Silk Road trade routes.

(continued)

Category	Scoring Criteria	Notes
Analysis and Reasoning (0–2 points)	Complexity of understanding and reasoning. The response shows historical reasoning to make an argument about the prompt. (1 point) OR The response demonstrates complex understanding, using evidence to support, qualify, or modify an argument about the prompt. (2 points)	Comparison, causation, or continuity and change over time should be incorporated into the overall argument about Afro-Eurasian trade networks. Example: A detailed description of one or more of the changes to trade networks listed above (continuity and change over time); an explanation of the causes that contributed to a change to trade networks, such as maritime technologies developing in the Golden Age of Islam and spreading through trade contacts and the Crusades (causation). OR A complex understanding should be incorporated into the overall argument about Afro-Eurasian trade networks. Examples: A description of both changes *and* continuities, such as the use of existing ports to transport the same types of luxury goods (silk, porcelain, etc.) and the continued connections between Indian Ocean trade and the Silk Road; an explanation of the developments in trade in later periods, such as the role of the Portuguese and later the English and Dutch in Indian Ocean trade.

3. *In the period 1450–1900, significant economic changes in the areas of agriculture and industry occurred throughout the world, impacting demand for labor.*

   Develop an argument that evaluates how labor systems changed as a result of increased demand for labor in this time period.

Category	Scoring Criteria	Notes
Thesis/Claim (0–1 points)	Historically defensible thesis/claim with a logical line of reasoning. The response must make a thesis or claim without restating the prompt itself. The thesis must consist of one or more sentences located in one place, either in the introduction or the conclusion.	This question assesses the skill of continuity and change over time. A strong thesis should make a claim about two or more changes to labor systems as a result of increased demand for labor. Examples: Slavery and other forms of involuntary labor in the Americas; many former European peasants working in factories; increased need for labor to extract raw materials for industrial production. A thesis might read: "In the period 1450–1900, slavery became more widespread and the slave trade was redirected across the Atlantic in order to meet the increased demand for labor on plantations."
Contextualization (0–1 points)	Broader historical context related to the prompt. The response must connect the topic to historical developments, events, or processes; these can occur before, during, or after the time frame of the prompt itself.	Contextualization for this prompt should explain, not merely mention, broader factors relevant to changes to labor systems. Examples: An examination of the European Age of Exploration, which led to the establishment of plantations in the Americas; an explanation of the decline of serfdom and how changes to agriculture decreased the need for farm labor while increasing agricultural output; a description of the Industrial Revolution.
Evidence (0–2 points)	Use of evidence to support the thesis. The response identifies specific examples *relevant to the topic* of the prompt. (1 point) OR The response uses specific examples to *support an argument* about the prompt. (2 points)	Evidence must be paraphrased, not merely quoted. To earn 2 points, the evidence must be used to support an argument about changes to labor systems. Examples: In the Americas, the decline in the population of Native Americans due to diseases that led to the importation of African slaves; the use of slave labor plantations for the production of cash crops; the expansion of the slave trade over the centuries as a result of mercantilist policies; the rise in indentured servitude. In industrializing nations, the improvements in agriculture and practices like enclosure that decreased the demand for farm labor; the development of industry that necessitated factory labor; the shift from cottage industry to wage labor. In nonindustrialized regions, the demand for labor to extract raw materials that often resulted in the exploitation of laborers.

(continued)

Category	Scoring Criteria	Notes
Analysis and Reasoning (0–2 points)	Complexity of understanding and reasoning. The response shows historical reasoning to make an argument about the prompt. (1 point) OR The response demonstrates complex understanding, using evidence to support, qualify, or modify an argument about the prompt. (2 points)	Comparison, causation, or continuity and change over time should be incorporated into the overall argument about changes to labor systems. Example: A detailed description of one or more of the changes to labor systems listed above (continuity and change over time); an explanation of how the Age of Exploration and/or Industrial Revolution impacted changes to labor systems (causation). OR A complex understanding should be incorporated into the overall argument about changes to labor systems. Examples: A description of changes *and* continuities in labor systems, such as the continued use of slavery from classical and medieval periods and the continuation of serfdom in Eastern Europe; an explanation of both causes *and* effects, such as the living conditions created by factory work prompting reform movements, unions, and communism.

4. *In the period 1750–1900, revolutions and rebellions began against existing governments, leading to the establishment of new nation-states around the world.*

Develop an argument that evaluates how Enlightenment ideas contributed to revolutions against imperial or monarchical rule in one or more regions in this time period.

Category	Scoring Criteria	Notes
Thesis/Claim (0–1 points)	Historically defensible thesis/claim with a logical line of reasoning. The response must make a thesis or claim without restating the prompt itself. The thesis must consist of one or more sentences located in one place, either in the introduction or the conclusion.	This question assesses the skill of causation. A strong thesis should make a claim about how Enlightenment ideas influenced revolutions. The claim could focus on two or more Enlightenment ideas or two or more revolutions. Example: "The Enlightenment idea of natural rights was used to support revolutions against governments that the revolutionaries claimed were violating their natural rights, as in the Haitian population rejecting French colonial rule and the people within France protesting the economic and social disparities created by the estate system and absolute monarchy."
Contextualization (0–1 points)	Broader historical context related to the prompt. The response must connect the topic to historical developments, events, or processes; these can occur before, during, or after the time frame of the prompt itself.	Contextualization for this prompt should explain, not merely mention, broader factors that contributed to the development of Enlightenment ideas or the political environment before revolutions. Examples: An explanation of how Enlightenment ideas developed in response to the consolidation of power by European absolute monarchs; a description of the technological and economic circumstances that led to European colonies in the Americas; an explanation of the role of the Seven Years' War in the American Revolution; a description of labor and social conditions that prompted rebellions in Latin America, Haiti, or France.
Evidence (0–2 points)	Use of evidence to support the thesis. The response identifies specific examples *relevant to the topic* of the prompt. (1 point) OR The response uses specific examples to *support an argument* about the prompt. (2 points)	Evidence must be paraphrased, not merely quoted. To earn 2 points, the evidence must be used to support an argument about the Enlightenment's impact on revolutions. Examples: The idea of consent of the governed as applied by American colonists to protest their lack of representation in British government in the Declaration of Independence; the idea of natural rights being incorporated into the French National Assembly's Declaration of the Rights of Man and of the Citizen; the application of the idea of natural rights to the call to abolish slavery in the Haitian Revolution.

(continued)

Category	Scoring Criteria	Notes
Analysis and Reasoning (0–2 points)	Complexity of understanding and reasoning. The response shows historical reasoning to make an argument about the prompt. (1 point) OR The response demonstrates complex understanding, using evidence to support, qualify, or modify an argument about the prompt. (2 points)	Comparison, causation, or continuity and change over time should be incorporated into the overall argument about the Enlightenment's impact on revolutions. Example: An explanation of how Enlightenment ideas such as constitutional government influenced Bolívar's Jamaica Letter (causation). OR A complex understanding should be incorporated into the overall argument about the Enlightenment's impact on revolutions. Examples: An explanation of both causes *and* effects, such as the impact of Bolívar's Jamaica Letter on Latin American independence movements and the creation of Gran Columbia, which eventually divided into new independent states; a comparison of causes *and* results of two revolutions, such as the American Revolution leading to the creation of the United States and the French Revolution eventually being followed by the rule of Napoleon.

References

The following content has been used with permission:

Murdoch, James and Isoh Yamagata. *A History of Japan During the Century of Early Foreign Intercourse (1542–1651)*, Kobe, Japan: Published at the office of The Chronicle, 1903. Used by permission.

From Bulliet, Richard et al, *The Earth and Its Peoples: A Global History, Volume II: Since 1500*, 6th ed. Stamford: Cengage, 2014. Permission conveyed through Copyright Clearance Center.

"The politics of Taíno revivalism: The insignificance of Amerindian mtDNA in the population history of Puerto Ricans. A comment on recent research," by Gabriel Hasplip-Viera (CENTRO: *Journal of the Center for Puerto Rican Studies* 18(1): 2006. Used by permission.

Travels in Asia & Africa Vol. 18, 1st Edition by Ibn Battuta (H.A.R. Gibb, trans), published by Routledge. © Routledge & Kegan Paul Ltd., 1929. Reproduced by arrangement with Taylor & Francis Books UK. Used by permission.

Republished with permission of University of Hawaii Press from Douglas M. Peers, "Is Humpty Dumpty Back Together Again?: The Revival of Imperial History and the Oxford History of the British Empire," *Journal of World History*. 13.2 (Fall 2002). Permission conveyed through Copyright Clearance Center, Inc.

Adapted from Payne, John, trans. *The Decameron of Giovanni Boccaccio, Volume One*; Florentine Edition. London, 1906. Privately printed.

Excerpt from *Discoveries and Opinions of Galileo* by Galileo, translated by Stillman Drake, translation © 1957 by Stillman Drake. Used by permission of Doubleday, an imprint of the Knopft Doubleday Publishing Group, a division of Penguin Random House LLC. All Rights Reserved.

From *China and Africa in the Middle Ages*, 1st Edition by Teobaldo Filesi, David Morison (trans.), published by Routledge. © Frank Cass, 1972. Reproduced by arrangement with Taylor & Francis Books UK.

"Memorandum from the International Department of the Central Committee of the CPSU to Alexander Yakovlev," February, 1989, History and Public Policy Program Digital Archive, Archive of the Gorbachev Foundation, Moscow; on file at the National Security Archive, donated by Professor Jacques Levesque. Translated by Svetlana Savranskaya and Gary Goldberg.

Madyibi, Ayanda (trans). The Arusha Declaration and TANU's Policy on Socialism and Self-Reliance. Courtesy Dr. Ayanda Madyibi. Reprinted with permission.

The Royal Danish Library, Copenhagen, *El primer nueva corónica y buen gobierno conpuesto por Don Phelipe Guaman Poma de Ayala, señor y príncipe*. Cover.

From Antonio Vasquez de Espinosa. Charles Upson Clark, trans. *Compendium and Description of the West Indies*. Smithsonian Miscellaneous Collections, Volume 102. Washington: Smithsonian Institution, September 1, 1942.

Excerpted from *The Wealth of Africa: The Swahili Coast* (Teacher's Notes). © The Trustees of the British Museum. Used with permission.

Adapted from Robert Brown, ed. *The History and Description of Africa and of the Notable Things Therein Contained* by Leo Africanus. Translated by John Pory. London: The Hakluyt Society (private printing), 1896.

Eversley, Lord George John Shaw-Lefevre. *The Turkish Empire, its Growth and Decay*. London: T. Fisher Unwin Ltd., 1917. Used with permission.

Republished with permission of University of Hawaii Press from Dennis O. Flynn and Arturo Giráldez, historians, "Born with a "Silver Spoon": The Origin of World Trade in 1571." *Journal of World History*, Vol. 6 No.2, Fall 1995. Permission conveyed through Copyright Clearance Center, Inc.

From Sherwell, Guillermo A. *Simón Bolívar (el libertador): Patriot, Warrior, Statesman, Father of Five Nations; a Sketch of His Life and His Work*. Washington, D.C.: Press of Byron S. Adams, 1921.

From Greenpeace International, "Twenty years of failure: Why GM crops have failed to deliver on their promises." November 5, 2015. © 2015 Greenpeace International. Used with permission.

From Marx, Karl and Frederick Engels, *Manifesto of the Communist Party* (Authorized English Translation). New York: New York Labor News Co., 1908.

From Ricardo, Davis. *On The Principles of Political Economy, and Taxation*. London: John Murray, Albemarle-Street, 1817.

Adapted from the British Factory Act of 1833, "An Act to regulate the Labour of Children and Young Persons in the Mills and Factories of the United Kingdom." 1833.

Vernadsky, George, ed. *A Source Book for Russian History From Early Times to 1917, vol. 2, Early Times to the Late Seventeenth Century*. New Haven and London: Yale U. Press, 1972. © 1972 Yale University Press.

International Food Policy Research Institute, "Green Revolution: Curse or Blessing?" © 2002 IFPRI. Reproduced with permission from the International Food Policy Research Institute.